POETR

POETRY

JILL P. BAUMGAERTNER
Wheaton College

Harcourt Brace Jovanovich, Publishers

San Diego   New York   Chicago   Austin   Washington, D.C.
London   Sydney   Tokyo   Toronto

PREFACE

Poetry is designed to make poetry accessible and inviting to college students. The introductory chapters (Part I) and the anthology (Part II) together present well over 500 poems, consisting of standard literary works as well as a strong representation of recent works by women and minority poets.

The introductory chapters are meant to engage the imagination and encourage the reader to become a part of the creative process which the poet began. Rather than jumping immediately into the techniques of sophisticated literary analysis, the reader learns first (in Chapters 1 through 3) to approach the poems aesthetically or intuitively—a process that leads more gradually into the interpretation of poetry. The intention is to encourage the student to approach poetry without fear and with self-confidence, establishing personal connections with a poem in early readings and refining those first ideas as the reading becomes more analytical. Chapters 4 through 7 define, respectively, the elements, sounds, rhythms, and forms of poetry. Chapter 8, "Careful Reading," suggests ways to avoid misinterpretation. And Chapter 9, "Writing about Poetry," introduces the literary journal and follows a student through the various stages of thinking about and preparing an analysis of a poem, culminating in the finished paper. Finally, the reader should be able to judge the quality of a given poem by measuring the poem's attributes, a process described in Chapter 10, "Becoming a Discriminating Reader."

The poems have been numbered consecutively through both the introductory chapters and the anthology. This has been done for ease of reference between *Poetry* and the Instructor's Manual, by Linda Dover, and to facilitate the typing of syllabi. The poems in the anthology are arranged alphabetically by author and by date of first publication under each author. Many of the poems are briefly annotated in footnotes. Study questions are provided for all the anthologized poems, either in the anthology itself or in the Instructor's Manual. The Instructor's Manual also provides explications for those anthologized poems accompanied by questions in the text.

I would like to express appreciation to my students at Wheaton College whose willing, enthusiastic responses have been the inspiration for my attempts to create a pedagogy based upon reader-response theory. I thank Donna Ray in particular for allowing me to use excerpts from her journal. I am indebted to my own professors, William Dillingham, Frank Manley, and Floyd Watkins, for teaching me both to read poetry and to trust myself. As always, my husband, Martin, has been my enabler in thought, word, and deed.

The following reviewers made helpful suggestions: Julius C. Feazell, Memphis State University; Gilbert Powell Findlay, Colorado State University; William Landau, Los Angeles Pierce College; and Michael Shapiro, University of Illinois, Champaign. At HBJ, Karl Yambert and Karen Allanson provided welcome support and advice in the preparation of the manuscript, and Mary Allen, Michael Biskup, Lynne Bush, Eleanor Garner, Diane Pella, and Robbie Shelburne contributed their several talents to convert the manuscript to finished book, for which I am grateful. For his interest, his discernment, and his encouragement, I owe special thanks to my editor, Bill McLane.

Jill P. Baumgaertner

CONTENTS

CHAPTER 7   THE ORGANIZATION OF POETRY

POETRY

PART I

HOW TO
READ POETRY

CHAPTER 1

WHAT IS A POEM?

What is a poem and what can it do? A poem, Dylan Thomas said, "makes your toenails twinkle." A poem transforms the ordinary, and in the process it may delight, surprise, and upset your usual way of seeing or hearing. Even though a poem may adopt a philosophic or religious or political stance, it is not a secret code to be deciphered or picked apart to uncover an obscure "message." Getting to know poems and becoming comfortable with them take patience and practice, but you must not look at poetry as you would look at a machine, which once mastered, acquires utilitarian significance. Poetry is simply a means of human expression that exists because there are readers and writers who are involved and engaged in human experience. Poetry, like all other artistic expression, is an attempt to name that experience, to create feeling, to express the otherwise inexpressible.

Poetry encourages you, the reader, to participate in the creative process. You will bring all of your life experiences with you as you read the poem. If you are in love, or have broken your arm, or are looking forward to a swim on a hot day—all of these experiences and the feelings connected with them will influence the way you read a poem. Likewise, your background, your culture, your sex, and your religion will be factors affecting and contributing to your reading of a particular poem on a particular day. Whoever you are and whatever your level of experience or inexperience with literature, you are equipped to be a reader of poetry.

In fact, without a reader to understand it, to "hear" it, a poem is much like a tree falling in an uninhabited forest. If no ears receive the sound waves of its crash, the sound does not exist. In other words, sound depends upon the existence of ears to receive the sound waves, and in much the same way, a poem depends upon the reader. A poet can create an artifact which is pleasing or disturbing to the poet alone, but each time it is placed before the eyes of a reader, its existence is reenacted; it *becomes* a poem. The reader, alongside the writer, creates the poem.

Unlike sound, however, poetry cannot be passively absorbed. You hear the distant whistle of a train in the still summer night, or the car screeching around the corner, or the dog barking in the yard next door—and usually you hear these sounds whether or not you want to hear them. With poetry, however, you must be more *actively* involved. You may hear a poem once and enjoy it, but the more you read it, the more intense your involvement will become, and the more you will feel as if you are a participant in the poem, not just an observer viewing an interesting phenomenon at a safe distance. As an active reader, you will, in other words, be in the middle of the forest, *creating* the sound of a tree crashing to the earth, just as you do now in your mind.

WHY READ POETRY?

Why is it that some poems have lasted through the years? Consider the following poem, written in 1851 but containing strong resonance for readers today.

MATTHEW ARNOLD

DOVER BEACH   1

The sea is calm tonight.
The tide is full, the moon lies fair
Upon the straits;—on the French coast the light
Gleams and is gone; the cliffs of England stand,
Glimmering and vast, out in the tranquil bay.   5
Come to the window, sweet is the night-air!
Only, from the long line of spray
Where the sea meets the moon-blanched land,
Listen! you hear the grating roar
Of pebbles which the waves draw back, and fling,   10
At their return, up the high strand,
Begin, and cease, and then again begin,
With tremulous cadence slow, and bring
The eternal note of sadness in.

Sophocles long ago   15
Heard it on the Aegean, and it brought
Into his mind the turbid ebb and flow
Of human misery; we
Find also in the sound a thought,
Hearing it by this distant northern sea.   20

The Sea of Faith
Was once, too, at the full, and round earth's shore
Lay like the folds of a bright girdle furled.
But now I only hear
Its melancholy, long, withdrawing roar,   25
Retreating, to the breath
Of the night-wind, down the vast edges drear
And naked shingles of the world.

Ah, love, let us be true
To one another! for the world, which seems   30
To lie before us like a land of dreams,
So various, so beautiful, so new,
Hath really neither joy, nor love nor light,
Nor certitude, nor peace, nor help for pain;
And we are here as on a darkling plain   35
Swept with confused alarms of struggle and flight,
Where ignorant armies clash by night.

1867

This poem, about the loss of faith and its accompanying feelings of disillusionment and sadness, catalogs all of our lost connections. In the face of uncertainty and hopelessness and a world which "hath really neither joy, nor love, nor light, / Nor certitude, nor peace, nor help for pain," human relationships alone seem to give identity and solace to the poem's speaker. The last three lines of this poem make the twentieth-century reader feel a kinship with Arnold's mid-nineteenth-century world because our world is also swept with terror. We, too, may feel that in the dark confusion of modern life it is often difficult to distinguish between allies and enemies. We read this poem and realize that Arnold, writing 150 years ago, created a poem which we, remarkably, can experience now, as if his world were our own. In fact, in reading a poem, we reconstruct a world the poet initially created—and that becomes our reading, our interpretation, of the poem.

Poetry endures because it expresses universal truths. This seriousness of intent occasionally intimidates students who discover that poetry is at times difficult to understand on first reading. But remember—a quick, first reading can begin to open a poem for you. You do not need to answer all the questions at once nor understand all the subtleties on a first reading. To jump immediately into informational, analytical reading would be a mistake in your first approach to a poem. You need, instead, to develop a more intuitive way of thinking. Poets themselves rarely begin poems with detailed, analytical plans. Instead, an image will capture a poet's imagination and almost before she is aware of it, she is playing with that image in a poem, examining it from different angles and allowing it to suggest other related images to her.

As a reader of poetry, then, you must not be afraid to let yourself participate in a poem in the same playful way—particularly in the first stages of reading it. Look at "Dover Beach" once again. Which are the words and lines that appeal most to you? Which call up your own personal associations? What does the poem allow you to visualize? Where does the poem take you in your imagination? You must learn to trust yourself as the co-creator of the poem, to explore personal connections with the poem and to pay careful attention to them. In other words, you must be creative. A poem requires more than just consciousness on the part of a recipient. It requires intense activity on the part of the reader.

Why bother? Is reading poetry really worth the effort? What will you miss if you never develop the skill? To begin with, you will have excluded yourself from one of life's purest pleasures. Poetry can be as enjoyable as music, as exhilarating as a tennis match, as challenging and absorbing as an excellent film. However, while you can compare its effects with that of other human activities, particularly other art forms, poetry is unique. It does what no other art form can do. It compresses experience; it intensifies language; it uses words to say the unsayable. To choose not to read poetry would be like choosing meal after meal of bread and water when fruit, fresh meat and fish, and garden vegetables were also available. It is not just that poetry is good for you; it is also enjoyable because it cracks open your everyday life, the mundane world in which you spend so much unconscious time, and it releases the extraordinary, bringing you to full consciousness.

THE POETIC LINE

Someone once said that the difference between poetry and prose is that poetry is jagged on one side of the page. Although this may seem a rather artificial distinction, it actually possesses a certain degree of validity because it says something about the importance of "line" in poetry. The poetic line announces itself as something to be read in a different way—more carefully than the way we might read a newspaper column or an essay. Consider the following excerpt from Roy A. Gallant's *Our Universe* (Washington, D.C.: National Geographic Society, 1980, p. 157).

> Jupiter is the largest planet in the Solar System. It is about five times farther from the Sun than Earth is. More than 11 Earths could be lined up along the giant planet's diameter and 1,300 Earths could easily be packed inside.

This prose passage is factual and informative. Look what happens to it, however, when it is put into poetic lines.

Jupiter

is the largest planet in the
Solar System. It is about five
times farther from the Sun than
Earth is. More than 11

Earths could be lined up along
the giant planet's diameter and 1,300
Earths could easily be packed
inside.

This is not, of course, a poem, but nonetheless, one tends to read it more slowly and carefully in this form. The words draw more attention to themselves—particularly those at the beginnings and the ends of the lines. Any word appearing alone on a line assumes a new significance. The stanza divisions also create emphasis where there was none in the prose version. Of course, the poetic line is only one device of many that a poet uses—and a reader heeds—in creating poetry. The point is that the poetic line changes emphasis and meaning, highlights words, arrests the reader's attention with surprises and insights, and in fact contributes much to the meaning of a poem.

WHAT POETRY CAN DO

A poem can simultaneously tell a story, describe a scene, express feelings, and provide entertainment. Sometimes the stories, scenes, and feelings will be well known to you, but the poetic retelling of even very familiar stories allows you to experience them in fresh ways. Consider, for example, this poem which encourages you to reconsider a familiar fairy tale.

ROBERT PACK

THE FROG PRINCE   2

(A Speculation on Grimm's Fairy Tale)

Imagine the princess' surprise!
Who would have thought a frog's cold frame
Could hold the sweet and gentle body
Of a prince? How can I name
The joy she must have felt to learn   5
His transformation was the wonder
Of her touch—that she too, in
Her way, had been transformed under
Those clean sheets? Such powers were
Like nothing she had ever read.   10
And in the morning when her mother
Came and saw them there in bed,
Heard how a frog became a prince;
What was it that her mother said?

1980

This poem puts you inside the princess' head, allows you to experience her surprise as she feels the transformation of the "frog's cold frame" into the warm body of a prince, and further provokes you to consider the physical implications of the presence of a frog-turned-prince in bed with a princess! Yes, we wonder after reading this poem, what *did* her mother say?

Poetry that tells a story is called **narrative poetry** and it has been written for centuries. In its most ambitious, lengthy form (as in *The Iliad, The Odyssey, The Aeneid, Beowulf,* and *Paradise Lost*), it is called **epic poetry.** Knowing about these and other classical types of poetry grants you a better understanding of the deep-seated traditions of poetry—traditions which have undergone constant redefinition through the years.

The **lyric,** for example, once referred to poetry meant to be sung to music. In more recent times, *lyric* describes any short, concentrated poem expressing personal feelings.

WALTER SAVAGE LANDOR

ROSE AYLMER   3

Ah, what avails the sceptred race,
   Ah, what the form divine!
What every virtue, every grace!
   Rose Aylmer, all were thine.

Rose Aylmer, whom these wakeful eyes   5
   May weep, but never see,
A night of memories and of sighs
   I consecrate to thee.

1806

The poem is brief but strong, evoking in only eight lines the feelings of loss and loneliness.

One type of lyric is the **ode** (from a Greek word for "song"). The ode is usually a long, complex lyric, expressing profound emotion. Its expression and style are usually more elaborate and exalted than other lyrics, as in John Keats' "Ode to a Nightingale," "Ode on a Grecian Urn," and "Ode on Melancholy" (poems 313–315).[1] The **elegy,** a long, ceremonious poem of mourning, is a lyric much more commonly used in English. In the elegy the speaker meditates at length on his feelings of grief and loss. See, for example, Gray's "Elegy Written in a Country Churchyard" (245), Milton's "Lycidas" (381), Auden's "In Memory of W. B. Yeats" (109), and Roethke's "Elegy for Jane" (449).

---

[1]These and similar numbers refer to poems as they are numbered throughout this book.

Poetry is not always serious, however. Poetry which entertains with humor or wit is called **light verse.** Nursery rhymes are forms of light verse, but there are also many other examples of light verse written for adults who simply enjoy a good laugh, ranging from Alexander Pope's "The Rape of the Lock" (424) to Anthony Hecht's "The Dover Bitch" (267—a parody of Arnold's "Dover Beach") to Dorothy Parker's "One Perfect Rose" (409) and "Résumé" (410). Some light verse—particularly satire—has an underlying serious intent, but notice that much light verse has the effect of a good one-liner.

R. P. DICKEY

MATERIALISM   4

Did you think all that stuff you gave me
would make me stay with you?
Well, it helped; and I'm still here,
and I want more stuff.

1986

OGDEN NASH

THE PERFECT HUSBAND   5

He tells you when you've got on too much lipstick,
And helps you with your girdle when your hips stick.

1945

THE SURPRISE OF POETRY

In some ways poetry is a game, calling upon you to play with wild impossibilities. In "A Valediction Forbidding Mourning" (28), John Donne uses the legs of a **V**-shaped compass to describe the relationship of separated lovers' souls.

If they be two, they are two so
    As stiff twin compasses are two;
Thy soul, the fixed foot, makes no show
    To move, but doth, if th'other do.

What could be logical or reasonable about this comparison between a compass and two souls? It is only through the play of the poem that this seemingly illogical comparison begins to make any sense at all. The one leg of the compass represents the soul of the lover who stays at home, and though "fixed" and stationary, follows the other foot, or the soul of the travelling lover, as he journeys. And suddenly, when the poem is taken in, absorbed, when the reader has become a player in the poem, upsetting all usual ways of seeing or hearing, then what was an ordinary occurrence (two lovers tearfully saying good-bye before one departs on a long journey) becomes surprisingly immediate and new.

Poetry upsets ordinary expectations and involves readers in familiar experiences in totally new ways. Consider, for example, the following poem:

LEWIS CARROLL

JABBERWOCKY

'Twas brillig, and the slithy toves
  Did gyre and gimble in the wabe;
All mimsy were the borogoves,
  And the mome raths outgrabe.

"Beware the Jabberwock, my son!   5
  The jaws that bite, the claws that catch!
Beware the Jubjub bird, and shun
  The frumious Bandersnatch!"

He took his vorpal sword in hand:
  Long time the manxome foe he sought—   10
So rested he by the Tumtum tree,
  And stood awhile in thought.

And as in uffish thought he stood,
  The Jabberwock, with eyes of flame,
Came whiffling through the tulgey wood,   15
  And burbled as it came!

One, two! One, two! And through and through
  The vorpal blade went snicker-snack!
He left it dead, and with its head
  He went galumphing back.   20

"And hast thou slain the Jabberwock?
  Come to my arms, my beamish boy!
O frabjous day! Callooh! Callay!"
  He chortled in his joy.

'Twas brillig, and the slithy toves   25
  Did gyre and gimble in the wabe;
All mimsy were the borogoves,
  And the mome raths outgrabe.

1871

The surprise of this poem is the language itself—an entirely new language which the poet created for the poem. Apart from anything else, Lewis Carroll was having a great deal of fun when he wrote this poem, and he expected that his readers would, too. The poem depends upon the *active* imaginations of its readers; one feels the meaning of certain words without really knowing how one knows these meanings: *frabjous, borogoves, burbled, mimsy*. These are not words one would find in any dictionary, but they are words which are similar in sound or appearance to other words we do know—and they are words which in the context of the poem, begin to make a sort of emotional, associational sense. The poem also presents these strange words in familiar grammatical structures, sentences in which the word order imposes a sense the words themselves do not contain. For example, "The Jabberwock, with eyes of flame, / Came whiffling through the tulgey wood, / And burbled as it came!" uses ordinary syntax which encourages the reader to imagine and to create the meanings of the words.

We have heard variations of the "Jabberwocky" plot since we were children. It is the classic initiation story in which a boy, cautioned by his father about dangers in the wilderness, kills a beast and proves himself a man. He has performed the deed almost without realizing what he has done. Lost in "uffish thought" ("offish"—or distant), the boy is surprised by the beast, responds with his sword, the "vorpal blade," slices off the creature's head, and then returns ungracefully but surely "galumphing back" home to his father who greets him with chortles[2] of joy and cries of "Callooh! Callay!"

The poem has created a language which the reader's experience allows him to "understand," even though the words are new, the vocabulary foreign, and the landscape vegetated by strange forms never before seen in nature.

Word meanings are also fluid in "Eve Names the Animals." Whereas in "Jabberwocky" the reader creates meaning in the poem through an intuitive understanding of certain newly created words and phrases, in "Eve Names the Animals," the speaker is a familiar figure from the Bible, and understanding the poem depends upon knowing the scriptural story of Adam and Eve.

SUSAN DONNELLY

EVE NAMES THE ANIMALS   7

To me, *lion* was sun on a wing
over the garden. *Dove,*
a burrowing, blind creature.

I swear that man
never knew animals. Words   5
he lined up according to size,

---

[2]Coined by Carroll for "Jabberwocky," the word *chortle* apparently so aptly struck an intuitive chord that it has since entered the language and can be found in any standard dictionary.

while elephants slipped flat-eyed
through water

and trout
hurtled from the underbrush, tusked   10
and ready for battle.

The name he gave me stuck
me to him. He did it to comfort me,
for not being first.

Mornings, while he slept,   15
I got away. Pickerel
hopped on the branches above me.
Only spider accompanied me,

nosing everywhere,
running up to lick my hand.   20

Poor finch. I suppose I was
woe to him—

the way he'd come looking for me,
not wanting either of us
to be ever alone.   25

But to myself I was
palomino
     raven
          fox . . .

I strung words   30
by their stems and wore them
as garlands on my long walks.

The next day
I'd find them withered.

I liked change.   35

1985

    Eve has decided that Adam does not understand language, a particular problem because Adam has been given the task of naming the animals. She feels Adam has mixed up trout and elephant, dog and spider, dove and mole, that Adam has not looked deeply enough into the meaning and feeling of words. Eve is a poet, in love with change, aware of the slipperiness of the meaning of words, and the appeal of the *sounds* of language. Eve likes to wear words as adornment—stringing them together as flower garlands—completely aware of their ephemeral qualities.

When you read this poem, you accept Eve's eyes as your own and begin to perceive the world of language and the act of naming in a different way. Words whose meaning you ordinarily take for granted—*lion, dove, elephant, trout, pickerel, spider, finch,*—suddenly become ambiguous. You begin to see the old story in a new way. Because we associate these animals' names with absolute animal forms, in a sense we become as intransigent as Adam, while we simultaneously are delighted by Eve's creativity. We are both Adam the absolutist, the powerful name-giver, and Eve the relativist, the name-changer—and suddenly in the final line ("I liked change") we hear hints of a distant but certain danger. Eve is rebelling against Adam's authority, and the snake, who will tempt both Adam and Eve to ignore God's authority, begins to rustle subtly in the grass. The poem presents the familiar story of the Fall in the Garden of Eden, but the poet has upset our usual way of remembering that story so that we can experience it as if for the very first time. In the process we also see the power that the act of naming gives—and its arbitrariness.

Poetry uses language to do more than present facts. If you attempt to paraphrase a poem, you will find that poetry does not translate into prose; a paraphrase of a poem will never be the same as the poem itself. In a short poem, Emily Dickinson has offered a definition of poetry more profound than any prose statement could hope to be.

EMILY DICKINSON

[TELL ALL THE TRUTH BUT TELL IT SLANT]   8

Tell all the Truth but tell it slant—
Success in Circuit lies
Too bright for our infirm Delight
The Truth's superb surprise

As Lightning to the Children eased   5
With explanation kind
The Truth must dazzle gradually
Or every man be blind—

1945

The methods of poetry are sometimes the methods of indirection—of telling the truth, but telling it slant—of presenting an old picture at a new angle—of looking carefully at a small section of experience rather than attempting to take in all of human experience in one huge breath. It is through the details, the particulars, the well-chosen examples in poetry that readers can recreate a poetic experience for themselves. Too much light all at once can blind, but a flash of light at just the right moment can reveal a portion of a landscape ordinarily not seen.

THE CONCRETENESS OF POETRY

A focus on the concrete is one way to "tell it slant." Poetry chooses the specific over the general, the concrete over the abstract. Feel the difference in the effects of the following poems—one of which presents experience in concrete language, and one of which relies on abstract expression.

EDGAR ALLAN POE

FROM DREAMS   9

Oh! that my young life were a lasting dream!
My spirit not awakening, till the beam
Of an Eternity should bring the morrow.
Yes! tho' that long dream were of hopeless sorrow,
'T were better than the cold reality   5
Of waking life, to him whose heart must be,
And hath been still, upon the lovely earth,
A chaos of deep passion, from his birth.
But should it be—that dream eternally
Continuing—as dreams have been to me   10
In my young boyhood—should it thus be given,
'T were folly still to hope for higher Heaven.

1827

ROBERT FROST

THE OFT-REPEATED DREAM   10

(*From* "The Hill Wife")

She had no saying dark enough
  For the dark pine that kept
Forever trying the window-latch
  Of the room where they slept.

The tireless, but ineffectual hands   5
  That with every futile pass
Made the great tree seem as a little bird
  Before the mystery of glass!

It never had been inside the room,
  And only one of the two   10
Was afraid in an oft-repeated dream
  Of what the tree might do.

1916

Notice that the poem by Poe relies almost completely on abstract words: *life, dream, spirit, Eternity, sorrow, reality, heart, chaos, passion, birth, boyhood,* and *heaven.* These words cannot be visualized; rather, they present general concepts that discourage you from experiencing the poem in any particular, specific way. In fact, you probably would push the poem aside after the third line because the poem does not invite you into an experience. Such a poem will never engage your imagination. Recall the tree falling in the forest, and consider whether a poem that excludes readers is really a poem. In order to "be," a poem must actively involve a reader.

Of course, you as the reader also have an obligation to attend fully to the poem's images, a task made easier in Frost's poem, which invites you directly into a nightmare. Notice the specific, concrete images: *the dark pine, the window-latch, the room where they slept, the tireless . . . hands, a little bird, glass.* The poem contains abstract words, too (notice, for example, *mystery*), but these are anchored by an association with the concrete images. The dark pine that brushes and scrapes across the glass of the window seems in the young woman's dreams like hands trying to open the window-latch, "tireless, but ineffectual," and like a small bird flying into the sky's reflection in a windowpane. The images of this poem should allow you to recreate the scene yourself, until in the final stanza, you actually feel the fear the poet describes.

T. S. Eliot described the way concrete language works in poetry. He said,

> the only way of expressing emotion in the form of art is by finding an "objective correlative"; in other words, a set of objects, a situation, a chain of events which shall be the formula of that particular emotion; such that when the external facts, which must terminate in a sensory experience, are given, the emotion is immediately evoked. (T. S. Eliot, *Selected Essays,* New York: Harcourt Brace, 1932)

Eliot's **objective correlative** is simply another way of saying that the emotion a poem evokes in a reader depends completely upon the concrete images in that poem. Of course, Eliot's emphasis in this statement is on the creative process experienced by the poet as he creates the poem. When we begin to consider the reader as co-creator of the poem, we must shift the emphasis slightly in Eliot's definition. The reader brings experience to the poem—his or her own set of associations with the images of the poem—and these may or may not be what the poet had in mind when writing the poem. What happens to a reader as he encounters a poem depends on his own set of personal circumstances, his background, his culture, the mood he is in at the moment. There are many variables, but if the poem contains concrete images, one thing is certain: the reader will see and respond to them—and it is at that point that a grouping of words, lines, and stanzas finally becomes a poem.

Often a writer will base a poem on an experience he knows is universally shared. The meaning of the following poem, for example, depends on the reader's experience of receiving junk mail.

FRANK MANLEY

DEAD LETTERS 11

The safety deposit box
Had a hole in it
Plugged up
With a note that said
There wasn't anything here in the first place 5

And that was it
Except for some used furniture
Only a drunk would haul away
Or St. Vincent de Paul's
Or a drunk working for St. Vincent de Paul's 10

I cleaned out the apartment
Had the mail forwarded
The unpaid last few months of his life
And then one night on the parapet—

No. 15
That's not right.
That was later.

The first letter I got from my father
After he died
Was from New Guinea 20
It said
The natives are starving Frank
Waiting for parachutes
Send five dollars
Quick 25

A week later from Guatemala
The letter said
This is no vacation Frank
I am in the mountains

With Camilo Torres   30
We have bombed the President's Palace
We sleep in ancient ruins
And wait for government trucks to pass
Send five dollars in care of the Melvilles

In Cuba   35
In Cuernavaca with Ivan Illich
In Baltimore at Jonah House
My father was there
Shuffling to Selma
Paying bond   40
Hustling votes in Mississippi
Getting killed and buried under a dam
Walking down a road alone
Tar hot under his feet
The do-rag tied in knots on his head   45
Waiting for the sniper

While ten nuns in Savannah Georgia
Discalced Carmelites eighty years old
Were praying in shifts
Perpetually   50
Twenty-four hours a day
For the repose of his soul
My father among them scribbling furiously

Send more money Frank
Wire it collect   55
Write a check on the back of this holy picture
On the calendar
Count the days of your life
The poor are bleeding to death
The poor are in jail with no one to help them   60
The children are dying Frank
They are brain damaged

They are burned to death in frying pans
By parents
Who were burned to death in frying pans   65
They are beaten by fathers
Who can't find work

While all the cars in the world
Creep up on New York City
The cars are brain damaged Frank   70
Send five dollars

Quick
Here's a scapular
Three hundred and sixty-five Masses a year
Visits to the Blessed Sacrament   75
Novenas litanies
Thirty years plenary indulgence

In every letter to the dead
From every otherwordly
Catholic charity   80
He ever sent five dollars to
My father's restless spirit
Roams the world
Crying
List list oh list   85

Like the other night on the parapet
Rumors of invasion
A blood-red moon
Carousing in the palace
Far below   90
Silence darkness
And there beyond the battlements
The very shape and gesture of his thought
He spoke to me in his native tongue

I could a tale unfold   95
He said
Whose lightest word
Would harrow up thy soul
Freeze thy young blood
Make thy two eyes   100
Like stars
To start from their spheres
Thy knotted and combined locks to part
And each particular hair
To stand on end   105
Like quills upon the fretful porcupine

> But this eternal blazon must not be
> To ears of flesh and blood
> List list oh list
> If ever thou didst thy dear father love   110
> Send five dollars
>
> And I said
> In the same language
> Rest, rest, perturbèd spirit
> But I thought to myself   115
> Oh cursed spite that ever I was born to set it right
> And then I thought
> Nay
> Come
> Let's go together
> *1980*

The son in this poem is settling the estate of his deceased father. He closes up the house, sells the furniture, and takes care of all the necessary business details (lines 1–13), and then one day feels that his father is attempting to communicate with him from beyond the grave, the "letters" from his father appearing in the form of personal appeals from charitable organizations his father had contributed to during his lifetime (lines 18ff. and 78–85). The letters keep coming, and they seem to be addressed now to the son (lines 22, 28, 54, 61).

The poem depends upon the reader's experience with mail—and even if you have never received a request from a charity, you certainly will have received computer-generated advertising flyers, insurance information, or subscription solicitations. You will know what this sort of experience feels like, and you will then most likely feel the same jolt the poet describes when suddenly these letters become personal—and in fact seem to be his father's own words telling him of the suffering in the world—the suffering to which he as a son must respond as the father evidently had—in five-dollar increments—throughout his life.

This poem requires even more from you than an understanding and experience with junk mail, however, for the son who speaks in "Dead Letters" alludes to another father and son—Shakespeare's Hamlet and his murdered father, the King. In act 1, scene 4, of the play, the father's ghost appears on a parapet to goad Hamlet into seeking revenge for his death. In Frank Manley's poem, the son feels a restlessness in his own father's spirit—a restlessness which forces him into seeing overt connections between himself and Hamlet:

> I cleaned out the apartment
> Had the mail forwarded
> The unpaid last few months of his life
> And then one night on the parapet—

Manley uses the experience of Hamlet to deepen his own understanding of the combination of feelings he is experiencing: his grief over his father's death, the frustration he feels in the face of it, and his inability to act according to his father's wishes. Although most readers would understand the poet's allusion to and pun on dead letters, not all readers would bring to the poem an experience with Shakespeare enabling them to be aware of these echoes of *Hamlet*. But even if you do not immediately understand the Hamlet allusions, you are still aware, if you are a careful reader, that Manley's language changes at certain points—that it partakes much less of twentieth-century idiom and speech patterns, that it is a language one normally associates with an older, more heroic age:

> In every letter to the dead
> From every otherworldly
> Catholic charity
> He ever sent five dollars to
> My father's restless spirit
> Roams the world
> Crying
> List list oh list

List is an archaic form of *listen* and serves as an indicator that the poem is about to veer in another direction, which it does immediately in the next stanza when the father's ghost appears on the parapet. Is this the narrator's father or Hamlet's? In a way, it is both, and the reader begins to understand that the narrator is using one experience to explain another. Finally, the ghost begins to speak Hamlet's words, straight from Shakespeare.

> I could a tale unfold
> He said
> Whose lightest word
> Would harrow up thy soul
> Freeze thy young blood
> Make thy two eyes
> Like stars
> To start from their spheres
> Thy knotted and combined locks to part
> And each particular hair
> To stand on end
> Like quills upon the fretful porcupine
> But this eternal blazon must not be
> To ears of flesh and blood
> List list oh list
> If ever thou didst thy dear father love
> Send five dollars

Notice how the twentieth-century phrase shows up in the last line, attaining an ironic, comic edge because it appears in the midst of Elizabethan English. The speaker now explains how he finally is able to relate to this ghost.

> And I said
> In the same language
> Rest, rest, perturbed spirit
> But I thought to myself
> Oh cursed spite that ever I was born to set it right
> And then I thought
> Nay
>
> Come
>
> Let's go together.

The speaker discovers new connections with his father and is finally reconciled to him and to his death in these last lines.

If you have lost your own father, you will read this poem more personally than someone who has not. As a reader you will always bring all of your life experiences to a reading of a literary text. A poem can be read on many levels, but the more you bring to it—other literature you have read, your own experience of life's joys and tragedies, biographical and historical information—the more likely you will be to create a solid and rich reading of a poetic text. At any rate, you experience a poem first through its concrete language, which opens your imagination and engages your intellect so that you can create a personal reading.

THE SUBJECTS OF POETRY

Any fact, image, or subject can find its way into a poetic line because the subjects of poetry include death, birth, love, hate, God, truth, beauty, good, evil, and anything else you can imagine. A poem does not consider these subjects in the abstract, however. It works instead by presenting one or more specific and concrete objects or situations.

There is no limit, therefore, to appropriate subjects for poetry. One can write about the death of a father, as Frank Manley did, or the uncurling of a single leaf in spring. On the one hand a poem like "Lines Composed a Few Miles above Tintern Abbey" (540), by William Wordsworth deals with the exalted subjects of nature and morality, but other poems—good poems—may present experiences which at first and even second glances do not seem at all exalted.

JOHN UPDIKE

DOG'S DEATH   12

She must have been kicked unseen or brushed by a car.
Too young to know much, she was beginning to learn
To use the newspapers spread on the kitchen floor
And to win, wetting there, the words, "Good dog! Good dog!"

We thought her shy malaise was a shot reaction.   5
The autopsy disclosed a rupture in her liver.
As we teased her with play, blood was filling her skin
And her heart was learning to lie down forever.

Monday morning, as the children were noisily fed
And sent to school, she crawled beneath the youngest's bed.   10
We found her twisted and limp but still alive.
In the car to the vet's, on my lap, she tried

To bite my hand and died. I stroked her warm fur
And my wife called in a voice imperious with tears.
Though surrounded by love that would have upheld her,   15
Nevertheless she sank and, stiffening, disappeared.

Back home, we found that in the night her frame
Drawing near to dissolution, had endured the shame
Of diarrhoea and had dragged across the floor
To a newspaper carelessly left there. Good dog.   20

1969

    The death of a pet is often the occasion for sentimental, clichéd verse, but Updike's approach is direct, even graphic, using what one would ordinarily consider "unpoetic language"—a plain style infused with an almost matter-of-fact tone. He presents the facts of the situation—that the dog was only recently house-trained, that her liver ruptured, that after the children had breakfast, the husband and wife found the dog under the bed, that she died in the car on the way to the veterinarian's office, that when they returned home, they discovered that the dog had been sick in the night and had been a "good dog," finding a stray newspaper. The poem reveals the irony of the dog's situation—that in learning to live with humans, she was also rehearsing her death. This is a poem, then, about "disappearing," a poem about death, but along the way Updike has used such prosaic words and phrases as "shot reaction" and "diarrhoea" to waylay any possible veering toward sentimentality, which always kills verse.

As another example of poetry's inclusive nature, "Walking in the Snow" is a poem which accepts the challenge posed by a phrase from an academic journal. Notice the way the epigraph from *College English*, a journal, provides the subject matter for the poem.

DAVID WAGONER

WALKING IN THE SNOW   13

". . . if the author had said, 'Let us put on appropriate galoshes,' there could, of course, have been no poem. . ."

— An analysis of Elinor Wylie's "Velvet Shoes,"
College English, March 1948, p. 319.

Let us put on appropriate galoshes, letting them flap open,
And walk in the snow.
The eyes have fallen out of the nearest snowman;
It slumps in its shadow,
And the slush at the curb is gray as the breasts of gulls.   5
As we slog together
Past arbors and stiff trees, all knocked out cold
At the broken end of winter,
No matter what may be falling out of the sky
Or blowing sideways   10
Against our hearts, we'll make up our own weather.
Love, stamping our galoshes,
Let's say something inappropriate, something flat
As a scholar's ear
And, since this can't be a poem, something loud   15
And pointless, leading nowhere
Like our foot prints ducking and draking in the snow
One after the other.

1976

The poem is, tongue-in-cheek, about how a poem cannot be written about "appropriate galoshes," but the poet seems to have managed handily to do the impossible. The point is, of course, that the subject matter of poetry is anything the poet writes and the reader reads. There was a time when this was not the case, but today almost anything is acceptable—so long as it is interesting and fresh.

CHAPTER 2

THE POEM AND THE SENSES

In everyday life, you are not always aware that your senses are receiving impressions. You read the morning newspaper in a bright kitchen filled with the aroma of coffee brewing. Turning the newspaper pages still damp from the dew, you sip a steaming mug of coffee and feel the sun warm the back of the chair. The dog begins to whine to be let out. Your senses are working—sight, hearing, touch, smell, taste—but sometimes you are hardly aware of them.

Poetry, on the other hand, relies on your conscious awareness of sensory response. Poetry awakens first your senses and then your feelings and thoughts. In fact, one could argue that your *senses* must actually awaken the *poem*, making it a personal, individual experience. For this reason, when approaching a poem for a quick, first-time read-through, you should be alert for the *sensory images* (mental pictures or vivid descriptions) to which your imagination will respond quickly, becoming gradually more emotionally and intellectually involved in the poem.

SIGHT

Visual images are of primary importance in helping you respond imaginatively to a poem. Notice how completely you can "see" the scene described in this poem.

WILLIAM CARLOS WILLIAMS

THE RED WHEELBARROW   14

so much depends
upon

a red wheel
barrow

glazed with rain   5
water

beside the white
chickens

1923

The poem possesses even more vibrancy than a color photograph. One sees the red wheelbarrow—shiny with slickness—and the bright, white chickens standing next to it. The colors splash across the page, making the picture seem starkly real. The second, third, and fourth stanzas each contain one image and in this way the poem has isolated and emphasized the various parts of a visual experience. Your imagination creates a unified mental picture of the scene. You see it as if it were a photograph.

But is the poem entirely visual? Does the poet merely present images and then stand back for the reader's recreation of the scene? Look again at the curious first stanza: "so much depends / upon" this juxtaposition of images and colors, it says. Just what depends upon it depends, of course, on the reader's experience. These first words, which present no images, indicate that the scene is significant for some reason, which may not be immediately apparent to the reader, but the reader is called upon to *make it significant.* The poem begins with an abstract assertion which challenges you to use the rest of the poem to clarify its initial statement. As you reread the poem, you begin to understand that merely entering the scene of the poem—seeing its color, life, and contrast, and letting its beauty and simplicity impress you—that alone is significant. The images, which in another context might seem ordinary, here in collaboration with each other become infused with something special, something that makes the moment insightful. The mere act of seeing this scene is what is so significant.

Most poems contain visual effects because the sense of sight, barring unusual handicaps on the part of the reader, is the primary means by which we experience the world around us. The poet who has had the most influence on literature written in English is Shakespeare, who fills his poetry with concrete, visual images.

WILLIAM SHAKESPEARE

SONNET 130   15
[MY MISTRESS' EYES ARE NOTHING LIKE THE SUN]

My mistress' eyes are nothing like the sun;
Coral is far more red than her lips' red:
If snow be white, why then her breasts are dun;
If hairs be wires, black wires grow on her head.
I have seen roses damasked, red and white,   5
But no such roses see I in her cheeks;
And in some perfumes is there more delight
Than in the breath that from my mistress reeks.
I love to hear her speak, yet well I know
That music hath a far more pleasing sound;   10
I grant I never saw a goddess go,
My mistress, when she walks, treads on the ground.
And yet, by heaven, I think my love as rare
As any she belied with false compare.

1609

    In describing his mistress, Shakespeare refuses to use any of the stock visual images that permeated the courtly love poetry of his day. Instead, he paints a realistic, nonidealized picture of her: her eyes do not sparkle, her lips are not red, and her hair is not gold wires (an image often used in Renaissance poetry) but black wires. But, he says, he loves her.

    The poem is built so much on visual images that by the last line the reader has created a surprisingly complete picture of the mistress in spite of the clichés, which ordinarily would exclude the reader from the experience. That is because Shakespeare uses the clichés ironically, showing how they are conventional but in some ways dishonest forms of human discourse. By reversing the usual, hackneyed comparisons, Shakespeare invites you as reader, based upon your own experience, to form a mental picture of a real woman, not one idealized into abstraction.

HEARING

    Poetry's "sound effects," its aural qualities, do not merely provide adornment but contribute in major ways to its meaning. Two different but related uses of sound effects deserve to be mentioned (see also Chapter 5).

SONNET 130 3 *dun:* dull, greyish brown. 5 *damasked:* woven with rich patterns of color. 8 *reeks:* exhales.

Poems often use various sounds as subject matter: the singing of birds, the crunch of boots on top of snow, or, as the following portion of a longer poem illustrates, the slurping of a dog drinking water.

DENISE LEVERTOV

FROM SIX VARIATIONS 16

III
Shlup, shlup, the dog
as it laps up
water
makes intelligent
music, resting   5
now and then to
take breath in irregular
measure.

1961

One hears the dog's "shlup" and his occasional breath before he begins drinking again. The "irregular measure" of the sound also echoes in the line length, which may seem erratic, but which suggests breaths irregularly taken.

But poems do more than describe sounds. When people speak of poetry's "music," they are usually referring to the *sounds* of poetic language. Most poets would much prefer for their poems to be read aloud, to be heard, because then the sounds of the words presenting the images can contribute to the listener's interpretation. This Updike poem is one that demands to be read aloud.

JOHN UPDIKE

PLAYER PIANO 17

My stick fingers click with a snicker
And, chuckling, they knuckle the keys;
Light-footed, my steel feelers flicker
And pluck from these keys melodies.

My paper can caper; abandon   5
Is broadcast by dint of my din,
And no man or band has a hand in
The tones I turn on from within.

At times I'm a jumble of tumbles,
At others I'm light like the moon,   10
But never my numb plunker fumbles,
Misstrums me, or tries a new tune.

1958

The poem is not just *about* a player piano; it *is* a player piano speaking in its clunky, thumping, plucky rhythms and sounds. The poem *becomes* the piano, and the reader's ear responds to the sound effects. Note, for example, the rhyme in each line: "My *stick* fingers *click* with a *snicker*," or "At *times I'm* a *jumble* of *tumbles*," or "My *paper* can *caper*." The playfulness of rhythm, rhyme, **alliteration** (repetition of an initial consonant sound) and **assonance** (the repetition of similar vowel sounds) pulls the lines forward until suddenly the poem stops and the room is left echoing with the final words that suggest the piano's artlessness. It may be perfect and precise in its music (just as the poem's rhyme and rhythm are even and predictable), but it can never vary its tune, express emotion, make interesting mistakes, or be anything other than a machine.

Sometimes a poet will purposely create irregular rhythms or imperfect rhymes. In the following poem, no two of the words rhyme perfectly; their effect is to unbalance the reader.

WILFRED OWEN

ARMS AND THE BOY   18

Let the boy try along this bayonet-blade
How cold steel is, and keen with hunger of blood;
Blue with all malice, like a madman's flash;
And thinly drawn with famishing for flesh.

Lend him to stroke these blind, blunt bullet-leads   5
Which long to nuzzle in the hearts of lads,
Or give him cartridges of fine zinc teeth,
Sharp with the sharpness of grief and death.

For his teeth seem for laughing round an apple.
There lurk no claws behind his fingers supple;   10
And God will grow no talons at his heels,
Nor antlers through the thickness of his curls.

1946

Blade and *blood, flash* and *flesh, bullet-leads* and *lads, teeth* and *death*—these are odd combinations of words, not rhyming exactly, and providing uneasy connections. Why does the poet use rhyme to link such odd words? What, for example do "bullet-leads" have to do with "lads," especially since "lads" suggests rollicking games and schooldays? The reader feels uncomfortable making these connections—precisely the point of the poem, which contrasts armed violence with the gentleness of the boy. The imperfect rhyme reinforces the mood created by the images and subtly works to unsettle the reader.

THE OTHER SENSES

Your eyes do more than record visual detail for you. They also encourage you to experience the world through your other senses—touch, smell, and taste. The visual image of a cow on a July afternoon, swatting the flies away with its tail, evokes other sensory memories and associations. You can imagine the drone of crickets, the pungent odor of cow and stagnant water, the heavy heat of the day—even though none of these details is described directly.

You read a description of a pitcher of lemonade, filled with ice and garnished with mint, and you can almost taste it and almost feel its coolness sliding down your throat, the moisture from the glass dampening your palms. You see a picture of a boy mowing a lawn and you can just about hear the rough hum of the mower and smell the freshly cut grass.

Although poetry involves sight and hearing most directly, the other senses—their associations and memories—also help you to experience a poem. Consider, for example, the beginning stanza of John Keats' "The Eve of St. Agnes" (316), considered by many to be one of the most successful poetic depictions of frigid weather in the English language.

> St. Agnes' Eve—Ah, bitter chill it was!
> The owl, for all his feathers, was a-cold;
> The hare limped trembling through the frozen grass,
> And silent was the flock in woolly fold:
> Numb were the Beadsman's fingers, while he told   5
> His rosary, and while his frosted breath,
> Like pious incense from a censer old,
> Seemed taking flight for heaven, without a death,
> Past the sweet Virgin's picture, while his prayer he saith.

Images of cold permeate this stanza: the freezing owl, the hare limping, not racing, through the stiff grass, the sheep silent and huddled, the Beadsman's numbed fingers, and the clouds of his frosty breath. Even if you read this poem on a hot August evening heavy with humidity and the smell of neighborhood barbecues, even then you can imagine the "bitter chill," because the images suggesting the feeling are concrete and appeal to your imagination.

The sensations experienced through touch, smell, and taste often cannot be described directly. Try, for example to describe the sensation of the wind against your hand held out the window of a moving car and you'll probably find yourself comparing it to what it feels *like*. For instance, you may say that it feels *as if* you had pushed your hand into water gushing from a hose. Or maybe your hand feels *as if* it were riding at the tail end of a kite. But notice how even the images which describe these feelings indirectly are anchored in concrete, visual detail.

In the following poem, one poet has tried to describe what it feels like to be a growing child. As a reader, you see and then feel the splitting of the thin pajamas, the cotton weak from frequent washings. You see and then feel what it must be like to have a body stretching in growth, reaching up, the neck craning. You see and then feel what it is like to be a six-year-old who is experiencing a growth-spurt, who is growing so fast that his mother cannot keep him in clothes. In fact, in this poem, the child seems to be growing out of his clothes as we watch.

SHARON OLDS

SIZE AND SHEER WILL   19

The fine, green pajama cotton,
washed so often it is paper-thin and
iridescent, has split like a sheath
and the glossy white naked bulbs of
Gabriel's toes thrust forth like crocus   5
this early Spring. The boy is growing
as fast as he can, elongated
wrists dangling, lean meat
showing between the shirt and the belt.
If there were a rack to stretch himself, he would   10
strap his slight body to it.
If there were a machine to enter,
skip the next ten years and be
sixteen immediately, this boy would
do it. All day long he cranes his   15
neck, like a plant in the dark with a single
light above it, or a sailor under
tons of green water, longing
for the surface, for his rightful life.

1984

Notice how the comparisons form essential links for the reader who may have forgotten exactly what it feels like to wear clothes too small: "the fine green pajama cotton . . . has split like a sheath" and the child's toes peek out "like crocus this early Spring," appropriate because crocus propels itself through half-frozen soil, pushing its sturdy leaves and small, hearty flower to emerge earlier than any other flower in the spring. The child "cranes his / neck, like a plant in the dark with a single / light above it." The reader becomes plant and child all at once in feeling the stretch in this image. At the end of the poem you can actually feel the terrible weight of water as you struggle for the surface and fresh air.

"A Knowledge of Water" is another poem in which the visual image contains within it other sensory associations central to the experience.

JUDSON MITCHAM

A KNOWLEDGE OF WATER   20

I love the way the cows go down to the water
and wade in deep, till the nostrils rest
on the pond's copper film. In July,
when the oak shade bakes like a shut loft,
all the cattle walk off into coolness, feel   5
their heavy meat lift.

        So the body
they drink from consumes them, becomes
a eucharist busy with flies. This stink
of pond slime, piss, and rotting possum   10
swallows till their giant taw eyes
gaze across the surface, where the light
changes every move.

        And I believe
they can nearly take it in, like a drink,   15
the ripple, slope, fence, pines, sky,
and they walk from the pond onto earth
with a knowledge they will bear,
crossing dry pastures at dusk, single file,
their wet flesh heavier than before.   20

1986

    This is what it must feel like to be a cow on a July day so hot that the shade from the oak tree feels like the stale, hot air of a windowless attic. The poem shows the cows walking into the pond until much of their weight is submerged, their nostrils resting on the surface of the water which not only dissipates the heat in the stagnant, slimy water, but also lightens the weight of the meat the cattle carry around with them. The reader feels the lightening of the heavy air and the heavy bodies in the cool of the pond, and later at dusk, the sudden heaviness of the flesh as the cows climb out of the pond and go home again.

Notice also the smells in this poem. A July day in the middle of a pond filled with cows smells like "pond slime, piss, and rotting possum." It also smells like wet cow and fresh dung, even though the smells are not directly described in the poem. But the reader's imagination fills in the gaps. It is this fundamental grounding in the senses that allows the reader to create the poem. In fact, you allow the poem to enter your consciousness through senses that ordinarily work unconsciously. But when you are reading a poem, these senses—and the images they evoke—are constantly at work. It is as difficult to imagine a poem without sensory images as it is to imagine life without the senses.

SYNESTHESIA

"All eyes be muffled," Keats writes in "The Eve of St. Agnes," suggesting the castle guards' lack of wariness on a night of feasting and revelry. By using the word *muffled* to describe eyes rather than using it in its ordinary association with ears, Keats appeals to two senses rather than one, upsetting your expectations, and thereby encouraging a new and more intense sensory experience—probably because the surprise of it has made you pay attention. This poetic device of using one sense to describe another is called **synesthesia.** In "The Bells," Edgar Allan Poe uses images of sight and perhaps touch to describe sound: the pealing of wedding bells—"molten-golden notes"—creates a "liquid ditty." In "Angel," James Merrill writes of "the cold sun pounding on the sea," stirring together images of sight, touch, and hearing.

Poets frequently claim that poems come to them not as ideas but as individual images which they shape and expand in order to discover meaning. As the reader, you must also begin with the sensory image, allowing it to work on the imagination, allowing it to adhere to other senses and other images, until finally it develops the world of the poem. In fact, you will not be ready to consider the meaning of poetry in a more formal sense until you have fully experienced it—and this experience depends on the extent of your sensory involvement as you read a poem.

CHAPTER 3

FIRST STEP
READING A POEM INTUITIVELY

It is important to read a poem first for its sensuous effects, for its play of images, for the concrete experience it allows you to create. Avoid thinking of poetry-reading as a mechanical exercise something like problem-solving in mathematics—a task to be accomplished quickly and then left behind. That is not the way poetry operates, although it is the way some readers operate on poetry. Eventually these readers push poetry aside because they have ceased to be re-creators of the poems they read, and the poems have, understandably, ceased to interest them.

Poets speak of the creation of poetry as a playful, frenetic, haphazard compulsion. Maxine Kumin describes the creative process this way:

> I set down everything I can think of, everything that flies into my head, even though it may seem terribly digressive. I try to get it all because I'm afraid that if I don't get it all down on the page, it will evanesce and blow away. I tend to get a whole chunk that looks like prose, maybe three or four pages of it. While that's going on, I can already sense that certain of those things are lines, and then the next time through, I can begin to pick out the lines. By the end of the second session with the poem, I can see the order, the stanzaic pattern, if there's going to be one, and so on. It can happen the other way, too. Once in a while a poem will start with a compelling rhythm or line or just a phrase that you can't get rid of, and the poem will come from there.[1]

In its early stages, writing poetry is usually not an orderly, rational, controlled process. Similarly, in your first reading of a poem, you should be alert for chances for involvement, allowing yourself the experience of discovery rather than immediately attempting to impose a premature inter-

[1]"An Interview at Interlochen," *To Make a Prairie* (Ann Arbor: University of Michigan Press, 1979), pp. 35–36.

pretation. Writing in 1817, the poet John Keats advised fellow writers to be the passive and objective recipients of truth and beauty. **Negative capability** is what he termed this poetic ability to accept whatever the senses receive. The reader must likewise learn to trust intuition.

A reader must also be flexible, because poems often defy expectations. An approach that helps you read one poem will not necessarily help you read another. The poems of John Ashbery, for example, may be read as if they were abstract paintings in which color, texture, sound, and line wash over the reader. In his acceptance speech for the National Book Award, Ashbery said that

> for as long as I have been publishing poetry, it has been criticized as "difficult" and "private," though I never meant for it to be. At least, I wanted its privateness to suggest the ways in which all of us are private and alone. . . . And I wanted the difficulty to reflect the difficulty of reading, any kind of reading, which is both a pleasant and a painful experience since we are temporarily giving ourselves to something which may change us.

Consider, for example, an Ashbery poem unsettling in its description of a stranger approaching through time and space to accost you at a certain moment in a certain way.

JOHN ASHBERY

AT NORTH FARM   21

Somewhere someone is traveling furiously toward you,
At incredible speed, traveling day and night,
Through blizzard and desert heat, across torrents, through narrow
    passes.
But will he know where to find you,
Recognize you when he sees you,   5
Give you the thing he has for you?

Hardly anything grows here,
Yet the granaries are bursting with meal,
The sacks of meal piled to the rafters.
The streams run with sweetness, fattening fish;   10
Birds darken the sky. Is it enough
That the dish of milk is set out at night,
That we think of him sometimes,
Sometimes and always, with mixed feelings?

1984

Is the stranger a future friend, lover, enemy? Is it perhaps Death? Or could it be Life in the form of an unborn child? None of these questions is answered. What is certain is that the images, which suggest feelings of loneliness and isolation in the midst of a landscape of great abundance (granaries bursting, fat fish, dish of milk), are eerily evocative, inviting the reader to sit in front of them for a while, reading and rereading, as one would sit in front of a painting at an art gallery, observing, allowing the images to collect and coalesce. After a while, the experience of reading the poem becomes something like the experience of dreaming, in which strangely juxtaposed images seem to defy analysis but do evoke feelings and contain private meaning for the individual reader.

A different kind of poem is William Blake's "The Sick Rose," which immediately forces the reader to begin to ask questions.

WILLIAM BLAKE

THE SICK ROSE   22

O Rose, thou art sick!
The invisible worm
That flies in the night,
In the howling storm,

the Chappy
Police

Has found out thy bed   5
Of crimson joy,
And his dark secret love
Does thy life destroy.

1794

The first emphatic line—"O Rose, thou art sick!"—provides a challenge to you to respond immediately to the poem's images. The rose is not ill or indisposed or diseased; it is *sick,* a word which suggests the rose's desperately critical condition. And the worm is not an ordinary worm, but an "invisible worm / That flies in the night." At this point the active reader should realize that the poem presents images which do not make perfect *literal* sense. You as reader must now begin to consider the implications, the associations and connotations of its images, and perhaps even go outside of the poem to search for other meanings of *rose* and *worm*. For example, the rose is a traditional symbol for youth, beauty, and female sexuality. The worm, on the other hand, is frequently associated with corruption from within, death, and male sexuality. The active reader begins to see that Blake is actually speaking of the destructive nature of sexual passion. The rose as a "bed / Of crimson joy" contains, then, the seeds of its own destruction, its beauty inviting that which will finally consume it. The poem's images will not make everyday sense to you, especially in a first or a second reading, but will force you to look beyond the literal to read the poem the third and fourth times in a different way.

The first readings of a poem, like warm-up exercises before a race, allow you to establish initial connections with the poem—connections that will lead to more analytical reading later. These first impressions do not have to be "correct." Without giving in to extreme fancifulness or eccentricity, they can and should be as individual as the person reading.

Consider the following poem, which was presented to a group of students for a first reading.

JOHN UPDIKE

WINTER OCEAN   23

Many-maned scud-thumper, tub
of male whales, maker of worn wood, shrub-
ruster, sky-mocker, rave!
portly pusher of waves, wind-slave.

1963

The students were asked to jot down their initial responses to the poem. They were cautioned not to be too analytical, just to write reactions, which proved to be varied and colorful. The responses of four students:

1. "Sailboat with weathered wood, pushing against the waves with the wind's strength. Filled with fat men."
2. "Moby-Dick. No—something more. Sailboats on water. Huge sea vessel on rough sea. Also those scrub men on commercials going down drains."
3. "A ship crashing through the water. Overwhelming. 'Big' feeling."
4. One student, who was reading Frederick Buechner's *The Book of Bebb* for another class, wrote: "Bebb. Fat blue whales in the ocean. Comic and a little pompous. Heavy, confusing."

Notice the variety of responses, and yet a certain consistency of theme and image. All students noted the fatness or expansiveness of the imagery, but at the same time they were bringing their individual readings, their current experiences, and their familiarities and ignorances of the sea with them as they responded honestly, directly, to the poem.

The same students were then asked to identify sections or qualities of the poem that touched them in some way, even if they were not sure exactly why or exactly what those sections, those lines, those images meant.

1. "The sounds of the words, the clashing, harsh noises, the terror of the winter ocean."

2. "The 'portly pusher of waves.' The strength."
3. "Defiance: the 'sky-mocker.' Why would one mock the sky? One may as well fight against the ocean."
4. "The 'male whales' and the thick, choppy words."

Notice how these students started from different positions, bringing with them differing experiences in life and in literature, yet seemed to be stirred by the same quality in the poem—the strength, defiance, terror, and underlying masculinity in the imagery.

At this point the students identified personal associations the images in the poem had for them. Notice that the students had already mentioned some personal connections with Bebb and Moby-Dick and even an image from a television commercial. Some other associations were:

1. "Tough-skinned dock workers, foul-mouthed and smelly from hard work and hard drink."
2. "A Winslow Homer painting of men in a boat in the midst of a storm."
3. "Sailing in summer on Lake Harriet."
4. "Ulysses and my dad, whom I see rarely."

These are not universal but particular, highly individual connections. These personal associations, no matter how peculiar or far-fetched, are essential for the first-time reader.

If, however, the students had stopped at this point, they really would not have *read* the poem because they had only just begun to enter into the creative process. They were beginning to form a response to the poem, but they probably did not yet really understand it.

It is helpful for you to consider just why certain words and images of a poem strike you more than others. Is it purely personal response, or could it be that the poem's meaning lies in its most compelling images? It is even possible at this point to speculate about the main idea of the poem—even before considering the elements of poetry (comparisons, rhythm, rhyme, and so on) that have helped this poem find expression. To this end, you need to identify certain words which stir you positively or negatively. The same students were asked to do just this.

1. "All the words turn me off. They seem unapproachable, sharp and cutting, too coarse as well. I don't like their sound, except for 'male whales.' "
2. "The images of decay bother me and yet I like the sounds of the words describing them: 'worn wood,' 'shrub-ruster.' "
3. " 'Wind-slave' is sad, helpless."
4. " 'Portly'—adds dignity or at least an odd pomposity."

These are four different but closely related observations. The first student says he does not like the sounds of the words because they are so harsh, and yet he immediately identifies something he does like: "male whales." Could it be that the student has, this early in his reading, begun to uncover some of the poem's subtleties? In the midst of the poem's heavy words is this liquid rhyme—male/whale—with a long vowel sound and soft consonants. Could the poem, in identifying negative, unpleasant qualities of a winter ocean, also be expressing a more ambivalent feeling? The second student shows an even more overt awareness of her contradictory responses to the words of the poem. The third student, who was impressed in earlier questions with the tone of defiance in certain phrases, now notices the helplessness in the image of "wind-slave." And the fourth student is impressed by the word *portly,* which adds dignity to a primarily destructive picture of the ocean.

What these students have discovered already in their initial, somewhat idiosyncratic responses—and long before they have been asked to write rational explications of the poem—is that the poem contains ambivalence, maybe even contradiction. A winter ocean is not an easy thing, the poem seems to say in its first readings. It is both master and slave, both defiant and helpless, both harsh and comic. For these readers at this point in their experience of the poem, this conclusion is purely speculative. Reading the poem now must become a more analytical testing and connecting of first impressions. Sometimes first impressions are wrong. But probably more often than you realize, you can trust yourself and your associations to point the way for you.

STEPS TO AN INTUITIVE RESPONSE

1. Quickly jot down initial responses to the poem. Do not analyze the poem.
2. What is the most striking part of the poem for you? Which image or quality contains the most interest?
3. With what do you ordinarily associate that image or quality? Any personal connections?
4. Does anything particularly please you or bother you about the poem? Do you react positively or negatively to any of the words or images?
5. What might be the main idea of the poem?

CHAPTER 4

ELEMENTS OF POETRY

Looking out on an expanse of green lawn, you see the roll of the land, the gentle curves around the shoreline of a pond, the shrubs distinctly placed, the line of trees on the horizon. The grass smooths the way for your eye, creating a feeling of order and gracefulness. Or perhaps you look across the street to a field strewn with rubble and weeds, the grass occasionally surfacing in straggles. Bushes grow out of control and under a lone tree is only dirt, no grass.

The individual elements of these scenes work together to create a feeling, an attitude, in the viewer, just as the elements of a poem work *together* to create the whole picture. Those elements can never be separated from the poem as a whole. Symbols or rhyme or meter are never just "put in." They are there to contribute to meaning and in fact *to become* part of the meaning of a poem.

Analysis, which begins with a close and careful reading of the poem, depends upon your familiarity with poetic elements. In an analysis, you identify the elements at work in a poem, separate them from each other, collate them, and observe the ways they are used. As you identify the major images, comparisons, and symbols, and uncover the patterns these elements form in the poem, you will also begin to appreciate other aspects of the poem—its sound effects, rhythm, and form. You will discover how these other elements also operate in the poem and contribute to your experience of the poem.

Formal analysis is neither the beginning nor the end of the creative reading process. It is instead the middle—what occurs between your first response to the poem and your creation of a reading. Your analysis of a poem depends upon what you have already experienced more informally in the poem. First, read the poem following the suggestions presented in Chapters 2 and 3. Then—and only then—will you be ready to proceed to this next stage.

In a way, analysis is the "scientific" stage of poetry reading, during which you will probably find yourself pushing your feelings aside and approaching the poem more objectively than you did at first. In a sense this process "unbuilds" the poem in order to rebuild it again, in much the same way a dressmaker may take apart a worn but favorite piece of clothing in order to create a pattern for a new suit. Once you understand the way a poem is put together, once you have analyzed its various parts, you will be able to see the whole poem more clearly and enjoy it more completely.

METAPHOR AND SIMILE

Comparisons in poetry usually take the form of metaphor or simile. **Metaphor** is an implicit comparison (for example, "the tomatoes are small, red bellies"), and **simile** uses *like* or *as* (for example, "the tomatoes are as fat as babies' bellies"). Metaphor and simile clarify one image, not by looking at it directly but by showing its similarities to another image, similarities which may not be immediately apparent. "All flesh is grass," the Scriptures say, and the reader who encounters that metaphor for the first time may find it puzzling. Clearly, the context of the metaphor means everything in its interpretation, and in this case, the surrounding text explains the comparison.

All flesh is grass,
And all its loveliness is like the flower of the field.
The grass withers, the flower fades,
Because the breath of the Lord blows upon it;
Surely the people are grass.   5
The grass withers, the flower fades,
But the word of our God stands forever.

(Isaiah 40:6–8)

The poet could have said, "people die, but the word of God does not," but that would have been a statement without concrete images, an abstraction without anchors. It would have been neither interesting, memorable, nor beautiful; it would not have contained meaning in quite the same way because it would not have appealed to the imagination of the reader. Through combinations as unlikely as flesh and grass, metaphor challenges the human mind to find connections.

Poets use metaphors and similes not just as clever displays of wit, but to encourage the reader to bring both the **tenor** (the object being described, as in *flesh*) and the **vehicle** (the object used to describe the tenor, as in *grass*) into a new relationship.

The following poem, complete in only two lines, contains one strong metaphor.

EZRA POUND

IN A STATION OF THE METRO 24

The apparition of these faces in the crowd;
Petals on a wet, black bough.

1926

As you read these lines, you may remember a spring morning after a heavy rain. The tree branches were sodden and black, the pale petals of the new blossoms standing out against the charcoal sweep of bark. And suddenly you understand the comparison of petals with pale and beautiful human faces— those few which also stand out in the press of a crowd on a busy morning.

Metaphor and simile force the mind to find similarities between dissimilar things, transferring qualities from the vehicle to the tenor in ways not possible in everyday language. This is a chief reason poetry is more expressive than ordinary language, and also one of the reasons that metaphor is often used to explain human mysteries—such as birth, death, or love—which cannot always be explained in everyday language. Consider the following poem.

W. S. MERWIN

FOR THE ANNIVERSARY OF MY DEATH 25

Every year without knowing it I have passed the day
When the last fires will wave to me
And the silence will set out
Tireless traveller
Like the beam of a lightless star   5

Then I will no longer
Find myself in life as in a strange garment
Surprised at the earth
And the love of one woman
And the shamelessness of men   10
As today writing after three days of rain
Hearing the wren sing and the falling cease
And bowing not knowing to what

1967

Merwin begins with expansive images—the silence of death, light travelling through space—and gradually narrows the focus of the poem to himself in the present. Notice how "silence" becomes a "tireless traveller," a metaphor suggesting the endlessness of the silence of death. The next line is a simile in which the "tireless traveller" is "like the beam of a lightless star." The light cast by stars still reaches earth, the poet says, even though many of the stars are long dead, just as he will be one day. In the next stanza he finds himself "in life as in a strange garment," another simile suggesting that life is not completely comfortable for him—that in fact, sometimes it feels as if he is wearing unfamiliar clothes. In attempting to describe the unimaginable (the mystery of death) and the inexpressible (the surprises of life), he uses metaphors and similes, which push language beyond its everyday meaning.

Try your hand at identifying the metaphors in the following poem. How many does the poem contain? Do they form a pattern of related images?

BABETTE DEUTSCH

FIREWORKS   26

Not guns, not thunder, but a flutter of clouded drums
That announce a fiesta: abruptly, fiery needles
Circumscribe on the night boundless chrysanthemums.
Softly, they break apart, they flake away, where
Darkness, on a svelte hiss, swallows them.   5
Delicate brilliance: a bellflower opens, fades,
In a sprinkle of falling stars.
Night absorbs them
With the sponge of her silence.

1962

EXTENDED METAPHOR AND CONCEIT

In some poems you will find that a poet is not content to use a metaphor once and drop it. Instead, the entire poem will become an elaboration of that metaphor, an **extended metaphor.** Notice how the following poem both describes a wreath and becomes one.

GEORGE HERBERT

A WREATH   27

A wreathed garland of deserved praise,
Of praise deserved unto thee I give,
I give to thee, who knowest all my wayes,
My crooked winding wayes, wherein I live,
Wherein I die, not live: for life is straight,   5

Straight as a line, and ever tends to thee,
To thee, who art more farre above deceit,
Then deceit seems above simplicitie.
Give me simplicitie, that I may live,
So live and like, that I may know, thy wayes,   10
Know them and practise them: then shall I give
For this poore wreath, give thee a crown of praise.

                                                   1633

One makes a wreath by weaving flowers over and around each other, as the poet here attempts to do with his words, repeating words from each line in the following line until the poem itself becomes a wreath. Notice also how the first four lines and the last four lines end with the same words in reverse order, linking beginning and end, making the poem not just a loose-ended garland, but a circle, the "crown of praise" referred to in the final line.

The metaphor of the wreath not only describes the words and structure of the poem, but also informs the content. The poet says he gives this wreath to God, "who knowest all my wayes."

My crooked winding wayes, wherein I live,
Wherein I die, not live: for life is straight,
Straight as a line, and ever tends to thee

Although he would like to go *straight* to God, he realizes that he cannot do that because as a mortal, he is destined to travel in "crooked winding wayes," which lead to death. The poet explores and develops the metaphor so thoroughly that the poem would simply not exist without it.

Another type of metaphor is the **conceit**, an exaggerated comparison, popularized in the seventeenth century by the metaphysical poets, of whom George Herbert and John Donne are the primary representatives. The following poem develops one of the best-known conceits in literature.

JOHN DONNE

A VALEDICTION; FORBIDDING MOURNING   28

As virtuous men passe mildly away,
    And whisper to their soules, to goe,
Whilst some of their sad friends doe say,
    The breath goes now, and some say, no.

So let us melt, and make no noise,   5
   No teare-floods, nor sigh-tempests move,
T'were prophanation of our joyes
   To tell the layetie our love.

Moving of th'earth brings harmes and feares,
   Men reckon what it did and meant,   10
But trepidation of the spheares,
   Though greater farre, is innocent.

Dull sublunary lovers love
   (Whose soule is sense) cannot admit
Absence, because it doth remove   15
   Those things which elemented it.

But we by a love, so much refin'd,
   That our selves know not what it is,
Inter-assured of the mind,
   Care lesse, eyes, lips, hands to misse.   20

Our two soules therefore, which are one,
   Though I must goe, endure not yet
A breach, but an expansion,
   Like gold to ayery thinnesse beate.

If they be two, they are two so   25
   As stiffe twin compasses are two,
Thy soule the fixt foot, makes no show
   To move, but doth, if the'other doe.

And though it in the center sit,
   Yet when the other far doth rome,   30
It leanes and hearkens after it,
   And growes erect, as that comes home.

Such wilt thou be to mee, who must
   Like th'other foot, obliquely runne.
Thy firmnes makes my circle just,   35
   And makes me end, where I begunne.

                                                        1633

A VALEDICTION; FORBIDDING MOURNING 11 *trepidation of the spheares:* quivering of the great concentric spheres that, in the Ptolemaic view of the universe, contained the planets and other heavenly bodies. 13 *sublunary:* literally, "beneath the moon," that is, earthly, and therefore unstable and transitory.

The speaker, in bidding farewell to his lover, cautions her not to cry. He attempts to stop her tears with reason, providing her with various learned metaphors, similes, and analogies which he hopes might convince her to stop crying. The speaker, however, saves the most convincing argument for last, using the conceit that compares himself and his love to the two legs of a geometrical compass. The woman's soul is "the fixt foot," which stays at home in the center, leaning toward the other leg as it "far doth rome." Because of the firmness of her soul, the speaker says, he, "who must / Like th'other foot, obliquely runne," will be able to return home to her once again. She is his support, his center, his beginning and end. This comparison, which seems at first so unpromising—even ridiculous—becomes, as it is explained and elaborated, absolutely convincing. In the context of the speaker's purpose, which is to encourage his lover not to cry, the conceit is also extremely effective. His cleverness, displayed in this conceit, was meant to distract her, to engage her mind so much with his wit that she would momentarily forget about her emotions.

SYNECDOCHE AND METONYMY

Whereas metaphor, simile, and conceit bring together vehicle and tenor, synecdoche and metonymy *divide* a term and replace it with a representative part. In the metaphor, "all flesh is grass," *flesh* stands for all of a person—the entire human body—and by extension all mortal beings. T. S. Eliot, in "The Love Song of J. Alfred Prufrock" (212), describes a crab as "a pair of ragged claws." In these cases the poets are using **synecdoche,** in which a part represents the whole.

WILLIAM BUTLER YEATS

FOR ANNE GREGORY   29

'Never shall a young man
Thrown into despair
By those great honey-coloured
Ramparts at your ear,
Love you for yourself alone   5
And not your yellow hair.'

'But I can get a hair-dye
And set such colour there,
Brown, or black, or carrot
That young men in despair   10
May love me for myself alone
And not my yellow hair.'

'I heard an old religious man
But yesternight declare
That he had found a text to prove   15
That only God, my dear,
Could love you for yourself alone
And not your yellow hair.'

1931

    The poem presents a dialogue between a young girl and an admirer, who insists that the girl's beauty is so extraordinary that it cannot be separated from her very identity. The girl would like to think that men will love her for something other than her physical beauty—that perhaps she could mask it in some way—but the admirer insists that only God could love her for herself.

    Notice how "yellow hair" is a synecdoche in this poem—one beautiful part of the girl standing for the whole of her beauty. Synecdoche allows the reader to focus on the particular and then to generalize from it.

    Metonymy is a related device, in which an object or characteristic associated with the subject is used in place of the subject, as in "the pen is mightier than the sword." Whenever a monarch is referred to as "the crown," or high-ranking military officers are referred to as "the brass," metonymy is at work. Notice how this poem begins:

RICHMOND LATTIMORE

RISE AND SHINE   30

At the big trumpet, we must all put on
our dentures, tie old strings to knees, adjust
shank upon socket, wig to cranium, bust
on ribbed architrave, fastidiously don
our properties, and blink to face the sun.   5
Farewell, dream image, cankered in our dust,
and sweets shrunk in the brain, farewell, we trust.
Uprise, O fragment brethren! We have won—
For, hallelujah, these dry graves are torn!
Thin bugles crash the valley of our bones   10
to rock the vultures wide away and scare
the griffin from his precipice as, worn
and damp, we crawl like grubs from under stones
to scarf our loves in paradisial air.

1957

RISE AND SHINE 4 *architrave:* molding around a door.

As an object associated with Judgment Day, "the big trumpet" operates here as metonymy.

PUN

Puns are useful devices in poetry because they are words and expressions which contain two or more meanings simultaneously, helpful in a genre which requires language to condense meanings in a compact space. Notice how puns pack this short poem with meaning.

A. E. HOUSMAN

EIGHT O'CLOCK   31

He stood, and heard the steeple
  Sprinkle the quarters on the morning town.
One, two, three, four, to market-place and people
  It tossed them down.

Strapped, noosed, nighing his hour,   5
  He stood and counted them and cursed his luck;
And then the clock collected in the tower
  Its strength, and struck.

1922

In describing a clock preparing to strike the hour of eight o'clock, Housman puns on *quarters,* which can refer both to quarter-hours and to the former British coin, the farthing, also called *quarter,* because it was worth one-quarter of a penny. The steeple chimes the familiar quarter-hour pattern of four sets of four notes as casually as quarters are tossed—inconsequential to all but one person who stands "strapped, noosed, nighing his hour" of execution. A miser with the time he has left, he counts the quarters one by one. What he has left the clock finally "collects" as it strikes the hour. Notice how Housman puns on *quarters, collected . . . its strength,* and even *strapped* (as in "strapped for time").

SYMBOL

A well-known poet was once approached by a younger writer seeking a critical reader for her own work. As the young woman handed her poems to the older poet, she apologized for them, saying that she had been so rushed in her preparation that she had not yet had the time to "put the symbols in."

    Unfortunately, that erroneous idea about how symbols operate in poetry is all too common. A poet cannot "put the symbols in" anymore than a reader can "take them out" again. A **symbol** is something that stands for something else. An effective symbol is so much a part of the poem that it cannot be separated from it. Recall, for example, William Blake's "The Sick Rose" (22), in which the rose and the worm must be read first as literal images but almost immediately also begin to operate as symbols. Without the symbols there would be no poem. They *are* the poem.

Certain symbols are familiar because they are used so often. The rose, for example, appears often in poetry as a sign or symbol of transitory beauty, as in "The Sick Rose" and also in the following poem.

WILLIAM CARLOS WILLIAMS

POEM   32

The rose fades
and is renewed again
by its seed, naturally
but where

save in the poem   5
shall it go
to suffer no diminution
of its splendor

1938

Some symbols have been repeated so often in literature, dream, and myth that they lead to immediate associations for the reader. For example, the desert or wasteland usually connotes spiritual barrenness; the sun, energy and power; and rain, fertility and growth, or grief. "Western Wind," a Middle English lyric, relies on these kinds of associations for its meaning.

ANONYMOUS

WESTERN WIND   33

Western wind, when will thou blow?
The small rain down can rain.
Christ, that my love were in my arms,
And I in my bed again.

The speaker requests what he does not have: wind, rain, his love, and his bed, suggesting that perhaps he is far from his home and his love, that the weather has been dry and the air still. He wants his life to start up again—the drought to break, the wind to blow (particularly the western wind, which in the British Isles is the moist wind off the ocean), human connections to return, passions to be experienced. Rain is a sign of life, of purification and of adversity. Here the speaker yearns for "the small rain"—not harsh but gently nourishing, bringing with it fertility, spiritual growth, and the possibility for love to flourish.

Another example of the strength of the symbol occurs in a poem with more frightening implications.

WILLIAM BLAKE

THE TYGER   34

Tyger! Tyger! burning bright
In the forests of the night,
What immortal hand or eye
Could frame thy fearful symmetry?

In what distant deeps or skies   5
Burnt the fire of thine eyes?
On what wings dare he aspire?
What the hand, dare seize the fire?

And what shoulder, & what art,
Could twist the sinews of thy heart?   10
And when thy heart began to beat,
What dread hand? & what dread feet?

What the hammer? what the chain?
In what furnace was thy brain?
What the anvil? What dread grasp   15
Dare its deadly terrors clasp?

When the stars threw down their spears,
And water'd heaven with their tears,
Did he smile his work to see?
Did he who made the Lamb make thee?   20

Tyger! Tyger! burning bright
In the forests of the night,
What immortal hand or eye
Dare frame thy fearful symmetry?

                                                                1794

The poem's power lies in the eerie and uncomfortable symbol of the tiger, traditionally associated with power, cruelty, and wrath. The "forests of the night," the "distant deeps," the "fearful symmetry" of the tiger's stripes, and the "fire" in the tiger's eyes reinforce those initial associations. This creature forged by the hammer, chain, furnace, and hand of some awesome force, inspires terror. While this force is never named directly, it is implied in the question, "Did he who made the Lamb make thee?" The creator of the lamb, traditional symbol of gentleness and meekness, also possesses the power to create something fearfully beautiful, and to smile at it.

Notice the "fearful symmetry" of the poem itself—in which the first and the last stanzas are identical except for one word. To begin with Blake asks, "What immortal hand or eye / *Could* frame thy fearful symmetry?" At the end of the poem he asks, "What immortal hand or eye / *Dare* frame thy fearful symmetry?" The suggestion is that the creator has willed this fearful creation—has in fact taken pride in its creation. The implications are terrifying largely because of the strong images which elaborate the symbol of the tiger.

In a companion poem Blake uses another symbol.

WILLIAM BLAKE

THE LAMB   35

Little Lamb, who made thee?
  Dost thou know who made thee?
Gave thee life & bid thee feed,
By the stream & o'er the mead;
Gave thee clothing of delight,   5
Softest clothing wooly bright;
Gave thee such a tender voice,
Making all the vales rejoice!
  Little Lamb who made thee?
  Dost thou know who made thee?   10

Little Lamb I'll tell thee,
  Little Lamb I'll tell thee!
He is called by thy name,
For he calls himself a Lamb:
He is meek & he is mild,   15
He became a little child:
I a child & thou a lamb,
We are called by his name.
  Little Lamb God bless thee.
  Little Lamb God bless thee.   20

1789

Blake is relying upon the reader's association of the lamb, traditional symbol for innocence and purity, with Christ, the *Agnus Dei,* the Lamb of God.

The two poems, "The Tyger" and "The Lamb," represent two different points of view, one of innocence and the other of terrifying power. The symbols of lamb and tiger directly influence the way you read the language, consider the form, and interpret the tone. Symbols encourage you to move beyond the superficial and experience the poems more fully.

Whether or not it has ever before been used as a symbol, just about any image which a poet uses will contain personal associations and symbolic potential for the individual reader.

WILLIAM BUTLER YEATS

THE SECOND COMING   36

Turning and turning in the widening gyre
The falcon cannot hear the falconer;
Things fall apart; the centre cannot hold;
Mere anarchy is loosed upon the world,
The blood-dimmed tide is loosed, and everywhere   5
The ceremony of innocence is drowned;
The best lack all conviction, while the worst
Are full of passionate intensity.

Surely some revelation is at hand;
Surely the Second Coming is at hand.   10
The Second Coming! Hardly are those words out
When a vast image out of *Spiritus Mundi*
Troubles my sight: somewhere in sands of the desert
A shape with lion body and the head of a man,
A gaze blank and pitless as the sun,   15
Is moving its slow thighs, while all about it
Reel shadows of the indignant desert birds.
The darkness drops again; but now I know
That twenty centuries of stony sleep
Were vexed to nightmare by a rocking cradle,   20
And what rough beast, its hour come round at last,
Slouches towards Bethlehem to be born?

1920

THE SECOND COMING 12 *Spiritus Mundi:* spirit of the world.

In the analysis of this poem it helps to be familiar with Yeats' private system of symbols, but it is not essential, for the poem itself explains and develops many of the symbols. In the first line of "The Second Coming," for example, Yeats refers to the "gyre," a private symbol for his time, his age's movement, which he describes as widening until it finally turns upon itself and breaks apart. The spiralling movement of the gyre appears in the first verse-paragraph in the flight of the falcon as it circles farther and farther from the falconer. The description of the state of the world as anarchic, as a circle whose "centre cannot hold" also echoes this movement, and in the second verse-paragraph the "indignant desert birds" trace similar motions in the air above the "rough beast" which now "slouches toward Bethlehem to be born." Yeats describes the violent wrenching and transformation of the old order, which now seems to be changing into a new era into which that bestial figure will soon be born.

Symbols such as the gyre ordinarily do not carry with them traditional literary associations. Instead, the poet creates a system of associations, sometimes within his work as a whole, but often within only one poem, so the burden of interpretation then rests on the individual reader confronting the individual poem. Symbols are like multifaceted gems, which flash reflected light back to the observer or the reader. You hold the gem in your hand and turn it whichever way it will capture the best light. And you may even see it slightly differently each time you look at it.

PERSONIFICATION

Whether we create personlike animals, such as the speaking, thinking rabbits in *Watership Down,* or endow inanimate objects with human characteristics, such as the stuffed bear, Winnie-the-Pooh, or embody an abstract quality with human form, such as the character of Sin in *Paradise Lost,* we never tire of giving human qualities to the nonhuman. **Personification** is the name of this device that endows inanimate objects or abstractions with human characteristics. It represents our attempt to explain the universe in terms of ourselves, in terms that we can understand most personally. For example, in this poem Keats describes autumn as if it were a person.

JOHN KEATS

TO AUTUMN   37

1

Season of mists and mellow fruitfulness,
    Close bosom-friend of the maturing sun;
Conspiring with him how to load and bless
    With fruit the vines that round the thatch-eaves run;

To bend with apples the mossed cottage-trees,   5
 And fill all fruit with ripeness to the core;
  To swell the gourd, and plump the hazel shells
 With a sweet kernel; to set budding more,
And still more, later flowers for the bees,
Until they think warm days will never cease,   10
  For Summer has o'er-brimmed their clammy cells.

2

Who hath not seen thee oft amid thy store?
 Sometimes whoever seeks abroad may find
Thee sitting careless on a granary floor,
 Thy hair soft-lifted by the winnowing wind;   15
Or on a half-reaped furrow sound asleep,
 Drowsed with the fume of poppies, while thy hook
  Spares the next swath and all its twined flowers:
And sometimes like a gleaner thou dost keep
 Steady thy laden head across a brook;   20
 Or by a cider-press, with patient look,
  Thou watchest the last oozings hours by hours.

3

Where are the songs of Spring? Aye, where are they?
 Think not of them, thou hast thy music too—
While barred clouds bloom the soft-dying day,   25
 And touch the stubble-plains with rosy hue;
Then in a wailful choir the small gnats mourn
 Among the river sallows, borne aloft
  Or sinking as the light wind lives or dies;
And full-grown lambs loud bleat from hilly bourn; 30
 Hedge crickets sing; and now with treble soft
 The redbreast whistles from a garden croft;
  And gathering swallows twitter in the skies.

1820

Autumn, who is a close friend of the sun, and conspires with him to ripen fruit, "to swell the gourd, and plump the hazel shells / With a sweet kernel," also has forced the flowers to bloom over and over again for the bees, whose hives were already filled ("o'er-brimmed") with honey by Summer's efforts. In the second stanza we see more of Autumn than just the results of her actions. Autumn dwells in the midst of an abundant nature, ready for the harvest, sometimes in the middle of it, watching "the last oozings hours by hours"—of the cider pressed from ripened apples and of the growing season itself.

An earlier season is also personified in this poem, as we hear of the fled "songs of Spring," and the speaker describes the music which maturing Autumn sings: "the small gnats mourn," the "full-grown lambs loud bleat," the "hedge crickets sing," "the redbreast whistles," and "gathering swallows twitter in the skies." Here are harbingers of change, hints of mourning, images of maturity, signs that the season is coming to an end and will leave with the swallows as they migrate to warmer climates. Keats personifies Autumn not only to make an appealing picture, but also to say something more insightful about the contending forces of life and death in nature.

PARADOX

Paradox occurs when language appears to contradict itself. In paradox, however, the contradiction is only *apparent*. A reader encountering paradox is immediately challenged to find the truth behind the statement, to understand that in the area of certain human experiences, language can only go so far—that the imagination must then take over and discover what it is the words are really trying to say. Paradox is not nonsense, but it depends upon an active reader to see beyond the words on the page.

Writing in the sixteenth century, Sir Thomas Wyatt used a series of paradoxes to describe being in love.

SIR THOMAS WYATT

I FIND NO PEACE   38

I find no peace and all my war is done,
I fear and hope, I burn and freeze like ice,
I fly above the wind, yet can I not arise,
And naught I have and all the world I seize on:
That looseth nor locketh holdeth me in prison,   5
And holdeth me not; yet can I 'scape nowise;
Nor letteth me live nor die at my devise,
And yet of death it giveth none occasion.
Without eyen I see; and without tongue I plain;
I desire to perish, and yet I ask health;   10
I love another, and thus I hate myself;
I feed me in sorrow, and laugh in all my pain.
Likewise displeaseth me both death and life,
And my delight is causer of this strife.

1557

I FIND NO PEACE 9 *eyen:* eyes; *plain:* complain.

Passion has thrown the speaker into disorder. He becomes all things at once, all feelings at once, hoping and fearing, blind and seeing, tongueless yet full of words. He has ceased to fight and yet he can find no peace. He wants to die, yet prays for health. Love brings him laughter and pain, joy and sorrow. He burns with passion and freezes "like ice." The woman he loves so intensely ("my delight") has thrown his spirit into turmoil and there seems to be no possibility for escape—an escape he does not really desire anyway.

In this poem paradox pulls you into the conflict until you also feel the tension between contradictory emotions and desires. You begin to understand that this attempt to describe a complex feeling *must necessarily* push language into paradox. In fact, language alone is inadequate. It is up to you, the reader, to hold these contradictory words and images in your mind simultaneously and allow them to work on your imagination. You will probably be motivated not so much to seek a resolution to the contradictions as to allow the contrary states of mind to continue to contend with each other, unresolved but understood.

The following poem also relies upon paradox.

JOHN DONNE

SONNET 10
[DEATH BE NOT PROUD]

39

Death, be not proud, though some have called thee
Mighty and dreadful, for thou art not so;
For those whom thou think'st thou dost overthrow
Die not, poor Death, nor yet canst thou kill me.
From rest and sleep, which but thy pictures be,   5
Much pleasure; then from thee much more must flow.
And soonest our best men with thee do go,
Rest of their bones, and soul's delivery.
Thou art slave to fate, chance, kings, and desperate men,
And dost with poison, war, and sickness dwell,   10
And poppy or charms can make us sleep as well
And better than thy stroke; why swell'st thou then?
One short sleep past, we wake eternally
And death shall be no more; Death, thou shalt die.

1633

"Death, thou shalt die" is a paradox. Donne crafts a carefully logical argument to reveal Death's weaknesses. The reputation of death is misleading, Donne says, for although many have called Death "mighty and dreadful,"

Death's appearances prove otherwise. Death looks like sleep, a welcome respite for good men whose souls will be delivered to God. Furthermore, Death is no sovereign—it is only a slave unable to initiate activity; it can respond only to the dictates of "fate, chance, kings, and desperate men." What looks like death is not really death but an entrance into eternal life—thus death is an opportunity for Death's own death.

The reader of this poem allows its images and its arguments to accumulate until finally the paradox expressed in the last line begins to make sense. The reader, in fact, uses logic to defy logic, and thus to create an understanding of the poem which goes beyond the sense of the final line.

The final line of the next poem operates in a similar fashion.

X. J. KENNEDY

ON A CHILD WHO LIVED ONE MINUTE   40

Into a world where children shriek like suns
sundered from other suns on their arrival,
she stared, and saw the waiting shape of evil,
but could not take its meaning in at once,
so fresh her understanding, and so fragile.   5

Her first breath drew a fragrance from the air
and put it back. However hard her agile
heart danced, however full the surgeon's satchel
of healing stuff, a blackness tiptoed in her
and snuffed the only candle of her castle.   10

Oh, let us do away with elegiac
drivel! Who can restore a thing so brittle,
so new in any jingle? Still I marvel
that, making light of mountainloads of logic,
so much could stay a moment in so little.   15

1958

The entire poem is directed toward the paradox in the final line which defines the dilemma so clearly that you do not read it as contradiction by the time you reach it. Unlike other newborns, this child does not utter its first gasping scream; she simply stares, and in her one minute of life, her only chance to acquire any understanding, she sees "the waiting shape of evil." When she does breathe, it is simply to take a bit of air in and then "put it back" again—breathe it out. The surgeon cannot help her, nor can her heart beat her into life. Her brief flame is snuffed out.

The poet insists that he can say no more, and he does not wish to trivialize the child's death with "elegiac drivel." Nonetheless, contradicting his stated intentions, he continues the poem, noting that he is amazed that "so much could stay a moment in so little." Life and breath and understanding have resided for a moment in a tiny, fragile being—and that alone is remarkable. The paradox, however, points to another reading also. Perhaps he means that he is surprised that so much could stay *only* a moment in so little—what a surprise that life does not have more power than it does, since all it had to do was inhabit such a small thing.

Paradox teases and challenges the mind. It allows the reader's mind to contain two opposing truths simultaneously—and to hold these truths in suspension, choosing neither one nor the other, but both at once, the two together pointing to something otherwise unsayable.

IRONY

Sometimes a poem will present a picture in which one element seems at odds with the rest of the scene—an ornate garden table, for example, set for a formal tea amidst the rubble of a dump. The juxtaposition of object and setting creates a tension that often results in the surprise of **irony.** In the following poem, notice how you are led in one direction, only to find your expectations violently reversed in the final line.

EDWIN ARLINGTON ROBINSON

RICHARD CORY   41

Whenever Richard Cory went down town
We people on the pavement looked at him;
He was a gentleman from sole to crown,
Clean favored, and imperially slim.

And he was always quietly arrayed,   5
And he was always human when he talked;
But still he fluttered pulses when he said,
"Good morning," and he glittered when he walked.

And he was rich—yes, richer than a king—
. And admirably schooled in every grace;   10
In fine, we thought that he was everything
To make us wish that we were in his place.

So on we worked, and waited for the light,
And went without the meat, and cursed the bread;
And Richard Cory, one calm summer night,   15
Went home and put a bullet through his head.

1897

Richard Cory had it all—the wealth of monarchs, the respect and adulation of the town, the physical appearance of a king (*"imperially* slim"), the quiet and self-confident demeanor, even the "glitter." What a surprise for both reader and townspeople when Richard Cory quietly puts a bullet through his head. Here the irony is situational, but notice how it is created not only by the situation itself, which leads the reader to believe one thing and then discover that another is the truth; the irony is underscored by the *form* of the poem. The poem is constructed with perfect rhymes in every first and third line and every second and fourth line. The regular rhythm and perfect rhymes combine to produce a slightly sing-song effect which lulls the reader into a false sense of predictability. Then comes the explosion at the end, shattering the reliable structure which seemed to control both the poem's direction and the social fabric of the town.

Reader expectation and reader surprise are at the heart of irony. Sometimes you will be forced to correct or revise your original expectations. Sometimes you will know from the beginning of the poem that what a speaker literally says is not what she really means. It can sting you, as it does in "Richard Cory." It can reveal a doubleness of character, as it does in Robert Browning's "My Last Duchess" (145). At any rate, irony relies on a fascinating dualism, sometimes even contradiction, and it is up to you to read it and to respond to it, as in this commentary on the arrogance of the powerful.

PERCY BYSSHE SHELLEY

OZYMANDIAS   42

I met a traveler from an antique land
Who said: Two vast and trunkless legs of stone
Stand in the desert . . . Near them, on the sand,
Half sunk, a shattered visage lies, whose frown,
And wrinkled lip, and sneer of cold command,   5
Tell that its sculptor well those passions read
Which yet survive, stamped on these lifeless things,
The hand that mocked them, and the heart that fed:
And on the pedestal these words appear:
"My name is Ozymandias, king of kings: 10

Look on my works, ye Mighty, and despair!"
Nothing beside remains. Round the decay
Of that colossal wreck, boundless and bare,
The lone and level sands stretch far away.

1818

Notice the irony in the inscription on the pedestal in lines 10–11. When originally inscribed, the words were intended to exalt the reputation of the "king of kings," but in the context of a wasteland of ruins—"the shattered visage," the "trunkless legs of stone," all "lifeless things"—they do quite the opposite. You look on Ozymandias' works and you do despair, not because they are so magnificent that they humble you but because there is nothing left of them. You see the scene from two different perspectives—that of Ozymandias and that of the later traveller—and that gives you a doubleness of vision that creates an ironic edge.

Occasionally a poet will use **understatement** or overstatement (**hyperbole**) for ironic effect. See, for example, Andrew Marvell's "To His Coy Mistress" (366), in which the speaker exaggerates in order to provoke a response from a young woman who is resisting his advances. "Had we but World enough, and Time," he says, he would spend hundreds, thousands of years adoring her.

An hundred years should go to praise
Thine eyes, and on thy forehead gaze;
Two hundred to adore each breast,
But thirty thousand to the rest.

Notice that once the speaker has set the ironic mood, hyperbole then gives way to understatement:

The Grave's a fine and private place,
But none I think do there embrace.

To say the grave is private is to deliberately understate the obvious. The effect is thoroughly ironic.

DICTION AND TONE

Diction is the choice and arrangement of words in poetry and is usually described as formal, informal, colloquial, or slang. The diction of John Milton's "Lycidas" (381), in which the speaker mourns the death of a friend, is serious and formal. That of Gwendolyn Brooks' "Beverly Hills, Chicago" (139) is more informal, although still decorous. Lucille Clifton's "Miss Rosie" (155), who used to be "the best looking gal in Georgia," uses a more colloquial or conversational diction. Lawrence Ferlinghetti's

"Sometime During Eternity" (217) is written almost entirely in the slang of the beat generation.

Diction contributes to **tone,** which is the mood of a poem, or the attitude expressed by the speaker toward the subject and toward the audience. To determine the tone, it is important to identify the speaker. Sometimes it is a **persona,** or character, the poet has created, sometimes it is the poet speaking, and sometimes you will barely be aware of the speaker's identity. In Tennyson's "Ulysses" (503) you will need to recognize the speaker as Ulysses himself if you are to interpret the tone correctly. The same would be true in Ezra Pound's "The River Merchant's Wife: A Letter" (428) or in Browning's "The Bishop Orders His Tomb at Saint Praxed's Church" (146), where the speakers are characters the authors have created. At the other extreme is the poetry of Sylvia Plath and Anne Sexton. Whenever these confessional poets use the first-person pronoun, you know they themselves are speaking. You should never automatically assume, however, that the speaker is the poet. Test it first and remember that often a poet uses a persona ironically, as in Robert Browning's "My Last Duchess" (145), in which the narrator dramatically but unwittingly reveals his own dark purposes and lack of character.

The **connotation,** or implied meaning, of words and phrases also helps to establish tone in a poem. Think of the differences in the connotations of *thin, scrawny, svelte,* and *skinny*—or on the other hand *plump, obese, hefty,* and *chubby.* The **denotations,** or dictionary meanings, of certain words may be almost identical, but their connotations may differ drastically, and these connotations create mood and tone.

Try to identify the words that contribute to the tone of the following poem. Don't be afraid to use your pencil to mark those images which establish the tone.

T. S. ELIOT

PRELUDES 43

I

The winter evening settles down
With smell of steaks in passageways.
Six o-clock.
The burnt-out ends of smoky days.
And now a gusty shower wraps
The grimy scraps
Of withered leaves about your feet
And newspapers from vacant lots;
The showers beat

5

On broken blinds and chimney-pots,   10
And at the corner of the street
A lonely cab-horse steams and stamps.
And then the lighting of the lamps.

II

The morning comes to consciousness
Of faint stale smells of beer   15
From the sawdust-trampled street
With all its muddy feet that press
To early coffee-stands.
With the other masquerades
That time resumes,   20
One thinks of all the hands
That are raising dingy shades
In a thousand furnished rooms.

III

You tossed a blanket from the bed,
You lay upon your back, and waited;   25
You dozed, and watched the night revealing
The thousand sordid images
Of which your soul was constituted;
They flickered against the ceiling.
And when all the world came back   30
And the light crept up between the shutters
And you heard the sparrows in the gutters,
You had such a vision of the street
As the street hardly understands;
Sitting along the bed's edge, where   35
You curled the papers from your hair,
Or clasped the yellow soles of feet
In the palms of both soiled hands.

IV

His soul stretched tight across the skies
That fade behind a city block,   40
Or trampled by insistent feet
At four and five and six o'clock;
And short square fingers stuffing pipes,

And evening newspapers, and eyes
Assured of certain certainties,   45
The conscience of a blackened street
Impatient to assume the world.

I am moved by fancies that are curled
Around these images, and cling:
The notion of some infinitely gentle   50
Infinitely suffering thing.

Wipe your hand across your mouth, and laugh;
The worlds revolve like ancient women
Gathering fuel in vacant lots.

                                                1917

CHAPTER 5

THE SOUNDS OF
POETRY

As Chapter 2, "The Poem and the Senses," points out, your ear and eye receive most of the sensory stimuli in poetry. A poem paints a picture in words, which you "hear" whether or not you pronounce them; nevertheless the careful reader will read a poem aloud, so as not to miss any of its sound effects. In fact, one of the real pleasures of poetry lies in the sounds of words and the ways in which they provide echoes, rhymes, and repetitions. The following poem, for example, read aloud, encourages you to linger over such sound effects.

EDNA ST. VINCENT MILLAY
COUNTING-OUT RHYME 44

Silver bark of beech, and sallow
Bark of yellow birch and yellow
   Twig of willow.

Stripe of green in moosewood maple,
Colour seen in leaf of apple,   5
   Bark of popple.

Wood of popple pale as moonbeam,
Wood of oak for yoke and barn-beam,
   Wood of hornbeam.

Silver bark of beech, and hollow   10
Stem of elder, tall and yellow
   Twig of willow.

                                       1928

Pronouncing the words of this poem is a pleasurable experience because of the repetitions, the near-rhymes, the alliterations, and the rhythm.

   Poetry, like music, can often mimic the various sounds in our lives. One poetic device which gives particular pleasure is **onomatopoeia,** words and phrases which sound like the object or action they name. For example, *cuckoo* mimics the sound the bird makes. Other examples are *splash, whisper, chirp*—words which sound like the action named—and *sluggish, quick,* and *zip*—words which mimic the speed or slowness of motion they describe.

   Phrases and lines can also be onomatopoeic. Notice in Herrick's poem the repeated *s*, which suggests the rustling of silk.

ROBERT HERRICK

UPON JULIA'S CLOTHES   45

Whenas in silks my Julia goes,
Then, then, methinks, how sweetly flows
That liquefaction of her clothes.

Next, when I cast mine eyes, and see
That brave vibration, each way free,   5
O, how that glittering taketh me!

                                       1648

The repetition of the *s* sound is an example of **consonance,** which refers to any repeated consonant sounds among several words. When similar consonant repetition occurs at the beginnings of words, it is referred to as **alliteration** (as in "Peter Piper picked a peck of pickled peppers," or as in the Herrick poem—in *silks, sweetly,* and *see*).

   It is, finally, various forms of *repetition* that create most of the interesting sound effects in poetry. Consonance and alliteration are repetitions of parts of words, as is **assonance,** the repetition of similar vowel sounds. In line 5 of "Upon Julia's Clothes," *brave vibration* repeats the long *a*, which is then echoed in *way*. Likewise, *each* and *free* repeat the long *e*. The assonance of line 5 emphasizes the long vowels, to draw the words out, appropriate in a line describing the free swinging of Julia's hips. The silks rustle, and Julia moves provocatively, "that brave vibration each way free." This is not a clipped, short motion, nor are the vowels of the words describing it.

Gerard Manley Hopkins' poems use sound particularly effectively. Consider the following poem, which is rich in all of the devices discussed so far, and several more.

GERARD MANLEY HOPKINS

GOD'S GRANDEUR   46

The world is charged with the grandeur of God.
  It will flame out, like shining from shook foil;
  It gathers to a greatness, like the ooze of oil
Crushed. Why do men then now not reck his rod?
Generations have trod, have trod, have trod;   5
  And all is seared with trade; bleared, smeared with toil;
  And wears man's smudge and shares man's smell: the soil
Is bare now, nor can foot feel, being shod.
And for all this, nature is never spent;
  There lives the dearest freshness deep down things;   10
And though the last lights off the black West went
  Oh, morning, at the brown brink eastward, springs—
Because the Holy Ghost over the bent
  World broods with warm breast and with ah! bright wings.

1918

Read this poem aloud, and you begin to pronounce the words more deliberately, to feel the connections and echoes of sound and syllable. The alliteration of words in each and every line creates a verbal melody.

line 1: grandeur . . . God
line 2: flame . . . foil; shining . . . shook
line 3: gathers . . . greatness
line 4: reck . . . rod
line 5: have trod . . . have trod . . . have trod
line 6: seared . . . smeared; trade . . . toil
line 7: smudge . . . smell . . . soil
line 8: bare . . . being; now . . . nor; foot . . . feel
line 9: nature . . . never
line 10: dearest . . . deep down
line 11: last . . . lights; West . . . went
line 12: brown . . . brink
line 13: Because . . . bent
line 14: World . . . with warm . . . with . . . wings; broods . . . breast
    . . . bright

Notice that the alliteration occurs not just inside every line but also spills over into subsequent lines, so that, for example, the word *black* in line 12 is preceded and followed by *b*'s in lines 11, 13, and 14. Like rhyme, alliteration is often pleasing to the ear—almost musical in effect. However, occasionally alliteration can produce cacophony, as in the following poem.

WILLIAM MEREDITH

WEATHER   47

> But swinging doesn't bend them down to stay.
> Ice storms do that.
> —"Birches," Robert Frost

The elm is turned to crystal
The tamarack is glass
An iridescent boneyard
Has taken the place of grass

Someone has piled old shakos   5
Where there was pine and spruce
The sentimental willows
Weep with no green excuse

But the birch trees stricken double
Cry to the sun click clack   10
Ours are the only natures
That you cannot give back.

1966

"Click clack" is an onomatopoeic phrase describing the sound of the ice-covered birches; it is also alliterative and draws attention to other hard *c* or *k* sounds in the poem: *cry, crystal, tamarack, shakos, stricken, back.* The sounds are harsh and as brittle as the ice they describe. Alliteration captures your ear, so that you are subtly drawn into the poem, senses first. It also unifies the poem, connecting word with word, image with image, improving the flow of language and idea.

Assonance works the same way in "God's Grandeur." Line 2, for example, contains *like* and *shining,* repeating the long *i* sound; lines 2 and 3 contain the long *a* echo in *flame* and *greatness,* and so on throughout the poem. Consonance also is at work, repeating internal consonant sounds such as the *l*'s in *world, will flame, like,* and *foil* in lines 1 and 2.

WEATHER 2 *tamarack:* a larch tree. 5 *shakos:* stiff, military dress hats.

The poem also uses onomatopoeia: *shining from shook foil,* for example, sounds like goldfoil being shaken out; the slowness of the words *ooze of oil* mimics the phenomenon they describe.

Hopkins also uses several different kinds of **rhyme. Perfect rhyme** appears in all the **end rhymes:** *God/rod/trod/shod, foil/oil/toil/soil, spent/ went/bent,* and *things/spring/wings.* Any rhymes which occur within a given line of poetry are called **internal rhymes;** notice that in line 6, *seared, bleared,* and *smeared* are internal rhymes. In addition, in lines 7 and 8, *wears, shares,* and *bare* rhyme. Notice that the end rhymes determine what is called the **rhyme scheme** of a poem. The final word of line 1, *God,* rhymes with the final words of lines 4, 5, and 8. Likewise, *foil* of line 2 rhymes with the ends of lines 3, 6, and 7. The initial rhyme in a poem is called *a,* the second *b,* and so on. Thus, the rhyme scheme of Hopkins' poem is *abbaabba, cdcdcd.*

Sometimes poets like to use **off-rhyme** or **slant-rhyme,** rhyme that is not full and perfect but that contains echoes of parts of words—for example, *last* and *West* in line 11, or *trade* and *trod* in lines 5 and 6. Notice that all the rhymes in Wilfred Owen's "Arms and the Boy" (Chapter 2) are slant-rhymes. All of these types of rhyme and various sound devices are examples of repetition and are used in poetry for their musical effects, for the ease with which they can mark off the poetic line, and even for unifying image and thought.

The repetition of whole words and images can be used for descriptive purposes (as the line "have trod, have trod, have trod" in Hopkins' poem describes repeated treading). It also can give a kind of rhythmical, musical pleasure, as it does when used as **anaphora,** the repetition of an initial word or phrase. Anaphora is rhetorical in tone, and usually appears as an emphatic device used for reflection, sermonizing, or prophecy, as in the following speech from Shakespeare's *Richard II.*

> This royal throne of kings, this scept'red isle,
> This earth of majesty, this seat of Mars,
> This other Eden, demi-paradise,
> This fortress built by Nature for herself
> Against infection and the hand of war,
> This happy breed of men, this little world,
> This precious stone set in the silver sea. . . .
> . . . This blessed plot, this earth, this realm, this England,
> This nurse, this teeming womb of royal kings. . . .
> . . . This land of such dear souls, this dear dear land,
> Dear for her reputation through the world. . . .

Notice how the repetition is not only of a single word, but also of a grammatical structure. In the case of this passage repetition creates suspense, piling subject on top of subject, postponing the verb almost indefinitely.

Entire lines can also be repeated in poetry. In this medieval poem, notice the repeated lines and phrases throughout.

ANONYMOUS

LORD RANDALL 48

"Oh where ha'e ye been, Lord Randall my son?
O where ha'e ye been, my handsome young man?"
  "I ha'e been to the wild wood: mother, make my bed soon,
  For I'm weary wi' hunting, and fain wald lie down."

"Where gat ye your dinner, Lord Randall my son? 5
Where gat ye your dinner, my handsome young man?"
  "I dined wi' my true love; mother, make my bed soon,
  For I'm weary wi' hunting, and fain wald lie down."

"What gat ye to your dinner, Lord Randall my son?
What gat ye to your dinner, my handsome young man?" 10
  "I gat eels boiled in broo: mother, make my bed soon,
  For I'm weary wi' hunting and fain wald lie down."

"What became of your bloodhounds, Lord Randall my son?
What became of your bloodhounds, my handsome young man?"
  "O they swelled and they died: mother, make my bed soon, 15
  For I'm weary wi' hunting and fain wald lie down."

"O I fear ye are poisoned, Lord Randall my son!
O I fear ye are poisoned, my handsome young man!"
  "O yes, I am poisoned: mother, make my bed soon,
  For I'm sick at the heart, and I fain wald lie down." 20

The poem is built upon repetition of a mother's questions and a son's answers, with the last line and a half of each stanza (with a significant variation in the last stanza) forming a **refrain** which helps to give the poem a form. Repetition here serves as a unifying device, closing out each stanza with the same or similar words. But notice what happens to the meaning of those words as they and entire lines and phrases are repeated over and over again. The first stanza's question and answer seem innocent and straightforward, but as the poem progresses, the questions the mother asks become more personal and the son's answers more bitter, even though many of the words and phrases are the same. The reader realizes by the last stanza that it is not weariness alone that the young man feels. He is not just tired but dying. The meaning of the words has changed with their repetition.

Various fixed verse forms considered in Chapter 7 also rely on the repetition of words, phrases, and lines. Repetition is a device which captures the ear, appeals to the sense of hearing, and helps to support rhythmical patterns, discussed in the next chapter. Repetition emphasizes the sound, the word, the phrase, and the line, intensifies their dramatic effect, and thereby both delights the ear and deepens the meaning of poetry.

LORD RANDALL 4 *fain wald:* gladly would. 11 *broo:* broth.

CHAPTER 6

THE RHYTHMS OF POETRY

It is a warm summer evening. You sit at your desk beside an open window, a glass of lemonade by your side, and you begin to listen to the sounds of the night. You hear distant thunder and the crickets' momentary pause in response to it. In the next room someone is typing, and the rapid key strokes and end-of-line bell create an almost predictable rhythm, now and then interrupted by silences of a minute or two. Someone else is walking down the sidewalk, and you hear her heels on the pavement, a rhythm as regular as the bass notes in the music being played on the stereo in the room above yours. The thunder is closer now and the rain begins, the first drops beating distinctly on the tin roof of your balcony. A friend knocks on your door and proposes a study break—a quick game of ping-pong.

The rhythms of poetry are taken from the rhythms of life. Whether it is a natural rhythm, such as waves relentlessly breaking against the shore, or a man-made rhythm, such as the clackety-clack of a train or the various time-signatures of music, we encounter rhythms daily and, in fact, are attracted to them—even mesmerized by them at times. Our everyday speech is filled with rhythms: pauses, stops, starts, rises, and falls. By its very nature language is rhythmical.

Poetry builds upon the natural rhythms of everyday speech, but then often adds extra degrees of regularity to those freer rhythms. Rhythm makes poetry more evocative, more readable, and more memorable and enjoyable. You will, however, find it difficult to enjoy poetry if the first thing you try to do with a poem is define its rhythmical pattern. If you have ever played a musical instrument, you know the advantages of occasionally playing to the beat of the metronome. But the first time you play a piece, as you learn the notes and the fingerings, as you become familiar with the direction of the music, the metronome's beat would only be intrusive. It is the same with poetry. In the first stages of reading, you must simply listen to the poem. Its rhythm will carry you along, as in the following. As you read this poem aloud, you will feel its jazzy rhythm and hear the alternation among jazz instruments.

CARL SANDBURG

JAZZ FANTASIA   49

Drum on your drums, batter on your banjos, sob on the long cool
    winding saxophones. Go to it, O jazzmen.

Sling your knuckles on the bottoms of the happy tin pans, let your
    trombones ooze, and go husha-husha-hush with the slippery
    sandpaper.

Moan like autumn wind high in the lonesome treetops, moan soft
    like you wanted somebody terrible, cry like a racing car slipping
    away from a motorcycle-cop, bang bang! you jazzmen, bang
    altogether drums, traps, banjos, horns, tin cans—make two
    people fight on the top of a stairway and scratch each other's
    eyes in a clinch tumbling down the stairs.

Can the rough stuff. . . Now a Mississippi steamboat pushes up the
    night river with a who-who-who-oo. . . and the green lanterns
    calling to the high soft stars. . . a red moon rides on the humps
    of the low river hills. . . . Go to it, O jazzmen.

1920

Rhythm, or **meter,** is often more regular than it is in this poem. In fact, the rest of this chapter deals with the ways in which poetic rhythms have been systematized and defined, much the way they have been in music. The time and place for using a metronome in practicing a piece of music is not, as noted above, in the first stages, but rather after you have achieved some familiarity with the piece and are now more interested in meeting its technical challenges. So it is with reading a poem. First be aware of the poem's beat and consider meter as you analyze a poem, but remember that being able to label a particular poem's meter is not the real end of the analytical process.

NUMBER OF FEET

Meter in poetry is usually measured in **feet,** regular combinations of stressed and unstressed syllables. When you beat time to your favorite tune, you do not thump out every note, but only those that are accented, or stressed.

You can do much the same thing in poetry, where stressed and unstressed syllables form the rhythmic pattern in each foot, and in the combinations of feet that make up each line of a poem.

Feet normally consist of a single accented (′) syllable with one or more unaccented (˘) syllables. A line of poetry may be analyzed by the number of feet it contains and it can be named accordingly. A line that consists of one foot would be called monometer, another with two feet would be dimeter, yet another containing three feet would be trimeter, and so on. A vertical line (|) is often used to mark the division between feet.

Prominent among the following examples are feet in which a single unstressed syllable is followed by a single stressed syllable, but keep in mind that many other unstressed–stressed combinations are possible.

Monometer (One Foot)

ROBERT HERRICK

UPON HIS DEPARTURE HENCE   50

Thŭs Í
Passe bý,
Ănd dié:
Ăs One,́
Ŭnknówn,   5
And gon:
I'm made
A shade,
And laid
I'th grave,   10
There have
My Cave,
Where tell
I dwell,
Farewell.   15

                                                               1648

Monometer is a rare pattern in English, but perfectly appropriate in this poem in which the few words in each line create a thin length, becoming a picture of the grave it describes, and also suggesting the brevity of life.

Dimeter (Two Feet)

BEN JONSON

FROM A HYMN TO GOD THE FATHER 51

Hĕar mé, | Ō Gód!
 Ā bró | kĕn heárt
 Ĭs mý | bĕst párt;
Ŭsē stíll | Thy̆ ród,
 Thāt Í | may̆ próve   5
 Thĕreiń, | Thy̆ Lóve.

If Thou hadst not
 Been stern to me,
 But left me free,
I had forgot   10
 My self and Thee.

1640

This poem contains no frills, no unnecessary adornment; the brief lines emphasize the speaker's straghtforward prayer.

Trimeter (Three Feet)

THEODORE ROETHKE

MY PAPA'S WALTZ 52

Thĕ whís | kĕy oń | yŏur bréath
Cŏuld máke | ă small | bŏy dizzy̆;
Bŭt Í | hŭng oń | likē déath;
Sŭch wáltz | ĭng wás | nŏt eásy̆.

We romped until the pans   5
Slid from the kitchen shelf;
My mother's countenance
Could not unfrown itself.

The hand that held my wrist
Was battered on one knuckle;   10
At every step you missed
My right ear scraped a buckle,

You beat time on my head
With a palm caked hard by dirt,
Then waltzed me off to bed   15
Still clinging to your shirt.

1948

The three feet in each line echo the ¾ waltz time of the father as he rolicks with
his child. Notice, however, the syllables which seem to add an extra fillip to
lines 2, 4, 10, and 12 in the final words, *dizzy, easy, knuckle,* and *buckle.* The
father has been drinking, so that his waltz is not completely graceful—and in
the **feminine endings** (extra, unaccented syllables at the ends of the lines) you
can hear the extra little steps he occasionally must take to keep his balance.
Masculine endings are those in which the last syllable is stressed, as in the
next poem.

Tetrameter (Four Feet)

ARCHIBALD MacLEISH
SEAFARER   53

And leárn | Ŏ vóy | āgĕr | tŏ wálk ,
Thĕ róll | ŏf eárth, | thĕ pítch | ănd fáll
Thăt swíngs | ăcróss | thĕse trées | thŏse stárs:
Thăt swíngs | thĕ sún | lĭght úp | thĕ wáll.

And learn upon these narrow beds   5
To sleep in spite of sea, in spite
Of sound the rushing planet makes:
And learn to sleep against this ground.

1933

The "seafarer" is one who walks upon the earth—an earth of huge
planetary motions—as it turns on its axis and rolls in its orbit. The human
who finally "sleeps" in a "narrow bed" (the grave) "learn[s] to sleep against
this ground" even though it is really as unstable as the sea. The regularity of
the meter holds the poem together, even in the face of the huge motions being
described. One feels stability at the core.

Pentameter (Five Feet)

ROBERT FROST

FORGIVE, O LORD   54

Forgíve, | Ŏ Lórd, | mў lĭt | tlĕ jŏkes | ŏn Thĕe
Ănd Ĭ'll | fŏrgíve | Thў gréat | bĭg óne | ŏn mĕe.

1962

Pentameter is the most commonly used measure in English verse. It seems equally well suited for very short poems (**epigrams**) such as "Forgive, O Lord" and longer, narrative pieces.

Hexameter (Six Feet)

KARL SHAPIRO

BUICK   55

Ăs ă sloóp | wĭth ă sweép | ŏf ĭmmác | ŭlăte wíngs | ŏn hĕr
  . dĕl | ĭcăte spíne
Ănd ă kĕel | ăs steel | ăs ă róot | thăt hólds | ĭn thĕ séa | ăs shĕ leáns,
Leaning and laughing, my warm hearted beauty, you ride, you ride,
You tack on the curves with parabola speed and a kiss of goodbye,
Like a thoroughbred sloop, my new high-spirited spirit, my kiss.   5

As my foot suggests that you leap in the air with your hips of a girl,
My finger that praises your wheel and announces your voices of
    song,
Flouncing your skirts, you blueness of joy, you flirt of politeness,
You leap, you intelligence, essence of wheelness with silvery nose,
And your platinum clocks of excitement stir like the hairs of a fern.   10

But now with your eyes that enter the future of roads you forget;
Where you turned on the stinging lathes of Detroit and Lansing at
    night
And shrieked at the torch in your secret parts and the amorous tests,
But now with your eyes that enter the future of roads you forget;
You are all instinct with your phosphorous glow and your streaking
    hair.   15

And now when we stop it is not as the bird from the shell that I
    leave
Or the leathery pilot who steps from his bird with a sneer of delight,
And not as the ignorant beast do you squat and watch me depart,
But with exquisite breathing you smile, with satisfaction of love,
And I touch you again as you tick in the silence and settle in sleep.   20

1941

Because this meter, which requires such long lines, is often awkward and
unwieldy, you will rarely find a poem written in hexameter that is as graceful
as this one. The length of the line describes the graceful sweep of the lines of
the car, the loving, almost sexual relationship the speaker feels with this car,
which he personifies, describing as human in its beauty and movement.

    Probably the best-known use of hexameter occurs in Edmund Spenser's
The Faerie Queene, in which each stanza, consisting primarily of pentametric
lines, ends with an **Alexandrine,** a six-foot, twelve-syllable line.

EDMUND SPENSER

FROM THE FAERIE QUEENE 56

A Gentle Knight was pricking on the plaine,
  Ycladd in mightie armes and silver shielde,
  Wherein old dints of deepe wounds did remaine,
  The cruell markes of many a bloudy fielde;
  Yet armes till that time did he never wield: 5
  His angry steede did chide his foming bitt,
  As much disdayning to the curbe to yield:
  Full jolly knight he seemed, and faire did sitt,
As one | for knight | ly giusts | and fierce | encoun | ters fitt.

1590

THE FAERIE QUEENE 1 *pricking:* galloping. 9 *giusts:* jousts.

Heptameter (Seven Feet)

WILLIAM WORDSWORTH

FROM STAR-GAZERS 57

What crowd | is this? | what have | we here! | we must | not pass | it
    by;
A Telescope upon its frame, and pointed to the sky:
Long is it as a barber's pole, or mast of little boat,
Some little pleasure-skill, that doth on Thames's waters float.

1807

As the number of feet increases in poetry, it becomes more difficult to both sustain a steady rhythm and avoid ridiculousness. In unskillful hands, the meter may begin to predominate, and the words become more and more inaudible behind the pounding rhythm of the poem's feet.

A poet will occasionally use this tendency to humorous advantage. Ogden Nash, who frequently plays with long-line meters, begins "Who Understands Who Anyhow?" with the following lines:

> There is one phase of life that I have never heard discussed in any
>   seminar,
> And that is that all women think men are funny and all men think
>   that weminar.

The rushed meter and the forced, triple-syllable rhyme establish the light tone. Nash indelicately wrenches the words to fit the meter, but it works because the poem is a joke.

KINDS OF FEET

Different kinds of feet are distinguished by their particular combinations of stressed and unstressed syllables, which confer upon each kind of feet a distinctive rhythmic pattern. The chief rhythmic patterns (with the names of their feet in parentheses) are the following.

Iambic (Iamb)

⌣ ′ unstressed–stressed

examples: forgive
           repeat
           the dog

WILLIAM BUTLER YEATS

THE WHEEL   58

Through win | ter-time | we call | on spring,
And through the spring on summer call,
And when abounding hedges ring
Declare that winter's best of all;
And after that there's nothing good   5
Because the spring-time has not come—
Nor know that what disturbs our blood
Is but its longing for the tomb.

1922

Trochaic (Trochee)

′ ‿ stressed–unstressed

examples: winter
                figure
                that way

HENRY WADSWORTH LONGFELLOW

FROM THE SONG OF HIAWATHA   59

Should you | ask me, | whence these | stories?
Whence these legends and traditions,
With the odors of the forest,
With the dew and damp of meadows,
With the curling smoke of wigwams,   5
With the rushing of great rivers,
With their frequent repetitions,
And their wild reverberations,
As of thunder in the mountains?

1855

Anapestic (Anapest)

‿ ‿ ′ unstressed–unstressed–stressed

examples: kangaroo
                bright blue eyes
                in the swamp

ROBERT BROWNING

FROM HOW THEY BROUGHT THE
GOOD NEWS FROM GHENT TO AIX 60

. . .Not a word | to each oth | er; we kept | the great pace
Neck by neck, stride by stride, never changing our place;
I turned in my saddle and made its girths tight,
Then shortened each stirrup, and set the pique right,
Rebuckled the cheek-strap, chained slacker the bit, 5
Nor galloped less steadily Roland a whit.

1845

This poem, describing a furious, 400-mile gallop, uses an anapestic meter to echo the rhythm of the galloping horse.

Dactylic (Dactyl)

′ ◡ ◡ stressed–unstressed–unstressed

examples: pocketbook
Washington
promise me

ALFRED, LORD TENNYSON

FROM THE CHARGE OF THE LIGHT BRIGADE 61

. . . Stormed at with | shot and shell,
White horse and | hero fell,
They that had fought so well
Came through the jaws of Death,
Back from the mouth of hell, 5
All that was left of them.
Left of six hundred.

1854

Spondaic (Spondee)

′ ′ stressed–stressed

examples: heartache
brown legs
green lawn

There are no poems in English written entirely in spondees; they are used only for variation within poems, as in this example from John Milton's *Paradise Lost:*

Rocks, caves, lakes, fens, bogs, dens, and shades of death.

METRICAL VARIATION

Scansion, or examining a poem to determine its meter, is not an exact science. Readers will at times scan poems with different results, to be expected because of regional differences in pronunciation and inflection, or maybe even because of differing interpretations of emphasis in a line of poetry. Nor should a reader expect poems in English to adhere to one meter only. A poem written in iambic pentameter, for example, will become monotonous very quickly if the writer does not vary the meter occasionally. Notice how in the third line of Browning's "How They Brought the Good News from Ghent to Aix," the established meter, anapestic tetrameter, varies slightly.

I turned in my saddle and made its girths tight. . . .

The first foot of the line is an *iamb* rather than an *anapest*. Such **substitution** creates welcome variation within regular rhythmic patterns, keeping them from becoming monotonous, and it draws attention to the words it undergirds. Compare, for example, the final line of this poem with the rhythmic pattern of the other lines.

R O B E R T   H E R R I C K
UPON A CHILD THAT DIED   62

Here she lies, a pretty bud,
Lately made of flesh and blood,
Who as soon fell fast asleep
As her little eyes did peep.
Give her strewing but not stir   5
The earth that lightly covers her.

1648

Notice how the trochaic meter of lines 1–5 is disturbed in the final line by the addition of an initial unstressed syllable, in effect creating a perfect iambic line. The heaviness and predictability of the trochaic rhythm throughout the poem is emphasized even more by the omission of the unaccented syllable of each

UPON A CHILD THAT DIED 5 *give her strewing:* cover her with flowers.

final trochee ("pretty bud," "flesh and blood," "fast asleep," "eyes did peep," "but not stir"). When the final line shifts into an iambic pattern, you can almost feel the lightness, the softening of "the earth that lightly covers her."

Another kind of variation, which provides relief within a predictable meter and emphasis within lines, among other functions, is **caesura,** a pause usually in the middle of a line. Caesura is often a creation of the grammar and punctuation in a line, and can be marked in scansion by a double vertical line (‖). Notice how frequently caesura occurs in this poem.

ROBERT FROST

"OUT, OUT—" 63

The buzz-saw snarled and rattled in the yard
And made dust and dropped stove-length sticks of wood,
Sweet-scented stuff when the breeze drew across it.
And from there those that lifted eyes could count
Five mountain ranges one behind the other   5
Under the sunset far into Vermont.
And the saw snarled and rattled, snarled and rattled,
As it ran light, or had to bear a load.
And nothing happened: day was all but done.
Call it a day, I wish they might have said   10
To please the boy by giving him the half hour
That a boy counts so much when saved from work.
His sister stood beside them in her apron
To tell them 'Supper.' At the word, the saw,
As if to prove saws knew what supper meant,   15
Leaped out at the boy's hand, or seemed to leap—
He must have given the hand. However it was,
Neither refused the meeting. But the hand!
The boy's first outcry was a rueful laugh,
As he swung toward them holding up the hand   20
Half in appeal, but half as if to keep
The life from spilling. Then the boy saw all—
Since he was old enough to know, big boy
Doing a man's work, though a child at heart—
He saw all spoiled. 'Don't let him cut my hand off—   25
The doctor, when he comes. Don't let him, sister!'
So. But the hand was gone already.
The doctor put him in the dark of ether.
He lay and puffed his lips out with his breath.

And then—the watcher at his pulse took fright.   30
No one believed. They listened at his heart.
Little—less—nothing!—and that ended it.
No more to build on there. And they, since they
Were not the one dead, turned to their affairs.

1916

The poem emphasizes physical fragility—how easy it is to lose a hand and then a life—how little it takes to interrupt the heartbeat and the breath. In telling this story of a young boy who loses his hand to a buzz-saw, Frost sometimes uses caesura to serve an onomatopoeic function, as in:

And the saw snarled and rattled, || snarled and rattled,
As it ran light, || or had to bear a load.

The rattling ceases for an instant and the snarl begins again as the line mimics its uneven sound. Its pitch is higher, then heavier, depending on the thickness of the wood, and echoing the interstices of time when it is not sawing anything but is being lifted to the next log. Notice also how light the words *as it ran light* sound compared to *had to bear a load,* which seems slower and heavier.

The use of caesura continues throughout the poem, often emphasized by punctuation as in:

And nothing happened: || day was all but done.
Call it a day, || I wish they might have said. . . .

or later:

His sister stood beside them in her apron
To tell them 'Supper.' || At the word, || the saw, ||
As if to prove saws knew what supper meant, ||
Leaped out at the boy's hand, || or seemed to leap—||
He must have given the hand. || However it was, || 5
Neither refused the meeting. || But the hand!

The word *Supper* causes the momentary pause—interrupting the action enough so that maybe the boy loses his concentration and then the saw leaps out, and in the stops and starts of the next few lines we see what has been sundered—the hand from the body—in the brokenness of the lines' rhythm.

Next, caesura suggests the irregular breathing and heartbeat of the child.

And then—|| the watcher at his pulse took fright.
No one believed. || They listened at his heart.
Little—|| less—|| nothing! ||—and that ended it.

Notice also how enjambment, or lines of poetry that run uninterruptedly into succeeding lines, also recreates the scene and its sounds. The first two lines of the poem continue without pause, one *and* leading naturally to the next, uninterrupted by line-end punctuation.

> The buzz-saw snarled *and* rattled in the yard
> *And* made dust *and* dropped stove length sticks of wood. . . .

The buzz-saw is described in continuous motion. Similarly, the continuity of the horizon, which seems to reach farther and farther back into space, is emphasized by the enjambment of three lines:

> And from there those that lifted eyes could count
> Five mountain ranges one behind the other
> Under the sunset far into Vermont.

A poet has many poetic devices to choose from, which together create the individual world of a poem. Rhythm, however, is an integral part of the music of poetry. It also is an ordering device, a way of containing and controlling the individual lines of a poem. Poems also use ordering devices of a larger sort, those provided by the traditional types and forms of poetry, which will be considered next.

CHAPTER 7

THE ORGANIZATION OF POETRY

METERED AND UNMETERED VERSE

You know that you are reading a poem because a poem's appearance on the page is different. Sometimes it is a narrow column of words, sometimes it is organized neatly into stanzas of consistent length, and sometimes its lines sprawl wildly across the paper. The poet's method of organizing verse depends on a number of factors, including subject matter and personality. The poet can choose to write in traditional poetic forms, create novel forms, or write **free verse.**

Although poets used free verse in earlier times, it is really only in the twentieth-century that it has become the predominant type of poetry written in English. Unlike poetry written in any of the fixed forms, free verse has no rules to guide its play, no predetermined structures such as rhyme patterns or regular meter or stanza arrangement to which it must conform. Robert Frost said that writing free verse is like playing tennis without a net. This is not to say that free verse entirely discards rhythm and rhyme as ordering factors. It is, instead, rather like playing music which emphasizes personal expressiveness over the regularity of the metronome.

Consider the following poem written in free verse. Notice the **syntax** (word order). Poets—not just those writing free verse—often distort ordinary syntax in order to emphasize certain words, images, and ideas, and in order to upset reader expectation so that a familiar scene or image can be apprehended in a new, fresh way. Free verse particularly encourages this kind of verbal play.

E. E. CUMMINGS

[ME UP AT DOES]   64

Me up at does

out of the floor
quietly Stare

a poisoned mouse

still who alive   5

is asking What
have i done that

You wouldn't have

1963

The scene is simple: on the floor a poisoned mouse, dying but still alive, stares up at the speaker and seems to be asking, "What have I done that you wouldn't have?" This moment of confrontation between mouse and man is unusual and disturbing, and the convoluted syntax reflects the disconcerting and suddenly sympathetic response of the man standing tall over the small creature on the floor.

Notice also the importance of *line break* (discussed under "The Poetic Line" in Chapter 1), which in free verse assumes even greater significance than in most other types of poetry. Even though free verse may seem to be completely "free" and without formal boundaries, it often uses lines and stanzas to divide a poem evenly into rhythmic and/or thematic sections. Notice, for example, how Cummings carefully divides the lines into four-syllable units and the poem into orderly stanzas, regularities which offset the convoluted syntax.

The lines of Cummings' poem are **enjambed,** requiring you not to pause but to keep going as you read the poem. Free verse may also be organized into **end-stopped lines,** poetic lines which end with a pause indicated by punctuation, as in the following.

WALT WHITMAN

A NOISELESS PATIENT SPIDER   65

A noiseless patient spider,
I marked where on a little promontory it stood isolated,
Marked how to explore the vacant vast surrounding,
It launched forth filament, filament, filament, out of itself,
Ever unreeling them, ever tirelessly speeding them.   5

And you O my soul where you stand,
Surrounded, detached, in measureless oceans of space,
Ceaselessly musing, venturing, throwing, seeking the spheres to
    connect them,
Till the bridge you will need be formed, till the ductile anchor hold,
Till the gossamer thread you fling catch somewhere, O my soul.   10

1881

Each line ends with a comma or a period, punctuation which divides the
two sentences of the poem into grammatical units. The first sentence, which
also forms the first five-line stanza, describes the spider. The second sentence
forms the second stanza, equal in length, describing the soul. Clearly, what
may seem at first glance to be formless verse, actually adheres to its own
internal rules. Free verse is rarely completely without form.

    Free verse may also be organized spatially, as it is in **concrete poetry,**
which uses the arrangement of typeface to create a visual effect.

ROGER MCGOUGH

40———LOVE

(66)

middle	aged
couple	playing
ten	nis
when	the
game	ends
and	they
go	home
the	net
will	still
be	be
tween	them

5

10

1971

    Concrete poetry needs to be seen to be appreciated. It can be recited or read
to an audience, but then its visual appeal disappears.

    Not all concrete poetry is written in free verse, however. Notice the shape
of the following poem, but notice also the pattern of rhyme and meter.

GEORGE HERBERT

THE ALTAR   67

A broken ALTAR, Lord, thy servant rears,
Made of a heart, and cemented with tears:
  Whose parts are as thy hand did frame;
  No workman's tool hath touched the same.
      A   HEART   alone   5
      Is   such   a   stone,
      As   nothing   but
      Thy power doth cut.
      Wherefore each part
      Of my hard heart   10
      Meets in this frame,
      To praise thy Name:
  That, if I chance to hold my peace,
  These stones to praise thee may not cease.
Oh let they blessed SACRIFICE be mine,   15
And sanctify this ALTAR to be thine.

1633

    In a poem of great subtlety and intricacy the poet describes an altar, using its form to organize his words. The altar he refers to is both literal and figurative. As a general symbol, the altar usually represents sacrifice and atonement, so in this poem the speaker says he constructs his altar from his broken heart, which he sacrifices to God. Anyone reading the poem, rather than just listening to it, can see that the poem is also written in the form of an altar. The poet, then, asks God in the last line to "sanctify this ALTAR to be thine"—to take his verse and purify it so it can serve as a sacrifice. Furthermore, the poet has written most of the poem in **couplets,** pairs of lines sharing the same meter, and in this case the same rhyme. Herbert has written a concrete poem, but he has also created his own set of rules, formal constraints within whose boundaries the poem is contained. This is not free verse.

    Why do some poets choose to write in poetic forms? Why do they make it so difficult for themselves? Part of the reason is that poetry is play, and the rules of the game make it both more challenging and more satisfying. Another reason is that the rules make the writer—and the reader—stretch for the unreachable, and in the process of reaching, both writer and reader discover surprises waiting for them in the language. These are often surprises and insights that never would have been discovered if the easiest and most immediate word or image or phrase had been used. Form provides a pattern, and the pattern must be appropriate or the poem will not work. Form and content are intimately related.

Metrical verse, poetry that is measured in stressed syllables, often is divided into regular stanzas. Some of these stanza forms take their names from their length. The couplet, as already noted, is a two-line stanza. When these two lines rhyme and are written in iambic pentameter, they are called a **heroic couplet.** Other stanza forms are the **tercet,** consisting of three lines; the **quatrain,** four; the **sestet,** six; and the **octave,** eight. In addition, stanzas of fixed length and rhyme patterns are the **Spenserian stanza** (*ababbcbcc,* eight iambic pentameter lines, one iambic hexameter line), the **rime royal** (*aabbbcc,* iambic pentameter), and the **ottava rima** (*abababcc,* iambic pentameter).

Syllabic verse is measured in syllables rather than in regularly accented feet. Marianne Moore is the chief proponent of syllabic verse in English.

MARIANNE MOORE

THE FISH 68

wade
through black jade.
   Of the crow-blue mussel shells, one keeps
   adjusting the ash heaps;
      opening and shutting itself like 5

an
injured fan.
   The barnacles which encrust the side
   of the wave, cannot hide
      there for the submerged shafts of the 10

sun,
split like spun
   glass, move themselves with spotlight swiftness
   into the crevices—
      in and out, illuminating 15

the
turquoise sea
   of bodies. The water drives a wedge
   of iron through the iron edge
      of the cliff; whereupon the stars, 20

pink
rice-grains, ink-
   bespattered jellyfish, crabs like green
   lilies, and submarine
      toadstools, slide each on the other. 25

All
external
   marks of abuse are present on this
   defiant edifice—
      all the physical features of   30

ac-
cident—lack
   of cornice, dynamite grooves, burns, and
   hatchet strokes, these things stand
      out on it; the chasm-side is   35

dead.
Repeated
   evidence has proved that it can live
   on what can not revive
      its youth. The sea grows old in it.   40

1921

Notice the symmetry of the stanzas—not just the way they appear on the page, but also the number of syllables per line in each stanza. The first line of every stanza has one syllable, the second line has three, the third has nine, and so on.

    Another way of organizing the poetic line is **blank verse,** unrhymed iambic pentameter, considered by many to be the poetic form closest to spoken English. It seems one of the most satisfying forms for poets, one of the most natural, and there is a strong tradition of excellent blank verse written in English. Milton chose it for *Paradise Lost,* Shakespeare for most of the dialogue in his plays, and the tradition continues to the twentieth century where it is the predominant form in the narrative poetry of Robert Frost, among many others.

ROBERT FROST

NOT TO KEEP   69

They sent him back to her. The letter came
Saying. . . And she could have him. And before
She could be sure there was no hidden ill
Under the formal writing, he was in her sight,
Living. They gave him back to her alive—   5
How else? They are not known to send the dead—
And not disfigured visibly. His face?
His hands? She had to look, to ask,
'What is it, dear?' And she had given all

And still she had all—*they* had—they the lucky!   10
Wasn't she glad now? Everything seemed won,
And all the rest for them permissible ease.
She had to ask, 'What was it, dear?'

                                   'Enough,
Yet not enough. A bullet through and through,
High in the breast. Nothing but what good care   15
And medicine and rest, and you a week,
Can cure me of to go again.' The same
Grim giving to do over for them both.
She dared no more than ask him with her eyes
How was it with him for a second trial.   20
And with his eyes he asked her not to ask.
They had given him back to her, but not to keep.

                                           1928

Line 13 appears to have only four feet, rather than the required five, but notice that the missing foot appears below it in a continuation of the line. This is called a **dropped line,** used here to indicate a change in speakers. For the most part this poem captures natural speech rhythms.

There are many other ways of organizing poems. Other fixed forms are more rigid in their strictures. A few of the more popular forms are described in the following sections.

TRADITIONAL FORMS

Ballad

The *folk ballad* is a short narrative poem, originally meant to be sung. Later poets, particularly the Romantics, chose the ballad form to create the *literary ballad* in which they imitated the early balladeers' simplicity of language and romantic themes. The ballad stanza consists of four lines with a rhyme scheme of *abcb* and alternating tetrameter and trimeter lines.

DUDLEY RANDALL

BALLAD OF BIRMINGHAM   70

(ON THE BOMBING OF A CHURCH IN BIRMINGHAM, ALABAMA, 1963)

"Mother dear, may I go downtown
Instead of out to play,
And march the streets of Birmingham
In a Freedom March today?"

"No, baby, no, you may not go,   5
For the dogs are fierce and wild,
And clubs and hoses, guns and jails
Aren't good for a little child."

"But, mother, I won't be alone.
Other children will go with me,   10
And march the streets of Birmingham
to make our country free."

"No, baby, no, you may not go,
For I fear those guns will fire.
but you may go to church instead   15
And sing in the children's choir."

She has combed and brushed her night-dark hair,
And bathed rose petal sweet,
And drawn white gloves on her small brown hands,
And white shoes on her feet.   20

The mother smiled to know her child
Was in the sacred place,
But that smile was the last smile
To come upon her face.

For when she heard the explosion,   25
Her eyes grew wet and wild.
She raced through the streets of Birmingham
Calling for her child.

She clawed through bits of glass and brick,
Then lifted out a shoe.   30
"O, here's the shoe my baby wore,
But, baby, where are you?"

1969

The traditional medieval ballad used dialogue and usually described feats of
physical courage and bouts with death. "Ballad of Birmingham," written in
the 1960s, uses traditional ballad stanzas to present conventional ballad themes
in a modern setting. Notice how similar the presentation and direction of this
contemporary ballad are to the medieval "The Wife of Usher's Well."

ANONYMOUS

THE WIFE OF USHER'S WELL

71

There lived a wife at Usher's Well,
　　And a wealthy wife was she;
She had three stout and stalwart sons,
　　And sent them o'er the sea.

They hadna' been a week from her,
　　A week but barely one
When word came to the carlin wife
　　That her three sons were gone.

They hadna' been a week from her,
　　A week but barely three,
When word came to the carlin wife
　　That her sons she'd never see.

"I wish the wind may never cease.
　　Nor fashes in the flood,
Till my three sons come home to me,
　　In earthly flesh and blood."

It fell about the Martinmas,
　　When nights are long and mirk
The carlin wife's three sons came home,
　　And their hats were o' the birk.

It neither grew in sike nor ditch,
　　Nor yet in any sheugh,
But at the gates o' Paradise
　　That birk grew fair eneugh.

"Blow up the fire, my maidens,
　　Bring water from the well:
For a' my house shall feast this night,
　　Since my three sons are well."

And she has made to them a bed,
　　She's made it large and wide,
And she's ta'en her mantle her about,
　　Sat down at the bedside.

5

10

15

20

25

30

THE WIFE OF USHER'S WELL 7 *carlin:* old woman. 14 *fashes:* trouble. 17 *Martinmas:* St. Martin's Day, November 11. 18. *mirk:* murky. 20 *birk:* birch. It was a common belief that the dead wore wreathes of leaves and branches when they returned to the living. 21 *sike:* meadow. 22 *sheugh:* furrow.

Up then crew the red, red cock,
    And up and crew the gray.
The eldest to the youngest said,   35
    "'Tis time we were away."

The cock he hadna' crawed but once,
    And clapped his wings at a',
When the youngest to the eldest said,
    "Brother, we must awa'.   40

"The cock doth craw, the day doth daw,
    The channerin worm doth chide:
Gin we be missed out o' our place,
    A sair pain we maun bide.

"Fare ye weel, my mother dear,   45
    Fareweel to barn and byre
And fare ye weel, the bonny lass
    That kindles my mother's fire."

In both ballads mothers bid farewell to children who set out on routine journeys that have fatal consequences. Notice, however, the tragic tone of "Ballad of Birmingham." "The Wife of Usher's Well" also contains tragedy, but the emphasis is not on the death of the sons so much as on the return of the ghosts. In "Ballad of Birmingham," the child's death, and the irony of the mother's futile attempt to protect her child from harm create the tone of desolation, a feeling that is particularly evident in the final image—the small shoe, the only sign she now has that the child ever existed. Five hundred years may separate the composition of these ballads, but they still involve the reader in similar ways. You do not need to know "The Wife of Usher's Well" in order to enjoy "Ballad of Birmingham," but reading the latter as a part of a tradition represented by the former enriches and deepens the experience.

Haiku

Haiku is a Japanese form. It is brief—usually three short lines or seventeen syllables—presenting one or two images and a sudden insight. In Japanese, haiku must also contain references to nature and to a season, and have some spiritual significance. Because of differences in the languages, traditional haiku cannot really be written in English. What we have done, however, is adapt the idea and the philosophy of the form to English use. Ezra Pound's "In the Station of the Metro" (24) captures some of the spirit of haiku. Robert Bly offers the following translation of one of the haiku masters of Japan, Kobayashi Issa.

41 *daw:* dawn. 42 *channerin:* murmuring. 43 *Gin:* if. 44 *A sair pain we maun bide:* a sore pain we must abide. 46 *byre:* cow house.

ROBERT BLY   72

The old dog bends his head listening . . .
I guess the singing
of the earthworms gets to him.

1969

Gary Snyder, another contemporary poet, has also experimented with the form.

GARY SNYDER   73

They didn't hire him
        so he ate his lunch alone:
the noon whistle

1965

Limerick

Another brief poetic form is the **limerick,** in which rhythm and rhyme create the humorous effect. It is a form of light verse.

HARVEY L. CARTER   74

'Tis a favorite project of mine
A new value of *pi* to assign.
        I would fix it at 3
        For it's simpler, you see,
Than 3 point 1 4 1 5 9.   5

1979

WELDON KEES   75

There was a French writer named Sartre
Who got off to a pretty good startre.
But as year followed year,
It got painfully clear
He was longer on wind than on artre.   5

1986

Limericks take their name from the city of Limerick, Ireland, where they first appeared as a party game in which participants took turns creating the lines.

Notice how rhyme, pun, rhythm, and visual effects combine to create the humor.

Sestina

One of the most complex poetic forms, the **sestina,** consists of six six-line stanzas and a final three-line stanza. The end words of the first six lines are repeated at the ends of all the succeeding lines in this prescribed order:

$$1, 2, 3, 4, 5, 6$$
$$6, 1, 5, 2, 4, 3$$
$$3, 6, 4, 1, 2, 5$$
$$5, 3, 2, 6, 1, 4$$
$$4, 5, 1, 3, 6, 2$$
$$2, 4, 6, 5, 3, 1$$
$$5, 3, 1$$

Poets often take liberty with the final stanza, which also uses words 2, 4, and 6 inside the lines or sometimes as substitutes for 5, 3, and 1.

RONALD WALLACE
GRANDMOTHER GRACE   76

I didn't give her a goodbye kiss
as I went off in the bus for the last time,
away from her house in Williamsburg, Iowa,
away from her empty house with Jesus
on all of the walls, with clawfoot tub and sink,   5
with the angular rooms that trapped my summers.

I remember going there every summer—
every day beginning with that lavender kiss,
that face sprayed and powdered at the upstairs sink,
then mornings of fragile teacups and old times,   10
afternoons of spit-moistened hankies and Jesus,
keeping me clean in Williamsburg, Iowa.

Cast off, abandoned, in Williamsburg, Iowa,
I sat in that angular house with summer
dragging me onward, hearing how Jesus   15
loved Judas despite his last kiss,
how he turned his other cheek time after time,
how God wouldn't let the good person sink.

Months later, at Christmas, my heart would sink
when that flowery letter from Williamsburg, Iowa   20
arrived, insistent, always on time,
stiff and perfumed as summer.
She always sealed it with a kiss,
a taped-over dime, and the words of Jesus.

I could have done without the words of Jesus;   25
the dime was there to make the message sink
in, I thought; and the violet kiss,
quavering and frail, all the way from Williamsburg, Iowa,
sealed some agreement we had for the next summer
as certain and relentless as time.   30

I didn't know this would be the last time.
If I had, I might even have prayed to Jesus
to let me see her once again next summer.
But how could I know she would sink
her feet fat boats of cancer, in Williamsburg, Iowa,   35
alone, forsaken, without my last kiss?

I was ten, Jesus, and the idea of a kiss
at that time made my young stomach sink.

Let it be summer. Let it be Williamsburg, Iowa.

1981

The sestina, like the ballad and the prose poem, invites narrative. The form is exact, but the poem is also long with much space to fill, so poets often will use it to tell a story or draw a character or evoke a time and a place in particular detail. The sestina particularly challenges the poet and the reader to create variation within repetition.

Sonnet

The **sonnet** is ordinarily a fourteen-line poem of a fixed rhyme pattern. Two traditional sonnet forms are the **Italian sonnet** and the **Shakespearean sonnet**. The rhyme scheme of the Italian sonnet is usually *abbaabba, cdecde*, divided into an octave, which presents a problem or asks a question, and a sestet, which offers a resolution, a further development, or an answer.

JOHN KEATS

ON THE GRASSHOPPER AND THE CRICKET   77

The poetry of earth is never dead:
  When all the birds are faint with the hot sun,
  And hide in cooling trees, a voice will run
From hedge to hedge about the new-mown mead;
That is the Grasshopper's—he takes the lead   5
  In summer luxury,—he has never done
  With his delights; for when tired out with fun
He rests at ease beneath some pleasant weed.
The poetry of earth is ceasing never:
  On a long winter evening, when the frost   10
    Has wrought a silence, from the stove there shrills
The Cricket's song, in warmth increasing ever,
  And seems to one in drowsiness half lost,
    The Grasshopper's among some grassy hills.

1817

The description of the grasshopper in summer fills the octave of the poem, and
with the ninth line one sees the *turn* in the poem—that point at which it begins
to change direction. Lines 9–14, the sestet, then describe another scene and
another creature—the hearth cricket in winter—and finally in the last line the
poem returns to the theme of the grasshopper.

    The Shakespearean sonnet usually has a rhyme scheme of *abab, cdcd, efef, gg.*
The three quatrains may present three variations of the same theme, although
there are important shifts from quatrain to quatrain in imagery and tone.

WILLIAM SHAKESPEARE

SONNET 73   78
[THAT TIME OF YEAR THOU MAYST IN ME BEHOLD]

That time of year thou mayst in me behold
When yellow leaves, or none, or few, do hang
Upon those boughs which shake against the cold,
Bare ruined choirs, where late the sweet birds sang.
In me thou see'st the twilight of such day   5
As after sunset fadeth in the west;
Which by and by black night doth take away,
Death's second self that seals up all in rest.

In me thou see'st the glowing of such fire,
That on the ashes of his youth doth lie,   10
As the deathbed whereon it must expire,
Consumed with that which it was nourished by.
This thou perceiv'st, which makes thy love more strong,
To love that well which thou must leave ere long.

1609

Notice how important the final couplet is in the Shakespearean sonnet. In this type of sonnet you will not actually experience a turn until the couplet, which serves both as a summarizing statement and a new direction, an expansion of the theme.

Wordsworth tackled the issue of poetic form in a poem which presents a series of metaphors to describe the poet who chooses the sonnet form.

WILLIAM WORDSWORTH

NUNS FRET NOT AT THEIR
CONVENT'S NARROW ROOM   79

Nuns fret not at their convent's narrow room:
And hermits are contented with their cells;
And students with their pensive citadels;
Maids at the wheel, the weaver at his loom,
Sit blithe and happy; bees that soar for bloom,   5
High as the highest Peak of Furness-fells,
Will murmur by the hour in foxglove bells:
In truth the prison, into which we doom
Ourselves, no prison is: and hence for me,
In sundry moods, 'twas pastime to be bound   10
Within the sonnet's scanty plot of ground;
Pleased if some soul (for some there needs must be)
Who have felt the weight of too much liberty.
Should find brief solace there, as I have found.

1807

These sparse and disciplined ways of life of nun, hermit, student, maid, and weaver do not require enormous expanses of space. Even the bee is happiest inside the small room of the flower. Just so, the speaker says, the sonnet is a form which encloses him in order to give him ground for creativity. The sonnet, that "scanty plot of ground," is fertile enough and provides space enough for the writer's happiness—and, furthermore, he chooses it freely. The sonnet's form is both the subject matter and the *modus operandi*.

Many variations of the sonnet form exist, particularly in contemporary poetry which often combines the Italian and the Shakespearean, or sometimes creates other hybrid forms. The sonnet remains a popular poetic form because it is long enough to allow the development of a major idea or experience, but it is short enough to encourage economy of expression.

Terza rima

Terza rima links three-line stanzas with the rhyme scheme, *aba, bcb, cdc, ded, efe*. Notice that the end word of the second line of each stanza provides the rhyme for the first and third lines of the following stanza.

PERCY BYSSHE SHELLEY

THE TOWER OF FAMINE   80

Amid the desolation of a city,
Which was the cradle, and is now the grave
Of an extinguished people—so that Pity

Weeps o'er the shipwrecks of Oblivion's wave,
There stands the Tower of Famine. It is built   5
Upon some prison-homes, whose dwellers rave

For bread, and gold, and blood: Pain, linked to Guilt,
Agitates the light flame of their hours,
Until its vital oil is spent or spilt.

There stands the pile, a tower amid the towers   10
And sacred domes; each marble-ribbed roof,
The brazen-gated temples, and the bowers

Of solitary wealth—the tempest-proof
Pavilions of the dark Italian air—
Are by its presence dimmed—they stand aloof,   15

And are withdrawn—so that the world is bare;
As if a specter wrapped in shapeless terror
Amid a company of ladies fair

Should glide and glow, till it became a mirror
Of all their beauty, and their hair and hue,   20
The life of their sweet eyes, with all its error,
Should be absorbed, till they to marble grew.

1829

Why would Shelley have chosen this particular form for this poem? It wasn't just happenstance, for in fact he is describing an incident at Pisa that Dante related in terza rima in his *Inferno*. The story is of a ruler who seizes control of Pisa and then with his sons and grandsons is locked into the tower and left to starve. The interwoven stanzas capture this feeling of confinement and desperation.

Villanelle

Originally a French form, the **villanelle** is composed of five three-line stanzas and a concluding quatrain. The first and third lines of the first stanza are repeated alternatingly as the final lines of the next four stanzas, and then they come together to form a final couplet in the concluding quatrain. The middle lines of each of the tercets rhyme, as do the repeated lines.

DYLAN THOMAS

DO NOT GO GENTLE INTO THAT GOOD NIGHT   81

Do not go gentle into that good night, A
Old age should burn and rave at close of day; b
Rage, rage against the dying of the light. A

Though wise men at their end know dark is right,
Because their words had forked no lightning they   5
Do not go gentle into that good night.

Good men, the last wave by, crying how bright
Their frail deeds might have danced in a green bay,
Rage, rage against the dying of the light.

Wild men who caught and sang the sun in flight,   10
And learn, too late, they grieved it on its way,
Do not go gentle into that good night.

Grave men, near death, who see with blinding sight
Blind eyes could blaze like meteors and be gay,
Rage, rage against the dying of the light.   15

And you, my father, there on the sad height,
Curse, bless, me now with your fierce tears, I pray.
Do not go gentle into that good night.
Rage, rage against the dying of the light.

1952

The two lines, repeated throughout as a refrain, create a tension resolved in the final couplet when they finally unite to form the one thought they have been pushing towards all along. This tension and the drive toward its ultimate resolution keep the poem moving until the rhyme of the opposites *night* and *light* in the final couplet satisfies both the ear and the intellect.

Improvisation

Occasionally, you will discover that the lines between poetry and prose blur. One type of poetry contains none of the traditional structural or thematic elements discussed so far. Neither free verse nor lyric nor epic, it is, nonetheless, a type of poetry.

The **prose poem** is not as contradictory as it may sound. On the page it looks like prose, but it possesses all of the other characteristics of poetry—sensory images, more particular attention to rhythms and cadences, sound effects, and so on. The following prose poem is a section from a longer piece, *The Letting Down of the Hair,* a modern rendition of the Rapunzel fairy tale.

ANNE SEXTON

THE WINDOW THAT WATCHED THE PRU
82

I have never cut my hair. That's something you ought to know right off. It fills the room the way ten giraffes would, twisting and twisting their long innocent necks. My hair is innocent, too. It knows no better.

I have one window in this room and from it can see over the countryside. The lilacs in April blushing like ten-year-old ballet dancers. The snows of Valentine's Day laid out as smooth and as humped as a dentist's chair. And then there is the clock tower, striking the hour as faithful as a town crier. But today, this May 25, the new leaves are green. They are my green ladies. They sing. They call out to me. They are the Christs of the grass.

But at night I watch the lights in the blackness. At night, along with the stars, those neon jacks. I watch the Pru and under it the skyline of Boston. The Pru stands up like an electrified totem pole. And the planes jet over from Chicago on their way to Logan Airport. In their bellies they carry one hundred and twenty people. I am alone. I am in my room. The room is my belly. It carries me.

1972

The woman in the poem watches the seasons from the window of the room where she lives alone. On this particular day, May 25th, she feels a strong stirring, a realized connection with the new season, the leaves, the outdoors.

THE WINDOW THAT WATCHED THE PRU title *Pru:* the Prudential Building in Boston.

At night she looks to the lights of the stars and of the city, but it is with the passengers in the planes flying overhead that she most identifies because they are encased in a room, as is she.

The prose poem gracefully contains narrative. It allows the reader the fluidity of prose while preserving the qualities of poetry that make it pleasing to the ear. It also, to a certain extent, represents a break with the traditions of formal poetry. While the prose poem finds its roots in Greek poetry, which did not use line breaks, the acknowledged beginning of prose poetry occurred much later, in nineteenth-century France among poets rebelling against the strict rules for versification which had developed over the centuries. The fixed forms of poetry still exist, however, in spite of the twentieth-century surge toward free verse and the development of types such as the prose poem.

The conventions of poetry are consistent but not invariable. Indeed, many poets play against the conventions, varying a rhyme scheme or a metrical pattern, truncating, inverting, or doubling forms. Wherever there is a form, there are exceptions and variations to those forms. Sometimes a poet will vary a form and that variation will become yet another form. Gerard Manley Hopkins, for example, created the **curtal sonnet,** a shortened version of the Italian sonnet (as *curtal* itself is a shortened version of *curtailed*). He wrote two of these sonnets, and other poets later used the form for their verse.

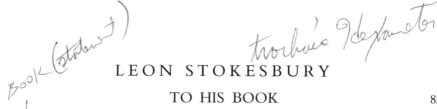

LEON STOKESBURY

TO HIS BOOK   83

Wafer; thin and hard and bitter pill I
   Take from time to time; pillow I have lain
      Too long on; holding the brief dreams, the styled
Dreams, the nightmares, shadows, red flames high
   High up on mountains; wilted zinnias, rain   5
      On dust, and great weight, the dead dog, and wild
Onions; mastodonic woman who knows how,—
   I'm tired of you, tired of your insane
      Acid eating in the brain. Sharp stones, piled
Particularly, I let you go. Sink, or float, or fly now,   10
      Bad child.

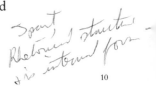

1976

This curtal sonnet consists of ten-and-a-half lines. The original octave of the Italian sonnet has become a sestet, describing the speaker's book. The original sestet of the Italian sonnet has become four-and-a-half lines, commenting and acting on the earlier description.

It should be clear, then, that the fixed forms of poetry do not necessarily constrain a poet or a reader, although they can provide a guiding framework for the images of a poetic experience. They not only provide challenge, they also introduce endless opportunity for development and variation. Like the rules of tennis—or the net on the playing court—the fixed forms of poetry provide the background and sometimes the obstacles which can make the game more exciting and satisfying for the participants.

CHAPTER 8

CAREFUL READING

Each time you read a poem, you will find something new. In fact, you will probably discover that each reading is slightly different from the last. Sometimes, however, you may bring to the poem certain biases and presuppositions which will limit your reading if you are not careful. Early in a poem you need to "suspend your disbelief," as the poet Samuel Coleridge once advised. In other words, you need to believe that any meaning is possible. As your reading progresses, and the poem develops, the words and images of the poem will begin to suggest possible meanings, and you need to be receptive and ready to go wherever the poem may take you.

An important first step in avoiding mistakes in reading is to be certain of the meaning of the words in the poem. While a poem contains meaning beyond the denotative definitions of its words, you still have an obligation to know these denotations in addition to the connotations of those words and any personal associations those connotations have for you.

Sometimes, in attempting to create personal connections with a poem in the first stages of reading it, you may find yourself tempted to completely rewrite the poem according to a particular experience you may have had. For example, for some students "My Papa's Waltz" (52) by Theodore Roethke triggers completely negative associations. Probably for personal reasons, *whiskey* and *papa* are words which these readers could never connect in an amusing way. It is difficult for these individuals to read the poem as anything other than a description of an abusive, alcoholic father who instills terror in his child. Personal connections with the theme and images of a poem are important in a first reading, but you should not allow your own experience to *replace* the experience the poem presents. Instead, use your own experience as an entry into the poem, but then, in the analytical stages of interpretation, look beyond purely personal associations. Remember that you must consider tone and word choice. Roethke's title should provide a hint of what is to come. *Waltz* is a key word, and its denotative and connotative meanings set the stage for the action in the rest of the poem. A waltz is not a violent dance—it is graceful and performed in gracious society. The irony, of course, is that the father is neither graceful nor a part of gracious society. He is unsteady on his feet, having drunk too much, and he does scare his child a bit with the raucousness of the dance. But the dance is still a "waltz," their activity is a "romp," and the child exits the poem "clinging" to his father. This is not a child being knocked around by a violent father. This is a father and child shown in relationship—the child somewhat overwhelmed, but still quite attached to a father whose actions are not gentle but are affectionate nonetheless.

So be careful about jumping to premature conclusions. Remember that you must find support for your reading in *all* of the words and images of a poem.

Another related problem arises when you limit yourself to discovering only what you *expect* to discover in a poem—perhaps only *one* object, situation, point-of-view, or character. Good poetry provides a rich reading experience, and you need to be ready for surprises and suddenly gained insights. If, for example, you read Karl Shapiro's "Buick" (55) to gather clues about the car's physical description so that you can determine its precise year and model, you will have engaged in an exercise which may be personally satisfying to you, but if you stop there you will have excluded the rest of the poem. You will have neglected to create the beauty of the car and will have ignored the complex relationship the speaker has with the machine. You will have missed most of the poem.

Poetry has a lot to offer you. It will take you to places you have never been and introduce you to experiences you have never had, if you keep your eyes open. But if you read a poem only to discover ways in which it supports your religious beliefs or your political stance—or if you read only for biographical data the author may reveal—or if you read only for the symbols—or only to discern the metrical pattern—you are reading with your eyes half-closed.

The problems discussed so far are symptoms of careless reading. You need to look carefully at the poem to discover what it is, bringing your own personal connections and associations with you, but not allowing them to sidetrack you or to blind you to the experience described in the poem. Careless reading, jumping to conclusions, and reading with closed eyes are in evidence in one student's response to the following poem.

WILLIAM WORDSWORTH
THE WORLD IS TOO MUCH WITH US 84

The world is too much with us; late and soon,
Getting and spending, we lay waste our powers;
Little we see in Nature that is ours;
We have given our hearts away, a sordid boon!
This sea that bares her bosom to the moon, 5

The winds that will be howling at all hours,
And are up-gathered now like sleeping flowers,
For this, for everything, we are out of tune;
It moves us not.—Great God! I'd rather be
A pagan suckled in a creed outworn;   10
So might I, standing on this pleasant lea,
Have glimpses that would make me less forlorn,
Have sight of Proteus rising from the sea;
Or hear old Triton blow his wreathèd horn.

1807

The poem emphasizes our materialism and mindless desecration of the natural world. The speaker points out that we have so disconnected ourselves from the natural world that we don't even see or hear it anymore. Such a separation from the power and rejuvenating effects of nature have hurt us immeasurably, and the speaker stands by the sea wishing for the connections that once linked us inexorably to nature, but that are now gone.

One student, attempting an analysis of the poem, wrote:

> The speaker of this poem, obsessed with nature's beauty, is distraught and spiritually disturbed. In fact, his faith in God is completely tainted by his obsession with nature.

The student's condemnation of the speaker's supposed philosophic stance led her to a mistaken reading. She allowed herself to be sidetracked by the exclamation, "Great God!" and the reference to the pagan gods. These references are images used to emphasize the degree of the speaker's distress, but the student was mistakenly scandalized by the speaker's statement: "I'd rather be / A pagan suckled in a creed outworn." The speaker is saying that he feels so dissociated from nature and its restorative powers that he looks back with some nostalgia to the outmoded beliefs of ancient times because at least the pagan gods were gods of nature. But the student's outrage blinded her to the poem and led her eventually off on a tangent. She continued:

> This individual is unsettled because he is spending too much time trying to discredit human economic efforts. "Getting and spending" are natural human activities. His idea that nature is the ultimate answer to every problem blinds him to his own faults.

The student fought the poem from the beginning. She limited it, she misread it, she forgot to consider denotative and connotative meanings of words. *Spending,* for example, also means "using up" or "depleting." The implication in the second line of the poem is that we have spent ourselves and we have no power left. The student, however, neglected to consider this. By the last paragraph of her paper she had discarded the poem entirely, and had turned the paper into a treatise on free trade.

Some readers are over-active symbol-hunters. For example, one student interpreted Williams' poem, "The Red Wheelbarrow" (14), as a poem about thwarted sexuality. His interpretation relied upon the tertiary meaning of *barrow:* a castrated pig. This initial error, in which he completely ignored the "*wheel*barrow," led to an extremely forced reading. He associated *red* with blood, thereby making "red . . . barrow" a particularly violent image of castration, which he then juxtaposed to the rain, a symbol of fertility. Because of the association of *white* with purity, the white chickens then became, in his convoluted reading, symbols of denied virginity, or rape. He concluded that the poem demonstrated the tension and ambiguity inherent in sexuality. At the best, this is an extremely forced interpretation which depends on obscure definitions and strained relationships between images. At the worst, it has ruined the poem, making it into an intellectual game of no real significance.

This misinterpretation of word meanings, which plagued both students in their reactions to the poems above is a particular danger in readings of medieval and Renaissance verse. The English language changes almost weekly, so be particularly careful in your assumptions about language when you read poetry from earlier eras. For example, a frequent misinterpretation of George Herbert's "The Collar" (86) occurs when readers assume that the author refers to a clerical collar a minister or priest might wear. However, during the seventeenth century, when Herbert wrote, clerics did not wear collars. A good reference work to consult in this case would be the *Oxford English Dictionary* (often referred to as the *O.E.D.*), which not only lists word meanings and records changes through the ages, but also gives examples of particular word usages from literature of the time.

Related to the problems of a changing vocabulary is poetry's frequent use of allusion to historical events, personages, other works of art, biblical stories, and so on.

W. H. AUDEN

MUSÉE DES BEAUX ARTS   85

About suffering they were never wrong,
The Old Masters: how well they understood
Its human position; how it takes place
While someone else is eating or opening a window or just walking
    dully along;
How, when the aged are reverently, passionately waiting   5
For the miraculous birth, there always must be
Children who did not specially want it to happen, skating
On a pond at the edge of the wood:

They never forgot
That even the dreadful martyrdom must run its course   10
Anyhow in a corner, some untidy spot
Where the dogs go on with their doggy life and the torturer's horse
Scratches its innocent behind on a tree.
In Brueghel's *Icarus,* for instance: how everything turns away
Quite leisurely from the disaster; the ploughman may   15
Have heard the splash, the forsaken cry,
But for him it was not an important failure; the sun shone
As it had to on the white legs disappearing into the green
Water; and the expensive delicate ship that must have seen
Something amazing, a boy falling out of the sky,   20
Had somewhere to get to and sailed calmly on.

1940

To understand this poem, you need to know that Brueghel was a sixteenth-century painter. It would enrich your reading if you also knew the painting, *The Fall of Icarus,* but if you are not familiar with that particular piece of art, you still should be able to visualize it from the details in the poem. You most certainly will have to know something about the myth of Daedalus and Icarus if the poem is to engage your imagination at all. You cannot ignore Auden's allusions and expect to be an active reader of the poem.

Avoid the trap of attempting to interpret a poem according to its author's intentions. Intentions are elusive. When Robert Frost said that he meant to do nothing more than describe a winter scene in "Stopping by Woods on a Snowy Evening" (226), and that he was not referring to death in the last two lines, he was probably truthfully describing his intentions. However, despite his stated intentions, the last two lines contain implications of death which most readers cannot ignore.

But though you need not consider an author's intentions, you need not ignore them either. Be cautious. Keep your eyes open. Accept whatever you find useful in interpreting a poem: the author's own words, pieces of the poet's biography, similar uses of imagery in other poems, but be sure that your reading of the poem is indeed supported by what is in the poem.

Sometimes paraphrase is helpful in your initial attempts to understand the organization and meaning of a poem, but do not make the mistake of reducing a poem to prose and then leaving it there. Too much is happening in a good poem for a paraphrase ever to capture it.

MUSEE DES BEAUX ARTS 14 *Brueghel:* Pieter Brueghel, a sixteenth-century Flemish painter. His work, *The Fall of Icarus,* hangs in a museum in Brussels. Icarus and his father, Daedalus, were figures from mythology, known for Daedalus' attempts to fashion wings for his son so that he could fly. The contraption worked until Icarus flew too close to the sun, the wax holding the wings to his body melted, and he fell into the sea.

Mistakes in reading are usually the result of either carelessness or too much tampering. Although the poem doesn't really exist until you read it, you still must read it attentively and you must not force it into directions it does not want to go. Test whether the *whole poem*—each image, metaphor, simile, and symbol—supports your reading of the poem. The tone of the poem and the connotations of words and phrases must be consistent with your reading. You must also understand the poem's allusions and the denotative meanings of its words. Be open to a poem's possibilities; allow it to enlarge your experience.

CHAPTER 9

WRITING ABOUT POETRY

Now that you know about rhyme, meter, and the forms of poetry, you need to push that knowledge aside for a moment and remember the suggestions from Chapter 3. Poetry reading is not a mechanical exercise, nor is a poem a collection of poetic devices. Once you have identified the form, the rhyme scheme, and the metrical pattern, once you have discovered the image patterns and identified the symbols, you still have not created a reading of a poem. You have responded personally to the poem and moved beyond that to more analytical concerns, but you must now put your scattered observations into a larger context. You must, as a reader, now re-create the poem.

Once you have come this far, it helps to have your pen in hand as you read. You need to order and test your responses, and that begins with underlinings, marginal notes, or scribbles on a notepad. Writing even random notes helps you to clarify and to organize your thoughts. Once you begin to translate your thinking into writing, you will begin to think more clearly. Writing will force you to articulate what you may have felt only vaguely. It will help you to test your ideas. Writing will help you to discover what it is you actually *do* think.

From your first sketchy notes you might further develop your thoughts in an informal journal or by providing short answers to questions presented later in this chapter. You eventually might even choose to present your conclusions in a polished paper. At any rate, remember that all forms of writing—from casual notes to formal, footnoted papers—can enhance your understanding of poetry. Your own writing will guide and form your re-creation of the poem.

THE LITERARY JOURNAL

You may find that keeping a literary journal is a helpful tool in understanding poetry because the journal allows—in fact, requires—you to become actively engaged by each poem you read. Journal-writing forces you to articulate concepts and to come to terms with the poetry you read in ways which you simply would not be challenged to do if you simply read a poem without a written response. Obviously, the key to a successful journal is commitment, for it is only through regular and sustained writing and thinking that the journal works.

The journal is a record of your readings and your reactions to the literature assigned to you. It is a place for you to present *and form* your responses to the literature, not necessarily a place for you to display your mastery of the finer points of writing. In other words, the journal is a place for you to reveal your own voice and your sincere, uncensored responses to the poetry, as one student demonstrates in her journal entry on the following poem.

GEORGE HERBERT

THE COLLAR   86

I struck the board, and cried, "No more.
    I will abroad.
What? shall I ever sigh and pine?
My lines and life are free; free as the road,
  Loose as the wind, as large as store.   5
    Shall I be still in suit?
Have I no harvest but a thorn
To let me blood, and not restore
What I have lost with cordial fruit?
    Sure there was wine   10
Before my sighs did dry it; there was corn
    Before my tears did drown it.
  Is the year only lost to me?
    Have I no bays to crown it?
No flowers, no garlands gay? all blasted?   15
    All wasted?
Not so, my heart; but there is fruit.
    And thou hast hands.
    Recover all thy sigh-blown age
On double pleasures: leave thy cold dispute   20
Of what is fit and not. Forsake thy cage,
    Thy rope of sands,
Which petty thoughts have made, and made to thee
  Good cable, to enforce and draw,
    And be thy law,   25
  While thou didst wink and wouldst not see.

Away! take heed;
        I will abroad.
Call in thy death's head there; tie up thy fears.
                He that forbears   30
        To suit and serve his need,
                Deserves his load."
But as I raved and grew more fierce and wild
                At every word,
        Methoughts I heard one calling, *Child!*   35
        And I replied, *My Lord.*

                                            1633

There is a lot in George Herbert's "The Collar"
that I don't understand, even after reading it several
times. On the other hand I think there is a lot I
understand by trying to read it more intuitively and
less objectively and trusting my intuitions. Here is
a man who is feeling trapped and stifled, either by
his own self-restraint or by some institutional
expectation, or both—and I think it is both. The
first two lines remind me of some of the beginnings of
John Donne's poems—dramatic and abrupt. Apparently
the speaker has been brooding over his feelings of
frustration, maybe for a few hours, and they come to a
head, and burst out into the beginning of the poem.

He seems to be trying to unshackle himself from
the burdens that come with being a religious person.
He is crying out against restraint: "What? shall I
ever sigh and pine? My lines and life are
free. . . ." He seems to be defensive about the
freedom that is inherently his but which he hasn't
been allowed to practice. It is terrific to realize
that you really are free as the road, loose as the
wind, as large as store. When I was growing up in a
small rural town, my family was criticized because my
brother's hair hung an inch over the top of his ear.
He was told discreetly that he could either drop out
of the church choir or push his hair behind his ears
when singing. That is when we decided to find another
church.

Realizing that we were "free indeed" came in a burst, as with the speaker in Herbert's poem. He realizes that his "harvest" has been only "thorns." He wants to restore his original joy and freedom, the cordial fruit, wine, and corn that have since been choked out by sighs and tears. How much better it is to look back on a year and see flowers——even the ones that grow out of pain——than to look back and realize you've somehow let yourself be defeated by the thorns. He is surprised and disappointed by his own blasted and wasted months. I'm not sure what Herbert means by recovering "double pleasures," but there might be shades of Job here. After a time of spiritual void and pain, he looks forward to a time of pleasure twice as great as it ever was before.

But then his ravings suddenly cease as he quietly answers the summons in the final line. What does this mean? What has all of this been about? This final response seems to negate everything else in the poem.

Notice the informal style, her sensitivity to her personal reactions based in her personal experience, and the focus on what she discovers as she reads. Notice also the importance of her final, unanswered questions. In these questions lies the beginning of her full understanding of the poem. Remember that often it is not your definite answers but your unanswered questions about a poem that need to be pursued.

Whether you are interested in beginning a journal but still uncertain about how to approach it, or whether you are preparing to write a paper, the following checklist should help guide your responses. In a journal entry, you will not necessarily have to organize your responses, although you will discover that the more you write, the more coherent, articulate, and organized you will become. Of course, a formal paper requires a much tighter organization, but you cannot begin to write a paper without preparing for it—and writing answers to the following questions will help you to do just that.

PREPARING TO WRITE A PAPER

The Personal Response

1. Quickly jot down initial responses to the poem. Do not analyze the poem.
2. What is the most striking part of the poem for you? Which element elicits the most interest?

3. With what do you ordinarily associate that element? Any personal connections?
4. Does anything particularly please you or bother you about the poem? Do you react positively or negatively to any of the words or images?
5. What puzzles you about the poem? Do you understand its syntax and words? Are its images clear to you?
6. What might be the main idea of the poem?
7. Do you consider the poem important, mildly affecting, or deeply moving?

The Analytical Response

8. What does the title lead you to expect?
9. List the "facts" of the poem: the speaker, the audience, the setting, the characters if any, any other information the poem gives you. List its images. Do they form categories or patterns or do they interconnect in any way?
10. Does the poem contain metaphors or similies? Do they relate thematically to one another? Any extended metaphors or conceits? synecdoche?
11. Do any images in the poem seem to be operating as symbols?
12. Does the poem use paradox? What other factors in the poem work to make the paradox seem "logical"?
13. Can you discern a difference between the speaker's words and his motives or intentions? Is there a surprise or sudden reversal?
14. Describe the tone of the poem. Is it cynical, joyful, excited, reverent, questioning, nostalgic, angry, contemplative?
15. How does the poem look on the page? Is it written in a traditional form or style? in a consistent meter? in syllabic verse? Does it depart from standard form at any point? Has the author created a stanzaic pattern unique to this poem?
16. What kinds of sound effects do you find? perfect or slant rhyme? internal rhyme? alliteration? consonance, assonance? onomatopoiea? repetition? caesura? enjambment? anaphora? convoluted syntax? Why are they present?
17. What seems to be the central action, subject, theme, and/or purpose of the poem? How do its individual elements relate to its subject and purpose? (Is there any discrepancy between this answer and your answer to #6 above? If so, have you gone off on a tangent? suffered from limited reader expectation? mistaken the tone? been an overly ambitious symbol-hunter? been certain of word meanings throughout? understood the allusions?)

In answering these questions you are participating in a significant prewriting activity. You are putting into words everything that you now know and everything that you are in the process of learning about the poem. All of these questions, and your answers to them, are important, even if you decide never to use the answers in a formal paper—so answer as many of them as you can. After you have established personal connections with a poem and analyzed its elements, you should be able to come up with a *thesis,* a statement indicating the main idea of the poem and the direction you are going to take in your discussion of it.

It may be helpful to observe the development of one student's response to a poem—a response she later developed into a paper.

T. R. HUMMER

THE RURAL CARRIER STOPS TO KILL A NINE-FOOT COTTONMOUTH 87

Lord God, I saw the son-of-a-bitch uncoil
In the road ahead of me, uncoil and squirm
For the ditch, squirm a hell of a long time.
Missed him with the car. When I got back to him, he was all
But gone, nothing left on the road but the tip-end   5
Of his tail, and that disappearing into Johnson grass.
I leaned over the ditch and saw him, balled up now, hiss.
I aimed for the mouth and shot him. And shot him again.

Then I got a good strong stick and dragged him out.
He was long and evil, thick as the top of my arm.   10
There are things in this world a man can't look at without
Wanting to kill. Don't ask me why. I was calm
Enough, I thought. But I felt my spine
Squirm, suddenly. I admit it. It was mine.

1982

THE PERSONAL RESPONSE

1. Quick, initial responses:

The snake is evil, deadly. I am assaulted by the language of the first line (it doesn't seem like "poetic" language at all), but it doesn't shock me because the title has alerted me to the presence of danger which will require a strong response. Exciting and violent. Something like a fairy-tale about the commoner who kills the dragon and becomes a hero.

2. Most striking part of the poem:

Aiming for the mouth of the snake and shooting it. The image with the most interest: the snake described as being as "thick as the top of my arm." This is a big snake.

3. Personal connections:

A childhood memory of a lake in Florida. I lay on the dock, sunning myself. My little brother, about age three, sat on the shore and reached forward to splash in the water. My mother sat a couple of yards from him. All of a sudden, screams. The other children ran out of the water. My brother sat transfixed, smiling at the snake that had just slithered next to him. My mother tentatively, slowly, cautiously reached for the child as a man raised a water-ski over his head. My mother jerked the child from the wet sand, and at the same time the man's arms came down and his ski sliced the snake in half.

4. Reactions to individual words or images:

I react negatively to every image. It's not that I dislike the poem, but the images in the poem make me shiver with revulsion. It's like walking barefoot at night and suddenly feeling something alive underfoot.

5. Parts that are unclear:

What is "Johnson grass"?

Why is the man's reaction so violent?

6. Main idea:

The main idea seems to be expressed in lines 11-12.

There are things in this world a man can't look
at without
Wanting to kill. Don't ask me why.

7. Effect of poem:

Terrifying.

THE ANALYTICAL RESPONSE

8. Title:

Leads me to expect a description which will make me squeamish.

9. The facts:

All of the information is in the title: a rural mail-carrier stops to kill a nine-foot cottonmouth. He is driving along a country road and sees a snake ahead. The snake uncoils and heads for the ditch, and the driver tries to hit it with the car but misses. He stops the car, goes back to the ditch, finds the snake, shoots it, and picks it up. He then gets a shiver down his spine.

There seems to be a connection between the squirming of the snake, which is emphasized in the first stanza, and the squirming of the man's spine. All of the images relate--and all of the words are connected in some way. For example, "uncoil," "squirm," "ditch," and "tail" make me think of worms, snakes, swampy areas. The swearing seems the only possible verbal response to a creature so long and evil. This poem is all of a piece--everything is connected, nothing is extraneous.

10. Metaphors or Similes?

The poem contains only one simile, which I have already quoted: "He was long and evil, thick as the top of my arm." This is a visual and tactile simile-- I can see and feel it. Comparing the snake to the top of his arm makes the snake seem more threatening, more alive than if the mail carrier were to say, for example, "The snake was as thick as a telephone cable." Also, this simile makes the connection between the snake and the man seem more personal.

Perhaps because the speaker is something of a "regular guy," the poem contains no other metaphors or similes. Only this one. Maybe he doesn't want to sound "literary." Or maybe there isn't time in the first few lines, since he seems to be describing a series of quick and fluid motions. A simile would

only interrupt the flow there. It's interesting that
only after the snake is dead and he picks it up does
he use a simile. He seems to be trying to describe
something more than just a surface reaction here--
something that goes deeper into the scariness of the
poem. Perhaps this is something that cannot be
described directly.

11. Symbols:

The snake is an archetypal symbol of evil. That
seemed immediately apparent to me the first time I
read the poem.

12. Paradox:

No obvious paradoxes in this poem.

13. Irony:

The poem is loaded with irony. That the snake's
killer should manifest behavior (the squirming)
similar to the snake's is certainly ironic. This is
the surprise at the end of the poem which contains
some enlightenment for the speaker. There is also the
difference between the words of the speaker, who
insists he is calm, and his response, which is to
shiver.

14. Tone:

The man acting against evil does it methodically
and emphatically, setting a tone of controlled excite-
ment. But the tone gives way in the end to pure
revulsion.

15. Form and Meter:

The poem is a sonnet, divided into an octave and
a sestet, a division that would seem to describe an
Italian sonnet, but the poem does not follow the

traditional Italian rhyme scheme. Instead, it has three quatrains and a concluding couplet, similar to the Shakespearean sonnet. This must be a hybrid form.

The octave describes the physical encounter with the snake and the sestet concentrates on the spiritual encounter or the metaphysical response to the reptile. The rhythm and meter are uneven, almost conversational. In fact, if this poem were read aloud, I might not even be aware of the sonnet form until the concluding couplet.

16. Sound Effects and Rhyme:

The rhyme scheme is <u>abbacddc, efefgg</u>. Most of the rhymes are slant rhymes (for example, "uncoil. . . all," "grass . . . hiss," etc.), used probably for the slightly unsettling effect they give. In other words, they fit the squirminess of the subject matter. One rhyme is simple repetition ("out. . . without"), and only the final couplet is a perfect rhyme ("spine. . . mine"), emphasizing the connected words.

Internal rhyme occurs with "bitch. . . ditch," "strong. . . long," and "thick. . . stick." All perfect rhymes, thereby putting particular emphasis on these words. Alliteration occurs infrequently: "strong stick," "thick. . . there. . . things." More prevalent, but still used subtly is consonance: "uncoil. . . squirm," "enough. . . felt," "kill. . . calm," and so on. Uncomfortable effect.

The poem uses frequent repetition: "uncoil" in lines 1 and 2; "squirm" in lines 2, 3, and 14; "ditch" in lines 3 and 7. It also occurs in line 8: "I aimed for the mouth and shot him. And shot him again." Here the repeated words describe a repeated action.

The enjambment of the first three lines is appropriate because the lines describe one complete action. The choppiness and caesura of line 4 introduce a casual tone and describe a shortened

action (the car moves quickly). Further enjambment of
the next two lines again describes the movement of the
snake, which is fluid. Also, the tail hangs out in
the road and on the page. The next few lines are all
end-stopped with frequent caesuras, as the man kills
the snake, picks him up, and reflects on him. The
choppiness picks up at the end, climaxing in the final
line which contains three caesuras. In this final
line the speaker makes an uncomfortable association
between himself and the snake. They both squirm. It
is enough to make him pause several times before
continuing and before admitting it.

17. Central Action, Theme, Subject:
     The snake is man's primeval enemy. Even for a
harmless mail-carrier, the urge to kill the snake is
overwhelming. In a way, then, the poem goes beyond
merely showing evil and one man's response to it. It
emphasizes human involvement with evil—both as a
subjugator of it and also as a participant in it. An
irony which suddenly occurs to me is that the poem
shows a man killing something evil—not because it has
threatened him personally, but simply because it
represented evil to him—and of course in the killing,
the killer himself is not completely innocent—thus
the final line in which the man squirms not just
because he is holding something disgusting, but
because he sees himself as playing a part in that
disgusting world.
     There seems to be no discrepancy between this
answer and my answer to #6—just an enlargement and
expansion of the original idea I had. I do not think
that I have gone off on an experiential tangent, even
though my first response to the poem was so intense
because of my childhood memory. In fact, I believe
the poem has allowed me to better understand the
reason I remember this incident with such clarity.

The only allusion I was uncertain about is the reference to "Johnson grass," which in the dictionary is defined as a coarse grass and a troublesome weed.

POSSIBLE THESIS FOR PAPER: The poem shows a snake-killer realizing his kinship with the snake he has just killed: in shooting a predator, the man has himself become a predator, linked in deed and intent with the archetypal symbol of evil.

At this point the student realized that it would help to organize her ideas into a brief, tentative outline for her paper. She reread the poem and her notes, and keeping her thesis statement in mind, she came up with the following informal outline:

1. Introduction
   Poem is a sonnet, but no love poem in the
      Renaissance tradition.
   Sinister turn.
   Statement of thesis: end of first paragraph

2. "Squirm"
   Used twice in first two lines
   Foreshadows final use in line 13
   creates "squirmy" feeling in reader
      other uncomfortable elements: rhyme
                                    rhythm
                                    (caesuras)

3. Man's response to snake
   At first: profanity
   then: shoots it
   then: uses <u>simile</u> which links man and snake
   then: attempts to explain his action but cannot

4. Insight
   Man sees he killed for satisfaction of seeing it
      dead
   Sees he has become the snake ("spine . . . mine")

```
5. Conclusion
   Sonnet moves from Physical
                  to Metaphysical
                  to Spiritual
```

After checking the thesis against the evidence of the poem one final time, the student was now ready to begin her paper. She used her notes and her rough outline as guides, but notice in the paper below that she added examples and occasionally shifted her emphasis. Writing the answers to the questions, jotting down a plan for the paper, and finally writing the paper allowed her to articulate what she had felt only vaguely before. In the process of writing about the poem, she was actually able to re-create the poem for herself.

PRESENTING THE PAPER

The student also followed the conventions of paper-writing, which are as follows:

1. Type the paper on 8½x11-inch sheets. Double-space, leaving 1-inch margins at the top, bottom, and sides of the page. Be sure the ribbon is black and the presentation clean and neat.
2. Begin the first page 1 inch from the top, flush with the left margin, with your name, the course, the instructor's name, and the date on separate lines.
3. Number all pages except for the first page. Page numbers should appear in the upper-right-hand margin, one-half inch from the top.
4. Always number the lines of a poem and cite line numbers as you quote from the text.
5. If you quote lines of poetry within one of your own sentences, indicate line breaks with a slash (/):

Up to this point all we have seen of the snake has been a distant coil, a squirming action, "the tip-end / Of his tail," and a hissing mouth.

```
            The Predator as Prey:


                  T. R. Hummer's
 "The Rural Carrier Stops to Kill a Nine-Foot Cottonmouth"


      Although the sonnet has remained a popular poetic
form for many centuries, one usually associates it
with Renaissance love poetry.  T. R. Hummer, however,
```

uses a contemporary version of the Italian sonnet to describe not a man in love but rather a man killing a snake. Although "The Rural Carrier Stops to Kill a Nine-Foot Cottonmouth" begins as a simple variation of the mythic quest story—in this case the medieval legend in which the man of modest means kills a dragon and frees the countryside from its evil influence, the poem ultimately takes a more sinister turn. The poem shows a snake-killer realizing his kinship with the snake he has just killed. In shooting a predator, the man himself becomes a predator, linked in deed and intent with the snake, the archetypal symbol of evil.

The poem opens with a startling, colloquial expression of disgust and surprise.

> Lord God, I saw the son-of-a-bitch uncoil
> In the road ahead of me, uncoil and squirm
> For the ditch, squirm a hell of a long time.
>
> (1–3)

The repetition of "squirm" emphasizes the snake's length as it takes several of these "squirms" to remove its entire nine-foot body from the road. In this beginning is also a foreshadowing of the end of the poem. By the time a third "squirm" appears in line 13 (this time describing the mail-carrier's reaction to the snake), the reader has also felt revulsion—not only because snakes seem to inspire this universal response, but also because other poetic elements have been at work throughout the poem to encourage and sustain an uneasy feeling.

For example, the word "squirm" introduces an action which finds an echo in the uncomfortable and imperfect end-rhymes throughout: "uncoil. . . all," "squirm. . . time," "tip-end. . . again," "grass. . . hiss," and "arm. . . calm." Likewise, the rhythm is uneven with frequent caesuras. Sometimes these pauses

or interruptions mimic a short silence between two
explosions as in:

> I aimed for the mouth and shot him. And shot him
> again.

(8)

But sometimes the choppy stop—and—go cadences make it
obvious that the speaker is struggling to understand
and finally to express something difficult, as in the
final lines of the poem. These imperfect rhymes and
uneven rhythms unsettle the reader, keeping him aware
that something important has not yet been resolved.

To begin with, we see the mail—carrier respond to
the snake not with action or philosophy but with
profanity. In the first few lines the speaker is not
so much describing the snake squirming off the road as
recording his hatred of it. He then translates this
emotion into action as he stops the car, finds the
snake, and shoots it, showing that he definitely has
the upper hand. Up to this point all we have seen of
the snake has been a distant coil, a squirming action,
"the tip—end / Of his tail," and a hissing mouth.
Only after the snake is dead does the speaker stop to
look at the whole snake, and he pulls him out with a
stick, noticing that "he was long and evil, thick as
the top of my arm." The simile in this line is the
only use of figurative language in the poem, and it
comes at a moment of profound awe as the speaker
reaches for some way to describe what he is feeling
about the creature. The simile comparing the snake to
a part of a living person makes the snake seem
threatening even in death and serves to link man and
snake in a more direct, personal way.

It is disconcerting for a man to realize his
connections with evil, and this provokes the next
response from the mail—carrier, who attempts to
explain his action:

> There are things in this world a man can't look
>   at without
> Wanting to kill. Don't ask me why. . . .
>
> (11-12)

He realizes, however, that he cannot really explain
why he killed the snake so methodically and
efficiently. What he did, of course, was kill
something for the satisfaction of seeing it dead. The
snake had not threatened him personally, but it
represented something evil, against which the man
violently responded. The irony is that in killing
this predator, the man himself becomes a predator,
too.

>   I was calm
>   Enough, I thought. But I felt my spine
>   Squirm, suddenly. I admit it. It was mine.
>
> (12-14)

He squirms because the snake is long and evil and
disgusting, but he also squirms because he realizes
that in his action, he has become no better than the
snake. How appropriate that the man's spine should
squirm, like the snake, which is all squirming
backbone and vertebrae.

  The final couplet of this sonnet rhymes "spine"
and "mine," the only perfect end-rhyme in the poem,
emphasizing the connection the speaker is making
between these words. "I admit it," he says. "It was
mine." His surface calmness has given way to an
involuntary shudder. He is in the presence of a
revolting carcass and cannot avoid recognizing his own
similarity to it.

  There are no surprises in the action of "The
Rural Carrier Stops to Kill a Nine-Foot Cottonmouth,"
especially since all of the "facts" of the poem are in
the lengthy title. In the octave of the sonnet the

```
speaker does describe a physical encounter, but in the
sestet we see the surprising and more important
metaphysical response which leads, finally, to
spiritual insight and a discomfiting resolution.
```

A formal paper is usually not the place for a reader to explore personal connections and associations with a poem. Notice, for example, that this student does not mention the childhood memory she described in response to preliminary question #3. But it should be clear that that memory conditioned her response to the poem, made her more sensitive to its implications, and prepared her to create a thorough and insightful reading of it. She brought her experience to her reading of the poem, but it did not replace the poem; instead it was the foundation for her understanding of it.

CHAPTER 10

BECOMING A
DISCRIMINATING READER

Reading poetry is like listening to music. When you were a child, you began with simple nursery songs, alphabet tunes, game chants, often perfectly rhymed and rhythmically predictable. As you grew older, you began to learn longer, more complex tunes; perhaps you began to sing in two-part harmonies; you might even have started to provide instrumental accompaniment. You learned more and more about the traditions and conventions of different kinds of music.

Of course, many people never become discriminating listeners of music, just as many people never advance to become critical readers of poetry. But one thing is certain: if you do not allow your musical or poetic tastes to mature by consciously listening or reading, you will never reach the highest levels of enjoyment. You can become stuck at an elementary and immature stage, thus cutting yourself off from some of life's most profound pleasures.

The more poetry you read, the more poetry you will want to read, and you will find yourself becoming more choosy as your tastes mature. You will have a firmer idea about what works in poetry and what doesn't. You will discover that not all poems are good poems. This chapter should help you to recognize some of those qualities which help to make a good poem good.

Remember that as with music, *good* poetry is not always *easy* poetry. A poem that is not completely clear the first time you read it is not necessarily a bad poem. On the other hand, obscurity can mar a poem, too. If after several attentive readings a poem's meaning is still unclear to you, the problem could be the fault of the poet.

Determining whether a poem is good or bad is not an exact science, but there are certain criteria that readers generally use to determine a poem's quality. In the eighteenth century, Alexander Pope wrote a lengthy poem

125

called *An Essay on Criticism*, in which he both instructed poets and writers and parodied some of the common problems in the verse of his day, problems which still crop up in twentieth-century verse.

ALEXANDER POPE

FROM AN ESSAY ON CRITICISM   88

But most by numbers judge a poet's song;
And smooth or rough, with them, is right or wrong:
In the bright muse though thousand charms conspire,
Her voice is all these tuneful fools admire;
Who haunt Parnassus but to please their ear,   5
Not mend their minds; as some to church repair,
Not for the doctrine, but the music there.
These equal syllables alone require,
Though oft the ear the open vowels tire;
While expletives their feeble aid do join;   10
And ten low words oft creep in one dull line:
While they ring round the same unvaried chimes,
With sure returns of still expected rhymes;
Where'er you find "the cooling western breeze,"
In the next line, it "whispers through the trees";   15
If crystal streams "with pleasing murmurs creep,"
The reader's threatened (not in vain) with "sleep":
Then, at the last and only couplet fraught
With some unmeaning thing they call a thought,
A needless Alexandrine ends the song,   20
That, like a wounded snake, drags its slow length along.
Leave such to tune their own dull rhymes, and know
What's roundly smooth, or languishingly slow;
And praise the easy vigor of a line,
Where Denham's strength and Waller's sweetness join.   25
True ease in writing comes from art, not chance,
As those move easiest who have learned to dance.
'Tis not enough no harshness gives offense,
The sound must seem an echo to the sense:
Soft is the strain when Zephyr gently blows,   30
And the smooth stream in smoother numbers flows;

AN ESSAY ON CRITICISM 5 *Parnassus:* a mountain in Greece, sacred to Apollo and the Muses. 25 *Denham's . . . Waller's:* John Denham and Edmund Waller, seventeenth-century English poets. 30 *Zephyr:* the west wind.

But when loud surges lash the sounding shore,
The hoarse, rough verse should like the torrent roar:
When Ajax strives some rock's vast weight to throw,
The line too labors, and the words move slow;   35
Not so, when swift Camilla scours the plain,
Flies o'er the unbending corn, and skims along the main.

1711

Pope criticizes both the reader who looks for nothing but correct meter in a poem and the poet who uses predictable rhymes, **clichés,** or any poetic devices just for the sake of convention. He provides examples of the devices he names and mimics the weaknesses he criticizes, and in the process seems to be having great fun.

Through the centuries poets have often written **parodies,** or satiric imitations, of bad poetry. In *The Adventures of Huckleberry Finn,* Mark Twain, with his tongue firmly in his cheek, had one of his characters write the following very bad poem.

MARK TWAIN

ODE TO STEPHEN DOWLING BOTS,
DEC'D.   89

And did young Stephen sicken,
  And did young Stephen die?
And did the sad hearts thicken,
  And did the mourners cry?

No; such was not the fate of   5
  Young Stephen Dowling Bots;
Though sad hearts round him thickened,
  'Twas not from sickness' shots.

No whooping-cough did rack his frame,
  Nor measles drear, with spots;   10
Not these impaired the sacred name
  Of Stephen Dowling Bots.

Despised love struck not with woe
  That head of curly knots,
Nor stomach troubles laid him low,   15
  Young Stephen Dowling Bots.

---

34 *Ajax:* Greek warrior who fought against Troy. 36 *Camilla:* ancient queen known for her swift running.

O no. Then list with tearful eye,
  Whilst I his fate do tell.
His soul did from this cold world fly,
  By falling down a well.   20

They got him out and emptied him;
  Alas it was too late;
His spirit was gone for to sport aloft
  In the realms of the good and great.

1885

How soon is it apparent that Twain is writing a parody of sentimental obituary verse? Probably as early as the title, with the strange abbreviation for *deceased.* Certainly, however, by the end of the first stanza, with its galloping rhythm and predictable rhyme, and the odd image of thickening hearts, you know you are in the presence of some pretty awful verse. Notice how the image which did not work in the first stanza is repeated in the second. Notice also how *shots* in line 8 makes no sense and is apparently used only for the rhyme. The humor is created by imprecise and hilariously inappropriate language combined with clichés and other signs of bad writing.

It isn't always fun, however, to encounter these problems in one's reading. A lot of poetry really is not good poetry at all. Look out for sentimentality, archaic language, clichés, ridiculous metaphors, abstract language, predictable rhyme, and sing-song rhythm. Be suspicious of any expression that is pretentious or seems purposely obscure. These are all signs of lazy writing.

The following checklist may help you to discern good poems from poor ones.

1. Look for strong images, and an emphasis on the particular rather than the general. *Abstract language* and *obscurity* may be indications that the writer is not being precise. Notice how the following poem uses only two images—"a ray of sun" and "the ripples of water"—and those are clichés.

CHARLES MacKAY

ONLY A THOUGHT   90

'Twas only a passing thought, my love,
  Only a passing thought,
That came o'er my mind like a ray of the sun
  In the ripples of waters caught;
And it seemed to me, and I say to thee,   5
  That sorrow and shame and sin

Might disappear from our happy sphere,
  If we knew but to begin;
If we knew but how to profit
  By wisdom dearly bought: 10
'Twas only a passing thought, my love,
  Only a passing thought.

c. 1867

The poem is so vague and the language so general *(thought, love, mind, sorrow, shame, sin, wisdom)* that it is impossible for a reader to feel engaged by it at all.

    Obscure, pedantic imagery and self-conscious philosophizing also create serious problems in poetry. Notice how the remote allusions and an obscure vocabulary practically exclude the reader from the following poem.

THOMAS HOLLEY CHIVERS

A CALL   91

In the music of the morns,
Blown through Conchimarian horns,
Down the dark vistas of the reboantic Norns,
To the Genius of Eternity,
Crying: "Come to me! Come to me!"   5

c. 1840

2. When a contemporary poem contains *archaic language,* the effect is usually pretentious or trite. Words such as *ne'er, thy, canst,* or *morn,* which appear frequently in older poetry, usually do not contribute to an effective diction in modern poetry unless they are used as parody.

The two young men on rafts struck from the shore
Their orders were to cross the river o'er.

3. *Clichés* are lazy and ineffectual uses of language, evidence of hackneyed expression and shallow thought. "As white as snow," "quick as a wink," "crying over spilled milk" are all clichés. Notice that they are images, phrases, and metaphors that have been used so often that they have become invisible. They are boring.

DANTE GABRIEL ROSSETTI

FROM ROSE MARY 92

And lo! on the ground Rose Mary lay,
With a cold brow like the snows ere May,
With a cold breast like the earth till Spring,
With such a smile as the June days bring
When the year grows warm for harvesting. 5

1881

4. *Mixed metaphors* are comparisons which appear close to each other in a poem and together create a contradictory or nonsensical picture. Notice, for example, how the following sentences mix the metaphors of glaciers and leaves across a grave, or monkeys and eggplants. The result is confusion.

The books, as old as glaciers, lay scattered on her desk, like leaves across a grave.

The baby, fat as an eggplant, grinned like a monkey.

Inappropriate metaphors are those which seem ridiculous because they do not fit the context of the phrase or they are exaggerated in some way. For example:

His tie was a river connecting throat to belt, crossing the bridge of his barrel chest.

In the following poem, notice how the metaphor introduced in the first line creates a far-fetched picture, pushing the rest of the stanza somewhat beyond credulity.

SIR RICHARD BLACKMORE

FROM POSSIBILITIES 93

In the wide womb of possibility
Lie many things, which ne'er may actual be;
And more productions, of a various kind,
Will cause no contradictions in the mind.
'Tis possible the things in Nature found, 5
Might different forms and different parts have own'd:

The bear might wear a trunk, the wolf a horn,
The peacock's train the bittern might adorn;
Strong tusks might in the horse's mouth have grown,
And lions might have spots, and leopards none.   10

c. 1700

5. *Sentimentality* is characterized by "cute" language and an excessive display
   of emotion. Greeting-card verse is often sentimental, as is "the tear-jerker,"
   which tempts the reader to sigh over the prettiness of sadness rather than to
   feel the deep stirrings of tragedy. Notice the exaggerated and false emotion
   in this poem. Notice also how many other problems the poem has besides
   its sentimentality.

ELIZA COOK

FROM THE OLD ARM-CHAIR   94

I love it, I love it; and who shall dare
To chide me for loving that old Arm-chair?
I've treasured it long as a sainted prize;
I've bedewed it with tears, and embalmed it with sighs.
'Tis bound by a thousand bands to my heart;   5
Not a tie will break, not a link will start.
Would ye learn the spell?—a mother sat there;
And a scared thing is that old Arm-chair.

1836

6. *Overwriting* is verbose, exaggerated, pompous language, filled with extrav-
   agant conceits, far-fetched metaphors, and intrusive sound effects. Notice
   how the adjectives overwhelm the following poem.

MARY ROBINSON

THE TEMPLE OF CHASTITY   95

High on a rock, coeval with the skies,
    A temple stands, reared by immortal powers
    To Chastity divine! Ambrosial flowers,
Twining round icicles, in columns rise,
Mingling with pendent gems of orient dyes!   5
    Piercing the air, a golden crescent towers,
    Veiled by transparent clouds; while smiling hours
Shake from their varying wings celestial joys!

The steps of spotless marble, scattered o'er
  With deathless roses armed with many a thorn,   10
Lead to the altar. On the frozen floor,
  Studded with tear-drops, petrified with scorn,
Pale vestals kneel the goddess to adore,
  While Love, his arrows broke, retires forlorn.

c. 1790

7. Words which appear in a line of poetry for the sole purpose of filling in a gap in the meter are called *metrical fillers*. The word *do* often appears in this role, as Pope points out in line 10 of his poem (where he calls these metrical fillers "expletives").

While expletives their feeble aid do join;
And ten low words oft creep in one dull line.

  Notice how extra words also fill in the rhythm at various points in Twain's poem, as in "His spirit was gone for to sport aloft."

8. A related problem is *predictable rhyme*. Pope points out the boring and unsubtle nature of the rhyme in these phrases:

While they ring round the same unvaried chimes,
With sure returns of still expected rhymes;
Where'er you find "the cooling western breeze,"
In the next line, it "whispers through the trees":
If crystal streams "with pleasing murmurs creep,"   5
The reader's threatened (not in vain) with "sleep."

  Such hackneyed rhyme would tend to overwhelm anything else the poet may be trying to say or do in the poem. Notice in the following example how the rhyme combines with a *sing-song meter,* and in the process drowns out everything else in the poem.

AMBROSE PHILIPS

ODE   96

TO MISS MARGARET PULTENEY, DAUGHTER OF DANIEL PULTENEY, ESP. IN THE NURSERY

Dimply damsel, sweetly smiling,
All caressing, none beguiling,
Bud of beauty, fairly blowing,
Every charm to nature owing,

This and that new thing admiring,   5
Much of this and that inquiring,
Knowledge by degrees attaining,
Day by day some virtue gaining,
Ten years hence, when I leave chiming,
Beardless poets, fondly rhyming   10
(Fescu'd now, perhaps, in spelling).
On thy riper beauties dwelling,
Shall accuse each killing feature
Of the cruel, charming creature,
Whom I know complying, willing,   15
Tender, and averse to killing.

c. 1714

Notice how common it is for a poem with one problem to also have many others. Besides the problems with rhyme and meter, this poem also contains abstract language and cliché.

9. *Wrenched accent* occurs when the meter is allowed to take complete control of the poem. Often in this case words are forced to fit into the metrical pattern, even though their natural accents may be distorted.

God bless the town that Thompson founded
So many years ago.
It sits up straight upon a hill
Just west of Chicago.

Sometimes the author will indicate with an accent mark that the word must be pronounced differently.

SAMUEL TAYLOR COLERIDGE

FROM THE RIME OF THE ANCIENT
MARINER   97

This Hermit good lives in that wood
    Which slopes down to the Sea.
How loudly his sweet voice he rears!
He loves to talk with Marineres
    That come from a far Countrée.   5

1798

ATTRIBUTES OF POETRY

A good poem has the following attributes:

1. Precise language that is specific rather than general
2. No redundancy or wordiness
3. Concrete imagery with sparing use of abstract words
4. Appropriate diction that is not pretentious or archaic
5. Fresh expression and the absence of clichés
6. Appropriate, clear metaphors
7. Rhythm and rhyme that do not wrench the rest of the poem to fit an imposed pattern
8. Avoidance of sentimentality
9. Something new to communicate

With these qualities in mind, read the following pairs of poems and compare them. Ask yourself whether they meet the criteria for good poetry and determine where their strengths and weaknesses lie.

I.

[SILENCE]   98

silence

.is
a
looking

bird:the   5

turn
ing;edge,of
life

(inquiry before snow

1958

SIMILES AND METAPHORS   99
AN EXERCISE

Silence is like an empty box.
Silence is an empty box.
I am in silence,
silence is in me.
I am like an empty box.   5

I am not an empty box.
I am full.
I am a full box,
Full of poems,
but I can't open it.   10

I need a knife.
No, this might hurt my poems.
I need an electric can opener.

It makes a humming sound.

What happened to Silence?   15
                                                            1980

II.

NOCTURNE   100

(FOR LISA)

The wind is playing fugues
    among the pines,
Bowing the tautened limbs
    to pure enchantment,
Throbbing through the trunks   5
    with ancient resonance.
There is mystery in the
    wind–sound of night—
A wild, elusive harmony
    of elements   10
That flows from every leaf
    and rock,
Swelling with abandon
To touch the silent stars,
Falling to a shimmering descant   15
    above the muted valley;
And then, with one last murmur,
Nature lays aside her violin. . .
And rests within her timeless
    repertoire.   20
The velvet hills stand silent—
Their secret melting
    in the fiery touch of dawn.

                                                            1984

THE DARK AND FALLING SUMMER 101

The rain was full of the freshness
  and the fresh fragrance of darkening grapes.
The rain was as the dark falling of hidden
And fabulous plums ripening—great blue thunderheads moving
    slowly.
The dark air was possessed by the fragrance of freshness, 5
By a scattered and confused profusion until,
After the tattering began, the pouring-down came,
And plenitude descended, multitudinous.
Everywhere was full of the pulsing of the loud and fallen dusk.

1958

CHAPTER 11

RE-CONSTRUCTING
POETRY

The first time you pick up a tennis racket, your muscles have not yet learned what to do. Your fingers are stiff and the racket is heavy, your strokes are choppy and uncontrolled, the rules governing the game are hazy and somewhat overwhelming. You are very aware of form, of movement, of your own awkwardness. Playing tennis is uncomfortable at this stage of learning the game, but you keep at it anyway until holding the racket and hitting the ball become natural. With practice, the sport becomes easier, more enjoyable. Your body learns how to respond without thinking of the various steps you must go through to hit a ball in a fluid motion.

But before it becomes a coordinated part of your everyday life, you need to practice your skill. So it is with writing and reading. If you do not practice regularly, you will never become skillful, no matter how much natural ability you may seem to have. Once you have learned how to read a poem—once you have identified its image patterns, the poetic devices at work, its themes and subtleties—then you are ready to return to the poem as if you were reading it for the very first time. You are ready to re-create it, to put it back together and let it speak to you again. When you think you have grasped a poem, read it a final time, nonstop, to experience it as a rich unity. In other words, play a game of tennis for the sheer enjoyment of it.

Return now to a poem you read last week or last month and reread it. Notice how it has changed. Notice how you have changed. What is on your mind now that was not there the first time you encountered the poem? What have you experienced since that encounter that has shifted your vision or grabbed your attention? These are important factors which will influence the way you read a poem. Now with your vision refreshed, the poem stands ready for you to step back to read it yet again.

Remember that reading poetry is not "decoding" an artifact. Reading a poem is re-creating a work of art. Reading a poem is living a more interesting life. Notice how many places you encounter poetry. In the past month, for example, I have heard poetry read at a wedding, quoted on a television news program, sung in church. I have found lines from Blake and Shakespeare and Dickinson in magazine advertisements. At a dinner honoring a friend, the emcee read three pages of limericks. On the same day both a high-school student and a third-grader showed me their most recent poems. A friend handed me some poems written after the death of a family member. On the radio I heard an interview with a woman who, because she was denied paper and pen, had to scratch her poems into bars of soap while she was imprisoned.

What *is* this impulse we have to fill our lives with poetry? It must come from deep within. I suspect that to ignore it would be to risk losing a part of what makes us human.

PART II

AN ANTHOLOGY

CONRAD AIKEN

(1889–1973)

SUMMER   102

Absolute zero: the locust sings:
summer's caught in eternity's rings:
the rock explodes, the planet dies,
we shovel up our verities.

The razor rasps across the face   5
and in the glass our fleeting race
lit by infinity's lightning wink
under the thunder tries to think.

In this frail gourd the granite pours
the timeless howls like all outdoors   10
the sensuous moment builds a wall
open as wind, no wall at all:

while still obedient to valves and knobs
the vascular jukebox throbs and sobs
expounding hope propounding yearning   15
proposing love, but never learning

or only learning at zero's gate
like summer's locust the final hate
formless ice on a formless plain
that was and is and comes again.   20

                                                    1949

QUESTIONS

1. What does the title lead you to expect? Is that what you find? How is it similar to or different from what you expected?
2. What are the characteristics of "the vascular jukebox" (line 14)? What is it?
3. What is "zero's gate" (line 17)?
4. What is the relationship between the abstract and the particular?
5. Does this poem provide an optimistic or a pessimistic statement?

A. R. AMMONS

(b. 1926)

THE CITY LIMITS   103

When you consider the radiance, that it does not withhold
itself but pours its abundance without selection into every
nook and cranny not overhung or hidden; when you consider

that birds' bones make no awful noise against the light but
lie low in the light as in a high testimony; when you consider   5
the radiance, that it will look into the guiltiest

swervings of the weaving heart and bear itself upon them,
not flinching into disguise or darkening; when you consider
the abundance of such resource as illuminates the glow-blue

bodies and gold-skeined wings of flies swarming the dumped   10
guts of a natural slaughter or the coil of shit and in no
way winces from its storms of generosity; when you consider

that air or vacuum, snow or shale, squid or wolf, rose or lichen,
each is accepted into as much light as it will take, then
the heart moves roomier, the man stands and looks about, the   15

leaf does not increase itself above the grass, and the dark
work of the deepest cells is of a tune with May bushes
and fear lit by the breadth of such calmly turns to praise.

1971

QUESTIONS

1. The poem is one long periodic sentence. What effect does this have on the way you
   would read it aloud? The way you approach creating a personal reading of it?
2. Identify the anaphora in this poem. What function does it serve?
3. Where does the turn toward a resolution of the tension occur?
4. Why is the poem filled with negatives? What happens to them?
5. How do you relate the pairings of opposites in line 13 to the poem as a whole?
6. The title introduces an urban theme. Is it carried throughout the poem? In what sense
   does the poem consider "limits" or limitations?

CUT THE GRASS   104

The wonderful workings of the world: wonderful,
wonderful: I'm surprised half the time:
ground up fine, I puff if a pebble stirs:

I'm nervous: my morality's intricate: if
a squash blossom dies, I feel withered as a stained   5
zucchini and blame my nature: and

when grassblades flop to the little red-ant
queens burring around trying to get aloft, I blame
my not keeping the grass short, stubble

firm: well, I learn a lot of useless stuff, meant   10
to be ignored: like when the sun sinking in the
west glares a plane invisible, I think how much

revelation concealment necessitates: and then I
think of the ocean, multiple to a blinding
oneness and realize that only total expression   15

expresses hiding: I'll have to say everything
to take on the roundness and withdrawal of the deep dark:
less than total is a bucketful of radiant toys.

                                                    1972

JOHN ASHBERY

(b. 1927)

THE INSTRUCTION MANUAL   105

As I sit looking out of a window of the building
I wish I did not have to write the instruction manual on the uses of a
    new metal.
I look down into the street and see people, each walking with an
    inner peace,
And envy them—they are so far away from me!
Not one of them has to worry about getting out this manual on
    schedule.   5
And, as my way is, I begin to dream, resting my elbows on the desk
    and leaning out of the window a little,
Of dim Guadalajara! City of rose-colored flowers!
City I wanted most to see, and most did not see, in Mexico!
But I fancy I see, under the press of having to write the instruction
    manual,
Your public square, city, with its elaborate little bandstand!   10
The band is playing *Scheherazade* by Rimsky-Korsakov.
Around stand the flower girls, handing out rose- and lemon-colored
    flowers,

Each attractive in her rose-and-blue striped dress (Oh! such shades of
    rose and blue),
And nearby is the little white booth where women in green serve you
    green and yellow fruit.
The couples are parading; everyone is in a holiday mood.   15
First, leading the parade, is a dapper fellow
Clothed in deep blue. On his head sits a white hat
And he wears a mustache, which has been trimmed for the occasion.
His dear one, his wife, is young and pretty; her shawl is rose, pink,
    and white.
Her slippers are patent leather, in the American fashion,   20
And she carries a fan, for she is modest, and does not want the
    crowd to see her face too often.
But everybody is so busy with his wife or loved one
I doubt they would notice the mustachioed man's wife.
Here come the boys! They are skipping and throwing little things on
    the sidewalk
Which is made of gray tile. One of them, a little older, has a
    toothpick in his teeth.   25
He is silenter than the rest, and affects not to notice the pretty young
    girls in white.
But his friends notice them, and shout their jeers at the laughing
    girls.
Yet soon all this will cease, with the deepening of their years,
And love bring each to the parade grounds for another reason.
But I have lost sight of the young fellow with the toothpick.   30
Wait—there he is—on the other side of the bandstand,
Secluded from his friends, in earnest talk with a young girl
Of fourteen or fifteen. I try to hear what they are saying
But it seems they are just mumbling something—shy words of love,
    probably.
She is slightly taller than he, and looks quietly down into his sincere
    eyes.   35
She is wearing white. The breeze ruffles her long fine black hair
    against her olive cheek.
Obviously she is in love. The boy, the young boy with the
    toothpick, he is in love too;
His eyes show it. Turning from this couple,
I see there is an intermission in the concert.
The paraders are resting and sipping drinks through straws   40
(The drinks are dispensed from a large glass crock by a lady in dark
    blue),

And the musicians mingle among them, in their creamy white
    uniforms, and talk
About the weather, perhaps, or how their kids are doing at school.
Let us take this opportunity to tiptoe into one of the side streets.
Here you may see one of those white houses with green trim   45
That are so popular here. Look—I told you!
It is cool and dim inside, but the patio is sunny.
An old woman in gray sits there, fanning herself with a palm leaf
    fan.
She welcomes us to her patio, and offers us a cooling drink.
"My son is in Mexico City," she says. "He would welcome you too   50
If he were here. But his job is with a bank there.
Look, here is a photograph of him."
And a dark-skinned lad with pearly teeth grins out at us from the
    worn leather frame.
We thank her for her hospitality, for it is getting late
And we must catch a view of the city, before we leave, from a good
    high place.   55
That church tower will do—the faded pink one, there against the
    fierce blue of the sky. Slowly we enter.
The caretaker, an old man dressed in brown and gray, asks us how
    long we have been in the city, and how we like it here.
His daughter is scrubbing the steps—she nods to us as we pass into
    the tower.
Soon we have reached the top, and the whole network of the city
    extends before us.
There is the rich quarter, with its houses of pink and white, and its
    crumbling, leafy terraces.   60
There is the poorer quarter, its homes a deep blue.
There is the market, where men are selling hats and swatting flies
And there is the public library, painted several shades of pale green
    and beige.
Look! There is the square we just came from, with the promenaders.
There are fewer of them, now that the heat of the day has increased, 65
But the young boy and girl still lurk in the shadows of the
    bandstand.
And there is the home of the little old lady—
She is still sitting in the patio, fanning herself.
How limited, but how complete withal, has been our experience of
    Guadalajara!
We have seen young love, married love, and the love of an aged
    mother for her son.   70

We have heard the music, tasted the drinks, and looked at colored
    houses.
What more is there to do, except stay? And that we cannot do.
And as a last breeze freshens the top of the weathered old tower, I
    turn my gaze
Back to the instruction manual which has made me dream of
    Guadalajara.

1956

PARADOXES AND OXYMORONS   106

This poem is concerned with language on a very plain level.
Look at it talking to you. You look out a window
Or pretend to fidget. You have it but you don't have it.
You miss it, it misses you. You miss each other.

The poem is sad because it wants to be yours, and cannot.   5
What's a plain level? It is that and other things,
Bringing a system of them into play. Play?
Well, actually, yes, but I consider play to be

A deeper outside thing, a dreamed role-pattern,
As in the division of grace these long August days   10
Without proof. Open-ended. And before you know
It gets lost in the steam and chatter of typewriters.

It has been played once more. I think you exist only
To tease me into doing it, on your level, and then you aren't there
Or have adopted a different attitude. And the poem   15
Has set me softly down beside you. The poem is you.

1981

QUESTIONS

1. What is the tone of the title? How does it affect the way you read the poem the first
    time?
2. Do you find any irony in the poem?
3. Where are the paradoxes and oxymorons?

MARGARET ATWOOD
(b. 1939)

THIS IS A PHOTOGRAPH OF ME   107

It was taken some time ago.
At first it seems to be
a smeared
print: blurred lines and gray flecks
blended with the paper;   5

then, as you scan
it, you see in the left-hand corner
a thing that is like a branch: part of a tree
(balsam or spruce) emerging
and, to the right, halfway up   10
what ought to be a gentle
slope, a small frame house.

In the background there is a lake,
and beyond that, some low hills.

(The photograph was taken   15
the day after I drowned.

I am in the lake, in the center
of the picture, just under the surface.

It is difficult to say where
precisely, or to say   20
how large or small I am:
the effect of water
on light is a distortion

but if you look long enough,
eventually   25
you will be able to see me.)

                                   1966

AT THE TOURIST CENTER IN BOSTON   108

There is my country under glass,
a white relief-
map with red dots for the cities,
reduced to the size of a wall
and beside it 10 blownup snapshots   5

one for each province,
in purple-browns and odd reds,
the green of the trees dulled;
all blues however
of an assertive purity.   10

Mountains and lakes and more lakes
(though Quebec is a restaurant and Ontario the empty
interior of the parliament buildings),
with nobody climbing the trails and hauling out
the fish and splashing in the water   15

but arrangements of grinning tourists—
look here, Saskatchewan
is a flat lake, some convenient rocks
where two children pose with a father
and the mother is cooking something   20
in immaculate slacks by a smokeless fire,
her teeth white as detergent.

Whose dream is this, I would like to know:
is this a manufactured
hallucination, a cynical fiction, a lure   25
for export only?

I seem to remember people,
at least in the cities, also slush,
machines and assorted garbage. Perhaps
that was my private mirage   30

which will just evaporate
when I go back. Or the citizens will be gone,
run off to the peculiarly-
green forests
to wait among the brownish mountains   35
for the platoons of tourists
and plan their odd red massacres.

Unsuspecting
window lady, I ask you:

Do you see nothing   40
watching you from under the water?

Was the sky ever that blue?

Who really lives there?

                                                    1968

QUESTIONS

1. What kinds of things do you recall seeing displayed under glass?
2. Identify the "country under glass" (line 1). What is this glass and where is it?
3. How do the colors used in the poem evoke feeling and support the theme?
4. Who is the "window lady" (line 39) and who is watching her?

W. H. AUDEN
(1907–1973)

IN MEMORY OF W. B. YEATS   109

(d. Jan. 1939)

I

He disappeared in the dead of winter:
The brooks were frozen, the airports almost deserted,
And snow disfigured the public statues;
The mercury sank in the mouth of the dying day.
What instruments we have agree   5
The day of his death was a dark cold day.

Far from his illness
The wolves ran on through the evergreen forests,
The peasant river was untempted by the fashionable quays;
By mourning tongues   10
The death of the poet was kept from his poems.

But for him it was his last afternoon as himself,
An afternoon of nurses and rumours;
The provinces of his body revolted,
The squares of his mind were empty,   15
Silence invaded the suburbs,
The current of his feeling failed; he became his admirers.

Now he is scattered among a hundred cities
And wholly given over to unfamiliar affections,
To find his happiness in another kind of wood   20
And be punished under a foreign code of conscience.
The words of a dead man
Are modified in the guts of the living.

But in the importance and noise of to-morrow
When the brokers are roaring like beasts on the floor of the Bourse,   25

IN MEMORY OF W. B. YEATS 25 *Bourse:* the stock exchange of Paris.

And the poor have the sufferings to which they are fairly accustomed,
And each in the cell of himself is almost convinced of his freedom,
A few thousand will think of this day
As one thinks of a day when one did something slightly unusual.　30
What instruments we have agree
The day of his death was a dark cold day.

II

You were silly like us; your gift survived it all:
The parish of rich women, physical decay,
Yourself. Mad Ireland hurt you into poetry.　35
Now Ireland has her madness and her weather still,
For poetry makes nothing happen: it survives
In the valley of its making where executives
Would never want to tamper, flows on south
From ranches of isolation and the busy griefs,　40
Raw towns that we believe and die in; it survives,
A way of happening, a mouth.

III

Earth, receive an honoured guest:
William Yeats is laid to rest.
Let the Irish vessel lie　45
Emptied of its poetry.

In the nightmare of the dark
All the dogs of Europe bark,
And the living nations wait,
Each sequestered in its hate;　50

Intellectual disgrace
Stares from every human face,
And the seas of pity lie
Locked and frozen in each eye.

Follow, poet, follow right　55
To the bottom of the night,
With your unconstraining voice
Still persuade us to rejoice;

With the farming of a verse
Make a vineyard of the curse,　60
Sing of human unsuccess
In a rapture of distress;

In the deserts of the heart
Let the healing fountain start,
In the prison of his days
Teach the free man how to praise.   65

                                                          1940

OUR BIAS   110

The hour-glass whispers to the lion's roar,
The clock-towers tell the gardens day and night
How many errors Time has patience for,
How wrong they are in being always right.

Yet Time, however loud its chimes or deep,   5
However fast its falling torrent flows,
Has never put one lion off his leap
Nor shaken the assurance of a rose.

For they, it seems, care only for success:
While we choose words according to their sound   10
And judge a problem by its awkwardness;

And Time with us was always popular.
When have we not preferred some going round
To going straight to where we are?

                                                          1940

THE UNKNOWN CITIZEN   111

(To JS/07/M/378 This Marble Monument Is Erected by the State)

He was found by the Bureau of Statistics to be
One against whom there was no official complaint,
And all the reports on his conduct agree
That, in the modern sense of an old-fashioned word, he was a saint,
For in everything he did he served the Greater Community.   5
Except for the War till the day he retired
He worked in a factory and never got fired,
But satisfied his employers, Fudge Motors Inc.
Yet he wasn't a scab or odd in his views,
For his Union reports that he paid his dues   10
(Our report on his Union shows it was sound),
And our Social Psychology workers found
That he was popular with his mates and liked a drink.

The Press are convinced that he bought a paper every day
And that his reactions to advertisements were normal in every way.   15
Policies taken out in his name prove that he was fully insured,
And his Health-card shows he was once in hospital but left it cured.
Both Producers Research and High-Grade Living declare
He was fully sensible to the advantages of the Installment Plan
And had everything necessary to the Modern Man,   20
A phonograph, a radio, a car and a frigidaire.
Our researchers into Public Opinion are content
That he held the proper opinions for the time of year;
When there was peace, he was for peace; when there was war, he
    went.
He was married and added five children to the population,   25
Which our Eugenist says was the right number for a parent of his
    generation,
And our teachers report that he never interfered with their education.
Was he free? Was he happy? The question is absurd:
Had anything been wrong, we should certainly have heard.

1940

AMIRI BARAKA (LEROI JONES)

(b. 1934)

IN MEMORY OF RADIO   112

Who has ever stopped to think of the divinity of Lamont Cranston?
(Only Jack Kerouac, that I know of: & me.
The rest of you probably had on WCBS and Kate Smith,
Or something equally unattractive.)

What can I say?   5
It is better to have loved and lost
Than to put linoleum in your living rooms?

Am I a sage or something?
Mandrake's hypnotic gesture of the week?
(Remember, I do not have the healing powers of Oral Roberts . . .   10
I cannot, like F. J. Sheen, tell you how to get saved & *rich!*
I cannot even order you to gaschamber satori like Hitler or Goody
    Knight

IN MEMORY OF RADIO 1 *Lamont Cranston:* radio drama hero. 2 *Jack Kerouac:* (1922–1969) novelist of the beat generation. 3 *Kate Smith:* popular entertainer, singer. 10 *Oral Roberts:* evangelist. 11 *F. J. Sheen:* American bishop. 12 *satori:* a state of spiritual enlightenment sought in Zen Buddhism.

& Love is an evil word.
Turn it backwards/see, what I mean?
An evol word. & besides   15
Who understands it?
I certainly wouldn't like to go out on that kind of limb.

Saturday mornings we listened to *Red Lantern* & his undersea folk.
At 11, *Let's Pretend*/& we did/& I, the poet, still do, Thank God!

What was it he used to say (after the transformation, when he was
     safe
                                                                20
& invisible & the unbelievers couldn't throw stones?) "Heh, heh, heh,
Who knows what evil lurks in the hearts of men? The Shadow
     knows."

O, yes he does
O, yes he does.
An evil word it is,   25
This Love.

                                                              1961

APHRA BEHN
(1640–1689)

SONG: LOVE ARMED   113

Love in fantastic triumph sate,
     Whilst bleeding hearts around him flowed,
For whom fresh pains he did create,
     And strange tyrannic power he showed:
From thy bright eyes he took his fire,   5
     Which round about in sport he hurled;
But 'twas from mine he took desire,
     Enough to undo the amorous world.

From me he took his sighs and tears;
     From thee, his pride and cruelty;   10
From me, his languishments and fears;
     And every killing dart from thee.
Thus thou and I the god have armed
     And set him up a deity;
But my poor heart alone is harmed,   15
     Whilst thine the victor is, and free.

                                                            c.1685

JOHN BERRYMAN
(1914–1972)

THE BALL POEM   114

What is the boy now, who has lost his ball,
What, what is he to do? I saw it go
Merrily bouncing, down the street, and then
Merrily over—there it is in the water!
No use to say 'O there are other balls':   5
An ultimate shaking grief fixes the boy
As he stands rigid, trembling, staring down
All his young days into the harbour where
His ball went. I would not intrude on him,
A dime, another ball, is worthless. Now   10
He senses first responsibility
In a world of possessions. People will take balls,
Balls will be lost always, little boy,
And no one buys a ball back. Money is external.
He is learning, well behind his desperate eyes,   15
The epistemology of loss, how to stand up
Knowing what every man must one day know
And most know many days, how to stand up.
And gradually light returns to the street,
A whistle blows, the ball is out of sight,   20
Soon part of me will explore the deep and dark
Floor of the harbour . . I am everywhere,
I suffer and move, my mind and my heart move
With all that move me, under the water
Or whistling, I am not a little boy.   25
1950

QUESTIONS

1. What evokes the memories of childhood experiences in the first few lines? Why does
   the poem begin this way?
2. How would you describe the relationship between the boy and the speaker? Does it
   stay the same or does it change within the poem?
3. What does the speaker's vocabulary—especially his use of the word *epistemology*
   —tell you about his level of involvement in the boy's loss? Is the experience
   immediate or distant for the speaker?
4. Who is the speaker?

THE DREAM SONGS   115

16

Henry's pelt was put on sundry walls
where it did much resemble Henry and
them persons was delighted.
Especially his long & glowing tail
by all them was admired, and visitors.   5
They whistled: This is *it!*

Golden, whilst your frozen daiquiris
whir at midnight, gleams on you his fur
& silky & black.
Mission accomplished, pal.   10
My molten yellow & moonless bag,
drained, hangs at rest.

Collect in the cold depths barracuda. Ay,
in Sealdah Station some possessionless
children survive to die.   15
The Chinese communes hum. Two daiquiris
withdrew into a corner of the gorgeous room
and one told the other a lie.

                                                    1964

ELIZABETH BISHOP
(1911–1979)

THE MAN-MOTH   116

Here, above,
cracks in the buildings are filled with battered moonlight.
The whole shadow of Man is only as big as his hat.
It lies at his feet like a circle for a doll to stand on,
and he makes an inverted pin, the point magnetized to the moon.   5
He does not see the moon; he observes only her vast properties,
feeling the queer light on his hands, neither warm nor cold,
of a temperature impossible to record in thermometers.

THE MAN-MOTH title: "Newspaper misprint for 'mammoth' " (Bishop's note).

But when the Man-Moth
pays his rare, although occasional, visits to the surface,   10
the moon looks rather different to him. He emerges
from an opening under the edge of one of the sidewalks
and nervously begins to scale the faces of the buildings.
He thinks the moon is a small hole at the top of the sky,
proving the sky quite useless for protection.   15
He trembles, but must investigate as high as he can climb.

    Up the façades,
his shadow dragging like a photographer's cloth behind him,
he climbs fearfully, thinking that this time he will manage
to push his small head through that round clean opening   20
and be forced through, as from a tube, in black scrolls on the light.
(Man, standing below him, has no such illusions.)
But what the Man-Moth fears most he must do, although
he fails, of course, and falls back scared but quite unhurt.

    Then he returns   25
to the pale subways of cement he calls his home. He flits,
he flutters, and cannot get aboard the silent trains
fast enough to suit him. The doors close swiftly.
The Man-Moth always seats himself facing the wrong way
and the train starts at once at its full, terrible speed,   30
without a shift in gears or a gradation of any sort.
He cannot tell the rate at which he travels backwards.

    Each night he must
be carried through artificial tunnels and dream recurrent dreams.
Just as the ties recur beneath his train, these underlie   35
his rushing brain. He does not dare look out the window,
for the third rail, the unbroken draught of poison,
runs there beside him. He regards it as a disease
he has inherited the susceptibility to. He has to keep
his hands in his pockets, as others must wear mufflers.   40

    If you catch him,
hold up a flashlight to his eye. It's all dark pupil,
an entire night itself, whose haired horizon tightens
as he stares back, and closes up the eye. Then from the lids
one tear, his only possession, like the bee's sting, slips.   45
Slyly he palms it, and if you're not paying attention
he'll swallow it. However, if you watch, he'll hand it over,
cool as from underground springs and pure enough to drink.

1946

THE MONUMENT

Now can you see the monument? It is of wood
built somewhat like a box. No. Built
like several boxes in descending sizes
one above the other.
Each is turned half-way round so that   5
its corners point toward the sides
of the one below and the angles alternate.
Then on the topmost cube is set
a sort of fleur-de-lys of weathered wood,
long petals of board, pierced with odd holes,   10
four-sided, stiff, ecclesiastical.
From it four thin, warped poles spring out,
(slanted like fishing-poles or flag-poles)
and from them jig-saw work hangs down,
four lines of vaguely whittled ornament   15
over the edges of the boxes
to the ground.
The monument is one-third set against
a sea; two-thirds against a sky.
The view is geared   20
(that is, the view's perspective)
so low there is no "far away,"
and we are far away within the view.
A sea of narrow, horizontal boards
lies out behind our lonely monument,   25
its long grains alternating right and left
like floor-boards—spotted, swarming-still,
and motionless. A sky runs parallel,
and it is palings, coarser than the sea's:
splintery sunlight and long-fibred clouds.   30
"Why does that strange sea make no sound?
Is it because we're far away?
Where are we? Are we in Asia Minor,
or in Mongolia?"
              An ancient promontory,
an ancient principality whose artist-prince   35
might have wanted to build a monument
to mark a tomb or boundary, or make
a melancholy or romantic scene of it . . .
"But that queer sea looks made of wood,

half-shining, like a driftwood sea. 40
And the sky looks wooden, grained with cloud.
It's like a stage-set; it is all so flat!
Those clouds are full of glistening splinters!
What is that?"
                    It is the monument.
"It's piled-up boxes, 45
outlined with shoddy fret-work, half-fallen off,
cracked and unpainted. It looks old."
— The strong sunlight, the wind from the sea,
all the conditions of its existence,
may have flaked off the paint, if ever it was painted, 50
and made it homelier than it was.
"Why did you bring me here to see it?
A temple of crates in cramped and crated scenery,
what can it prove?
I am tired of breathing this eroded air, 55
this dryness in which the monument is cracking."
It is an artifact
of wood. Wood holds together better
than sea or cloud or sand could by itself,
much better than real sea or sand or cloud. 60
It chose that way to grow and not to move.
The monument's an object, yet those decorations,
carelessly nailed, looking like nothing at all,
give it away as having life, and wishing;
wanting to be a monument, to cherish something. 65
The crudest scroll-work says "commemorate,"
while once each day the light goes around it
like a prowling animal,
or the rain falls on it, or the wind blows into it.
It may be solid, may be hollow. 70
The bones of the artist-prince may be inside
or far away on even drier soil.
But roughly but adequately it can shelter
what is within (which after all
cannot have been intended to be seen). 75
It is the beginning of a painting,
a piece of sculpture, or poem, or monument,
and all of wood. Watch it closely.

1946

THE FISH

I caught a tremendous fish
and held him beside the boat
half out of water, with my hook
fast in a corner of his mouth.
He didn't fight.
He hadn't fought at all.
He hung a grunting weight,
battered and venerable
and homely. Here and there
his brown skin hung in strips
like ancient wallpaper,
and its pattern of darker brown
was like wallpaper:
shapes like full-blown roses
stained and lost through age.
He was speckled with barnacles,
fine rosettes of lime,
and infested
with tiny white sea-lice,
and underneath two or three
rags of green weed hung down.
While his gills were breathing in
the terrible oxygen
—the frightening gills,
fresh and crisp with blood,
that can cut so badly—
I thought of the coarse white flesh
packed in like feathers,
the big bones and the little bones,
the dramatic reds and blacks
of his shiny entrails,
and the pink swim-bladder
like a big peony.
I looked into his eyes
which were far larger than mine
but shallower, and yellowed,
the irises backed and packed
with tarnished tinfoil
seen through the lenses

5
10
15
20
25
30
35

of old scratched isinglass.   40
They shifted a little, but not
to return my stare.
—It was more like the tipping
of an object toward the light.
I admired his sullen face,   45
the mechanism of his jaw,
and then I saw
that from his lower lip
—if you could call it a lip—
grim, wet, and weaponlike,   50
hung five old pieces of fish-line,
or four and a wire leader
with the swivel still attached,
with all their five big hooks
grown firmly in his mouth.   55
A green line, frayed at the end
where he broke it, two heavier lines,
and a fine black thread
still crimped from the strain and snap
when it broke and he got away.   60
Like medals with their ribbons
frayed and wavering,
a five-haired beard of wisdom
trailing from his aching jaw.
I stared and stared   65
and victory filled up
the little rented boat,
from the pool of bilge
where oil had spread a rainbow
around the rusted engine   70
to the bailer rusted orange,
the sun-cracked thwarts,
the oarlocks on their strings,
the gunnels—until everything
was rainbow, rainbow, rainbow!   75
And I let the fish go.

1946

THE FISH 40 *isinglass:* a translucent form of mica used before plastics were common.

AT THE FISHHOUSES   119

Although it is a cold evening,
down by one of the fishhouses
an old man sits netting,
his net, in the gloaming almost invisible
a dark purple-brown,   5
and his shuttle worn and polished.
The air smells so strong of codfish
it makes one's nose run and one's eyes water.
The five fishhouses have steeply peaked roofs
and narrow, cleated gangplanks slant up   10
to storerooms in the gables
for the wheelbarrows to be pushed up and down on.
All is silver: the heavy surface of the sea,
swelling slowly as if considering spilling over,
is opaque, but the silver of the benches,   15
the lobster pots, and masts, scattered
among the wild jagged rocks,
is of an apparent translucence
like the small old buildings with an emerald moss
growing on their shoreward walls.   20
The big fish tubs are completely lined
with layers of beautiful herring scales
and the wheelbarrows are similarly plastered
with creamy iridescent coats of mail,
with small iridescent flies crawling on them.   25
Up on the little slope behind the houses,
set in the sparse bright sprinkle of grass,
is an ancient wooden capstan,
cracked, with two long bleached handles
and some melancholy stains, like dried blood,   30
where the ironwork has rusted.
The old man accepts a Lucky Strike.
He was a friend of my grandfather.
We talk of the decline in the population
and of codfish and herring   35
while he waits for a herring boat to come in.

AT THE FISHHOUSES 28 *capstan:* a nautical apparatus, around which are wound cables for anchors.

There are sequins on his vest and on his thumb.
He has scraped the scales, the principal beauty,
from unnumbered fish with that black old knife,
the blade of which is almost worn away.   40

Down at the water's edge, at the place
where they haul up the boats, up the long ramp
descending into the water, thin silver
tree trunks are laid horizontally
across the gray stones, down and down   45
at intervals of four or five feet.
Cold dark deep and absolutely clear,
element bearable to no mortal,
to fish and to seals . . . One seal particularly
I have seen here evening after evening.   50
He was curious about me. He was interested in music;
like me a believer in total immersion,
so I used to sing him Baptist hymns.
I also sang "A Mighty Fortress Is Our God."
He stood up in the water and regarded me   55
steadily, moving his head a little.
Then he would disappear, then suddenly emerge
almost in the same spot, with a sort of shrug
as if it were against his better judgment.
Cold dark deep and absolutely clear,   60
the clear gray icy water . . . Back, behind us,
the dignified tall firs begin.
Bluish, associating with their shadows,
a million Christmas trees stand
waiting for Christmas. The water seems suspended   65
above the rounded gray and blue-gray stones.
I have seen it over and over, the same sea, the same,
slightly, indifferently swinging above the stones,
icily free above the stones,
above the stones and then the world.   70
If you should dip your hand in,
your wrist would ache immediately,
your bones would begin to ache and your hand would burn
as if the water were a transmutation of fire
that feeds on stones and burns with a dark gray flame.   75
If you tasted it, it would first taste bitter,
then briny, then surely burn your tongue.

It is like what we imagine knowledge to be:
dark, salt, clear, moving, utterly free,
drawn from the cold hard mouth   80
of the world, derived from the rocky breasts
forever, flowing and drawn, and since
our knowledge is historical, flowing, and flown.

1955

THE ARMADILLO   120

FOR ROBERT LOWELL

This is the time of year
when almost every night
the frail, illegal fire balloons appear.
Climbing the mountain height,

rising toward a saint   5
still honored in these parts,
the paper chambers flush and fill with light
that comes and goes, like hearts.

Once up against the sky it's hard
to tell them from the stars—   10
planets, that is—the tinted ones:
Venus going down, or Mars,

or the pale green one. With a wind,
they flare and falter, wobble and toss;
but if it's still they steer between   15
the kite sticks of the Southern Cross,

receding, dwindling, solemnly
and steadily forsaking us,
or, in the downdraft from a peak,
suddenly turning dangerous.   20

Last night another big one fell.
It splattered like an egg of fire
against the cliff behind the house.
The flame ran down. We saw the pair

THE ARMADILLO 16 *Southern Cross:* a constellation whose stars appear as the four brightest tips of a cross, visible in the Southern hemisphere.

of owls who nest there flying up   25
and up, their whirling black–and–white
stained bright pink underneath, until
they shrieked up out of sight.

The ancient owls' nest must have burned.
Hastily, all alone,   30
a glistening armadillo left the scene,
rose-flecked, head down, tail down,

and then a baby rabbit jumped out,
short-eared, to our surprise.
So soft!—a handful of intangible ash   35
with fixed, ignited eyes.

Too pretty, dreamlike mimicry!
O falling fire and piercing cry
and panic, and a weak mailed fist
clenched ignorant against the sky!   40

                                                                    1965

SESTINA   121

September rain falls on the house.
In the failing light, the old grandmother
sits in the kitchen with the child
beside the Little Marvel Stove,
reading the jokes from the almanac,   5
laughing and talking to hide her tears.

She thinks that her equinoctial tears
and the rain that beats on the roof of the house
were both foretold by the almanac,
but only known to a grandmother.   10
The iron kettle sings on the stove.
She cuts some bread and says to the child,

It's time for tea now; but the child
is watching the teakettle's small hard tears
dance like mad on the hot black stove,   15
the way the rain must dance on the house.
Tidying up, the old grandmother
hangs up the clever almanac

SESTINA 4 *Little Marvel Stove:* a wood-burning stove.

on its string. Birdlike, the almanac
hovers half open above the child,   20
hovers above the old grandmother
and her teacup full of dark brown tears.
She shivers and says she thinks the house
feels chilly, and puts more wood in the stove.

It was to be, says the Marvel Stove.   25
I know what I know, says the almanac.
With crayons the child draws a rigid house
and a winding pathway. Then the child
puts in a man with buttons like tears
and shows it proudly to the grandmother.   30

But secretly, while the grandmother
busies herself about the stove,
the little moons fall down like tears
from between the pages of the almanac
into the flower bed the child   35
has carefully placed in the front of the house.

Time to plant tears, says the almanac.
The grandmother sings to the marvelous stove
and the child draws another inscrutable house.

1965

QUESTIONS

1. Who are the speakers in this poem and what do they say?
2. What do they suggest about the relationship between the child and the grandmother?
3. Which words are repeated throughout the poem? Why?
4. How does the repetition of words relate to the theme of the poem? What effect does this repetition have on the tone?
5. What constraints does the sestina form put on the reader?
6. Why do you think personification is such a central part of this poem? What is its effect on the way you read the poem aloud?

WILLIAM BLAKE

(1757–1827)

SONG   122

How sweet I roam'd from field to field,
    And tasted all the summer's pride,
'Till I the prince of love beheld,
    Who in the sunny beams did glide!

He shew'd me lilies for my hair,   5
   And blushing roses for my brow;
He led me through his gardens fair,
   Where all his golden pleasures grow.

With sweet May dews my wings were wet,
   And Phoebus fir'd my vocal rage;   10
He caught me in his silken net,
   And shut me in his golden cage.

He loves to sit and hear me sing,
   Then, laughing, sports and plays with me;
Then stretches out my golden wing,   15
   And mocks my loss of liberty.

1783

THE CHIMNEY SWEEPER   123

When my mother died I was very young,
And my father sold me while yet my tongue
Could scarcely cry " 'weep! 'weep! 'weep! 'weep!"
So your chimneys I sweep, and in soot I sleep.

There's little Tom Dacre, who cried when his head,   5
That curled like a lamb's back, was shaved; so I said,
"Hush, Tom! never mind it, for, when your head's bare,
You know that the soot cannot spoil your white hair."

And so he was quiet, and that very night,
As Tom was asleeping, he had such a sight!   10
That thousands of sweepers, Dick, Joe, Ned, and Jack,
Were all of them locked up in coffins of black.

And by came an Angel who had a bright key,
And he opened the coffins and set them all free;
Then down a green plain leaping, laughing, they run,   15
And wash in a river, and shine in the sun.

Then naked and white, all their bags left behind,
They rise upon clouds and sport in the wind;
And the Angel told Tom, if he'd be a good boy,
He'd have God for his father, and never want joy.   20

SONG 10 *Phoebus:* Apollo, god of the sun and poetry.

And so Tom awoke, and we rose in the dark,
And got with our bags and our brushes to work.
Though the morning was cold, Tom was happy and warm;
So if all do their duty they need not fear harm.

1789

LONDON   124

I wander thro' each charter'd street,
Near where the charter'd Thames does flow,
And mark in every face I meet
Marks of weakness, marks of woe.

In every cry of every man,   5
In every Infant's cry of fear,
In every voice, in every ban,
The mind-forg'd manacles I hear.

How the Chimney-sweeper's cry
Every blackning Church appalls;   10
And the hapless Soldier's sigh
Runs in blood down Palace walls.

But most thro' midnight streets I hear
How the youthful Harlot's curse
Blasts the new-born Infant's tear,   15
And blights with plagues the Marriage hearse.

1794

ETERNITY   125

He who binds to himself a joy
Does the wingéd life destroy
But he who kisses the joy as it flies
Lives in eternity's sun rise.

1863

LONDON 7 *ban:* a public order forbidding something.

ROBERT BLY
(b. 1926)

WAKING FROM SLEEP   126

Inside the veins there are navies setting forth,
Tiny explosions at the water lines,
And seagulls weaving in the wind of the salty blood.

It is the morning. The country has slept the whole winter.
Window seats were covered with fur skins, the yard was full   5
Of stiff dogs, and hands that clumsily held heavy books.

Now we wake, and rise from bed, and eat breakfast!—
Shouts rise from the harbor of the blood,
Mist, and masts rising, the knock of wooden tackle in the sunlight.

Now we sing, and do tiny dances on the kitchen floor.   10
Our whole body is like a harbor at dawn;
We know that our master has left us for the day.

                                                        1962

QUESTIONS

1. How does it feel to wake from sleep? Which images in this poem capture that feeling
   most effectively for you? To which sense do these images appeal?
2. Who or what awakens in this poem? Which image patterns connect the various types
   of awakenings?
3. There are two possible puns in this poem. Where are they and how do they work to
   link image patterns and unify the poem?
4. What does the repetition of the word *rise* in stanza three contribute to your personal
   experience of the poem? How does the repetition contribute to meaning?

DRIVING THROUGH MINNESOTA
DURING THE HANOI BOMBINGS   127

We drive between lakes just turning green;
Late June. The white turkeys have been moved
To new grass.
How long the seconds are in great pain!
Terror just before death,   5
Shoulders torn, shot
From helicopters, the boy
Tortured with the telephone generator,

"I felt sorry for him,
And blew his head off with a shotgun."   10
These instants become crystals,
Particles
The grass cannot dissolve. Our own gaiety
Will end up
In Asia, and in your cup you will look down   15
And see
Black Starfighters.
We were the ones we intended to bomb!
Therefore we will have
To go far away   20
To atone
For the sufferings of the stringy-chested
And the small rice-fed ones, quivering
In the helicopter like wild animals,
Shot in the chest, taken back to be questioned.   25

1967

LOUISE BOGAN
(1897–1970)

MEDUSA   128

I had come to the house, in a cave of trees,
Facing a sheer sky.
Everything moved,—a bell hung ready to strike,
Sun and reflection wheeled by.

When the bare eyes were before me   5
And the hissing hair,
Held up at a window, seen through a door.
The stiff bald eyes, the serpents on the forehead
Formed in the air.

This is a dead scene forever now.   10
Nothing will ever stir.
The end will never brighten it more than this,
Nor the rain blur.

MEDUSA title: Medusa was one of the Gorgons in Greek mythology; her hair was made of snakes and her glance turned people to stone.

The water will always fall, and will not fall,
And the tipped bell make no sound.   15
The grass will always be growing for hay
Deep on the ground.

And I shall stand here like a shadow
Under the great balanced day,
My eyes on the yellow dust, that was lifting in the wind,   20
And does not drift away.

                                                                    1921

QUESTIONS

1. Which images are most startling the first or second time you read the poem? How
   does their strong effect on you mirror the action being described?
2. What is the basic contrast explored by the poem? Which images seem to express this
   contrast most effectively?
3. Where is paradox operative?

NIGHT   129

The cold remote islands
And the blue estuaries
Where what breathes, breathes
The restless wind of the inlets,
And what drinks, drinks   5
The incoming tide;

Where shell and weed
Wait upon the salt of the sea,
And the clear nights of stars
Swing their lights westward   10
To set behind the land;

Where the pulse clinging to the rocks
Renews itself forever;
Where, again on cloudless nights,
The water reflects   15
The firmament's partial setting;

—O remember
In your narrowing dark hours
That more things move
Than blood in the heart.   20

                                                                    1923

NIGHT 2 *estuaries:* inlets of the sea.

THE DRAGONFLY   130

You are made of almost nothing
But of enough
To be great eyes
And diaphanous double vans;
To be ceaseless movement,   5
Unending hunger
Grappling love.

Link between water and air,
Earth repels you.
Light touches you only to shift into iridescence   10
Upon your body and wings.

Twice-born, predator,
You split into the heat.
Swift beyond calculation or capture
You dart into the shadow   15
Which consumes you.

You rocket into the day.
But at last, when the wind flattens the grasses,
For you, the design and purpose stop.
And you fall   20
With the other husks of summer.

1968

ANNE BRADSTREET
(c. 1612–1672)

THE AUTHOR TO HER BOOK   131

Thou ill-formed offspring of my feeble brain,
Who after birth didst by my side remain,
Till snatched from thence by friends, less wise than true,
Who thee abroad, exposed to public view,
Made thee in rags, halting to th' press to trudge,   5
Where errors were not lessened (all may judge).
At thy return my blushing was not small,

THE DRAGONFLY 4 *vans:* wings.

My rambling brat (in print) should mother call,
I cast thee by as one unfit for light,
Thy visage was so irksome in my sight;   10
Yet being mine own, at length affection would
Thy blemishes amend, if so I could:
I washed thy face, but more defects I saw,
And rubbing off a spot still made a flaw.
I stretched thy joints to make thee even feet,   15
Yet still thou run'st more hobbling than is meet;
In better dress to trim thee was my mind,
But nought save homespun cloth i' th' house I find.
In this array 'mongst vulgars may'st thou roam.
In critic's hands beware thou dost not come,   20
And take thy way where yet thou art not known;
If for thy father asked, say thou hadst none;
And for thy mother, she alas is poor,
Which caused her thus to send thee out of door.

1678

HERE FOLLOWS SOME VERSES UPON THE
BURNING OF OUR HOUSE JULY 10TH, 1666   132

COPIED OUT OF A LOOSE PAPER

In silent night when rest I took
For sorrow near I did not look
I wakened was with thund'ring noise
And piteous shrieks of dreadful voice.
That fearful sound of "Fire!" and "Fire!"   5
Let no man know is my desire.
I, starting up, the light did spy,
And to my God my heart did cry
To strengthen me in my distress
And not to leave me succorless.   10
Then, coming out, beheld a space
The flame consume my dwelling place.
And when I could no longer look,
I blest His name that gave and took,
That laid my goods now in the dust.   15
Yea, so it was, and so 'twas just.
It was His own, it was not mine,
Far be it that I should repine;

He might of all justly bereft
But yet sufficient for us left.   20
When by the ruins oft I past
My sorrowing eyes aside did cast,
And here and there the places spy
Where oft I sat and long did lie:
Here stood that trunk, and there that chest,   25
There lay that store I counted best.
My pleasant things in ashes lie,
And them behold no more shall I.
Under thy roof no guest shall sit,
Nor at thy table eat a bit.   30
No pleasant tale shall e'er be told,
Nor things recounted done of old.
No candle e'er shall shine in thee,
Nor bridegroom's voice e'er heard shall be.
In silence ever shall thou lie,   35
Adieu, Adieu, all's vanity.
Then straight I 'gin my heart to chide,
And did thy wealth on earth abide?
Didst fix thy hope on mold'ring dust?
The arm of flesh didst make thy trust?   40
Raise up thy thoughts above the sky
That dunghill mists away may fly.
Thou hast an house on high erect,
Framed by that mighty Architect,
With glory richly furnished,   45
Stands permanent though this be fled.
It's purchaséd and paid for too
By Him who hath enough to do.
A price so vast as is unknown
Yet by His gift is made thine own;   50
There's wealth enough, I need no more,
Farewell, my pelf, farewell my store.
The world no longer let me love,
My hope and treasure lies above.

1867

HERE FOLLOWS SOME VERSES . . . 52 *pelf:* ill-gotten wealth.

ROBERT BRIDGES
(1844–1930)

LOW BAROMETER   133

The south-wind strengthens to a gale,
Across the moon the clouds fly fast,
The house is smitten as with a flail,
The chimney shudders to the blast.

On such a night, when Air has loosed   5
Its guardian grasp on blood and brain,
Old terrors then of god or ghost
Creep from their caves to life again;

And Reason kens he herits in
A haunted house. Tenants unknown   10
Assert their squalid lease of sin
With earlier title than his own.

Unbodied presences, the pack'd
Pollution and remorse of Time,
Slipp'd from oblivion reënact   15
The horrors of unhouseld crime.

Some men would quell the thing with prayer
Whose sightless footsteps pad the floor,
Whose fearful trespass mounts the stair
Or bursts the lock'd forbidden door.   20

Some have seen corpses long interr'd
Escape from hallowing control,
Pale charnel forms—nay ev'n have heard
The shrilling of a troubled soul,

That wanders till the dawn hath cross'd   25
The dolorous dark, or Earth hath wound
Closer her storm-spredd cloke, and thrust
The baleful phantoms underground.

1925

QUESTIONS

1. Which words do you find strange? Why does the author use such an odd vocabulary?
2. Identify the elements of horror. Does the poem have a more serious purpose than just to scare?

LOW BAROMETER 16 *unhouseld:* having nothing to do with the bread and wine of the Eucharist.

EMILY BRONTË
(1818–1848)

REMEMBRANCE 134

Cold in the earth—and the deep snow piled above thee,
Far, far removed, cold in the dreary grave!
Have I forgot, my only Love, to love thee,
Severed at last by Time's all-severing wave?

Now, when alone, do my thoughts no longer hover   5
Over the mountains, on that northern shore,
Resting their wings where heath and fern leaves cover
Thy noble heart forever, ever more?

Cold in the earth—and fifteen wild Decembers,
From those brown hills, have melted into spring;   10
Faithful, indeed, is the spirit that remembers
After such years of change and suffering!

Sweet Love of youth, forgive, if I forget thee,
While the world's tide is bearing me along;
Other desires and other hopes beset me,   15
Hopes which obscure, but cannot do thee wrong!

No later light has lightened up my heaven,
No second morn has ever shone for me;
All my life's bliss from thy dear life was given,
All my life's bliss is in the grave with thee.   20

But, when the days of golden dreams had perished,
And even Despair was powerless to destroy,
Then did I learn how existence could be cherished,
Strengthened, and fed without the aid of joy.

Then did I check the tears of useless passion—   25
Weaned my young soul from yearning after thine;
Sternly denied its burning wish to hasten
Down to that tomb already more than mine.

And, even yet, I dare not let it languish,
Dare not indulge in memory's rapturous pain;   30
Once drinking deep of that divinest anguish,
How could I seek the empty world again?

1846

GWENDOLYN BROOKS
(b. 1917)

KITCHENETTE BUILDING   135

We are things of dry hours and the involuntary plan,
Grayed in, and gray. "Dream" makes a giddy sound, not strong
Like "rent," "feeding a wife," "satisfying a man."

But could a dream send up through onion fumes
Its white and violet, fight with fried potatoes   5
And yesterday's garbage ripening in the hall,
Flutter, or sing an aria down these rooms

Even if we were willing to let it in,
Had time to warm it, keep it very clean,
Anticipate a message, let it begin?   10

We wonder. But not well! not for a minute!
Since Number Five is out of the bathroom now,
We think of lukewarm water, hope to get in it.

                                                        1945

THE SUNDAYS OF SATIN-LEGS SMITH   136

Inamoratas, with an approbation,
Bestowed his title. Blessed his inclination.

He wakes, unwinds, elaborately: a cat
Tawny, reluctant, royal. He is fat
And fine this morning. Definite. Reimbursed.   5

He waits a moment, he designs his reign,
That no performance may be plain or vain.
Then rises in a clear delirium.

He sheds, with his pajamas, shabby days.
And his desertedness, his intricate fear, the   10
Postponed resentments and the prim precautions.

Now, at his bath, would you deny him lavender
Or take away the power of his pine?
What smelly substitute, heady as wine,
Would you provide? life must be aromatic.   15

THE SUNDAYS OF SATIN-LEGS SMITH 1 *Inamoratas:* his female lovers.

There must be scent, somehow there must be some.
Would you have flowers in his life? suggest
Asters? a Really Good geranium?
A white carnation? would you prescribe a Show
With the cold lilies, formal chrysanthemum   20
Magnificence, poinsettias, and emphatic
Red of prize roses? might his happiest
Alternative (you muse) be, after all,
A bit of gentle garden in the best
Of taste and straight tradition? Maybe so.   25
But you forget, or did you ever know,
His heritage of cabbage and pigtails,
Old intimacy with alleys, garbage pails,
Down in the deep (but always beautiful) South
Where roses blush their blithest (it is said)   30
And sweet magnolias put Chanel to shame.

No! He has not a flower to his name.
Except a feather one, for his lapel.
Apart from that, if he should think of flowers
It is in terms of dandelions or death.   35
Ah, there is little hope. You might as well—
Unless you care to set the world a-boil
And do a lot of equalizing things,
Remove a little ermine, say, from kings,
Shake hands with paupers and appoint them men,   40
For instance—certainly you might as well
Leave him his lotion, lavender and oil.

Let us proceed. Let us inspect, together
With his meticulous and serious love,
The innards of this closet. Which is a vault   45
Whose glory is not diamonds, not pearls,
Not silver plate with just enough dull shine.
But wonder-suits in yellow and in wine,
Sarcastic green and zebra-striped cobalt.
With shoulder padding that is wide   50
And cocky and determined as his pride;
Ballooning pants that taper off to ends
Scheduled to choke precisely.
                                    Here are hats
Like bright umbrellas; and hysterical ties
Like narrow banners for some gathering war.   55

People are so in need, in need of help.
People want so much that they do not know.

Below the tinkling trade of little coins
The gold impulse not possible to show
Or spend. Promise piled over and betrayed.   60

These kneaded limbs receive the kiss of silk.
Then they receive the brave and beautiful
Embrace of some of that equivocal wool.
He looks into his mirror, loves himself—
The neat curve here; the angularity   65
That is appropriate at just its place;
The technique of a variegated grace.

Here is all his sculpture and his art
And all his architectural design.
Perhaps you would prefer to this a fine   70
Value of marble, complicated stone.
Would have him think with horror of baroque,
Rococo. You forget and you forget.

He dances down the hotel steps that keep
Remnants of last night's high life and distress.   75
As spat-out purchased kisses and spilled beer.
He swallows sunshine with a secret yelp.
Passes to coffee and a roll or two.
Has breakfasted.
                        Out. Sounds about him smear,
Become a unit. He hears and does not hear   80
The alarm clock meddling in somebody's sleep;
Children's governed Sunday happiness;
The dry tone of a plane; a woman's oath;
Consumption's spiritless expectoration;
An indignant robin's resolute donation   85
Pinching a track through apathy and din;
Restaurant vendors weeping; and the L
That comes on like a slightly horrible thought.

Pictures, too, as usual, are blurred.
He sees and does not see the broken windows   90
Hiding their shame with newsprint; little girl
With ribbons decking wornness, little boy
Wearing the trousers with the decentest patch,
To honor Sunday; women on their way

From "service," temperate holiness arranged   95
Ably on asking faces; men estranged
From music and from wonder and from joy
But far familiar with the guiding awe
Of foodlessness.
             He loiters.
                           Restaurant vendors
Weep, or out of them rolls a restless glee.   100
The Lonesome Blues, the Long-lost Blues, I Want A
Big Fat Mama. Down these sore avenues
Comes no Saint-Saëns, no piquant elusive Grieg,
And not Tschaikovsky's wayward eloquence
And not the shapely tender drift of Brahms.   105
But could he love them? Since a man must bring
To music what his mother spanked him for
When he was two: bits of forgotten hate,
Devotion: whether or not his mattress hurts:
The little dream his father humored: the thing   110
His sister did for money: what he ate
For breakfast—and for dinner twenty years
Ago last autumn: all his skipped desserts.

The pasts of his ancestors lean against
Him. Crowd him. Fog out his identity.   115
Hundreds of hungers mingle with his own,
Hundreds of voices advise so dexterously
He quite considers his reactions his,
Judges he walks most powerfully alone,
That everything is—simply what it is.   120

But movie-time approaches, time to boo
The hero's kiss, and boo the heroine
Whose ivory and yellow it is sin
For his eye to eat of. The Mickey Mouse,
However, is for everyone in the house.   125

Squires his lady to dinner at Joe's Eats.
His lady alters as to leg and eye,
Thickness and height, such minor points as these,
From Sunday to Sunday. But no matter what
Her name or body positively she's   130
In Queen Lace stockings with ambitious heels
That strain to kiss the calves, and vivid shoes
Frontless and backless, Chinese fingernails,

Earrings, three layers of lipstick, intense hat
Dripping with the most voluble of veils.   135
Her affable extremes are like sweet bombs
About him, whom no middle grace or good
Could gratify. He had no education
In quiet arts of compromise. He would
Not understand your counsels on control, nor   140
Thank you for your late trouble.
       At Joe's Eats
You get your fish or chicken on meat platters.
With coleslaw, macaroni, candied sweets,
Coffee and apple pie. You go out full.
(The end is—isn't it?—all that really matters.)   145

   And even and intrepid come
   The tender boots of night to home.

Her body is like new brown bread
Under the Woolworth mignonette.
Her body is a honey bowl   150
Whose waiting honey is deep and hot.
Her body is like summer earth,
Receptive, soft, and absolute . . .

            1945

[POEM 4 *FROM* "THE WOMANHOOD"]   137

First fight. Then fiddle. Ply the slipping string
With feathery sorcery; muzzle the note
With hurting love; the music that they wrote
Bewitch, bewilder. Qualify to sing
Threadwise. Devise no salt, no hempen thing   5
For the dear instrument to bear. Devote
The bow to silks and honey. Be remote
A while from malice and from murdering.
But first to arms, to armor. Carry hate
In front of you and harmony behind.   10
Be deaf to music and to beauty blind.
Win war. Rise bloody, maybe not too late
For having first to civilize a space
Wherein to play your violin with grace.

            1949

149 *mignonette:* lace or net.

BEVERLY HILLS, CHICAGO 138

"AND THE PEOPLE LIVE TILL THEY HAVE WHITE HAIR"
— E. M. PRICE

The dry brown coughing beneath their feet,
(Only a while, for the handyman is on his way)
These people walk their golden gardens.
We say ourselves fortunate to be driving by today.

That we may look at them, in their gardens where   5
The summer ripeness rots. But not raggedly.
Even the leaves fall down in lovelier patterns here.
And the refuse, the refuse is a neat brilliancy.

When they flow sweetly into their houses
With softness and slowness touched by that everlasting gold,   10
We know what they go to. To tea. But that does not mean
They will throw some little black dots into some water and add sugar
        and the juice of the cheapest lemons that are sold,

While downstairs that woman's vague phonograph bleats, "Knock
        me a kiss."
And the living all to be made again in the sweatingest physical
        manner
Tomorrow. . . . Not that anybody is saying that these people have
        no trouble.   15
Merely that it is trouble with a gold-flecked beautiful banner.

Nobody is saying that these people do not ultimately cease to be.
        And
Sometimes their passings are even more painful than ours.
It is just that so often they live till their hair is white.
They make excellent corpses, among the expensive flowers. . . .   20

Nobody is furious. Nobody hates these people.
At least, nobody driving by in this car.
It is only natural, however, that it should occur to us
How much more fortunate they are than we are.

It is only natural that we should look and look   25
At their wood and brick and stone
And think, while a breath of pine blows,
How different these are from our own.

We do not want them to have less.
But it is only natural that we should think we have not enough. 30
We drive on, we drive on.
When we speak to each other our voices are a little gruff.

1949

WE REAL COOL 139

THE POOL PLAYERS.
SEVEN AT THE GOLDEN SHOVEL.

We real cool. We
Left school. We

Lurk late. We
Strike straight. We

Sing sin. We 5
Thin gin. We

Jazz June. We
Die soon.

1960

QUESTIONS

1. How does the poem succeed despite the predominance of rhyme and rhythm?
2. Identify the following poetic devices in the poem and show how they either reinforce
   or undercut the poem's rhythmic regularity.

   enjambment
   internal rhyme
   repetition
   alliteration
   assonance

3. Do you see any movement or development in the meaning of the verbs?
4. Why is the last line two feet shorter than the first line and one foot shorter than the
   rest of the lines?

THE BEAN EATERS 140

They eat beans mostly, this old yellow pair.
Dinner is a casual affair.
Plain chipware on a plain and creaking wood,
Tin flatware.

Two who are Mostly Good.   5
Two who have lived their day,
But keep on putting on their clothes
And putting things away.

And remembering . . .
Remembering, with twinklings and twinges,   10
As they lean over the beans in their rented back room that is full of
    beads and receipts and dolls and clothes, tobacco crumbs, vases
    and fringes.

1960

THE LOVERS OF THE POOR   141

        arrive. The Ladies from the Ladies' Betterment
   League
Arrive in the afternoon, the late light slanting
In diluted gold bars across the boulevard brag
Of proud, seamed faces with mercy and murder hinting   5
Here, there, interrupting, all deep and debonair,
The pink paint on the innocence of fear;
Walk in a gingerly manner up the hall.
Cutting with knives served by their softest care,
Served by their love, so barbarously fair.   10
Whose mothers taught: You'd better not be cruel!
You had better not throw stones upon the wrens!
Herein they kiss and coddle and assault
Anew and dearly in the innocence
With which they baffle nature. Who are full,   15
Sleek, tender-clad, fit, fiftyish, a-glow, all
Sweetly abortive, hinting at fat fruit,
Judge it high time that fiftyish fingers felt
Beneath the lovelier planes of enterprise.
To resurrect. To moisten with milky chill.   20
To be a random hitching-post or plush.
To be, for wet eyes, random and handy hem.
        Their guild is giving money to the poor.
The worthy poor. The very very worthy
And beautiful poor. Perhaps just not too swarthy?   25
Perhaps just not too dirty nor too dim
Nor—passionate. In truth, what they could wish
Is—something less than derelict or dull.

Not staunch enough to stab, though, gaze for gaze!
God shield them sharply from the beggar-bold!   30
The noxious needy ones whose battle's bald
Nonetheless for being voiceless, hits one down.
        But it's all so bad! and entirely too much for them.
The stench; the urine, cabbage, and dead beans,
Dead porridges of assorted dusty grains,   35
The old smoke, *heavy* diapers, and, they're told,
Something called chitterlings. The darkness. Drawn
Darkness, or dirty light. The soil that stirs.
The soil that looks the soil of centuries.
And for that matter the *general* oldness. Old   40
Wood. Old marble. Old tile. Old old old.
Not homekind Oldness! Not Lake Forest, Glencoe.
Nothing is sturdy, nothing is majestic,
There is no quiet drama, no rubbed glaze, no
Unkillable infirmity of such   45
A tasteful turn as lately they have left,
Glencoe, Lake Forest, and to which their cars
Must presently restore them. When they're done
With dullards and distortions of this fistic
Patience of the poor and put-upon.   50
        They've never seen such a make-do-ness as
Newspaper rugs before! In this, this "flat,"
Their hostess is gathering up the oozed, the rich
Rugs of the morning (tattered! the bespattered. . . .)
Readies to spread clean rugs for afternoon.   55
Here is a scene for you. The Ladies look,
In horror, behind a substantial citizeness
Whose trains clank out across her swollen heart.
Who, arms akimbo, almost fills a door.
All tumbling children, quilts dragged to the floor   60
And tortured thereover, potato peelings, soft-
Eyed kitten, hunched-up, haggard, to-be-hurt.
        Their League is allotting largesse to the Lost.
But to put their clean, their pretty money, to put
Their money collected from delicate rose-fingers   65
Tipped with their hundred flawless rose-nails seems . . .

THE LOVERS OF THE POOR 42 *Lake Forest, Glencoe:* affluent suburbs of Chicago.

They own Spode, Lowestoft, candelabra,
Mantels, and hostess gowns, and sunburst clocks,
Turtle soup, Chippendale, red satin "hangings,"
Aubussons and Hattie Carnegie. They Winter   70
In Palm Beach; cross the Water in June; attend,
When suitable, the nice Art Institute;
Buy the right books in the best bindings; saunter
On Michigan, Easter mornings, in sun or wind.
Oh Squalor! This sick four-story hulk, this fibre   75
With fissures everywhere! Why, what are bringings
Of loathe-love largesse? What shall peril hungers
So old old, what shall flatter the desolate?
Tin can, blocked fire escape and chitterling
And swaggering seeking youth and the puzzled wreckage   80
Of the middle passage, and urine and stale shames
And, again, the porridges of the underslung
And children children children. Heavens! That
Was a rat, surely, off there, in the shadows? Long
And long-tailed? Gray? The Ladies from the Ladies'   85
Betterment League agree it will be better
To achieve the outer air that rights and steadies,
To hie to a house that does not holler, to ring
Bells elsetime, better presently to cater
To no more Possibilities, to get   90
Away. Perhaps the money can be posted.
Perhaps they two may choose another Slum!
Some serious sooty half-unhappy home!—
Where loathe-love likelier may be invested.

           Keeping their scented bodies in the center   95
Of the hall as they walk down the hysterical hall,
They allow their lovely skirts to graze no wall,
Are off at what they manage of a canter,
And, resuming all the clues of what they were,
Try to avoid inhaling the laden air.   100

1960

---

67 *Spode, Lowestoft:* fine English china. 69 *Chippendale:* eighteenth-century English furniture. 70
Aubussons: French tapestries; *Hattie Carnegie:* American dress designer. 74 *Michigan:* Chicago's
Michigan Avenue.

THE CHICAGO DEFENDER SENDS A MAN TO LITTLE ROCK

142

FALL, 1957

In Little Rock the people bear
Babes, and comb and part their hair
And watch the want ads, put repair
To roof and latch. While wheat toast burns
A woman waters multiferns.   5

Time upholds or overturns
The many, tight, and small concerns.

In Little Rock the people sing
Sunday hymns like anything,
Through Sunday pomp and polishing.   10

And after testament and tunes,
Some soften Sunday afternoons
With lemon tea and Lorna Doones.

I forecast
And I believe   15
Come Christmas Little Rock will cleave
To Christmas tree and trifle, weave,
From laugh and tinsel, texture fast.

In Little Rock is baseball; Barcarolle.
That hotness in July . . . the uniformed figures raw and implacable   20
And not intellectual,
Batting the hotness or clawing the suffering dust.
The Open Air Concert, on the special twilight green. . . .
When Beethoven is brutal or whispers to lady-like air.
Blanket-sitters are solemn, as Johann troubles to lean   25
To tell them what to mean. . . .

There is love, too, in Little Rock. Soft women softly
Opening themselves in kindness,
Or, pitying one's blindness,
Awaiting one's pleasure   30
In azure
Glory with anguished rose at the root. . . .

THE CHICAGO DEFENDER SENDS A MAN TO LITTLE ROCK 19 *Barcarolle:* a song in the style of those sung by Venetian gondoliers.

To wash away old semi-discomfitures.
They re-teach purple and unsullen blue.
The wispy soils go. And uncertain   35
Half-havings have they clarified to sures.

In Little Rock they know
Not answering the telephone is a way of rejecting life,
That it is our business to be bothered, is our business
To cherish bores or boredom, be polite   40
To lies and love and many-faceted fuzziness.
I scratch my head, massage the hate-I-had.
I blink across my prim and pencilled pad.
The saga I was sent for is not down.
Because there is a puzzle in this town.   45
The biggest News I do not dare
Telegraph to the Editor's chair:
"They are like people everywhere."

The angry Editor would reply
In hundred harryings of Why.   50

And true, they are hurling spittle, rock,
Garbage and fruit in Little Rock.
And I saw coiling storm a-writhe
On bright madonnas. And a scythe
Of men harassing brownish girls.   55
(The bows and barrettes in the curls
And braids declined away from joy.)

I saw a bleeding brownish boy. . . .

The lariat lynch-wish I deplored.

The loveliest lynchee was our Lord.   60

1960

ELIZABETH BARRETT BROWNING

(1806–1861)

SONNET 43
[HOW DO I LOVE THEE?]   143

How do I love thee? Let me count the ways.
I love thee to the depth and breadth and height
My soul can reach, when feeling out of sight
For the ends of Being and ideal Grace.

I love thee to the level of everyday's   5
Most quiet need, by sun and candle-light.
I love thee freely, as men strive for Right;
I love thee purely, as they turn from Praise.
I love thee with the passion put to use
In my old griefs, and with my childhood's faith.   10
I love thee with a love I seemed to lose
With my lost saints,—I love thee with the breath,
Smiles, tears, of all my life!—and, if God choose,
I shall but love thee better after death.

1850

QUESTIONS

1. When you read this poem, what are the various activities you visualize?
2. Where is hyperbole in this poem?
3. Where are the images?
4. How does the speaker's past help her to define her present emotion?

A MUSICAL INSTRUMENT   144

What was he doing, the great god Pan,
    Down in the reeds by the river?
Spreading ruin and scattering ban,
Splashing and paddling with hoofs of a goat,
And breaking the golden lilies afloat   5
    With the dragonfly on the river.

He tore out a reed, the great god Pan,
    From the deep cool bed of the river;
The limpid water turbidly ran,
And the broken lilies a-dying lay,   10
And the dragonfly had fled away,
    Ere he brought it out of the river.

High on the shore sat the great god Pan
    While turbidly flowed the river;
And hacked and hewed as a great god can,   15
With his hard bleak steel at the patient reed,
Till there was not a sign of the leaf indeed
    To prove it fresh from the river.

A MUSICAL INSTRUMENT 1 *Pan:* the Greek god of fields, forests and shepherds, Pan had the legs of a
goat and body of a man. He pursued the nymph Syrinx, rescued by the river-nymphs who
transformed her into a reed-bed.

He cut it short, did the great god Pan
  (How tall it stood in the river!),
Then drew the pith, like the heart of a man,
Steadily from the outside ring,
And notched the poor dry empty thing
  In holes, as he sat by the river.   20

"This is the way," laughed the great god Pan
  (Laughed while he sat by the river),   25
"The only way, since gods began
To make sweet music, they could succeed."
Then, dropping his mouth to a hole in the reed,
  He blew in power by the river.   30

Sweet, sweet, sweet, O Pan!
  Piercing sweet by the river!
Blinding sweet, O great god Pan!
The sun on the hill forgot to die,
And the lilies revived, and the dragonfly   35
  Came back to dream on the river.

Yet half a beast is the great god Pan,
  To laugh as he sits by the river,
Making a poet out of a man;
The true gods sigh for the cost and pain—   40
For the reed which grows nevermore again
  As a reed with the reeds in the river.

                                                                      1862

ROBERT BROWNING
(1812–1889)

MY LAST DUCHESS   145

FERRARA

That's my last Duchess painted on the wall,
Looking as if she were alive. I call
That piece a wonder, now; Frà Pandolf's hands
Worked busily a day, and there she stands.
Will 't please you sit and look at her? I said   5
"Frà Pandolf" by design, for never read
Strangers like you that pictured countenance,

The depth and passion of its earnest glance,
But to myself they turned (since none puts by
The curtain I have drawn for you, but I)   10
And seemed as they would ask me, if they durst,
How such a glance came there; so, not the first
Are you to turn and ask thus. Sir, 'twas not
Her husband's presence only, called that spot
Of joy into the Duchess' cheek; perhaps   15
Frà Pandolf chanced to say, "Her mantle laps
Over my lady's wrist too much," or "Paint
Must never hope to reproduce the faint
Half-flush that dies along her throat." Such stuff
Was courtesy, she thought, and cause enough   20
For calling up that spot of joy. She had
A heart—how shall I say?—too soon made glad.
Too easily impressed; she liked whate'er
She looked on, and her looks went everywhere.
Sir, 'twas all one! My favor at her breast,   25
The dropping of the daylight in the West,
The bough of cherries some officious fool
Broke in the orchard for her, the white mule
She rode with round the terrace—all and each
Would draw from her alike the approving speech,   30
Or blush, at least. She thanked men,—good! but thanked
Somehow—I know not how—as if she ranked
My gift of a nine-hundred-years' old name
With anybody's gift. Who'd stoop to blame
This sort of trifling? Even had you skill   35
In speech—which I have not—to make your will
Quite clear to such an one, and say "Just this
Or that in you disgusts me; here you miss,
Or there exceed the mark"—and if she let
Herself be lessoned so, nor plainly set   40
Her wits to yours, forsooth, and made excuse—
E'en then would be some stooping; and I choose
Never to stoop. Oh, sir, she smiled, no doubt,
Whene'er I passed her; but who passed without
Much the same smile? This grew; I gave commands;   45
Then all smiles stopped together. There she stands
As if alive. Will 't please you rise? We'll meet
The company below, then. I repeat,
The Count your master's known munificence

Is ample warrant that no just pretense 50
Of mine for dowry will be disallowed;
Though his fair daughter's self, as I avowed
At starting, is my object. Nay, we'll go
Together down, sir. Notice Neptune, though,
Taming a sea-horse, thought a rarity, 55
Which Claus of Innsbruck cast in bronze for me!

1842

QUESTIONS

1. What do you see and hear in the first five lines? What does the speaker reveal about himself right away?
2. Who is speaking? To whom?
3. What were the Duchess' attributes?
4. What are the complaints the speaker has about the Duchess' behavior?
5. What does the speaker value most in other people?
6. Where is the irony in the poem?

THE BISHOP ORDERS HIS TOMB AT SAINT PRAXED'S CHURCH 146

ROME, 15—

Vanity, saith the preacher, vanity!
Draw round my bed: is Anselm keeping back?
Nephews—sons mine . . . ah God, I know not! Well—
She, men would have to be your mother once,
Old Gandolf envied me, so fair she was! 5
What's done is done, and she is dead beside,
Dead long ago, and I am Bishop since,
And as she died so must we die ourselves,
And thence ye may perceive the world's a dream.
Life, how and what is it? As here I lie 10
In this state-chamber, dying by degrees,
Hours and long hours in the dead night, I ask
"Do I live, am I dead?" Peace, peace seems all.
Saint Praxed's ever was the church for peace;
And so, about this tomb of mine. I fought 15
With tooth and nail to save my niche, ye know:
—Old Gandolf cozened me, despite my care;
Shrewd was that snatch from out the corner south
He graced his carrion with, God curse the same!
Yet still my niche is not so cramped but thence 20

One sees the pulpit o' the epistle-side,
And somewhat of the choir, those silent seats,
And up into the aery dome where live
The angels, and a sunbeam's sure to lurk:
And I shall fill my slab of basalt there,   25
And 'neath my tabernacle take my rest,
With those nine columns round me, two and two,
The odd one at my feet where Anselm stands:
Peach-blossom marble all, the rare, the ripe
As fresh-poured red wine of a mighty pulse.   30
—Old Gandolf with his paltry onion-stone,
Put me where I may look at him! True peach,
Rosy and flawless: how I earned the prize!
Draw close: that conflagration of my church
—What then? So much was saved if aught were missed!   35
My sons, ye would not be my death? Go dig
The white-grape vineyard where the oil-press stood,
Drop water gently till the surface sink,
And if ye find . . . Ah God, I know not, I! . . .
Bedded in store of rotten fig-leaves soft,   40
And corded up in a tight olive-frail,
Some lump, ah God, of *lapis lazuli,*
Big as a Jew's head cut off at the nape,
Blue as a vein o'er the Madonna's breast . . .
Sons, all have I bequeathed you, villas, all,   45
That brave Frascati villa with its bath,
So, let the blue lump poise between my knees,
Like God the Father's globe on both his hands
Ye worship in the Jesu Church so gay,
For Gandolf shall not choose but see and burst!   50
Swift as a weaver's shuttle fleet our years:
Man goeth to the grave, and where is he?
Did I say basalt for my slab, sons? Black—
'Twas ever antique-black I meant! How else
Shall ye contrast my frieze to come beneath?   55
The bas-relief in bronze ye promised me,
Those Pans and Nymphs ye wot of, and perchance
Some tripod, thyrsus, with a vase or so,
The Saviour at his sermon on the mount,

THE BISHOP ORDERS HIS TOMB . . . *26 tabernacle:* a niche with a canopy. 41 *olive-frail:* olive basket. 42
lapis lazuli: a brilliant blue stone. 49 *Jesu Church:* the church, Il Gesù, which contains the sculpture
described here. The globe is made from a large block of lapis lazuli. 58 *thyrsus:* a staff entwined
with ivy or vine leaves, carried by Dionysus, the god of wine and boisterous festivity.

Saint Praxed in a glory, and one Pan   60
Ready to twitch the Nymph's last garment off,
And Moses with the tables . . . but I know
Ye mark me not! What do they whisper thee,
Child of my bowels, Anselm? Ah, ye hope
To revel down my villas while I gasp   65
Bricked o'er with beggar's moldy travertine
Which Gandolf from his tomb-top chuckles at!
Nay, boys, ye love me—all of jasper, then!
'T is jasper ye stand pledged to, lest I grieve
My bath must needs be left behind, alas!   70
One block, pure green as a pistachio-nut,
There's plenty jasper somewhere in the world—
And have I not Saint Praxed's ear to pray
Horses for ye, and brown Greek manuscripts,
And mistresses with great smooth marbly limbs?   75
—That's if ye carve my epitaph aright,
Choice Latin, picked phrase, Tully's every word,
No gaudy ware like Gandolf's second line—
Tully, my masters? Ulpian serves his need!
And then how I shall lie through centuries,   80
And hear the blessed mutter of the mass,
And see God made and eaten all day long,
And feel the steady candle-flame, and taste
Good strong thick stupefying incense-smoke!
For as I lie here, hours of the dead night,   85
Dying in state and by such slow degrees,
I fold my arms as if they clasped a crook,
And stretch my feet forth straight as stone can point,
And let the bedclothes, for a mortcloth, drop
Into great laps and folds of sculptor's-work: 90
And as yon tapers dwindle, and strange thoughts
Grow, with a certain humming in my ears,
About the life before I lived this life,
And this life too, popes, cardinals and priests,
Saint Praxed at his sermon on the mount,   95
Your tall pale mother with her talking eyes,
And new-found agate urns as fresh as day,
And marble's language, Latin pure, discreet,

---

66 *travertine:* limestone. 77 *Tully:* familiar name for Marcus Tullius Cicero, Roman statesman, orator, and philosopher. 79 *Ulpian:* Roman jurist whose Latin would be less sophisticated than that of Cicero.

—Aha, ELUCESCEBAT quoth our friend?

No Tully, said I, Ulpian at the best!   100

Evil and brief hath been my pilgrimage.

All *lapis,* all, son! Else I give the Pope

My villas! Will ye ever eat my heart?

Ever your eyes were as a lizard's quick,

They glitter like your mother's for my soul,   105

Or ye would heighten my impoverished frieze,

Piece out its starved design, and fill my vase

With grapes, and add a vizor and a Term,

And to the tripod ye would tie a lynx

That in his struggle throws the thyrsus down,   110

To comfort me on my entablature

Whereon I am to lie till I must ask

"Do I live, am I dead?" There, leave me, there!

For ye have stabbed me with ingratitude

To death—ye wish it—God, ye wish it! Stone—   115

Gritstone, a-crumble! Clammy squares which sweat

As if the corpse they keep were oozing through—

And no more *lapis* to delight the world!

Well, go! I bless ye. Fewer tapers there,

But in a row: and, going, turn your backs   120

—Ay, like departing altar-ministrants,

And leave me in my church, the church for peace,

That I may watch at leisure if he leers—

Old Gandolf, at me, from his onion-stone,

As still he envied me, so fair she was!   125

1849

ROBERT BURNS
(1759–1796)

A RED, RED ROSE   147

O my luve's like a red, red rose,

   That's newly sprung in June;

O my luve's like the melodie

   That's sweetly played in tune.

---

99 *elucescebat:* Latin for "shines forth," a word from Gandolf's tomb. 108 *vizor:* a mask. 108 *Term:* a pedestal topped by a bust. 111 *entablature:* horizontal superstructure supported by columns.

As fair art thou, my bonnie lass,
   So deep in luve am I;
And I will luve thee still, my dear,
   Till a' the seas gang dry.

        5

Till a' the seas gang dry, my dear,
   And the rocks melt wi' the sun:
O I will love thee still, my dear,
   While the sands o' life shall run.

        10

And fare thee weel, my only luve,
   And fare thee weel awhile!
And I will come again, my luve,
   Though it were ten thousand mile.

        15

1796

QUESTIONS

1. How does each stanza of the poem develop the theme of time?
2. What connections exist between time, space, and the speaker's love?

GEORGE GORDON, LORD BYRON

(1788–1824)

PROMETHEUS

148

Titan! to whose immortal eyes
   The sufferings of mortality,
   Seen in their sad reality,
Were not as things that gods despise;
What was thy pity's recompense?

        5

A silent suffering, and intense;
The rock, the vulture, and the chain,
All that the proud can feel of pain,
The agony they do not show,
The suffocating sense of woe,

        10

   Which speaks but in its loneliness,
And then is jealous lest the sky
Should have a listener, nor will sigh
   Until its voice is echoless.

PROMETHEUS title: also called "Titan," Prometheus stole fire from heaven for humans. Zeus punished him by chaining him to a rock where vultures devoured his liver daily.

Titan! to thee the strife was given   15
    Between the suffering and the will,
    Which torture where they cannot kill;
And the inexorable heaven,
And the deaf tyranny of fate,
The ruling principle of hate,   20
Which for its pleasure doth create
The things it may annihilate,
Refused thee even the boon to die:
The wretched gift eternity
Was thine—and thou hast borne it well.   25
All that the Thunderer wrung from thee
Was but the menace which flung back
On him the torments of thy rack;
The fate thou didst so well foresee,
But would not to appease him tell;   30
And in thy silence was his sentence,
And in his soul a vain repentance,
And evil dread so ill dissembled,
That in his hand the lightnings trembled.

Thy godlike crime was to be kind,   35
    To render with thy precepts less
    The sum of human wretchedness,
And strengthen man with his own mind;
But baffled as thou wert from high,
Still in thy patient energy,   40
In the endurance, and repulse
    Of thine impenetrable spirit,
Which earth and heaven could not convulse,
    A mighty lesson we inherit:
Thou art a symbol and a sign   45
    To mortals of their fate and force;
Like thee, man is in part divine,
    A troubled stream from a pure source;
And Man in portions can foresee
His own funereal destiny;   50
His wretchedness, and his resistance,
And his sad unallied existence;
To which his spirit may oppose
Itself—and equal to all woes,

26 *the Thunderer*: Zeus, chief of the Olympian gods.

And a firm will, and a deep sense,   55
Which even in torture can descry
  Its own concentered recompense,
Triumphant where it dares defy,
And making death a victory.

                                        1816

STANZAS   149

WHEN A MAN HATH NO FREEDOM TO FIGHT FOR AT HOME

When a man hath no freedom to fight for at home,
  Let him combat for that of his neighbors;
Let him think of the glories of Greece and of Rome,
  And get knocked on his head for his labors.

To do good to mankind is the chivalrous plan,   5
  And is always as nobly requited;
Then battle for freedom wherever you can,
  And, if not shot or hanged, you'll get knighted.

                                        1824

SO WE'LL GO NO MORE A-ROVING   150

1

So we'll go no more a-roving
  So late into the night,
Though the heart be still as loving,
  And the moon be still as bright.

2

For the sword outwears its sheath,   5
  And the soul wears out the breast,
And the heart must pause to breathe,
  And Love itself have rest.

3

Though the night was made for loving,
  And the day returns too soon,   10
Yet we'll go no more a-roving
  By the light of the moon.

                                        1836

QUESTIONS

1. Which words and images do you find yourself drawn to at first? Why?
2. Why has the speaker decided to "go no more a-roving"?
3. What is permanent and what is not?

THOMAS CAMPION
(1567–1620)

THERE IS A GARDEN IN HER FACE   151

There is a garden in her face,
Where roses and white lilies grow,
A heavenly paradise is that place,
Wherein all pleasant fruits do flow.
There cherries grow, which none may buy   5
Till "Cherry ripe!" themselves do cry.

Those cherries fairly do enclose
Of orient pearl a double row,
Which when her lovely laughter shows,
They look like rosebuds filled with snow.   10
Yet them nor peer nor prince can buy,
Till "Cherry ripe!" themselves do cry.

Her eyes like angels watch them still;
Her brows like bended bows do stand,
Threatening with piercing frowns to kill   15
All that attempt with eye or hand
Those sacred cherries to come nigh,
Till "Cherry ripe!" themselves do cry.

1617

QUESTIONS

1. When you imagine a garden, what do you see? How is the poem's garden similar or different?
2. Who cries "cherry ripe"? When?
3. How does the refrain change in meaning from the first to the last stanza?
4. Identify all similes and metaphors in the poem. What do they have in common?
5. Which images are traditional symbols?

LORNA DEE CERVANTES
(b. 1954)

PARA UN REVOLUCIONARIO   152

You speak of art
and your soul is like snow,
a soft powder raining from your
mouth,
covering my breasts and hair.   5
You speak of your love of mountains,
freedom,
and your love for a sun
whose warmth is like *una liberación*
pouring down upon brown bodies.   10
Your books are of the souls of men,
carnales with a spirit
that no army, pig or *ciudad*
could ever conquer.
You speak of a new way,   15
a new life.

When you speak like this
I could listen forever.

Pero your voice is lost to me, *carnal,*
in the wail of *tus hijos,*   20
in the clatter of dishes
and the pucker of beans upon the stove.
Your conversations come to me
de la sala where you sit,
spreading your dream to brothers,   25
where you spread that dream like damp clover
for them to trod upon,
when I stand here reaching
para ti con manos bronces that spring
from *mi espíritu*   30
(for I too am Raza).

PARA UN REVOLUCIONARIO title: For a Revolutionary. 9 *una liberación:* a liberation. 12 *carnales:* flesh. 13 *ciudad:* city. 19 *pero . . . carnal:* but . . . brother. 20 *tus hijos:* your children. 24 *de la sala:* from the room. 29 *para ti con manos bronces:* for you with bronze hands. 30 *mi espíritu:* my soul. 31 *Raza:* clan or family.

Pero, it seems I can only touch you
with my body.
You lie with me
and my body *es la hamaca*   35
that spans the void between us.
Hermano Raza,
I am afraid that you will lie with me
and awaken too late
to find that you have fallen   40
and my hands will be left groping
for you and your dream
in the midst of *la revolución.*

1975

AMY CLAMPITT
(b. 1920)

A PROCESSION AT CANDLEMAS   153

1

Moving on or going back to where you came from,
bad news is what you mainly travel with:
a breakup or a breakdown, someone running off

or walking out, called up or called home:
death in the family. Nudged from their stanchions   5
outside the terminal, anonymous of purpose

as a flock of birds, the bison of the highway
funnel westward onto Route 80, mirroring
an entity that cannot look into itself and know

what makes it what it is. Sooner or later   10
every trek becomes a funeral procession.
The mother curtained in Intensive Care—

a scene the mind leaves blank, fleeing instead
toward scenes of transhumance, the belled sheep
moving up the Pyrenees, red-tasseled pack llamas   15

---

32 *Pero:* but. 35 *es la hamaca:* is the hammock. 37 *Hermano Raza:* blood brother. 43 *la revolución:* the revolution.

A PROCESSION AT CANDLEMAS title *Candlemas:* February 2, a church feast celebrating the purification of the virgin Mary. 14 *transhumance:* seasonal movement of livestock from region to region.

footing velvet-green precipices, the Kurdish
women, jingling with bangles, gorgeous
on their rug-piled mounts—already lying dead,

bereavement altering the moving lights
to a processional, a feast of Candlemas.   20
Change as child-bearing, birth as a kind

of shucking off: out of what began
as a Mosaic insult—such a loathing
of the common origin, even a virgin,

having given birth, needs purifying—   25
to carry fire as though it were a flower,
the terror and the loveliness entrusted

into naked hands, supposing God might have,
might actually need a mother: people have
at times found this a way of being happy.   30

A Candlemas of moving lights along Route 80;
lighted candles in a corridor from Arlington
over the Potomac, for every carried flame

the name of a dead soldier: an element
fragile as ego, frightening as parturition,   35
necessary and intractable as dreaming.

The lapped, wheelborne integument, layer
within layer, at the core a dream of
something precious, ripped: Where are we?

The sleepers groan, stir, rewrap themselves   40
about the self's imponderable substance,
or clamber down, numb-footed, half in a drowse

of freezing dark, through a Stonehenge
of fuel pumps, the bison hulks slantwise
beside them, drinking. What is real except   45

what's fabricated? The jellies glitter
cream-capped in the cafeteria showcase:
gumball globes, Life Savers cinctured

in parcel gilt, plop from their housings
perfect, like miracles. Comb, nail clipper,   50
lip rouge, mirrors and emollients embody,

16 *Kurdish:* nomadic Moslem people.

niched into the washroom wall case,
the pristine seductiveness of money.
Absently, without inhabitants, this

nowhere oasis wears the place name
of Indian Meadows. The westward-trekking
transhumance, once only, of a people who,

in losing everything they had, lost even
the names they went by, stumbling past
like caribou, perhaps camped here. Who

can assign a trade-in value to that sorrow?
The monk in sheepskin over tucked-up saffron
intoning to a drum becomes the metronome

of one more straggle up Pennsylvania Avenue
in falling snow, a whirl of tenderly
remorseless corpuscles, street gangs

amok among magnolias' pregnant wands,
a stillness at the heart of so much whirling:
beyond the torn integument of childbirth,

sometimes, wrapped like a papoose into a grief
not merely of the ego, you rediscover almost
the rest-in-peace of the placental coracle.

2

Of what the dead were, living, one knows
so little as barely to recognize
the fabric of the backward-ramifying

antecedents, half-noted presences
in darkened rooms: the old, the feared,
the hallowed. Never the same river

drowns the unalterable doorsill. An effigy
in olive wood or pear wood, dank
with the sweat of age, walled in the dark

at Brauron, Argos, Samos: even the unwed
Athene, who had no mother, born—it's declared—
of some man's brain like every other pure idea,

55

60

65

70

75

80

---

72 *coracle:* a short, wide boat. 82 *Brauron:* city in Greece, once associated with a religious festival in which Artemis was worshipped; *Argos:* ancient Greek city; *Samos:* Greek island. 83 *Athene:* goddess of wisdom who sprang from the head of Zeus.

had her own wizened cult object, kept   85
out of sight like the incontinent whimperer
in the backstairs bedroom, where no child

ever goes—to whom, year after year,
the fair linen of the sacred peplos
was brought in ceremonial procession—   90

flutes and stringed instruments, wildflower-
hung cattle, nubile Athenian girls, young men
praised for the beauty of their bodies. Who

can unpeel the layers of that seasonal
returning to the dark where memory fails,   95
as birds re-enter the ancestral flyway?

Daylight, snow falling, knotting of gears:
Chicago. Soot, the rotting backsides
of tenements, grimed trollshapes of ice

underneath the bridges, the tunnel heaving   100
like a birth canal. Disgorged, the infant
howling in the restroom; steam-table cereal,

pale coffee; wall-eyed TV receivers, armchairs
of molded plastic: the squalor of the day
resumed, the orphaned litter taken up again   105

unloved, the spawn of botched intentions,
grief a mere hardening of the gut,
a set piece of what can't be avoided:

parents by the tens of thousands living
unthanked, unpaid but in the sour coin   110
of resentment. Midmorning gray as zinc

along Route 80, corn-stubble quilting
the underside of snowdrifts, the cadaverous
belvedere of windmills, the sullen stare

of feedlot cattle; black creeks puncturing   115
white terrain, the frozen bottomland
a mush of willow tops; dragnetted in ice,

---

89 *peplos:* a large shawl worn by women in ancient Greece. 114 *belvedere:* an open, roofed gallery.

the Mississippi. Westward toward the dark,
the undertow of scenes come back to, fright
riddling the structures of interior history: 120

Where is it? Where, in the shucked-off
bundle, the hampered obscurity that has been
for centuries the mumbling lot of women,

did the thread of fire, too frail
ever to discover what it meant, to risk   125
even the taking of a shape, relinquish

the seed of possibility, unguessed-at
as a dream of something precious? Memory,
that exquisite blunderer, stumbling

like a migrant bird that finds the flyway   130
it hardly knew it knew except by instinct,
down the long-unentered nave of childhood,

late on a midwinter afternoon, alone
among the snow-hung hollows of the windbreak
on the far side of the orchard, encounters   135

sheltering among the evergreens, a small
stilled bird, its cap of clear yellow
slit by a thread of scarlet—the untouched

nucleus of fire, the lost connection
hallowing the wizened effigy, the mother   140
curtained in Intensive Care: a Candlemas

of moving lights along Route 80, at nightfall,
in falling snow, the stillness and the sorrow
of things moving back to where they came from.

1983

QUESTIONS

1. What do you associate with westward movement? What is or has moved west in the poem? Is there any symbolic significance?
2. How do the allusions to Candlemas expand the poem's meaning for you?
3. Stanzas 19 and 20 refer to Indians. How is their presence developed into a theme in the poem? Where does the first image connected with this theme appear?
4. How does the theme of "transhumance" organize the poem? How does it relate to the central purpose of the poem?
5. Identify individual references to women. What do these statements imply?

JOHN CLARE
(1793–1864)

BADGER 154

When midnight comes a host of dogs and men
Go out and track the badger to his den,
And put a sack within the hole, and lie
Till the old grunting badger passes by.
He comes and hears—they let the strongest loose. 5
The old fox hears the noise and drops the goose.
The poacher shoots and hurries from the cry,
And the old hare half wounded buzzes by.
They get a forkéd stick to bear him down
And clap the dogs and take him to the town, 10
And bait him all the day with many dogs,
And laugh and shout and fright the scampering hogs.
He runs along and bites at all he meets:
They shout and hollo down the noisy streets.

He turns about to face the loud uproar 15
And drives the rebels to their very door.
The frequent stone is hurled where'er they go;
When badgers fight, then everyone's a foe.
The dogs are clapped and urged to join the fray;
The badger turns and drives them all away. 20
Though scarcely half as big, demure and small,
He fights with dogs for hours and beats them all.
The heavy mastiff, savage in the fray,
Lies down and licks his feet and turns away.
The bulldog knows his match and waxes cold, 25
The badger grins and never leaves his hold.
He drives the crowd and follows at their heels
And bites them through—the drunkard swears and reels.

The frighted women take the boys away,
The blackguard laughs and hurries on the fray. 30
He tries to reach the woods, an awkward race,
But sticks and cudgels quickly stop the chase.
He turns again and drives the noisy crowd
And beats the many dogs in noises loud.
He drives away and beats them every one, 35
And then they loose them all and set them on.
He falls as dead and kicked by boys and men,

Then starts and grins and drives the crowd again;
Till kicked and torn and beaten out he lies
And leaves his hold and cackles, groans, and dies.   40

1920

LUCILLE CLIFTON
(b. 1936)

MISS ROSIE   155

When I watch you
wrapped up like garbage
sitting, surrounded by the smell
of too old potato peels
or   5
when I watch you
in your old man's shoes
with the little toe cut out
sitting, waiting for your mind
like next week's grocery   10
I say
when I watch you
you wet brown bag of a woman
who used to be the best looking gal in Georgia
used to be called the Georgia Rose   15
I stand up
through your destruction
I stand up

1969

QUESTIONS

1. What sensory images do you find in this poem?
2. What emotion is expressed at the end of the poem? How?

HOMAGE TO MY HIPS   156

these hips are big hips.
they need space to
move around in.
they don't fit into little
petty places. these hips   5

are free hips.
they don't like to be held back.
these hips have never been enslaved,
they go where they want to go
they do what they want to do.   10
these hips are mighty hips.
these hips are magic hips.
i have known them
to put a spell on a man and
spin him like a top!   15

1980

I ONCE KNEW A MAN   157

i once knew a man who had wild horses killed.
when he told about it
the words came galloping out of his mouth
and shook themselves and headed off in
every damn direction. his tongue   5
was wild and wide and spinning when he talked
and the people he looked at closed their eyes
and tore the skins off their backs as they walked away
and stopped eating meat.
there was no holding him once he got started;   10
he had had wild horses killed one time and
they rode him to his grave.

1980

SAMUEL TAYLOR COLERIDGE
(1772–1834)

FROST AT MIDNIGHT   158

The Frost performs its secret ministry,
Unhelped by any wind. The owlet's cry
Came loud—and hark, again! loud as before.
The inmates of my cottage, all at rest,
Have left me to that solitude, which suits   5
Abstruser musings: save that at my side
My cradled infant slumbers peacefully.
'Tis calm indeed! so calm, that it disturbs

And vexes meditation with its strange
And extreme silentness. Sea, hill, and wood,   10
This populous village! Sea, and hill, and wood,
With all the numberless goings-on of life,
Inaudible as dreams! the thin blue flame
Lies on my low-burnt fire, and quivers not;
Only that film, which fluttered on the grate,   15
Still flutters there, the sole unquiet thing.
Methinks, its motion in this hush of nature
Gives it dim sympathies with me who live,
Making it a companionable form,
Whose puny flaps and freaks the idling Spirit   20
By its own moods interprets, every where
Echo or mirror seeking of itself,
And makes a toy of Thought.

                    But O! how oft,
How oft, at school, with most believing mind,
Presageful, have I gazed upon the bars,   25
To watch that fluttering *stranger*! and as oft
With unclosed lids, already had I dreamt
Of my sweet birth-place, and the old church-tower,
Whose bells, the poor man's only music, rang
From morn to evening, all the hot Fair-day,   30
So sweetly, that they stirred and haunted me
With a wild pleasure, falling on mine ear
Most like articulate sounds of things to come!
So gazed I, till the soothing things, I dreamt,
Lulled me to sleep, and sleep prolonged my dreams!   35
And so I brooded all the following morn,
Awed by the stern preceptor's face, mine eye
Fixed with mock study on my swimming book:
Save if the door half opened, and I snatched
A hasty glance, and still my heart leaped up,   40
For still I hoped to see the *stranger's* face,
Townsman, or aunt, or sister more beloved,
My play-mate when we both were clothed alike!

   Dear Babe, that sleepest cradled by my side,
Whose gentle breathings, heard in this deep calm,   45
Fill up the interspersed vacancies
And momentary pauses of the thought!
My babe so beautiful! it thrills my heart

With tender gladness, thus to look at thee,
And think that thou shalt learn far other lore,   50
And in far other scenes! For I was reared
In the great city, pent 'mid cloisters dim,
And saw nought lovely but the sky and stars.
But *thou,* my babe! shalt wander like a breeze
By lakes and sandy shores, beneath the crags   55
Of ancient mountain, and beneath the clouds,
Which image in their bulk both lakes and shores
And mountain crags: so shalt thou see and hear
The lovely shapes and sounds intelligible
Of that eternal language, which thy God   60
Utters, who from eternity doth teach
Himself in all, and all things in himself.
Great universal Teacher! he shall mould
Thy spirit, and by giving make it ask.

Therefore all seasons shall be sweet to thee,   65
Whether the summer clothe the general earth
With greenness, or the redbreast sit and sing
Betwixt the tufts of snow on the bare branch
Of mossy apple-tree, while the nigh thatch
Smokes in the sun-thaw; whether the eave-drops fall   70
Heard only in the trances of the blast,
Or if the secret ministry of frost
Shall hang them up in silent icicles,
Quietly shining to the quiet Moon.

1798

KUBLA KHAN   159

OR A VISION IN A DREAM. A FRAGMENT

In Xanadu did Kubla Khan
A stately pleasure dome decree:
Where Alph, the sacred river, ran
Through caverns measureless to man
  Down to a sunless sea.   5
So twice five miles of fertile ground
With walls and towers were girdled round:

And there were gardens bright with sinuous rills,   10
Where blossomed many an incense-bearing tree;
And here were forests ancient as the hills,
Enfolding sunny spots of greenery.

But oh! that deep romantic chasm which slanted
Down the green hill athwart a cedarn cover!   15
A savage place! as holy and enchanted
As e'er beneath a waning moon was haunted
By woman wailing for her demon lover!
And from this chasm, with ceaseless turmoil seething,
As if this earth in fast thick pants were breathing,   20
A mighty fountain momently was forced:
Amid whose swift half-intermitted burst
Huge fragments vaulted like rebounding hail,
Or chaffy grain beneath the thresher's flail:
And 'mid these dancing rocks at once and ever   25
It flung up momently the sacred river.
Five miles meandering with a mazy motion
Through wood and dale the sacred river ran,
Then reached the caverns measureless to man,
And sank in tumult to a lifeless ocean: 30
And 'mid this tumult Kubla heard from far
Ancestral voices prophesying war!

   The shadow of the dome of pleasure
   Floated midway on the waves;
   Where was heard the mingled measure   35
   From the fountain and the caves.
It was a miracle of rare device,
A sunny pleasure dome with caves of ice!

   A damsel with a dulcimer
   In a vision once I saw: 40
   It was an Abyssinian maid,
   And on her dulcimer she played,
   Singing of Mount Abora.
   Could I revive within me
   Her symphony and song,   45
   To such a deep delight 'twould win me,
That with music loud and long,
I would build that dome in air,
That sunny dome! those caves of ice!

And all who heard should see them there,
And all should cry, Beware! Beware!   50
His flashing eyes, his floating hair!
Weave a circle round him thrice,
And close your eyes with holy dread,
For he on honey-dew hath fed,
And drunk the milk of Paradise.   55

1816

QUESTIONS

1. Jot down your initial responses to the poem. After you consider the following
   questions, return to your first responses to consider how much you "knew" about
   the poem before you really knew it.
2. In the last stanza what does the shift to the first person indicate to you? Do you
   receive encouragement as a reader to enter the imaginative experience of the poem
   in a new way?
3. Coleridge prefaced the poem with the following statement:

> The following fragment is here published at the request of a poet of great
> and deserved celebrity [Lord Bryon], and, as far as the Author's own opinions
> are concerned, rather as a psychological curiosity, than on the ground of any
> supposed poetic merits. In the summer of the year 1797, the Author, then in
> ill health, had returned to a lonely farm-house between Porlock and Linton, on
> the Exmoor confines of Somerset and Devonshire. In consequence of a slight
> indisposition, an anodyne had been prescribed, from the effects of which he
> fell asleep in his chair at that moment that he was reading the following sen-
> tence, or words of the same substance, in "Purchas's Pilgrimage": "Here the
> Khan Kubla commanded a palace to be built, and a stately garden thereunto.
> And thus ten miles of fertil ground were inclosed with a wall." The Author
> continued for about three hours in a profound sleep, at least of the external
> senses, during which time he has the most vivid confidence, that he could not
> have composed less than from two to three hundred lines; if that indeed can be
> called composition in which all the images rose up before him as things, with
> a parallel production of the correspondent expression, without any sensation or
> consciousness of effort. On awaking he appeared to himself to have a distinct
> recollection of the whole, and taking his pen, ink, and paper, instantly and
> eagerly wrote down the lines that are here preserved. At this moment he was
> unfortunately called out by a person on business from Porlock, and detained
> by him above an hour, and on his return to his room, found, to his no small
> surprise and mortification, that though he still retained some vague and dim
> recollection of the general purport of the vision, yet, with the exception of
> some eight or ten scattered lines and images, all the rest had passed away like
> the images on the surface of a stream into which a stone has been cast, but,
> alas! without the after restoration of the latter!
>
>   Then all the charm
>   Is broken—all that phantom-world so fair
>   Vanishes, and a thousand circlets spread,
>   And each mis-shape['s] the other. Stay awhile,

Poor youth! who scarcely dar'st lift up thine eyes—
The stream will soon renew its smoothness, soon
The visions will return! And lo, he stays,
And soon the fragments dim of lovely forms
Come trembling back, unite and now once more
The pool becomes a mirror.

Yet from the still surviving recollections in his mind, the Author has
frequently purposed to finish for himself what had been originally, as it were,
given to him . . . but the tomorrow is yet to come.

Does this explanation change the way you might read the poem? How do you
measure an author's statement of intent?
4. The existence of "opium dreams" has been questioned by modern medical
authorities. Does the possibility that Coleridge's preface might be erroneous in some
way affect your reading of the poem?
5. Does the poem have rational content?

FROM METRICAL FEET   160

LESSON FOR A BOY

Trŏchĕe trīps frŏm lōng tŏ shŏrt;
From long to long in solemn sort
Slōw Spōndēe stālks; strōng fŏot! yet ill able
Ēvĕr tŏ cōme ŭp wĭth Dāctўl trĭsȳllăblĕ.
Ĭāmbĭcs mārch frŏm shŏrt tŏ lōng—   5
Wĭth ă lēap ănd ă bōund thĕ swĭft Ānăpĕsts thrōng.

1817

GREGORY CORSO

(b. 1930)

THE VESTAL LADY ON BRATTLE   161

Within a delicate grey ruin
the vestal lady on Brattle
is up at dawn, as is her custom,
with the raise of a shade.

Swan-boned slippers revamp her aging feet;   5
she glides within an outer room . . .
pours old milk for an old cat.

THE VESTAL LADY ON BRATTLE title *Vestal:* sacred virgin priestess in ancient Rome; *Brattle:* Brattle Street
near Harvard University.

Full-bodied and randomly young she clings,
peers down; hovers over a wine-filled vat,
and with outstretched arms like wings,   10
revels in the forming image of child below.

Despaired, she ripples a sunless finger
across the liquid eyes; in darkness
the child spirals down; drowns.
Pain leans her forward—face absorbing all—   15
mouth upon broken mouth, she drinks . . .

Within a delicate grey ruin
the vestal lady on Brattle
is up and about, as is her custom,
drunk with child.   20

                                                         1955

QUESTIONS

1. What picture do you have of "the vestal lady on Brattle" after the first reading?
   Which details first attract your eye?
2. Describe the contrasts in the poem. Are they contradictions? Paradoxes?
3. What feelings do you have for the woman?
4. Why are the first and last stanzas so similar? What do the differences tell you?

HART CRANE
(1899–1932)

MY GRANDMOTHER'S LOVE LETTERS   162

There are no stars to-night
But those of memory.
Yet how much room for memory there is
In the loose girdle of soft rain.

There is even room enough   5
For the letters of my mother's mother,
Elizabeth,
That have been pressed so long
Into a corner of the roof
That they are brown and soft,
And liable to melt as snow.   10

Over the greatness of such space
Steps must be gentle.
It is all hung by an invisible white hair.
It trembles as birch limbs webbing the air.   15

And I ask myself:

"Are your fingers long enough to play
Old keys that are but echoes:
Is the silence strong enough
To carry back the music to its source   20
And back to you again
As though to her?"

Yet I would lead my grandmother by the hand
Through much of what she would not understand;
And so I stumble. And the rain continues on the roof   25
With such a sound of gently pitying laughter.

                                                              1926

QUESTIONS

1. What works on the senses to stir memory in this poem?
2. What do space and time have to do with each other throughout the poem, but most
   particularly in lines 12–15? How are the concerns of those lines developed in the last
   four lines?
3. How do alliteration, consonance, and assonance help you create a reading of this
   poem?

THE BROKEN TOWER   163

The bell-rope that gathers God at dawn
Dispatches me as though I dropped down the knell
Of a spent day—to wander the cathedral lawn
From pit to crucifix, feet chill on steps from hell.

Have you not heard, have you not seen that corps   5
Of shadows in the tower, whose shoulders sway
Antiphonal carillons launched before
The stars are caught and hived in the sun's ray?

The bells, I say, the bells break down their tower;
And swing I know not where. Their tongues engrave   10
Membrane through marrow, my long-scattered score
Of broken intervals . . . And I, their sexton slave!

Oval encyclicals in canyons heaping
The impasse high with choir. Banked voices slain!
Pagodas, campaniles with reveilles outleaping— 15
O terraced echoes prostrate on the plain! . . .

And so it was I entered the broken world
To trace the visionary company of love, its voice
An instant in the wind (I know not whither hurled)
But not for long to hold each desperate choice. 20

My word I poured. But was it cognate, scored
Of that tribunal monarch of the air
Whose thigh embronzes earth, strikes crystal Word
In wounds pledged once to hope—cleft to despair?

The steep encroachments of my blood left me 25
No answer (could blood hold such a lofty tower
As flings the question true?)—or is it she
Whose sweet mortality stirs latent power?—

And through whose pulse I hear, counting the strokes
My veins recall and add, revived and sure 30
The angelus of wars my chest evokes:
What I hold healed, original now, and pure . . .

And builds, within, a tower that is not stone
(Not stone can jacket heaven)—but slip
Of pebbles,—visible wings of silence sown 35
In azure circles, widening as they dip

The matrix of the heart, lift down the eye
That shrines the quiet lake and swells a tower . . .
The commodious, tall decorum of that sky
Unseals her earth, and lifts love in its shower. 40

1933

ROBERT CREELEY
(b. 1926)

A WICKER BASKET   164

Comes the time when it's later
and onto your table the headwaiter
puts the bill, and very soon after
rings out the sound of lively laughter—

Picking up change, hands like a walrus,   5
and a face like a barndoor's,
and a head without any apparent size,
nothing but two eyes—

So that's you, man,
or me. I make it as I can,   10
I pick up, I go
faster than they know—

Out the door, the street like a night,
any night, and no one in sight,
but then, well, there she is,   15
old friend Liz—

And she opens the door of her cadillac,
I step in back,
and we're gone.
She turns me on—   20

There are very huge stars, man, in the sky,
and from somewhere very far off someone hands me a slice of apple
        pie,
with a gob of white, white ice cream on top of it,
and I eat it—

Slowly. And while certainly   25
they are laughing at me, and all around me is racket
of these cats not making it, I make it

in my wicker basket.

                                                                    1959

IF YOU   165

If you were going to get a pet
what kind of animal would you get.

A soft bodied dog, a hen—
feathers and fur to begin it again.

When the sun goes down and it gets dark   5
I saw an animal in a park.

Bring it home, to give it to you.
I have seen animals break in two.

You were hoping for something soft
and loyal and clean and wondrously careful—   10

a form of otherwise vicious habit
can have long ears and be called a rabbit.

Dead. Died. Will die. Want.
Morning, midnight. I asked you

if you were going to get a pet   15
what kind of animal would you get.

1959

MOTHER'S VOICE   166

In these few years
since her death I hear
mother's voice say
under my own, I won't

want any more of that.   5
My cheekbones resonate
with her emphasis. Nothing
of not wanting only

but the distance there from
common fact of others   10
frightens me. I look out
at all this demanding world

and try to put it quietly back,
from me, say, thank you,
I've already had some   15
though I haven't

and would like to
but I've said no, she has,
it's not my own voice anymore.
It's higher as hers was   20

and accommodates too simply
its frustrations when
I at least think I want more
and must have it.

1983

QUESTIONS

1. How do you respond to your mother's voice?
2. How does the speaker respond?
3. What is the conflict the speaker's response creates?
4. Where is the irony in the situation he describes?

COUNTEE CULLEN
(1903–1946)

INCIDENT   167

(FOR ERIC WALROND)

Once riding in old Baltimore,
   Heart-filled, head-filled with glee,
I saw a Baltimorean
   Keep looking straight at me.

Now I was eight and very small,   5
   And he was no whit bigger,
And so I smiled, but he poked out
   His tongue, and called me, "Nigger."

I saw the whole of Baltimore
   From May until December;   10
Of all the things that happened there
   That's all that I remember.

1925

HERITAGE   168

(FOR HAROLD JACKMAN)

What is Africa to me:
Copper sun or scarlet sea,
Jungle star or jungle track,
Strong bronzed men, or regal black
Women from whose loins I sprang   5
When the birds of Eden sang?
One three centuries removed
From the scenes his fathers loved,
Spicy grove, cinnamon tree,
What is Africa to me?   10

So I lie, who all day long
Want no sound except the song
Sung by wild barbaric birds
Goading massive jungle herds,
Juggernauts of flesh that pass   15
Trampling tall defiant grass
Where young forest lovers lie,
Plighting troth beneath the sky.
So I lie, who always hear,
Though I cram against my ear   20
Both my thumbs, and keep them there,
Great drums throbbing through the air.
So I lie, whose fount of pride,
Dear distress, and joy allied,
Is my somber flesh and skin,   25
With the dark blood dammed within
Like great pulsing tides of wine
That, I fear, must burst the fine
Channels of the chafing net
Where they surge and foam and fret.   30

Africa? A book one thumbs
Listlessly, till slumber comes.
Unremembered are her bats
Circling through the night, her cats
Crouching in the river reeds,   35
Stalking gentle flesh that feeds
By the river brink; no more
Does the bugle-throated roar
Cry that monarch claws have leapt
From the scabbards where they slept.   40
Silver snakes that once a year
Doff the lovely coats you wear,
Seek no covert in your fear
Lest a mortal eye should see;
What's your nakedness to me?   45
Here no leprous flowers rear
Fierce corollas in the air;
Here no bodies sleek and wet,
Dripping mingled rain and sweat,
Tread the savage measures of   50
Jungle boys and girls in love.

What is last year's snow to me,
Last year's anything? The tree
Budding yearly must forget
How its past arose or set—   55
Bough and blossom, flower, fruit,
Even what shy bird with mute
Wonder at her travail there,
Meekly labored in its hair.
One three centuries removed   60
From the scenes his fathers loved,
Spicy grove, cinnamon tree,
What is Africa to me?

So I lie, who find no peace
Night or day, no slight release   65
From the unremittent beat
Made by cruel padded feet
Walking through my body's street.
Up and down they go, and back,
Treading out a jungle track.   70
So I lie, who never quite
Safely sleep from rain at night—
I can never rest at all
When the rain begins to fall;
Like a soul gone mad with pain   75
I must match its weird refrain;
Ever must I twist and squirm,
Writhing like a baited worm,
While its primal measures drip
Through my body, crying, "Strip!   80
Doff this new exuberance.
Come and dance the Lover's Dance!"
In an old remembered way
Rain works on me night and day.

Quaint, outlandish heathen gods   85
Black men fashion out of rods,
Clay, and brittle bits of stone,
In a likeness like their own,
My conversion came high-priced;
I belong to Jesus Christ,   90
Preacher of humility;
Heathen gods are naught to me.

Father, Son, and Holy Ghost,
So I make an idle boast;
Jesus of the twice-turned cheek,   95
Lamb of God, although I speak
With my mouth thus, in my heart
Do I play a double part.
Ever at Thy glowing altar
Must my heart grow sick and falter,   100
Wishing He I served were black,
Thinking then it would not lack
Precedent of pain to guide it,
Let who would or might deride it;
Surely then this flesh would know   105
Yours had borne a kindred woe.
Lord, I fashion dark gods, too,
Daring even to give You
Dark despairing features where,
Crowned with dark rebellious hair,   110
Patience wavers just so much as
Mortal grief compels, while touches
Quick and hot, of anger, rise
To smitten cheek and weary eyes.
Lord, forgive me if my need   115
Sometimes shapes a human creed.
All day long and all night through,
One thing only must I do:
Quench my pride and cool my blood,
Lest I perish in the flood.   120
Lest a hidden ember set
Timber that I thought was wet
Burning like the dryest flax,
Melting like the merest wax,
Lest the grave restore its dead.   125
Not yet has my heart or head
In the least way realized
They and I are civilized.

1927

QUESTIONS

1. How can a reader who is not black or who has never been to Africa recreate this poem? What does Cullen give such a reader to build upon?
2. The poem begins with a question that is repeated throughout the poem. How does it change every time it is asked?

3. In its last section, what does the poem become? Is this a surprising turn or is there preparation for it earlier?
4. Are the final three lines triumphant or despairing?

E. E. CUMMINGS
(1894–1962)

[THE CAMBRIDGE LADIES WHO LIVE IN FURNISHED SOULS]   169

the Cambridge ladies who live in furnished souls
are unbeautiful and have comfortable minds
(also, with the church's protestant blessings
daughters, unscented shapeless spirited)
they believe in Christ and Longfellow, both dead,   5
are invariably interested in so many things—
at the present writing one still finds
delighted fingers knitting for the is it Poles?
perhaps. While permanent faces coyly bandy
scandal of Mrs. N and Professor D   10
. . . . the Cambridge ladies do not care, above
Cambridge if sometimes in its box of
sky lavender and cornerless, the
moon rattles like a fragment of angry candy

1923

QUESTIONS

1. Who are the Cambridge ladies and what do they do? What are they not, what don't they have, and what don't they do? What do they believe? What do they choose to ignore?
2. When you read this poem, what scene do you envision? If an artist were to draw it, would it be realistic or surrealistic?
3. What does Cummings' treatment of the sonnet form add to your understanding of the poem?

[O SWEET SPONTANEOUS]   170

O sweet spontaneous
earth how often have
the
doting

      fingers of   5
prurient philosophers pinched
and
poked

thee
,has the naughty thumb   10
of science prodded
thy

      beauty   .how
often have religions taken
thee upon their scraggy knees   15
squeezing and

buffeting thee that thou mightest conceive
gods
      (but
true   20

to the incomparable
couch of death thy
rhythmic
lover

      thou answerest   25

them only with

          spring)

1923

QUESTIONS

1. What demands do the typographical idiosyncrasies make upon the reader? How can you use them to help you create a solid reading?
2. What do the personifications of philosophy, science, and religion have in common? Are their intentions toward earth honorable?
3. In what sense must earth remain true to her lover, death?
4. If spring is the answer, what is the question?

CHANSONS INNOCENTES, I
[IN JUST-]   171

in Just-
spring   when the world is mud-
luscious the little
lame balloonman

whistles   far   and wee   5

and eddieandbill come
running from marbles and
piracies and it's
spring

when the world is puddle-wonderful   10

the queer
old balloonman whistles
far   and   wee
and bettyandisbel come dancing

from hop-scotch and jump-rope and   15

it's
spring
and
    the

      goat-footed   20

balloonMan   whistles
far
and
wee

1923

QUESTIONS

1. When does "Just-spring" occur? What are the characteristics of the season mentioned in the poem?
2. How do the descriptions of the balloonman change as the poem progresses? Does the tone change, too?
3. What is the effect of the balloonman's whistles?
4. Is the title at all ironic?

CHANSONS INNOCENTES title: innocent songs.

[SOMEWHERE I HAVE NEVER TRAVELLED, GLADLY BEYOND]   172

somewhere i have never travelled,gladly beyond
any experience, your eyes have their silence:
in your most frail gesture are things which enclose me,
or which i cannot touch because they are too near

your slightest look easily will unclose me   5
though i have closed myself as fingers,
you open always petal by petal myself as Spring opens
(touching skilfully,mysteriously) her first rose

or if your wish be to close me,i and
my life will shut very beautifully,suddenly,   10
as when the heart of this flower imagines
the snow carefully everywhere descending;

nothing which we are to perceive in this world equals
the power of your intense fragility:whose texture
compels me with the colour of its countries,   15
rendering death and forever with each breathing

(i do not know what it is about you that closes
and opens;only something in me understands
the voice of your eyes is deeper than all roses)
nobody,not even the rain,has such small hands   20

1931

[ANYONE LIVED IN A PRETTY HOW TOWN]   173

anyone lived in a pretty how town
(with up so floating many bells down)
spring summer autumn winter
he sang his didn't he danced his did.

Women and men (both little and small)   5
cared for anyone not at all
they sowed their isn't they reaped their same
sun moon stars rain

children guessed (but only a few
and down they forgot as up they grew   10
autumn winter spring summer)
that noone loved him more by more

when by now and tree by leaf
she laughed his joy she cried his grief
bird by snow and stir by still   15
anyone's any was all to her

someones married their everyones
laughed their cryings and did their dance
(sleep wake hope and then)they
said their nevers they slept their dream   20

stars rain sun moon
(and only the snow can begin to explain
how children are apt to forget to remember
with up so floating many bells down)

one day anyone died i guess   25
(and noone stooped to kiss his face)
busy folk buried them side by side
little by little and was by was

all by all and deep by deep
and more by more they dream their sleep   30
noone and anyone earth by april
wish by spirit and if by yes.

Women and men (both dong and ding)
summer autumn winter spring
reaped their sowing and went their came   35
sun moon stars rain

1940

[A SALESMAN IS AN IT THAT STINKS EXCUSE]   174

a salesman is an it that stinks Excuse

Me whether it's president of the you were say
or a jennelman name misder finger isn't
important whether it's millions of other punks
or just a handful absolutely doesn't   5
matter and whether it's in lonjewray

or shrouds is immaterial it stinks

a salesman is an it that stinks to please

but whether to please itself or someone else
makes no more difference than if it sells   10
hate condoms education snakeoil vac
uumcleaners terror strawberries democ
ra(caveat emptor)cy superfluous hair

or Think We've Met subhuman rights Before

                                                          1944

WALTER DE LA MARE
(1873–1956)

THE LISTENERS   175

'Is there anybody there?' said the Traveller,
   Knocking on the moonlit door;
And his horse in the silence champed the grasses
   Of the forest's ferny floor:
And a bird flew up out of the turret,   5
   Above the Traveller's head:
And he smote upon the door again a second time;
   'Is there anybody there?' he said.
But no one descended to the Traveller;
   No head from the leaf-fringed sill   10
Leaned over and looked into his grey eyes,
   Where he stood perplexed and still.
But only a host of phantom listeners
   That dwelt in the lone house then
Stood listening in the quiet of the moonlight   15
   To that voice from the world of men:
Stood thronging the faint moonbeams on the dark stair,
   That goes down to the empty hall,
Hearkening in an air stirred and shaken
   By the lonely Traveller's call.   20
And he felt in his heart their strangeness,
   Their stillness answering his cry,
While his horse moved, cropping the dark turf,
   'Neath the starred and leafy sky;
For he suddenly smote on the door, even   25
   Louder, and lifted his head:—
'Tell them I came, and no one answered,

A SALESMAN IS AN IT THAT STINKS EXCUSE 13 *caveat emptor:* let the buyer beware (Latin).

That I kept my word,' he said.
Never the least stir made the listeners,
   Though every word he spake   30
Fell echoing through the shadowiness of the still house
   From the one man left awake:
Ay, they heard his foot upon the stirrup,
   And the sound of iron on stone,
And how the silence surged softly backward,   35
   When the plunging hoofs were gone.

1912

QUESTIONS

1. Which concrete details create and emphasize the mood of this piece?
2. How are absence and silence made palpable?
3. As a reader, where do you stand as you create a reading: outside the door with the Traveller or inside with the listeners?
4. Who are the listeners? Are they real?

SCHOLARS   176

    Logic does well at school;
And Reason answers every question right;
Poll-parrot Memory unwinds her spool;
And Copy-cat keeps Teacher well in sight:

The Heart's a truant; nothing does by rule;   5
Safe in its wisdom, is taken for a fool;
Nods through the morning on the dunce's stool;
    And wakes to dream all night.

1945

JAMES DICKEY
(b. 1923)

CHERRYLOG ROAD   177

Off Highway 106
At Cherrylog Road I entered
The '34 Ford without wheels,
Smothered in kudzu,
With a seat pulled out to run   5
Corn whiskey down from the hills,

And then from the other side
Crept into an Essex
With a rumble seat of red leather
And then out again, aboard   10
A blue Chevrolet, releasing
The rust from its other color,

Reared up on three building blocks.
None had the same body heat;
I changed with them inward, toward   15
The weedy heart of the junkyard,
For I knew that Doris Holbrook
Would escape from her father at noon

And would come from the farm
To seek parts owned by the sun   20
Among the abandoned chassis,
Sitting in each in turn
As I did, leaning forward
As in a wild stock-car race

In the parking lot of the dead.   25
Time after time, I climbed in
And out the other side, like
An envoy or movie star
Met at the station by crickets.
A radiator cap raised its head,   30

Become a real toad or a kingsnake
As I neared the hub of the yard,
Passing through many states,
Many lives, to reach
Some grandmother's long Pierce-Arrow   35
Sending platters of blindness forth

From its nickel hubcaps
And spilling its tender upholstery
On sleepy roaches,
The glass panel in between   40
Lady and colored driver
Not all the way broken out,

The back-seat phone
Still on its hook.
I got in as though to exclaim,   45

"Let us go to the orphan asylum,
John; I have some old toys
For children who say their prayers."

I popped with sweat as I thought
I heard Doris Holbrook scrape   50
Like a mouse in the southern-state sun
That was eating the paint in blisters
From a hundred car tops and hoods.
She was tapping like code,

Loosening the screws,   55
Carrying off headlights,
Sparkplugs, bumpers,
Cracked mirrors and gear-knobs,
Getting ready, already,
To go back with something to show   60

Other than her lips' new trembling
I would hold to me soon, soon,
Where I sat in the ripped back seat
Talking over the interphone,
Praying for Doris Holbrook   65
To come from her father's farm

And to get back there
With no trace of me on her face
To be seen by her red-haired father
Who would change, in the squalling barn,   70
Her back's pale skin with a strop,
Then lay for me

In a bootlegger's roasting car
With a string-triggered 12-gauge shotgun
To blast the breath from the air.   75
Not cut by the jagged windshields,
Through the acres of wrecks she came
With a wrench in her hand,

Through dust where the blacksnake dies
Of boredom, and the beetle knows   80
The compost has no more life.
Someone outside would have seen
The oldest car's door inexplicably
Close from within:

I held her and held her and held her,   85
Convoyed at terrific speed
By the stalled, dreaming traffic around us,
So the blacksnake, stiff
With inaction, curved back
Into life, and hunted the mouse   90

With deadly overexcitement,
The beetles reclaimed their field
As we clung, glued together,
With the hooks of the seat springs
Working through to catch us red-handed   95
Amidst the gray breathless batting

That burst from the seat at our backs.
We left by separate doors
Into the changed, other bodies
Of cars, she down Cherrylog Road   100
And I to my motorcycle
Parked like the soul of the junkyard

Restored, a bicycle fleshed
With power, and tore off
Up Highway 106, continually   105
Drunk on the wind in my mouth,
Wringing the handlebar for speed,
Wild to be wreckage forever.

                                                                        1963

QUESTIONS

1. What does your experience with junkyards, old cars, or old garages contribute to
   your first reading of this poem? If you do not have any experiences with old, rusty
   machines or engine parts, which images help to provide you with that experience?
2. Explain the lines:

   For I knew that Doris Holbrook
   Would escape from her father at noon
   And would come from the farm
   To seek parts owned by the sun
   Among the abandoned chassis. . . .

3. Which car does the narrator choose for the rendezvous? What do each of the car's
   remaining parts — and the narrator's response to them — tell you about the narrator?
4. Why is the narrator "wild to be wreckage forever"? What is the tone of this final
   statement?

THE LEAP   178

The only thing I have of Jane MacNaughton
Is one instant of a dancing-class dance.
She was the fastest runner in the seventh grade,
My scrapbook says, even when boys were beginning
To be as big as the girls,   5
But I do not have her running in my mind,
Though Frances Lane is there, Agnes Fraser,
Fat Betty Lou Black in the boys-against-girls
Relays we ran at recess: she must have run

Like the other girls, with her skirts tucked up   10
So they would be like bloomers,
But I cannot tell; that part of her is gone.
What I do have is when she came,
With the hem of her skirt where it should be
For a young lady, into the annual dance   15
Of the dancing class we all hated, and with a light
Grave leap, jumped up and touched the end
Of one of the paper-ring decorations

To see if she could reach it. She could.
And reached me now as well, hanging in my mind   20
From a brown chain of brittle paper, thin
And muscular, wide-mouthed, eager to prove
Whatever it proves when you leap
In a new dress, a new womanhood, among the boys
Whom you easily left in the dust   25
Of the passionless playground. If I said I saw
In the paper where Jane MacNaughton Hill,

Mother of four, leapt to her death from a window
Of a downtown hotel, and that her body crushed-in
The top of a parked taxi, and that I held   30
Without trembling a picture of her lying cradled
In that papery steel as though lying in the grass,
One shoe idly off, arms folded across her breast,
I would not believe myself. I would say
The convenient thing, that it was a bad dream   35
Of maturity, to see that eternal process

Most obsessively wrong with the world
Come out of her light, earth-spurning feet
Grown heavy: would say that in the dusty heels
Of the playground some boy who did not depend   40
On speed of foot, caught and betrayed her.
Jane, stay where you are in my first mind:
It was odd in that school, at that dance.
I and the other slow-footed yokels sat in corners
Cutting rings out of drawing paper   45

Before you leapt in your new dress
And touched the end of something I began,
Above the couples struggling on the floor,
New men and women clutching at each other
And prancing foolishly as bears: hold on   50
To that ring I made for you, Jane—
My feet are nailed to the ground
By dust I swallowed thirty years ago—
While I examine my hands.

                                                      1967

EMILY DICKINSON
(1830–1886)

[MY LIFE HAD STOOD—A LOADED GUN]   179

My Life had stood—a Loaded Gun—
In Corners—till a Day
The Owner passed—identified—
And carried Me away—

And now We roam in Sovereign Woods—   5
And now We hunt the Doe—
And every time I speak for Him—
The Mountains straight reply—

And do I smile, such cordial light
Upon the Valley glow—   10
It is as a Vesuvian face
Had let its pleasure through—

And when at Night—Our good Day done—
I guard My Master's Head—

'Tis better than the Eider-Duck's   15
Deep Pillow—to have shared—

To foe of His—I'm deadly foe—
None stir the second time—
On whom I lay a Yellow Eye—
Or an emphatic Thumb—   20

Though I than He—may longer live
He longer must—than I—
For I have but the power to kill,
Without—the power to die—

                                           1929

[A NARROW FELLOW IN THE GRASS]   180

A narrow Fellow in the Grass
Occasionally rides—
You may have met Him—did you not
His notice sudden is—

The Grass divides as with a Comb—   5
A spotted shaft is seen—
And then it closes at your feet
And opens further on—

He likes a Boggy Acre
A Floor too cool for Corn—   10
Yet when a Boy, and Barefoot—
I more than once at Noon

Have passed, I thought, a Whip lash
Unbraiding in the Sun
When stooping to secure it   15
It wrinkled, and was gone—

Several of Nature's People
I know, and they know me—
I feel for them a transport
Of cordiality—   20

But never met this Fellow
Attended, or alone
Without a tighter breathing
And Zero at the Bone—

                                           1866

[BECAUSE I COULD NOT STOP FOR DEATH]   181

Because I could not stop for Death—
He kindly stopped for me—
The Carriage held but just Ourselves—
And Immortality.

We slowly drove—He knew no haste   5
And I had put away
My labor and my leisure too,
For His Civility—

We passed the School, where Children strove
At Recess—in the Ring—   10
We passed the Fields of Gazing Grain—
We passed the Setting Sun—

Or rather—He passed Us—
The Dews drew quivering and chill—
For only Gossamer, my Gown—   15
My Tippet—only Tulle—

We paused before a House that seemed
A Swelling of the Ground—
The Roof was scarcely visible—
The Cornice—in the Ground—   20

Since then—'tis Centuries—and yet
Feels shorter than the Day
I first surmised the Horses' Heads
Were toward Eternity—

1890

QUESTIONS

1. How does personification contribute to the poem's story-quality?
2. The speaker describes a journey through a landscape. What are the implications and significance of the various sights along the way: the children, the fields, the setting sun, the house?
3. Most journeys have a beginning, middle, and end. Does this one?
4. Do you feel the ballad stanza is appropriate? Do you sense any irony?

BECAUSE I COULD NOT STOP FOR DEATH 16: *Tippet:* shoulder cape; *Tulle:* thin silk net.

[THERE'S A CERTAIN SLANT OF LIGHT]   182

There's a certain Slant of light,
Winter Afternoons—
That oppresses, like the Heft
Of Cathedral Tunes—

Heavenly Hurt, it gives us—   5
We can find no scar,
But internal difference,
Where the Meanings, are—

None may teach it—Any—
'Tis the Seal Despair—   10
An imperial affliction
Sent us of the Air—

When it comes, the Landscape listens—
Shadows—hold their breath—
When it goes, 'tis like the Distance   15
On the look of Death—

1890

[THIS IS MY LETTER TO THE WORLD]   183

This is my letter to the World
That never wrote to Me—
The simple News that Nature told—
With tender Majesty

Her Message is committed   5
To Hands I cannot see—
For love of Her—Sweet—countrymen—
Judge tenderly—of Me

1890

[THE SOUL SELECTS HER OWN SOCIETY]   184

The Soul selects her own Society—
Then—shuts the Door—
To her divine Majority—
Present no more—

Unmoved—she notes the Chariots—pausing— 5
At her low Gate—
Unmoved—an Emperor be kneeling
Upon her Mat—

I've known her—from an ample nation—
Choose One— 10
Then—close the Valves of her attention—
Like Stone—

1890

[MUCH MADNESS IS DIVINEST SENSE] 185

Much Madness is divinest Sense—
To a discerning Eye—
Much Sense—the starkest Madness—
'Tis the Majority
In this, as All, prevail— 5
Assent—and you are sane—
Demur—you're straightway dangerous—
And handled with a Chain—

1890

[APPARENTLY WITH NO SURPRISE] 186

Apparently with no surprise
To any happy Flower
The Frost beheads it at its play—
In accidental power—
The blonde Assassin passes on— 5
The Sun proceeds unmoved
To measure off another Day
For an Approving God.

1890

[WILD NIGHTS—WILD NIGHTS!] 187

Wild Nights—Wild Nights!
Were I with thee
Wild Nights should be
Our luxury!

Futile—the Winds—   5
To a Heart in port—
Done with the Compass—
Done with the Chart!

Rowing in Eden—
Ah, the Sea!   10
Might I but moor—Tonight—
In Thee!

1891

[I HEARD A FLY BUZZ—WHEN I DIED]   188

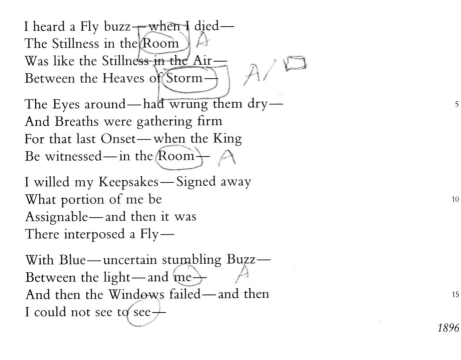

I heard a Fly buzz—when I died—
The Stillness in the Room
Was like the Stillness in the Air—
Between the Heaves of Storm—

The Eyes around—had wrung them dry—   5
And Breaths were gathering firm
For that last Onset—when the King
Be witnessed—in the Room—

I willed my Keepsakes—Signed away
What portion of me be   10
Assignable—and then it was
There interposed a Fly—

With Blue—uncertain stumbling Buzz—
Between the light—and me—
And then the Windows failed—and then   15
I could not see to see—

1896

QUESTIONS

1. What setting do you imagine for this poem? Who is present?
2. What prepares you to hear the loudness of the fly's buzzing?
3. What purpose does the fly have?
4. One usually speaks of lights failing, not windows. What is suggested by the final two lines?

[MY LIFE CLOSED TWICE BEFORE ITS CLOSE]   189

My life closed twice before its close;
It yet remains to see
If Immortality unveil
A third event to me,

So huge, so hopeless to conceive   5
As these that twice befell.
Parting is all we know of heaven,
And all we need of hell.

1896

[THE BRAIN—IS WIDER THAN THE SKY]   190

The Brain—is wider than the Sky—
For—put them side by side—
The one the other will contain
With ease—and You—beside—

The Brain is deeper than the sea—   5
For—hold them—Blue to Blue—
The one the other will absorb
As Sponges—Buckets—do—

The Brain is just the weight of God—
For—Heft them—Pound for Pound—   10
And they will differ—if they do—
As Syllable from Sound—

1896

[I FELT A FUNERAL, IN MY BRAIN]   191

I felt a Funeral, in my Brain,
And Mourners to and fro
Kept treading—treading—till it seemed
That Sense was breaking through—

And when they all were seated,   5
A Service, like a Drum—
Kept beating—beating—till I thought
My Mind was going numb—

And then I heard them lift a Box
And creak across my Soul   10
With those same Boots of Lead, again,
Then Space—began to toll,

As all the Heavens were a Bell,
And Being, but an Ear,
And I, and Silence, some strange Race   15
Wrecked, solitary, here—

And then a Plank in Reason, broke,
And I dropped down, and down—
And hit a World, at every plunge,
And Finished knowing—then—   20

1896

[IN WINTER IN MY ROOM]   192

In Winter in my Room
I came upon a Worm—
Pink, lank and warm—
But as he was a worm
And worms presume   5
Not quite with him at home—
Secured him by a string
To something neighboring
And went along.

A Trifle afterward   10
A thing occurred
I'd not believe it if I heard
But state with creeping blood—
A snake with mottles rare
Surveyed my chamber floor   15
In feature as the worm before
But ringed with power—

The very string with which
I tied him— too
When he was mean and new   20
That string was there—

IN WINTER IN MY ROOM 14 *mottles:* blotches.

I shrank—"How fair you are"!
Propitiation's claw—
"Afraid," he hissed
"Of me"?   25
"No cordiality"—
He fathomed me—
Then to a Rhythm *Slim*
Secreted in his Form
As Patterns swim   30
Projected him.

That time I flew
Both eyes his way
Lest he pursue
Nor ever ceased to run   35
Till in a distant Town
Towns on from mine
I set me down
This was a dream.

1914

[AFTER GREAT PAIN, A FORMAL FEELING COMES]   193

After great pain, a formal feeling comes—
The Nerves sit ceremonious, like Tombs—
The stiff Heart questions was it He, that bore,
And Yesterday, or Centuries before?

The Feet, mechanical, go round—   5
Of Ground, or Air, or Ought—
A Wooden way
Regardless grown,
A Quartz contentment, like a stone—

This is the Hour of Lead—   10
Remembered, if outlived,
As Freezing persons, recollect the Snow—
First—Chill—then Stupor—then the letting go—

1929

AFTER GREAT PAIN, A FORMAL FEELING COMES 6 *Ought:* nothing.

[I DWELL IN POSSIBILITY]   194

I dwell in Possibility—
A fairer House than Prose—
More numerous of Windows—
Superior—for Doors—

Of Chambers as the Cedars—   5
Impregnable of Eye—
And for an Everlasting Roof
The Gambrels of the Sky—

Of Visitors—the fairest—
For Occupation—This—   10
The spreading wide my narrow Hands
To gather Paradise—

1929

[TELL ALL THE TRUTH BUT TELL IT SLANT]   195

Tell all the Truth but tell it slant—
Success in Circuit lies
Too bright for our infirm Delight
The Truth's superb surprise

As Lightning to the Children eased   5
With explanation kind
The Truth must dazzle gradually
Or every man be blind—

1945

JOHN DONNE
(1572–1631)

OH MY BLACK SOUL   196

Oh my black Soul! now thou art summoned
By sickness, death's herald, and champion;
Thou art like a pilgrim, which abroad hath done
Treason, and durst not turn to whence he is fled,
Or like a thief, which till death's doom be read,   5

I DWELL IN POSSIBILITY 8 *Gambrels:* curved roofs.

Wisheth himself delivered from prison;
But damn'd and hal'd to execution,
Wisheth that still he might be imprisoned;
Yet grace, if thou repent, thou canst not lack;
But who shall give thee that grace to begin?   10
Oh make thy self with holy mourning black,
And red with blushing, as thou art with sin;
Or wash thee in Christ's blood, which hath this might
That being red, it dyes red souls to white.

                                                          1633

BATTER MY HEART, THREE-PERSONED
GOD, FOR YOU   197

Batter my heart, three-personed God, for You
As yet but knock, breathe, shine, and seek to mend.
That I may rise and stand, o'erthrow me, and bend
Your force to break, blow, burn, and make me new.
I, like an usurped town to another due,   5
Labor to admit You, but Oh! to no end.
Reason, Your viceroy in me, me should defend,
But is captived, and proves weak or untrue.
Yet dearly I love You, and would be lovèd fain,
But am betrothed unto Your enemy;   10
Divorce me, untie or break that knot again;
Take me to You, imprison me, for I,
Except You enthrall me, never shall be free,
Nor ever chaste, except You ravish me.

                                                          1633

THE FLEA   198

Mark but this flea, and mark in this
How little that which thou deny'st me is;
It sucked me first, and now sucks thee,
And in this flea our two bloods mingled be;
Thou know'st that this cannot be said   5
A sin, nor shame, nor loss of maidenhead,
   Yet this enjoys before it woo,
   And pampered swells with one blood made of two,
   And this, alas, is more than we would do.

Oh stay, three lives in one flea spare,   10
Where we almost, yea more than married are.
This flea is you and I, and this
Our marriage bed, and marriage temple is;
Though parents grudge, and you, we're met
And cloistered in these living walls of jet.   15
   Though use make you apt to kill me,
   Let not to that, self-murder added be,
   And sacrilege, three sins in killing three.

Cruel and sudden, hast thou since
Purpled thy nail in blood of innocence?   20
Wherein could this flea guilty be,
Except in that drop it sucked from thee?
Yet thou triumph'st, and say'st that thou
Find'st not thyself, nor me, the weaker now;
   'Tis true; then learn how false, fears be;   25
   Just so much honor, when thou yield'st to me,
   Will waste, as this flea's death took life from thee.

1633

THE SUN RISING   199

   Busy old fool, unruly sun,
   Why dost thou thus,
Through windows and through curtains call on us?
Must to thy motions lovers' seasons run?
   Saucy pedantic wretch, go chide   5
   Late school boys and sour prentices,
  Go tell court huntsmen that the king will ride,
  Call country ants to harvest offices;
Love, all alike, no season knows nor clime,
Nor hours, days, months, which are the rags of time.   10

   Thy beams, so reverend and strong
   Why shouldst thou think?
I could eclipse and cloud them with a wink,
But that I would not lose her sight so long;
   If her eyes have not blinded thine,   15
   Look, and tomorrow late tell me,
  Whether both th' Indias of spice and mine
  Be where thou leftst them, or lie here with me.

THE SUN RISING 17 *both th' Indias:* India and the West Indies.

Ask for those kings whom thou saw'st yesterday,
And thou shalt hear, All here in one bed lay. 20

    She's all states, and all princes, I,
      Nothing else is.
Princes do but play us; compared to this,
All honor's mimic, all wealth alchemy.
    Thou, sun, art half as happy as we, 25
      In that the world's contracted thus;
  Thine age asks ease, and since thy duties be
  To warm the world, that's done in warming us.
Shine here to us, and thou art everywhere;
This bed thy center is, these walls, thy sphere. 30

1633

QUESTIONS

1. Who is speaking and why is he irritated?
2. Why does he feel he should not be subject to the sun's power?
3. What proof does the speaker give of his superiority to the sun?
4. The speaker is willing to grant a favor to the sun. What is it?
5. What is the speaker's attitude? Is he serious? ironic? bitter? humorous? Do you see indications that he is addressing someone other than the sun?
6. In the seventeenth century, *wit* was defined as intellectual cleverness. Where is the wit in this poem and for whom is it intended?

THE GOOD-MORROW   200

I wonder, by my troth, what thou and I
Did, till we loved? were we not weaned till then?
But sucked on country pleasures, childishly?
Or snorted we in the Seven Sleepers' den?
'Twas so; but this, all pleasures fancies be. 5
If ever any beauty I did see,
Which I desired, and got, 'twas but a dream of thee.

And now good-morrow to our waking souls,
Which watch not one another out of fear;
For love, all love of other sights controls, 10
And makes one little room an everywhere.
Let sea-discoverers to new worlds have gone,
Let maps to others, worlds on worlds have shown,
Let us possess one world, each hath one, and is one.

THE GOOD-MORROW 4 *the Seven Sleepers' den:* a legend about seven Christian youths who hid in a cave to escape persecution and slept for almost two hundred years.

My face in thine eye, thine in mine appears,   15
And true plain hearts do in the faces rest;
Where can we find two better hemispheres,
Without sharp north, without declining west?
Whatever dies was not mixed equally;
If our two loves be one, or, thou and I   20
Love so alike that none do slacken, none can die.

1633

RITA DOVE
(b. 1952)

GEOMETRY   201

I prove a theorem and the house expands:
the windows jerk free to hover near the ceiling,
the ceiling floats away with a sigh.

As the walls clear themselves of everything
but transparency, the scent of carnations   5
leaves with them. I am out in the open

and above the windows have hinged into butterflies,
sunlight glinting where they've intersected.
They are going to some point true and unproven.

1980

DUSTING   202

Every day a wilderness—no
shade in sight. Beulah
patient among knicknacks,
the solarium a rage
of light, a grainstorm   5
as her gray cloth brings
dark wood to life.

Under her hand scrolls
and crests gleam
darker still. What   10
was his name, that
silly boy at the fair with

the rifle booth? And his kiss and
the clear bowl with one bright
fish, rippling   15
wound!

Not Michael—
something finer. Each dust
stroke a deep breath and
the canary in bloom.   20
Wavery memory: home
from a dance, the front door
blown open and the parlor
in snow, she rushed
the bowl to the stove, watched   25
as the locket of ice
dissolved and he
swam free.

That was years before
Father gave her up   30
with her name, years before
her name grew to mean
Promise, then
Desert-in-Peace.
Long before the shadow and   35
sun's accomplice, the tree.

Maurice.

                                                        1983

QUESTIONS

1. What do you see emerging as Beulah dusts? What does Beulah see?
2. Which images fit the wilderness motif?
3. What does this motif have to do with the specific memory Beulah has?
4. How are names and the art of naming worked out?

THE FISH IN THE STONE   203

The fish in the stone
would like to fall
back into the sea.

He is weary
of analysis, the small   5
predictable truths.

He is weary of waiting
in the open,
his profile stamped
by a white light.   10

In the ocean the silence
moves and moves

and so much is unnecessary!
Patient, he drifts
until the moment comes   15
to cast his
skeletal blossom.

The fish in the stone
knows to fail is
to do the living   20
a favor.

He knows why the ant
engineers a gangster's
funeral, garish
and perfectly amber.   25
He knows why the scientist
in secret delight
strokes the fern's
voluptuous braille.

1983

THE ZEPPELIN FACTORY   204

The zeppelin factory
needed workers, all right—
but, standing in the cage
of the whale's belly, sparks
flying off the joints   5
and noise thundering,
Thomas wanted to sit
right down and cry.

That spring the third
largest airship was dubbed   10
the biggest joke
in town, though they all
turned out for the launch.

Wind caught,
"The Akron" floated
out of control,   15

three men in tow—
one dropped
to safety, one
hung on but the third,   20
muscles and adrenalin
failing, fell
clawing
six hundred feet.

Thomas at night   25
in the vacant lot:
    Here I am, intact
    and faint-hearted.

Thomas hiding
his heart with his hat   30
at the football game, eyeing
the Goodyear blimp overhead:
    Big boy I know
    you're in there.

1986

ROAST POSSUM   205

The possum's a greasy critter
that lives on persimmons and what
the Bible calls carrion.
So much from the 1909 Werner
Encyclopedia, three rows of deep green   5
along the wall. A granddaughter
propped on each knee,
Thomas went on with his tale—

but it was for Malcolm, little
Red Delicious, that he invented   10
embellishments: *We shined that possum*
with a torch and I shinnied up,
being the smallest,
to shake him down. He glared at me,
teeth bared like a shark's
15

in that torpedo snout.
Man he was tough but no match
for old-time know-how.

Malcolm hung back, studying them
with his gold hawk eyes. When the girls   20
got restless, Thomas talked horses:
Strolling Jim, who could balance
a glass of water on his back
and trot the village square
without spilling a drop. Who put   25
Wartrace on the map and was buried
under a stone, like a man.

They liked that part.
He could have gone on to tell them
that the Werner admitted Negro children   30
to be intelligent, though briskness
clouded over at puberty, bringing
indirection and laziness. Instead,
he added: *You got to be careful*
with a possum when he's on the ground;   35
he'll turn on his back and play dead
till you give up looking. That's
what you'd call sullin'.

Malcolm interrupted to ask
who owned Strolling Jim,   40
and who paid for the tombstone.
They stared each other down
man to man, before Thomas,
as a grandfather, replied:
                      Yessir,
we enjoyed that possum. We ate him   45
real slow, with sweet potatoes.

                                 1986

THOMAS AT THE WHEEL   206

This, then, the river he had to swim.
Through the wipers the drugstore
shouted, lit up like a casino,
neon script leering from the shuddering asphalt.

Then the glass doors flew apart 5
and a man walked out to the curb
to light a cigarette. Thomas thought
the sky was emptying itself as fast
as his chest was filling with water.

Should he honk? What a joke— 10
he couldn't ungrip the steering wheel.
The man looked him calmly in the eye
and tossed the match away.

And now the street dark, not a soul
nor its brother. He lay down across 15
the seat, a pod set to sea,
a kiss unpuckering. He watched
the slit eye of the glove compartment,
the prescription inside,

he laughed as he thought *Oh* 20
the writing on the water. Thomas imagined
his wife as she awoke missing him,
cracking a window. He heard sirens
rise as the keys swung, ticking.

1986

QUESTIONS

1. Where is Thomas and why?
2. In the first two stanzas, what exaggerates the images Thomas sees?
3. What are the feelings Thomas exhibits at various points in the poem?
4. In the last line, why are the keys "ticking"?

JOHN DRYDEN

(1631–1700)

MAC FLECKNOE

207

OR A SATIRE UPON THE
TRUE-BLUE-PROTESTANT
POET, T.S.

All human things are subject to decay,
And when fate summons, monarchs must obey.
This Flecknoe found, who, like Augustus, young

MAC FLECKNOE subtitle *T.S.*: Thomas Shadwell (1640 – 1692), a comic playwright whom Dryden names "Mac" (son of) "Flecknoe" (an inept dramatist, poet, and priest of the time). 3 *Augustus:* became Roman emperor at the age of thirty-three and reigned for forty-four years.

Was called to empire, and had governed long;
In prose and verse, was owned, without dispute,   5
Through all the realms of Nonsense, absolute.
This aged prince, now flourishing in peace,
And blest with issue of a large increase,
Worn out with business, did at length debate
To settle the succession of the state;   10
And, pondering which of all his sons was fit
To reign, and wage immortal war with wit,
Cried: " 'Tis resolved; for nature pleads that he
Should only rule, who most resembles me.
Sh— alone my perfect image bears,   15
Mature in dullness from his tender years:
Sh— alone, of all my sons, is he
Who stands confirmed in full stupidity.
The rest to some faint meaning make pretense,
But Sh— never deviates into sense.   20
Some beams of wit on other souls may fall,
Strike through, and make a lucid interval;
But Sh—'s genuine night admits no ray,
His rising fogs prevail upon the day.
Besides, his goodly fabric fills the eye,   25
And seems designed for thoughtless majesty:
Thoughtless as monarch oaks that shade the plain,
And, spread in solemn state, supinely reign.
Heywood and Shirley were but types of thee,
Thou last great prophet of tautology.   30
Even I, a dunce of more renown than they,
Was sent before but to prepare thy way;
And, coarsely clad in Norwich drugget, came
To teach the nations in thy greater name.
My warbling lute, the lute I whilom strung,   35
When to King John of Portugal I sung,
Was but the prelude to that glorious day,
When thou on silver Thames didst cut thy way,
With well-timed oars before the royal barge,
Swelled with the pride of thy celestial charge;   40
And big with hymn, commander of a host,
The like was ne'er in Epsom blankets tossed.

15 *Sh—*: Shadwell. 29 *Heywood and Shirley*: Thomas Heywood and James Shirley, poorly regarded dramatists of the time. 30 *tautology*: repetition of the same idea in different words. 33 *Norwich drugget*: coarse wool. 35 *whilom*: formerly. 36 *King John of Portugal*: Flecknoe claimed the king of Portugal as a patron. 42 *Epsom blankets*: allusion to Shadwell's *Epsom Wells* and *The Virtuoso* in which a false wit is tossed in a blanket.

Methinks I see the new Arion sail,
The lute still trembling underneath thy nail.
At thy well-sharpened thumb from shore to shore   45
The treble squeaks for fear, the basses roar;
Echoes from Pissing Alley Sh— call,
And Sh— they resound from Aston Hall.
About thy boat the little fishes throng,
As at the morning toast that floats along.   50
Sometimes, as prince of thy harmonious band,
Thou wield'st thy papers in thy threshing hand.
St. André's feet ne'er kept more equal time,
Not ev'n the feet of thy own *Psyche's* rhyme;
Though they in number as in sense excel: 55
So just, so like tautology, they fell,
That, pale with envy, Singleton forswore
The lute and sword, which he in triumph bore,
And vowed he ne'er would act Villerius more."
Here stopped the good old sire, and wept for joy   60
In silent raptures of the hopeful boy.
All arguments, but most his plays, persuade,
That for anointed dullness he was made.
　　Close to the walls which fair Augusta bind
(The fair Augusta much to fears inclined),   65
An ancient fabric raised to inform the sight,
There stood of yore, and Barbican it hight:
A watchtower once; but now, so fate ordains,
Of all the pile an empty name remains.
From its old ruins brothel houses rise,   70
Scenes of lewd loves, and of polluted joys,
Where their vast courts the mother-strumpets keep,
And, undisturbed by watch, in silence sleep.
Near these a Nursery erects its head,
Where queens are formed, and future heroes bred;   75
Where unfledged actors learn to laugh and cry,
Where infant punks their tender voices try,
And little Maximins the gods defy.

---

43 *Arion:* Greek musician–poet who was cast into the sea and saved by dolphins enthralled by his music. 50 *morning toast:* sewage. 53 *St. André:* a French dancing-master who choreographed Shadwell's opera, *Psyche.* 57 *Singleton:* John Singleton, a leading musician to Charles II. 59 *Villerius:* a character in Sir William D'Avenant's opera *The Siege of Rhodes* in which battles were presented in recitative, requiring the actor to use both lute and sword. 64 *Augusta:* Roman name for London. 66 *fabric:* building. 74 *Nursery:* training-school for actors. 77 *punks:* prostitutes. 78 *little Maximins:* the ranting Roman emperor in Dryden's *Tyrannic Love.*

Great Fletcher never treads in buskins here,
Nor greater Jonson dares in socks appear;   80
But gentle Simkin just reception finds
Amidst this monument of vanished minds:
Pure clinches the suburban Muse affords,
And Panton waging harmless war with words.
Here Flecknoe, as a place to fame well known,   85
Ambitiously designed his Sh—'s throne;
For ancient Dekker prophesied long since,
That in this pile would reign a mighty prince,
Born for a scourge of wit, and flail of sense;
To whom true dullness should some *Psyches* owe,   90
But worlds of *Misers* from his pen should flow;
Humorists and *Hypocrites* it should produce,
Whole Raymond families, and tribes of Bruce.
   Now Empress Fame had published the renown
Of Sh—'s coronation through the town.   95
Roused by report of Fame, the nations meet,
From near Bunhill, and distant Watling Street.
No Persian carpets spread the imperial way,
But scattered limbs of mangled poets lay;
From dusty shops neglected authors come,   100
Martyrs of pies, and relics of the bum.
Much Heywood, Shirley, Ogilby there lay,
But loads of Sh— almost choked the way.
Bilked stationers for yeomen stood prepared,
And Herringman was captain of the guard.   105
The hoary prince in majesty appeared,
High on a throne of his own labors reared.
At his right hand our young Ascanius sate,
Rome's other hope, and pillar of the state.
His brows thick fogs, instead of glories, grace,   110
And lambent dullness played around his face.

---

79 *Fletcher:* John Fletcher, popular dramatist; *buskins:* thick-soled half-boots worn by classical
actors in tragedy. 80 *Jonson:* Ben Jonson, popular dramatist and poet; *socks:* light shoes worn by
comic actors. 81 *Simkin:* a fool or clown. 83 *clinches:* puns. 84 *Panton:* a punster. 87 *Dekker:*
Thomas Dekker, dramatist regarded by Jonson as inept. 90–92 *Psyches . . . Misers . . . Humorists
. . . Hypocrites:* works by Shadwell. 93 *Raymond . . . Bruce:* characters in *The Humorists* and *The
Virtuoso.* 97 *Bunhill:* a field in which the victims of the plague were buried; *Watling Street:* a street
in an unfashionable part of London. 100–101 *authors . . . bum:* old discarded books, the pages of
which lined pie-tins or were used as toilet paper. 102 *Ogilby:* John Ogilby or Ogelby, translator
of Virgil and Homer. 104 *Bilked . . . prepared:* cheated publishers who stocked the works of
Shadwell guard their investment. 105 *Herringman:* Shadwell's and Dryden's publisher. 108
Ascanius: Aeneas' son (thus, like Shadwell, the heir).

As Hannibal did to the altars come,
Sworn by his sire a mortal foe to Rome,
So Sh— swore, nor should his vow be vain,
That he till death true dullness would maintain;   115
And, in his father's right, and realm's defense,
Ne'er to have peace with wit, nor truce with sense.
The king himself the sacred unction made,
As king by office, and as priest by trade.
In his siníster hand, instead of ball,   120
He placed a mighty mug of potent ale;
Love's Kingdom to his right he did convey,
At once his scepter, and his rule of sway;
Whose righteous lore the prince had practiced young,
And from whose loins recorded *Psyche* sprung.   125
His temples, last, with poppies were o'erspread,
That nodding seemed to consecrate his head.
Just at that point of time, if fame not lie,
On his left hand twelve reverend owls did fly.
So Romulus, 'tis sung, by Tiber's brook,   130
Presage of sway from twice six vultures took.
The admiring throng loud acclamations make,
And omens of his future empire take.
The sire then shook the honors of his head,
And from his brows damps of oblivion shed   135
Full on the filial dullness: long he stood,
Repelling from his breast the raging god;
At length burst out in this prophetic mood:
    "Heavens bless my son, from Ireland let him reign
To far Barbadoes on the western main;   140
Of his dominion may no end be known,
And greater than his father's be his throne;
Beyond *Love's Kingdom* let his stretch his pen!"
He paused, and all the people cried, "Amen."
Then thus continued he: "My son, advance   145
Still in new imprudence, new ignorance.
Success let others teach, learn thou from me

112 *Hannibal:* the Carthagenian general who invaded Italy. His father made him swear to his
hatred of Rome when he was nine years old. 118 *unction:* anointing oil. 120 *siníster:* left; 120 *ball:*
during the English coronation the king holds a globe in his left hand. 122 *Love's Kingdom:* one of
Flecknoe's plays held here in the right hand instead of a scepter. 126 *poppies:* suggests sleep and
Shadwell's opium addiction. 130 *Romulus:* the founder of Rome on the river Tiber. Twelve
vultures visited the site he chose for Rome, compared to six vultures at his brother Remas's site.
134 *honors:* locks. 135 *damps:* vapors. 139–140 *Ireland . . . Barbadoes:* nothing but a long expanse
of water exists between them.

Pangs without birth, and fruitless industry.
Let *Virtuosos* in five years be writ;
Yet not one thought accuse thy toil of wit.   150
Let gentle George in triumph tread the stage,
Make Dorimant betray, and Loveit rage;
Let Cully, Cockwood, Fopling, charm the pit,
And in their folly show the writer's wit.
Yet still thy fools shall stand in thy defense,   155
And justify their author's want of sense.
Let 'em be all by thy own model made
Of dullness, and desire no foreign aid;
That they to future ages may be known,
Not copies drawn, but issue of thy own.   160
Nay, let thy men of wit too be the same,
All full of thee, and differing but in name.
But let no alien S—dl—y interpose,
To lard with wit thy hungry *Epsom* prose.
And when false flowers of rhetoric thou wouldst cull,   165
Trust nature, do not labor to be dull;
But write thy best, and top; and, in each line,
Sir Formal's oratory will be thine:
Sir Formal, though unsought, attends thy quill,
And does thy northern dedications fill.   170
Nor let false friends seduce thy mind to fame,
By arrogating Jonson's hostile name.
Let father Flecknoe fire thy mind with praise,
And uncle Ogilby thy envy raise.
Thou art my blood, where Jonson has no part: 175
What share have we in nature, or in art?
Where did his wit on learning fix a brand,
And rail at arts he did not understand?
Where made he love in Prince Nicander's vein,
Or swept the dust in *Psyche's* humble strain?   180
Where sold he bargains, 'whip-stitch, kiss my arse,'
Promised a play and dwindled to a farce?
When did his Muse from Fletcher scenes purloin,
As thou whole Eth'rege dost transfuse to thine?

---

151 *George:* George Etherege, Restoration playwright. Five of his characters are named in succeeding lines. 163 *S—dl—y:* Sir Charles Sedley, court wit thought to have written the prologue and several lines of Shadwell's *Epsom's Wells.* 168 *Sir Formal:* Sir Formal Trifle, an exaggerated orator in *The Virtuoso.* 170 *northern dedications:* Shadwell dedicated plays to the Duke and Duchess of Newcastle in the north of England. 179 *Nicander:* the character who pursues Psyche in Shadwell's opera. 181 *sold he bargains:* wrote obscene replies to innocent questions.

But so transfused, as oil on water's flow,　　　　　185
His always floats above, thine sinks below.
This is thy province, this thy wondrous way,
New humors to invent for each new play:
This is that boasted bias of thy mind,
By which one way, to dullness, 'tis inclined;　　　190
Which makes thy writings lean on one side still,
And, in all changes, that way bends thy will.
Nor let thy mountain-belly make pretense
Of likeness; thine's a tympany of sense.
A tun of man in thy large bulk is writ,　　　　　195
But sure thou'rt but a kilderkin of wit.
Like mine, thy gentle numbers feebly creep;
Thy tragic Muse gives smiles, thy comic sleep.
With whate'er gall thou sett'st thyself to write,
Thy inoffensive satires never bite.　　　　　　　200
In thy felonious heart though venom lies,
It does but touch thy Irish pen, and dies.
Thy genius calls thee not to purchase fame
In keen iambics, but mild anagram.
Leave writing plays, and choose for thy command　　205
Some peaceful province in acrostic land.
There thou may'st wings display and altars raise,
And torture one poor word ten thousand ways.
Or, if thou wouldst thy different talent suit,
Set thy own songs, and sing them to thy lute."　　210
　　He said: but his last words were scarcely heard
For Bruce and Longville had a trap prepared,
And down they sent the yet declaiming bard.
Sinking he left his drugget robe behind,
Borne upwards by a subterranean wind.　　　　　215
The mantle fell to the young prophet's part,
With double portion of his father's art.

　　　　　　　　　　　　　　　　　　　　　　1682

---

194 *tympany:* swelling caused by air or an emptiness as in a drum. 195 *tun:* a large wine cask. 196 *kilderkin:* small wine cask. 204 *keen iambics:* the meter of Greek satire; *anagrams:* rearrangement of the letters in a word to form new words. 206 *acrostic:* a poem in which the first letters of each line form the name of the person or thing written about. 212 *Bruce and Longville:* characters in *The Virtuoso* who drop Sir Formal through a trap door. 216 *the mantle . . . prophet's part:* like the prophet Elijah's mantle falling upon Elisha.

TO THE MEMORY OF MR. OLDHAM   208

Farewell, too little, and too lately known,
Whom I began to think and call my own:
For sure our souls were near allied, and thine
Cast in the same poetic mold with mine.
One common note on either lyre did strike,   5
And knaves and fools we both abhorred alike.
To the same goal did both our studies drive;
The last set out the soonest did arrive.
Thus Nisus fell upon the slippery place,
While his young friend performed and won the race.   10
O early ripe! to thy abundant store
What could advancing age have added more?
It might (what nature never gives the young)
Have taught the numbers of thy native tongue.
But satire needs not those, and wit will shine   15
Through the harsh cadence of a rugged line:
A noble error, and but seldom made,
When poets are by too much force betrayed.
Thy generous fruits, though gathered ere their prime,
Still showed a quickness, and maturing time   20
But mellows what we write to the dull sweets of rhyme.
Once more, hail and farewell; farewell, thou young,
But ah too short, Marcellus of our tongue;
Thy brows with ivy, and with laurels bound;
But fate and gloomy night encompass thee around.   25

1684

QUESTIONS

1. Which lines give you the general meaning of the poem most directly and clearly in your first reading? Which allusions are obstacles for you?
2. To what does the paradox in line 8 refer?
3. After establishing a form, the author departs from it. Where does this occur and why at that point?

TO THE MEMORY OF MR. OLDHAM title *Mr. Oldham:* John Oldham (1653–1683), best known for *Satyrs upon the Jesuits.* Dryden's poem appeared as an introduction to a posthumous volume of Oldham's works. 9 *Nisus:* in Virgil's *Aeneid,* Nisus and the young Euryalus entered a foot race, during which Nisus slipped and inadvertently tripped Salius, the front-runner. Euryalus then won the race. 23 *Marcellus:* nephew and heir of Augustus Caesar, Marcellus died at the age of twenty.

ALAN DUGAN

(b. 1923)

FUNERAL ORATION FOR A MOUSE   209

This, Lord, was an anxious brother and
a living diagram of fear: full of health himself,
   he brought diseases like a gift
to give his hosts. Masked in a cat's moustache
   but sounding like a bird, he was a ghost   5
   of lesser noises and a kitchen pest
for whom some ladies stand on chairs. So,
Lord, accept our felt though minor guilt
   for an ignoble foe and ancient sin:
   the murder of a guest   10
who shared our board: just once he ate
   too slowly, dying in our trap
from necessary hunger and a broken back.

Humors of love aside, the mousetrap was our own
   opinion of the mouse, but for the mouse   15
   it was the tree of knowledge with
   its consequential fruit, the true cross
   and the gate of hell. Even to approach
   it makes him like or better than
   its maker: his courage as a spoiler never once   20
impressed us, but to go out cautiously at night,
   into the dining room;—what bravery, what
   hunger! Younger by far, in dying he
was older than us all: his mobile tail and nose
spasmed in the pinch of our annoyance. Why,   25
then, at that snapping sound, did we, victorious,
   begin to laugh without delight?

Our stomachs, deep in an analysis
   of their own stolen baits
(and asking, "Lord, Host, to whom are we the pests?"),   30
   contracted and demanded a retreat
from our machine and its effect of death,
   as if the mouse's fingers, skinnier
than hairpins and as breakable as cheese,
   could grasp our grasping lives, and in   35
their drowning movement pull us under too,
into the common death beyond the mousetrap.

1961

QUESTIONS

1. What is your initial response to the title? How does it influence your first reading of the poem?
2. Identify the religious allusions. Are they serious? comic? ironic?
3. What connections from the first line to the last does the narrator see between himself and the mouse?
4. What attitude does the narrator have toward the mouse? Does it change within the poem?

ROBERT DUNCAN
(b. 1919)

MY MOTHER WOULD BE A FALCONRESS   210

My mother would be a falconress,
And I, her gay falcon treading her wrist,
would fly to bring back
from the blue of the sky to her, bleeding, a prize,
where I dream in my little hood with many bells   5
jangling when I'd turn my head.

My mother would be a falconress,
and she sends me as far as her will goes.
She lets me ride to the end of her curb
where I fall back in anguish.   10
I dread that she will cast me away,
for I fall, I mis-take, I fail in her mission.

She would bring down the little birds.
And I would bring down the little birds.
When will she let me bring down the little birds,   15
pierced from their flight with their necks broken,
their heads like flowers limp from the stem?

I tread my mother's wrist and would draw blood.
Behind the little hood my eyes are hooded.
I have gone back into my hooded silence,   20
talking to myself and dropping off to sleep.

For she has muffled my dreams in the hood she has made me,
sewn round with bells, jangling when I move.
She rides with her little falcon upon her wrist.
She uses a barb that brings me to cower.   25
She sends me abroad to try my wings

and I come back to her. I would bring down
the little birds to her
I may not tear into, I must bring back perfectly.

I tear at her wrist with my beak to draw blood,   30
and her eye holds me, anguisht, terrifying.
She draws a limit to my flight.
Never beyond my sight, she says.
She trains me to fetch and to limit myself in fetching.
She rewards me with meat for my dinner.   35
But I must never eat what she sends me to bring her.

Yet it would have been beautiful, if she would have carried me,
always, in a little hood with the bells ringing,
at her wrist, and her riding
to the great falcon hunt, and me   40
flying up to the curb of my heart from her heart
to bring down the skylark from the blue to her feet,
straining, and then released for the flight.

My mother would be a falconress,
and I her gerfalcon, raised at her will,   45
from her wrist sent flying, as if I were her own
pride, as if her pride
knew no limits, as if her mind
sought in me flight beyond the horizon.

Ah, but high, high in the air I flew.   50
And far, far beyond the curb of her will,
were the blue hills where the falcons nest.
And then I saw west to the dying sun—
it seemed my human soul went down in flames.

I tore at her wrist, at the hold she had for me,   55
until the blood ran hot and I heard her cry out,
far, far beyond the curb of her will

to horizons of stars beyond the ringing hills of the world where the
        falcons nest
I saw, and I tore at her wrist with my savage beak.
I flew, as if sight flew from the anguish in her eye beyond her sight, 60
sent from my striking loose, from the cruel strike at her wrist,
striking out from the blood to be free of her.

MY MOTHER WOULD BE A FALCONRESS 45 *gerfalcon:* large falcon.

My mother would be a falconress,
and even now, years after this,
when the wounds I left her had surely heald,   65
and the woman is dead,
her fierce eyes closed, and if her heart
were broken, it is stilld

I would be a falcon and go free.
I tread her wrist and wear the hood,   70
talking to myself, and would draw blood.

                                                        1966

RICHARD EBERHART
(b. 1904)

ANALOGUE OF UNITY IN MULTEITY   211

A man of massive meditation
Is like a man looking at death,
Looking at death as at a bull's-eye.
He watches before he crosses the tracks.

   Every day a man is in a box,   5
   Hourly he watches the trains go by,
   Opening and closing the wooden gates,
   As one who is interested in the world.

The man who is massive in thought,
As it were of mountainous fortitude,   10
Whom decades have seasoned in male beauty,
Whose clarity is an age of harmony,

A man of intellectual power
Will not be killed by a ribboned artifice.
He is too full of deaths to be undone,   15
Death is his hourly communion.

   Who will say what the gate-keeper thinks?
   A man necessary to the metropolis,
   Comfort he knows, he keeps a comfort station,
   As decades pass on shining steel.   20

   The meditative man, a power of eye,
   Big shouldered, with the torso of a Jove,
   Is master of a world of action,
   An actor in a world of masks.

In complex thought he walks along   25
The most fearless man to be seen,
For with animal nature he is one,
Who looks ever death in the bull's-eye.

Far in the sky another eye
Beholds these creatures in their ways,   30
Indifferent to their differences,
A point of agate reference.

1957

QUESTIONS

1. What are your first reactions to the title? After you have read the poem several times, do you find the title descriptive or ironic?
2. What role does repetition play? How is it connected with the profession of the man and the theme of the poem?
3. What attitude toward death do you find in the poem?
4. How does the final stanza affect the tone of the poem?

T. S. ELIOT
(1888–1965)

THE LOVE SONG OF J. ALFRED PRUFROCK   212

> *S'io credesse che mia risposta fosse*
> *A persona che mai tornasse al mondo,*
> *Questa fiamma staria senza più scosse.*
> *Ma perciocche giammai di questo fondo*
> *Non tornò vivo alcun, s'i'odo il vero,*
> *Senza tema d'infamia ti rispondo.*

Let us go then, you and I,
When the evening is spread out against the sky
Like a patient etherized upon a table;
Let us go, through certain half-deserted streets,
The muttering retreats   5
Of restless nights in one-night cheap hotels
And sawdust restaurants with oyster-shells:
Streets that follow like a tedious argument

THE LOVE SONG OF J. ALFRED PRUFROCK epigraph: "If I thought my answer were given to anyone who would ever return to the world, this flame would stand still without moving any further. But since never from this abyss has anyone ever returned alive, if what I hear is true, without fear of infamy I answer thee." From Dante's *Inferno,* these words are spoken by Guido da Montelfeltro who has been shut inside a flame, the punishment for false counselors.

Of insidious intent
To lead you to an overwhelming question. . .   10
Oh, do not ask, "What is it?"
Let us go and make our visit.

In the room the women come and go
Talking of Michelangelo.

The yellow fog that rubs its back upon the window-panes   15
The yellow smoke that rubs its muzzle on the window-panes
Licked its tongue into the corners of the evening,
Lingered upon the pools that stand in drains,
Let fall upon its back the soot that falls from chimneys,
Slipped by the terrace, made a sudden leap,   20
And seeing that it was a soft October night,
Curled once about the house, and fell asleep.

And indeed there will be time
For the yellow smoke that slides along the street,
Rubbing its back upon the window-panes;   25
There will be time, there will be time
To prepare a face to meet the faces that you meet;
There will be time to murder and create,
And time for all the works and days of hands
That lift and drop a question on your plate;   30
Time for you and time for me,
And time yet for a hundred indecisions,
And for a hundred visions and revisions,
Before the taking of a toast and tea.

In the room the women come and go   35
Talking of Michelangelo.

And indeed there will be time
To wonder, "Do I dare?" and, "Do I dare?"
Time to turn back and descend the stair,
With a bald spot in the middle of my hair—   40
[They will say: "How his hair is growing thin!"]
My morning coat, my collar mounting firmly to the chin,
My necktie rich and modest, but asserted by a simple pin—
[They will say: "But how his arms and legs are thin!"]
Do I dare   45
Disturb the universe?
In a minute there is time
For decisions and revisions which a minute will reverse.

For I have known them all already, known them all:
Have known the evenings, mornings, afternoons,   50
I have measured out my life with coffee spoons;
I know the voices dying with a dying fall
Beneath the music from a farther room.
    So how should I presume?

And I have known the eyes already, known them all—   55
The eyes that fix you in a formulated phrase,
And when I am formulated, sprawling on a pin,
When I am pinned and wriggling on the wall,
Then how should I begin
To spit out all the butt-ends of my days and ways?   60
    And how should I presume?

And I have known the arms already, known them all—
Arms that are braceleted and white and bare
[But in the lamplight, downed with light brown hair!]
Is it perfume from a dress   65
That makes me so digress?
Arms that lie along a table, or wrap about a shawl.
    And should I then presume?
    And how should I begin?

                    . . . . .

Shall I say, I have gone at dusk through narrow streets   70
And watched the smoke that rises from the pipes
Of lonely men in shirt-sleeves, leaning out of windows? . . .

I should have been a pair of ragged claws
Scuttling across the floors of silent seas.

                    . . . . .

And the afternoon, the evening, sleeps so peacefully!   75
Smoothed by long fingers,
Asleep . . . tired . . . or it malingers,
Stretched on the floor, here beside you and me.
Should I, after tea and cakes and ices,
Have the strength to force the moment to its crisis?   80
But though I have wept and fasted, wept and prayed,
Though I have seen my head [grown slightly bald] brought in upon a
        platter,
I am no prophet—and here's no great matter;

---

82 *head . . . brought in upon a platter:* the prophet John the Baptist was beheaded and his head was
presented on a platter to Salome.

I have seen the moment of my greatness flicker,
And I have seen the eternal Footman hold my coat, and snicker,   85
And in short, I was afraid.

And would it have been worth it, after all,
After the cups, the marmalade, the tea,
Among the porcelain, among some talk of you and me,
Would it have been worth while,   90
To have bitten off the matter with a smile,
To have squeezed the universe into a ball
To roll it toward some overwhelming question,
To say: "I am Lazarus, come from the dead,
Come back to tell you all, I shall tell you all"—   95
If one, settling a pillow by her head,
    Should say: "That is not what I meant at all.
    That is not it, at all."

And would it have been worth it, after all,
Would it have been worth while,   100
After the sunsets and the dooryards and the sprinkled streets,
After the novels, after the teacups, after the skirts that trail along the
    floor—
And this, and so much more?—
It is impossible to say just what I mean!
But as if a magic lantern threw the nerves in patterns on a screen: 105
Would it have been worth while
If one, settling a pillow or throwing off a shawl,
And turning toward the window, should say:
    "That is not it at all,
    That is not what I meant, at all."   110

                    . . . . .

No! I am not Prince Hamlet, nor was meant to be;
Am an attendant lord, one that will do
To swell a progress, start a scene or two,
Advise the prince; no doubt, an easy tool,
Deferential, glad to be of use,   115
Politic, cautious, and meticulous;
Full of high sentence, but a bit obtuse;
At times, indeed, almost ridiculous—
Almost, at times, the Fool.

I grow old . . . I grow old . . .   120
I shall wear the bottoms of my trousers rolled.

94 *Lazarus:* Jesus raised Lazarus from the dead.

Shall I part my hair behind? Do I dare to eat a peach?
I shall wear white flannel trousers, and walk upon the beach.
I have heard the mermaids singing, each to each.

I do not think that they will sing to me.   125

I have seen them riding seaward on the waves
Combing the white hair of the waves blown back
When the wind blows the water white and black.

We have lingered in the chambers of the sea
By sea-girls wreathed with seaweed red and brown   130
Till human voices wake us, and we drown.

1917

QUESTIONS

1. Eliot said the "you" of the poem referred to Prufrock's male friend. Read the epigraph and first twelve lines with this in mind:

   • Reread those lines, identifying the "you" as a female companion.
   • Read again, this time identifying the "you" with yourself, the reader.

   Which reading is most convincing for you? Reread the entire poem with your choice in mind.
2. Characterize Prufrock. What does he want? What is he afraid of? What has he done already with his life?
3. Identify all of the questions throughout the poem. Do you see a developing pattern of questioning? Does he answer all of his questions?
4. Are the mermaids at the end of the poem a sign of hope or despair?

SWEENEY AMONG THE NIGHTINGALES   213

ὤμοι, πέπληγμαι καιρίαν πληγὴν ἔσω.

Apeneck Sweeney spreads his knees
Letting his arms hang down to laugh,
The zebra stripes along his jaw
Swelling to maculate giraffe.

   The circles of the stormy moon   5
Slide westward toward the River Plate,
Death and the Raven drift above
And Sweeney guards the hornèd gate.

SWEENEY AMONG THE NIGHTINGALES epigraph: "Oh, I have been struck a direct deadly blow, within!" from Aeschylus' *Agamemnon*. 4 *maculate*: spotted. 6 *River Plate*: Rio de la Plata on the southeast coast of South America, extending between Argentina and Uruguay. 7 *the Raven*: Corvus, a southern constellation. 8 *the hornèd gate*: according to Greek legend, dreams could enter through two gates: ivory gates for untrue dreams or gates of horn for true dreams.

Gloomy Orion and the Dog
Are veiled; and hushed the shrunken seas;   10
The person in the Spanish cape
Tries to sit on Sweeney's knees

    Slips and pulls the table cloth
Overturns a coffee-cup,
Reorganized upon the floor   15
She yawns and draws a stocking up;

    The silent man in mocha brown
Sprawls at the window-sill and gapes;
The waiter brings in oranges
Bananas figs and hothouse grapes;   20

    The silent vertebrate in brown
Contracts and concentrates, withdraws;
Rachel *née* Rabinovitch
Tears at the grapes with murderous paws;

    She and the lady in the cape   25
Are suspect, thought to be in league;
Therefore the man with heavy eyes
Declines the gambit, shows fatigue,

    Leaves the room and reappears
Outside the window, leaning in,   30
Branches of wistaria
Circumscribe a golden grin;

    The host with someone indistinct
Converses at the door apart,
The nightingales are singing near   35
The Convent of the Sacred Heart,

    And sang within the bloody wood
When Agamemnon cried aloud,
And let their liquid siftings fall
To stain the stiff dishonored shroud.   40

    1919

9 *Orion:* a constellation containing a hunter and his dog-star, Sirius.

JOURNEY OF THE MAGI   214

'A cold coming we had of it,
Just the worst time of the year
For a journey, and such a long journey:
The ways deep and the weather sharp,
The very dead of winter.'   5
And the camels galled, sore-footed, refractory,
Lying down in the melting snow.
There were times we regretted
The summer palaces on slopes, the terraces,
And the silken girls bringing sherbet.   10
Then the camel men cursing and grumbling
And running away, and wanting their liquor and women,
And the night-fires going out, and the lack of shelters,
And the cities hostile and the towns unfriendly
And the villages dirty and charging high prices: 15
A hard time we had of it.
At the end we preferred to travel all night,
Sleeping in snatches,
With the voices singing in our ears, saying
That this was all folly.   20

Then at dawn we came down to a temperate valley,
Wet, below the snow line, smelling of vegetation;
With a running stream and a water-mill beating the darkness,
And three trees on the low sky,
And an old white horse galloped away in the meadow.   25
Then we came to a tavern with vine-leaves over the lintel,
Six hands at an open door dicing for pieces of silver,
And feet kicking the empty wine-skins.
But there was no information, and so we continued
And arrived at evening, not a moment too soon   30
Finding the place; it was (you may say) satisfactory.

All this was a long time ago, I remember,
And I would do it again, but set down
This set down
This: were we led all that way for   35
Birth or Death? There was a Birth, certainly,
We had evidence and no doubt. I had seen birth and death,
But had thought they were different; this Birth was
Hard and bitter agony for us, like Death, our death.

We returned to our places, these Kingdoms,   40
But no longer at ease here, in the old dispensation,
With an alien people clutching their gods.
I should be glad of another death.

                                                                 1927

QUEEN ELIZABETH I
(1533–1603)

WHEN I WAS FAIR AND YOUNG   215

When I was fair and young, and favor gracéd me,
Of many was I sought, their mistress for to be;
But I did scorn them all, and answered them therefore,
   "Go, go, go seek some otherwhere!
     Importune me no more!"   5

How many weeping eyes I made to pine with woe,
How many sighing hearts, I have no skill to show;
Yet I the prouder grew, and answered them therefore,
   "Go, go, go seek some otherwhere!
     Importune me no more!"   10

Then spake fair Venus' son, that proud victorious boy,
And said, "Fine dame, since that you be so coy,
I will so pluck your plumes that you shall say no more,
   'Go, go, go seek some otherwhere!
     Importune me no more!' "   15

When he had spake these words, such change grew in my breast
That neither night nor day since that, I could take any rest.
Then lo! I did repent that I had said before,
   "Go, go, go seek some otherwhere!
     Importune me no more!"   20

                                                              c. 1585

LAWRENCE FERLINGHETTI
(b. 1919)

[CONSTANTLY RISKING ABSURDITY]   216

Constantly risking absurdity
             and death
   whenever he performs
        above the heads

of his audience

the poet like an acrobat   5
climbs on rime
to a high wire of his own making

and balancing on eyebeams
above a sea of faces

paces his way   10
to the other side of day

performing entrechats
and sleight-of-foot tricks

and other high theatrics
and all without mistaking   15
any thing
for what it may not be

For he's the super realist
who must perforce perceive

taut truth   20
before the taking of each stance or step

in his supposed advance
toward that still higher perch

where Beauty stands and waits
with gravity   25
to start her death-defying leap

And he
a little charleychaplin man
who may or may not catch

her fair eternal form   30
spreadeagled in the empty air

of existence
1955

QUESTIONS

1. How does Ferlinghetti describe readers of poetry and what is his attitude toward them?
2. At what point does the simile begin to turn into allegory?
3. What do you associate with "little charleychaplin man" (line 29)? How do those associations also describe the poet?
4. Does the poem present the poet as a hero or as a ridiculous figure?

CONSTANTLY RISKING ABSURDITY 13 *entrechats:* a leap in ballet during which the dancer crosses the feet a number of times, often beating them together.

[SOMETIME DURING ETERNITY]   217

Sometime during eternity
                    some guys show up
and one of them
            who shows up real late
                        is a kind of carpenter   5
    from some square-type place
                        like Galilee
        and he starts wailing
                    and claiming he is hip
            to who made heaven   10
                        and earth
                            and that the cat
            who really laid it on us
                        is his Dad

And moreover   15
    he adds
            It's all writ down
                        on some scroll-type parchments
        which some henchmen
                    leave lying around the Dead Sea somewheres 20
        a long time ago
                    and which you won't even find
for a coupla thousand years or so
                    or at least for
nineteen hundred and fortyseven   25
                        of them
            to be exact
                    and even then
nobody really believes them
                        or me   30
                        for that matter

You're hot
            they tell him

And they cool him

They stretch him on the Tree to cool   35

SOMETIME DURING ETERNITY 20 *Dead Sea:* the Dead Sea Scrolls, discovered in 1947, provide evidence for the historical life of Christ.

And everybody after that
　　　　　　　　is always making models
　　of this Tree
　　　　with Him hung up
and always crooning His name　　　　　　　　　　　40
　　　　　　　and calling Him to come down
　　　and sit in
　　　　　on their combo
　　as if he is *the* king cat
　　　　　　　who's got to blow　　　　　　　　45
　　or they can't quite make it

Only he don't come down
　　　　　　from His Tree

Him just hang there
　　　　　on His Tree　　　　　　　　　　　　　50
　　　　　　looking real Petered out
　　and real cool
　　　　　and also
　　according to a roundup
　　　　　　　of late world news　　　　　　55
from the usual unreliable sources
　　　　　　real dead

1958

ANNE FINCH, COUNTESS OF WINCHILSEA

(1661–1720)

A NOCTURNAL REVERIE　　　　　　　218

In such a night, when every louder wind
Is to its distant cavern safe confined;
And only gentle Zephyr fans his wings,
And lonely Philomel, still waking, sings;
Or from some tree, famed for the owl's delight,　　　5
She, hollowing clear, directs the wanderer right:
In such a night, when passing clouds give place,
Or thinly veil the heavens' mysterious face;
When in some river, overhung with green,
The waving moon and trembling leaves are seen;　　10

A NOCTURNAL REVERIE 4 *Philomel:* nightingale.

When freshened grass now bears itself upright,
And makes cool banks to pleasing rest invite,
Whence springs the woodbind, and the bramble-rose,
And where the sleepy cowslip sheltered grows;
Whilst now a paler hue the foxglove takes,   15
Yet checkers still with red the dusky brakes.
When scattered glow-worms, but in twilight fine,
Show trivial beauties watch their hour to shine;
Whilst Salisbury stands the test of every light,
In perfect charms, and perfect virtue bright: 20
When odors, which declined repelling day,
Through temperate air uninterrupted stray;
When darkened groves their softest shadows wear,
And falling waters we distinctly hear;
When through the gloom more venerable shows   25
Some ancient fabric, awful in repose,
While sunburnt hills their swarthy looks conceal,
And swelling haycocks thicken up the vale:
When the loosed horse now, as his pasture leads,
Comes slowly grazing through the adjoining meads,   30
Whose stealing pace, and lengthened shade we fear,
Till torn-up forage in his teeth we hear:
When nibbling sheep at large pursue their food,
And unmolested kine rechew the cud;
When curlews cry beneath the village walls,   35
And to her straggling brood the partridge calls;
Their shortlived jubilee the creatures keep,
Which but endures, whilst tyrant man does sleep;
When a sedate content the spirit feels,
And no fierce light disturbs, whilst it reveals;   40
But silent musings urge the mind to seek
Something, too high for syllables to speak;
Till the free soul to a composedness charmed,
Finding the elements of rage disarmed,
O'er all below a solemn quiet grown,   45
Joys in the inferior world, and thinks it like her own:
In such a night let me abroad remain,
Till morning breaks, and all's confused again;
Our cares, our toils, our clamors are renewed,
Or pleasures, seldom reached, again pursued.   50

1713

---

16 *brakes:* thickets. 19 *Salisbury:* Lady Salisbury. 26 *fabric:* building. 34 *kine:* cattle. 35 *curlews:* long-legged shore birds. 46 *inferior:* lower.

CAROLYN FORCHÉ
(b. 1950)

SELECTIVE SERVICE   219

We rise from the snow where we've
lain on our backs and flown like children,
from the imprint of perfect wings and cold gowns,
and we stagger together wine-breathed into town
where our people are building   5
their armies again, short years after
body bags, after burnings. There is a man
I've come to love after thirty, and we have
our rituals of coffee, of airports, regret.
After love we smoke and sleep   10
with magazines, two shot glasses
and the black and white collapse of hours.
In what time do we live that it is too late
to have children? In what place
that we consider the various ways to leave?   15
There is no list long enough
for a selective service card shriveling
under a match, the prison that comes of it,
a flag in the wind eaten from its pole
and boys sent back in trash bags.   20
We'll tell you. You were at that time
learning fractions. We'll tell you
about fractions. Half of us are dead or quiet
or lost. Let them speak for themselves.
We lie down in the fields and leave behind   25
the corpses of angels.

1977

CITY WALK-UP, WINTER 1969   220

There is the morning shuffle of traffic confined
to a window, the blue five p.m. of a street
light, a yellow supper left untouched.
A previous month is pinned to the wall where
days are numbered differently and described by   5
the photograph of a dead season. If I could
move from the bed I would clear the window
and cold-palmed watch myself at twenty, walking

in frozen socks with sacks of clothes and letters,
wearing three winter coats from Goodwill,   10
keeping a footing on the slick silence
of the hysterical deaf. When I tell of my life
now it is not this version.

I would see her climb three flights
of a condemned house with her bags   15
because she is still awakened
by a wrecking ball swung to the attic ribs
and the shelled daylight that followed her
everywhere after that: a silent implosion
of rooms, the xylophone bells as a fire   20
escape plummeted toward the ice.
Even now the house itself is etched
on the hard black air where it had been.
No one knew about it then: meals
of raw egg and snow, rolls of insulation   25
in which she wrapped herself, a blanket
of brown paper and spun glass.
From Kosinski she took the idea of a tin
can, its white lard given to birds, small
holes of punched light on her face.   30
She wrote names on walls and was aware
of her hands, chewing the skin into small
white scraps around each nail. She still
eats her hands and steals bread: street
screamer, housewife, supermarket thief.   35

We do not rid ourselves of these things
even when we are cured of personal silence
when for no reason one morning
we begin to hear the noise of the world again.

1977

ROBERT FROST
(1874–1963)

MENDING WALL   221

Something there is that doesn't love a wall,
That sends the frozen-ground-swell under it,
And spills the upper boulders in the sun;
And makes gaps even two can pass abreast.

The work of hunters is another thing: 5
I have come after them and made repair
Where they have left not one stone on a stone,
But they would have the rabbit out of hiding,
To please the yelping dogs. The gaps I mean,
No one has seen them made or heard them made,   10
But at spring mending-time we find them there.
I let my neighbor know beyond the hill;
And on a day we meet to walk the line
And set the wall between us once again.
We keep the wall between us as we go.   15
To each the boulders that have fallen to each.
And some are loaves and some so nearly balls
We have to use a spell to make them balance:
"Stay where you are until our backs are turned!"
We wear our fingers rough with handling them.   20
Oh, just another kind of outdoor game,
One on a side. It comes to little more:
There where it is we do not need the wall:
He is all pine and I am apple orchard.
My apple trees will never get across   25
And eat the cones under his pines, I tell him.
He only says, "Good fences make good neighbors."
Spring is the mischief in me, and I wonder
If I could put a notion in his head:
'Why do they make good neighbors? Isn't it   30
Where there are cows? But here there are no cows.
Before I built a wall I'd ask to know
What I was walling in or walling out,
And to whom I was like to give offense.
Something there is that doesn't love a wall,   35
That wants it down.' I could say "Elves" to him,
But it's not elves exactly, and I'd rather
He said it for himself. I see him there
Bringing a stone grasped firmly by the top
In each hand, like an old-stone savage armed.   40
He moves in darkness as it seems to me,
Not of woods only and the shade of trees.
He will not go behind his father's saying,
And he likes having thought of it so well
He says again, "Good fences make good neighbors."   45

1914

QUESTIONS

1. What comes to mind as you read:

    Oh, just another kind of outdoor game,
    One on a side. . . .

    Does your experience with outdoor games help you see more clearly the relationship
    between these two men? How?
2. What are the various reasons for the gaps in the wall? What does the narrator want
    to say to his neighbor? Does he say it?
3. "Good fences make good neighbors" is often represented as a piece of Robert Frost's
    homespun philosophy. Does examining it in the context of this poem change its
    meaning for you?

AFTER APPLE-PICKING   222

My long two-pointed ladder's sticking through a tree
Toward heaven still,
And there's a barrel that I didn't fill
Beside it, and there may be two or three
Apples I didn't pick upon some bough.   5
But I am done with apple-picking now.
Essence of winter sleep is on the night,
The scent of apples: I am drowsing off.
I cannot rub the strangeness from my sight
I got from looking through a pane of glass   10
I skimmed this morning from the drinking trough
And held against the world of hoary grass.
It melted, and I let it fall and break.
But I was well
Upon my way to sleep before it fell,   15
And I could tell
What form my dreaming was about to take.
Magnified apples appear and disappear,
Stem end and blossom end,
And every fleck of russet showing clear.   20
My instep arch not only keeps the ache,
It keeps the pressure of a ladder-round.
I feel the ladder sway as the boughs bend.
And I keep hearing from the cellar bin
The rumbling sound   25
Of load on load of apples coming in.
For I have had too much
Of apple-picking: I am overtired

Of the great harvest I myself desired.
There were ten thousand thousand fruit to touch,   30
Cherish in hand, lift down, and not let fall.
For all
That struck the earth,
No matter if not bruised or spiked with stubble,
Went surely to the cider-apple heap   35
As of no worth.
One can see what will trouble
This sleep of mine, whatever sleep it is.
Were he not gone,
The woodchuck could say whether it's like his   40
Long sleep, as I describe its coming on,
Or just some human sleep.

1914

THE ROAD NOT TAKEN   223

Two roads diverged in a yellow wood,
And sorry I could not travel both
And be one traveler, long I stood
And looked down one as far as I could
To where it bent in the undergrowth;   5

Then took the other, as just as fair,
And having perhaps the better claim,
Because it was grassy and wanted wear;
Though as for that, the passing there
Had worn them really about the same,   10

And both that morning equally lay
In leaves no step had trodden black.
Oh, I kept the first for another day!
Yet knowing how way leads on to way,
I doubted if I should ever come back.   15

I shall be telling this with a sigh
Somewhere ages and ages hence:
Two roads diverged in a wood, and I—
I took the one less traveled by,
And that has made all the difference.   20

1916

QUESTIONS

1. If you studied this poem in junior high or high school, what do you remember about your conclusions?
2. Why did the speaker choose the road he did?
3. What is the effect of his observation in lines 9 and 10 on the way you read his previous assertion?
4. Are there any contradictions between his description in lines 11–12 and earlier descriptions of the roads?
5. What makes his exclamation in line 13 lose credibility?
6. Is there any irony in the poem?

RANGE-FINDING   224

The battle rent a cobweb diamond-strung
And cut a flower beside a ground bird's nest
Before it stained a single human breast.
The stricken flower bent double and so hung.
And still the bird revisited her young.   5
A butterfly its fall had dispossessed
A moment sought in air his flower of rest,
Then lightly stooped to it and fluttering clung.
On the bare upland pasture there had spread
O'ernight 'twixt mullein stalks a wheel of thread   10
And straining cables wet with silver dew.
A sudden passing bullet shook it dry.
The indwelling spider ran to greet the fly,
But finding nothing, sullenly withdrew.

1916

BIRCHES   225

When I see birches bend to left and right
Across the lines of straighter darker trees,
I like to think some boy's been swinging them.
But swinging doesn't bend them down to stay.
As ice-storms do. Often you must have seen them   5
Loaded with ice a sunny winter morning
After a rain. They click upon themselves
As the breeze rises, and turn many-colored

RANGE-FINDING 10 *mullein:* woolly leaved plant with yellow flowers.

As the stir cracks and crazes their enamel.
Soon the sun's warmth makes them shed crystal shells   10
Shattering and avalanching on the snow-crust—
Such heaps of broken glass to sweep away
You'd think the inner dome of heaven had fallen.
They are dragged to the withered bracken by the load,
And they seem not to break; though once they are bowed   15
So low for long, they never right themselves:
You may see their trunks arching in the woods
Years afterwards, trailing their leaves on the ground
Like girls on hands and knees that throw their hair
Before them over their heads to dry in the sun.   20
But I was going to say when Truth broke in
With all her matter-of-fact about the ice-storm
I should prefer to have some boy bend them
As he went out and in to fetch the cows—
Some boy too far from town to learn baseball,   25
Whose only play was what he found himself,
Summer or winter, and could play alone.
One by one he subdued his father's trees
By riding them down over and over again
Until he took the stiffness out of them,   30
And not one but hung limp, not one was left
For him to conquer. He learned all there was
To learn about not launching out too soon
And so not carrying the tree away
Clear to the ground. He always kept his poise   35
To the top branches, climbing carefully
With the same pains you use to fill a cup
Up to the brim, and even above the brim.
Then he flung outward, feet first, with a swish,
Kicking his way down through the air to the ground.   40
So was I once myself a swinger of birches.
And so I dream of going back to be.
It's when I'm weary of considerations,
And life is too much like a pathless wood
Where your face burns and tickles with the cobwebs   45
Broken across it, and one eye is weeping
From a twig's having lashed across it open.
I'd like to get away from earth awhile
And then come back to it and begin over.

May no fate willfully misunderstand me 50
And half grant what I wish and snatch me away
Not to return. Earth's the right place for love:
I don't know where it's likely to go better.
I'd like to go by climbing a birch tree,
And climb black branches up a snow-white trunk 55
Toward heaven, till the tree could bear no more,
But dipped its top and set me down again.
That would be good both going and coming back.
One could do worse than be a swinger of birches.

1916

STOPPING BY WOODS ON A SNOWY EVENING 226

Whose woods these are I think I know
His house is in the village though;
He will not see me stopping here
To watch his woods fill up with snow.

My little horse must think it queer 5
To stop without a farmhouse near
Between the woods and frozen lake
The darkest evening of the year.

He gives his harness bells a shake
To ask if there is some mistake. 10
The only other sound's the sweep
Of easy wind and downy flake.

The woods are lovely, dark and deep.
But I have promises to keep,
And miles to go before I sleep, 15
And miles to go before I sleep.

1923

QUESTIONS

1. This is a poem you probably have read before. How must you read it to make it a fresh experience once again?
2. Why does the speaker stop? Who and what is he aware of as he stops? What does this awareness tell you about him?
3. Why does he decide to move on?
4. What do you think is intended by the repetition of the final two lines?

FIRE AND ICE   227

Some say the world will end in fire,
Some say in ice.
From what I've tasted of desire
I hold with those who favor fire.
But if it had to perish twice,   5
I think I know enough of hate
To say that for destruction ice
Is also great
And would suffice.

                                                        1923

NOTHING GOLD CAN STAY   228

Nature's first green is gold,
Her hardest hue to hold.
Her early leaf's a flower;
But only so an hour.
Then leaf subsides to leaf.   5
So Eden sank to grief,
So dawn goes down to day.
Nothing gold can stay.

                                                        1923

ACQUAINTED WITH THE NIGHT   229

I have been one acquainted with the night.
I have walked out in rain—and back in rain.
I have outwalked the furthest city light.

I have looked down the saddest city lane.
I have passed by the watchman on his beat   5
And dropped my eyes, unwilling to explain.

I have stood still and stopped the sound of feet
When far away an interrupted cry
Came over houses from another street,

But not to call me back or say good-by;   10
And further still at an unearthly height
One luminary clock against the sky

Proclaimed the time was neither wrong nor right.
I have been one acquainted with the night.

1928

PROVIDE, PROVIDE   230

The witch that came (the withered hag)
To wash the steps with pail and rag,
Was once the beauty Abishag,

The picture pride of Hollywood.
Too many fall from great and good   5
For you to doubt the likelihood.

Die early and avoid the fate.
Or if predestined to die late,
Make up your mind to die in state.

Make the whole stock exchange your own!   10
If need be occupy a throne,
Where nobody can call *you* crone.

Some have relied on what they knew;
Others on being simple true.
What worked for them might work for you.   15

No memory of having starred
Atones for later disregard,
Or keeps the end from being hard.

Better to go down dignified
With boughten friendship at your side   20
Than none at all. Provide, provide!

1936

DESIGN   231

I found a dimpled spider, fat and white,
On a white heal-all, holding up a moth
Like a white piece of rigid satin cloth—
Assorted characters of death and blight

PROVIDE, PROVIDE 3 *Abishag:* in the Old Testament, a beautiful girl brought to comfort King David
in his old age.
DESIGN 2 *heal-all:* a plant thought to have healing powers.

Mixed ready to begin the morning right, 5
Like the ingredients of a witches' broth—
A snow-drop spider, a flower like froth,
And dead wings carried like a paper kite.

What had that flower to do with being white,
The wayside blue and innocent heal-all? 10
What brought the kindred spider to that height,
Then steered the white moth thither in the night?
What but design of darkness to appall?—
If design govern in a thing so small.

1936

QUESTIONS

1. The original version of this poem was as follows:

> A dented spider like a snowdrop white
> On a white Heal-all, holding up a moth
> Like a white peace of lifeless satin cloth—
> Saw ever curious eye so strange a sight?
> Portent in little, assorted death and blight
> Like the ingredients of a witches' broth?
> The beady spider, the flower like a froth,
> And the moth carried like a paper kite.
> What had that flower to do with being white,
> The blue Brunnella every child's delight?
> What brought the kindred spider to that height?
> (Make we no thesis of the miller's plight.)
> What but design of darkness and of night?
> Design, design! Do I use the word aright?

Which do you think is the better poem? Why?
2. How does the form of the poem contribute to its meaning?
3. How do the similes unify the poem?

NEITHER OUT FAR NOR IN DEEP   232

The people along the sand
All turn and look one way.
They turn their back on the land.
They look at the sea all day.

As long as it takes to pass 5
A ship keeps raising its hull;
The wetter ground like glass
Reflects a standing gull.

The land may vary more;
But wherever the truth may be—   10
The water comes ashore,
And the people look at the sea.

They cannot look out far.
They cannot look in deep.
But when was that ever a bar   15
To any watch they keep?

                                                        1936

THE SUBVERTED FLOWER   233

She drew back; he was calm;
'It is this that had the power.'
And he lashed his open palm
With the tender-headed flower.
He smiled for her to smile,   5
But she was either blind
Or willfully unkind.
He eyed her for a while
For a woman and a puzzle.
He flicked and flung the flower,   10
And another sort of smile
Caught up like finger tips
The corners of his lips
And cracked his ragged muzzle.
She was standing to the waist   15
In goldenrod and brake,
Her shining hair displaced.
He stretched her either arm
As if she made it ache
To clasp her—not to harm;   20
As if he could not spare
To touch her neck and hair.
'If this has come to us
And not to me alone—'
So she thought she heard him say;   25
Though with every word he spoke
His lips were sucked and blown
And the effort made him choke

THE SUBVERTED FLOWER 16 *brake:* fern.

Like a tiger at a bone.
She had to lean away.   30
She dared not stir a foot,
Lest movement should provoke
The demon of pursuit
That slumbers in a brute.
It was then her mother's call   35
From inside the garden wall
Made her steal a look of fear
To see if he could hear
And would pounce to end it all
Before her mother came.   40
She looked and saw the shame:
A hand hung like a paw,
An arm worked like a saw
As if to be persuasive,
An ingratiating laugh   45
That cut the snout in half,
An eye become evasive.
A girl could only see
That a flower had marred a man,
But what she could not see   50
Was that the flower might be
Other than base and fetid:
That the flower had done but part,
And what the flower began
Her own too meager heart   55
Had terribly completed.
She looked and saw the worst.
And the dog or what it was,
Obeying bestial laws,
A coward save at night,   60
Turned from the place and ran.
She heard him stumble first
And use his hands in flight.
She heard him bark outright.
And oh, for one so young   65
The bitter words she spit
Like some tenacious bit
That will not leave the tongue.
She plucked her lips for it,
And still the horror clung.   70

Her mother wiped the foam
From her chin, picked up her comb,
And drew her backward home.

1942

THE GIFT OUTRIGHT

234

The land was ours before we were the land's.
She was our land more than a hundred years
Before we were her people. She was ours
In Massachusetts, in Virginia,
But we were England's, still colonials,   5
Possessing what we still were unpossessed by,
Possessed by what we now no more possessed.
Something we were withholding made us weak
Until we found it was ourselves
We were withholding from our land of living,   10
And forthwith found salvation in surrender.
Such as we were we gave ourselves outright
(The deed of gift was many deeds of war)
To the land vaguely realizing westward,
But still unstoried, artless, unenhanced,   15
Such as she was, such as she would become.

1942

ISABELLA GARDNER
(1915–1981)

THE WIDOW'S YARD

235

FOR MYRA

"Snails lead slow idyllic lives . . ."
The rose and the laurel leaves
in the raw young widow's yard
were littered with silver. Hard-
ly a leaf lacked the decimal scale   5
of the self of a snail. Frail
in friendship I observed with care
these creatures (meaning to spare
the widow's vulnerable eyes
the hurting pity in my gaze).   10

Snails, I said, are tender skinned.
Excess in nature . . . sun rain wind
are killers. To save themselves
snails shrink to shelter in their shells
where they wait safe and patient   15
until the elements are gent-
ler. And do they not have other foes?
the widow asked. Turtles crows
foxes rats, I replied, and canned
heat that picnickers aband-   20
on. Also parasites invade
their flesh and alien eggs are laid
inside their skins. Their mating
too is perilous. The meeting
turns their faces blue with bliss   25
and consummation of this
absolute embrace is so
extravagantly slow
in coming that love begun
at dawn may end in fatal sun.   30

The widow told me that her
husband knew snails' ways and his gar-
den had been Eden for them. He
said the timid snail could lift three
times his weight straight up and haul   35
a wagon toy loaded with a whole
two hundred times his body's burden.
Then as we left the garden
she said that at the first faint chill
the first premonition of fall   40
the snails go straight to earth . . . excrete
the lime with which they then secrete
the openings in their shells . . . and wait for spring.
It is those little doors which sing,
she said, when they are boiled.   45
She smiled at me when I recoiled.

1980

ALLEN GINSBERG

(b. 1926)

AMERICA   236

America I've given you all and now I'm nothing.
America two dollars and twentyseven cents January 17, 1956.
I can't stand my own mind.
America when will we end the human war?
Go fuck yourself with your atom bomb.   5
I don't feel good don't bother me.
I won't write my poem till I'm in my right mind.
America when will you be angelic?
When will you take off your clothes?
When will you look at yourself through the grave?   10
When will you be worthy of your million Trotskyites?
America why are your libraries full of tears?
America when will you send your eggs to India?
I'm sick of your insane demands.
When can I go into the supermarket and buy what I need with my
    good looks?   15
America after all it is you and I who are perfect not the next world.
Your machinery is too much for me.
You made me want to be a saint.
There must be some other way to settle this argument.
Burroughs is in Tangiers I don't think he'll come back it's sinister.   20
Are you being sinister or is this some form of practical joke?
I'm trying to come to the point.
I refuse to give up my obsession.
America stop pushing I know what I'm doing.
America the plum blossoms are falling.   25
I haven't read the newspapers for months, everyday somebody goes
    on trial for murder.
America I feel sentimental about the Wobblies.
America I used to be a communist when I was a kid I'm not sorry.
I smoke marijuana every chance I get.
I sit in my house for days on end and stare at the roses in the closet. 30
When I go to Chinatown I get drunk and never get laid.
My mind is made up there's going to be trouble.

AMERICA 11 *Trotskyites:* followers of Leon Trotsky (1879–1940), Russian revolutionary and Soviet
statesman. 20 *Burroughs:* William S. Burroughs, author of *Naked Lunch* and *Junkie.* 27 *Wobblies:*
members of the Industrial Workers of the World, many of whom were arrested and imprisoned
from 1919–1921.

You should have seen me reading Marx.
My psychoanalyst thinks I'm perfectly right.
I won't say the Lord's Prayer.   35
I have mystical visions and cosmic vibrations.
America I still haven't told you what you did to Uncle Max after he
    came over from Russia.

I'm addressing you.
Are you going to let your emotional life be run by Time Magazine?
I'm obsessed by Time Magazine.   40
I read it every week.
Its cover stares at me every time I slink past the corner candystore.
I read it in the basement of the Berkeley Public Library.
It's always telling me about responsibility. Businessmen are serious.
    Movie producers are serious. Everybody's serious but me.
It occurs to me that I am America.   45
I am talking to myself again.

Asia is rising against me.
I haven't got a chinaman's chance.
I'd better consider my national resources.
My national resources consist of two joints of marijuana millions of
    genitals an unpublishable private literature that goes 1400 miles
    an hour and twenty-five-thousand mental institutions.   50
I say nothing about my prisons nor the millions of underprivileged
    who live in my flowerpots under the light of five hundred suns.
I have abolished the whorehouses of France, Tangiers is the next to
    go.
My ambition is to be President despite the fact that I'm a Catholic.
America how can I write a holy litany in your silly mood?
I will continue like Henry Ford my strophes are as individual as his
    automobiles more so they're all different sexes.   55
America I will sell you strophes $2500 apiece $500 down on your old
    strophe
America free Tom Mooney
America save the Spanish Loyalists
America Sacco & Vanzetti must not die

57 *Tom Mooney:* radical labor organizer who received the death penalty on charges that he set a
bomb during a San Francisco parade. His sentence was commuted and he was freed after 23 years
in prison. 58 *Spanish Loyalists:* those who fought on the side of the Socialist government of Spain
and against the revolution led by General Francisco Franco. 59 *Sacco & Vanzetti:* Nicola Sacco and
Bartolomeo Vanzetti, anarchists many believe were executed for their radical views rather than for
the crime they committed.

America I am the Scottsboro boys.   60

America when I was seven momma took me to Communist Cell
    meetings they sold us garbanzos a handful per ticket a ticket
    costs a nickel and the speeches were free everybody was angelic
    and sentimental about the workers it was all so sincere you have
    no idea what a good thing the party was in 1835 Scott Nearing
    was a grand old man a real mensch Mother Bloor made me cry I
    once saw Israel Amter plain. Everybody must have been a spy.

America you don't really want to go to war.

America it's them bad Russians.

Them Russians them Russians and them Chinamen. And them
    Russians.

The Russia wants to eat us alive. The Russia's power mad. She wants
    to take our cars from out our garages.   65

Her wants to grab Chicago. Her needs a Red Readers' Digest. Her
    wants our auto plants in Siberia. Him big bureaucracy running
    our fillingstations.

That no good. Ugh. Him make Indians learn read. Him need big
    black niggers. Hah. Her make us all work sixteen hours a day.
    Help.

America this is quite serious.

America this is the impression I get from looking in the television
    set.

America is this correct?   70

I'd better get right down to the job.

It's true I don't want to join the Army or turn lathes in precision
    parts factories, I'm nearsighted and psychopathic anyway.

America I'm putting my queer shoulder to the wheel.

                                                                    1956

QUESTIONS

1. How do you read this poem differently from a poem by, for example, Emily
   Dickinson? How early in the poem do you find clues that this will be a different kind
   of reading experience?
2. Who are the "I" and the "you"?
3. To what extent is this an "insider's" poem—that is, a poem in which a reader *must*
   understand the allusions in order to create a reading? ˙
4. Do you find any attempt to use *form* in this poem?
5. What similarities do you find between this poem and any by Walt Whitman?

60 *Scottsboro boys:* blacks executed in Alabama after an unfair trial during which they were
convicted of raping two white girls. 61 *Scott Nearing:* communist author of *The Conscience of a
Radical; Mother Bloor:* Ella Reeve Bloor, feminist socialist; *Amter:* Israel Amter, leader of the
underground Communist party.

MY SAD SELF

TO FRANK O'HARA

Sometimes when my eyes are red
I go up on top of the RCA Building
    and gaze at my world, Manhattan—
        my buildings, streets I've done feats in,
            lofts, beds, coldwater flats
—on Fifth Ave below which I also bear in mind,
        its ant cars, little yellow taxis, men
            walking the size of specks of wool—
Panorama of the bridges, sunrise over Brooklyn machine,
        sun go down over New Jersey where I was born
            & Paterson where I played with ants—
my later loves on 15th Street,
        my greater loves of Lower East Side,
            my once fabulous amours in the Bronx
                faraway—
paths crossing in these hidden streets,
        my history summed up, my absences
            and ecstasies in Harlem —
        — sun shining down on all I own
            in one eyeblink to the horizon
                in my last eternity—
                    matter is water.

Sad,
    I take the elevator and go
        down, pondering,
and walk on the pavements staring into all man's
                plateglass, faces,
        questioning after who loves,
    and stop, bemused
        in front of an automobile shopwindow
standing lost in calm thought,
        traffic moving up & down 5th Avenue blocks
            behind me
        waiting for a moment when. . . .
Time to go home & cook supper & listen to
        the romantic war news on the radio

            . . . all movement stops
& I walk in the timeless sadness of existence,
    tenderness flowing thru the buildings,
        my fingertips touching reality's face,

my own face streaked with tears in the mirror
　　of some window—at dusk—
　　　　　　where I have no desire—
for bonbons—or to own the dresses or Japanese
　　lampshades of intellection—   45

Confused by the spectacle around me,
　　Man struggling up the street
　　　　with packages, newspapers,
　　　　　　　　ties, beautiful suits
　　　　toward his desire   50
Man, woman, streaming over the pavements
　　　　red lights clocking hurried watches &
　　　　　movements at the curb—

And all these streets leading
　　so crosswise, honking, lengthily,   55
　　　　　by avenues
stalked by high buildings or crusted into slums
　　　　thru such halting traffic
　　　　　　　　screaming cars and engines
so painfully to this   60
　　countryside, this graveyard
　　　　this stillness
　　　　　　　　on deathbed or mountain
　　once seen
　　　　　never regained or desired   65
　　　　　　in the mind to come
where all Manhattan that I've seen must disappear.

1963

NIKKI GIOVANNI
(b. 1943)

KIDNAP POEM   238

ever been kidnapped
by a poet
if i were a poet
i'd kidnap you
put you in my phrases and meter   5
you to jones beach
or maybe coney island
or maybe just to my house

lyric you in lilacs
dash you in the rain 10
blend into the beach
to complement my see
play the lyre for you
ode you with my love song
anything to win you 15
wrap you in the red Black green
show you off to mama
yeah if i were a poet i'd kid
nap you

1970

QUESTIONS

1. What does the rhythm of the first four lines tell you about the speaker's tone of voice?
2. The speaker says "if i were a poet." Is she? What evidence does she give that she is or is not?
3. Where is the irony?
4. "Kidnap" or "kidnapped" appears four times in this poem. How is it different each time?

LOUISE GLÜCK

(b. 1943)

THE SCHOOL CHILDREN 239

The children go forward with their little satchels.
And all morning the mothers have labored
to gather the late apples, red and gold,
like words of another language.

And on the other shore 5
are those who wait behind great desks
to receive these offerings.

How orderly they are—the nails
on which the children hang
their overcoats of blue or yellow wool. 10

And the teachers shall instruct them in silence
and the mothers shall scour the orchards for a way out,
drawing to themselves the gray limbs of the fruit trees
bearing so little ammunition.

1975

QUESTIONS

1. Are there any words or images that surprise you on your first reading?
2. Discuss contrasting images. Does the contrast indicate conflict?
3. What do the colors tell you about the several environments described?
4. What is the "ammunition" in the final line?

POEM   240

In the early evening, as now, a man is bending
over his writing table.
Slowly he lifts his head; a woman
appears, carrying roses.
Her face floats to the surface of the mirror,   5
marked with the green spokes of rose stems.

It is a form
of suffering: then always the transparent page
raised to the window until its veins emerge
as words finally filled with ink.   10

And I am meant to understand
what binds them together
or to the gray house held firmly in place by dusk

because I must enter their lives:
it is spring, the pear tree   15
filming with weak, white blossoms.

                                                            1975

JORIE GRAHAM
(b. 1951)

MY GARDEN, MY DAYLIGHT   241

My neighbor brings me bottom fish—
        tomcod, rockcod—
a fist of ocean. He comes out
        from the appletrees between us
holding his gift like a tight   5
        spool of thread.

Once a week he brings me fresh-catch,
    boned and skinned
and rolled up like a tongue. I freeze them,
    speechless, angelic   10
instruments. I have a choir of them.
    Alive, they feed

driving their bodies through the mud,
    mud through their flesh.
See how white they become. High above,   15
    the water thins
to blue, then air, then less. . . .
    These aren't as sweet

as those that shine up there,
    quick schools   20
forever trying to slur over, become water.
    But these belong to us
who cannot fall out of this world
    but only deeper

into it, driving it into the white   25
    of our eyes. Muddy
daylight, we utter it, we drown in it.
    You can stay dry
if you can step between the raindrops
    mother's mother   30

said. She's words now you can't hear.
    I try to wind my way
between what's here: chalk, lily, milk,
    titanium, snow—
as far as I can say   35
    these appleblossoms house

five shades of white, and yet
    I know there's more.
Between my held breath and its small hot
    death, a garden,   40
Whiteness, grows. Its icy fruit
    seems true,

it glows. *For free* he says
    so that I can't refuse.

1983

QUESTIONS

1. After reading the poem a couple of times, quickly describe its beginning, middle, and end. Do you see a possible thematic development?
2. What connections does the speaker see between bottom fish and herself?
3. What is white in this poem? What connections do you see between and among these images? Does a theme emerge?
4. What part does speech play in the world the speaker describes? Why does she say "as far as I can say" instead of "as far as I can see" in line 35?

MIND   242

The slow overture of rain,
each drop breaking
without breaking into
the next, describes
the unrelenting, syncopated   5
mind. Not unlike
the hummingbirds
imagining their wings
to be their heart, and swallows
believing the horizon   10
to be a line they lift
and drop. What is it
they cast for? The poplars,
advancing or retreating,
lose their stature   15
equally, and yet stand firm,
making arrangements
in order to become
imaginary. The city
draws the mind in streets,   20
and streets compel it
from their intersections
where a little
belongs to no one. It is
what is driven through   25
all stationary portions
of the world, gravity's
stake in things. The leaves,
pressed against the dank
window of November   30
soil, remain unwelcome

till transformed, parts
of a puzzle unsolvable
till the edges give a bit
and soften. See how   35
then the picture becomes clear,
the mind entering the ground
more easily in pieces,
and all the richer for it.

                                                              1983

ROBERT GRAVES
(1895–1985)

THE COOL WEB   243

Children are dumb to say how hot the day is,
How hot the scent is of the summer rose,
How dreadful the black wastes of evening sky,
How dreadful the tall soldiers drumming by.

But we have speech, to chill the angry day,   5
And speech, to dull the rose's cruel scent.
We spell away the overhanging night,
We spell away the soldiers and the fright.

There's a cool web of language winds us in,
Retreat from too much joy or too much fear: 10
We grow sea-green at last and coldly die
In brininess and volubility.

But if we let our tongues lose self-possession,
Throwing off language and its watery clasp
Before our death, instead of when death comes,   15
Facing the wide glare of the children's day,
Facing the rose, the dark sky and the drums,
We shall go mad no doubt and die that way.

                                                              1927

QUESTIONS

1. Does the poem remind you of any childhood fears?
2. What are the characteristics of the child's world?
3. What are the characteristics of the adult's world?
4. What happens when the adult world predominates? What happens
   when the child's world predominates?
5. To what extent is the poem self-critical?

DOWN, WANTON, DOWN!   244

Down, wanton, down! Have you no shame
That at the whisper of Love's name,
Or Beauty's, presto! up you raise
Your angry head and stand at gaze?

Poor bombard-captain, sworn to reach   5
The ravelin and effect a breach—
Indifferent what you storm or why,
So be that in the breach you die!

Love may be blind, but Love at least
Knows what is man and what mere beast;   10
Or Beauty wayward, but requires
More delicacy from her squires.

Tell me, my witless, whose one boast
Could be your staunchness at the post,
When were you made a man of parts   15
To think fine and profess the arts?

Will many-gifted Beauty come
Bowing to your bald rule of thumb,
Or Love swear loyalty to your crown?
Be gone, have done! Down, wanton, down!   20

1933

THOMAS GRAY
(1716–1771)

ELEGY WRITTEN IN A COUNTRY
CHURCHYARD   245

The curfew tolls the knell of parting day,
  The lowing herd wind slowly o'er the lea,
The plowman homeward plods his weary way,
  And leaves the world to darkness and to me.

Now fades the glimmering landscape on the sight,   5
  And all the air a solemn stillness holds,
Save where the beetle wheels his droning flight,
  And drowsy tinklings lull the distant folds;

DOWN, WANTON, DOWN! 5 *bombard-captain*: operator of an early form of cannon that threw stone balls.
6 *ravelin*: a railing or fence.

Save that from yonder ivy-mantled tower
   The moping owl does to the moon complain   10
Of such, as wandering near her secret bower,
   Molest her ancient solitary reign.

Beneath those rugged elms, that yew tree's shade,
   Where heaves the turf in many a moldering heap,
Each in his narrow cell forever laid,   15
   The rude forefathers of the hamlet sleep.

The breezy call of incense-breathing morn,
   The swallow twittering from the straw-built shed,
The cock's shrill clarion, or the echoing horn,
   No more shall rouse them from their lowly bed.   20

For them no more the blazing hearth shall burn,
   Or busy housewife ply her evening care;
No children run to lisp their sire's return,
   Or climb his knees the envied kiss to share.

Oft did the harvest to their sickle yield,   25
   Their furrow oft the stubborn glebe has broke;
How jocund did they drive their team afield!
   How bowed the woods beneath their sturdy stroke!

Let not Ambition mock their useful toil,
   Their homely joys, and destiny obscure;   30
Nor Grandeur hear with a disdainful smile
   The short and simple annals of the poor.

The boast of heraldry, the pomp of power,
   And all that beauty, all that wealth e'er gave,
Awaits alike the inevitable hour.   35
   The paths of glory lead but to the grave.

Nor you, ye proud, impute to these the fault,
   If Memory o'er their tomb no trophies raise,
Where through the long-drawn aisle and fretted vault
   The pealing anthem swells the note of praise.   40

Can storied urn or animated bust
   Back to its mansion call the fleeting breath?
Can Honor's voice provoke the silent dust,
   Or Flattery soothe the dull cold ear of Death?

Elegy Written in a Country Churchyard 16 *rude:* rustic. 26 *glebe:* soil. 39 *fretted:* ornamented. 41
storied urn or animated bust: a funeral urn with a story or epitaph on it; lifelike sculptures.

Perhaps in this neglected spot is laid   45
   Some heart once pregnant with celestial fire;
Hands that the rod of empire might have swayed,
   Or waked to ecstasy the living lyre.

But Knowledge to their eyes her ample page
   Rich with the spoils of time did ne'er unroll;   50
Chill Penury repressed their noble rage,
   And froze the genial current of the soul.

Full many a gem of purest ray serene,
   The dark unfathomed caves of ocean bear:
Full many a flower is born to blush unseen,   55
   And waste its sweetness on the desert air.

Some village Hampden, that with dauntless breast
   The little tyrant of his fields withstood;
Some mute inglorious Milton here may rest,
   Some Cromwell guiltless of his country's blood.   60

The applause of listening senates to command,
   The threats of pain and ruin to despise,
To scatter plenty o'er a smiling land,
   And read their history in a nation's eyes,

Their lot forbade: nor circumscribed alone   65
   Their growing virtues, but their crimes confined;
Forbade to wade through slaughter to a throne,
   And shut the gates of mercy on mankind,

The struggling pangs of conscious truth to hide,
   To quench the blushes of ingenuous shame,   70
Or heap the shrine of Luxury and Pride
   With incense kindled at the Muse's flame.

Far from the madding crowd's ignoble strife,
   Their sober wishes never learned to stray;
Along the cool sequestered vale of life   75
   They kept the noiseless tenor of their way.

Yet even these bones from insult to protect
   Some frail memorial still erected nigh,
With uncouth rhymes and shapeless sculpture decked,
   Implores the passing tribute of a sigh.   80

57 *Hampden:* John Hampden (1594–1643), leader of the opposition to Charles I. 60 *Cromwell:* Oliver Cromwell (1599–1658), leader of the English Civil Wars against Charles I. 73 *madding:* frenzied.

Their name, their years, spelt by the unlettered Muse,
    The place of fame and elegy supply:
And many a holy text around she strews,
    That teach the rustic moralist to die.

For who to dumb Forgetfulness a prey,   85
    This pleasing anxious being e'er resigned,
Left the warm precincts of the cheerful day,
    Nor cast one longing lingering look behind?

On some fond breast the parting soul relies,
    Some pious drops the closing eye requires;   90
Even from the tomb the voice of Nature cries,
    Even in our ashes live their wonted fires.

For thee, who mindful of the unhonored dead
    Dost in these lines their artless tale relate;
If chance, by lonely contemplation led,   95
    Some kindred spirit shall inquire thy fate,

Haply some hoary-headed swain may say,
    "Oft have we seen him at the peep of dawn
Brushing with hasty steps the dews away
    To meet the sun upon the upland lawn.   100

"There at the foot of yonder nodding beech
    That wreathes its old fantastic roots so high,
His listless length at noontide would he stretch,
    And pore upon the brook that babbles by.

"Hard by yon wood, now smiling as in scorn,   105
    Muttering his wayward fancies he would rove,
Now drooping, woeful wan, like one forlorn,
    Or crazed with care, or crossed in hopeless love.

"One morn I missed him on the customed hill,
    Along the heath and near his favorite tree;   110
Another came; nor yet beside the rill,
    Nor up the lawn, nor at the wood was he;

"The next with dirges due in sad array
    Slow through the churchway path we saw him borne.
Approach and read (for thou canst read) the lay,   115
    Graved on the stone beneath yon aged thorn."

The Epitaph

Here rests his head upon the lap of Earth
* A youth to Fortune and to Fame unknown.*
Fair Science frowned not on his humble birth,
* And Melancholy marked him for her own.*   120

Large was his bounty, and his soul sincere,
* Heaven did a recompense as largely send:*
He gave to Misery all he had, a tear,
* He gained from Heaven ('twas all he wished) a friend.*

No farther seek his merits to disclose,   125
* Or draw his frailties from their dread abode*
(There they alike in trembling hope repose),
* The bosom of his Father and his God.*

1751

QUESTIONS

1. How does the word *elegy* influence your first reading of the first four quatrains? Which words and images assume a stronger meaning as a result?
2. Is the lack of opportunity described in lines 45–76 presented as a positive or a negative situation?
3. What do the allusions of lines 57–60 add to this attitude?
4. The speaker does not use the first-person pronoun to refer to himself, yet the poem can be read as a personal statement. What devices does he use to characterize himself and how does he manage to present a vivid picture of himself anyway?

THOM GUNN

(b. 1929)

MOLY   246

Nightmare of beasthood, snorting, how to wake.
I woke. What beasthood skin she made me take?

Leathery toad that ruts for days on end,
Or cringing dribbling dog, man's servile friend,

---

119 *Science:* learning.

MOLY *title:* a magic herb with black roots and white flowers, which protected Odysseus from being turned into a pig as his shipmates had been by the enchantress Circe.

Or cat that prettily pounces on its meat,   5
Tortures it hours, then does not care to eat:

Parrot, moth, shark, wolf, crocodile, ass, flea.
What germs, what jostling mobs there were in me.

   These seem like bristles, and the hide is tough.
No claw or web here: each foot ends in hoof.   10

Into what bulk has method disappeared?
Like ham, streaked. I am gross—grey, gross, flap-eared.

The pale-lashed eyes my only human feature.
My teeth tear, tear. I am the snouted creature

That bites through anything, root, wire, or can.   15
If I was not afraid I'd eat a man.

Oh a man's flesh already is in mine.
Hand and foot poised for risk. Buried in swine.

   I root and root, you think that it is greed,
It is, but I seek out a plant I need.   20

Direct me gods, whose changes are all holy,
To where it flickers deep in grass, the moly:

Cool flesh of magic in each leaf and shoot,
From milk flower to the black forked root.

From this fat dungeon I could rise to skin   25
And human title, putting pig within.

I push my big grey wet snout through the green,
Dreaming the flower I have never seen.

                                                                                        1971

QUESTIONS

1. When do you first realize the identity of the animal speaking?
2. What hints does he unwittingly give earlier in the poem before he really knows
   himself?
3. "What germs, what jostling mobs there were in me," the speaker says in line 8. How
   is this idea developed?
4. How does the speaker feel about himself?

MARILYN HACKER

(b. 1942)

PART OF A TRUE STORY

FOR MARGARET DELANY

"We dress UP!"—NTOZAKE SHANGE

My dear Mrs. Bloomer:
                  The exigencies
of my life demand rational costume.
I noticed recently upon perusal
of a number of your interesting
journal, *The Lily,* that your radical   5
bifurcate garment for gentlewomen
is beyond suggestion; not to mince words,
for sale.
       My people, Mrs. Bloomer, are
as well, south of the District, and until
the last and least of us no longer is   10
chattel, this woman must be radical
to be rational. A woman of color
is gentle as yourself, until provoked.
I have been, since the age of six.
              When I,   15
aged twenty-some, returned to the scene
of my truncated childhood, with the goal
—which I achieved—of bringing forth my mother
and my father from bondage, as I had
my brothers, many of my sisters and   20
brothers, I was obliged, for my safety
and theirs, to come to them in male attire.
(Does *attire* have gender?) I cannot pass
as other than I am in one respect;
nor would I wish to. It was curious   25
passing that other way, where I had passed
before: "This gal can haul as heavy a
load as three men or a mule," et cetera.
A black man is only marginally
more anonymous on a Southern road   30

PART OF A TRUE STORY 1 *Mrs. Bloomer:* Amelia Bloomer, feminist, inventor of "bloomers," editor of *The Lily,* a feminist publication. The letter is written to Bloomer by Harriet Tubman, American abolitionist, nurse, and conductor on the Underground Railroad. 6 *bifurcate:* divided into two parts. 11 *chattel:* a piece of property or a slave.

than a black woman. Dare I confess, I
liked that marginal anonymity?
Crop-headed in a neutral suit of clothes,
I sat, a stranger at my mother's table,
bearing good news she could not bear to hear   35
who bore me, till I bared myself as well,
scarred as I was, to loving scrutiny.
Later, I also bore the scrutiny
of the spouse whom I had reluctantly
left; who, free, had forbidden me to go   40
to freedom. Newly wived, he did not know
me at all, either as woman, or as
myself. It's a peculiar thing: to pass
easily, anonymously, from one
life, or mode of life, to another: done   45
with a forked suit? Night, starvation, a gun
to scare stragglers to courage, sleep in snow
or straw or not at all are what I know
as passage-rites. I do what I can,
but I do not wish to be thought a man   50
again.
        Tonight, four hundred human souls,
still embodied, disembondaged, lie wakeful
or sleep in this rough but hospitable
hospice, this time, taken across water
to free land. You know the name I am called.   55
The straits do not. We cross them nonetheless.
I have another name now: General;
a task I had first as a nursling: Nurse.
We intend to bring out four hundred more.
I wish to be there. It is efficacious   60
that I be there. I must be recognized
though: black, female, and old, or nearly old.
Still, I am of scant use immobilized.
I wish to be relieved of the woolen gown
whose waterlogged skirts and underskirts hold   65
me so, as well as the Confederate
Army would wish. I was nearly drowned.
Thus, Mrs. Bloomer, my request. Disguise
is not wished, or called for. Compromise,
though unaccustomed, is appropriate   70

---

57 *General:* after one operation which freed eight hundred slaves, Harriet Tubman began to call
herself "General Moses."

on this occasion. So is the connection
of our aims. I entertain reflection
that, free and black, I am still disfranchised,
female; a condition I first realized
espoused: bondwoman and freedman, we   75
embodied it. I transcend limitation.
I am a black woman, whose education
was late and little: necessity
of adulthood vowed to emancipation
of my people; the larger limitation   80
imposed by childhood spent in servitude,
leave me comparatively unlettered.
You will receive this missive, dictated
by me to my adjutant, from her
hand, to which I pray you will deliver   85
the costume I desire.
                    Awaiting your
kind reply, I remain,
                    Yours faithfully,
Harriet Tubman   United States Army
Medical Division   Port Royal Island

                                        1985

OPEN WINDOWS   248

1

This isn't about unrequited love
although I'm warmed by your proximity.
I don't yearn for you, wish you wanted me
a different way. I want you to approve
my life, my person: insecurity   5
hamstrings me without reassuring strokes.
Earned trust some careless clumsiness revokes,
some fervid overstatement nullifies:
that's happened. When I'm with you, something ties
me to your mood, should not. You're not my child.   10
I think of feeling absolutely free
outside the Gare Routière, in a blue-tiled
café, alone in France, morning haze, mild
light in my brown hands, cupping it like a prize.

                                        1985

---

84 *adjutant:* a staff officer who helps a commanding officer with administrative affairs. Tubman dictates this letter because she herself is illiterate.

OPEN WINDOWS 249

2

Tonight when I cup my hand beneath your breast
(fountain and pillow of felicity)
your womb shudders with possibility
suctioned from you, and your sigh is pain. Pressed
even gently against me, you ache; the best   5
choice, made, presses us both. How will it be
held between us, this complicity
in what we can't repeat? Silken, we nest
aloft, sleep curled. Reflected from the snow,
a dawn lamp glints up through your tall window.   10
Uptown, my child will wake, ask where's her mother.
Promised, I inhale you, descend from you, gather
scattered woolens, gather my wits to go
from one hard choice, love chosen, to the other.

1985

THOMAS HARDY
(1840– 1928)

HAP 250

If but some vengeful god would call to me
From up the sky, and laugh: "Thou suffering thing,
Know that thy sorrow is my ecstasy,
That thy love's loss is my hate's profiting!"

Then would I bear it, clench myself, and die,   5
Steeled by the sense of ire unmerited;
Half-eased in that a Powerfuller than I
Had willed and meted me the tears I shed.

But not so. How arrives it joy lies slain,
And why unblooms the best hope ever sown?   10
—Crass Casualty obstructs the sun and rain,
And dicing Time for gladness casts a moan. . . .
These purblind Doomsters had as readily strown
Blisses about my pilgrimage as pain.

1898

DRUMMER HODGE

I

They throw in Drummer Hodge, to rest
    Uncoffined—just as found:
His landmark is a kopje-crest
    That breaks the veldt around;
And foreign constellations west   5
    Each night above his mound.

II

Young Hodge the Drummer never knew—
    Fresh from his Wessex home—
The meaning of the broad Karoo,
    The Bush, the dusty loam,   10
And why uprose to nightly view
    Strange stars amid the gloam.

III

Yet portion of that unknown plain
    Will Hodge for ever be;
His homely Northern breast and brain   15
    Grow to some Southern tree,
And strange-eyed constellations reign
    His stars eternally.

1902

THE SUBALTERNS

I

"Poor wanderer," said the leaden sky,
    "I fain would lighten thee,
But there are laws in force on high
    Which say it must not be."

II

—"I would not freeze thee, shorn one," cried   5
    The North, "knew I but how
To warm my breath, to slack my stride;
    But I am ruled as thou."

DRUMMER HODGE title: A soldier killed in the Boer War (1899–1902) in South Africa. 3 *kopje-crest:* a small hill. 4 *veldt:* open grazing areas of southern Africa. 8 *Wessex:* ancient Anglo-Saxon kingdom of southern England. 9 *Karoo:* arid plateau of southern Africa. 10 *Bush:* land covered with dense growth of shrubs; *loam:* soil consisting of sand, clay, and silt. 12 *gloam:* twilight.

THE SUBALTERNS title *subalterns:* subordinates.

III

—"To-morrow I attack thee, wight,"
 Said Sickness.   "Yet I swear
I bear thy little ark no spite,   10
 But am bid enter there."

IV

—"Come hither, Son," I heard Death say;
 "I did not will a grave
Should end thy pilgrimage to-day,   15
 But I, too, am a slave!"

V

We smiled upon each other then,
 And life to me had less
Of that fell look it wore ere when
 They owned their passiveness.   20

                  1902

THE DARKLING THRUSH   253

I leant upon a coppice gate
 When Frost was specter-gray,
And Winter's dregs made desolate
 The weakening eye of day.
The tangled bine-stems scored the sky   5
 Like strings of broken lyres,
And all mankind that haunted nigh
 Had sought their household fires.

The land's sharp features seemed to be
 The Century's corpse outleant,   10
His crypt the cloudy canopy,
 The wind his death-lament.
The ancient pulse of germ and birth
 Was shrunken hard and dry,
And every spirit upon earth   15
 Seemed fervorless as I.

At once a voice arose among
 The bleak twigs overhead
In a full-hearted evensong
 Of joy illimited;   20

THE DARKLING THRUSH 1 *coppice:* thicket. 5 *bine-stems:* climbing plants. 10 *outleant:* laid out.

An aged thrush, frail, gaunt, and small,
      In blast-beruffled plume,
Had chosen thus to fling his soul
      Upon the growing gloom.

So little cause for carolings   25
      Of such ecstatic sound
Was written on terrestrial things
      Afar or nigh around,
That I could think there trembled through
      His happy good-night air   30
Some blessed Hope, whereof he knew
      And I was unaware.

                                                                1902

QUESTIONS

1. Do the first two stanzas contain any images of light, hope, or promise?
2. Which senses do each of the first two stanzas rely upon? What is implied about the function of the senses in the setting described?
3. How do the "broken lyres" of line 6 assume greater significance later in the poem?
4. How do you read the narrator's final statement? Is it hopeful or ironic, serious or flippant?

THE MAN HE KILLED   254

Had he and I but met
   By some old ancient inn,
We should have sat us down to wet
   Right many a nipperkin!

But ranged as infantry,   5
   And staring face to face,
I shot at him as he at me,
   And killed him in his place.

I shot him dead because—
   Because he was my foe,   10
Just so: my foe of course he was;
   That's clear enough; although

He thought he'd 'list, perhaps,
   Off-hand-like—just as I—
Was out of work—had sold his traps—   15
   No other reason why.

THE MAN HE KILLED 4 *nipperkin:* half-pint cup. 15 *traps:* personal belongings.

Yes; quaint and curious war is!
You shoot a fellow down
You'd treat, if met where any bar is,
Or help to half-a-crown.   20

                                                                1902

THE CONVERGENCE OF THE TWAIN   255

LINES ON THE LOSS OF THE TITANIC

1

In a solitude of the sea
Deep from human vanity,
And the Pride of Life that planned her, stilly couches she.

2

Steel chambers, late the pyres
Of her salamandrine fires,   5
Cold currents thrid, and turn to rhythmic tidal lyres.

3

Over the mirrors meant
To glass the opulent
The sea-worm crawls—grotesque, slimed, dumb, indifferent.

4

Jewels in joy designed   10
To ravish the sensuous mind
Lie lightless, all their sparkles bleared and black and blind.

5

Dim moon-eyed fishes near
Gaze at the gilded gear
And query: "What does this vaingloriousness down here?"   15

6

Well: while was fashioning
This creature of cleaving wing,
The Immanent Will that stirs and urges everything

THE CONVERGENCE OF THE TWAIN subtitle *Titanic:* ship sunk after hitting an iceberg on April 15, 1912.
5 *salamandrine:* The salamander, a mythical creature resembling a lizard, was capable of withstanding fire. 6 *thrid:* thread.

7

Prepared a sinister mate
For her—so gaily great—   20
A Shape of Ice, for the time far and dissociate.

8

And as the smart ship grew
In stature, grace, and hue,
In shadowy silent distance grew the Iceberg too.

9

Alien they seemed to be: 25
No mortal eye could see
The intimate welding of their later history,

10

Or sign that they were bent
By paths coincident
On being anon twin halves of one august event,   30

11

Till the Spinner of the Years
Said "Now!" And each one hears,
And consummation comes, and jars two hemispheres.

1912

CHANNEL FIRING   256

That night your great guns, unawares,
Shook all our coffins as we lay,
And broke the chancel window-squares,
We thought it was the Judgment-day

And sat upright. While drearisome   5
Arose the howl of wakened hounds:
The mouse let fall the altar-crumb,
The worms drew back into the mounds,

The glebe cow drooled. Till God called, "No;
It's gunnery practice out at sea   10
Just as before you went below;
The world is as it used to be:

CHANNEL FIRING 9 *glebe cow:* cow which grazes on land granted to a clergyman.

"All nations striving strong to make
Red war yet redder. Mad as hatters
They do no more for Christés sake 15
Than you who are helpless in such mattérs.

"That this is not the judgment-hour
For some of them's a blessed thing,
For if it were they'd have to scour
Hell's floor for so much threatening. . . . 20

"Ha, ha. It will be warmer when
I blow the trumpet (if indeed
I ever do; for you are men,
And rest eternal sorely need)."

So down we lay again. "I wonder, 25
Will the world ever saner be,"
Said one, "than when He sent us under
In our indifferent century!"

And many a skeleton shook his head.
"Instead of preaching forty year," 30
My neighbor Parson Thirdly said,
"I wish I had stuck to pipes and beer."

Again the guns disturbed the hour,
Roaring their readiness to avenge,
As far inland as Stourton Tower, 35
And Camelot, and starlit Stonehenge.

1914

QUESTIONS

1. Who and what are disturbed by the channel firing? Does anyone or anything seem untouched or undisturbed?
2. How many speakers are there in this poem? Describe their attributes and attitudes.
3. How is time handled? What time is it? How much time has passed? What other references to time does the poem contain? Are the final allusions time-related?

THE VOICE 257

Woman much missed, how you call to me, call to me,
Saying that now you are not as you were
When you had changed from the one who was all to me,
But as at first, when our day was fair.

Can it be you that I hear? Let me view you, then, 5
Standing as when I drew near to the town
Where you would wait for me: yes, as I knew you then,
Even to the original air-blue gown!

Or is it only the breeze, in its listlessness
Traveling across the wet mead to me here, 10
You being ever dissolved to wan wistlessness,
Heard no more again far or near?

    Thus I; faltering forward,
    Leaves around me falling,
Wind oozing thin through the thorn from norward, 15
    And the woman calling.

1914

THE OXEN 258

Christmas Eve, and twelve of the clock.
    "Now they are all on their knees,"
An elder said as we sat in a flock
    By the embers in hearthside ease.

We pictured the meek mild creatures where 5
    They dwelt in their strawy pen,
Nor did it occur to one of us there
    To doubt they were kneeling then.

So fair a fancy few would weave
    In these years! Yet, I feel, 10
If someone said on Christmas Eve,
    "Come; see the oxen kneel,

"In the lonely barton by yonder coomb
    Our childhood used to know,"
I should go with him in the gloom, 15
    Hoping it might be so.

1916

THE VOICE 11 *wistlessness:* inattentiveness.

THE OXEN 13 *barton:* farmyard; *coomb:* valley.

IN TIME OF "THE BREAKING OF NATIONS" 259

I

Only a man harrowing clods
  In a slow silent walk
With an old horse that stumbles and nods
  Half asleep as they stalk.

II

Only thin smoke without flame
  From the heaps of couch-grass;
Yet this will go onward the same
  Though Dynasties pass.

III

Yonder a maid and her wight
  Come whispering by:
War's annals will fade into night
  Ere their story die.

1916

ROBERT HAYDEN

(1913–1980)

THOSE WINTER SUNDAYS 260

Sundays too my father got up early
and put his clothes on in the blueblack cold,
then with cracked hands that ached
from labor in the weekday weather made
banked fires blaze. No one ever thanked him.

I'd wake and hear the cold splintering, breaking.
When the rooms were warm, he'd call,
and slowly I would rise and dress,
fearing the chronic angers of that house,

Speaking indifferently to him,
who had driven out the cold
and polished my good shoes as well.
What did I know, what did I know
of love's austere and lonely offices?

1962

IN TIME OF "THE BREAKING OF NATIONS" title *The Breaking of Nations:* from Jeremiah 51:20: "Thou art my battle axe and weapons of war: for with thee will I break in pieces the nations, and with thee will I destroy kingdoms." 6 *couch-grass:* a troublesome weed.

QUESTIONS

1. Does line 9 surprise you? Are you prepared for it in any way in earlier lines?
2. How are the first two words significant?
3. What keeps this poem from becoming sentimental?
4. Where do the abstract or more general statements appear? Why?

MONET'S "WATERLILIES" 261

(FOR BILL AND SONJA)

Today as the news from Selma and Saigon
poisons the air like fallout,
   I come again to see
the serene great picture that I love.

Here space and time exist in light 5
the eye like the eye of faith believes.
   The seen, the known
dissolve in iridescence, become
illusive flesh of light
   that was not, was, forever is. 10

O light beheld as through refracting tears.
Here is the aura of that world
   each of us has lost.
Here is the shadow of its joy.

1966

H. D. (HILDA DOOLITTLE)
(1886–1961)

OREAD 262

Whirl up, sea—
whirl your pointed pines,
splash your great pines
on our rocks,
hurl your green over us, 5
cover us with your pools of fir.

1924

OREAD title: a nymph of the mountains.

QUESTIONS

1. What is the informing metaphor of this poem? How does it operate?
2. Which qualities of the sea appeal most to Oread?
3. Oread is not described directly, but from what you hear in her request, what can you surmise about her own nature? Which part of speech does she seem most drawn to?
4. What type of sentence does Oread speak?

"WE HAVE SEEN HER"   263

We have seen her
the world over,

Our Lady of the Goldfinch,
Our Lady of the Candelabra,

Our Lady of the Pomegranate,   5
Our Lady of the Chair;

we have seen her, an empress,
magnificent in pomp and grace,

and we have seen her
with a single flower   10

or a cluster of garden-pinks
in a glass beside her;

we have seen her snood
drawn over her hair,

or her face set in profile   15
with the blue hood and stars;

we have seen her head bowed down
with the weight of a domed crown,

or we have seen her, a wisp of a girl
trapped in a golden halo;   20

we have seen her with arrow, with doves
and a heart like a valentine;

we have seen her in fine silks imported
from all over the Levant,

"WE HAVE SEEN HER" 24 *Levant:* countries bordering the eastern Mediterranean Sea.

and hung with pearls brought   25
from the city of Constantine;

we have seen her sleeve
of every imaginable shade

of damask and figured brocade;
it is true,   30

the painters did very well by her;
it is true, they missed never a line

of the suave turn of the head
or subtle shade of lowered eye-lid

or eye-lids half-raised; you find   35
her everywhere (or did find),

in cathedral, museum, cloister,
at the turn of the palace stair.

1945

S E A M U S   H E A N E Y
(b. 1939)

WATERFALL   264

The burn drowns steadily in its own downpour,
A helter-skelter of muslin and glass
That skids to a halt, crashing up suds.

Simultaneous acceleration
And sudden braking; water goes over   5
Like villains dropped screaming to justice.

It appears an athletic glacier
Has reared into reverse: is swallowed up
And regurgitated through this long throat.

My eye rides over and downwards, falls with   10
Hurtling tons that slabber and spill,
Falls, yet records the tumult thus standing still.

1966

WATERFALL 1 *burn:* small stream.

DOCKER

There, in the corner, staring at his drink.
The cap juts like a gantry's crossbeam,
Cowling plated forehead and sledgehead jaw.
Speech is clamped in the lips' vice.

That fist would drop a hammer on a Catholic—   5
Oh yes, that kind of thing could start again;
The only Roman collar he tolerates
Smiles all round his sleek pint of porter.

Mosaic imperatives bang home like rivets;
God is a foreman with certain definite views   10
Who orders life in shifts of work and leisure.
A factory horn will blare the Resurrection.

He sits, strong and blunt as a Celtic cross,
Clearly used to silence and an armchair:
Tonight the wife and children will be quiet   15
At slammed door and smoker's cough in the hall.

1966

Q U E S T I O N S

1. Does the docker remind you of anyone you have ever seen before? Is he a universal type or a particular individual?
2. What two image patterns develop the picture of the docker? Where do these patterns coincide?
3. What do the frequent end-stopped lines contribute to the tone?
4. What does his image of God tell you about the docker?

DOCKER 2 *gantry:* a bridgelike frame over which a traveling crane moves. 3 *Cowling:* a removable metal covering for an aircraft engine; also the hooded robe of a monk. 8 *porter:* dark beer.

ANTHONY HECHT

(b. 1923)

"MORE LIGHT! MORE LIGHT!" 266

FOR HEINRICH BLÜCHER AND HANNAH ARENDT

Composed in the Tower before his execution
These moving verses, and being brought at that time
Painfully to the stake, submitted, declaring thus:
"I implore my God to witness that I have made no crime."

Nor was he forsaken of courage, but the death was horrible, 5
The sack of gunpowder failing to ignite.
His legs were blistered sticks on which the black sap
Bubbled and burst as he howled for the Kindly Light.

And that was but one, and by no means one of the worst;
Permitted at least his pitiful dignity; 10
And such as were by made prayers in the name of Christ,
That shall judge all men, for his soul's tranquillity.

We move now to outside a German wood.
Three men are there commanded to dig a hole
In which the two Jews are ordered to lie down 15
And be buried alive by the third, who is a Pole.

Not light from the shrine at Weimar beyond the hill
Nor light from heaven appeared. But he did refuse.
A Lüger settled back deeply in its glove.
He was ordered to change places with the Jews. 20

Much casual death had drained away their souls.
The thick dirt mounted toward the quivering chin.
When only the head was exposed the order came
To dig him out again and to get back in.

No light, no light in the blue Polish eye. 25
When he finished a riding boot packed down the earth.
The Lüger hovered lightly in its glove.
He was shot in the belly and in three hours bled to death.

"MORE LIGHT! MORE LIGHT!" dedication *Heinrich Blücher and Hannah Arendt:* husband and wife philosophers. Arendt wrote about totalitarianism and Nazi Germany in particular. Germany's best-known author is Goethe, whose last words were purported to be, "More light. . . ."
1 *Tower:* the Tower of London, where many executions took place, particularly during the religious controversies of the sixteenth and seventeenth centuries. 8 *Kindly Light:* "Lead, Kindly Light" is a hymn. 19 *Lüger:* a German pistol.

No prayers or incense rose up in those hours
Which grew to be years, and every day came mute   30
Ghosts from the ovens, sifting through crisp air,
And settled upon his eyes in a black soot.

1968

QUESTIONS

1. What is your immediate response to the first execution? Does your response to this
   incident prepare you for the next one? Are you more shocked or less shocked as a
   result?
2. Hecht's note on this poem reads: "The details are conflated from several executions,
   including Latimer and Ridley whose deaths at the stake are described by Foxe in *Acts
   and Monuments*. But neither of them wrote poems just before their deaths, as others
   did." Look up Latimer and Ridley to determine when and why they died. What are
   the implications for the modern reader?
3. What are the differences between the two incidents?
4. Explain the title.

THE DOVER BITCH, A CRITICISM OF LIFE   267

FOR ANDREWS WANNING

So there stood Matthew Arnold and this girl
With the cliffs of England crumbling away behind them,
And he said to her, "Try to be true to me,
And I'll do the same for you, for things are bad
All over, etc., etc."   5
Well now, I knew this girl. It's true she had read
Sophocles in a fairly good translation
And caught that bitter allusion to the sea,
But all the time he was talking she had in mind
The notion of what his whiskers would feel like   10
On the back of her neck. She told me later on
That after a while she got to looking out
At the lights across the channel, and really felt sad,
Thinking of all the wine and enormous beds
And blandishments in French and the perfumes.   15
And then she got really angry. To have been brought
All the way down from London, and then be addressed
As a sort of mournful cosmic last resort
Is really tough on a girl, and she was pretty.
Anyway, she watched him pace the room   20

THE DOVER BITCH, A CRITICISM OF LIFE title: see Matthew Arnold's "Dover Beach."

And finger his watch-chain and seem to sweat a bit,
And then she said one or two unprintable things.
But you mustn't judge her by that. What I mean to say is,
She's really all right. I still see her once in a while
And she always treats me right. We have a drink   25
And I give her a good time, and perhaps it's a year
Before I see her again, but there she is,
Running to fat, but dependable as they come.
And sometimes I bring her a bottle of *Nuit d'Amour.*

1968

A LOT OF NIGHT MUSIC   268

Even a Pyrrhonist
Who knows only that he can never know
          (But adores a paradox)
Would admit it's getting dark. Pale as a wrist-
          Watch numeral glow,   5
Fireflies build a sky among the phlox,

          Imparting their faint light
Conservatively only to themselves.
          Earthmurk and flowerscent
Sweeten the homes of ants. Comes on the night   10
          When the mind rockets and delves
In blind hyperbolas of its own bent.

          Above, the moon at large,
Muse-goddess, slightly polluted by the runs
          Of American astronauts,   15
(Poor, poxed Diana, laid open to the charge
          Of social Actaeons)
Mildly solicits our petty cash and thoughts.

          At once with their votive mites,
Out of the woods and woodwork poets come,   20
          Hauling their truths and booty,
Each one a Phosphor, writing by his own lights,
          And with a diesel hum
Of mosquitoes or priests, proffer their wordy duty.

29 *Nuit d'Amour:* French for "night of love."

A LOT OF NIGHT MUSIC 1 *Pyrrhonist:* skeptic. 16–17 *Diana . . . Actaeons:* bathing one day, Diana,
goddess of hunting and the moon, was surprised by Actaeon, a hunter. Diana changed him to a
stag and he was killed by his dogs. 22 *Phosphor:* the morning star.

        They speak in tongues, no doubt;   25
High glossolalia, runic gibberish.
        Some are like desert saints,
Wheat-germ ascetics, draped in pelt and clout.
        Some come in schools, like fish.
These make their litany of dark complaints;   30
        Those laugh and rejoice
At liberation from the bonds of gender,
        Race, morals and mind,
As well as meter, rhyme and the human voice.
        Still others strive to render   35
The cross-word world in perfectly declined

        Pronouns, starting with ME.
Yet there are honest voices to be heard:
        The crickets keep their vigil
Among the grass; in some invisible tree   40
        Anonymously a bird
Whistles a fioritura, a light, vestigial

        Reminder of a time,
An Aesopic Age when all the beasts were moral
        And taught their ways to men;   45
Some herbal dream, some chlorophyll sublime
        In which Apollo's laurel
Blooms in a world made innocent again.

                                             1977

GEORGE HERBERT

(1593–1633)

REDEMPTION   269

Having been tenant long to a rich lord,
        Not thriving, I resolvéd to be bold,
        And make a suit unto him, to afford
A new small-rented lease, and cancel the old.
In heaven at his manor I him sought;   5
        They told me there thât he was lately gone
        About some land, which he had dearly bought
Long since on earth, to take possessïon.

---

26 *glossolalia:* the gift of tongues; *runic:* magic. 42 *fioritura:* an ornament or embellishment in music. 44 *Aesopic Age . . . moral:* Aesop was a writer of animal fables. 47 *Apollo's laurel:* Apollo was the god of poetry and music. His laurel would be given only to excellent poets.
REDEMPTION 3 *afford:* provide.

I straight returned, and knowing his great birth,
    Sought him accordingly in great resorts;   10
    In cities, theaters, gardens, parks, and courts;
At length I heard a ragged noise and mirth
    Of thieves and murderers; there I him espied,
    Who straight, *Your suit is granted,* said, and died.

1633

EASTER WINGS   270

Lord, who createdst man in wealth and store,
    Though foolishly he lost the same,
        Decaying more and more
            Till he became
              Most poor: 5
              With thee
            O let me rise
        As larks, harmoniously,
    And sing this day thy victories:
Then shall the fall further the flight in me.   10

My tender age in sorrow did begin;
    And still with sickness and shame
        Thou didst so punish sin,
            That I became
              Most thin.   15
              With thee
            Let me combine,
        And feel this day thy victory;
    For, if I imp my wing on thine,
Affliction shall advance the flight in me.   20

1633

QUESTIONS

1. Early versions of this poem show the lines running vertically rather than horizontally. How would that change your reading experience? Would it provide obstacles or enhance your creation of a reading?
2. In what specific ways are form and content related?
3. How does the content of the first stanza mirror the second? For what reasons?
4. Does the poem's form help to resolve the paradoxes of lines 10 and 20, or does it make them more mysterious?

EASTER WINGS 1 *store:* abundance. 19 *imp:* in falconry, to graft new feathers on the wing of a bird.

JORDAN (I)   271

Who says that fictions only and false hair
Become a verse? Is there in truth no beauty?
Is all good structure in a winding stair?
May no lines pass, except they do their duty
    Not to a true, but painted chair?   5

Is it no verse, except enchanted groves
And sudden arbors shadow coarse-spun lines?
Must purling streams refresh a lover's loves?
Must all be veiled while he that reads, divines,
    Catching the sense at two removes?   10

Shepherds are honest people; let them sing:
Riddle who list, for me, and pull for prime:
I envy no man's nightingale or spring;
Nor let them punish me with loss of rhyme,
    Who plainly say, *My God, My King*.   15

1633

ROBERT HERRICK
(1591–1674)

DELIGHT IN DISORDER   272

A sweet disorder in the dress
Kindles in clothes a wantonness.
A lawn about the shoulders thrown
Into a fine distraction;
An erring lace, which here and there   5
Enthralls the crimson stomacher;
A cuff neglectful, and thereby
Ribbons to flow confusedly;
A winning wave, deserving note,
In the tempestuous petticoat;   10
A careless shoestring, in whose tie
I see a wild civility;
Do more bewitch me than when art
Is too precise in every part.

1648

DELIGHT IN DISORDER 6 *stomacher:* a decorative garment worn over the chest and stomach.

QUESTIONS

1. As you read this aloud, where do you notice departures from regular rhythm and perfect rhyme?
2. How do irregularities of rhyme and rhythm contribute to the theme of the poem? Do perfect rhyme and meter play any part in the poem?
3. Is there a discernible method of organization?
4. What are the implications of the final statement of the poem?

TO THE VIRGINS, TO MAKE MUCH OF TIME   273

Gather ye rosebuds while ye may,
   Old time is still a-flying;
And this same flower that smiles today
   Tomorrow will be dying.

The glorious lamp of heaven, the sun,   5
   The higher he's a-getting,
The sooner will his race be run,
   And nearer he's to setting.

That age is best which is the first,
   When youth and blood are warmer;   10
But being spent, the worse, and worst
   Times still succeed the former.

Then be not coy, but use your time,
   And, while ye may, go marry;
For, having lost but once your prime,   15
   You may forever tarry.

1648

JOHN HOLLANDER
(b. 1929)

HELICON   274

Allen said, *I am searching for the true cadence.* Gray
Stony light had flashed over Morningside Drive since noon,
Mixing high in the east with a gray smoky darkness,
Blackened steel trusses of Hell-Gate faintly etched into it,

HELICON title: in Greek mythology, Helicon was the mountain on which two fountains were found —one for poetic and one for artistic inspiration. 1 *Allen:* Allen Ginsberg, American poet, who was Hollander's fellow student at Columbia University. 4 *Hell-Gate:* Hell-Gate Bridge in Manhattan, close to Columbia.

Gray visionary gleam, revealing the clarity of   5
Harlem's grid, like a glimpse of a future city below:
When the fat of the land shall have fallen into the dripping pan,
The grill will still be stuck with brown crusts, clinging to
Its bars, and neither in the fire nor out of it.
So is it coming about. But in my unguessing days   10
Allen said, *They still give you five dollars a pint at St. Luke's,*
No kickback to the interne, either; and I leaned out
Over the parapet and dug my heel in the hard,
Unyielding concrete below, and kicked again, and missed
The feeling of turf with water oozing its way to the top   15
Or of hard sand, making way for life. And was afraid,
Not for the opening of vessels designed to keep
Their rich dark cargo from the air, but for the kind
Of life that led from this oldest of initiations
Ending in homelessness, despondency and madness,   20
And for the moment itself when I should enter through
Those dirty-gray stone portals into the hospital
Named for the Greek doctor, abandoning all hope
Of home or of self-help. The heights of Morningside
Sloped downward, to the north, under the iron line   25
The subway holds to above it, refusing to descend
Under the crashing street. St. John the Divine's gray bulk
Posed, in its parody of history, just in the south.
Dry in the mouth and tired after a night of love
I followed my wild-eyed guide into the darkening door.   30

Inquiries and directions. Many dim rooms, and the shades
Of patient ghosts in the wards, caught in the privileged
Glimpses that the hurrying visitor always gets;
Turnings; errors; wanderings; while Allen chattered on:
I mean someday to cry out against the cities, but first   35
I must find the true cadence. We finally emerged
Into a dismal chamber, bare and dusty, where, suddenly,
Sunlight broke over a brown prospect of whirling clouds
And deepening smoke to plummet down, down to the depths
Of the darknesses, where, recessed in a tiny glory of light   40
A barely-visible man made his way in a boat
Along an amber chasm closing in smoke above him—
Two huge paintings by Thomas Cole opened, like airshaft
Windows, on darkening hearts, there by the blood bank.
We waited then and the dead hospital-white of the cots   45

---

43 *Thomas Cole:* American landscape painter (1801–1848).

Blinded my eyes for a while, and filled my ears with the silence
Of blanketing rushes of blood. Papers and signatures. Waiting;
And then being led by the hand into a corner across
The narrow room from Allen. We both lay down in the whiteness.
The needle struck. There was no pain, and as Allen waved,   50
I turned to the bubbling fountain, welling down redly beside me
And vanishing into the plasma bottle. My life drained of richness
As the light outside seemed to darken.
                              Darker and milder the stream
Of blood was than the flashing, foaming spray I remembered   55
Just then, when, the summer before, with some simple souls who
     knew
Not Allen, I'd helped to fill Columbia's public fountains
With some powdered detergent and concentrated essence of grape,
Having discovered the circulation of water between them
To be a closed system. The sun of an August morning fired   60
Resplendently overhead; maiden teachers of English
From schools in the south were moving whitely from class to class
When the new, bubbling wine burst from the fountain's summits
Cascading down to the basins. The air was full of grapes
And little birds from afar clustered about their rims,   65
Not daring to drink, finally, and all was light and wine.
I forgot what we'd felt or said. My trickle of blood had died,
As the light outside seemed to brighten.
                              Then rest; then five dollars. Then Allen
Urged us out onto the street. The wind sang around the corner,   70
Blowing in from the sound and a siren screeched away
Up Amsterdam Avenue. *Now you have a chocolate malted*
And then you're fine, he said, and the wind blew his hair like feathers,
And we both dissolved into nineteen forty-eight, to be whirled
Away into the wildwood of time, I to leave the city   75
For the disorganized plain, spectre of the long drink
Taken of me that afternoon. *Turning a guy*
On, said Allen last year to the hip psychiatrists
Down in Atlantic City, *that's the most intimate thing*
You can ever do to him. Perhaps. I have bled since   80
To many cadences, if not to the constant tune
Of the heart's yielding and now I know how hard it is
To turn the drops that leaky faucets make in unquiet
Nights, the discrete tugs of love in its final scene,
Into a stream, whether thicker or thinner than blood, and I know   85
That opening up at all is harder than meeting a measure:
With night coming on like a death, a ruby of blood is a treasure.

                                                      1965

QUESTIONS

1. Does the speaker describe any experiences similar to your own as a college student?
2. Could his activity at St. Luke's be repeated in the same way today? Does that enhance or detract from the experience of reading about it?
3. Where is Helicon for Allen and the speaker? How does the speaker develop the allusion?
4. How does the prank the speaker played the previous summer relate to the experience at hand?
5. What does the speaker conclude about the way in which the incident at St. Luke's related to the rest of his life?

GERARD MANLEY HOPKINS
(1844–1889)

SPRING AND FALL   275

TO A YOUNG CHILD

Márgarét, áre you gríeving
Over Goldengrove unleaving?
Leáves, líke the things of man, you
With your fresh thoughts care for, can you?
Áh! ás the heart grows older   5
It will come to such sights colder
By and by, nor spare a sigh
Though worlds of wanwood leafmeal lie;
And yet you *will* weep and know why.
Now no matter, child, the name: 10
Sórrow's spríngs áre the same.
Nor mouth had, no nor mind, expressed
What heart heard of, ghost guessed:
It ís the blight man was born for,
It is Margaret you mourn for.   15

1893

THE HABIT OF PERFECTION   276

Elected Silence, sing to me
And beat upon my whorlèd ear,
Pipe me to pastures still and be
The music that I care to hear.

SPRING AND FALL 8 *wanwood*: pale, dim; *leafmeal*: as in "piecemeal"; also "meal" as in "finely ground." 13 *ghost*: soul.
THE HABIT OF PERFECTION 2 *whorlèd*: spiraled, convoluted.

Shape nothing, lips; be lovely-dumb: 5
It is the shut, the curfew sent
From there where all surrenders come
Which only makes you eloquent.

Be shellèd, eyes, with double dark
And find the uncreated light: 10
This ruck and reel which you remark
Coils, keeps, and teases simple sight.

Palate, the hutch of tasty lust,
Desire not to be rinsed with wine:
The can must be so sweet, the crust   15
So fresh that come in fasts divine!

Nostrils, your careless breath that spend
Upon the stir and keep of pride,
What relish shall the censers send
Along the sanctuary side!   20

O feel-of-primrose hands, O feet
That want the yield of plushy sward,
But you shall walk the golden street
And you unhouse and house the Lord.

And, Poverty, be thou the bride   25
And now the marriage feast begun,
And lily-coloured clothes provide
Your spouse not laboured-at nor spun.

          1918

THE WINDHOVER   277

TO CHRIST OUR LORD

I caught this morning morning's minion, king-
  dom of daylight's dauphin, dapple-dawn-drawn Falcon, in his
    riding
  Of the rolling level underneath him steady air, and striding
High there, how he rung upon the rein of a wimpling wing
In his ecstasy! then off, off forth on swing,   5

15 *can:* cup. 19 *censers:* incense burners. 22 *sward:* grassy turf.

THE WINDHOVER title: a small hawk. 1 *minion:* favorite (in the sense of a favorite at court). 2 *dauphin:* eldest son of the king of France. 4 *wimpling:* rippling.

As a skate's heel sweeps smooth on a bow-bend: the hurl and
    gliding
Rebuffed the big wind. My heart in hiding
Stirred for a bird,—the achieve of, the mastery of the thing!

Brute beauty and valour and act, oh, air, pride, plume, here
    Buckle! AND the fire that breaks from thee then, a billion   10
Times told lovelier, more dangerous, O my chevalier!

    No wonder of it: shéer plód makes plough down sillion
Shine, and blue-bleak embers, ah my dear,
    Fall, gall themselves, and gash gold-vermilion.

1918

PIED BEAUTY   278

Glory be to God for dappled things —
   For skies of couple-colour as a brinded cow;
      For rose-moles all in stipple upon trout that swim;
Fresh-firecoal chestnut-falls; finches' wings;
      Landscape plotted and pieced—fold, fallow, and plough;   5
      And áll trádes, their gear and tackle and trim.
All things counter, original, spare, strange;
      Whatever is fickle, freckled (who knows how?)
      With swift, slow; sweet, sour; adazzle, dim;
He fathers-forth whose beauty is past change: 10
            Praise him.

1918

FELIX RANDAL   279

Felix Randal the farrier, O is he dead then? my duty all ended,
Who have watched his mould of man, big-boned and
    hardy-handsome
Pining, pining, till time when reason rambled in it and some
Fatal four disorders, fleshed there, all contended?

Sickness broke him. Impatient, he cursed at first, but mended   5
Being anointed and all; though a heavenlier heart began some
Months earlier, since I had our sweet reprieve and ransom
Tendered to him. Ah well, God rest him all road ever he offended!

10 *Buckle:* to unite, to give way, to yield. 11 *chevalier:* knight. 12 *sillion:* furrow.
PIED BEAUTY title *pied:* spotted or patched. 2 *brinded:* streaked.
FELIX RANDAL 1 *farrier:* blacksmith.

This seeing the sick endears them to us, us too it endears.
My tongue had taught thee comfort, touch had quenched thy tears,   10
Thy tears that touched my heart, child, Felix, poor Felix Randal;

How far from then forethought of, all thy more boisterous years,
When thou at the random grim forge, powerful amidst peers,
Didst fettle for the great grey drayhorse his bright and battering
　　sandal!

1918

[NO WORST, THERE IS NONE]   280

No worst, there is none. Pitched past pitch of grief,
More pangs will, schooled at forepangs, wilder wring.
Comforter, where, where is your comforting?
Mary, mother of us, where is your relief?

My cries heave, herds-long; huddle in a main, a chief-   5
woe, world-sorrow; on an age-old anvil wince and sing—
Then lull, then leave off. Fury had shrieked 'No ling-
ering! Let me be fell: force I must be brief'.

O the mind, mind has mountains; cliffs of fall
Frightful, sheer, no-man-fathomed. Hold them cheap   10
May who ne'er hung there. Nor does long our small
Durance deal with that steep or deep. Here! creep,
Wretch, under a comfort serves in a whirlwind: all
Life death does end and each day dies with sleep.

1918

A. E. HOUSMAN
(1859–1936)

LOVELIEST OF TREES, THE CHERRY NOW   281

Loveliest of trees, the cherry now
Is hung with bloom along the bough,
And stands about the woodland ride
Wearing white for Eastertide.

---

14 *fettle:* to line with loose sand before filling with molten metal.
NO WORST, THERE IS NONE 8 *fell:* capable of destroying; *force:* by necessity.

Now, of my threescore years and ten, 5
Twenty will not come again,
And take from seventy springs a score,
It only leaves me fifty more.

And since to look at things in bloom
Fifty springs are little room, 10
About the woodlands I will go
To see the cherry hung with snow.

1896

QUESTIONS

1. How is the way you read the second stanza different from the way you may have read the first stanza?
2. Which season begins and which ends the poem? Why?
3. How does the middle stanza influence the direction you take as a reader of the last stanza?
4. Why does line 4 contain a reference to Easter?

TO AN ATHLETE DYING YOUNG 282

The time you won your town the race
We chaired you through the market-place;
Man and boy stood cheering by,
And home we brought you shoulder-high.

Today, the road all runners come, 5
Shoulder-high we bring you home,
And set you at your threshold down,
Townsman of a stiller town.

Smart lad, to slip betimes away
From fields where glory does not stay 10
And early though the laurel grows
It withers quicker than the rose.

Eyes the shady night has shut
Cannot see the record cut,
And silence sounds no worse than cheers 15
After earth has stopped the ears:

Now you will not swell the rout
Of lads that wore their honors out,
Runners whom renown outran
And the name died before the man. 20

So set, before its echoes fade,
The fleet foot on the sill of shade,
And hold to the low lintel up
The still-defended challenge-cup.

And round that early-laureled head   25
Will flock to gaze the strengthless dead,
And find unwithered on its curls
The garland briefer than a girl's.

1896

QUESTIONS

1. Which stanza most nearly captures the mood and meaning of this poem for you?
2. Which traditional symbols appear in this poem? How are they related and how do they function to help you create a reading?
3. Describe and compare the actions in stanza 1 and stanza 2. How are they similar and different?
4. Which of the five senses seem most receptive in this poem? Why?
5. Explain the last stanza. Why "strengthless dead"? Why a "garland briefer than a girl's"?

IS MY TEAM PLOWING   283

"Is my team plowing,
    That I was used to drive
And hear the harness jingle
    When I was man alive?"

Ay, the horses trample,   5
    The harness jingles now;
No change though you lie under
    The land you used to plow.

"Is football playing
    Along the river shore,   10
With lads to chase the leather,
    Now I stand up no more?"

Ay, the ball is flying,
    The lads play heart and soul;
The goal stands up, the keeper   15
    Stands up to keep the goal.

"Is my girl happy,
    That I thought hard to leave,
And has she tired of weeping
    As she lies down at eve?"   20

Ay, she lies down lightly,
    She lies not down to weep:
Your girl is well contented.
    Be still, my lad, and sleep.

"Is my friend hearty,   25
    Now I am thin and pine,
And has he found to sleep in
    A better bed than mine?"

Yes, lad, I lie easy,
    I lie as lads would choose;   30
I cheer a dead man's sweetheart,
    Never ask me whose

                                                                    1896

WITH RUE MY HEART IS LADEN   284

With rue my heart is laden
    For golden friends I had,
For many a rose-lipt maiden
    And many a lightfoot lad.

By brooks too broad for leaping   5
    The lightfoot boys are laid;
The rose-lipt girls are sleeping
    In fields where roses fade.

                                                                    1896

"TERENCE, THIS IS STUPID STUFF . . ."   285

    "Terence, this is stupid stuff:
You eat your victuals fast enough;
There can't be much amiss, 'tis clear,
To see the rate you drink your beer.
But oh, good Lord, the verse you make,   5
It gives a chap the belly-ache.
The cow, the old cow, she is dead;

It sleeps well, the horned head:
We poor lads, 'tis our turn now
To hear such tunes as killed the cow.   10
Pretty friendship 'tis to rhyme
Your friends to death before their time
Moping melancholy mad:
Come, pipe a tune to dance to, lad."

   Why, if 'tis dancing you would be,   15
There's brisker pipes than poetry.
Say, for what were hop-yards meant,
Or why was Burton built on Trent?
Oh many a peer of England brews
Livelier liquor than the Muse,   20
And malt does more than Milton can
To justify God's ways to man.
Ale, man, ale's the stuff to drink
For fellows whom it hurts to think:
Look into the pewter pot   25
To see the world as the world's not.
And faith, 'tis pleasant till 'tis past:
The mischief is that 'twill not last.
Oh I have been to Ludlow fair
And left my necktie God knows where,   30
And carried halfway home, or near,
Pints and quarts of Ludlow beer:
Then the world seemed none so bad,
And I myself a sterling lad;
And down in lovely muck I've lain,   35
Happy till I woke again.
Then I saw the morning sky:
Heigho, the tale was all a lie;
The world, it was the old world yet,
I was I, my things were wet,   40
And nothing now remained to do
But begin the game anew.

   Therefore, since the world has still
Much good, but much less good than ill,
And while the sun and moon endure   45
Luck's a chance, but trouble's sure,

"TERENCE, THIS IS STUPID STUFF . . ." 17–18 *hop-yards . . . Trent:* Burton-on-Trent is a town in England known for its brewing of ale. 29 *Ludlow:* town in Shropshire.

I'd face it as a wise man would,
And train for ill and not for good.
'Tis true, the stuff I bring for sale
Is not so brisk a brew as ale: 50
Out of a stem that scored the hand
I wrung it in a weary land.
But take it: if the smack is sour,
The better for the embittered hour;
It should do good to heart and head   55
When your soul is in my soul's stead;
And I will friend you, if I may,
In the dark and cloudy day.

   There was a king reigned in the East:
There, when kings will sit to feast,   60
They get their fill before they think
With poisoned meat and poisoned drink.
He gathered all that springs to birth
From the many-venomed earth;
First a little, thence to more,   65
He sampled all her killing store;
And easy, smiling, seasoned sound,
Sate the king when healths went round.
They put arsenic in his meat
And stared aghast to watch him eat;   70
They poured strychnine in his cup
And shook to see him drink it up:
They shook, they stared as white's their shirt:
Them it was their poison hurt.
—I tell the tale that I heard told.   75
Mithridates, he died old.

                                              1896

76 *Mithridates:* (132–163 B.C.), king of Pontus, who gave himself a little poison every day to inure himself to its effects.

LANGSTON HUGHES

(1902–1967)

THE NEGRO SPEAKS OF RIVERS

286

(TO W. E. B. DU BOIS)

I've known rivers:
I've known rivers ancient as the world and older than the
    flow of human blood in human veins.

My soul has grown deep like the rivers.

I bathed in the Euphrates when dawns were young.   5
I built my hut near the Congo and it lulled me to sleep.
I looked upon the Nile and raised the pyramids above it.
I heard the singing of the Mississippi when Abe Lincoln
    went down to New Orleans, and I've seen its muddy
    bosom turn all golden in the sunset.   10

I've known rivers:
Ancient, dusky rivers.

My soul has grown deep like the rivers.

1926

BRASS SPITTOONS

287

Clean the spittoons, boy.
    Detroit,
    Chicago,
    Atlantic City,
    Palm Beach.   5
Clean the spittoons.
The steam in hotel kitchens,
And the smoke in hotel lobbies,
And the slime in hotel spittoons:
Part of my life.   10
    Hey, boy!
    A nickel,
    A dime,
    A dollar,
Two dollars a day.   15

THE NEGRO SPEAKS OF RIVERS dedication *W. E. B. DuBois:* American sociologist (1868–1963),
educator, author, founder of the NAACP.

Hey, boy!
A nickel,
A dime,
A dollar,
Two dollars   20
Buy shoes for the baby.
House rent to pay.
Gin on Saturday,
Church on Sunday.
    My God!   25
Babies and gin and church
And women and Sunday
All mixed with dimes and
Dollars and clean spittoons
And house rent to pay.   30
    Hey, boy!
A bright bowl of brass is beautiful to the Lord.
Bright polished brass like the cymbals
Of King David's dancers,
Like the wine cups of Solomon.   35
    Hey, boy!
A clean spittoon on the altar of the Lord.
A clean bright spittoon all newly polished—
At least I can offer that.
    Com'mere, boy!   40

1927

SYLVESTER'S DYING BED   288

I woke up this mornin'
'Bout half-past three.
All the womens in town
Was gathered round me.

Sweet gals was a-moanin',   5
"Sylvester's gonna die!"
And a hundred pretty mamas
Bowed their heads to cry.

I woke up little later
'Bout half-past fo',   10
The doctor 'n' undertaker's
Both at ma do'.

Black gals was a-beggin',
"You can't leave us here!"
Brown-skins cryin', "Daddy!   15
Honey! Baby! Don't go, dear!"

But I felt ma time's a-comin',
And I know'd I's dyin' fast.
I seed the River Jerden
A-creepin' muddy past—   20
But I's still Sweet Papa 'Vester,
Yes, sir! Long as life do last!

So I hollers, "Com'ere, babies,
Fo' to love yo' daddy right!"
And I reaches up to hug 'em—   25
When the Lawd put out the light.

Then everything was darkness
In a great . . . big . . . night.

                                     1942

HARLEM   289

What happens to a dream deferred?

   Does it dry up
   like a raisin in the sun?
   Or fester like a sore—
   And then run?   5
   Does it stink like rotten meat?
   Or crust and sugar over—
   like a syrupy sweet?

   Maybe it just sags
   like a heavy load.   10

   Or does it explode?

                                     1951

QUESTIONS

1. What do you expect after reading the first line? Does the rest of the poem surprise
   you or satisfy those first expectations?
2. Show how the poem relies on all five senses.
3. What kinds of human response do the similes suggest?

THEME FOR ENGLISH B   290

The instructor said,

> *Go home and write*
> *a page tonight.*
> *And let that page come out of you—*
> *Then, it will be true.*   5

I wonder if it's that simple?
I am twenty-two, colored, born in Winston-Salem.
I went to school there, then Durham, then here
to this college on the hill above Harlem.
I am the only colored student in my class.   10
The steps from the hill lead down into Harlem,
through a park, then I cross St. Nicholas,
Eighth Avenue, Seventh, and I come to the Y,
the Harlem Branch Y, where I take the elevator
up to my room, sit down, and write this page: 15

It's not easy to know what is true for you or me
at twenty-two, my age. But I guess I'm what
I feel and see and hear, Harlem, I hear you:
hear you, hear me—we two—you, me, talk on this page.
(I hear New York, too.) Me—who?   20
Well, I like to eat, sleep, drink, and be in love.
I like to work, read, learn, and understand life.
I like a pipe for a Christmas present,
or records—Bessie, bop, or Bach.
I guess being colored doesn't make me *not* like   25
The same things other folks like who are other races.
So will my page be colored that I write?
Being me, it will not be white.
But it will be
a part of you, instructor.   30
You are white—
yet a part of me, as I am a part of you.
That's American.
Sometimes perhaps you don't want to be a part of me.
Nor do I often want to be a part of you.   35
But we are, that's true!
I guess you learn from me—
although you're older—and white—
and somewhat more free.

This is my page for English B.   40

1951

TED HUGHES

(b. 1930)

THE THOUGHT-FOX   291

I imagine this midnight moment's forest:
Something else is alive
Beside the clock's loneliness
And this blank page where my fingers move.

Through the window I see no star: 5
Something more near
Though deeper within darkness
Is entering the loneliness:

Cold, delicately as the dark snow,
A fox's nose touches twig, leaf;   10
Two eyes serve a movement, that now
And again now, and now, and now

Sets neat prints into the snow
Between trees, and warily a lame
Shadow lags by stump and in hollow   15
Of a body that is bold to come

Across clearings, an eye,
A widening deepening greenness,
Brilliantly, concentratedly,
Coming about its own business   20

Till, with a sudden sharp hot stink of fox
It enters the dark hole of the head.
The window is starless still; the clock ticks,
The page is printed.

1957

QUESTIONS

1. What gives you a strong sense of immediacy in this poem? What poetic devices help you to become a more active reader than you might ordinarily?
2. What is the informing metaphor? What process does it describe?
3. Reread the first and last stanzas. What has actually happened in between?

WIND   292

This house has been far out at sea all night,
The woods crashing through darkness, the booming hills,
Winds stampeding the fields under the window
Floundering black astride and blinding wet

Till day rose; then under an orange sky   5
The hills had new places, and wind wielded
Blade-like, luminous black and emerald,
Flexing like the lens of a mad eye.

At noon I scaled along the house-side as far as
The coal-house door. I dared once to look up—   10
Through the brunt wind that dented the balls of my eyes
The tent of the hills drummed and strained its guyrope,

The fields quivering, the skyline a grimace,
At any second to bang and vanish with a flap:
The wind flung a magpie away and a black-   15
Back gull bent like an iron bar slowly. The house

Rang like some fine green goblet in the note
That any second would shatter it. Now deep
In chairs, in front of the great fire, we grip
Our hearts and cannot entertain book, thought,   20

Or each other. We watch the fire blazing,
And feel the roots of the house move, but sit on,
Seeing the window tremble to come in,
Hearing the stones cry out under the horizons.

1959

THE BULL MOSES   293

A hoist up and I could lean over
The upper edge of the high half-door,
My left foot ledged on the hinge, and look in at the byre's
Blaze of darkness: a sudden shut-eyed look
Backward into the head.   5
                    Blackness is depth
Beyond star. But the warm weight of his breathing,
The ammoniac reek of his litter, the hotly-tongued

THE BULL MOSES 3 *byre:* cowshed's.

Mash of his cud, steamed against me.
Then, slowly, as onto the mind's eye—
The brow like masonry, the deep-keeled neck: 10
Something come up there onto the brink of the gulf,
Hadn't heard of the world, too deep in itself to be called to,
Stood in sleep. He would swing his muzzle at a fly
But the square of sky where I hung, shouting, waving,
Was nothing to him; nothing of our light   15
Found any reflection in him.
                             Each dusk the farmer led him
Down to the pond to drink and smell the air,
And he took no pace but the farmer
Led him to take it, as if he knew nothing
Of the ages and continents of his fathers,   20
Shut, while he wombed, to a dark shed
And steps between his door and the duckpond;
The weight of the sun and the moon and the world hammered
To a ring of brass through his nostrils.
                                 He would raise
His streaming muzzle and look out over the meadows,   25
But the grasses whispered nothing awake, the fetch
Of the distance drew nothing to momentum
In the locked black of his powers. He came strolling gently back,
Paused neither toward the pigpens on his right,
Nor toward the cow-byres on his left: something   30
Deliberate in his leisure, some beheld future
Founding in his quiet.
                        I kept the door wide,
Closed it after him and pushed the bolt.

                                      1960

RICHARD HUGO
(1923–1982)

THE HILLTOP   294

I like bars close to home and home run down,
a signal to the world, I'm weak. I like a bar
to be a home. Take this one. Same men every night.
Same jokes. Traffic going by

fifteen feet away and punchboards never paying off.   5
Churn of memory and ulcer. Most of all
the stale anticipation of the girl
sure to walk in someday fresh from '39,
not one day older, holding out her arms.

Soon, I say to no one late each night,   10
I'll be all right. I put five dollars
in the jukebox and never hear a tune.
I take pride drinking alone and being kind.
When I walk in, people say my name.
By ten, the loveliest girl in Vegas   15
swims about the room, curving in and counter
to the flow of smoke. Her evil sister
swings her legs and giggles in my drink.

When I'm at home, the kitchen light stays on.
Help me, friend. By dawn, a hundred dogs   20
are gnawing at my throat. My gnarled phlegm
chokes up yellow. My empty room
revolves tornado and my relatives
are still unnamed. A dozen practiced gestures
get me through the day. By five, I'm crawling   25
up the hill, certain I'll live, my Hilltop smile
perfected and my coin naïve.

                                                        1975

FOR SUSAN ZWINGER

RANDALL JARRELL
(1914–1965)

THE DEATH OF THE BALL TURRET
GUNNER   295

From my mother's sleep I fell into the State,
And I hunched in its belly till my wet fur froze.
Six miles from earth, loosed from its dream of life,
I woke to black flak and the nightmare fighters.
When I died they washed me out of the turret with a hose.   5

                                                        1945

THE HILLTOP 5 *punchboards:* game of chance.

QUESTIONS

1. Are the images in this poem of birth or of death?
2. The poet wrote this explanation:

> A ball turret was a plexiglass sphere set into the belly of a B-17 or B-24, and inhabited by two .50 caliber machine-guns and one man, a short small man. When this gunner tracked with his machine guns a fighter attacking his bomber from below, he revolved with the turret; hunched upside-down in his little sphere, he looked like the foetus in the womb. The fighters which attacked him were armed with cannon firing explosive shells. The hose was a steam hose.

Does this information clarify or complicate? Does it change your experience of the poem?

NEXT DAY   296

Moving from Cheer to Joy, from Joy to All,
I take a box
And add it to my wild rice, my Cornish game hens.
The slacked or shorted, basketed, identical
Food-gathering flocks   5
Are selves I overlook. Wisdom, said William James,

Is learning what to overlook. And I am wise
If that is wisdom.
Yet somehow, as I buy All from these shelves
And the boy takes it to my station wagon,   10
What I've become
Troubles me even if I shut my eyes.

When I was young and miserable and pretty
And poor, I'd wish
What all girls wish: to have a husband,   15
A house and children. Now that I'm old, my wish
Is womanish:
That the boy putting groceries in my car

See me. It bewilders me he doesn't see me.
For so many years   20
I was good enough to eat: the world looked at me
And its mouth watered. How often they have undressed me,
The eyes of strangers!
And, holding their flesh within my flesh, their vile

Imaginings within my imagining,   25
I too have taken
The chance of life. Now the boy pats my dog
And we start home. Now I am good.
The last mistaken,
Ecstatic, accidental bliss, the blind   30

Happiness that, bursting, leaves upon the palm
Some soap and water—
It was so long ago, back in some Gay
Twenties, Nineties, I don't know . . . Today I miss
My lovely daughter   35
Away at school, my sons away at school,

My husband away at work—I wish for them.
The dog, the maid,
And I go through the sure unvarying days
At home in them. As I look at my life,   40
I am afraid
Only that it will change, as I am changing:

I am afraid, this morning, of my face.
It looks at me
From the rear-view mirror, with the eyes I hate,   45
The smile I hate. Its plain, lined look
Of gray discovery
Repeats to me: "You're old." That's all, I'm old.

And yet I'm afraid, as I was at the funeral
I went to yesterday.   50
My friend's cold made-up face, granite among its flowers,
Her undressed, operated-on, dressed body
Were my face and body.
As I think of her I hear her telling me

How young I seem; I *am* exceptional;   55
I think of all I have.
But really no one is exceptional,
No one has anything, I'm anybody,
I stand beside my grave
Confused with my life, that is commonplace and solitary.   60

1965

ROBINSON JEFFERS
(1887–1962)

ROCK AND HAWK   297

Here is a symbol in which
Many high tragic thoughts
Watch their own eyes.

This gray rock, standing tall
On the headland, where the seawind   5
Lets no tree grow,

Earthquake-proved, and signatured
By ages of storms: on its peak
A falcon has perched.

I think, here is your emblem   10
To hang in the future sky;
Not the cross, not the hive,

But this; bright power, dark peace;
Fierce consciousness joined with final
Disinterestedness;   15

Life with calm death; the falcon's
Realist eyes and act
Married to the massive

Mysticism of stone,
Which failure cannot cast down   20
Nor success make proud.

                                                          1935

QUESTIONS

1. What do you associate with rocks and hawks?
2. How is the symbol which is announced in the first line developed throughout the
   poem? What are its components?
3. Has its meaning been simplified by the end of the poem or is it more complex?
4. Is the poem successful? Why or why not?

THE PURSE-SEINE

Our sardine fishermen work at night in the dark of the moon;
    daylight or moonlight
They could not tell where to spread the net, unable to see the
    phosphorescence of the shoals of fish.
They work northward from Monterey, coasting Santa Cruz; off New
    Year's Point or off Pigeon Point
The look-out man will see some lakes of milk-color light on the sea's
    night-purple; he points, and the helmsman
Turns the dark prow, the motorboat circles the gleaming shoal and
    drifts out her seine-net. They close the circle   5
And purse the bottom of the net, then with great labor haul it in.

                        I cannot tell you
How beautiful the scene is, and a little terrible, then, when the
    crowded fish
Know they are caught, and wildly beat from one wall to the other of
    their closing destiny the phosphorescent
Water to a pool of flame, each beautiful slender body sheeted with
    flame, like a live rocket   10
A comet's tail wake of clear yellow flame; while outside the
    narrowing
Floats and cordage of the net great sea-lions come up to watch,
    sighing in the dark; the vast walls of night
Stand erect to the stars.

                Lately I was looking from a night mountain-top
On a wide city, the colored splendor, galaxies of light: how could I
    help but recall the seine-net   15
Gathering the luminous fish? I cannot tell you how beautiful the city
    appeared, and a little terrible.
I thought, We have geared the machines and locked all together into
    interdependence; we have built the great cities; now
There is no escape. We have gathered vast populations incapable of
    free survival, insulated
From the strong earth, each person in himself helpless, on all depen-
    dent. The circle is closed, and the net
Is being hauled in. They hardly feel the cords drawing, yet they shine
    already. The inevitable mass-disasters   20
Will not come in our time nor in our children's, but we and our
    children

THE PURSE-SEINE title: a purse-shaped fishing net.

Must watch the net draw narrower, government take all powers — or
    revolution, and the new government
Take more than all, add to kept bodies kept souls — or anarchy, the
    mass-disasters.

            These things are Progress;
Do you marvel our verse is troubled or frowning, while it keeps its
    reason? Or it lets go, lets the mood flow   25
In the manner of the recent young men into mere hysteria, splintered
    gleams, crackled laughter. But they are quite wrong.
There is no reason for amazement: surely one always knew that cul-
    tures decay, and life's end is death.

                                                  1937

BEN JONSON
(1573–1637)

STILL TO BE NEAT   299

Still to be neat, still to be dressed,
As you were going to a feast;
Still to be powdered, still perfumed;
Lady, it is to be presumed,
Though art's hid causes are not found,   5
All is not sweet, all is not sound.

Give me a look, give me a face
That makes simplicity a grace;
Robes loosely flowing, hair as free;
Such sweet neglect more taketh me   10
Then all th' adulteries of art.
They strike mine eyes, but not my heart.

                                                  1609

ON MY FIRST SON   300

Farewell, thou child of my right hand, and joy;
My sin was too much hope of thee, loved boy:
Seven years thou'wert lent to me, and I thee pay,
Exacted by thy fate, on the just day.
O could I lose all father now! for why   5
Will man lament the state he should envý,

To have so soon 'scaped world's and flesh's rage,
And, if no other misery, yet age?
Rest in soft peace, and asked, say, "Here doth lie
Ben Jonson his best piece of poetry."   10
For whose sake henceforth all his vows be such
As what he loves may never like too much.

1616

QUESTIONS

1. What keeps the poem from becoming sentimental?
2. What does the author mean in the final two lines? Does this statement support or develop any earlier statements in the poem?
3. Explore all levels of the father/son relationship present in this poem.

EPITAPH ON ELIZABETH, L. H.   301

Woudst thou hear what man can say
In a little? Reader, stay.
Underneath this stone doth lie
As much beauty as could die;
Which in life did harbor give   5
To more virtue than doth live.
If at all she had a fault,
Leave it buried in this vault.
One name was Elizabeth;
Th' other, let it sleep with death: 10
Fitter, where it died, to tell,
Than that it lived at all. Farewell.

1616

JAMES JOYCE
(1882–1941)

[THOUGH I THY MITHRIDATES WERE]   302

Though I thy Mithridates were,
    Framed to defy the poison-dart,
Yet must thou fold me unaware
    To know the rapture of thy heart,
And I but render and confess   5
The malice of thy tenderness.

THOUGH I THY MITHRIDATES WERE title *Mithridates:* (132–163 B.C.), king of Pontus, who gave himself a little poison every day to inure himself to its effects.

For elegant and antique phrase,
   Dearest, my lips wax all too wise;
Nor have I known a love whose praise
   Our piping poets solemnize,   10
Neither a love where may not be
Ever so little falsity.

1907

QUESTIONS

1. What is the effect of the allusion to Mithridates? Does encountering it in the first line
   create a particular attitude in you, the reader? Could you create a near-valid reading
   of the poem without knowing the precise identity of Mithridates?
2. Is the speaker's attitude cynical? fatalistic? romantic? serious? witty?
3. Discuss the paradox present in the poem. Do contradiction, contrast, and paradox
   retard the focus or create unity?

[I HEAR AN ARMY CHARGING UPON THE LAND] 303

I hear an army charging upon the land,
   And the thunder of horses plunging, foam about their knees:
Arrogant, in black armour, behind them stand,
   Disdaining the reins, with fluttering whips, the charioteers.

They cry unto the night their battle-name: 5
   I moan in sleep when I hear afar their whirling laughter.
They cleave the gloom of dreams, a blinding flame,
   Clanging, clanging upon the heart as upon an anvil.

They come shaking in triumph their long, green hair:
   They come out of the sea and run shouting by the shore.   10
My heart, have you no wisdom thus to despair?
   My love, my love, my love, why have you left me alone?

1907

DONALD JUSTICE
(b. 1925)

TALES FROM A FAMILY ALBUM   304

How shall I speak of doom, and ours in special,
But as of something altogether common?
No house of Atreus ours, too humble surely,
The family tree a simple chinaberry

TALES FROM A FAMILY ALBUM 3 *Atreus:* King of Mycenae, father of Menelaus and Agamemnon, and
brother of Thyestes, three of whose sons he slew and served to him at a banquet.

Such as springs up in Georgia in a season.   5
(Under it sags the farmer's broken wagon.)
Nor may I laud it much for shade or beauty,
But praise that tree for being prompt to flourish,
Despite the worm and weather out of heaven.

I publish of my folk how they have prospered   10
With something in the eyes, perhaps inherent,
Or great-winged nose, bespeaking an acquaintance
Not casual and not recent with a monster,
Citing, as an example of some courage,
That aunt, long gone, who kept one in a birdcage   15
Thirty-odd years in shape of a green parrot,
Nor overcame her fears, yet missed no feeding,
Thrust in the crumbs with thimbles on her fingers.

I had an uncle, long of arm and hairy,
Who seldom spoke in any lady's hearing   20
For fear his tongue should light on aught unseemly,
Yet he could treat most kindly with us children
Touching that beast, wholly imaginary,
Which, hunting once, his hounds had got the wind of.
And even of this present generation   25
There is a cousin of no great removal
On whom the mark is printed of a forepaw.

How shall I speak of doom and not the shadow
Caught in the famished cheeks of those few beauties
My people boast of, being flushed and phthisic?   30
Of my own childhood I remember dimly
One who died young, though as a hag most toothless,
Her fine hair wintry, from a hard encounter
By moonlight in a dark wood with a stranger,
Who had as well been unicorn or centaur   35
For all she might recall of him thereafter.

There was a kinsman took up pen and paper
To write our history, at which he perished,
Calling for water and the holy wafer,
Who had, till then, resisted all persuasion.   40
I pray your mercy on a leaf so shaken,

---

30 *phthisic:* consumptive.

And mercy likewise on these other fallen,
Torn from the berry-tree in heaven's fashion,
For there was something in their way of going
Put doom upon my tongue and bade me utter.   45

                                                                    1960

THE SNOWFALL   305

The classic landscapes of dreams are not
More pathless, though footprints leading nowhere
Would seem to prove that a people once
Survived for a little even here.

Fragments of a pathetic culture   5
Remain, the lost mittens of children,
And a single, bright, detasseled snow cap,
Evidence of some frantic migration.

The landmarks are gone. Nevertheless,
There is something familiar about this country.   10
Slowly now we begin to recall

The terrible whispers of our elders
Falling softly about our ears
In childhood, never believed till now.

                                                                    1960

MEN AT FORTY   306

Men at forty
Learn to close softly
The doors to rooms they will not be
Coming back to.

At rest on a stair landing,   5
They feel it
Moving beneath them now like the deck of a ship,
Though the swell is gentle.

And deep in mirrors
They rediscover   10
The face of the boy as he practices tying
His father's tie there in secret

And the face of that father,
Still warm with the mystery of lather.
They are more fathers than sons themselves now.   15
Something is filling them, something

That is like the twilight sound
Of the crickets, immense,
Filling the woods at the foot of the slope
Behind their mortgaged houses.   20

1965

THE MISSING PERSON   307

He has come to report himself
A missing person.

The authorities
Hand him the forms.

He knows how they have waited   5
With the learned patience of barbers

In small shops, idle,
Stropping their razors.

But now that these spaces in his life
Stare up at him blankly,   10

Waiting to be filled in,
He does not know how to begin.

Afraid that he may not answer
To his description of himself,

He asks for a mirror.   15
They reassure him

That he can be nowhere
But wherever he finds himself

From moment to moment
Which, for the moment, is here.   20

And he might like to believe them.
But in the mirror

He sees what is missing.
It is himself

He sees there emerging   25
Slowly, as from the dark

Of a furnished room
Only by darkness,

One who receives no mail
And is known to the landlady only   30

For keeping himself to himself,
And for whom it will be years yet

Before he can trust to the light
This last disguise, himself.

                                                    1965

QUESTIONS

1. Which of your five senses do you find emphasized in this poem? Why and where?
2. What do the verbs indicate about the central issue of the poem? Consider tense, type, and repetition.
3. How many characters are described in the poem? How are they significant? What do the other characters know that "he" does not know?
4. How is the poem's form inseparable from the content?

THE SUICIDES   308

If we recall your voices
As softer now, it's only
That they must have drifted back

A long way to have reached us
Here, and upon such a wind   5
As crosses the high passes.

Nor does the blue of your eyes
(Remembered) cast much light on
The page ripped from the tablet.

                        ———

Once there in the labyrinth,   10
You were safe from your reasons.
We stand, now, at the threshold,

Peering in, but the passage,
For us, remains obscure; the
Corridors are still bloody.   15

——————

What you meant to prove you have
Proved—we did not care for you
Nearly enough. Meanwhile the

Bay was preparing herself
To receive you, the for once   20
Wholly adequate female

To your dark inclinations;
Under your care the pistol
Was slowly learning to flower

In the desired explosion,   25
Disturbing the careful part
And the briefly recovered

Fixed smile of a forgotten
Triumph; deep within the black
Forest of childhood that tree   30

Was already rising which,
With the length of your body,
Would cast the double shadow.

——————

The masks by which we knew you
Have been torn from you. Even   35
Those mirrors, to which always

You must have turned to confide,
Cannot have recognized you,
Stripped, as you were, finally.

At the end of your shadow   40
There sat another, waiting,
Whose back was always to us.

——————

When the last door had been closed,
You watched, inwardly raging,
For the first glimpse of your selves   45
Approaching, jangling their keys.

Musicians of the black keys,
At last you compose yourselves.
We hear the music raging
Under the lids we have closed.   50

                                                                  1967

                    IN MEMORY OF J. AND G. AND J.

PATRICK KAVANAGH
(1904–1967)

INNISKEEN ROAD: JULY EVENING   309

The bicycles go by in twos and threes—
There's a dance in Billy Brennan's barn to-night,
And there's the half-talk code of mysteries
And the wink-and-elbow language of delight.
Half-past eight and there is not a spot   5
Upon a mile of road, no shadow thrown
That might turn out a man or woman, not
A footfall tapping secrecies of stone.

I have what every poet hates in spite
Of all the solemn talk of contemplation.   10
Oh, Alexander Selkirk knew the plight
Of being king and government and nation.
A road, a mile of kingdom, I am king
Of banks and stones and every blooming thing.

                                                                  1936

QUESTIONS

1. Have you ever experienced a tension similar to that expressed in the poem? What
   about this one is new for you?
2. Explain the stanza division. What does it do?
3. What does every poet hate (line 9)?
4. Discuss the tone of the final line. Is it consistent with or at odds with the rest of the
   poem?

INNISKEEN ROAD: JULY EVENING title: Inniskeen was Kavanagh's native town. 11 *Alexander Selkirk:* the
historical figure upon whose adventures Daniel Defoe based *Robinson Crusoe.*

COME DANCE WITH KITTY STOBLING   310

No, no, no, I know I was not important as I moved
Through the colourful country, I was but a single
Item in the picture, the namer not the beloved.
O tedious man with whom no gods commingle.
Beauty, who has described beauty? Once upon a time   5
I had a myth that was a lie but it served:
Trees walking across the crests of hills and my rhyme
Cavorting on mile-high stilts and the unnerved
Crowds looking up with terror in their rational faces.
O dance with Kitty Stobling I outrageously   10
Cried out-of-sense to them, while their timorous paces
Stumbled behind Jove's page boy paging me.
I had a very pleasant journey, thank you sincerely
For giving me my madness back, or nearly.

1960

JOHN KEATS
(1795–1821)

ON FIRST LOOKING INTO CHAPMAN'S HOMER   311

Much have I traveled in the realms of gold,
  And many goodly states and kingdoms seen;
  Round many western islands have I been
Which bards in fealty to Apollo hold.
Oft of one wide expanse had I been told   5
  That deep-browed Homer ruled as his demesne;
  Yet did I never breathe its pure serene
Till I heard Chapman speak out loud and bold:
Then felt I like some watcher of the skies
  When a new planet swims into his ken;   10
Or like stout Cortez when with eagle eyes
  He stared at the Pacific—and all his men
Looked at each other with a wild surmise—
  Silent, upon a peak in Darien.

1816

ON FIRST LOOKING INTO CHAPMAN'S HOMER title: George Chapman (1559–1634), translator of Homer.
4 *fealty:* loyalty; *Apollo:* god of the sun and of poetry. 6 *demesne:* domain. 11 *Cortez:* Spanish
explorer and conqueror of Mexico. 14 *Darien:* the point in Panama from which Balboa and his
men first saw the Pacific Ocean. (Notice the confusion of identities here.)

ODE TO A NIGHTINGALE   312

1

My heart aches, and a drowsy numbness pains
  My sense, as though of hemlock I had drunk,
Or emptied some dull opiate to the drains
  One minute past, and Lethe-wards had sunk:
'Tis not through envy of thy happy lot,   5
  But being too happy in thine happiness—
    That thou, light-winged Dryad of the trees,
      In some melodious plot
  Of beechen green, and shadows numberless,
    Singest of summer in full-throated ease.   10

2

O, for a draught of vintage! that hath been
  Cooled a long age in the deep-delved earth,
Tasting of Flora and the country green,
  Dance, and Provençal song, and sunburnt mirth!
O for a beaker full of the warm South,   15
  Full of the true, the blushful Hippocrene,
    With beaded bubbles winking at the brim,
      And purple-stained mouth;
  That I might drink, and leave the world unseen,
    And with thee fade away into the forest dim: 20

3

Fade far away, dissolve, and quite forget
  What thou among the leaves hast never known,
The weariness, the fever, and the fret
  Here, where men sit and hear each other groan;
Where palsy shakes a few, sad, last gray hairs,   25
  Where youth grows pale, and specter-thin, and dies,
    Where but to think is to be full of sorrow
      And leaden-eyed despairs,
  Where Beauty cannot keep her lustrous eyes,
    Or new Love pine at them beyond tomorrow.   30

ODE TO A NIGHTINGALE 2 *hemlock:* a poisonous herb. 4 *Lethe-wards:* Lethe is the river of forgetfulness in Hades. 7 *Dryad:* wood nymphs. 13 *Flora:* goddess of springtime. 14 *Provençal song:* songs of Provence (southern France), famous for its medieval love poets. 16 *Hippocrene:* fountain of the Muses.

4

Away! away! for I will fly to thee,
  Not charioted by Bacchus and his pards,
But on the viewless wings of Poesy,
  Though the dull brain perplexes and retards:
Already with thee! tender is the night,   35
  And haply the Queen-Moon is on her throne,
    Clustered around by all her starry Fays;
      But here there is no light,
  Save what from heaven is with the breezes blown
    Through verdurous glooms and winding mossy ways.   40

5

I cannot see what flowers are at my feet,
  Nor what soft incense hangs upon the boughs,
But, in embalmed darkness, guess each sweet
  Wherewith the seasonable month endows
The grass, the thicket, and the fruit tree wild;   45
  White hawthorn, and the pastoral eglantine;
    Fast fading violets covered up in leaves;
      And mid-May's eldest child,
  The coming musk-rose, full of dewy wine,
    The murmurous haunt of flies on summer eves.   50

6

Darkling I listen; and for many a time
I have been half in love with easeful Death,
Called him soft names in many a mused rhyme,
  To take into the air my quiet breath;
Now more than ever seems it rich to die,   55
  To cease upon the midnight with no pain,
    While thou art pouring forth thy soul abroad
      In such an ecstasy!
  Still wouldst thou sing, and I have ears in vain—
    To thy high requiem become a sod.   60

7

Thou wast not born for death, immortal Bird!
  No hungry generations tread thee down;
The voice I hear this passing night was heard
  In ancient days by emperor and clown:

---

32 *Bacchus and his pards:* the god of wine, whose chariot was drawn by leopards. 33 *viewless:* invisible. 37 *Fays:* fairies. 43 *embalmed:* perfumed. 46 *eglantine:* sweetbriar. 51 *darkling:* in darkness.

Perhaps the selfsame song that found a path 65
  Through the sad heart of Ruth, when, sick for home,
    She stood in tears amid the alien corn;
      The same that ofttimes hath
  Charmed magic casements, opening on the foam
  Of perilous seas, in faery lands forlorn. 70

8

Forlorn! the very word is like a bell
  To toll me back from thee to my sole self!
Adieu! the fancy cannot cheat so well
  As she is famed to do, deceiving elf.
Adieu! adieu! thy plaintive anthem fades 75
  Past the near meadows, over the still stream,
    Up the hill side; and now 'tis buried deep
      In the next valley-glades:
  Was it a vision, or a waking dream?
  Fled is that music:—Do I wake or sleep? 80

1820

ODE ON A GRECIAN URN   313

1

Thou still unravished bride of quietness,
  Thou foster child of silence and slow time,
Sylvan historian, who canst thus express
  A flowery tale more sweetly than our rhyme:
What leaf-fringed legend haunts about thy shape 5
  Of deities or mortals, or of both,
    In Tempe or the dales of Arcady?
  What men or gods are these? What maidens loath?
What mad pursuit? What struggle to escape?
    What pipes and timbrels? What wild ecstasy? 10

2

Heard melodies are sweet, but those unheard
  Are sweeter; therefore, ye soft pipes, play on;
Not to the sensual ear, but, more endeared,
  Pipe to the spirit ditties of no tone:

---

66 *Ruth:* the book of Ruth in the Old Testament tells the story of this woman who, as a stranger in Judah, worked in the fields and won the love of Boaz.

ODE ON A GRECIAN URN 7 *Tempe or . . . Arcady:* in ancient Greece, places of beauty representing ideal pastoral landscapes.

Fair youth, beneath the trees, thou canst not leave   15
   Thy song, nor ever can those trees be bare;
     Bold Lover, never, never canst thou kiss,
Though winning near the goal—yet, do not grieve;
     She cannot fade, though thou hast not thy bliss,
   Forever wilt thou love, and she be fair!   20

3

Ah, happy, happy boughs! that cannot shed
   Your leaves, nor ever bid the Spring adieu;
And, happy melodist, unweariéd,
   Forever piping songs forever new;
More happy love! more happy, happy love!   25
   Forever warm and still to be enjoyed,
     Forever panting, and forever young;
All breathing human passion far above,
   That leaves a heart high-sorrowful and cloyed,
     A burning forehead, and a parching tongue.   30

4

Who are these coming to the sacrifice?
   To what green altar, O mysterious priest,
Lead'st thou that heifer lowing at the skies,
   And all her silken flanks with garlands dressed?
What little town by river or sea shore,   35
   Or mountain-built with peaceful citadel,
     Is emptied of this folk, this pious morn?
And, little town, thy streets forevermore
   Will silent be; and not a soul to tell
     Why thou art desolate, can e'er return.   40

5

O Attic shape! Fair attitude! with brede
   Of marble men and maidens overwrought,
With forest branches and the trodden weed;
   Thou, silent form, dost tease us out of thought
As doth eternity: Cold Pastoral!   45
   When old age shall this generation waste,
     Thou shalt remain, in midst of other woe
Than ours, a friend to man, to whom thou say'st,
   "Beauty is truth, truth beauty,"—that is all
     Ye know on earth, and all ye need to know.   50

1820

41 *Attic:* from Attica, a region of Greece; *brede:* embroidered pattern.

QUESTIONS

1. Describe the urn you see after reading this poem the first time. Reread, adding detail to your description.
2. What connections do you see between reading the poem and viewing the urn? Between writing the poem and making the urn? Between reading the poem and writing the poem?
3. Where are the paradoxes in the poem?
4. What is the relationship between concrete detail and abstract statement?

ODE ON MELANCHOLY   314

1

No, no, go not to Lethe, neither twist
   Wolfsbane, tight-rooted, for its poisonous wine;
Nor suffer thy pale forehead to be kissed
   By nightshade, ruby grape of Proserpine;
Make not your rosary of yew-berries,   5
   Nor let the beetle, nor the death-moth be
      Your mournful Psyche, nor the downy owl
A partner in your sorrow's mysteries;
   For shade to shade will come too drowsily,
      And drown the wakeful anguish of the soul.   10

2

But when the melancholy fit shall fall
   Sudden from heaven like a weeping cloud,
That fosters the droop-headed flowers all,
   And hides the green hill in an April shroud;
Then glut thy sorrow on a morning rose,   15
   Or on the rainbow of the salt sand-wave,
      Or on the wealth of globéd peonies;
Or if thy mistress some rich anger shows,
   Imprison her soft hand, and let her rave,
      And feed deep, deep upon her peerless eyes.   20

3

She dwells with Beauty—Beauty that must die;
   And Joy, whose hand is ever at his lips
Bidding adieu; and aching Pleasure nigh,
   Turning to Poison while the bee-mouth sips:

ODE ON MELANCHOLY 1 *Lethe:* river of forgetfulness in Hades. 2 *Wolfsbane:* poisonous plant. 4 *nightshade:* poisonous plant; *Proserpine:* queen of Hades. 5 *yew-berries:* yew trees are often found in cemeteries. 7 *Psyche:* the soul, often symbolized by a moth.

Aye, in the very temple of Delight   25
   Veiled Melancholy has her sov'reign shrine,
     Though seen of none save him whose strenuous tongue
   Can burst Joy's grape against his palate fine;
His soul shall taste the sadness of her might,
     And be among her cloudy trophies hung.   30

1820

THE EVE OF ST. AGNES   315

I

St. Agnes' Eve—Ah, bitter chill it was!
The owl, for all his feathers, was a-cold;
The hare limp'd trembling through the frozen grass,
And silent was the flock in woolly fold:
Numb were the Beadsman's fingers, while he told   5
His rosary, and while his frosted breath,
Like pious incense from a censer old,
Seem'd taking flight for heaven, without a death,
Past the sweet Virgin's picture, while his prayer he saith.

II

His prayer he saith, this patient, holy man;   10
Then takes his lamp, and riseth from his knees,
And back returneth, meagre, barefoot, wan,
Along the chapel aisle by slow degrees:
The sculptur'd dead, on each side, seem to freeze,
Emprison'd in black, purgatorial rails: 15
Knights, ladies, praying in dumb orat'ries,
He passeth by; and his weak spirit fails
To think how they may ache in icy hoods and mails.

III

Northward he turneth through a little door,
And scarce three steps, ere Music's golden tongue   20
Flatter'd to tears this aged man and poor;
But no—already had his deathbell rung:
The joys of all his life were said and sung:

THE EVE OF ST. AGNES title *St. Agnes:* fourth-century martyr, patron saint of young virgins. It was believed that if on St. Agnes' Eve (January 20) a young girl went to bed without supper, and lay on her back, she would dream of her future husband. 5 *Beadsman:* man who was paid to offer prayers for his patron. 16 *orat'ries:* small chapels within the larger church building.

His was harsh penance on St. Agnes' Eve:
Another way he went, and soon among   25
Rough ashes sat he for his soul's reprieve,
And all night kept awake, for sinners' sake to grieve.

IV

That ancient Beadsman heard the prelude soft;
And so it chanc'd, for many a door was wide,
From hurry to and fro. Soon, up aloft,   30
The silver, snarling trumpets 'gan to chide:
The level chambers, ready with their pride,
Were glowing to receive a thousand guests:
The carvèd angels, ever eager-eyed,
Star'd, where upon their heads the cornice rests,   35
With hair blown back, and wings put cross-wise on their breasts.

V

At length burst in the argent revelry,
With plume, tiara, and all rich array,
Numerous as shadows haunting faerily
The brain, new stuff'd, in youth, with triumphs gay   40
Of old romance. These let us wish away,
And turn, sole-thoughted, to one Lady there,
Whose heart had brooded, all that wintry day,
On love, and wing'd St. Agnes' saintly care,
As she had heard old dames full many times declare.   45

VI

They told her how, upon St. Agnes' Eve,
Young virgins might have visions of delight,
And soft adorings from their loves receive
Upon the honey'd middle of the night,
If ceremonies due they did aright;   50
As, supperless to bed they must retire,
And couch supine their beauties, lilly white;
Nor look behind, nor sideways, but require
Of Heaven with upward eyes for all that they desire.

VII

Full of this whim was thoughtful Madeline: 55
The music, yearning like a God in pain,
She scarcely heard: her maiden eyes divine,
Fix'd on the floor, saw many a sweeping train
Pass by—she heeded not at all: in vain

Came many a tiptoe, amorous cavalier,   60
And back retir'd; not cool'd by high disdain,
But she saw not: her heart was otherwhere:
She sigh'd for Agnes' dreams, the sweetest of the year.

VIII

She danc'd along with vague, regardless eyes,
Anxious her lips, her breathing quick and short: 65
The hallow'd hour was near at hand: she sighs
Amid the timbrels, and the throng'd resort
Of whisperers in anger, or in sport;
'Mid looks of love, defiance, hate, and scorn,
Hoodwink'd with faery fancy; all amort,   70
Save to St. Agnes and her lambs unshorn,
And all the bliss to be before to-morrow morn.

IX

So, purposing each moment to retire,
She linger'd still. Meantime, across the moors,
Had come young Porphyro, with heart on fire   75
For Madeline. Beside the portal doors,
Buttress'd from moonlight, stands he, and implores
All saints to give him sight of Madeline,
But for one moment in the tedious hours,
That he might gaze and worship all unseen;   80
Perchance speak, kneel, touch, kiss—in sooth such things have been.

X

He ventures in: let no buzz'd whisper tell:
All eyes be muffled, or a hundred swords
Will storm his heart, Love's fev'rous citadel:
For him, those chambers held barbarian hordes,   85
Hyena foemen, and hot-blooded lords,
Whose very dogs would execrations howl
Against his lineage: not one breast affords
Him any mercy, in that mansion foul,
Save one old beldame, weak in body and in soul.   90

XI

Ah, happy chance! the agèd creature came,
Shuffling along with ivory-headed wand,
To where he stood, hid from the torch's flame,
Behind a broad hall-pillar, far beyond

---

70 *amort:* dead. 71 *lambs unshorn:* lambs were traditionally associated with St. Agnes (*agnus* in Latin means "lamb"). 90 *beldame:* old woman.

The sound of merriment and chorus bland: 95
He startled her; but soon she knew his face,
And grasp'd his fingers in her palsied hand,
Saying, "Mercy, Porphyro! hie thee from this place;
They are all here to-night, the whole blood-thirsty race!

XII

"Get hence! get hence! there's dwarfish Hildebrand;   100
He had a fever late, and in the fit
He cursèd thee and thine, both house and land:
Then there's that old Lord Maurice, not a whit
More tame for his gray hairs—Alas me! flit!
Flit like a ghost away."—"Ah, Gossip dear,   105
We're safe enough; here in this arm-chair sit,
And tell me how"—"Good Saints! not here, not here;
Follow me, child, or else these stones will be thy bier."

XIII

He follow'd through a lowly archèd way,
Brushing the cobwebs with his lofty plume,   110
And as she mutter'd "Well-a—well-a-day!"
He found him in a little moonlight room,
Pale, lattic'd, chill, and silent as a tomb.
"Now tell me where is Madeline," said he,
'O tell me, Angela, by the holy loom   115
Which none but secret sisterhood may see,
When they St. Agnes' wool are weaving piously."

XIV

"St. Agnes! Ah! it is St. Agnes' Eve—
Yet men will murder upon holy days:
Thou must hold water in a witch's sieve,   120
And be liege-lord of all the Elves and Fays,
To venture so: it fills me with amaze
To see thee, Porphyro!—St. Agnes' Eve!
God's help! my lady fair the conjuror plays
This very night: good angels her deceive!   125
But let me laugh awhile, I've mickle time to grieve."

XV

Feebly she laugheth in the languid moon,
While Porphyro upon her face doth look,
Like puzzled urchin on an aged crone
Who keepeth clos'd a wond'rous riddle-book,   130

95 *bland:* in harmony. 121 *Fays:* fairies. 126 *mickle:* great amount.

As spectacled she sits in chimney nook.
But soon his eyes grew brilliant, when she told
His lady's purpose; and he scarce could brook
Tears, at the thought of those enchantments cold,
And Madeline asleep in lap of legends old.   135

XVI

Sudden a thought came like a full-blown rose,
Flushing his brow, and in his painèd heart
Made purple riot: then doth he propose
A stratagem, that makes the beldame start:
"A cruel man and impious thou art: 140
Sweet lady, let her pray, and sleep, and dream
Alone with her good angels, far apart
From wicked men like thee. Go, go!—I deem
Thou canst not surely be the same that thou didst seem."

XVII

"I will not harm her, by all saints I swear,"   145
Quoth Porphyro: "O may I ne'er find grace
When my weak voice shall whisper its last prayer,
If one of her soft ringlets I displace,
Or look with ruffian passion in her face:
Good Angela, believe me by these tears;   150
Or I will, even in a moment's space,
Awake, with horrid shout, my foemen's ears,
And beard them, though they be more fang'd than wolves and
    bears."

XVIII

"Ah! why wilt thou affright a feeble soul?
A poor, weak, palsy-stricken, churchyard thing,   155
Whose passing-bell may ere the midnight toll;
Whose prayers for thee, each morn and evening,
Were never miss'd."—Thus plaining, doth she bring
A gentler speech from burning Porphyro;
So woful, and of such deep sorrowing,   160
That Angela gives promise she will do
Whatever he shall wish, betide her weal or woe.

133 *brook:* check. 156 *passing-bell:* death knell.

XIX

Which was, to lead him, in close secrecy,
Even to Madeline's chamber, and there hide
Him in a closet, of such privacy   165
That he might see her beauty unespied,
And win perhaps that night a peerless bride,
While legion'd faeries pac'd the coverlet,
And pale enchantment held her sleepy-eyed.
Never on such a night have lovers met,   170
Since Merlin paid his Demon all the monstrous debt.

XX

"It shall be as thou wishest," said the Dame:
"All cates and dainties shall be storèd there
Quickly on this feast-night: by the tambour frame
Her own lute thou wilt see: no time to spare,   175
For I am slow and feeble, and scarce dare
On such a catering trust my dizzy head.
Wait here, my child, with patience; kneel in prayer
The while: Ah! thou must needs the lady wed,
Or may I never leave my grave among the dead."   180

XXI

So saying, she hobbled off with busy fear.
The lover's endless minutes slowly pass'd;
The dame return'd, and whisper'd in his ear
To follow her; with aged eyes aghast
From fright of dim espial. Safe at last,   185
Through many a dusky gallery, they gain
The maiden's chamber, silken, hush'd, and chaste;
Where Porphyro took covert, pleas'd amain.
His poor guide hurried back with agues in her brain.

XXII

Her falt'ring hand upon the balustrade,   190
Old Angela was feeling for the stair,
When Madeline, St. Agnes' charmèd maid,
Rose, like a mission'd spirit, unaware:
With silver taper's light, and pious care,

---

171 *Merlin . . . debt:* In Arthurian legend, Merlin, a great magician, was tricked by love into
subjugation to an evil woman. 173 *cates:* choice or dainty food. 174 *tambour frame:* embroidery
frame. 188 *amain:* greatly. 189 *agues:* fever and chills.

She turn'd, and down the agèd gossip led   195
  To a safe level matting. Now prepare,
  Young Porphyro, for gazing on that bed;
She comes, she comes again, like ring-dove fray'd and fled.

XXIII

Out went the taper as she hurried in;
  Its little smoke, in pallid moonshine, died: 200
  She clos'd the door, she panted, all akin
To spirits of the air, and visions wide:
No uttered syllable, or, woe betide!
  But to her heart, her heart was voluble,
  Paining with eloquence her balmy side;   205
As though a tongueless nightingale should swell
Her throat in vain, and die, heart-stifled, in her dell.

XXIV

A casement high and triple-arch'd there was,
  All garlanded with carven imag'ries
  Of fruits, and flowers, and bunches of knot-grass,   210
And diamonded with panes of quaint device,
Innumerable of stains and splendid dyes,
  As are the tiger-moth's deep-damask'd wings;
  And in the midst, 'mong thousand heraldries,
  And twilight saints, and dim emblazonings,   215
A shielded scutcheon blush'd with blood of queens and kings.

XXV

Full on this casement shone the wintry moon,
  And threw warm gules on Madeline's fair breast,
  As down she knelt for heaven's grace and boon;
Rose-bloom fell on her hands, together prest,   220
And on her silver cross soft amethyst,
  And on her hair a glory, like a saint:
  She seem'd a splendid angel, newly drest,
  Save wings, for heaven:—Porphyro grew faint:
She knelt, so pure a thing, so free from mortal taint.   225

---

198 *ring-dove:* pigeon; *fray'd:* afraid. 216 *scutcheon:* a shield bearing a coat of arms. 218 *gules:* red.
219 *boon:* favor.

XXVI

Anon his heart revives: her vespers done,
Of all its wreathèd pearls her hair she frees;
Unclasps her warmèd jewels one by one;
Loosens her fragrant boddice; by degrees
Her rich attire creeps rustling to her knees: 230
Half-hidden, like a mermaid in sea-weed,
Pensive awhile she dreams awake, and sees,
    In fancy, fair St. Agnes in her bed,
But dares not look behind, or all the charm is fled.

XXVII

Soon, trembling in her soft and chilly nest,   235
In sort of wakeful swoon, perplex'd she lay,
Until the poppied warmth of sleep oppress'd
Her soothèd limbs, and soul fatigued away;
Flown, like a thought, until the morrow-day;
Blissfully haven'd both from joy and pain;   240
Clasp'd like a missal where swart Paynims pray;
    Blinded alike from sunshine and from rain,
As though a rose should shut, and be a bud again.

XXVIII

Stol'n to this paradise, and so entranced,
Porphyro gazed upon her empty dress,   245
And listen'd to her breathing, if it chanced
To wake into a slumberous tenderness;
Which when he heard, that minute did he bless,
And breath'd himself: then from the closet crept,
Noiseless as fear in a wide wilderness,   250
    And over the hush'd carpet, silent, stept,
And 'tween the curtains peep'd, where, lo!—how fast she slept.

XXIX

Then by the bed-side, where the faded moon
Made a dim, silver twilight, soft he set
A table, and, half anguish'd, threw thereon   255
A cloth of woven crimson, gold, and jet:—
O for some drowsy Morphean amulet!

241 *swart Paynims:* dark pagans. 257 *Morphean amulet:* Morpheus was the god of sleep. An amulet is an object worn as a charm.

The boisterous, midnight, festive clarion,
The kettle-drum, and far-heard clarinet,
Affray his ears, though but in dying tone:— 260
The hall door shuts again, and all the noise is gone.

XXX

And still she slept an azure-lidded sleep,
In blanchèd linen, smooth, and lavender'd,
While he from forth the closet brought a heap
Of candied apple, quince, and plum, and gourd; 265
With jellies soother than the creamy curd,
And lucent syrops, tinct with cinnamon;
Manna and dates, in argosy transferr'd
From Fez; and spicèd dainties, every one,
From silken Samarcand to cedar'd Lebanon. 270

XXXI

These delicates he heap'd with glowing hand
On golden dishes and in baskets bright
Of wreathèd silver: sumptuous they stand
In the retired quiet of the night,
Filling the chilly room with perfume light.— 275
"And now, my love, my seraph fair, awake!
Thou art my heaven, and I thine eremite:
Open thine eyes, for meek St. Agnes' sake,
Or I shall drowse beside thee, so my soul doth ache."

XXXII

Thus whispering, his warm, unnerved arm 280
Sank in her pillow. Shaded was her dream
By the dusk curtains:—'twas a midnight charm
Impossible to melt as icèd stream:
The lustrous salvers in the moonlight gleam;
Broad golden fringe upon the carpet lies: 285
It seem'd he never, never could redeem
From such a stedfast spell his lady's eyes;
So mus'd awhile, entoil'd in woofèd phantasies.

XXXIII

Awakening up, he took her hollow lute,—
Tumultuous,—and, in chords that tenderest be, 290
He play'd an ancient ditty, long since mute,
In Provence call'd, "La belle dame sans mercy:"

267 tinct: infused. 269–270 Fez. . .Samarcand. . .Lebanon: exotic places. 284 salvers: serving
trays. 288 woofèd: woven. 292 La belle dame sans merci: "the beautiful lady without mercy."

Close to her ear touching the melody;—
Wherewith disturb'd, she utter'd a soft moan:
He ceased—she panted quick—and suddenly   295
Her blue affrayed eyes wide open shone:
Upon his knees he sank, pale as smooth-sculptured stone.

XXXIV

Her eyes were open, but she still beheld,
Now wide awake, the vision of her sleep:
There was a painful change, that nigh expell'd   300
The blisses of her dream so pure and deep,
At which fair Madeline began to weep,
And moan forth witless words with many a sigh;
While still her gaze on Porphyro would keep;
Who knelt, with joinèd hands and piteous eye,   305
Fearing to move or speak, she look'd so dreamingly.

XXXV

"Ah, Porphyro!" said she, "but even now
Thy voice was at sweet tremble in mine ear,
Made tuneable with every sweetest vow;
And those sad eyes were spiritual and clear: 310
How chang'd thou art! how pallid, chill, and drear!
Give me that voice again, my Porphyro,
Those looks immortal, those complainings dear!
Oh leave me not in this eternal woe,
For if thou diest, my Love, I know not where to go."   315

XXXVI

Beyond a mortal man impassion'd far
At these voluptuous accents, he arose,
Ethereal, flush'd, and like a throbbing star
Seen mid the sapphire heaven's deep repose;
Into her dream he melted, as the rose   320
Blendeth its odour with the violet,—
Solution sweet: meantime the frost-wind blows
Like Love's alarum pattering the sharp sleet
Against the window-panes; St. Agnes' moon hath set.

323 *alarum*: signal.

XXXVII

'Tis dark: quick pattereth the flaw-blown sleet: 325
"This is no dream, my bride, my Madeline!"
'Tis dark: the icèd gusts still rave and beat:
"No dream, alas! alas! and woe is mine!
Porphyro will leave me here to fade and pine.—
Cruel! what traitor could thee hither bring?   330
I curse not, for my heart is lost in thine,
Though thou forsakest a deceivèd thing;—
A dove forlorn and lost with sick unprunèd wing."

XXXVIII

"My Madeline! sweet dreamer! lovely bride!
Say, may I be for aye thy vassal blest?   335
Thy beauty's shield, heart-shap'd and vermeil dyed?
Ah, silver shrine, here will I take my rest
After so many hours of toil and quest,
A famish'd pilgrim,—sav'd by miracle.
Though I have found, I will not rob thy nest   340
Saving of thy sweet self; if thou think'st well
To trust, fair Madeline, to no rude infidel.

XXXIX

"Hark! 'tis an elfin-storm from faery land,
Of haggard seeming, but a boon indeed:
Arise—arise! the morning is at hand;—   345
The bloated wassaillers will never heed:—
Let us away, my love, with happy speed;
There are no ears to hear, or eyes to see,—
Drown'd all in Rhenish and the sleepy mead:
Awake! arise! my love, and fearless be,   350
For o'er the southern moors I have a home for thee."

XL

She hurried at his words, beset with fears,
For there were sleeping dragons all around,
At glaring watch, perhaps, with ready spears—
Down the wide stairs a darkling way they found.—   355
In all the house was heard no human sound.

---

325 *flaw-blown:* gust-blown. 336 *vermeil:* vermilion. 346 *bloated wassailers:* drunken party-goers.
349 *Rhenish and the sleepy mead:* Rhine wine and an alcoholic beverage made from fermented honey
and water.

A chain-droop'd lamp was flickering by each door;
The arras, rich with horseman, hawk, and hound,
Flutter'd in the besieging wind's uproar;
And the long carpets rose along the gusty floor.   360

XLI

They glide, like phantoms, into the wide hall;
Like phantoms, to the iron porch, they glide;
Where lay the Porter, in uneasy sprawl,
With a huge empty flaggon by his side:
The wakeful bloodhound rose, and shook his hide,   365
But his sagacious eye an inmate owns:
By one, and one, the bolts full easy slide:—
The chains lie silent on the footworn stones;—
The key turns, and the door upon its hinges groans.

XLII

And they are gone: aye, ages long ago   370
These lovers fled away into the storm.
That night the Baron dreamt of many a woe,
And all his warrior-guests, with shade and form
Of witch, and demon, and large coffin-worm,
Were long be-nightmar'd. Angela the old   375
Died palsy-twitch'd, with meagre face deform;
The Beadsman, after thousand aves told,
For aye unsought for slept among his ashes cold.

1820

WHEN I HAVE FEARS   316

When I have fears that I may cease to be
  Before my pen has gleaned my teeming brain,
Before high-piled books, in charact'ry,
  Hold like rich garners the full-ripened grain;
When I behold, upon the night's starred face,   5
  Huge cloudy symbols of a high romance,
And think that I may never live to trace
  Their shadows, with the magic hand of chance;
And when I feel, fair creature of an hour,
  That I shall never look upon thee more,   10

377 *aves:* prayers addressed to the Virgin Mary.
WHEN I HAVE FEARS 3 *charact'ry:* written symbols.

Never have relish in the faery power
   Of unreflecting love!—then on the shore
Of the wide world I stand alone, and think
Till Love and Fame to nothingness do sink.

1848

LA BELLE DAME SANS MERCI   317

O what can ail thee, Knight at arms,
   Alone and palely loitering?
The sedge has withered from the Lake
   And no birds sing!

O what can ail thee, Knight at arms,   5
   So haggard, and so woebegone?
The squirrel's granary is full
   And the harvest's done.

I see a lily on thy brow
   With anguish moist and fever dew,   10
And on thy cheeks a fading rose
   Fast withereth too.

"I met a Lady in the Meads,
   Full beautiful, a faery's child,
Her hair was long, her foot was light   15
   And her eyes were wild.

"I made a Garland for her head,
   And bracelets too, and fragrant Zone;
She looked at me as she did love
   And made sweet moan.   20

"I set her on my pacing steed
   And nothing else saw all day long,
For sidelong would she bend and sing
   A faery's song.

"She found me roots of relish sweet,   25
   And honey wild, and manna dew,
And sure in language strange she said
   'I love thee true.'

LA BELLE DAME SANS MERCI title: "the beautiful lady without mercy." 13 *Meads:* meadows. 18 *Zone:* a belt.

"She took me to her elfin grot
  And there she wept and sighed full sore,   30
And there I shut her wild wild eyes
  With kisses four.

"And there she lullèd me asleep,
  And there I dreamed, Ah Woe betide!
The latest dream I ever dreamt   35
  On the cold hill side.

"I saw pale Kings, and Princes too,
  Pale warriors, death-pale were they all;
They cried, 'La belle dame sans merci
  Hath thee in thrall!'   40

"I saw their starved lips in the gloam
  With horrid warning gapèd wide,
And I awoke, and found me here
  On the cold hill's side.

"And this is why I sojourn here,   45
  Alone and palely loitering;
Though the sedge is withered from the Lake
  And no birds sing."

                                   1888

GALWAY KINNELL
(b. 1927)

FIRST SONG   318

Then it was dusk in Illinois, the small boy
After an afternoon of carting dung
Hung on the rail fence, a sapped thing
Weary to crying. Dark was growing tall
And he began to hear the pond frogs all   5
Calling on his ear with what seemed their joy.

Soon their sound was pleasant for a boy
Listening in the smoky dusk and the nightfall
Of Illinois, and from the fields two small
Boys came bearing cornstalk violins   10
And they rubbed the cornstalk bows with resins
And the three sat there scraping of their joy.

It was now fine music the frogs and the boys
Did in the towering Illinois twilight make
And into dark in spite of a shoulder's ache   15
A boy's hunched body loved out of a stalk
The first song of his happiness, and the song woke
His heart to the darkness and into the sadness of joy.

1960

FOR WILLIAM CARLOS WILLIAMS   319

When you came and you talked and you read with your
Private zest from the varicose marble
Of the podium, the lovers of literature
Paid you the tribute of their almost total
Inattention, although someone when you spoke of a pig   5
Did squirm, and it is only fair to report another gig-

gled. But you didn't even care. You seemed
Above remarking we were not your friends.
You hung around inside the rimmed
Circles of your heavy glasses and smiled and   10
So passed a lonely evening. In an hour
Of talking your honesty built you a tower.

When it was over and you sat down and the chair-
man got up and smiled and congratulated
You and shook your hand, I watched a professor   15
In neat bow tie and enormous tweeds, who patted
A faint praise of the sufficiently damned,
Drained spittle from his pipe, then scrammed.

1960

QUESTIONS

1. When do you first realize the attitude of "the lovers of literature"?
2. What does the second stanza tell you about Williams' attitude and position?
3. Where does perfect rhyme appear? Why? Describe the effect.

THE RIVER THAT IS EAST   320

1

Buoys begin clanging like churches
And peter out. Sunk to the gunwhales
In their shapes tugs push upstream.
A carfloat booms down, sweeping past
Illusory suns that blaze in puddles   5
On the shores where it rained, past the Navy Yard,
Under the Williamsburg Bridge
That hangs facedown from its strings
Over which the Jamaica Local crawls,
Through white-winged gulls which shriek   10
And flap from the water and sideslip in
Over the chaos of illusions, dangling
Limp red hands, and screaming as they touch.

2

A boy swings his legs from the pier,
His days go by, tugs and carfloats go by,   15
Each prow pushing a whitecap. On his deathbed
Kane remembered the abrupt, missed Grail
Called Rosebud, Gatsby must have flashed back
To his days digging clams in Little Girl Bay
In Minnesota, Nick fished in dreamy Michigan,   20
Gant had his memories, Griffiths, those
Who went baying after the immaterial
And whiffed its strange dazzle in a blonde
In a canary convertible, who died
Thinking of the Huck Finns of themselves   25
On the old afternoons, themselves like this boy
Swinging his legs, who sees the *Ile de France*
Come in, and wonders if in some stateroom
There is not a sick-hearted heiress sitting
Drink in hand, saying to herself his name.   30

THE RIVER THAT IS EAST 2 *gunwhales:* the upper edge of a ship's side. 4 *carfloat:* car ferry. 17–18 *Kane . . . Rosebud:* the character Charles Foster Kane from Orson Welles' film, *Citizen Kane.* In medieval legend the "Grail," the chalice which Christ used at the Last Supper, was the object of many quests. The word has come to mean any object of dedicated search. In *Citizen Kane,* Rosebud is the name of a sled Kane played with as a child and then forgot until his deathbed. 18 *Gatsby:* Jay Gatsby, the hero of F. Scott Fitzgerald's novel, *The Great Gatsby,* who grew up in the Midwest, but attempted to adopt the lifestyle of a wealthy Long Islander. 20 *Nick:* Ernest Hemingway's character from *The Nick Adams Stories.* 21 *Gant:* Eugene Gant, hero of Thomas Wolfe's *Look Homeward, Angel* and *Of Time and the River; Griffiths:* Clyde Griffiths, the hero of Theodore Dreiser's *An American Tragedy,* attracted to the dazzling lifestyle of the rich, but condemned to death for the murder of his pregnant girlfriend.

3

A man stands on the pier.
He has long since stopped wishing his heart were full
Or his life dear to him.
He watches the snowfall hitting the dirty water.
He thinks: Beautiful. Beautiful.   35
If I were a gull I would be one with white wings,
I would fly out over the water, explode, and
Be beautiful snow hitting the dirty water.

4

And thou, River of Tomorrow, flowing . . .
We stand on the shore, which is mist beneath us,   40
And regard the onflowing river. Sometimes
It seems the river stops and the shore
Flows into the past. Nevertheless, its leaked promises
Hopping in the bloodstream, we strain for the future,
Sometimes even glimpse it, a vague, scummed thing   45
We dare not recognize, and peer again
At the cabled shroud out of which it came,
We who have no roots but the shifts of our pain,
No flowering but our own strange lives.

What is this river but the one   50
Which drags the things we love,
Processions of debris like floating lamps,
Toward the radiance in which they go out?
No, it is the River that is East, known once
From a high window in Brooklyn, in agony—river   55
On which a door locked to the water floats,
A window sash paned with brown water, a whiskey crate,
Barrel staves, sun spokes, feathers of the birds,
A breadcrust, a rat, spittle, butts, and peels,
The immaculate stream, heavy, and swinging home again.   60

                                                          1964

THE BURN   321

Twelve years ago I came here
to wander across burnt land,
I had only begun to know
the kind of pain others endure,
I was too full of sorrows.   5
Now, on the dirt road

that winds beside the Kilchis River
to the sea, saplings
on all the hills, I go deep
into the first forest of Douglas firs   10
shimmering out of prehistory,
a strange shine up where the tops
shut out the sky, whose roots
feed in the waters of the rainbow trout.
And here, at my feet, in the grain   15
of a burnt log opened by a riverfall,
the clear
swirls of the creation. At the
San Francisco airport, Charlotte,
where yesterday my arms   20
died around you like old snakeskins, the puffed
needletracks on your arms
marked how the veins wander.
I see you walking like a somnambulist
through a poppy field, blind   25
as myself on this dirt road, tiny
flowers brightening about you,
the skills of fire, of fanning
the blossoms until they die,
perfected; only the power to nurture   30
and make whole, only love,
impossible. The mouth of the river.
On these beaches
the sea throws itself down, in flames.

1968

THE MILK BOTTLE   322

A tiny creature moves
through the tide pool, holding up
its little fortress foretelling
our tragedies; another clamps
itself down to the stone. A sea anemone   5
sucks at my finger, mildly, I can just
feel it, though it may mean to kill—no,
it would probably say, to eat
and flow, for all these creatures
even half made of stone seem to thrill   10

to altered existences. As do we ourselves,
who advance so far, then stop, then creep
a little, stop again, suddenly gasp—breath
is the bright shell
of our life-wish encasing us—gasp   15
it all back in, on seeing that any time
would be OK
to go, to vanish back into things—as when
lovers wake up at night and see
they both are crying and think, *Yes,*   20
but it doesn't matter, already
we will have lived forever. And yes,
if we could do that: separate out
time from happiness, remove
the molecules scattered   25
throughout our flesh that remember, skim them off,
throw them at non-conscious things,
who may even crave them . . . It's funny,
I imagine I can actually remember one certain
quart of milk which has just finished clinking   30
against three of its brethren
in the milkman's great hand and stands,
freeing itself from itself, on the rotting
doorstep in Pawtucket circa 1932,
to be picked up and taken inside   35
by one in whom time hasn't yet completely
woven all its tangles, and not ever set down . . .
So that here, by the tide pool,
where a sea eagle rings its glass voice
above us, I remember myself back there,   40
and first dreams easily untangling
themselves rise in me, flow from me in waves,
as if they felt ready now to be fulfilled
out there where there is nothing.
The old bottle will shatter   45
in the decay of its music, the sea eagle
will cry itself back down into the sea
the sea's creatures transfigure over and over.
And now everything changes. Look:
Ahead of us the meantime is overflowing.   50
Around us its own almost-invisibility
streams and sparkles over everything.

1980

CAROLYN KIZER

(b. 1925)

AFTERNOON HAPPINESS

At a party I spy a handsome psychiatrist,
And wish, as we all do, to get her advice for free.
Doctor, I'll say, I'm supposed to be a poet.
All life's awfulness has been grist to me.
We learn that happiness is a Chinese meal,   5
While sorrow is a nourishment forever.
My new environment is California Dreamer.
I'm fearful I'm forgetting how to brood.
And, Doctor, another thing has got me worried:
I'm not drinking as much as I should. . . .   10

At home, I want to write a happy poem
On love, or a love poem of happiness.
But they won't do, the tensions of everyday,
The rub, the minor abrasions of any two
Who share one space. Ah, there's no substitute for tragedy!   15
But in this chapter, tragedy belongs
To that other life, the old life before *us*.
Here is my aphorism of the day:
Happy people are monogamous,
Even in California. So how does the poem play   20

Without the paraphernalia of betrayal and loss?
I don't have a jealous eye or fear
And neither do you. In truth, I'm fond
Of your ex-mate, whom I name, "my wife-in-law."
My former husband, that old disaster, is now just funny,   25
So laugh we do, in what Cyril Connolly
Has called the endless, nocturnal conversation
Of marriage. Which may be the best part.
Darling, must I love you in light verse
Without the tribute of profoundest art?   30

Of course it won't last. You will break my heart
Or I yours, by dying. I could weep over that.
But now it seems forced, here in these heaven hills,
The mourning doves mourning, the squirrels mating,
My old cat warm in my lap, here on our terrace   35

AFTERNOON HAPPINESS 26 *Cyril Connolly:* (1903–1974) English author of *The Unquiet Grave,* a
collection of essays and maxims.

As from below comes a musical cursing
As you mend my favorite plate. Later of course
I could pick a fight; there is always material in that.
But we don't come from fighting people, those
Who scream out red-hot iambs in their hate.   40

No, love, the heavy poem will have to come
From *temps perdu,* fertile with pain, or perhaps
Detonated by terrors far beyond this place
Where the world rends itself, and its tainted waters
Rise in the east to erode our safety here.   45
Much as I want to gather a lifetime thrift
And craft, my cunning skills tied in a knot for you,
There is only this useless happiness as gift.

                                                              1984

QUESTIONS

1. Does the poet's complaint in the first stanza coincide with your ideas about the sources of poetry?
2. Who is the person addressed in the first stanza? in the third stanza?
3. Does the tone of the poem shift at any point or is it consistent throughout?
4. What are the dichotomies explored in the poem?

SEMELE RECYCLED   324

After you left me forever,
I was broken into pieces,
and all the pieces flung into the river.
Then the legs crawled ashore
and aimlessly wandered the dusty cow-track.   5
They became, for a while, a simple roadside shrine:
A tiny table set up between the thighs
held a dusty candle, weed, and fieldflower chains
placed reverently there by children and old women.
My knees were hung with tin triangular medals   10
to cure all forms of hysterical disease.

After I died forever in the river,
my torso floated, bloated in the stream,
catching on logs or stones among the eddies.
White water foamed around it, then dislodged it;   15

---

42 *temps perdu:* lost times.
SEMELE RECYCLED title *Semele:* paramour of Zeus; she demanded Zeus appear before her in all his splendor and was destroyed by his lightnings.

after a whirlwind trip, it bumped ashore.
A grizzled old man who scavenged along the banks
had already rescued my arms and put them by,
knowing everything has its uses, sooner or later.

When he found my torso, he called it his canoe,   20
and, using my arms as paddles,
he rowed me up and down the scummy river.
When catfish nibbled my fingers, he scooped them up
and blessed his re-usable bait.
Clumsy but serviceable, that canoe!   25
The trail of blood that was its wake
attracted the carp and eels, and the river turtle,
easily landed, dazed by my tasty red.

A young lad found my head among the rushes
and placed it on a dry stone.   30
He carefully combed my hair with a bit of shell
and set small offerings before it
which the birds and rats obligingly stole at night,
so it seemed I ate.
And the breeze wound through my mouth and empty sockets   35
so my lungs would sigh and my dead tongue mutter.
Attached to my throat like a sacred necklace
was a circlet of small snails.
Soon the villagers came to consult my oracular head
with its waterweed crown.   40
Seers found occupation, interpreting sighs,
and their papyrus rolls accumulated.

Meanwhile, young boys retrieved my eyes
they used for marbles in a simple game
—till somebody's pretty sister snatched at them   45
and set them, for luck, in her bridal diadem.
Poor girl! When her future groom caught sight of her,
all eyes, he crossed himself in horror,
and stumbled away in haste
through her dowered meadows.   50

What then of my heart and organs,
my sacred slit
which loved you best of all?
They were caught in a fisherman's net
and tossed at night into a pen for swine.   55
But they shone so by moonlight that the sows stampeded,

trampled each other in fear, to get away.
And the fisherman's wife, who had 13 living children
and was contemptuous of holy love,
raked the rest of me onto the compost heap.   60

Then in their various places and helpful functions,
the altar, oracle, offal, canoe, and oars
learned the wild rumor of your return.
The altar leapt up and ran to the canoe,
scattering candle grease and wilted grasses.   65
Arms sprang to their sockets, blind hands with nibbled nails
groped their way, aided by loud lamentation,
to the bed of the bride, snatched up those unlucky eyes
from her discarded veil and diadem,
and rammed them home. O what a bright day it was!   70
This empty body danced on the river bank.
Hollow, it called and searched among the fields
for those parts that steamed and simmered in the sun,
and never would have found them.

But then your great voice rang out under the skies   75
my name!—and all those private names
for the parts and places that had loved you best.
And they stirred in their nest of hay and dung.
The distraught old ladies chasing their lost altar,
and the seers pursuing my skull, their lost employment,   80
and the tumbling boys, who wanted the magic marbles,
and the runaway groom, and the fisherman's 13 children
set up such a clamor with their cries of "Miracle!"
that our two bodies met like a thunderclap
in mid-day—right at the corner of that wretched field   85
with its broken fenceposts and startled, skinny cattle.
We fell in a heap on the compost heap
and all our loving parts made love at once,
while the bystanders cheered and prayed and hid their eyes
and then went decently about their business.   90

And here it is, moonlight again; we've bathed in the river
and are sweet and wholesome once more.
We kneel side by side in the sand;
we worship each other in whispers.
But the inner parts remember fermenting hay,   95
the comfortable odor of dung, the animal incense,
and passion, its bloody labor,
its birth and rebirth and decay.

1984

THE BLESSING   325

I.

Daughter-my-mother,
you have observed my worst.
Holding me together at your expense
has made you burn cool.

So did I in childhood: 5
nursed her old hurts and doubts,
myself made cool to shallowness.
She grew out as I grew in.
At mid-point, our furies met.

My mother's dust has rested   10
for fifteen years
in the front hall closet
because we couldn't bear to bury it.
Her dust-lined, dust-coated urn
squats among the size-eleven overshoes.   15
My father, who never forgets
his overshoes,
has forgotten that.

Hysterical-tongued daughter
of a dead marriage,   20
you shed hot tears in the bed
of that benign old woman
whose fierce joy you were:
tantrums in the closet
taking upon yourself the guilt   25
the split parents never felt.

Child and old woman
soothing each other,
sharing the same face
in a span of seventy years,   30
the same mother wit.

II.

I must go home, says my father,
his mind straying;
this is a hard time
for your mother. But she's been dead   35
these fifteen years.

Daughter and daughter, we sit
on either side.
Whose? Which? He's not sure.
After long silence,   40
don't press me, he says.

Mother, hysterical-tongued,
age and grace burned away
your excesses, left
that lavender-sweet child   45
who turned up the thermostat
on her electric blanket, folded
her hands on her breast.
You had dreamed death
as a silver prince: 50
like marrying Nehru, you said.

Dearest, does your dust hum
in the front hall closet—
this is a hard time for me—
among the umbrella points,   55
the canes, and overshoes
of that cold climate?

Each week she denies it,
my blithe mother
in that green, cloud-free landscape   60
where we whisper our dream-secrets
to each other.

III.

Daughter, you lived through
my difficult affairs
as I tried to console   65
your burnt-out childhood.
We coped with our fathers,
compared notes
on the old one and the cold one,
learned to moderate our hates.   70
Risible in suffering,
we grew up together.

THE BLESSING 51 *Nehru:* Indian leader and statesman.

Mother-my-daughter,
I have been blessed
on both sides of my life.   75
Forgive me if sometimes
like my fading father
I see you as one.

Not that I confuse
your two identities   80
as he does, taking off
or putting on his overshoes,
but my own role:

I lean on the bosom
of that double mother,   85
the ghost by night, the girl by day;
I between my
two mild furies,
alone but comforted.

And I will whisper blithely   90
in your dreams
when you are as old as I,
my hard time over.
Meanwhile, keep warm
your love, your bed,   95
and your wise heart and head,
my good daughter.

1984

FOR ASHLEY

THE COPULATING GODS   326

Brushing back the curls from your famous brow,
Lingering over the prominent temple vein
Purple as Aegean columns in the dawn,
Calm now, I ponder how self-consciously
The gods must fornicate.   5
It is that sense of unseen witness:
Those mortals with whom we couple or have coupled,
Clinging to our swan-suits, our bull-skins,
Our masquerades in coin and shrubbery.

We were their religion before they were born.   10
The spectacle of our carnality
Confused them into spiritual lust.
The headboard of our bed became their altar;
Rare nectar, shared, a common sacrament.
The wet drapery of our sheets, molded   15
To noble thighs, is made the basis
For a whole new aesthetic:
God is revealed as the first genius.

Men continue to invent our histories,
Deny our equal pleasure in each other.   20
Club-foot, nymphomanic, they dub us,
Then fabricate the net that God will cast
Over our raptures: we, trussed up like goats,
Paraded past the searchlights of the sky
By God himself, the ringmaster and cuckold,   25
Amidst a thunderous laughter and applause.

Tracing again the bones of your famous face,
I know we are not their history but our myth.
Heaven prevents time; and our astral raptures
Float buoyant in the universe. Come, kiss!   30
Come, swoon again, we who invented dying
And the whole alchemy of resurrection.
They will concoct a scripture explaining this.

1984

FOOD OF LOVE   327

Eating is touch carried to the bitter end.
—SAMUEL BUTLER II

I'm going to murder you with love;
I'm going to suffocate you with embraces;
I'm going to hug you, bone by bone,
Till you're dead all over.
Then I will dine on your delectable marrow.   5

You will become my personal Sahara;
I'll sun myself in you, then with one swallow
Drain your remaining brackish well.

With my female blade I'll carve my name
In your most aspiring palm   10
Before I chop it down.
Then I'll inhale your last oasis whole.

But in the total desert you become
You'll see me stretch, horizon to horizon,
Opulent mirage!   15
Wisteria balconies dripping cyclamen.
Vistas ablaze with crystal, laced in gold.

So you will summon each dry grain of sand
And move towards me in undulating dunes
Till you arrive at sudden ultramarine: 20
A Mediterranean to stroke your dusty shores;
Obstinate verdure, creeping inland, fast renudes
Your barrens; succulents spring up everywhere,
Surprising life! And I will be that green.

When you are fed and watered, flourishing   25
With shoots entwining trellis, dome and spire,
Till you are resurrected field in bloom,
I will devour you, my natural food,
My host, my final supper on the earth,
And you'll begin to die again.   30

1984

MAXINE KUMIN

(b. 1925)

WOODCHUCKS   328

Gassing the woodchucks didn't turn out right.
The knockout bomb from the Feed and Grain Exchange
was featured as merciful, quick at the bone
and the case we had against them was airtight,
both exits shoehorned shut with puddingstone,   5
but they had a sub-sub-basement out of range.

Next morning they turned up again, no worse
for the cyanide than we for our cigarettes
and state-store Scotch, all of us up to scratch.
They brought down the marigolds as a matter of course   10
and then took over the vegetable patch
nipping the broccoli shoots, beheading the carrots.

The food from our mouths, I said, righteously thrilling
to the feel of the .22, the bullets' neat noses.
I, a lapsed pacifist fallen from grace   15
puffed with Darwinian pieties for killing,
now drew a bead on the littlest woodchuck's face.
He died down in the everbearing roses.

Ten minutes later I dropped the mother. She
flipflopped in the air and fell, her needle teeth   20
still hooked in a leaf of early Swiss chard.
Another baby next. O one-two-three
the murderer inside me rose up hard,
the hawkeye killer came on stage forthwith.

There's one chuck left. Old wily fellow, he keeps   25
me cocked and ready day after day after day.
All night I hunt his humped-up form. I dream
I sight along the barrel in my sleep.
If only they'd all consented to die unseen
gassed underground the quiet Nazi way.   30

1971

HOW IT IS   329

Shall I say how it is in your clothes?
A month after your death I wear your blue jacket.
The dog at the center of my life recognizes
you've come to visit, he's ecstatic.
In the left pocket, a hole.   5
In the right, a parking ticket
delivered up last August on Bay State Road.
In my heart, a scatter like milkweed,
a flinging from the pods of the soul.
My skin presses your old outline.   10
It is hot and dry inside.

I think of the last day of your life,
old friend, how I would unwind it, paste
it together in a different collage,
back from the death car idling in the garage,   15
back up the stairs, your praying hands unlaced,

WOODCHUCKS 16 *Darwinian pieties:* Charles Darwin was responsible for the theory of evolution and the idea of the survival of the fittest.

reassembling the bites of bread and tuna fish
into a ceremony of sandwich,
running the home movie backward to a space
we could be easy in, a kitchen place   20
with vodka and ice, our words like living meat.

Dear friend, you have excited crowds
with your example. They swell
like wine bags, straining at your seams.
I will be years gathering up our words,   25
fishing out letters, snapshots, stains,
leaning my ribs against this durable cloth
to put on the dumb blue blazer of your death.

1978

MORNING SWIM   330

Into my empty head there come
a cotton beach, a dock wherefrom

I set out, oily and nude ♨
through mist, in chilly solitude.

There was no line, no roof or floor   5
to tell the water from the air.

Night fog thick as terry cloth
closed me in its fuzzy growth.

I hung my bathrobe on two pegs.
I took the lake between my legs.   10

Invaded and invader, I
went overhand on that flat sky.

Fish twitched beneath me, quick and tame.
In their green zone they sang my name

and in the rhythm of the swim   15
I hummed a two-four-time slow hymn.

I hummed *Abide with Me*. The beat
rose in the fine thrash of my feet,

MORNING SWIM 17 *Abide with Me:* a popular hymn.

rose in the bubbles I put out
slantwise, trailing through my mouth.   20

My bones drank water; water fell
through all my doors. I was the well

that fed the lake that met my sea
in which I sang *Abide with Me.*

1982

QUESTIONS

1. Why is the speaker's head "empty" in line 1? When have you experienced a similar feeling?
2. Which words and images help develop the feeling of unity the speaker feels with the scene she describes?
3. What is the connection between "Abide with Me" and the form of the poem?
4. Find the hymn text and explore the connections between it and the theme of the poem.

STANLEY KUNITZ
(b. 1905)

FATHER AND SON   331

Now in the suburbs and the falling light
I followed him, and now down sandy road
Whiter than bone-dust, through the sweet
Curdle of fields, where the plums
Dropped with their load of ripeness, one by one.   5
Mile after mile I followed, with skimming feet,
After the secret master of my blood,
Him, steeped in the odor of ponds, whose indomitable love
Kept me in chains. Strode years; stretched into bird;
Raced through the sleeping country where I was young,   10
The silence unrolling before me as I came,
The night nailed like an orange to my brow.

How should I tell him my fable and the fears,
How bridge the chasm in a casual tone,
Saying, "The house, the stucco one you built,   15
We lost. Sister married and went from home,
And nothing comes back, it's strange, from where she goes.
I lived on a hill that had too many rooms:

Light we could make, but not enough of warmth,
And when the light failed, I climbed under the hill.   20
The papers are delivered every day;
I am alone and never shed a tear."

At the water's edge, where the smothering ferns lifted
Their arms, "Father!" I cried, "Return! You know
The way. I'll wipe the mudstains from your clothes;   25
No trace, I promise, will remain. Instruct
Your son, whirling between two wars,
In the Gemara of your gentleness,
For I would be a child to those who mourn
And brother to the foundlings of the field   30
And friend of innocence and all bright eyes.
O teach me how to work and keep me kind."
Among the turtles and the lilies he turned to me
The white ignorant hollow of his face.

1944

QUESTIONS

1. What surprises you or upsets your initial expectations? How can you use the surprises as focal points as you create a reading?
2. What are the differences between the two speeches (stanzas 2 and 3)? Which is more effective?
3. How soon do you first realize what is actually going on between father and son? Looking back at the poem, do you find earlier hints that the encounters bridge time and space?

PHILIP LARKIN

(1922–1985)

CHURCH GOING   332

Once I am sure there's nothing going on
I step inside, letting the door thud shut.
Another church: matting, seats, and stone,
And little books; sprawlings of flowers, cut
For Sunday, brownish now; some brass and stuff   5
Up at the holy end; the small neat organ;
And a tense, musty, unignorable silence,
Brewed God knows how long. Hatless, I take off
My cycle-clips in awkward reverence,

FATHER AND SON 28 *Gemara*: the second part of the Talmud, much of which is obscure.

Move forward, run my hand around the font.   10
From where I stand, the roof looks almost new—
Cleaned, or restored? Someone would know: I don't.
Mounting the lectern, I peruse a few
Hectoring large-scale verses, and pronounce
'Here endeth' much more loudly than I'd meant.   15
The echoes snigger briefly. Back at the door
I sign the book, donate an Irish sixpence,
Reflect the place was not worth stopping for.

Yet stop I did: in fact I often do,
And always end much at a loss like this,   20
Wondering what to look for; wondering, too,
When churches fall completely out of use
What we shall turn them into, if we shall keep
A few cathedrals chronically on show,
Their parchment, plate and pyx in locked cases,   25
And let the rest rent-free to rain and sheep.
Shall we avoid them as unlucky places?

Or, after dark, will dubious women come
To make their children touch a particular stone;
Pick simples for a cancer; or on some   30
Advised night see walking a dead one?
Power of some sort or other will go on
In games, in riddles, seemingly at random;
But superstition, like belief, must die,
And what remains when disbelief has gone?   35
Grass, weedy pavement, brambles, buttress, sky,

A shape less recognisable each week,
A purpose more obscure. I wonder who
Will be the last, the very last, to seek
This place for what it was; one of the crew   40
That tap and jot and know what rood-lofts were?
Some ruin-bibber, randy for antique,
Or Christmas-addict, counting on a whiff
Of gown-and-bands and organ-pipes and myrrh?
Or will he be my representative,   45

CHURCH GOING 25 *pyx:* the container in which the communion wafer is kept. 30 *simples:* medicinal herbs. 41 *rood-lofts:* a loft or gallery in a church on which the cross is set up. 42 *ruin-bibber:* a bibber is a drinker.

Bored, uninformed, knowing the ghostly silt
Dispersed, yet tending to this cross of ground
Through suburb scrub because it held unspilt
So long and equably what since is found
Only in separation—marriage, and birth,   50
And death, and thoughts of these—for whom was built
This special shell? For, though I've no idea
What this accoutred frowsty barn is worth,
It pleases me to stand in silence here;

A serious house on serious earth it is,   55
In whose blent air all our compulsions meet,
Are recognised, and robed as destinies.
And that much never can be obsolete,
Since someone will forever be surprising
A hunger in himself to be more serious,   60
And gravitating with it to this ground,
Which, he once heard, was proper to grow wise in,
If only that so many dead lie round.

1955

QUESTIONS

1. What does the title lead you to expect? Is that what you find?
2. How does the first line relate to the rest of the poem?
3. Why does the speaker stop at this church? Has he done such a thing before?
4. Is the speaker a believer or a skeptic?
5. What does the speaker believe will eventually happen to the church and the beliefs it represents? What is his attitude toward that anticipated result?
6. What does he finally realize about himself?

TOADS   333

Why should I let the toad *work*
    Squat on my life?
Can't I use my wit as a pitchfork
    And drive the brute off?

Six days of the week it soils   5
    With its sickening poison—
Just for paying a few bills!
    That's out of proportion.

---

53 *accoutred:* outfitted or equipped; *frowsty:* musty.

Lots of folk live on their wits:
    Lecturers, lispers,
Losels, loblolly-men, louts—
    They don't end as paupers;

Lots of folk live up lanes
    With fires in a bucket,
Eat windfalls and tinned sardines—
    They seem to like it.

Their nippers have got bare feet,
    Their unspeakable wives
Are skinny as whippets—and yet
    No one actually *starves*.

Ah, were I courageous enough
    To shout *Stuff your pension!*
But I know, all too well, that's the stuff
    That dreams are made on:

For something sufficiently toad-like
    Squats in me, too;
Its hunkers are heavy as hard luck,
    And cold as snow,

And will never allow me to blarney
    My way to getting
The fame and the girl and the money
    All at one sitting.

I don't say, one bodies the other
    One's spiritual truth;
But I do say it's hard to lose either,
    When you have both.

1955

TOADS 11 *losels:* worthless people; *loblolly men:* louts. 17 *nippers:* small boys. 27 *hunkers:* haunches.

D. H. LAWRENCE
(1885–1930)

PIANO   334

Softly, in the dusk, a woman is singing to me;
Taking me back down the vista of years, till I see
A child sitting under the piano, in the boom of the tingling strings
And pressing the small, poised feet of a mother who smiles as she
    sings.

In spite of myself, the insidious mastery of song   5
Betrays me back, till the heart of me weeps to belong
To the old Sunday evenings at home, with winter outside
And hymns in the cosy parlour, the tinkling piano our guide.

So now it is vain for the singer to burst into clamour
With the great black piano appassionato. The glamour   10
Of childish days is upon me, my manhood is cast
Down in the flood of remembrance, I weep like a child for the past.

1918

QUESTIONS

1. How many "characters" are in this poem? Describe the conflicts and affinities
   between them.
2. To which character(s) do you, as the reader, find your sympathies drawn?
3. The narrator expresses his feelings. Do you see evidence of other feelings he may
   have but not name?
4. Consider an earlier version of this poem:

The Piano

Somewhere beneath that piano's superb sleek black
Must hide my mother's piano, little and brown, with the back
That stood close to the wall, and the front's faded silk both torn,
And the keys with little hollows, that my mother's fingers had worn.

Softly, in the shadows, a woman is singing to me
Quietly, through the years I have crept back to see
A child sitting under the piano, in the boom of the shaking strings
Pressing the little poised feet of the mother who smiles as she sings.

The full throated woman has chosen a winning, living song
And surely the heart that is in me must belong
To the old Sunday evenings, when darkness wandered outside
And hymns gleamed on our warm lips, as we watched mother's fingers glide.

Or this is my sister at home in the old front room
Singing love's first surprised gladness, alone in the gloom.
She will start when she sees me, and blushing, spread out her hands
To cover my mouth's raillery, till I'm bound in her shame's heartspun bands.

A woman is singing me a wild Hungarian air
And her arms, and her bosom, and the whole of her soul is bare.
And the great black piano is clamouring as my mother's never could clamour
And my mother's tunes are devoured of this music's ravaging glamour.

What is added or excised in the later version? How has the theme changed? Which
do you like better?

SNAKE   335

A snake came to my water-trough
On a hot, hot day, and I in pyjamas for the heat,
To drink there.

In the deep, strange-scented shade of the great dark carob-tree
I came down the steps with my pitcher   5
And must wait, must stand and wait, for there he was at the trough
    before me.

He reached down from a fissure in the earth-wall in the gloom
And trailed his yellow-brown slackness soft-bellied down, over the
    edge of the stone trough
And rested his throat upon the stone bottom,
And where the water had dripped from the tap, in a small clearness,   10
He sipped with his straight mouth,
Softly drank through his straight gums, into his slack long body,
Silently.

Someone was before me at my water-trough,
And I, like a second comer, waiting.   15

He lifted his head from his drinking, as cattle do,
And looked at me vaguely, as drinking cattle do,
And flickered his two-forked tongue from his lips, and mused a
    moment,
And stooped and drank a little more,
Being earth-brown, earth-golden from the burning bowels of the
    earth   20
On the day of Sicilian July, with Etna smoking.

The voice of my education said to me
He must be killed,
For in Sicily the black, black snakes are innocent, the gold are
    venomous.

And voices in me said, If you were a man   25
You would take a stick and break him now, and finish him off.

But must I confess how I liked him,
How glad I was he had come like a guest in quiet, to drink at my
    water-trough
And depart peaceful, pacified, and thankless,
Into the burning bowels of this earth?   30

Was it cowardice, that I dared not kill him?
Was it perversity, that I longed to talk to him?
Was it humility, to feel so honoured?
I felt so honoured.

And yet those voices: 35
If you were not afraid, you would kill him!

And truly I was afraid, I was most afraid,
But even so, honoured still more
That he should seek my hospitality
From out the dark door of the secret earth.   40

He drank enough
And lifted his head, dreamily, as one who has drunken,
And flickered his tongue like a forked night on the air, so black;
Seeming to lick his lips,

And looked around like a god, unseeing, into the air,   45
And slowly turned his head,
And slowly, very slowly, as if thrice adream,
Proceeded to draw his slow length curving round
And climb again the broken bank of my wall-face.

And as he put his head into that dreadful hole,   50
And as he slowly drew up, snake-easing his shoulders, and entered
    farther,
A sort of horror, a sort of protest against his withdrawing into that
    horrid black hole,
Deliberately going into the blackness, and slowly drawing himself
    after,
Overcame me now his back was turned.

I looked round, I put down my pitcher,   55
I picked up a clumsy log
And threw it at the water-trough with a clatter.

I think it did not hit him,
But suddenly that part of him that was left behind convulsed in
    undignified haste,
Writhed like lightning, and was gone   60
Into the black hole, the earth-lipped fissure in the wall-front,
At which, in the intense still noon, I stared with fascination.

And immediately I regretted it.
I thought how paltry, how vulgar, what a mean act!
I despised myself and the voices of my accursed human education.   65

And I thought of the albatross,
And I wished he would come back, my snake.

For he seemed to me again like a king,
Like a king in exile, uncrowned in the underworld,
Now due to be crowned again.   70

And so, I missed my chance with one of the lords
Of life.
And I have something to expiate;
A pettiness.

                                                                                1923

BAVARIAN GENTIANS   336

Not every man has gentians in his house
in Soft September, at slow, sad Michaelmas.

Bavarian gentians, big and dark, only dark
darkening the day-time, torch-like with the smoking blueness of
    Pluto's gloom,
ribbed and torch-like, with their blaze of darkness spread blue   5
down flattening into points, flattened under the sweep of white day
torch-flower of the blue-smoking darkness, Pluto's dark-blue daze,

---

SNAKE 66 *albatross:* in *The Rime of the Ancient Mariner,* by Coleridge, a sailor kills an albatross and
falls under a curse.
BAVARIAN GENTIANS title *gentians:* blue flowers. 2 *Michaelmas:* the feast of the archangel Michael,
celebrated on September 29th. 4 *Pluto's:* (also called Dis) the god of the underworld.

black lamps from the halls of Dis, burning dark blue,
giving off darkness, blue darkness, as Demeter's pale lamps give off
    light,
lead me then, lead the way.   10

Reach me a gentian, give me a torch!
let me guide myself with the blue, forked torch of this flower
down the darker and darker stairs, where blue is darkened on
    blueness
even where Persephone goes, just now, from the frosted September
to the sightless realm where darkness is awake upon the dark   15
and Persephone herself is but a voice
or a darkness invisible enfolded in the deeper dark
of the arms Plutonic, and pierced with the passion of dense gloom,
among the splendour of torches of darkness, shedding darkness on
    the lost bride and her groom.

1932

EDWARD LEAR
(1812–1888)

THERE WAS AN OLD MAN
WITH A BEARD   337

There was an Old Man with a beard,
Who said, "It is just as I feared!—
Two Owls and a Hen, four Larks and a Wren,
Have all built their nests in my beard!"

1846

THERE WAS AN OLD MAN IN A TREE   338

There was an Old Man in a tree,
Who was horribly bored by a Bee;
When they said, "Does it buzz?" he replied, "Yes, it does!"
"It's a regular brute of a Bee!"

1846

9 *Demeter:* Demeter, the goddess of agriculture, went to Hades to rescue her daughter Persephone,
the goddess of springtime, who had been kidnapped by Pluto. Persephone was allowed to return
to the earth for six months, but every fall she returns to the underworld.

THERE WAS AN OLD MAN WHO SUPPOSED   339

There was an Old Man who supposed,
That the street door was partially closed;
But some very large rats, ate his coats and his hats,
While that futile old gentleman dozed.

1846

DENISE LEVERTOV
(b. 1923)

PLEASURES   340

I like to find
what's not found
at once, but lies

within something of another nature,
in repose, distinct.   5
Gull feathers of glass, hidden

in white pulp: the bones of squid
which I pull out and lay
blade by blade on the draining board—

    tapered as if for swiftness, to pierce   10
    the heart, but fragile, substance
    belying design.   Or a fruit, *mamey,*

cased in rough brown peel, the flesh
rose-amber, and the seed:
the seed a stone of wood, carved and   15

polished, walnut-colored, formed
like a brazilnut, but large,
large enough to fill
the hungry palm of a hand.

I like the juicy stem of grass that grows   20
within the coarser leaf folded round,
and the butteryellow glow

in the narrow flute from which the morning-glory
opens blue and cool on a hot morning.

1959

QUESTIONS

1. Which details allow you to experience the pleasures described? Which senses are involved?
2. Does the poem move from particular to abstract or vice versa? What constraints does that put upon the poem and upon you as a reader?
3. What do the objects described (squid bones, *mamey* fruit, grass stem, morning-glory) have in common?
4. What do the metaphors and similes add to the pleasures described?

MATINS   341

i

The authentic! Shadows of it
sweep past in dreams, one could say imprecisely,
evoking the almost-silent
ripping apart of giant
sheets of cellophane. No.   5
It thrusts up close. Exactly in dreams
it has you off-guard, you
recognize it before you have time.
For a second before waking
the alarm bell is a red conical hat, it   10
takes form.

ii

The authentic! I said
rising from the toilet seat.
The radiator in rhythmic knockings
spoke of the rising steam.   15
The authentic, I said
breaking the handle of my hairbrush as I
brushed my hair in
rhythmic strokes: That's it,
that's joy, it's always   20
a recognition, the known
appearing fully itself, and
more itself than one knew.

iii

The new day rises
as heat rises,   25
knocking in the pipes
with rhythms it seizes for its own

MATINS title: morning prayers.

to speak of its invention—
the real, the new-laid
egg whose speckled shell   30
the poet fondles and must break
if he will be nourished.

iv

A shadow painted where
yes, a shadow must fall.
The cow's breath   35
not forgotten in the mist, in the
words. Yes,
verisimilitude draws up
heat in us, zest
to follow through,   40
follow through,
follow
transformations of day
in its turning, in its becoming.

v

Stir the holy grains, set   45
the bowls on the table and
call the child to eat.

While we eat we think,
as we think an undercurrent
of dream runs through us   50
faster than thought
towards recognition.

Call the child to eat,
send him off, his mouth
tasting of toothpaste, to go down   55
into the ground, into a roaring train
and to school.

His cheeks are pink
his black eyes hold his dreams, he has left
forgetting his glasses.   60

Follow down the stairs at a clatter
to give them to him and save
his clear sight.

Cold air
comes in at the street door.   65

vi

The authentic! It rolls
just out of reach, beyond
running feet and
stretching fingers, down
the green slope and into   70
the black waves of the sea.
Speak to me, little horse, beloved,
tell me
how to follow the iron ball,
how to follow through to the country   75
beneath the waves
to the place where I must kill you and you step out
of your bones and flystrewn meat
tall, smiling, renewed,
formed in your own likeness.   80

vii

Marvelous Truth, confront us
at every turn,
in every guise, iron ball,
egg, dark horse, shadow,
cloud   85
of breath on the air,

dwell
in our crowded hearts
our steaming bathrooms, kitchens full of
things to be done, the   90
ordinary streets.

Thrust close your smile
that we know you, terrible joy.

1962

STEPPING WESTWARD   342

What is green in me
darkens, muscadine.

If woman is inconstant,
good, I am faithful to

STEPPING WESTWARD 2 *muscadine:* a type of grape.

ebb and flow, I fall   5
in season and now

is a time of ripening.
If her part

is to be true,
a north star,   10

good, I hold steady
in the black sky

and vanish by day,
yet burn there

in blue or above   15
quilts of cloud.

There is no savor
more sweet, more salt

than to be glad to be
what, woman,   20

and who, myself,
I am, a shadow

that grows longer as the sun
moves, drawn out

on a thread of wonder.   25
If I bear burdens

they begin to be remembered
as gifts, goods, a basket

of bread that hurts
my shoulders but closes me   30

in fragrance. I can
eat as I go.

1963

THE ACHE OF MARRIAGE   343

The ache of marriage:

thigh and tongue, beloved,
are heavy with it,
it throbs in the teeth

We look for communion   5
and are turned away, beloved,
each and each

It is leviathan and we
in its belly
looking for joy, some joy   10
not to be known outside it

two by two in the ark of
the ache of it.

1964

THE SECRET   344

Two girls discover
the secret of life
in a sudden line of
poetry.

I who don't know the   5
secret wrote
the line. They
told me

(through a third person)
they had found it   10
but not what it was
not even

what line it was. No doubt
by now, more than a week
later, they have forgotten   15
the secret,

the line, the name of the poem. I love them
for finding what
I can't find,

and for loving me   20
for the line I wrote,
and for forgetting it
so that

THE ACHE OF MARRIAGE 8 *leviathan:* a sea monster which swallowed Jonah.

a thousand times, till death
finds them, they may   25
discover it again, in other
lines

in other
happenings. And for
wanting to know it,   30
for

assuming there is
such a secret, yes,
for that
most of all.   35
                                                        1964

PHILIP LEVINE
(b. 1928)

TO A CHILD TRAPPED IN A
BARBER SHOP   345

You've gotten in through the transom
        and you can't get out
till Monday morning or, worse,
        till the cops come.

That six-year-old red face   5
        calling for mama
is yours; it won't help you
        because your case

is closed forever, hopeless.
        So don't drink   10
the Lucky Tiger, don't
        fill up on grease

because that makes it a lot worse,
        that makes it a crime
against property and the state   15
        and that costs time.

TO A CHILD TRAPPED IN A BARBER SHOP 1 *transom:* a small window directly over a door.

We've all been here before,
       we took our turn
under the electric storm
       of the vibrator   20

and stiffened our wills to meet
       the close clippers
and heard the true blade mowing
       back and forth

on a strip of dead skin,   25
       and we stopped crying.
You think your life is over?
       It's just begun.

1968

QUESTIONS

1. What in this poem awakens your memories of childhood fears or nightmares?
2. Why is it important to know that the child is six years old?
3. Show how the poem uses the particular to move toward a more general observation. Is it predictable or does it provide a new angle for an old dilemma?
4. What does "the true blade mowing / back and forth" bring to mind? How does that contribute to your reading?

ANIMALS ARE PASSING FROM OUR LIVES   346

It's wonderful how I jog
on four honed-down ivory toes
my massive buttocks slipping
like oiled parts with each light step.

I'm to market. I can smell   5
the sour, grooved block, I can smell
the blade that opens the hole
and the pudgy white fingers

that shake out the intestines
like a hankie. In my dreams   10
the snouts drool on the marble,
suffering children, suffering flies,

suffering the consumers
who won't meet their steady eyes
for fear they could see. The boy   15
who drives me along believes

that any moment I'll fall
on my side and drum my toes
like a typewriter or squeal
and shit like a new housewife   20

discovering television,
or that I'll turn like a beast
cleverly to hook his teeth
with my teeth. No. Not this pig.

1968

C. DAY LEWIS
(1904–1972)

SONG   347

Come, live with me and be my love,
And we will all the pleasures prove
Of peace and plenty, bed and board,
That chance employment may afford.

I'll handle dainties on the docks   5
And thou shalt read of summer frocks:
At evening by the sour canals
We'll hope to hear some madrigals.

Care on thy maiden brow shall put
A wreath of wrinkles, and thy foot   10
Be shod with pain: not silken dress
But toil shall tire thy loveliness.

Hunger shall make thy modest zone
And cheat fond death of all but bone—
If these delights thy mind may move,   15
Then live with me and be my love.

1935

SONG 13 *zone:* belt.

A U D R E   L O R D E
(b. 1934)

CONVERSATIONS IN CRISIS   348

I speak to you as a friend speaks
or a true lover
not out of friendship nor love
but for a clear meeting
of self upon self   5
in sight of our hearth
but without fire.

I cherish your words that ring
like late summer thunders
to sing without octave   10
and fade, having spoken the season.
But I hear the false heat of this voice
as it dries up the sides of your words
coaxing melodies from your tongue
and this curled music is treason.   15

Must I die in your fever—
or, as the flames wax, take cover
in your heart's culverts
crouched like a stranger
under scorched leaves of your other burnt loves   20
until the storm passes over?

                                                    1962

NOW THAT I AM FOREVER WITH CHILD   349

How the days went
while you were blooming within me
I remember each upon each—
the swelling changed planes of my body
and how you first fluttered, then jumped   5
and I thought it was my heart.

How the days wound down
and the turning of winter
I recall, with you growing heavy
against the wind. I thought   10
now her hands

are formed, and her hair
has started to curl
now her teeth are done
now she sneezes.   15
Then the seed opened
I bore you one morning just before spring
My head rang like a fiery piston
my legs were towers between which
A new world was passing.   20

Since then
I can only distinguish
one thread within running hours
You, flowing through selves
toward You.   25

                                                              1963

GENERATION   350

How the young attempt and are broken
differs from age to age
We were brown free girls
love singing beneath our skin
sun in our hair in our eyes   5
sun our fortune
and the wind had made us golden
made us gay.

In a season of limited power
we wept out our promises   10
And these are the children we try now
for temptations that wear our face.
But who comes back from our latched cities of falsehood
to warn them the road to nowhere
is slippery with our blood   15
to warn them
they need not drink the river to get home
since we have purchased bridges
with our mothers' bloody gold;—
now we are more than kin   20
who come to share
not only blood
but the bloodiness of failure.

How the young are tempted and betrayed
into slaughter or conformity   25
is a turn of the mirror
time's question only.

1966

REVOLUTION IS ONE FORM OF
SOCIAL CHANGE   351

When the man is busy
making niggers
it doesn't matter
much
what shade   5
you are.

If he runs out of one
particular color
he can always switch
to size   10
and when he's finished
off the big ones
he'll just change
to sex
which is   15
after all
where it all began.

1968

PAPERWEIGHT   352

Paper is neither kind nor cruel
merely white in its neutrality
I have for reality now
the brown bar of my arm
moving in broken rhythm   5
across this dead place.

All the poems I have ever written
are historical reviews of some now-absorbed country
a small judgment

hawking and coughing them up   10
I have ejected them not unlike children.
Now my throat is clear
and perhaps I shall speak again.

All the poems I have ever written
make a small book shaped like another me   15
called by yesterday's names
the shedding of a past in patched conceits
molted like snake skin—
a book of leavings.
I can do anything with them I wish   20
I can love them or hate them
use them for comfort or warmth
tissues or decoration
dolls or japanese baskets
blankets or spells.   25
I can use them for magic
lanterns or music
advice or small counsel
for napkins or past-times or
disposable diapers   30
I can make fire from them
or kindling
songs or paper chains

Or fold them all into a paper fan
with which to cool my husband's dinner.   35
                                                              1969

LOVE, MAYBE   353

Always
in the middle
of our bloodiest battles
you lay down your arms
like flowering mines   5

to conqueror me home.
                                                              1970

BLACK MOTHER WOMAN 354

I cannot recall you gentle
yet through your heavy love
I have become
an image of your once delicate flesh
split with deceitful longings.   5

When strangers come and compliment me
your aged spirit takes a bow
jingling with pride
but once you hid that secret
in the center of furies   10
hanging me
with deep breasts and wiry hair
with your own split flesh
and long suffering eyes
buried in myths of little worth.   15
But I have peeled away your anger
down to the core of love
and look mother
I Am
a dark temple where your true spirit rises   20
beautiful
and tough as chestnut
stanchion against your nightmare of weakness
and if my eyes conceal
a squadron of conflicting rebellions   25
I learned from you
to define myself
through your denials.

                                                                1971

HANGING FIRE 355

I am fourteen
and my skin has betrayed me
the boy I cannot live without
still sucks his thumb
in secret   5
how come my knees are

always so ashy
what if I die
before morning
and momma's in the bedroom   10
with the door closed.

I have to learn how to dance
in time for the next party
my room is too small for me
suppose I die before graduation   15
they will sing sad melodies
but finally
tell the truth about me
There is nothing I want to do
and too much   20
that has to be done
and momma's in the bedroom
with the door closed.

Nobody even stops to think
about my side of it   25
I should have been on Math Team
my marks were better than his
why do I have to be
the one
wearing braces   30
I have nothing to wear tomorrow
will I live long enough
to grow up
and momma's in the bedroom
with the door closed.   35

                                                                        1978

RICHARD LOVELACE

(1618–1658)

TO LUCASTA, GOING TO THE WARS   356

Tell me not, sweet, I am unkind
That from the nunnery
Of thy chaste breast and quiet mind,
To war and arms I fly.

True, a new mistress now I chase,   5
The first foe in the field;
And with a stronger faith embrace
A sword, a horse, a shield.

Yet this inconstancy is such
As you too shall adore;   10
I could not love thee, dear, so much,
Loved I not honor more.

                                                                        1649

QUESTIONS

1. What challenge do the last two lines present as you attempt to create a fresh reading
   of this poem?
2. Describe all facets of the extended metaphor at work in this poem.
3. Is the resolution convincing?

ROBERT LOWELL

(1917–1977)

THE QUAKER GRAVEYARD
IN NANTUCKET   357

(FOR WARREN WINSLOW, DEAD AT SEA)

*Let man have dominion over the fishes of the sea and the fowls of the air and the beasts
and the whole earth, and every creeping creature that moveth upon the earth.*

I

A brackish reach of shoal off Madaket,—
The sea was still breaking violently and night
Had steamed into our North Atlantic Fleet,
When the drowned sailor clutched the drag-net. Light
Flashed from his matted head and marble feet,   5
He grappled at the net
With the coiled, hurdling muscles of his thighs:
The corpse was bloodless, a botch of reds and whites,
Its open, staring eyes
Were lustreless dead-lights   10
Or cabin-windows on a stranded hulk
Heavy with sand. We weight the body, close
Its eyes and heave it seaward whence it came,

THE QUAKER GRAVEYARD AT NANTUCKET dedication *Warren Winslow:* Lowell's cousin.

Where the heel-headed dogfish barks its nose
On Ahab's void and forehead; and the name   15
Is blocked in yellow chalk.
Sailors, who pitch this portent at the sea
Where dreadnaughts shall confess
Its hell-bent deity,
When you are powerless   20
To sand-bag this Atlantic bulwark, faced
By the earth-shaker, green, unwearied, chaste
In his steel scales: ask for no Orphean lute
To pluck life back. The guns of the steeled fleet
Recoil and then repeat   25
The hoarse salute.

II

Whenever winds are moving and their breath
Heaves at the roped-in bulwarks of this pier,
The terns and sea-gulls tremble at your death
In these home waters. Sailor, can you hear   30
The Pequod's sea wings, beating landward, fall
Headlong and break on our Atlantic wall
Off 'Sconset, where the yawing S-boats splash
The bellbuoy, with ballooning spinnakers,
As the entangled, screeching mainsheet clears   35
The blocks: off Madaket, where lubbers lash
The heavy surf and throw their long lead squids
For blue-fish? Sea-gulls blink their heavy lids
Seaward. The winds' wings beat upon the stones,
Cousin, and scream for you and the claws rush   40
At the sea's throat and wring it in the slush
Of this old Quaker graveyard where the bones
Cry out in the long night for the hurt beast
Bobbing by Ahab's whaleboats in the East.

III

All you recovered from Poseidon died   45
With you, my cousin, and the harrowed brine
Is fruitless on the blue beard of the god,
Stretching beyond us to the castles in Spain,
Nantucket's westward haven. To Cape Cod

15 *Ahab:* the hero of Melville's *Moby Dick,* Ahab was a crazed hunter of the white whale. 23
Orphean lute: Orpheus married Eurydice who died soon afterwards. He followed her to the
underworld where his music persuaded Persephone to allow Eurydice to return with him. 31
Pequod: Ahab's ship, destroyed by Moby Dick. 33 *'Sconset:* Siasconset on Nantucket; *S-boats:* large
sailing boats. 36 *lubbers:* landlubbers. 45 *Poseidon:* Neptune, god of the sea.

Guns, cradled on the tide,   50
Blast the eelgrass about a waterclock
Of bilge and backwash, roil the salt and sand
Lashing earth's scaffold, rock
Our warships in the hand
Of the great God, where time's contrition blues   55
Whatever it was these Quaker sailors lost
In the mad scramble of their lives. They died
When time was open-eyed,
Wooden and childish; only bones abide
There, in the nowhere, where their boats were tossed   60
Sky-high, where mariners had fabled news
Of IS, the whited monster. What it cost
Them is their secret. In the sperm-whale's slick
I see the Quakers drown and hear their cry:
"If God himself had not been on our side,   65
If God himself had not been on our side,
When the Atlantic rose against us, why,
Then it had swallowed us up quick."

IV

This is the end of the whaleroad and the whale
Who spewed Nantucket bones on the thrashed swell   70
And stirred the troubled waters to whirlpools
To send the Pequod packing off to hell:
This is the end of them, three-quarters fools,
Snatching at straws to sail
Seaward and seaward on the turntail whale,   75
Spouting out blood and water as it rolls,
Sick as a dog to these Atlantic shoals:
Clamavimus, O depths. Let the sea-gulls wail

For water, for the deep where the high tide
Mutters to its hurt self, mutters and ebbs.   80
Waves wallow in their wash, go out and out,
Leave only the death-rattle of the crabs,
The beach increasing, its enormous snout
Sucking the ocean's side.
This is the end of running on the waves;   85
We are poured out like water. Who will dance
The mast-lashed master of Leviathans
Up from this field of Quakers in their unstoned graves?

78 *Clamavimus:* Latin for "We have cried." 87 *Leviathans:* Leviathan was a sea monster which swallowed Jonah.

V

When the whale's viscera go and the roll
Of its corruption overruns this world   90
Beyond tree-swept Nantucket and Wood's Hole
And Martha's Vineyard, Sailor, will your sword
Whistle and fall and sink into the fat?
In the great ash-pit of Jehoshaphat
The bones cry for the blood of the white whale,   95
The fat flukes arch and whack about its ears,
The death-lance churns into the sanctuary, tears
The gun-blue swingle, heaving like a flail,
And hacks the coiling life out: it works and drags
And rips the sperm-whale's midriff into rags,   100
Gobbets of blubber spill to wind and weather,
Sailor, and gulls go round the stoven timbers
Where the morning stars sing out together
And thunder shakes the white surf and dismembers
The red flag hammered in the mast-head. Hide,   105
Our steel, Jonas Messias, in Thy side.

VI

Our Lady of Walsingham

There once the penitents took off their shoes
And then walked barefoot the remaining mile;
And the small trees, a stream and hedgerows file
Slowly along the munching English lane,   110
Like cows to the old shrine, until you lose
Track of your dragging pain.
The stream flows down under the druid tree,
Shiloah's whirlpools gurgle and make glad
The castle of God. Sailor, you were glad   115
And whistled Sion by that stream. But see:

Our Lady, too small for her canopy,
Sits near the altar. There's no comeliness
At all or charm in that expressionless
Face with its heavy eyelids. As before,   120
This face, for centuries a memory,

---

94 *Jehoshaphat:* "Let the heathen be wakened, and come up to the valley of Jehosophat: for there will I sit to judge all the heathen round about" (Joel 3:12). 98 *swingle:* a wooden, swordlike tool. 101 *gobbets:* lumps. 105 *red flag:* at the end of *Moby Dick,* Ahab's flag is nailed to the sinking *Pequod's* mast. 106 *Jonas Messias:* Jonah, identified with the Messiah. VI *Our Lady of Walsingham:* an image of the Virgin Mary frequently visited by pilgrims. 114 *Shiloah:* ancient town of Israel, site of the Tabernacle. 116 *Sion:* Zion.

Non est species, neque decor,
Expressionless, expresses God: it goes
Past castled Sion. She knows what God knows,
Not Calvary's Cross nor crib at Bethlehem   125
Now, and the world shall come to Walsingham.

VII

The empty winds are creaking and the oak
Splatters and splatters on the cenotaph,
The boughs are trembling and a gaff
Bobs on the untimely stroke   130
Of the greased wash exploding on a shoal-bell
In the old mouth of the Atlantic. It's well;
Atlantic, you are fouled with the blue sailors,
Sea-monsters, upward angel, downward fish:
Unmarried and corroding, spare of flesh   135
Mart once of supercilious, wing'd clippers,
Atlantic, where your bell-trap guts its spoil
You could cut the brackish winds with a knife
Here in Nantucket, and cast up the time
When the Lord God formed man from the sea's slime   140
And breathed into his face the breath of life,
And blue-lung'd combers lumbered to the kill.
The Lord survives the rainbow of His will.

1946

SKUNK HOUR   358

(FOR ELIZABETH BISHOP)

Nautilus Island's hermit
heiress still lives through winter in her Spartan cottage;
her sheep still graze above the sea.
Her son's a bishop. Her farmer
is first selectman in our village;   5
she's in her dotage.

Thirsting for
the hierarchic privacy
of Queen Victoria's century,

---

122 *Non est species, neque decor:* "There is no comeliness or beauty" (Latin). 128 *cenotaph:* a monument honoring a dead person whose body is elsewhere. 129 *gaff:* a large, strong hook on a pole. 131 *shoal-bell:* bell-buoy. 142 *combers:* large waves.
SKUNK HOUR dedication "Skunk Hour" is influenced by Elizabeth Bishop's "The Armadillo."

she buys up all₁₀　　　　　　　　　　　　　　　　　　10
the eyesores facing her shore,
and lets them fall.

The season's ill—
we've lost our summer millionaire,
who seemed to leap from an L. L. Bean　　　　　　15
catalogue. His nine-knot yawl
was auctioned off to lobstermen.
A red fox stain covers Blue Hill.

And now our fairy
decorator brightens his shop for fall;　　　　　　20
his fishnet's filled with orange cork,
orange, his cobbler's bench and awl;
there is no money in his work,
he'd rather marry.

One dark night,　　　　　　　　　　　　　　　　25
my Tudor Ford climbed the hill's skull;
I watched for love-cars. Lights turned down,
they lay together, hull to hull,
where the graveyard shelves on the town. . . .
My mind's not right.　　　　　　　　　　　　　30

A car radio bleats,
"Love, O careless Love. . . ." I hear
my ill-spirit sob in each blood cell,
as if my hand were at its throat. . . .
I myself am hell;　　　　　　　　　　　　　35
nobody's here—

only skunks, that search
in the moonlight for a bite to eat.
They march on their soles up Main Street:
white stripes, moonstruck eyes' red fire　　　40
under the chalk-dry and spar spire
of the Trinitarian Church.

I stand on top
of our back steps and breathe the rich air—
a mother skunk with her column of kittens swills the garbage pail.　　45
She jabs her wedge-head in a cup
of sour cream, drops her ostrich tail,
and will not scare.

1959

QUESTIONS

1. Read Elizabeth Bishop's poem, "The Armadillo," which served as the model for "Skunk Hour." What similarities, if any, do you find in the structures of the two poems? In the theme? In the tone? In the direction?
2. Identify the various settings and characters described throughout the poem. In what order do they appear? What are the implications?
3. Line 35 is an allusion to Milton's *Paradise Lost* (IV:75), where Lucifer says, "Which way I fly is Hell; myself am Hell." What does the allusion contribute to the meaning of the poem?
4. What quality do the skunks exhibit? Does this provide a resolution?

FOR THE UNION DEAD   359

"RELINQUUNT OMNIA SERVARE REM PUBLICAM."

The old South Boston Aquarium stands
in a Sahara of snow now. Its broken windows are boarded.
The bronze weathervane cod has lost half its scales.
The airy tanks are dry.

Once my nose crawled like a snail on the glass;   5
my hand tingled
to burst the bubbles
drifting from the noses of the cowed, compliant fish.

My hand draws back. I often sigh still
for the dark downward and vegetating kingdom   10
of the fish and reptile. One morning last March,
I pressed against the new barbed and galvanized

fence on the Boston Common. Behind their cage,
yellow dinosaur steamshovels were grunting
as they cropped up tons of mush and grass   15
to gouge their underworld garage.

Parking spaces luxuriate like civic
sandpiles in the heart of Boston.
A girdle of orange, Puritan-pumpkin colored girders
braces the tingling Statehouse,   20

FOR THE UNION DEAD epigraph *Relinquunt Omnia Servare Rem Publicam:* "They give up everything to serve the Republic" (Latin).

shaking over the excavations, as it faces Colonel Shaw
and his bell-cheeked Negro infantry
on St. Gaudens' shaking Civil War relief,
propped by a plank splint against the garage's earthquake.

Two months after marching through Boston, 25
half the regiment was dead;
at the dedication,
William James could almost hear the bronze Negroes breathe.

Their monument sticks like a fishbone
in the city's throat. 30
Its Colonel is as lean
as a compass-needle.

He has an angry wrenlike vigilance,
a greyhound's gentle tautness;
he seems to wince at pleasure, 35
and suffocate for privacy.

He is out of bounds now. He rejoices in man's lovely,
peculiar power to choose life and die—
when he leads his black soldiers to death,
he cannot bend his back. 40

On a thousand small town New England greens,
the old white churches hold their air
of sparse, sincere rebellion; frayed flags
quilt the graveyards of the Grand Army of the Republic.

The stone statues of the abstract Union Soldier 45
grow slimmer and younger each year—
wasp-wasted, they doze over muskets
and muse through their sideburns . . .

Shaw's father wanted no monument
except the ditch, 50
where his son's body was thrown
and lost with his "niggers."

21–23: *Colonel Shaw . . . relief:* Lowell describes a monument by Augustus Saint-Gaudens which is on Boston Commons. It depicts the commander of a Negro regiment, Robert Gould Shaw, killed in battle. 28 *William James:* (1842–1910) Harvard psychologist and philosopher.

The ditch is nearer.
There are no statues for the last war here;
on Boylston Street, a commercial photograph   55
shows Hiroshima boiling

over a Mosler Safe, the "Rock of Ages"
that survived the blast. Space is nearer.
When I crouch to my television set,
the drained faces of Negro school-children rise like balloons.   60

Colonel Shaw
is riding on his bubble,
he waits
for the blessèd break.

The Aquarium is gone. Everywhere,   65
giant finned cars nose forward like fish;
a savage servility
slides by on grease.

1959

ROBERT FROST   360

Robert Frost at midnight, the audience gone
to vapor, the great act laid on the shelf in mothballs,
his voice musical, raw and raw—he writes in the flyleaf:
"Robert Lowell from Robert Frost, his friend in the art."
"Sometimes I feel too full of myself," I say.   5
And he, misunderstanding, "When I am low,
I stray away. My son wasn't your kind. The night
we told him Merrill Moore would come to treat him,
he said, 'I'll kill him first.' One of my daughters thought things,
knew every male she met was out to make her;   10
the way she dresses, she couldn't make a whorehouse."
And I, "Sometimes I'm so happy I can't stand myself."
And he, "When I am too full of joy, I think
how little good my health did anyone near me."

1969

54 *the last war:* World War II.
ROBERT FROST 8 *Merrill Moore:* psychoanalyst and poet.

CLAUDE McKAY
(1890–1948)

IF WE MUST DIE   361

If we must die, let it not be like hogs
Hunted and penned in an inglorious spot,
While round us bark the mad and hungry dogs,
Making their mock at our accursed lot.
If we must die, O let us nobly die,   5
So that our precious blood may not be shed
In vain; then even the monsters we defy
Shall be constrained to honor us though dead!
O kinsmen! we must meet the common foe!
Though far outnumbered let us show us brave,   10
And for their thousand blows deal one deathblow!
What though before us lies the open grave?
Like men we'll face the murderous, cowardly pack,
Pressed to the wall, dying, but fighting back!

1922

QUESTIONS

1. Claude McKay wrote this poem initially in response to the 1919 Harlem race riots. How does that affect your reading?
2. Later in World War II the poem was used by Winston Churchill and Senator Henry Cabot Lodge, Sr., to rally Englishmen and Americans to the cause of the war. How does that change or expand your reading?
3. Identify the metaphor used throughout the poem. Does it change?
4. How do form and content relate?

ARCHIBALD MacLEISH
(1892–1982)

ARS POETICA   362

A poem should be palpable and mute
As a globed fruit,

Dumb
As old medallions to the thumb,

Silent as the sleeve-worn stone   5
Of casement ledges where the moss has grown—

ARS POETICA title: "The Art of Poetry" (Latin).

A poem should be wordless
As the flight of birds.

A poem should be motionless in time
As the moon climbs,   10

Leaving, as the moon releases
Twig by twig the night-entangled trees,

Leaving, as the moon behind the winter leaves,
Memory by memory the mind—

A poem should be motionless in time   15
As the moon climbs.

A poem should be equal to:
Not true.

For all the history of grief
An empty doorway and a maple leaf.   20

For love
The leaning grasses and two lights above the sea—

A poem should not mean
But be.

                                                                       1926

QUESTIONS

1. Disregarding the rest of the poem, speculate about what the final two lines of the
   poem might mean.
2. Identify the similes in the poem. What do they describe?
3. How does the poem present the sensory experience of poetry?
4. Identify the concrete images and the abstract statements. How do they support each
   other?

YOU, ANDREW MARVELL   363

And here face down beneath the sun
And here upon earth's noonward height
To feel the always coming on
The always rising of the night

To feel creep up the curving east   5
The earthy chill of dusk and slow
Upon those under lands the vast
And ever climbing shadow grow

And strange at Ecbatan the trees
Take leaf by leaf the evening strange 10
The flooding dark about their knees
The mountains over Persia change

And now at Kermanshah the gate
Dark empty and the withered grass
And through the twilight now the late 15
Few travelers in the westward pass

And Baghdad darken and the bridge
Across the silent river gone
And through Arabia the edge
Of evening widen and steal on 20

And deepen on Palmyra's street
The wheel rut in the ruined stone
And Lebanon fade out and Crete
High through the clouds and overblown

And over Sicily the air 25
Still flashing with the landward gulls
And loom and slowly disappear
The sails above the shadowy hulls

And Spain go under and the shore
Of Africa the gilded sand 30
And evening vanish and no more
The low pale light across that land

Nor now the long light on the sea
And here face downward in the sun
To feel how swift how secretly 35
The shadow of the night comes on. . . .

1930

LOUIS MacNEICE
(1907–1963)

LONDON RAIN 364

The rain of London pimples
The ebony street with white
And the neon-lamps of London

Stain the canals of night
And the park becomes a jungle 5
In the alchemy of night.

My wishes turn to violent
Horses black as coal—
The randy mares of fancy,
The stallions of the soul— 10
Eager to take the fences
That fence about my soul.

Across the countless chimneys
The horses ride and across
The country to the channel 15
Where warning beacons toss,
To a place where God and No-God
Play at pitch and toss.

Whichever wins I am happy
For God will give me bliss 20
But No-God will absolve me
From all I do amiss
And I need not suffer conscience
If the world was made amiss.

Under God we can reckon 25
On pardon when we fall
But if we are under No-God
Nothing will matter at all,
Adultery and murder
Will count for nothing at all. 30

So reinforced by logic
As having nothing to lose
My lust goes riding horseback
To ravish where I choose,
To burgle all the turrets 35
Of beauty as I choose.

But now the rain gives over
Its dance upon the town,
Logic and lust together
Come dimly tumbling down, 40
And neither God nor No-God
Is either up or down.

The argument was wilful,
The alternatives untrue,
We need no metaphysics   45
To sanction what we do
Or to muffle us in comfort
From what we did not do.

Whether the living river
Began in bog or lake,   50
The world is what was given,
The world is what we make.
And we only can discover
Life in the life we make.

So let the water sizzle   55
Upon the gleaming slates,
There will be sunshine after
When the rain abates
And rain returning duly
When the sun abates.   60

My wishes now come homeward,
Their gallopings in vain,
Logic and lust are quiet
And again it starts to rain;
Falling asleep I listen   65
To the falling London rain.

                                                        1941

CHRISTOPHER MARLOWE
(1564–1593)

THE PASSIONATE SHEPHERD TO HIS LOVE   365

Come live with me and be my love,
And we will all the pleasures prove
That valleys, groves, hills, and fields,
Woods, or steepy mountain yields.

And we will sit upon the rocks,   5
Seeing the shepherds feed their flocks,
By shallow rivers to whose falls
Melodious birds sing madrigals.

THE PASSIONATE SHEPHERD TO HIS LOVE 2 *prove:* try.

And I will make thee beds of roses
And a thousand fragrant posies,   10
A cap of flowers, and a kirtle
Embroidered all with leaves of myrtle;

A gown made of the finest wool
Which from our pretty lambs we pull;
Fair lined slippers for the cold,   15
With buckles of the purest gold;

A belt of straw and ivy buds,
With coral clasps and amber studs:
And if these pleasures may thee move,
Come live with me, and be my love.   20

The shepherds' swains shall dance and sing
For thy delight each May morning:
If these delights thy mind may move,
Then live with me and be my love.

                                                                1600

QUESTIONS

1. What are the initial challenges this poem provides for you as a reader? How can you meet these challenges?
2. How does the shepherd's passion affect his rhetoric?
3. How does he attempt to appeal to his love? What kinds of gifts does he promise her? What does this tell you about her?
4. Is this only a springtime love?

ANDREW MARVELL
(1621–1678)

TO HIS COY MISTRESS   366

  Had we but world enough, and time,
This coyness, lady, were no crime.
We would sit down, and think which way
To walk, and pass our long love's day.
Thou by the Indian Ganges' side   5
Shoudst rubies find; I by the tide
Of Humber would complain. I would
Love you ten years before the flood,

---

11 *kirtle:* dress.
TO HIS COY MISTRESS 7 *Humber:* the Humber River flows through Marvell's home town.

And you should, if you please, refuse
Till the conversion of the Jews.   10
My vegetable love should grow
Vaster than empires and more slow;
An hundred years should go to praise
Thine eyes, and on thy forehead gaze;
Two hundred to adore each breast,   15
But thirty thousand to the rest;
An age at least to every part,
And the last age should show your heart.
For, lady, you deserve this state,
Nor would I love at lower rate.   20
    But at my back I always hear
Time's wingèd chariot hurrying near;
And yonder all before us lie
Deserts of vast eternity.
Thy beauty shall no more be found;   25
Nor, in thy marble vault, shall sound
My echoing song; then worms shall try
That long-preserved virginity,
And your quaint honor turn to dust,
And into ashes all my lust: 30
The grave's a fine and private place,
But none, I think, do there embrace.
    Now therefore, while the youthful hue
Sits on thy skin like morning glow,
And while thy willing soul transpires   35
At every pore with instant fires,
Now let us sport us while we may,
And now, like amorous birds of prey,
Rather at once our time devour
Than languish in his slow-chapped power.   40
Let us roll all our strength and all
Our sweetness up into one ball,
And tear our pleasures with rough strife
Thorough the iron gates of life:
Thus, though we cannot make our sun   45
Stand still, yet we will make him run.

1681

---

11 *vegetable love:* in the Great Chain of Being, plants were considered a lower and more primitive form of life than animals and their superiors, humans. 19 *state:* high rank or position. 29 *quaint:* clever or ingenious. 40 *slow-chapped:* slow-jawed.

QUESTIONS

1. What has occurred before the beginning of the poem?
2. Describe the way the poem's three sections structure the argument. If you were the coy mistress, would the speaker's argument convince you? What would appeal to you? What would you resist?
3. Considering the purpose of the speaker's monologue, how do you explain his gruesome references to death? Why the serious turn at the end?
4. What would you say is the real theme of the poem?

THE GARDEN   367

How vainly men themselves amaze
To win the palm, the oak, or bays,
And their incessant labors see
Crowned from some single herb, or tree,
Whose short and narrow-vergéd shade   5
Does prudently their toils upbraid;
While all flowers and all trees do close
To weave the garlands of repose!

Fair Quiet, have I found thee here,
And Innocence, thy sister dear?   10
Mistaken long, I sought you then
In busy companies of men.
Your sacred plants, if here below,
Only among the plants will grow;
Society is all but rude   15
To this delicious solitude.

No white nor red was ever seen
So amorous as this lovely green.
Fond lovers, cruel as their flame,
Cut in these trees their mistress' name: 20
Little, alas, they know or heed
How far these beauties hers exceed!
Fair trees, wheresoe'er your barks I wound,
No name shall but your own be found.

When we have run our passion's heat,   25
Love hither makes his best retreat.
The gods, that mortal beauty chase,
Still in a tree did end their race:

THE GARDEN 1 *amaze:* bewilder. 2 *the palm, the oak, or bays:* awards for athletic prowess, civic acts, and poetic excellence. 7 *close:* gather.

Apollo hunted Daphne so,
Only that she might laurel grow;   30
And Pan did after Syrinx speed,
Not as a nymph, but for a reed.

    What wondrous life is this I lead!
Ripe apples drop about my head;
The luscious clusters of the vine   35
Upon my mouth do crush their wine;
The nectarine and curious peach
Into by hands themselves do reach;
Stumbling on melons, as I pass,
Insnared with flowers, I fall on grass.   40

    Meanwhile the mind, from pleasure less,
Withdraws into its happiness;
The mind, that ocean where each kind
Does straight its own resemblance find;
Yet it creates, transcending these,   45
Far other worlds and other seas,
Annihilating all that's made
To a green thought in a green shade.

    Here at the fountain's sliding foot,
Or at some fruit tree's mossy root,   50
Casting the body's vest aside,
My soul into the boughs does glide:
There, like a bird, it sits and sings,
Then whets and combs its silver wings,
And, till prepared for longer flight,   55
Waves in its plumes the various light.

    Such was that happy garden-state,
While man there walked without a mate:
After a place so pure and sweet,
What other help could yet be meet!   60
But 'twas beyond a mortal's share
To wander solitary there:
Two paradises 'twere in one
To live in paradise alone.

29–32 *Apollo . . . Daphne . . . Pan . . . Syrinx*: Apollo pursued Daphne who escaped by turning
into a laurel tree. Pan pursued Syrinx who escaped by turning into a reed-bed. 37 *curious*: excellent.
43–44 *The mind . . . find*: the belief that all creatures on earth have counterparts in the sea. 54
whets: sharpens its beak. 56 *various*: many-colored.

How well the skillful gardener drew   65
Of flowers and herbs this dial new,
Where, from above, the milder sun
Does through a fragrant zodiac run;
And as it works, th' industrious bee
Computes its time as well as we!   70
How could such sweet and wholesome hours
Be reckoned but with herbs and flowers?

                                                                        1681

WILLIAM MEREDITH

(b. 1919)

A MAJOR WORK   368

Poems are hard to read
Pictures are hard to see
Music is hard to hear
And people are hard to love

But whether from brute need   5
Or divine energy
At last mind eye and ear
And the great sloth heart will move.

                                                                        1958

RECOLLECTION OF BELLAGIO   369

(FOR JOHN AND CHARLOTTE MARSHALL)

On the dark lake below, the fishermen's bells
are calling to one another from their nets.
Who is here on the dark promontory at night?
Tossed by the April wind,
a horizontal pine, warped to the cliff,   5
married to the limestone cliff by the east wind,
rises and falls, rises and falls.
And who sees, against the stars,
the needled tufts change and exchange
like dancers, gracious dependents?   10

---

66 *dial:* a sundial made from flowers.

The fixed stars are a commodious dancing-
floor, at any moment the pine-tufts
know where their home-places are
on the polished floor of the marble constellations.   15

How long has this been going on, this *allemande,*
before a man's thoughts climbed up to sit
on the limestone knob and watch (briefly,
as man's thoughts' eyes watch) the needles
keeping time to the bells which the same wind rocks   20
on the water below, marking the fishermen's nets—
thoughts he would haul in later from the lake
of time, feeling himself drawn clumsy
back into time's figure, hand over hand,
by the grace of pine boughs? And who   25
is saying these words, now that that man
is a shade, has become his own shade?
I see the shade rise slow and ghostly from its seat
on the soft, grainy stone, I watch it descend
by the gravelled paths of the promontory,   30
under a net of steady stars, in April,
from the boughs' rite and the bells'—quiet,
my shade, and long ago, and still going on.

                                                                                                    1980

QUESTIONS

1. Who is speaking and to whom?
2. Who *is* "on the dark promontory at night" (line 3)?
3. Explore the references to time (past, present, and future).

IDEOGRAM   370

(FOR WILLIAM AND EMMY MAXWELL)

I am trying to describe to you a river at first light.
The water is glassy, under a scud of mist.
It is taking the color of the new sky
but the mist has something else in mind than pink—
a force of discoloration, it would have everything white.   5
On the far bank are serried low hills, tree-clusters,
occasionally the lights of a car.

RECOLLECTION OF BELLAGIO 16 *allemande:* a stately German dance.

IDEOGRAM title: a symbol or character representing an idea or an object without using its name. 2
scud: wind-driven clouds. 6 *serried:* crowded together.

This river I want you to see is being remembered.
I tell you this not to make us self-conscious
or conscious of words, but hoping to heighten   10
the peculiar vividness of a thing imagined.
I put no water-bird or craft on the surface:
the poem is absolutely quiet at about 5 a.m.
Rose-grey water slips away to left and right, silky,
upstream and downstream, just before sunrise,   15
just before we are called away,
you who don't know me, I who don't know you.

Soon it will be full light. We will blink this river away
and my talking to you, a stranger, as if I knew you,
as if our partaking a strange river at the edge of light   20
had been no impertinence—this will yield to another subject.
A river talked away, may be the new subject, or,
Mist burned off by the sun, an ancient, common figure,
a nearly dead metaphor, for enlightenment, and
it occurs to me now that someone may have already   25
accomplished this for you, hundreds of years ago,
someone deft with a brush, in China.

1980

A BOTANICAL TROPE   371

Regret, a bright meander on the nights
Of the driver coming always to the turn
Where the child was killed, regret is a design
As repetitious as the dogwood's veined
Descent, in autumn, from the twig to root.   5

At night, for all the world as if it mattered,
The bankrupt tries to fix his first mistake;
His thoughts concenter there monotonously,
As the commerce of the dogwood centers where
It borrows blossoms: at the rich black bole.   10

And all night long the embezzler reviews
The diagram of greed that pulled him under.
How could he hope to see, involved like that,
That his was not unlike the dogwood's scheme
To pay back all its foliage in the spring.   15

A BOTANICAL TROPE title *trope:* a figure of speech.

Unwittingly a tossing man will draw
The family of his guilt as a thick tree.
That is the winter time. The sap goes down
In grave, unhoping penance to the root,
And neither tree nor man knows to what end.   20

The ruined nights of men are no less praise
Than slopes of dogwood on a winter day,
Suggesting springtime only to the blind
Or sentimental—trees of the cross, some say—
Soughing together in divine remorse.   25

1985

A KOREAN WOMAN SEATED BY A WALL   372

Suffering has settled like a sly disguise
On her cheerful old face. If she dreams beyond
Rice and a roof, now toward the end of winter,
Is it of four sons gone, the cries she has heard,
A square farm in the south, soured by tents?   5
Some alien and untranslatable loss
Is a mask she smiles through at the weak sun
That is moving north to invade the city again.

A poet penetrates a dark disguise
After his own conception, little or large.   10
Crossing the scaleless asia of trouble
Where it seems no one could give himself away,
He gives himself away, he sets a scale.
Hunger and pain and death, the sorts of loss,
Dispute our comforts like peninsulas   15
Of no particular value, places to fight.
And what is it in suffering dismays us more:
The capriciousness with which it is dispensed
Or the unflinching way we see it borne?

She may be dreaming of her wedding gift,   20
A celadon bowl of a good dynasty
With cloud and heron cut in its green paste,
It sleeps in a hollow bed of pale blue silk.
The rice it bought was eaten the second winter.

A KOREAN WOMAN SEATED BY A WALL 21 *celadon:* pale green.

And by what happier stove is it unwrapped   25
In the evening now and passed around like a meat,
Making a foliage in the firelight?

She shifts the crate she sits on as the March
Wind mounts from the sea. The sun moves down the sky
Perceptibly, like the hand of a public clock,   30
In increments of darkness though ablaze.
Ah, now she looks at me. We are unmasked
And exchange what roles we guess at for an instant.
The questions Who comes next and Why not me
Rage at and founder my philosophy.   35
Guilt beyond my error and a grace past her grief
Alter the coins I tender cowardly,
Shiver the porcelain fable to green shards.

                                                                    1985

W. S. MERWIN
(b. 1927)

THE DRUNK IN THE FURNACE   373

        For a good decade
The furnace stood in the naked gully, fireless
And vacant as any hat. Then when it was
No more to them than a hulking black fossil
To erode unnoticed with the rest of the junk-hill   5
By the poisonous creek, and rapidly to be added
        To their ignorance.

        They were afterwards astonished
To confirm, one morning, a twist of smoke like a pale
Resurrection, staggering out of its chewed hole,   10
And to remark then other tokens that someone,
Cozily bolted behind the eye-holed iron
Door of the drafty burner, had there established
        His bad castle.

        Where he gets his spirits   15
It's a mystery. But the stuff keeps him musical:
Hammer-and-anviling with poker and bottle
To his jugged bellowings, till the last groaning clang
As he collapses onto the rioting
Springs of a litter of car-seats ranged on the grates,   20
        To sleep like an iron pig.

> In their tar-paper church
> On a text about stoke-holes that are sated never
> Their Reverend lingers. They nod and hate trespassers.   25
> When the furnace wakes, though, all afternoon
> Their witless offspring flock like piped rats to its siren
> Crescendo, and agape on the crumbling ridge
> Stand in a row and learn.

1960

QUESTIONS

1. Which parts of the poem do you initially find easiest to experience? Why?
2. Discuss the movement from the "ignorance" of line 7 to the "learn[ing]" of the final line. What is learned?
3. What do the images in the first stanza have in common?
4. How does the quality suggested by the first stanza's images begin to change in stanza two? By stanza three, what sensory emphasis is found in the images?
5. How do the religious images contribute to meaning?

JOSEPHINE MILES
(b. 1911)

REASON   374

Said, Pull her up a bit will you, Mac, I want to unload there.
Said, Pull her up my rear end, first come first serve.
Said, Give her the gun, Bud, he needs a taste of his own bumper.
Then the usher came out and got into the act:

Said, Pull her up, pull her up a bit, we need this space, sir.   5
Said, For God's sake, is this still a free country or what?
You go back and take care of Gary Cooper's horse
And leave me handle my own car.

Saw them unloading the lame old lady,
Ducked out under the wheel and gave her an elbow,   10
Said, All you needed to do was just explain;
Reason, Reason is my middle name.

1955

QUESTIONS

1. Imagine the setting. Describe what you imagine. What do so few details about setting appear in the poem?

2. The author said, " 'Reason' is a favorite one of my poems because I like the idea of speech—not images, not ideas, not music, but people talking—as the material from which poetry is made." Are there no images, ideas, or music in the poem?
3. How many speakers are there? Is it important to know who they are?
4. How do cliches work in this poem?

[AS DIFFERENCE BLENDS INTO IDENTITY]   375

As difference blends into identity
    Or blurs into obliteration, we give
    To zero our position at the center,
    Withdraw our belief and baggage.

As rhyme at the walls lapses, at frontiers   5
    Customs scatter like a flight of snow,
    And boundaries moonlike draw us out, our opponents
    Join us, we are their refuge.

As barriers between us melt, I may treat you
    Unkindly as myself, I may forget   10
    Your name as my own. Then enters
    Our anonymous assailant.

As assonance by impulse burgeons
    And that quaver shakes us by which we are spent,
    We may move to consume another with us,   15
    Stir into parity another's cyphers.

Then when our sniper steps to a window
    In the brain, starts shooting, and we fall surprised,
    Of what we know not do we seek forgiveness
    From ourselves, for ourselves?   20

1967

EDNA ST. VINCENT MILLAY
(1892–1950)

RECUERDO   376

We were very tired, we were very merry—
We had gone back and forth all night on the ferry.
It was bare and bright, and smelled like a stable—

RECUERDO title: "memory" (Spanish).

But we looked into a fire, we leaned across a table,   5
We lay on a hill-top underneath the moon;
And the whistles kept blowing, and the dawn came soon.

We were very tired, we were very merry—
We had gone back and forth all night on the ferry;
And you ate an apple, and I ate a pear,   10
From a dozen of each we had bought somewhere;
And the sky went wan, and the wind came cold,
And the sun rose dripping, a bucketful of gold.

We were very tired, we were very merry—
We had gone back and forth all night on the ferry.   15
We hailed, "Good morrow, mother!" to a shawl-covered head
And bought a morning paper, which neither of us read;
And she wept, "God bless you!" for the apples and pears,
And we gave her all our money but our subway fares.

                                                                         1920

[HEARING YOUR WORDS, AND NOT A WORD AMONG THEM]   377

Hearing your words, and not a word among them
Tuned to my liking, on a salty day
When inland woods were pushed by winds that flung them
Hissing to leeward like a ton of spray,
I thought how off Matinicus the tide   5
Came pounding in, came running through the Gut,
While from the Rock the warning whistle cried,
And children whimpered, and the doors blew shut;
There in the autumn when the men go forth,
With slapping skirts the island women stand   10
In gardens stripped and scattered, peering north,
With dahlia tubers dripping from the hand:
The wind of their endurance, driving south,
Flattened your words against your speaking mouth.

                                                                         1931

HEARING YOUR WORDS 5–7 *Matinicus . . . Gut . . . Rock:* an island off the coast of Maine and sites thereon.

[OH, SLEEP FOREVER IN THE
LATMIAN CAVE]   378

Oh, sleep forever in the Latmian cave,
Mortal Endymion, darling of the Moon!
Her silver garments by the senseless wave
Shouldered and dropped and on the shingle strewn,
Her fluttering hand against her forehead pressed,   5
Her scattered looks that trouble all the sky,
Her rapid footsteps running down the west—
Of all her altered state, oblivious lie!
Whom earthen you, by deathless lips adored,
Wild-eyed and stammering to the grasses thrust,   10
And deep into her crystal body poured
The hot and sorrowful sweetness of the dust:
Whereof she wanders mad, being all unfit
For mortal love, that might not die of it.

1931

THE RETURN   379

Earth does not understand her child,
   Who from the loud gregarious town
Returns, depleted and defiled,
   To the still woods, to fling him down.

Earth can not count the sons she bore: 5
   The wounded lynx, the wounded man
Come trailing blood unto her door;
   She shelters both as best she can.

But she is early up and out,
   To trim the year or strip its bones;   10
She has no time to stand about
   Talking of him in undertones

Who has no aim but to forget,
   Be left in peace, be lying thus
For days, for years, for centuries yet,   15
   Unshaven and anonymous;

OH, SLEEP FOREVER IN THE LATMIAN CAVE 1–2: *Latmian . . . Endymion . . . Moon:* Endymion fell asleep
in a cave in Mount Latmos where the goddess of the moon visited him. Zeus then allowed him
to sleep forever.

Who, marked for failure, dulled by grief,
  Has traded in his wife and friend
For this warm ledge, this alder leaf:
  Comfort that does not comprehend.   20

1934

QUESTIONS

1. Who is returning? To what?
2. How many times are negative words used in this poem? Why? Is there any positive statement?
3. What is Earth's general attitude toward her children?
4. Does this parent–child relationship ring true to your experience?

MAY MILLER

(b. 1899)

THE SCREAM   380

I am a woman controlled.
Remember this: I never scream.
Yet I stood a form apart
Watching my other frenzied self
Beaten by words and wounds   5
Make in silence a mighty scream—
A scream that the wind took up
And thrust through the bars of night
Beyond all reason's final rim.

Out where the sea's last murmur dies   10
And the gull's cry has no sound,
Out where city voices fade,
Stilled in a lyric sleep
Where silence is its own design,
My scream hovered a ghost denied   15
Wanting the shape of lips.

1975

JOHN MILTON

(1608–1674)

LYCIDAS   381

In this monody the author bewails a learned friend, unfortunately drowned in his passage from
Chester on the Irish Seas, 1637. And by occasion foretells the ruin of our corrupted clergy,
then in their height.

Yet once more, O ye laurels and once more
Ye myrtles brown, with ivy never sere,
I come to pluck your berries harsh and crude,
And with forced fingers rude,
Shatter your leaves before the mellowing year.   5
Bitter constraint, and sad occasion dear,
Compels me to disturb your season due;
For Lycidas is dead, dead ere his prime,
Young Lycidas, and hath not left his peer.
Who would not sing for Lycidas? He knew   10
Himself to sing, and build the lofty rhyme.
He must not float upon his watery bier
Unwept, and welter to the parching wind,
Without the meed of some melodious tear.
  Begin then, sisters of the sacred well   15
That from beneath the seat of Jove doth spring,
Begin, and somewhat loudly sweep the string.
Hence with denial vain, and coy excuse;
So may some gentle Muse
With lucky words favor my destined urn,   20
And as he passes turn,
And bid fair peace be to my sable shroud.
For we were nursed upon the selfsame hill,
Fed the same flock, by fountain, shade, and rill.
  Together both, ere the high lawns appeared   25
Under the opening eyelids of the morn,
We drove afield, and both together heard
What time the grayfly winds her sultry horn,
Battening our flocks with the fresh dews of night,
Oft till the star that rose at evening bright   30
Toward Heaven's descent had sloped his westering wheel.

LYCIDAS epigraph *monody:* a song sung by a single voice; usually a lament or a dirge; *learned friend:*
Milton's friend was Edward King, fellow Cambridge student. 1–2 *laurel . . . myrtles . . . ivy:*
traditional garlands for poets. 2 *sere:* withered. 3 *crude:* unripe. 6 *dear:* heartfelt. 13 *welter:* tumble.
14 *meed:* tribute. 15 *sisters of the sacred well:* the Muses and their well at the foot of Mt. Helicon. 25
lawns: pastures. 29 *Battening:* fattening.

Meanwhile the rural ditties were not mute,
Tempered to th' oaten flute,
Rough satyrs danced, and fauns with cloven heel
From the glad sound would not be absent long,   35
And old Damoetas loved to hear our song.
   But O the heavy change, now thou art gone,
Now thou art gone, and never must return!
Thee, shepherd, thee the woods and desert caves,
With wild thyme and the gadding vine o'ergrown,   40
And all their echoes mourn.
The willows and the hazel copses green
Shall now no more be seen,
Fanning their joyous leaves to thy soft lays.
As killing as the canker to the rose,   45
Or taint-worm to the weanling herds that graze,
Or frost to flowers that their gay wardrobe wear,
When first the white thorn blows;
Such, Lycidas, thy loss to shepherd's ear.
   Where were ye, nymphs, when the remorseless deep   50
Closed o'er the head of your loved Lycidas?
For neither were ye playing on the steep,
Where your old Bards, the famous Druids lie,
Nor on the shaggy top of Mona high,
Nor yet where Deva spreads her wizard stream: 55
Ay me! I fondly dream—
Had ye been there—for what could that have done?
What could the Muse herself that Orpheus bore,
The Muse herself, for her inchanting son
Whom universal Nature did lament,   60
When by the rout that made the hideous roar,
His gory visage down the stream was sent,
Down the swift Hebrus to the Lesbian shore?
   Alas! What boots it with uncessant care
To tend the homely slighted shepherd's trade,   65
And strictly meditate the thankless Muse?
Were it not better done as others use,
To sport with Amaryllis in the shade,
Or with the tangles of Neaera's hair?

---

36 *Damoetas:* conventional pastoral name, referring probably to a Cambridge tutor. 40 *gadding:* wandering. 48 *blows:* blooms. 53–54 *Druids . . . Mona:* Mona was a Druid burial ground. 55 *Deva:* changes in the course of the River Dee were considered omens for the future. 56 *fondly:* foolishly. 58 *Muse . . . Orpheus:* Calliope was the muse of epic poetry. Her son, Orpheus, a great poet and musician, was torn apart by a group of Thracian women, who threw his head into the River Hebrus. It floated across the sea to Lesbos. 64 *boots:* profits. 68–69 *Amaryllis . . . Neaera:* conventional pastoral names for girls.

Fame is the spur that the clear spirit doth raise   70
(That last infirmity of noble mind)
To scorn delights, and live laborious days;
But the fair guerdon when we hope to find,
And think to burst out into sudden blaze,
Comes the blind Fury with th' abhorréd shears,   75
And slits the thin spun life. "But not the praise,"
Phoebus replied, and touched my trembling ears;
"Fame is no plant that grows on mortal soil,
Nor in the glistering foil
Set off to th' world, nor in broad rumor lies,   80
But lives and spreads aloft by those pure eyes,
And perfect witness of all-judging Jove;
As he pronounces lastly on each deed,
Of so much fame in Heaven expect thy meed."
    O fountain Arethuse, and thou honored flood,   85
Smooth-sliding Mincius, crowned with vocal reeds,
That strain I heard was of a higher mood.
But now my oat proceeds,
And listens to the herald of the sea
That came in Neptune's plea.   90
He asked the waves, and asked the felon winds,
"What hard mishap hath doomed this gentle swain?"
And questioned every gust of rugged wings
That blows from off each beakèd promontory;
They knew not of his story,   95
And sage Hippotades their answer brings,
That not a blast was from his dungeon strayed,
The air was calm, and on the level brine,
Sleek Panope with all her sisters played.
It was that fatal and perfidious bark   100
Built in th' eclipse, and rigged with curses dark,
That sunk so low that sacred head of thine.
    Next Camus, reverend sire, went footing slow,
His mantle hairy, and his bonnet sedge,
Inwrought with figures dim, and on the edge   105

73 *guerdon:* reward. 75 *Fury:* Atropos, the third of the three Fates, who cuts the thread of life spun by the other two. 77 *Phoebus:* Apollo, god of poetry. 79 *glistering foil:* setting which enhances the jewel placed in it. 85 *Arethuse:* fountain in Sicily associated with the pastoral poetry of Theocritus. 86 *Mincius:* river in Italy associated with the pastoral poetry of Virgil. 88 *oat:* oaten pipe. 89 *herald of the sea:* Triton, blowing on a shell trumpet, arrives to defend Neptune, the god of the sea, against accusations of responsibility for Lycidas' death. 96 *Hippotades:* god of the winds. 99 *Panope:* one of the sea-nymphs. 103 *Camus:* god of the river Cam; associated with Cambridge. 104 *sedge:* water-plants.

Like to that sanguine flower inscribed with woe.
"Ah! who hath reft," quoth he, "my dearest pledge?"
Last came and last did go
The pilot of the Galilean lake,
Two massy keys he bore of metals twain   110
(The golden opes, the iron shuts amain).
He shook his mitered locks, and stern bespake:
"How well could I have spared for thee, young swain,
Enow of such as for their bellies' sake,
Creep and intrude, and climb into the fold!   115
Of other care they little reckoning make,
Than how to scramble at the shearers' feast,
And shove away the worthy bidden guest.
Blind mouths! That scarce themselves know how to hold
A sheep-hook, or have learned aught else the least   120
That to the faithful herdsman's art belongs!
What recks it them? What need they? They are sped;
And when they list, their lean and flashy songs
Grate on their scrannel pipes of wretched straw.
The hungry sheep look up, and are not fed,   125
But swoln with wind, and the rank mist they draw,
Rot inwardly, and foul contagion spread,
Besides what the grim wolf with privy paw
Daily devours apace, and nothing said.
But that two-handed engine at the door   130
Stands ready to smite once, and smite no more."
   Return, Alpheus, the dread voice is past,
That shrunk thy streams; return, Sicilian muse,
And call the vales, and bid them hither cast
Their bells and flowerets of a thousand hues.   135
Ye valleys low where the mild whispers use,
Of shades and wanton winds, and gushing brooks,
On whose fresh lap the swart star sparely looks,
Throw hither all your quaint enameled eyes,

---

106 *that sanguine flower inscribed with woe:* the hyacincth, which grew from the blood of a young man accidentally killed by Apollo. Its markings were supposed to spell Al Al ("Alas, alas!"). 109 *pilot of the Galilean lake:* St. Peter, who carries the keys to heaven and wears a bishop's miter. 114 *enow:* enough. 122 *What recks it them?:* What does it matter to them? 123 *flashy:* trifling. 124 *scrannel:* meager. 128 *grim wolf with privy paw:* the Roman Catholic Church or anti-Protestant forces. 130 *two-handed-engine:* instrument of retribution against corrupt clergy. 132 *Alpheus:* Greek river god who fell in love with the nymph Arethuse (see line 85). She fled from him and he pursued her by diving under the sea and surfacing on Sicily, where she was hiding. She was turned into a fountain and their waters mingled. 136 *use:* go frequently. 138 *swart star:* Sirius, the dog-star, considered to have a dark influence.

That on the green turf suck the honeyed showers,   140
And purple all the ground with vernal flowers.
Bring the rathe primrose that forsaken dies,
The tufted crow-toe, and pale jessamine,
The white pink, and the pansy freaked with jet,
The glowing violet,   145
The musk-rose, and the well attired woodbine.
With cowslips wan that hang the pensive head,
And every flower that sad embroidery wears:
Bid amaranthus all his beauty shed,
And daffadillies fill their cups with tears,   150
To strew the laureate hearse where Lycid lies.
For so to interpose a little ease,
Let our frail thoughts dally with false surmise.
Ay me! Whilst thee the shores and sounding seas
Wash far away, where'er thy bones are hurled,   155
Whether beyond the stormy Hebrides,
Where thou perhaps under the whelming tide
Visit'st the bottom of the monstrous world;
Or whether thou, to our moist vows denied,
Sleep'st by the fable of Bellerus old,   160
Where the great vision of the guarded mount
Looks toward Namancos and Bayona's hold;
Look homeward angel now, and melt with ruth:
And, O ye dolphins, waft the hapless youth.
    Weep no more, woeful shepherds, weep no more,   165
For Lycidas your sorrow is not dead,
Sunk though he be beneath the watery floor,
So sinks the day-star in the ocean bed,
And yet anon repairs his drooping head,
And tricks his beams, and with new-spangled ore,   170
Flames in the forehead of the morning sky:
So Lycidas sunk low, but mounted high,
Through the dear might of him that walked the waves,
Where other groves, and other streams along,
With nectar pure his oozy locks he laves,   175
And hears the unexpressive nuptial song,
In the blest kingdoms meek of joy and love.
There entertain him all the saints above,

142 *rathe:* early. 144 *freaked:* streaked. 149 *amaranthus:* imaginary flower, believed never to fade. 160 *Bellerus:* figure invented by Milton and supposedly buried at Land's End in Cornwall. The mount is St. Michael's Mount and is named for the angel which is mentioned in line 163. 163 *ruth:* pity. 168 *day-star:* sun. 170 *tricks:* arranges; *ore:* gold.

In solemn troops and sweet societies
That sing, and singing in their glory move,   180
And wipe the tears forever from his eyes.
Now, Lycidas, the shepherds weep no more;
Henceforth thou art the genius of the shore,
In thy large recompense, and shalt be good
To all that wander in that perilous flood.   185
   Thus sang the uncouth swain to th' oaks and rills,
While the still morn went out with sandals gray;
He touched the tender stops of various quills,
With eager thought warbling his Doric lay:
And now the sun had stretched out all the hills,   190
And now was dropped into the western bay;
At last he rose, and twitched his mantle blue:
Tomorrow to fresh woods, and pastures new.

1637

WHEN I CONSIDER HOW MY
LIGHT IS SPENT   382

When I consider how my light is spent
  Ere half my days, in this dark world and wide,
  And that one talent which is death to hide
  Lodged with me useless, though my soul more bent
To serve therewith my Maker, and present   5
  My true account, lest he returning chide;
  "Doth God exact day-labor, light denied?"
  I fondly ask; but Patience to prevent
That murmur, soon replies, "God doth not need
  Either man's work or his own gifts; who best   10
  Bear his mild yoke, they serve him best. His state
Is kingly. Thousands at his bidding speed
  And post o'er land and ocean without rest:
  They also serve who only stand and wait."

1673

---

183 *genius:* guardian spirit. 186 *uncouth:* unknown. 188 *tender stops of various quills:* finger-holes of
the pipes. 189 *Doric lay:* dialect of the pastoral poets.

WHEN I CONSIDER HOW MY LIGHT IS SPENT 1: Milton was completely blind when he wrote this poem. 3
talent: parable of the talents (Matthew 25:14–30) in which a servant buries the talents (money) his
master gives him rather than investing them for his master. 8 *fondly:* foolishly.

QUESTIONS

1. Even if you are not blind, you need to identify with Milton's struggle if you are to create a reading of this poem. What personal connections do you find with the dilemma described here?
2. What do *spent, talent, account,* and *day-labor* have in common? How do they organize the poem and focus the vision?
3. Is this poem organized as a Petrarchan or an Elizabethan sonnet? Explain.
4. What is the tone of the final lines?

ON THE LATE MASSACRE IN PIEDMONT 383

Avenge, O Lord, thy slaughtered saints, whose bones
   Lie scattered on the Alpine mountains cold,
   Even them who kept thy truth so pure of old
   When all our fathers worshiped stocks and stones,
Forget not: in thy book record their groans   5
   Who were thy sheep and in their ancient fold
   Slain by the bloody Piedmontese that rolled
   Mother with infant down the rocks. Their moans
The vales redoubled to the hills, and they
   To Heaven. Their martyred blood and ashes sow   10
   O'er all th' Italian fields where still doth sway
The triple tyrant: that from these may grow
   A hundredfold, who having learnt thy way
   Early may fly the Babylonian woe.

1673

MARIANNE MOORE
(1887–1972)

POETRY 384

I, too, dislike it: there are things that are important beyond all this
   fiddle.
   Reading it, however, with a perfect contempt for it, one discovers
     in
   it after all, a place for the genuine.
     Hands that can grasp, eyes
      that can dilate, hair that can rise   5
       if it must, these things are important not because a

ON THE LATE MASSACRE IN PIEDMONT title: on Easter Day, 1655, almost 2000 Protestants were killed in a vicious attack in the Piedmont in Italy. 4 *stocks and stone:* gods of wood and stone; idols. 12 *the triple tyrant:* the pope. 14 *the Babylonian woe:* the destruction of Babylon prophesied in Revelation.

high-sounding interpretation can be put upon them but because they
are
useful. When they become so derivative as to become
unintelligible,
the same thing may be said for all of us, that we
do not admire what   10
we cannot understand: the bat
holding on upside down or in quest of something to

eat, elephants pushing, a wild horse taking a roll, a tireless wolf
under
a tree, the immovable critic twitching his skin like a horse that feels
a flea, the base-
ball fan, the statistician—   15
nor is it valid
to discriminate against 'business documents and

school-books'; all these phenomena are important. One must make a
distinction
however: when dragged into prominence by half poets, the result is
not poetry,
nor till the poets among us can be   20
'literalists of
the imagination'—above
insolence and triviality and can present

for inspection, 'imaginary gardens with real toads in them', shall we
have
it. In the meantime, if you demand on the one hand,   25
the raw material of poetry in
all its rawness and
that which is on the other hand
genuine, you are interested in poetry.

1921

CRITICS AND CONNOISSEURS   385

There is a great amount of poetry in unconscious
fastidiousness. Certain Ming
products, imperial floor coverings of coach-
wheel yellow, are well enough in their way but I have seen
something
that I like better—a   5

mere childish attempt to make an imperfectly bal-
    lasted animal stand up,
  similar determination to make a pup
    eat his meat from the plate.

I remember a swan under the willows in Oxford,   10
  with flamingo-colored, maple-
    leaflike feet. It reconnoitered like a battle-
ship. Disbelief and conscious fastidiousness were
      ingredients in its
        disinclination to move. Finally its hardihood was   15
        not proof against its
      proclivity to more fully appraise such bits
      of food as the stream

bore counter to it; it made away with what I gave it
  to eat. I have seen this swan and   20
    I have seen you; I have seen ambition without
understanding in a variety of forms. Happening to stand
    by an ant-hill, I have
      seen a fastidious ant carrying a stick north, south,
        east, west, till it turned on   25
      itself, struck out from the flower bed into the lawn,
      and returned to the point

from which it had started. Then abandoning the stick as
  useless and overtaxing its
    jaws with a particle of whitewash—pill-like but   30
heavy—it again went through the same course of procedure.
        What is
    there in being able
      to say that one has dominated the stream in an attitude of
        self-defense;   35
      in proving that one has had the experience
      of carrying a stick?

1924

A GRAVE   386

Man looking into the sea,
taking the view from those who have as much right to it as you have
  to yourself,
it is human nature to stand in the middle of a thing,

but you cannot stand in the middle of this;
the sea has nothing to give but a well excavated grave.   5
The firs stand in a procession, each with an emerald turkey-foot at
    the top,
reserved as their contours, saying nothing;
repression, however, is not the most obvious characteristic of the sea;
the sea is a collector, quick to return a rapacious look.
There are others besides you who have worn that look—   10
whose expression is no longer a protest; the fish no longer investigate
    them
for their bones have not lasted:
men lower nets, unconscious of the fact that they are desecrating a
    grave,
and row quickly away—the blades of the oars
moving together like the feet of water-spiders as if there were no
    such thing as death.   15
The wrinkles progress among themselves in a phalanx—beautiful
    under networks of foam,
and fade breathlessly while the sea rustles in and out of the seaweed;
the birds swim through the air at top speed, emitting catcalls as
    heretofore—
the tortoise-shell scourges about the feet of the cliffs, in motion
    beneath them;
and the ocean, under the pulsation of lighthouses and noise of bell-
    buoys,   20
advances as usual, looking as if it were not that ocean in which
    dropped things are bound to sink—
in which if they turn and twist, it is neither with volition nor
    consciousness.

1924

THE PANGOLIN   387

Another armored animal—scale
    lapping scale with spruce-cone regularity until they
form the uninterrupted central
    tail-row! This near artichoke with head and legs and grit-equipped
      gizzard,
    the night miniature artist engineer is,   5
        yes, Leonardo da Vinci's replica—
           impressive animal and toiler of whom we seldom hear.

THE PANGOLIN title *pangolin:* scaly anteater.

Armor seems extra. But for him,
 the closing ear-ridge—
  or bare ear lacking even this small   10
  eminence and similarly safe

contracting nose and eye apertures
 impenetrably closable, are not; a true ant-eater,
not cockroach-eater, who endures
 exhausting solitary trips through unfamiliar ground at night,   15
 returning before sunrise; stepping in the moonlight,
  on the moonlight peculiarly, that the outside
   edges of his hands may bear the weight and save the claws
 for digging. Serpentined about
  the tree, he draws   20
   away from danger unpugnaciously,
   with no sound but a harmless hiss; keeping

the fragile grace of the Thomas-
 of-Leighton Buzzard Westminster Abbey wrought-iron vine, or
rolls himself into a ball that has   25
 power to defy all effort to unroll it; strongly intailed, neat
head for core, on neck not breaking off, with curled-in feet.
  Nevertheless he has sting-proof scales; and nest
   of rocks closed with earth from inside, which he can thus
   darken.
  Sun and moon and day and night and man and beast   30
   each with a splendor
    which man in all his vileness cannot
   set aside; each with an excellence!

"Fearful yet to be feared," the armored
 ant-eater met by the driver-ant does not turn back, but   35
engulfs what he can, the flattened sword-
 edged leafpoints on the tail and artichoke set leg- and body-plates
 quivering violently when it retaliates
  and swarms on him. Compact like the furled fringed frill
   on the hat-brim of Gargallo's hollow iron head of a   40
 matador, he will drop and will
  then walk away
   unhurt, although if unintruded on,
   he cautiously works down the tree, helped

23–24 *Thomas-of-Leighton Buzzard Westminster Abbey wrought-iron vine:* Moore indicates in her notes that she is referring to a bit of ironwork in Westminster Abbey. 40 *Gargallo:* Pablo Gargallo (1881–1934), Spanish sculptor.

by his tail. The giant-pangolin-   45
    tail, graceful tool, as prop or hand or broom or ax, tipped like
an elephant's trunk with special skin,
      is not lost on this ant- and stone-swallowing uninjurable
      artichoke which simpletons thought a living fable
          whom the stones had nourished, whereas ants had done   50
            so. Pangolins are not aggressive animals; between
          dusk and day they have the not unchain-like machine-like
              form and frictionless creep of a thing
              made graceful by adversities, con-

versities. To explain grace requires   55
    a curious hand. If that which is at all were not forever,
why would those who graced the spires
      with animals and gathered there to rest, on cold luxurious
      low stone seats—a monk and monk and monk—between the thus
          ingenious roof supports, have slaved to confuse   60
            grace with a kindly manner, time in which to pay a debt,
          the cure for sins, a graceful use
              of what are yet
              approved stone mullions branching out across
              the perpendiculars? A sailboat   65

was the first machine. Pangolins, made
    for moving quietly also, are models of exactness,
on four legs; on hind feet plantigrade,
      with certain postures of a man. Beneath sun and moon, man
          slaving
      to make his life more sweet, leaves half the flowers worth having,   70
          needing to choose wisely how to use his strength;
            a paper-maker like the wasp; a tractor of foodstuffs,
          like the ant; spidering a length
               of web from bluffs
              above a stream; in fighting, mechanicked   75
              like the pangolin; capsizing in

disheartenment. Bedizened or stark
    naked, man, the self, the being we call human, writing-
master to this world, griffons a dark
      "Like does not like like that is obnoxious"; and writes error with
      four   80
      r's. Among animals, *one* has a sense of humor.
          Humor saves a few steps, it saves years. Unignorant,

---

68 *plantigrade:* walking with the entire lower surface of the foot on the ground. 77 *Bedizened:*
dressed tastelessly. 79 *griffons:* scribbles.

modest and unemotional, and all emotion,
   he has everlasting vigor,
      power to grow,   85
         though there are few creatures who can make one
         breathe faster and make one erecter.

Not afraid of anything is he,
   and then goes cowering forth, tread paced to meet an obstacle
at every step. Consistent with the   90
   formula—warm blood, no gills, two pairs of hands and a few
   hairs —
      that
is a mammal; there he sits in his own habitat,
   serge-clad, strong-shod. The prey of fear, he, always
   . .   curtailed, extinguished, thwarted by the dusk, work partly
         done,
   says to the alternating blaze,   95
      "Again the sun!
         anew each day; and new and new and new,
         that comes into and steadies my soul."

                                                                  1936

QUESTIONS

1. Why is the poem so long? Do you think it could be shortened or is its length
   necessary? What does its length require of you as a reader?
2. What function does the scientific detail serve?
3. Where does the poem depart from being purely informational?
4. What do the definitions of grace (lines 55–65) have to do with the pangolin?
5. Create a reading that considers the implications of the following lines:

   Sun and moon and day and night and man and beast
      each with a splendor
         Which man in all his vileness cannot
   set aside; each with an excellence!

THE STEEPLE-JACK   388

REVISED, 1961

Dürer would have seen a reason for living
   in a town like this, with eight stranded whales
to look at; with the sweet sea air coming into your house
on a fine day, from water etched
      with waves as formal as the scales   5
on a fish.

THE STEEPLE-JACK 1 *Dürer:* Albrecht Dürer (1471–1528), German artist.

One by one in two's and three's, the seagulls keep
    flying back and forth over the town clock,
or sailing around the lighthouse without moving their wings—
rising steadily with a slight   10
    quiver of the body—or flock
mewing where

a sea the purple of the peacock's neck is
    paled to greenish azure as Dürer changed
the pine green of the Tyrol to peacock blue and guinea   15
gray. You can see a twenty-five-
    pound lobster; and fish nets arranged
to dry. The

whirlwind fife-and-drum of the storm bends the salt
    marsh grass, disturbs stars in the sky and the   20
star on the steeple; it is a privilege to see so
much confusion. Disguised by what
    might seem the opposite, the sea-
side flowers and

trees are favored by the fog so that you have   25
    the tropics at first hand: the trumpet vine,
foxglove, giant snapdragon, a salpiglossis that has
spots and stripes; morning-glories, gourds,
    or moon-vines trained on fishing twine
at the back door: 30

cattails, flags, blueberries and spiderwort,
    striped grass, lichens, sunflowers, asters, daisies—
yellow and crab-claw ragged sailors with green bracts—toad-plant,
petunias, ferns; pink lilies, blue
    ones, tigers; poppies; black sweet-peas.   35
The climate

is not right for the banyan, frangipani, or
    jack-fruit trees; or for exotic serpent
life. Ring lizard and snakeskin for the foot, if you see fit;
but here they've cats, not cobras, to   40
    keep down the rats. The diffident
little newt

with white pin-dots on black horizontal spaced-
    out bands lives here; yet there is nothing that
ambition can buy or take away. The college student   45

named Ambrose sits on the hillside
    with his not-native books and hat
and sees boats

at sea progress white and rigid as if in
    a groove. Liking an elegance of which   50
the source is not bravado, he knows by heart the antique
sugar-bowl shaped summerhouse of
    interlacing slats, and the pitch
of the church

spire, not true, from which a man in scarlet lets   55
    down a rope as a spider spins a thread;
he might be part of a novel, but on the sidewalk a
sign says C. J. Poole, Steeple Jack,
    in black and white; and one in red
and white says   60

Danger. The church portico has four fluted
    columns, each a single piece of stone, made
modester by whitewash. This would be a fit haven for
waifs, children, animals, prisoners,
    and presidents who have repaid   65
sin-driven

senators by not thinking about them. The
    place has a schoolhouse, a post-office in a
store, fish-houses, hen-houses, a three-masted schooner on
the stocks. The hero, the student,   70
    the steeple jack, each in his way,
is at home.

It could not be dangerous to be living
    in a town like this, of simple people,
who have a steeple-jack placing danger signs by the church   75
while he is gilding the solid-
    pointed star, which on a steeple
stands for hope.

1935, 1961

EDWIN MUIR

(1887–1959)

THE HORSES   389

Barely a twelvemonth after
The seven days war that put the world to sleep,
Late in the evening the strange horses came.
By then we had made our covenant with silence,
But in the first few days it was so still   5
We listened to our breathing and were afraid.
On the second day
The radios failed; we turned the knobs; no answer.
On the third day a warship passed us, heading north,
Dead bodies piled on the deck. On the sixth day   10
A plane plunged over us into the sea. Thereafter
Nothing. The radios dumb;
And still they stand in corners of our kitchens,
And stand, perhaps, turned on, in a million rooms
All over the world. But now if they should speak,   15
If on a sudden they should speak again,
If on the stroke of noon a voice should speak,
We would not listen, we would not let it bring
That old bad world that swallowed its children quick
At one great gulp. We would not have it again.   20
Sometimes we think of the nations lying asleep,
Curled blindly in impenetrable sorrow,
And then the thought confounds us with its strangeness.
The tractors lie about our fields; at evening
They look like dank sea-monsters couched and waiting.   25
We leave them where they are and let them rust:
"They'll molder away and be like other loam."
We make our oxen drag our rusty plows,
Long laid aside. We have gone back
Far past our fathers' land.   30
                    And then, that evening
Late in the summer the strange horses came.
We heard a distant tapping on the road,
A deepening drumming; it stopped, went on again
And at the corner changed to hollow thunder.   35
We saw the heads
Like a wild wave charging and were afraid.
We had sold our horses in our fathers' time

To buy new tractors. Now they were strange to us
As fabulous steeds set on an ancient shield   40
Or illustrations in a book of knights.
We did not dare go near them. Yet they waited,
Stubborn and shy, as if they had been sent
By an old command to find our whereabouts
And that long-lost archaic companionship.   45
In the first moment we had never a thought
That they were creatures to be owned and used.
Among them were some half a dozen colts
Dropped in some wilderness of the broken world,
Yet new as if they had come from their own Eden.   50
Since then they have pulled our plows and borne our loads,
But that free servitude still can pierce our hearts.
Our life is changed; their coming our beginning.

                                                               1952

QUESTIONS

1. What is the state of the world before the horses appear? Where do the horses come
   from? What feelings do they evoke in you the first time you read the poem?
2. Where is fear expressed in the poem? Awe? Resoluteness? Do you find any signs of
   maturing emotional development? Intellectual? Spiritual?
3. Why is line 30 a dropped line?
4. The word *strange* is repeated several times throughout the poem. Why? Does it
   change meaning?
5. Discuss the way personification is used in the poem.
6. Identify the similes. Do you see any development of them from the first simile to the
   last?

HOWARD NEMEROV

(b. 1920)

THE GOOSE FISH   390

On the long shore, lit by the moon
To show them properly alone,
Two lovers suddenly embraced
So that their shadows were as one.
The ordinary night was graced   5
For them by the swift tide of blood
That silently they took at flood,
And for a little time they prized
    Themselves emparadised.

Then, as if shaken by stage-fright   10
Beneath the hard moon's bony light,
They stood together on the sand
Embarrassed in each other's sight
But still conspiring hand in hand,
Until they saw, there underfoot,   15
As though the world had found them out,
The goose fish turning up, though dead,
  His hugely grinning head.

There in the china light he lay,
Most ancient and corrupt and gray   20
They hesitated at his smile,
Wondering what it seemed to say
To lovers who a little while
Before had thought to understand,
By violence upon the sand,   25
The only way that could be known
  To make a world their own.

It was a wide and moony grin
Together peaceful and obscene;
They knew not what he would express,   30
So finished a comedian
He might mean failure or success,
But took it for an emblem of
Their sudden, new and guilty love
To be observed by, when they kissed,   35
  That rigid optimist.

So he became their patriarch,
Dreadfully mild in the half-dark.
His throat that the sand seemed to choke,
His picket teeth, these left their mark   40
But never did explain the joke
That so amused him, lying there
While the moon went down to disappear
Along the still and tilted track
  That bears the zodiac.   45

1960

QUESTIONS

1. What do you imagine a goose fish looks like? Use details from the poem to construct
   a mental picture.

2. What do the following words and phrases taken *together* present as a motif of this poem?

> emparadised (9)
> the world had found them out (16)
> new and guilty love (34)

Which other words and images support that motif?
3. What kind of language describes the lovers' love?
4. Why the sudden movement from the fish to the zodiac in the final stanza?

THE BLUE SWALLOWS   391

Across the millstream below the bridge
Seven blue swallows divide the air
In shapes invisible and evanescent,
Kaleidoscopic beyond the mind's
Or memory's power to keep them there.   5

"History is where tensions were,"
"Form is the diagram of forces."
Thus, helplessly, there on the bridge,
While gazing down upon those birds—
How strange, to be above the birds!—   10
Thus helplessly the mind in its brain
Weaves up relation's spindrift web,
Seeing the swallows' tails as nibs
Dipped in invisible ink, writing . . .

Poor mind, what would you have them write?   15
Some cabalistic history
Whose authorship you might ascribe
To God? to Nature? Ah, poor ghost,
You've capitalized your Self enough.
That villainous William of Occam   20
Cut out the feet from under that dream
Some seven centuries ago.
It's taken that long for the mind
To waken, yawn and stretch, to see
With opened eyes emptied of speech   25
The real world where the spelling mind
Imposes with its grammar book
Unreal relations on the blue
Swallows. Perhaps when you will have
Fully awakened, I shall show you   30

THE BLUE SWALLOWS 16 *cabalistic:* occult. 20 *William of Occam:* (1300–1349) English scholastic philosopher who felt that the simplest explanation was always the best.

A new thing: even the water
Flowing away beneath those birds
Will fail to reflect their flying forms,
And the eyes that see become as stones
Whence never tears shall fall again.   35

O swallows, swallows, poems are not
The point. Finding again the world,
That is the point, where loveliness
Adorns intelligible things
Because the mind's eye lit the sun.   40

                                                    1967

THE MAY DAY DANCING   392

The kindergarten children first come forth
In couples dressed as little brides and grooms.
By dancing in, by dancing round and out,
They braid the Maypole with a double thread;
Keep time, keep faith, is what the music says.   5

The corporal piano now leads out
Successively the older boys and girls,
Grade after grade, all for the dancing paired,
All dressed in the fashion of forgotten folk;
Those nymphs and shepherds, maybe, never were.   10

And all the parents standing in a ring,
With cameras some, and some with only eyes,
Attend to the dancing's measurable rule
Bemused, or hypnotized, so that they see
Not seven classes of children, but only one,   15

One class of children seven times again
That ever enters on the dancing floor
One year advanced in their compliant skill
To patterns ever with more varied styles
Clothing the naked order of the bass.   20

Some here relate the May with wanton rites,
Some with the Haymarket Riots, some with nothing
Beyond the present scene and circumstance
Which by the camera's thin incisive blade
They hope to take a frozen section through,   25

THE MAY DAY DANCING 22 *Haymarket Riots:* battle between police and workers in Chicago on May 4, 1886, following a demonstration for the eight-hour day. Several policemen were killed.

Keeping their child with one foot on the ground
And one foot off, and with a solemn face
Or one bewildered between grin and tears,
As many times repeating time and faith
He follows the compulsions of the dance   30

Around the brilliant morning with the sun,
The dance that leads him out to bring him home,
The May Day dance that tramples down the grass
And raises dust, that braids a double thread
Around the pole, in the great room of the sun.   35

1967

LEARNING BY DOING   393

They're taking down a tree at the front door,
The power saw is snarling at some nerves,
Whining at others. Now and then it grunts,
And sawdust falls like snow or a drift of seeds.

Rotten, they tell us, at the fork, and one   5
Big wind would bring it down. So what they do
They do, as usual, to do us good.
Whatever cannot carry its own weight
Has got to go, and so on; you expect
To hear them talking next about survival   10
And the values of a free society.
For in the explanations people give
On these occasions there is generally some
Mean-spirited moral point, and everyone
Privately wonders if his neighbors plan   15
To saw him up before he falls on them.

Maybe a hundred years in sun and shower
Dismantled in a morning and let down
Out of itself a finger at a time
And then an arm, and so down to the trunk,   20
Until there's nothing left to hold on to
Or snub the splintery holding rope around,
And where those big green divagations were
So loftily with shadows interleaved
The absent-minded blue rains in on us.   25
Now that they've got it sectioned on the ground

LEARNING BY DOING 23 *divagations:* wanderings.

It looks as though somebody made a plain
Error in diagnosis, for the wood
Looks sweet and sound throughout. You couldn't know,
Of course, until you took it down. That's what   30
Experts are for, and these experts stand round
The giant pieces of tree as though expecting
An instruction booklet from the factory
Before they try to put it back together.

Anyhow, there it isn't, on the ground.   35
Next come the tractor and the crowbar crew
To extirpate what's left and fill the grave.
Maybe tomorrow grass seed will be sown.
There's some mean-spirited moral point in that
As well: you learn to bury your mistakes,   40
Though for a while at dusk the darkening air
Will be with many shadows interleaved,
And pierced with a bewilderment of birds.

1977

THE HISTORICAL JUDAS   394

He too has an eternal part to play,
What did he understand? that good has scope
Only from evil, flowering in filth?
Did he go smiling, kissing, to betray
Out of a fine conviction of his truth,   5
Or some original wreckage of our hope?

If merely mistaken, at any rate,
He had a talent for the grand mistake,
The necessary one, without which not,
And managed to incur eternal hate   10
For triggering what destiny had got
Arranged from the beginning, for our sake.

Let us consider, then, if not forgive
This most distinguished of our fellow sinners,
Who sponsored our redemption with his sin,   15
And whose name, more than ours, shall surely live
To make our meanness look like justice in
All histories commissioned by the winners.

1980

FRANK O'HARA

(1926–1966)

POEM   395

The eager note on my door said "Call me,
call when you get in!" so I quickly threw
a few tangerines into my overnight bag,
straightened my eyelids and shoulders, and

headed straight for the door. It was autumn   5
by the time I got around the corner, oh all
unwilling to be either pertinent or bemused, but
the leaves were brighter than grass on the sidewalk!

Funny, I thought, that the lights are on this late
and the hall door open; still up at this hour, a   10
champion jai-alai player like himself? Oh fie!
for shame! What a host, so zealous! And he was

there in the hall, flat on a sheet of blood that
ran down the stairs. I did appreciate it. There are few
hosts who so thoroughly prepare to greet a guest   15
only casually invited, and that several months ago.

                                                       1952

THE DAY LADY DIED   396

It is 12:20 in New York a Friday
three days after Bastille day, yes
it is 1959 and I go get a shoeshine
because I will get off the 4:19 in Easthampton
at 7:15 and then go straight to dinner   5
and I don't know the people who will feed me

I walk up the muggy street beginning to sun
and have a hamburger and a malted and buy
and ugly NEW WORLD WRITING to see what the poets
in Ghana are doing these days   10
                              I go on to the bank
and Miss Stillwagon (first name Linda I once heard)
doesn't even look up my balance for once in her life

THE DAY LADY DIED title *Lady:* Billie Holiday (1915–1959), popular blues singer, also known as
"Lady Day." 2 *Bastille day:* July 14; French Independence Day. 4 *Easthampton:* a village on the
eastern end of Long Island.

and in the GOLDEN GRIFFIN I get a little Verlaine
for Patsy with drawings by Bonnard although I do   15
think of Hesiod, trans. Richmond Lattimore or
Brendan Behan's new play or *Le Balcon* or *Les Nègres*
of Genet, but I don't, I stick with Verlaine
after practically going to sleep with quandariness

and for Mike I just stroll into the PARK LANE   20
Liquor Store and ask for a bottle of Strega and
then I go back where I came from to 6th Avenue
and the tobacconist in the Ziegfeld Theatre and
casually ask for a carton of Gauloises and a carton
of Picayunes, and a NEW YORK POST with her face on it   25

and I am sweating a lot by now and thinking of
leaning on the john door in the 5 SPOT
while she whispered a song along the keyboard
to Mal Waldron and everyone and I stopped breathing

1964

QUESTIONS

1. Why all the precision about time and date? What effect does this have on your first reading?
2. What other compulsion for detail does the speaker display? How does this help you create a coherent reading of the poem?
3. What is the speaker's reaction to the news he reads?
4. How is the speaker's memory both similar to and different from the day he has described so far?
5. What is ironic about the final line?

WHY I AM NOT A PAINTER   397

I am not a painter, I am a poet.
Why? I think I would rather be
a painter, but I am not. Well,

for instance, Mike Goldberg
is starting a painting. I drop in.   5
"Sit down and have a drink" he
says. I drink; we drink. I look

14 *Verlaine:* Paul Verlaine (1844–1896), French poet. 15 *Bonnard:* Pierre Bonnard (1867–1947), French impressionist painter. 16 *Hesiod:* (eighth century B.C.) Greek poet. 17 *Brendan Behan:* (1923–1964) Irish author. 17–18 *Le Balcon . . . Genet:* Jean Genet, French author of *The Balcony* and *The Blacks.* 29 *Mal Waldron:* Billie Holiday's accompanist.
WHY I AM NOT A PAINTER 4 *Mike Goldberg:* New York artist.

up. "You have SARDINES in it."
"Yes, it needed something there."
"Oh." I go and the days go by   10
and I drop in again. The painting
is going on, and I go, and the days
go by. I drop in. The painting is
finished. "Where's SARDINES?"
All that's left is just   15
letters, "It was too much," Mike says.
But me? One day I am thinking of
a color: orange. I write a line
about orange. Pretty soon it is a
whole page of words, not lines.   20
Then another page. There should be
so much more, not of orange, of
words, of how terrible orange is
and life. Days go by. It is even in
prose, I am a real poet. My poem   25
is finished and I haven't mentioned
orange yet. It's twelve poems, I call
it ORANGES. And one day in a gallery
I see Mike's painting, called SARDINES.

1971

SHARON OLDS
(b. 1942)

SEX WITHOUT LOVE   398

How do they do it, the ones who make love
without love? Beautiful as dancers,
gliding over each other like ice-skaters
over the ice, fingers hooked
inside each other's bodies, faces   5
red as steak, wine, wet as the
children at birth whose mothers are going to
give them away. How do they come to the
come to the   come to the   God   come to the
still waters, and not love   10
the one who came there with them, light
rising slowly as steam off their joined

skin? These are the true religious,
the purists, the pros, the ones who will not
accept a false Messiah, love the   15
priest instead of the God. They do not
mistake the lover for their own pleasure,
they are like great runners: they know they are alone
with the road surface, the cold, the wind,
the fit of their shoes, their over-all cardio-   20
vascular health—just factors, like the partner
in the bed, and not the truth, which is the
single body alone in the universe
against its own best time.

1984

QUESTIONS

1. Identify the images that are the most vivid after your first reading of the poem. What
   do they have in common? How are they different?
2. How do running and skating relate to the theme of the poem?
3. How is the theme of solitude developed in the poem?
4. What is the attitude of the speaker toward the people she describes?

WHY MY MOTHER MADE ME   399

Maybe I am what she always wanted,
my father as a woman,
maybe I am what she wanted to be
when she first saw him, tall and smart,
standing there in the college yard with the   5
hard male light of 1937
shining on his black hair. She wanted that
power. She wanted that size. She pulled and
pulled through him as if he were dark
bourbon taffy, she pulled and pulled and   10
pulled through his body until she drew me out,
rubbery and gleaming, her life after her life.
Maybe I am the way I am
because she wanted exactly that,
wanted there to be a woman   15
a lot like her, but who would not hold back, so she
pressed herself hard against him,
pressed and pressed the clear soft
ball of herself like a stick of beaten cream

against his stained sour steel grater 20
until I came out the other side of his body,
a big woman, stained, sour, sharp,
but with that milk at the center of my nature.
I lie here now as I once lay
in the crook of her arm, her creature, 25
and I feel her looking down into me the way the
maker of a sword gazes at his face in the
steel of the blade.

1987

AFTER 37 YEARS MY MOTHER APOLOGIZES FOR MY CHILDHOOD 400

When you tilted toward me, arms out
like someone trying to walk through a fire,
when you swayed toward me, crying out you were
sorry for what you had done to me, your
eyes filling with terrible liquid like 5
balls of mercury from a broken thermometer
skidding on the floor, when you quietly screamed
Where else could I turn? Who else did I have?, the
chopped crockery of your hands swinging toward me, the
water cracking from your eyes like moisture from 10
stones under heavy pressure, I could not
see what I would do with the rest of my life.
The sky seemed to be splintering like a window
someone is bursting into or out of, your
tiny face glittered as if with 15
shattered crystal, with true regret, the
regret of the body. I could not see what my
days would be with you sorry, with
you wishing you had not done it, the
sky falling around me, its shards 20
glistening in my eyes, your old soft
body fallen against me in horror I
took you in my arms, I said *It's all right,
don't cry, it's all right,* the air filled with
flying glass, I hardly knew what I 25
said or who I would be now that I had forgiven you.

1987

THAT MOMENT   401

It is almost too long ago to remember—
when I was a woman without children,
a person, really, like a figure standing in a field,
alone, dark against the pale crop.
The children were there, they were shadowy figures   5
outside the fence, indistinct as
distant blobs of faces at twilight.
I can't remember, anymore,
the moment I turned to take them, my heel
turning on the earth, grinding the heads of the   10
stalks of grain under my foot, my
body suddenly swinging around as the
flat figure on a weathervane will
swerve when the wind changes. I can't
remember the journey from the center of the field to the edge   15
or the cracking of the fence like the breaking down of the
borders of the world, or my stepping out of the
ploughed field altogether and
taking them in my arms as you'd take the
whites and yolks of eggs in your arms running   20
over you glutinous, streaked, slimy,
glazing you. I cannot remember that
instant when I gave my life to them
the way someone will suddenly give her life over to God
and I stood with them outside the universe   25
and then like a god I turned and brought them in.

1987

MARY OLIVER
(b. 1935)

LIGHTNING   402

The oaks shone
gaunt gold
on the lip
of the storm before
the wind rose,   5
the shapeless mouth
opened and began

its five-hour howl;
the lights
went out fast, branches   10
sidled over
the pitch of the roof, bounced
into the yard
that grew black
within minutes, except   15
for the lightning—the landscape
bulging forth like a quick
lesson in creation, then
thudding away. Inside,
as always,   20
it was hard to tell
fear from excitement:
how sensual
the lightning's
poured stroke! and still,   25
what a fire and a risk!
As always the body
wants to hide,
wants to flow toward it—strives
to balance while   30
fear shouts,
excitement shouts, back
and forth—each
bolt a burning river
tearing like escape through the dark   35
field of the other.

1983

IN THE PINEWOODS, CROWS AND OWL   403

Great bumble. Sleek
slicer. How the crows
dream of you, caught at last
in their black beaks. Dream of you
leaking your life away. Your wings   5
crumbling like old bark. Feathers
falling from your breast like leaves,
and your eyes two bolts
of lightning gone to sleep.

Eight of them   10
fly over the pinewoods looking down
into the branches. They know you are
there somewhere, fat and drowsy
from your night of rabbits and rats. Once
this month you caught a crow. Scraps of him   15
flew far and wide, the news
rang all day through the woods. The cold
river of their hatred roils
day and night: you are their dream, their waking,
their quarry, their demon. You   20
are the pine god who never speaks but holds
the keys to everything while they fly
morning after morning against the shut doors. You
will have a slow life, and eat them, one by one.
They know it. They hate you. Still   25
when one of them spies you out, all stream
straight toward violence and confrontation.
As though it helped to see the living proof.
The bone-crushing prince of dark days, gloomy
at the interruption of his rest. Hissing   30
and snapping, grabbing about him, dreadful
as death's drum; mournful, unalterable fact.

1983

QUESTIONS

1. Which words help to establish the tone of the poem the first time you read it?
2. Who is addressed as "you" in this poem?
3. Who is the "bone-crushing prince" of the last four lines?
4. Which words describe the owl?
5. What are the various activities of the crows?
6. What is the "unalterable fact" (line 32)?

GHOSTS   404

1

Have you noticed?

2

Where so many millions of powerful bawling beasts
lay down on the earth and died
it's hard to tell now
what's bone, and what merely   5
was once.

The golden eagle, for instance,
has a bit of heaviness in him;
moreover the huge barns
seem ready, sometimes, to ramble off   10
toward deeper grass.

3

1805
near the Bitterroot Mountains:
a man named Lewis kneels down
on the prairie watching   15

a sparrow's nest cleverly concealed in the wild hyssop
and lined with buffalo hair. The chicks,
not more than a day hatched, lean
quietly into the thick wool as if
content, after all,   20
to have left the perfect world and fallen,
helpless and blind
into the flowered fields and the perils
of this one.

4

In the book of the earth it is written: 25
nothing can die.

In the book of the Sioux it is written:
they have gone away into the earth to hide.
Nothing will coax them out again
but the people dancing.   30

5

Said the old-timers:
the tongue
is the sweetest meat.

Passengers shooting from train windows
could hardly miss, they were   35
that many.

Afterward the carcasses
stank unbelievably, and sang with flies, ribboned
with slopes of white fat,
black ropes of blood—hellhunks   40
in the prairie heat.

GHOSTS 14 *Lewis:* Meriwether Lewis (1774–1809), American explorer and leader of the Lewis and Clark expedition (1804–1806) to the Northwest. The Bitterroot Mountains form a range of the Rocky Mountains along the Idaho–Montana border.

6

Have you noticed? how the rain
falls soft as the fall
of moccasins. *Have you noticed?*
how the immense circles still,   45
stubbornly, after a hundred years,
mark the grass where the rich droppings
from the roaring bulls
fell to the earth as the herd stood
day after day, moon after moon   50
in their tribal circle, outwaiting
the packs of yellow-eyed wolves that are also
have you noticed? gone now.

7

Once only, and then in a dream,
I watched while, secretly   55
and with the tenderness of any caring woman,
a cow gave birth
to a red calf, tongued him dry and nursed him
in a warm corner
of the clear night   60
in the fragrant grass
in the wild domains
of the prairie spring, and I asked them,
in my dream I knelt down and asked them
to make room for me.   65

1983

MAY   405

May, and among the miles of leafing,
blossoms storm out of the darkness—
windflowers and moccasin flowers. The bees
dive into them and I too, to gather
their spiritual honey. Mute and meek, yet theirs   5
is the deepest certainty that this existence too—
this sense of well-being, the flourishing
of the physical body—rides
near the hub of the miracle that everything
is a part of, is as good   10
as a poem or a prayer, can also make
luminous any dark place on earth.

1983

CLIMBING THE CHAGRIN RIVER   406

We enter
the green river,
heron harbor,
mud-basin lined
with snagheaps, where turtles   5
sun themselves—we push
through the falling
silky weight
striped warm and cold
bounding down   10
through the black flanks
of wet rocks—we wade
under hemlock
and white pine—climb
stone steps into   15
the timeless castles
of emerald eddies,
swirls, channels
cold as ice tumbling
out of a white flow—   20
sheer sheets
flying off rocks,
frivolous and lustrous,
skirting the secret pools—
cradles   25
full of the yellow hair
of last year's leaves
where grizzled fish
hang halfway down,
like tarnished swords,   30
while around them
fingerlings sparkle
and descend,
nails of light
in the loose   35
racing waters.

1983

WILFRED OWEN
(1893–1918)

ANTHEM FOR DOOMED YOUTH   407

What passing-bells for these who die as cattle?
  Only the monstrous anger of the guns.
  Only the stuttering rifles' rapid rattle
Can patter out their hasty orisons.
No mockeries now for them; no prayers nor bells,   5
  Nor any voice of mourning save the choirs,—
The shrill, demented choirs of wailing shells;
  And bugles calling for them from sad shires.

What candles may be held to speed them all?
  Not in the hands of boys, but in their eyes   10
Shall shine the holy glimmers of good-byes.
  The pallor of girls' brows shall be their pall;
Their flowers the tenderness of patient minds,
And each slow dusk a drawing-down of blinds.

1920

QUESTIONS

1. How does the title prepare you for the extended metaphor you find in the poem?
2. What feelings does the extended metaphor evoke? Are any of these feelings contradictory?
3. What is the effect of the word-play in line 12? The rhyme "cattle/rattle"? "guns/orisons"?
4. Do you find any irony?

DULCE ET DECORUM EST   408

Bent double, like old beggars under sacks,
Knock-kneed, coughing like hags, we cursed through sludge,
Till on the haunting flares we turned our backs
And towards our distant rest began to trudge.
Men marched asleep. Many had lost their boots   5
But limped on, blood-shod. All went lame; all blind;
Drunk with fatigue; deaf even to the hoots
Of tired, outstripped Five-Nines that dropped behind.

ANTHEM FOR DOOMED YOUTH 4 *orisons:* prayers.

DULCE ET DECORUM EST title and last two lines: from Horace, "Sweet and fitting it is to die for the fatherland" (Latin).

Gas! GAS! Quick, boys!—An ecstasy of fumbling,
Fitting the clumsy helmets just in time;   10
But someone still was yelling out and stumbling
And flound'ring like a man in fire or lime . . .
Dim, through the misty panes and thick green light,
As under a green sea, I saw him drowning.

In all my dreams, before my helpless sight,   15
He plunges at me, guttering, choking, drowning.

If in some smothering dreams you too could pace
Behind the wagon that we flung him in,
And watch the white eyes writhing in his face,
His hanging face, like a devil's sick of sin;   20
If you could hear, at every jolt, the blood
Come gargling from the froth-corrupted lungs,
Obscene as cancer, bitter as the cud
Of vile, incurable sores on innocent tongues,—
My friend, you would not tell with such high zest   25
To children ardent for some desperate glory,
The old Lie: Dulce et decorum est
Pro patria mori.

1920

D O R O T H Y   P A R K E R
(1893–1967)

ONE PERFECT ROSE   409

A single flow'r he sent me, since we met.
    All tenderly his messenger he chose;
Deep-hearted, pure, with scented dew still wet—
    One perfect rose.

I knew the language of the floweret;   5
    "My fragile leaves," it said, "his heart enclose."
Love long has taken for his amulet
    One perfect rose.

Why is it no one ever sent me yet
    One perfect limousine, do you suppose?   10
Ah no, it's always just my luck to get
    One perfect rose.

1926

QUESTIONS

1. What do the title and first stanza lead you to expect?
2. In the second stanza which word hints at a tone shift?
3. How does the diction change in the third stanza? Is the shift appropriate? What is the effect?

RÉSUMÉ 410

Razors pain you;
Rivers are damp;
Acids stain you;
And drugs cause cramp.
Guns aren't lawful;   5
Nooses give;
Gas smells awful;
You might as well live.

1926

MARGE PIERCY
(b. 1936)

THE FRIEND 411

We sat across the table.
he said, cut off your hands.
they are always poking at things.
they might touch me.
I said yes.   5

Food grew cold on the table.
he said, burn your body.
it is not clean and smells like sex.
it rubs my mind sore.
I said yes.   10

I love you, I said.
That's very nice, he said
I like to be loved,
that makes me happy.
Have you cut off your hands yet?   15

1969

BARBIE DOLL 412

This girlchild was born as usual
and presented dolls that did pee-pee
and miniature GE stoves and irons
and wee lipsticks the color of cherry candy.
Then in the magic of puberty, a classmate said: 5
You have a great big nose and fat legs.

She was healthy, tested intelligent,
possessed strong arms and back,
abundant sexual drive and manual dexterity.
She went to and fro apologizing.   10
Everyone saw a fat nose on thick legs.

She was advised to play coy,
exhorted to come on hearty,
exercise, diet, smile and wheedle.
Her good nature wore out   15
like a fan belt.
So she cut off her nose and her legs
and offered them up.

In the casket displayed on satin she lay
with the undertaker's cosmetics painted on,   20
a turned-up putty nose,
dressed in a pink and white nightie.
Doesn't she look pretty? everyone said.
Consummation at last.
To every woman a happy ending.   25

1969

QUESTIONS

1. Where does the poem surprise you?
2. What are the girl's attributes?
3. In the first stanza, what is she taught? In the third stanza?
4. When she acts, what does she do?
5. Where is the irony?

SYLVIA PLATH
(1932–1963)

POINT SHIRLEY   413

From Water-Tower Hill to the brick prison
The shingle booms, bickering under
The sea's collapse.
Snowcakes break and welter. This year
The gritted wave leaps   5
The seawall and drops onto a bier
Of quahog chips,
Leaving a salty mash of ice to whiten

In my grandmother's sand yard. She is dead,
Whose laundry snapped and froze here, who   10
Kept house against
What the sluttish, rutted sea could do.
Squall waves once danced
Ship timbers in through the cellar window;
A thresh-tailed, lanced   15
Shark littered in the geranium bed—

Such collusion of mulish elements
She wore her broom straws to the nub.
Twenty years out
Of her hand, the house still hugs in each drab   20
Stucco socket
The purple egg-stones: from Great Head's knob
To the filled-in Gut
The sea in its cold gizzard ground those rounds.

Nobody wintering now behind   25
The planked-up windows where she set
Her wheat loaves
And apple cakes to cool. What is it
Survives, grieves
So, over this battered, obstinate spit   30
Of gravel? The waves'
Spewed relics clicker masses in the wind,

POINT SHIRLEY title: Point Shirley in Winthrop, Massachusetts. The prison in line 1 is located on Deer Island in Boston Harbor. 7 *quahog:* an edible clam, having a very hard, solid shell.

Gray waves the stub-necked eiders ride.
A labor of love, and that labor lost.
Steadily the sea   35
Eats at Point Shirley. She died blessed,
And I come by
Bones, bones only, pawed and tossed,
A dog-faced sea.
The sun sinks under Boston, bloody red.   40

I would get from these dry-papped stones
The milk your love instilled in them.
The black ducks dive.
And though your graciousness might stream,
And I contrive,   45
Grandmother, stones are nothing of home
To that spumiest dove.
Against both bar and tower the black sea runs.

                                                   1960

THE COLOSSUS   414

I shall never get you put together entirely,
Pieced, glued, and properly jointed.
Mule-bray, pig-grunt and bawdy cackles
Proceed from your great lips.
It's worse than a barnyard.   5

Perhaps you consider yourself an oracle,
Mouthpiece of the dead, or of some god or other.
Thirty years now I have labored
To dredge the silt from your throat.
I am none the wiser.   10

Scaling little ladders with gluepots and pails of lysol
I crawl like an ant in mourning
Over the weedy acres of your brow
To mend the immense skull plates and clear
The bald, white tumuli of your eyes.   15

33 *eiders:* sea ducks.

THE COLOSSUS title: The Colossus was a gigantic statue of Apollo set at the entrance to the harbor of Rhodes.

A blue sky out of the Oresteia
Arches above us. O father, all by yourself
You are pithy and historical as the Roman Forum.
I open my lunch on a hill of black cypress.
Your fluted bones and acanthine hair are littered   20

In their old anarchy to the horizon-line.
It would take more than a lightning-stroke
To create such a ruin.
Nights, I squat in the cornucopia
Of your left ear, out of the wind,   25

Counting the red stars and those of plum-color.
The sun rises under the pillar of your tongue.
My hours are married to shadow.
No longer do I listen for the scrape of a keel
On the blank stones of the landing.   30

1960

METAPHORS   415

I'm a riddle in nine syllables,
An elephant, a ponderous house,
A melon strolling on two tendrils.
O red fruit, ivory, fine timbers!
This loaf's big with its yeasty rising.   5
Money's new-minted in this fat purse.
I'm a means, a stage, a cow in calf.
I've eaten a bag of green apples,
Boarded the train there's no getting off.

1961

THE BEE MEETING   416

Who are these people at the bridge to meet me? They are the
       villagers——
The rector, the midwife, the sexton, the agent for bees.
In my sleeveless summery dress I have no protection,
And they are all gloved and covered, why did nobody tell me?
They are smiling and taking out veils tacked to ancient hats.   5

16 *Oresteia:* three plays by Aeschylus (525–456 B.C.), Greek writer of tragedies. The plays present the story of Agamemnon, Clytemnestra, and Orestes. 20 *acanthine:* in architecture and sculpture, an ornament patterned after the curled acanthus leaves, used especially at the top of Corinthian columns.

I am nude as a chicken neck, does nobody love me?
Yes, here is the secretary of bees with her white shop smock,
Buttoning the cuffs at my wrists and the slit from my neck to my
    knees.
Now I am milkweed silk, the bees will not notice.
They will not smell my fear, my fear, my fear.   10

Which is the rector now, is it that man in black?
Which is the midwife, is that her blue coat?
Everybody is nodding a square black head, they are knights in visors,
Breastplates of cheesecloth knotted under the armpits.
Their smiles and their voices are changing. I am led through a
    beanfield.   15

Strips of tinfoil winking like people,
Feather dusters fanning their hands in a sea of bean flowers,
Creamy bean flowers with black eyes and leaves like bored hearts.
Is it blood clots the tendrils are dragging up that string?
No, no, it is scarlet flowers that will one day be edible.   20

Now they are giving me a fashionable white straw Italian hat
And a black veil that molds to my face, they are making me one of
    them.
They are leading me to the shorn grove, the circle of hives.
Is it the hawthorn that smells so sick?
The barren body of hawthorn, etherizing its children.   25

Is it some operation that is taking place?
It is the surgeon my neighbors are waiting for,
This apparition in a green helmet,
Shining gloves and white suit.
Is it the butcher, the grocer, the postman, someone I know?   30

I cannot run, I am rooted, and the gorse hurts me
With its yellow purses, its spiky armory.
I could not run without having to run forever.
The white hive is snug as a virgin,
Sealing off her brood cells, her honey, and quietly humming.   35

Smoke rolls and scarves in the grove.
The mind of the hive thinks this is the end of everything.
Here they come, the outriders, on their hysterical elastics.
If I stand very still, they will think I am cow-parsley,
A gullible head untouched by their animosity,   40

Not even nodding, a personage in a hedgerow.
The villagers open the chambers, they are hunting the queen.
Is she hiding, is she eating honey? She is very clever.
She is old, old, old, she must live another year, and she knows it.
While in their fingerjoint cells the new virgins   45

Dream of a duel they will win inevitably,
A curtain of wax dividing them from the bride flight,
The upflight of the murderess into a heaven that loves her.
The villagers are moving the virgins, there will be no killing.
The old queen does not show herself, is she so ungrateful?   50

I am exhausted, I am exhausted——
Pillar of white in a blackout of knives.
I am the magician's girl who does not flinch.
The villagers are untying their disguises, they are shaking hands.
Whose is that long white box in the grove, what have they
      accomplished, why am I cold.   55

                                                                  1961

NICK AND THE CANDLESTICK   417

I am a miner. The light burns blue.
Waxy stalactites
Drip and thicken, tears

The earthen womb
Exudes from its dead boredom.   5
Black bat airs

Wrap me, raggy shawls,
Cold homicides.
They weld to me like plums.

Old cave of calcium   10
Icicles, old echoer.
Even the newts are white,

Those holy Joes.
And the fish, the fish——
Christ! they are panes of ice,   15

A vice of knives,
A piranha
Religion, drinking

Its first communion out of my live toes.
The candle   20
Gulps and recovers its small altitude,

Its yellows hearten.
O love, how did you get here?
O embryo

Remembering, even in sleep,   25
Your crossed position.
The blood blooms clean

In you, ruby.
The pain
You wake to is not yours.   30

Love, love,
I have hung our cave with roses,
With soft rugs——

The last of Victoriana.
Let the stars   35
Plummet to their dark address,

Let the mercuric
Atoms that cripple drip
Into the terrible well,

You are the one   40
Solid the spaces lean on, envious.
You are the baby in the barn.

1963

LADY LAZARUS   418

I have done it again.
One year in every ten
I manage it——

A sort of walking miracle, my skin
Bright as a Nazi lampshade,   5
My right foot

A paperweight,
My face a featureless, fine
Jew linen.

Peel off the napkin   10
O my enemy.
Do I terrify?——

The nose, the eye pits, the full set of teeth?
The sour breath
Will vanish in a day.   15

Soon, soon the flesh
The grave cave ate will be
At home on me

And I a smiling woman.
I am only thirty.   20
And like the cat I have nine times to die.

This is Number Three.
What a trash
To annihilate each decade.

What a million filaments.   25
The peanut-crunching crowd
Shoves in to see

Them unwrap me hand and foot——
The big strip tease.
Gentlemen, ladies   30

These are my hands
My knees.
I may be skin and bone,

Nevertheless, I am the same, identical woman.
The first time it happened I was ten.   35
It was an accident.

The second time I meant
To last it out and not come back at all.
I rocked shut

As a seashell.   40
They had to call and call
And pick the worms off me like sticky pearls.

Dying
Is an art, like everything else.
I do it exceptionally well.   45

I do it so it feels like hell.
I do it so it feels real.
I guess you could say I've a call.

It's easy enough to do it in a cell.
It's easy enough to do it and stay put.   50
It's the theatrical

Comeback in broad day
To the same place, the same face, the same brute
Amused shout:

'A miracle!'   55
That knocks me out.
There is a charge

For the eyeing of my scars, there is a charge
For the hearing of my heart——
It really goes.   60

And there is a charge, a very large charge
For a word or a touch
Or a bit of blood

Or a piece of my hair or my clothes.
So, so, Herr Doktor.   65
So, Herr Enemy.

I am your opus,
I am your valuable,
The pure gold baby

That melts to a shriek.   70
I turn and burn.
Do not think I underestimate your great concern.

Ash, ash—
You poke and stir.
Flesh, bone, there is nothing there——   75

A cake of soap,
A wedding ring,
A gold filling.

Herr God, Herr Lucifer
Beware   80
Beware.

Out of the ash
I rise with my red hair
And I eat men like air.

1963

WORDS 419

Axes
After whose stroke the wood rings,
And the echoes!
Echoes traveling
Off from the center like horses.   5

The sap
Wells like tears, like the
Water striving
To re-establish its mirror
Over the rock   10

That drops and turns,
A white skull,
Eaten by weedy greens.
Years later I
Encounter them on the road——   15

Words dry and riderless,
The indefatigable hoof-taps.
While
From the bottom of the pool, fixed stars
Govern a life.   20

1963

ELM 420

FOR RUTH FAINLIGHT

I know the bottom, she says. I know it with my great tap root:
It is what you fear.
I do not fear it: I have been there.

Is it the sea you hear in me,
Its dissatisfactions?   5
Or the voice of nothing, that was your madness?

Love is a shadow.
How you lie and cry after it.
Listen: these are its hooves: it has gone off, like a horse.

All night I shall gallop thus, impetuously,   10
Till your head is a stone, your pillow a little turf,
Echoing, echoing.

Or shall I bring you the sound of poisons?
This is rain now, this big hush.
And this is the fruit of it: tin-white, like arsenic.   15

I have suffered the atrocity of sunsets.
Scorched to the root
My red filaments burn and stand, a hand of wires.

Now I break up in pieces that fly about like clubs.
A wind of such violence   20
Will tolerate no bystanding: I must shriek.

The moon, also, is merciless: she would drag me
Cruelly, being barren.
Her radiance scathes me. Or perhaps I have caught her.

I let her go. I let her go   25
Diminished and flat, as after radical surgery.
How your bad dreams possess and endow me.

I am inhabited by a cry.
Nightly it flaps out
Looking, with its hooks, for something to love.   30

I am terrified by this dark thing
That sleeps in me;
All day I feel its soft, feathery turnings, its malignity.

Clouds pass and disperse.
Are those the faces of love, those pale irretrievables?   35
Is it for such I agitate my heart?

I am incapable of more knowledge.
What is this, this face
So murderous in its strangle of branches?——

Its snaky acids kiss.   40
It petrifies the will. These are the isolate, slow faults
That kill, that kill, that kill.

1965

DADDY

You do not do, you do not do
Any more, black shoe
In which I have lived like a foot
For thirty years, poor and white,
Barely daring to breathe or Achoo.   5

Daddy, I have had to kill you.
You died before I had time——
Marble-heavy, a bag full of God,
Ghastly statue with one gray toe
Big as a Frisco seal   10

And a head in the freakish Atlantic
Where it pours bean green over blue
In the waters off beautiful Nauset.
I used to pray to recover you.
Ach, du.   15

In the German tongue, in the Polish town
Scraped flat by the roller
Of wars, wars, wars.
But the name of the town is common.
My Polack friend   20

Says there are a dozen or two.
So I never could tell where you
Put your foot, your root,
I never could talk to you.
The tongue stuck in my jaw.   25

It stuck in a barb wire snare.
Ich, ich, ich, ich,
I could hardly speak.
I thought every German was you.
And the language obscene   30

An engine, an engine
Chuffing me off like a Jew.
A Jew to Dachau, Auschwitz, Belsen.
I began to talk like a Jew.
I think I may well be a Jew.   35

DADDY 15 *Ach, du:* German for "Oh, you." 27 *Ich:* German for "I."

The snows of the Tyrol, the clear beer of Vienna
Are not very pure or true.
With my gypsy ancestress and my weird luck
And my Taroc pack and my Taroc pack
I may be a bit of a Jew.   40

I have always been scared of *you*,
With your Luftwaffe, your gobbledygoo.
And your neat moustache
And your Aryan eye, bright blue.
Panzer-man, panzer-man, O You——   45

Bit my pretty red heart in two.
I was ten when they buried you.
At twenty I tried to die
And get back, back, back to you.
I thought even the bones would do.   50

But they pulled me out of the sack,
And they stuck me together with glue,
And then I knew what to do.
I made a model of you,
A man in black with a Meinkampf look   55

And a love of the rack and the screw.
And I said I do, I do.
So daddy, I'm finally through.
The black telephone's off at the root,
The voices just can't worm through.   60

If I've killed one man, I've killed two——
The vampire who said he was you
And drank my blood for a year,
Seven years, if you want to know.
Daddy, you can lie back now.   65

There's a stake in your fat black heart
And the villagers never liked you.
They are dancing and stamping on you.
They always *knew* it was you.
Daddy, daddy, you bastard, I'm through.   70

1965

---

39 *Taroc:* Tarot, fortune-telling cards. 42 *Luftwaffe:* Nazi air force in World War II. 45 *Panzer-man:* a soldier manning an armored tank. 55 *Meinkampf: Mein Kampf* is a book by Adolf Hitler.

QUESTIONS

1. What does the title lead you to expect? Is that what you find? What surprises you or puzzles you at first?
2. What is the effect of the repeated rhyme throughout? How does it contribute to the tone of the poem?
3. What are the obstacles between the speaker and "daddy"?
4. How is the dilemma resolved? Who kills whom?

ARIEL   422

Stasis in darkness.
Then the substanceless blue
Pour of tor and distances.

God's lioness,
How one we grow,   5
Pivot of heels and knees!—The furrow

Splits and passes, sister to
The brown arc
Of the neck I cannot catch,

Nigger-eye   10
Berries cast dark
Hooks—

Black sweet blood mouthfuls,
Shadows.
Something else   15

Hauls me through air—
Thighs, hair;
Flakes from my heels.

White
Godiva, I unpeel—   20
Dead hands, dead stringencies.

And now I
Foam to wheat, a glitter of seas.
The child's cry

Melts in the wall.   25
And I
Am the arrow,

ARIEL title: Ariel is the spirit in Shakespeare's *The Tempest*. It is also the name of Sylvia Plath's horse. 3 *tor:* pile of rocks on a hilltop.

The dew that flies
Suicidal, at once with the drive
Into the red   30

Eye, the cauldron of morning.

                                                               1965

BLACK ROOK IN RAINY WEATHER   423

On the stiff twig up there
Hunches a wet black rook
Arranging and rearranging its feathers in the rain.
I do not expect miracle
Or an accident   5

To set the sight on fire
In my eye, nor seek
Any more in the desultory weather some design,
But let spotted leaves fall as they fall,
Without ceremony, or portent   10

Although, I admit, I desire,
Occasionally, some backtalk
From the mute sky, I can't honestly complain:
A certain minor light may still
Leap incandescent   15

Out of kitchen table or chair
As if a celestial burning took
Possession of the most obtuse objects now and then—
Thus hallowing an interval
Otherwise inconsequent   20

By bestowing largesse, honor,
One might say love. At any rate, I now walk
Wary (for it could happen
Even in this dull, ruinous landscape); skeptical,
Yet politic; ignorant   25

Of whatever angel may choose to flare
Suddenly at my elbow. I only know that a rook
Ordering its black feathers can so shine
As to seize my senses, haul
My eyelids up, and grant   30

A brief respite from fear
Of total neutrality. With luck,
Trekking stubborn through this season
Of fatigue, I shall
Patch together a content   35

Of sorts. Miracles occur,
If you care to call those spasmodic
Tricks of radiance miracles. The wait's begun again,
The long wait for the angel,
For that rare, random descent.   40

                                                            1971

ALEXANDER POPE
(1688–1744)

THE RAPE OF THE LOCK   424
AN HEROI-COMICAL POEM

Nolueram, Belinda, tuos violare capillos;
sed juvat hoc precibus me tribuisse tuis.
                                    —MARTIAL

Canto I

What dire offense from amorous causes springs,
What mighty contests rise from trivial things,
I sing—This verse to Caryll, Muse! is due:
This, even Belinda may vouchsafe to view:
Slight is the subject, but not so the praise,   5
If she inspire, and he approve my lays.
    Say what strange motive, Goddess! could compel
A well-bred lord to assault a gentle belle?
Oh, say what stranger cause, yet unexplored,
Could make a gentle belle reject a lord?   10
In tasks so bold can little men engage,
And in soft bosoms dwells such mighty rage?

THE RAPE OF THE LOCK subtitle: this poem is a mock-epic, or "heroi-comical poem." It is based on an incident that occurred in 1711 when Robert, Baron Petre, cut off a lock of Arabella Fermor's hair. Pope's friend, John Caryll (line 3), asked the poet if he would mediate in the quarrel which then arose between the families. Pope's response was this poem. epigraph: Latin from Martial: "Belinda, I did not want to violate your locks, but it pleases me to have paid this tribute to your prayers."

Sol through white curtains shot a timorous ray,
And oped those eyes that must eclipse the day.
Now lapdogs give themselves the rousing shake,   15
And sleepless lovers just at twelve awake:
Thrice rung the bell, the slipper knocked the ground,
And the pressed watch returned a silver sound.
Belinda still her downy pillow pressed,
Her guardian Sylph prolonged the balmy rest: 20
'Twas he had summoned to her silent bed
The morning dream that hovered o'er her head.
A youth more glittering than a birthnight beau
(That even in slumber caused her cheek to glow)
Seemed to her ear his winning lips to lay,   25
And thus in whispers said, or seemed to say:
   "Fairest of mortals, thou distinguished care
Of thousand bright inhabitants of air!
If e'er one vision touched thy infant thought,
Of all the nurse and all the priest have taught,   30
Of airy elves by moonlight shadows seen,
The silver token, and the circled green,
Or virgins visited by angel powers,
With golden crowns and wreaths of heavenly flowers,
Hear and believe! thy own importance know,   35
Nor bound thy narrow views to things below.
Some secret truths, from learned pride concealed,
To maids alone and children are revealed:
What though no credit doubting wits may give?
The fair and innocent shall still believe.   40
Know, then, unnumbered spirits round thee fly,
The light militia of the lower sky:
These, though unseen, are ever on the wing,
Hang o'er the box, and hover round the Ring.
Think what an equipage thou hast in air,   45
And view with scorn two pages and a chair.
As now your own, our beings were of old,
And once enclosed in woman's beauteous mold;
Thence, by a soft transition, we repair
From earthly vehicles to these of air.   50
Think not, when woman's transient breath is fled,

---

20 *Sylph:* air spirit. 23 *birthnight beau:* a courtier dressed for the birthday of royalty. 31–32 *airy elves
. . . circled green:* coin left by fairies and circle left in grass where the fairies danced. 44 *the box . . .
the Ring:* a theater box and the circular path in Hyde park. 46 *chair:* sedan chair in which one is
carried.

That all her vanities at once are dead:
Succeeding vanities she still regards,
And though she plays no more, o'erlooks the cards.
Her joy in gilded chariots, when alive,   55
And love of ombre, after death survive.
For when the Fair in all their pride expire,
To their first elements their souls retire:
The sprites of fiery termagants in flame
Mount up, and take a Salamander's name.   60
Soft yielding minds to water glide away,
And sip, with Nymphs, their elemental tea.
The graver prude sinks downward to a Gnome,
In search of mischief still on earth to roam.
The light coquettes in Sylphs aloft repair,   65
And sport and flutter in the fields of air.
    "Know further yet; whoever fair and chaste
Rejects mankind, is by some Sylph embraced:
For spirits, freed from mortal laws, with ease
Assume what sexes and what shapes they please.   70
What guards the purity of melting maids,
In courtly balls, and midnight masquerades,
Safe from the treacherous friend, the daring spark,
The glance by day, the whisper in the dark,
When kind occasion prompts their warm desires,   75
When music softens, and when dancing fires?
'Tis but their Sylph, the wise Celestials know,
Though Honor is the word with men below.
    "Some nymphs there are, too conscious of their face,
For life predestined to the Gnomes' embrace.   80
These swell their prospects and exalt their pride,
When offers are disdained, and love denied:
Then gay ideas crowd the vacant brain,
While peers, and dukes, and all their sweeping train,
And garters, stars, and coronets appear,   85
And in soft sounds, 'your Grace' salutes their ear.
'Tis these that early taint the female soul,
Instruct the eyes of young coquettes to roll,
Teach infant cheeks a bidden blush to know,
And little hearts to flutter at a beau.   90

---

56 *ombre:* a card game. 58 *elements:* fire, earth, water, and air—the four elements of the ancient world which corresponded to the personality-determining spirits. 59 *termagants:* shrews. 60 *Salamander:* it was commonly believed that the salamander could live in the fire. 73 *spark:* a young dandy. 85 *garter, stars, and coronets:* symbols of rank.

"Oft, when the world imagine women stray,
The Sylphs through mystic mazes guide their way,
Through all the giddy circle they pursue,
And old impertinence expel by new.
What tender maid but must a victim fall   95
To one man's treat, but for another's ball?
When Florio speaks what virgin could withstand,
If gentle Damon did not squeeze her hand?
With varying vanities, from every part,
They shift the moving toyshop of their heart;   100
Where wigs with wigs, with sword-knots sword-knots strive,
Beaux banish beaux, and coaches coaches drive.
This erring mortals levity may call;
Oh, blind to truth! the Sylphs contrive it all.
      "Of these am I, who thy protection claim,   105
A watchful sprite, and Ariel is my name.
Late, as I ranged the crystal wilds of air,
In the clear mirror of thy ruling star
I saw, alas! some dread event impend,
Ere to the main this morning sun descend,   110
But Heaven reveals not what, or how, or where:
Warned by the Sylph, O pious maid, beware!
This to disclose is all thy guardian can:
Beware of all, but most beware of Man!"
      He said; when Shock, who thought she slept too long, 115
Leaped up, and waked his mistress with his tongue.
'Twas then, Belinda, if report say true,
Thy eyes first opened on a billet-doux;
Wounds, charms, and ardors were no sooner read,
But all the vision vanished from thy head.   120
      And now, unveiled, the toilet stands displayed,
Each silver vase in mystic order laid.
First, robed in white, the nymph intent adores,
With head uncovered, the cosmetic powers.
A heavenly image in the glass appears;   125
To that she bends, to that her eyes she rears.
The inferior priestess, at her altar's side,
Trembling begins the sacred rites of pride.
Unnumbered treasures ope at once, and here

---

101 *Where wigs . . . sword-knots strive:* the vying suitors become nothing more than "wig against wig" or "sword-knot against sword-knot" (ribbons tied to the hilts of their swords). 115 *Shock:* her lapdog. 118 *billet-doux:* love letter.

The various offerings of the world appear;   130
From each she nicely culls with curious toil,
And decks the goddess with the glittering spoil.
This casket India's glowing gems unlocks,
And all Arabia breathes from yonder box.
The tortoise here and elephant unite,   135
Transformed to combs, the speckled and the white.
Here files of pins extend their shining rows,
Puffs, powders, patches, Bibles, billet-doux.
Now awful Beauty put on all its arms;
The fair each moment rises in her charms,   140
Repairs her smiles, awakens every grace,
And calls forth all the wonders of her face;
Sees by degrees a purer blush arise,
And keener lightnings quicken in her eyes.
The busy Sylphs surround their darling care,   145
These set the head, and those divide the hair,
Some fold the sleeve, whilst others plait the gown;
And Betty's praised for labors not her own.

Canto II

Not with more glories, in the ethereal plain,
The sun first rises o'er the purpled main,
Than, issuing forth, the rival of his beams
Launched on the bosom of the silver Thames.
Fair nymphs and well-dressed youths around her shone,   5
But every eye was fixed on her alone.
On her white breast a sparkling cross she wore,
Which Jews might kiss, and infidels adore.
Her lively looks a sprightly mind disclose,
Quick as her eyes, and as unfixed as those: 10
Favors to none, to all she smiles extends;
Oft she rejects, but never once offends.
Bright as the sun, her eyes the gazers strike,
And, like the sun, they shine on all alike.
Yet graceful ease, and sweetness void of pride,   15
Might hide her faults, if belles had faults to hide:
If to her share some female errors fall,
Look on her face, and you'll forget 'em all.

134 *Arabia:* noted for its perfumes.
Canto II. 4 *Thames:* the Thames River in London. Belinda takes a boat to Hampton Court, a
twelve-mile journey.

This nymph, to the destruction of mankind,
Nourished two locks which graceful hung behind   20
In equal curls, and well conspired to deck
With shining ringlets the smooth ivory neck.
Love in these labyrinths his slaves detains,
And mighty hearts are held in slender chains.
With hairy springes we the birds betray,   25
Slight lines of hair surprise the finny prey,
Fair tresses man's imperial race ensnare,
And beauty draws us with a single hair.
    The adventurous Baron the bright locks admired,
He saw, he wished, and to the prize aspired.   30
Resolved to win, he meditates the way,
By force to ravish, or by fraud betray;
For when success a lover's toil attends,
Few ask if fraud or force attained his ends.
    For this, ere Phoebus rose, he had implored   35
Propitious Heaven, and every power adored,
But chiefly Love—to Love an altar built,
Of twelve vast French romances, neatly gilt.
There lay three garters, half a pair of gloves,
And all the trophies of his former loves.   40
With tender billet-doux he lights the pyre,
And breathes three amorous sighs to raise the fire.
Then prostrate falls, and begs with ardent eyes
Soon to obtain, and long possess the prize:
The powers gave ear, and granted half his prayer,   45
The rest the winds dispersed in empty air.
    But now secure the painted vessel glides,
The sunbeams trembling on the floating tides,
While melting music steals upon the sky,
And softened sounds along the waters die.   50
Smooth flow the waves, the zephyrs gently play,
Belinda smiled, and all the world was gay.
All but the Sylph—with careful thoughts oppressed,
The impending woe sat heavy on his breast.
He summons straight his denizens of air;   55
The lucid squadrons round the sails repair:
Soft o'er the shrouds aërial whispers breathe
That seemed but zephyrs to the train beneath.
Some to the sun their insect-wings unfold,
Waft on the breeze, or sink in clouds of gold.   60

25 *springes*: snares. 35 *Phoebus*: Apollo, god of the sun. 51 *zephyrs*: gentle breezes. 55 *denizens*: inhabitants. 56 *repair*: gather. 57 *shrouds*: ropes.

Transparent forms too fine for mortal sight,
Their fluid bodies half dissolved in light,
Loose to the wind their airy garments flew,
Thin glittering textures of the filmy dew,
Dipped in the richest tincture of the skies,   65
Where light disports in ever-mingling dyes,
While every beam new transient colors flings,
Colors that change whene'er they wave their wings.
Amid the circle, on the gilded mast,
Superior by the head was Ariel placed;   70
His purple pinions opening to the sun,
He raised his azure wand, and thus begun:
    "Ye Sylphs and Sylphids, to your chief give ear!
Fays, Fairies, Genii, Elves, and Daemons, hear!
Ye know the spheres and various tasks assigned   75
By laws eternal to the aërial kind.
Some in the fields of purest ether play,
And bask and whiten in the blaze of day.
Some guide the course of wandering orbs on high,
Or roll the planets through the boundless sky.   80
Some less refined, beneath the moon's pale light
Pursue the stars that shoot athwart the night,
Or suck the mists in grosser air below,
Or dip their pinions in the painted bow,
Or brew fierce tempests on the wintry main,   85
Or o'er the glebe distill the kindly rain.
Others on earth o'er human race preside,
Watch all their ways, and all their actions guide:
Of these the chief the care of nations own,
And guard with arms divine the British Throne.   90
    "Our humbler province is to tend the Fair,
Not a less pleasing, though less glorious care:
To save the powder from too rude a gale,
Nor let the imprisoned essences exhale;
To draw fresh colors from the vernal flowers;   95
To steal from rainbows e'er they drop in showers
A brighter wash; to curl their waving hairs,
Assist their blushes, and inspire their airs;
Nay oft, in dreams invention we bestow,
To change a flounce, or add a furbelow.   100
    "This day black omens threat the brightest fair,
That e'er deserved a watchful spirit's care;

---

84 *painted bow:* rainbow. 86 *glebe:* cultivated land. 97 *brighter wash:* cosmetic rinse. 100 *furbelow:* a
ruffle.

Some dire disaster, or by force or slight,
But what, or where, the Fates have wrapped in night:
Whether the nymph shall break Diana's law,　　　　　　105
Or some frail china jar receive a flaw,
Or stain her honor or her new brocade,
Forget her prayers, or miss a masquerade,
Or lose her heart, or necklace, at a ball;
Or whether Heaven has doomed that Shock must fall.　　110
Haste, then, ye spirits! to your charge repair:
The fluttering fan be Zephyretta's care;
The drops to thee, Brillante, we consign;
And, Momentilla, let the watch be thine;
Do thou, Crispissa, tend her favorite Lock;　　　　　115
Ariel himself shall be the guard of Shock.
　　"To fifty chosen Sylphs, of special note,
We trust the important charge, the petticoat;
Oft have we known that sevenfold fence to fail,
Though stiff with hoops, and armed with ribs of whale.　120
Form a strong line about the silver bound,
And guard the wide circumference around.
　　"Whatever spirit, careless of his charge,
His post neglects, or leaves the fair at large,
Shall feel sharp vengeance soon o'ertake his sins,　　125
Be stopped in vials, or transfixed with pins,
Or plunged in lakes of bitter washes lie,
Or wedged whole ages in a bodkin's eye;
Gums and pomatums shall his flight restrain,
While clogged he beats his silken wings in vain,　　　130
Or alum styptics with contracting power
Shrink his thin essence like a riveled flower:
Or, as Ixion fixed, the wretch shall feel
The giddy motion of the whirling mill,
In fumes of burning chocolate shall glow,　　　　　135
And tremble at the sea that froths below!"
　　He spoke; the spirits from the sails descend;
Some, orb in orb, around the nymph extend;
Some thread the mazy ringlets of her hair;
Some hang upon the pendants of her ear:　　　　　140
With beating hearts the dire event they wait,
Anxious, and trembling for the birth of Fate.

---

105 *Diana's law:* chastity. 113 *drops:* earrings. 128 *bodkin:* needle. 131 *alum styptics:* astringents. 132
riveled: shriveled. 133 *Ixion:* for trying to seduce Juno, Ixion was tied to an eternally revolving
wheel. 134 *whirling mill:* device for making hot chocolate.

Canto III

Close by those meads, forever crowned with flowers,
Where Thames with pride surveys his rising towers,
There stands a structure of majestic frame,
Which from the neighboring Hampton takes its name.
Here Britain's statesmen oft the fall foredoom   5
Of foreign tyrants and of nymphs at home;
Here thou, great Anna! whom three realms obey,
Dost sometimes counsel take—and sometimes tea.
    Hither the heroes and the nymphs resort,
To taste awhile the pleasures of a court;   10
In various talk the instructive hours they passed,
Who gave the ball, or paid the visit last;
One speaks the glory of the British Queen,
And one describes a charming Indian screen;
A third interprets motions, looks, and eyes;   15
At every word a reputation dies.
Snuff, or the fan, supply each pause of chat,
With singing, laughing, ogling, and all that.
    Meanwhile, declining from the noon of day,
The sun obliquely shoots his burning ray;   20
The hungry judges soon the sentence sign,
And wretches hang that jurymen may dine;
The merchant from the Exchange returns in peace,
And the long labors of the toilet cease.
Belinda now, whom thirst of fame invites,   25
Burns to encounter two adventurous knights,
At ombre singly to decide their doom,
And swells her breast with conquests yet to come.
Straight the three bands prepare in arms to join,
Each band the number of the sacred nine.   30
Soon as she spreads her hand, the aërial guard
Descend, and sit on each important card:
First Ariel perched upon a Matadore,
Then each according to the rank they bore;
For Sylphs, yet mindful of their ancient race,   35
Are, as when women, wondrous fond of place.

Canto III. 7 *Anna:* Queen Anne. 23 *Exchange:* stock exchange. 27 *ombre:* card game played by three persons holding nine cards (the 8's, 9's, and 10's have been removed from the deck). Thirteen cards are placed in a central pool. The player who tries to win by taking the most tricks is called the ombre and he or she names the trumps. 30 *the sacred nine:* the nine cards. 33 *Matadore:* one of the three highest cards.

Behold, four Kings in majesty revered,
With hoary whiskers and a forky beard;
And four fair Queens whose hands sustain a flower,
The expressive emblem of their softer power;   40
Four Knaves in garbs succinct, a trusty band,
Caps on their heads, and halberts in their hand;
And parti-colored troops, a shining train,
Draw forth to combat on the velvet plain.
 The skillful nymph reviews her force with care;   45
"Let Spades be trumps!" she said, and trumps they were.
 Now move to war her sable Matadores,
In show like leaders of the swarthy Moors.
Spadillio first, unconquerable lord!
Led off two captive trumps, and swept the board.   50
As many more Manillio forced to yield,
And marched a victor from the verdant field.
Him Basto followed, but his fate more hard
Gained but one trump and one plebeian card.
With his broad saber next, a chief in years,   55
The hoary Majesty of Spades appears,
Puts forth one manly leg, to sight revealed,
The rest his many-colored robe concealed.
The rebel Knave, who dares his prince engage,
Proves the just victim of his royal rage.   60
Even mighty Pam, that kings and queens o'erthrew
And mowed down armies in the fights of loo,
Sad chance of war! now distitute of aid,
Falls undistinguished by the victor Spade.
 Thus far both armies to Belinda yield;   65
Now to the Baron fate inclines the field.
His warlike amazon her host invades,
The imperial consort of the crown of Spades.
The Club's black tyrant first her victim died,
Spite of his haughty mien and barbarous pride.   70
What boots the regal circle on his head,
His giant limbs, in state unwieldy spread?
That long behind he trails his pompous robe.
And of all monarchs only grasps the globe?

---

41 *succinct:* short and close fitting. 42 *halberts:* weapon consisting of a blade and a steel spike. 49
Spadillio: ace of spades. 51 *Manillio:* deuce of spades. 53 *Basto:* ace of clubs. 59 *rebel Knave:* jack of
spades. 61 *Pam:* jack of clubs, highest card in the game of loo. 67 *amazon:* queen of spades. 74 *globe:*
only the king of clubs holds the ball in English decks.

The Baron now his Diamonds pours apace;   75
The embroidered King who shows but half his face,
And his refulgent Queen, with powers combined
Of broken troops an easy conquest find.
Clubs, Diamonds, Hearts, in wild disorder seen,
With throngs promiscuous strew the level green.   80
Thus when dispersed a routed army runs,
Of Asia's troops, and Afric's sable sons,
With like confusion different nations fly,
Of various habit, and of various dye,
The pierced battalions disunited fall   85
In heaps on heaps; one fate o'erwhelms them all.
    The Knave of Diamonds tries his wily arts,
And wins (oh, shameful chance!) the Queen of Hearts.
At this, the blood the virgin's cheek forsook,
A livid paleness spreads o'er all her look;   90
She sees, and trembles at the approaching ill,
Just in the jaws of ruin, and Codille,
And now (as oft in some distempered state)
On one nice trick depends the general fate.
An Ace of Hearts steps forth: the King unseen   95
Lurked in her hand, and mourned his captive Queen.
He springs to vengeance with an eager pace,
And falls like thunder on the prostrate Ace.
The nymph exulting fills with shouts the sky,
The walls, the woods, and long canals reply.   100
    O thoughtless mortals! ever blind to fate,
Too soon dejected, and too soon elate:
Sudden these honors shall be snatched away,
And cursed forever this victorious day.
    For lo! the board with cups and spoons is crowned,   105
The berries crackle, and the mill turns round;
On shining altars of Japan they raise
The silver lamp; the fiery spirits blaze:
From silver spouts the grateful liquors glide,
While China's earth receives the smoking tide.   110
At once they gratify their scent and taste,
And frequent cups prolong the rich repast.
Straight hover round the fair her airy band;
Some, as she sipped, the fuming liquor fanned,

---

84 *habit:* dress; *dye:* color. 92 *Codille:* although the Baron and Belinda are tied, she is on the verge of losing and will have to pay a stake to the winner. 106 *mill turns round:* for coffee. 107 *altars of Japan:* lacquered tables. 110 *China's earth:* China cups.

Some o'er her lap their careful plumes displayed,   115
Trembling, and conscious of the rich brocade.
Coffee (which makes the politician wise,
And see through all things with his half-shut eyes)
Sent up in vapors to the Baron's brain
New stratagems, the radiant Lock to gain.   120
Ah, cease, rash youth! desist ere 'tis too late,
Fear the just Gods, and think of Scylla's fate!
Changed to a bird, and sent to flit in air,
She dearly pays for Nisus' injured hair!
But when to mischief mortals bend their will,   125
How soon they find fit instruments of ill!
Just then, Clarissa drew with tempting grace
A two-edged weapon from her shining case:
So ladies in romance assist their knight,
Present the spear, and arm him for the fight.   130
He takes the gift with reverence, and extends
The little engine on his fingers' ends;
This just behind Belinda's neck he spread,
As o'er the fragrant steams she bends her head.
Swift to the Lock a thousand sprites repair,   135
A thousand wings, by turns, blow back the hair,
And thrice they twitched the diamond in her ear,
Thrice she looked back, and thrice the foe drew near.
Just in that instant, anxious Ariel sought
The close recesses of the virgin's thought;   140
As on the nosegay in her breast reclined,
He watched the ideas rising in her mind,
Sudden he viewed, in spite of all her art,
An earthly lover lurking at her heart.
Amazed, confused, he found his power expired,   145
Resigned to fate, and with a sigh retired.
The Peer now spreads the glittering forfex wide,
To enclose the Lock; now joins it, to divide.
Even then, before the fatal engine closed,
A wretched Sylph too fondly interposed;   150
Fate urged the shears, and cut the Sylph in twain
(But airy substance soon unites again):
The meeting points the sacred hair dissever
From the fair head, forever, and forever!

122 *Scylla:* knowing that the life of her father, Nisus, would be threatened by her action, Scylla cut a lock from his hair and gave it to her lover and her father's enemy, Minos. Shocked by her action, which had killed Nisus, Minos refused to accept it. Scylla was then transformed into a sea-bird. 128 *two-edged weapon:* scissors. 147 *forfex:* scissors.

Then flashed the living lightning from her eyes,   155
And screams of horror rend the affrighted skies.
Not louder shrieks to pitying heaven are cast,
When husbands; or when lapdogs breathe their last;
Or when rich china vessels fallen from high,
In glittering dust and painted fragments lie!   160
"Let wreaths of triumph now my temples twine,"
The victor cried, "the glorious prize is mine!
While fish in streams, or birds delight in air,
Or in a coach and six the British Fair,
As long as *Atalantis* shall be read,   165
Or the small pillow grace a lady's bed,
While visits shall be paid on solemn days,
When numerous wax-lights in bright order blaze,
While nymphs take treats, or assignations give,
So long my honor, name, and praise shall live!   170
What Time would spare, from Steel receives its date,
And monuments, like men, submit to fate!
Steel could the labor of the Gods destroy,
And strike to dust the imperial towers of Troy;
Steel could the works of mortal pride confound,   175
And hew triumphal arches to the ground.
What wonder then, fair nymph! thy hairs should feel,
The conquering force of unresisted Steel?"

Canto IV

But anxious cares the pensive nymph oppressed,
And secret passions labored in her breast.
Not youthful kings in battle seized alive,
Not scornful virgins who their charms survive,
Not ardent lovers robbed of all their bliss,   5
Not ancient ladies when refused a kiss,
Not tyrants fierce that unrepenting die,
Not Cynthia when her manteau's pinned awry,
E'er felt such rage, resentment, and despair,
As thou, sad virgin! for thy ravished hair.   10
For, that sad moment, when the Sylphs withdrew
And Ariel weeping from Belinda flew,
Umbriel, a dusky, melancholy sprite
As ever sullied the fair face of light,
Down to the central earth, his proper scene,   15
Repaired to search the gloomy Cave of Spleen.

165 *Atalantis:* scandalous book by Mary de la Riviere Manly. 171 *date:* end.
Canto IV. 8 *manteau:* robe. 13 *Umbriel: umbra* means "shadow" in Latin. 16 *Spleen:* the seat of melancholy.

Swift on his sooty pinions flits the Gnome,
And in a vapor reached the dismal dome.
No cheerful breeze this sullen region knows,
The dreaded east is all the wind that blows.   20
Here in a grotto, sheltered close from air,
And screened in shades from day's detested glare,
She sighs forever on her pensive bed,
Pain at her side, and Megrim at her head.
    Two handmaids wait the throne: alike in place,   25
But differing far in figure and in face.
Here stood Ill-Nature like an ancient maid,
Her wrinkled form in black and white arrayed;
With store of prayers for mornings, nights, and noons,
Her hand is filled; her bosom with lampoons.   30
    There Affectation, with a sickly mien,
Shows in her cheek the roses of eighteen,
Practiced to lisp, and hang the head aside,
Faints into airs, and languishes with pride,
On the rich quilt sinks with becoming woe,   35
Wrapped in a gown, for sickness and for show.
The fair ones feel such maladies as these,
When each new nightdress gives a new disease.
    A constant vapor o'er the palace flies,
Strange phantoms rising as the mists arise;   40
Dreadful as hermit's dreams in haunted shades,
Or bright as visions of expiring maids.
Now glaring fiends, and snakes on rolling spires,
Pale specters, gaping tombs, and purple fires;
Now lakes of liquid gold, Elysian scenes,   45
And crystal domes, and angels in machines.
    Unnumbered throngs on every side are seen
Of bodies changed to various forms by Spleen.
Here living teapots stand, one arm held out,
One bent; the handle this, and that the spout: 50
A pipkin there, like Homer's tripod, walks;
Here sighs a jar, and there a goose pie talks;
Men prove with child, as powerful fancy works,
And maids, turned bottles, call aloud for corks.
    Safe passed the Gnome through this fantastic band,   55
A branch of healing spleenwort in his hand.
Then thus addressed the Power: "Hail, wayward Queen!

---

24 *Megrim:* migraine. 45 *Elysian:* heavenly. 46 *angels in machines:* as in stage effects. 51 *pipkin:* earthen pot, which walks like the tripods in the *Iliad.* 56 *spleenwort:* herb thought to cure spleen disorders.

Who rule the sex to fifty from fifteen:
Parent of vapors and of female wit,
Who give the hysteric or poetic fit,   60
On various tempers act by various ways,
Make some take physic, others scribble plays;
Who cause the proud their visits to delay,
And send the godly in a pet to pray.
A nymph there is that all thy power disdains,   65
And thousands more in equal mirth maintains.
But oh! if e'er thy Gnome could spoil a grace,
Or raise a pimple on a beauteous face,
Like citron-waters matrons' cheeks inflame,
Or change complexions at a losing game;   70
If e'er with airy horns I planted heads,
Or rumpled petticoats, or tumbled beds,
Or caused suspicion when no soul was rude,
Or discomposed the headdress of a prude,
Or e'er to costive lapdog gave disease,   75
Which not the tears of brightest eyes could ease,
Hear me, and touch Belinda with chagrin:
That single act gives half the world the spleen."
    The Goddess with a discontented air
Seems to reject him though she grants his prayer.   80
A wondrous bag with both her hands she binds,
Like that where once Ulysses held the winds;
There she collects the force of female lungs,
Sighs, sobs, and passions, and the war of tongues.
A vial next she fills with fainting fears,   85
Soft sorrows, melting griefs, and flowing tears.
The Gnome rejoicing bears her gifts away,
Spreads his black wings, and slowly mounts to day.
    Sunk in Thalestris' arms the nymph he found,
Her eyes dejected and her hair unbound.   90
Full o'er their heads the swelling bag he rent,
And all the Furies issued at the vent.
Belinda burns with more than mortal ire,
And fierce Thalestris fans the rising fire.
"O wretched maid!" she spreads her hands, and cried   95
(While Hampton's echoes, "Wretched maid!" replied),
"Was it for this you took such constant care

---

62 *physic:* medication. 69 *citron-waters:* lemon-flavored brandy. 71 *airy horns:* of the cuckold. 75 *costive:* constipated. 82 *Ulysses . . . winds:* the wind-god allowed Ulysses to tie up all of the adverse winds in a bag. 89 *Thalestris:* Queen of the Amazons.

The bodkin, comb, and essence to prepare?
For this your locks in paper durance bound,
For this with torturing irons wreathed around?   100
For this with fillets strained your tender head,
And bravely bore the double loads of lead?
Gods! shall the ravisher display your hair,
While the fops envy, and the ladies stare!
Honor forbid! at whose unrivaled shrine   105
Ease, pleasure, virtue, all, our sex resign.
Methinks already I your tears survey,
Already hear the horrid things they say,
Already see you a degraded toast,
And all your honor in a whisper lost!   110
How shall I, then, your helpless fame defend?
'Twill then be infamy to seem your friend!
And shall this prize, the inestimable prize,
Exposed through crystal to the gazing eyes,
And heightened by the diamond's circling rays,   115
On that rapacious hand forever blaze?
Sooner shall grass in Hyde Park Circus grow,
And wits take lodgings in the sound of Bow;
Sooner let earth, air, sea, to chaos fall,
Men, monkeys, lapdogs, parrots, perish all!"   120
    She said; then raging to Sir Plume repairs,
And bids her beau demand the precious hairs
(Sir Plume of amber snuffbox justly vain,
And the nice conduct of a clouded cane).
With earnest eyes, and round unthinking face,   125
He first the snuffbox opened, then the case,
And thus broke out —"My Lord, why, what the devil!
Zounds! damn the lock! 'fore Gad, you must be civil!
Plague on't! 'tis past a jest—nay prithee, pox!
Give her the hair"—he spoke, and rapped his box.   130
    "It grieves me much," replied the Peer again,
"Who speaks so well should ever speak in vain.
But by this Lock, this sacred Lock I swear
(Which never more shall join its parted hair;
Which never more its honors shall renew,   135
Clipped from the lovely head where late it grew),
That while my nostrils draw the vital air,

---

98 *bodkin:* hairpin. 101 *fillets:* headbands. 117 *Hyde Park Circus:* same as line 44 in Canto I. 118 *Bow:* within the sound of Bowchurch in an unfashionable area of London. 124 *nice conduct:* expert handling.

This hand, which won it, shall forever wear."
He spoke, and speaking, in proud triumph spread
The long-contended honors of her head.   140
    But Umbriel, hateful Gnome, forbears not so;
He breaks the vial whence the sorrows flow.
Then see! the nymph in beauteous grief appears,
Her eyes half languishing, half drowned in tears;
On her heaved bosom hung her drooping head,   145
Which with a sigh she raised, and thus she said:
    "Forever cursed be this detested day,
Which snatched my best, my favorite curl away!
Happy! ah, ten times happy had I been,
If Hampton Court these eyes had never seen!   150
Yet am not I the first mistaken maid,
By love of courts to numerous ills betrayed.
Oh, had I rather unadmired remained
In some lone isle, or distant northern land;
Where the gilt chariot never marks the way,   155
Where none learn ombre, none e'er taste bohea!
There kept my charms concealed from mortal eye,
Like roses that in deserts bloom and die.
What moved my mind with youthful lords to roam?
Oh, had I stayed, and said my prayers at home!   160
'Twas this the morning omens seemed to tell,
Thrice from my trembling hand the patch box fell;
The tottering china shook without a wind,
Nay, Poll sat mute, and Shock was most unkind!
A Sylph too warned me of the threats of fate,   165
In mystic visions, now believed too late!
See the poor remnants of these slighted hairs!
My hands shall rend what e'en thy rapine spares.
These in two sable ringlets taught to break,
Once gave new beauties to the snowy neck;   170
The sister lock now sits uncouth, alone,
And in its fellow's fate foresees its own;
Uncurled it hangs, the fatal shears demands,
And tempts once more thy sacrilegious hands.
Oh, hadst thou, cruel! been content to seize   175
Hairs less in sight, or any hairs but these!"

---

156 *bohea:* tea. 162 *patch box:* box of cosmetic patches for the face.

Canto V

She said: the pitying audience melt in tears.
But Fate and Jove had stopped the Baron's ears.
In vain Thalestris with reproach assails,
For who can move when fair Belinda fails?
Not half so fixed the Trojan could remain,   5
While Anna begged and Dido raged in vain.
Then grave Clarissa graceful waved her fan;
Silence ensued, and thus the nymph began:
    "Say why are beauties praised and honored most,
The wise man's passion, and the vain man's toast?   10
Why decked with all that land and sea afford,
Why angels called, and angel-like adored?
Why round our coaches crowd the white-gloved beaux,
Why bows the side box from its inmost rows?
How vain are all these glories, all our pains,   15
Unless good sense preserve what beauty gains;
That men may say when we the front box grace,
'Behold the first in virtue as in face!'
Oh! if to dance all night, and dress all day,
Charmed the smallpox, or chased old age away,   20
Who would not scorn what housewife's cares produce,
Or who would learn one earthly thing of use?
To patch, nay ogle, might become a saint,
Nor could it sure be such a sin to paint.
But since, alas! frail beauty must decay,   25
Curled or uncurled, since locks will turn to gray;
Since painted, or not painted, all shall fade,
And she who scorns a man must die a maid;
What then remains but well our power to use,
And keep good humor still whate'er we lose?   30
And trust me, dear, good humor can prevail
When airs, and flights, and screams, and scolding fail.
Beauties in vain their pretty eyes may roll;
Charms strike the sight, but merit wins the soul."
    So spoke the dame, but no applause ensued;   35
Belinda frowned, Thalestris called her prude.
"To arms, to arms!" the fierce virago cries,
And swift as lightning to the combat flies.
All side in parties, and begin the attack;

Canto V. 6 *Anna . . . Dido:* Anna and Dido begged Aeneas to remain in Carthage; when he left, Dido killed herself. 37 *virago:* noisy, domineering woman.

Fans clap, silks rustle, and tough whalebones crack;   40
Heroes' and heroines' shouts confusedly rise,
And bass and treble voices strike the skies.
No common weapons in their hands are found,
Like Gods they fight, nor dread a mortal wound.
   So when bold Homer makes the Gods engage,   45
And heavenly breasts with human passions rage;
'Gainst Pallas, Mars; Latona, Hermes arms;
And all Olympus rings with loud alarms:
Jove's thunder roars, heaven trembles all around,
Blue Neptune storms, the bellowing deeps resound: 50
Earth shakes her nodding towers, the ground gives way,
And the pale ghosts start at the flash of day!
   Triumphant Umbriel on a sconce's height
Clapped his glad wings, and sat to view the fight:
Propped on the bodkin spears, the sprites survey   55
The growing combat, or assist the fray.
   While through the press enraged Thalestris flies,
And scatters death around from both her eyes,
A beau and witling perished in the throng,
One died in metaphor, and one in song.   60
"O cruel nymph! a living death I bear,"
Cried Dapperwit, and sunk beside his chair.
A mournful glance Sir Fopling upwards cast,
"Those eyes are made so killing"—was his last.
Thus on Maeander's flowery margin lies   65
The expiring swan, and as he sings he dies.
   When bold Sir Plume had drawn Clarissa down,
Chloe stepped in, and killed him with a frown;
She smiled to see the doughty hero slain,
But, at her smile, the beau revived again.   70
   Now Jove suspends his golden scales in air,
Weighs the men's wits against the lady's hair;
The doubtful beam long nods from side to side;
At length the wits mount up, the hairs subside.
   See, fierce Belinda on the Baron flies,   75
With more than usual lightning in her eyes;
Nor feared the chief the unequal fight to try,
Who sought no more than on his foe to die.

---

47 *Pallas, Mars; Latona, Hermes:* Mars fights Pallas Athene, and Hermes fights Latona. 65
Maeander: the swan on the Maeander River sings as he dies.

But this bold lord with manly strength endued,
She with one finger and a thumb subdued: 80
Just where the breath of life his nostrils drew,
A charge of snuff the wily virgin threw;
The Gnomes direct, to every atom just,
The pungent grains of titillating dust.
Sudden, with starting tears each eye o'erflows,   85
And the high dome re-echoes to his nose.
    "Now meet thy fate," incensed Belinda cried,
And drew a deadly bodkin from her side.
(The same, his ancient personage to deck,
Her great-great-grandsire wore about his neck,   90
In three seal rings; which after, melted down,
Formed a vast buckle for his widow's gown:
Her infant grandame's whistle next it grew,
The bells she jingled, and the whistle blew;
Then in a bodkin graced her mother's hairs,   95
Which long she wore, and now Belinda wears.)
    "Boast not my fall," he cried, "insulting foe!
Thou by some other shalt be laid as low.
Nor think to die dejects my lofty mind:
All that I dread is leaving you behind!   100
Rather than so, ah, let me still survive,
And burn in Cupid's flames—but burn alive."
    "Restore the Lock!" she cries; and all around
"Restore the Lock!" the vaulted roofs rebound.
Not fierce Othello in so loud a strain   105
Roared for the handkerchief that caused his pain.
But see how oft ambitious aims are crossed,
And chiefs contend till all the prize is lost!
The lock, obtained with guilt, and kept with pain,
In every place is sought, but sought in vain: 110
With such a prize no mortal must be blessed,
So Heaven decrees! with Heaven who can contest?
    Some thought it mounted to the lunar sphere,
Since all things lost on earth are treasured there.
There heroes' wits are kept in ponderous vases,   115
And beaux' in snuffboxes and tweezer cases.
There broken vows and deathbed alms are found,
And lovers' hearts with ends of riband bound,
The courtier's promises, and sick man's prayers,
The smiles of harlots, and the tears of heirs,   120

Cages for gnats, and chains to yoke a flea,
Dried butterflies, and tomes of casuistry.
    But trust the Muse—she saw it upward rise,
Though marked by none but quick, poetic eyes
(So Rome's great founder to the heavens withdrew,   125
To Proculus alone confessed in view);
A sudden star, it shot through liquid air,
And drew behind a radiant trail of hair.
Not Berenice's locks first rose so bright,
The heavens bespangling with disheveled light.   130
The Sylphs behold it kindling as it flies,
And pleased pursue its progress through the skies.
    This the beau monde shall from the Mall survey,
And hail with music its propitious ray.
This the blest lover shall for Venus take,   135
And send up vows from Rosamonda's Lake.
This Partridge soon shall view in cloudless skies,
When next he looks through Galileo's eyes;
And hence the egregious wizard shall foredoom
The fate of Louis, and the fall of Rome.   140
    Then cease, bright nymph! to mourn thy ravished hair,
Which adds new glory to the shining sphere!
Not all the tresses that fair head can boast,
Shall draw such envy as the Lock you lost.
For, after all the murders of your eye,   145
When, after millions slain, yourself shall die:
When those fair suns shall set, as set they must,
And all those tresses shall be laid in dust,
This Lock the Muse shall consecrate to fame,
And 'midst the stars inscribe Belinda's name.   150

1714

125–126 *Rome's great founder . . . Proculus:* Romulus' ascent to heaven was witnessed only by Proculus. 127 *liquid:* clear. 129 *Berenice:* the Egyptian queen offered her locks to Aphrodite for her husband's safe return. The locks were turned into a constellation. 133 *beau monde . . . Mall:* fashionable people walking in St. James Park. 136 *Rosamonda's Lake:* in St. James Park, associated with unhappy lovers. 137 *Partridge:* astrologer who predicted absurd events such as the fall of the pope. 138 *Galileo's eyes:* telescope.

EZRA POUND

(1885–1972)

PORTRAIT D'UNE FEMME   425

Your mind and you are our Sargasso Sea,
London has swept about you this score years
And bright ships left you this or that in fee:
Ideas, old gossip, oddments of all things,
Strange spars of knowledge and dimmed wares of price.   5
Great minds have sought you—lacking someone else.
You have been second always. Tragical?
No. You preferred it to the usual thing:
One dull man, dulling and uxorious,
One average mind—with one thought less, each year.   10
Oh, you are patient, I have seen you sit
Hours, where something might have floated up.
And now you pay one. Yes, you richly pay.
You are a person of some interest, one comes to you
And takes strange gain away.   15
Trophies fished up; some curious suggestions;
Fact that leads nowhere; and a tale or two,
Pregnant with mandrakes, or with something else
That might prove useful and yet never proves,
That never fits a corner or shows use,   20
Or finds its hour upon the loom of days:
The tarnished, gaudy, wonderful old work;
Idols and ambergris and rare inlays,
These are your riches, your great store; and yet
For all this sea-hoard of deciduous things,   25
Strange woods half sodden, and new brighter stuff:
In the slow float of differing light and deep,
No! there is nothing! In the whole and all,
Nothing that's quite your own.
          Yet this is you.   30

1912

PORTRAIT D'UNE FEMME title: "Portrait of a Woman" (French). 1 *Sargasso Sea:* region of calms in the North Atlantic, noted for its abundance of sargassum, a floating, brown seaweed. 18 *mandrakes:* plant whose root resembles a human figure. 23 *ambergris:* substance found in the intestines of sperm whales and used in perfume.

A VIRGINAL   426

No, no! Go from me. I have left her lately.
I will not spoil my sheath with lesser brightness,
For my surrounding air hath a new lightness;
Slight are her arms, yet they have bound me straitly
And left me cloaked as with a gauze of æther;   5
As with sweet leaves; as with subtle clearness.
Oh, I have picked up magic in her nearness
To sheathe me half in half the things that sheathe her.
No, no! Go from me. I have still the flavour,
Soft as spring wind that's come from birchen bowers.   10
Green come the shoots, aye April in the branches,
As winter's wound with her sleight hand she staunches,
Hath of the trees a likeness of the savour;
As white their bark, so white this lady's hours.

1912

THE RETURN   427

See, they return; ah, see the tentative
        Movements, and the slow feet,
        The trouble in the pace and the uncertain
        Wavering!

See, they return, one, and by one,   5
With fear, as half-awakened;
As if the snow should hesitate
And murmur in the wind,
        and half turn back;
These were the "Wing'd-with-Awe,"   10
        Inviolable.

Gods of the wingèd shoe!
With them the silver hounds,
        sniffing the trace of air!

A VIRGINAL title: a harpsichord.
THE RETURN 12 *Gods of the wingèd shoe:* Hermes, the messenger of the gods, wore winged shoes.

Haie! Haie!   15
        These were the swift to harry;
These the keen-scented;
These were the souls of blood.

Slow on the leash,
        pallid the leash-men!   20

1915

THE RIVER-MERCHANT'S WIFE:
A LETTER   428

While my hair was still cut straight across my forehead
I played about the front gate, pulling flowers.
You came by on bamboo stilts, playing horse,
You walked about my seat, playing with blue plums.
And we went on living in the village of Chokan: 5
Two small people, without dislike or suspicion.

At fourteen I married My Lord you.
I never laughed, being bashful.
Lowering my head, I looked at the wall.
Called to, a thousand times, I never looked back.   10

At fifteen I stopped scowling,
I desired my dust to be mingled with yours
Forever and forever and forever.
Why should I climb the look out?

At sixteen you departed,   15
You went into far Ku-tō-en, by the river of swirling eddies,
And you have been gone five months.
The monkeys make sorrowful noise overhead.

You dragged your feet when you went out.
By the gate now, the moss is grown, the different mosses,   20
Too deep to clear them away!
The leaves fall early this autumn, in wind.
The paired butterflies are already yellow with August

Over the grass in the West garden;
They hurt me. I grow older.   25
If you are coming down through the narrows of the river Kiang,
Please let me know beforehand,
And I will come out to meet you
                    As far as Chō-fū-Sa.

                                                                     1915

Q U E S T I O N S

1. How does the fact that this is a *translation* of a poem by the Chinese poet Li-Po
   influence your reading?
2. Ezra Pound could not read Chinese at the time he translated this poem. He relied on
   notes made by another man, who also could not read Chinese, but who had access
   to the notes of Japanese scholars on the Chinese poem. Does or should that
   knowledge influence your reading in any way?
3. How old is the letter writer? What does she chronicle?
4. Describe her direct and indirect means of presenting her feelings.

SIR WALTER RALEGH
(ca. 1552–1618)

THE NYMPH'S REPLY TO THE SHEPHERD   429

If all the world and love were young,
And truth in every shepherd's tongue,
These pretty pleasures might me move
To live with thee and be thy love.

Time drives the flocks from field to fold   5
When rivers rage and rocks grow cold,
And Philomel becometh dumb;
The rest complains of cares to come.

The flowers do fade, and wanton fields
To wayward winter reckoning yields;   10
A honey tongue, a heart of gall,
Is fancy's spring, but sorrow's fall.

Thy gowns, thy shoes, thy beds of roses,
Thy cap, thy kirtle, and thy posies
Soon break, soon wither, soon forgotten—   15
In folly ripe, in reason rotten.

THE NYMPH'S REPLY TO THE SHEPHERD title: written in reply to Christopher Marlowe's "The Passionate
Shepherd to His Love." 7 *Philomel:* the nightingale. 14 *kirtle:* dress.

Thy belt of straw and ivy buds,
Thy coral clasps and amber studs,
All these in me no means can move
To come to thee and be thy love.   20

But could youth last and love still breed,
Had joys no date nor age no need,
Then these delights my mind might move
To live with thee and be thy love.

1600

QUESTIONS

1. What do you imagine it is that the shepherd has asked to provoke such a reply from the nymph?
2. Read Christopher Marlowe's "The Passionate Shepherd to His Love." Do you find evidence *within* the poems that one was written as a response to the other?
3. How does the nymph construct her argument?
4. What similarities and differences do you find between the structure and the substance of the argument in this poem and that in Marvell's "To His Coy Mistress"?
5. What is the mood of the final stanza?
6. Are your sympathies with the nymph or with the shepherd?

JOHN CROWE RANSOM
(1888–1974)

BELLS FOR JOHN WHITESIDE'S
DAUGHTER   430

There was such speed in her little body,
And such lightness in her footfall,
It is no wonder her brown study
Astonishes us all.

Her wars were bruited in our high window.   5
We looked among orchard trees and beyond
Where she took arms against her shadow,
Or harried unto the pond

The lazy geese, like a snow cloud
Dripping their snow on the green grass,   10
Tricking and stopping, sleepy and proud,
Who cried in goose, Alas,

22 *date:* end.

For the tireless heart within the little
Lady with rod that made them rise
From their noon apple-dreams and scuttle   15
Goose-fashion under the skies!

But now go the bells, and we are ready,
In one house we are sternly stopped
To say we are vexed at her brown study,
Lying so primly propped.   20

                                                    1924

QUESTIONS

1. What distance do you as a reader feel from the girl? From the "we" of the poem? Where do you stand as an observer of the scene? As you create a reading of the poem, with whom do you identify most strongly?
2. The fourth line announces a reaction before the situation that provokes it is presented. Is this an obstacle for you or does the subject for some reason warrant such treatment?
3. If "brown study" is an expression unfamiliar to you, attempt to come to an understanding of its general meaning by contrasting it with other images throughout the poem.
4. What function does enjambment serve in stanzas 2–4?
5. In the final stanza how do sound effects and word choice help you to create a reading?

PIAZZA PIECE   431

—I am a gentleman in a dustcoat trying
To make you hear. Your ears are soft and small
And listen to an old man not at all,
They want the young men's whispering and sighing.
But see the roses on your trellis dying   5
And hear the spectral singing of the moon;
For I must have my lovely lady soon,
I am a gentleman in a dustcoat trying.

—I am a lady young in beauty waiting
Until my truelove comes, and then we kiss.   10
But what gray man among the vines is this
Whose words are dry and faint as in a dream?
Back from my trellis, Sir, before I scream!
I am a lady young in beauty waiting.

                                                    1927

PIAZZA PIECE title *piazza:* veranda.

JANET WAKING   432

Beautifully Janet slept
Till it was deeply morning. She woke then
And thought about her dainty-feathered hen,
To see how it had kept.

One kiss she gave her mother,   5
Only a small one gave she to her daddy
Who would have kissed each curl of his shining baby;
No kiss at all for her brother.

"Old Chucky, old Chucky!" she cried,
Running across the world upon the grass   10
To Chucky's house, and listening. But alas,
Her Chucky had died.

It was a transmogrifying bee
Came droning down on Chucky's old bald head
And sat and put the poison. It scarcely bled,   15
But how exceedingly

And purply did the knot
Swell with the venom and communicate
Its rigor! Now the poor comb stood up straight
But Chucky did not.   20

So there was Janet
Kneeling on the wet grass, crying her brown hen
(Translated far beyond the daughters of men)
To rise and walk upon it.

And weeping fast as she had breath   25
Janet implored us, "Wake her from her sleep!"
And would not be instructed in how deep
Was the forgetful kingdom of death.

1927

JANET WAKING 13 *transmogrifying:* changing or altering in a grotesque manner.

HENRY REED

(b. 1914)

FROM LESSONS OF THE WAR   433

TO ALAN MITCHELL

*Vixi duellis nuper idoneus
Et militavi non sine gloria*

1. *Naming of Parts*

Today we have naming of parts. Yesterday,
We had daily cleaning. And tomorrow morning,
We shall have what to do after firing. But today,
Today we have naming of parts. Japonica
Glistens like coral in all of the neighboring gardens,   5
    And today we have naming of parts.

This is the lower sling swivel. And this
Is the upper sling swivel, whose use you will see,
When you are given your slings. And this is the piling swivel,
Which in your case you have not got. The branches   10
Hold in the gardens their silent, eloquent gestures,
    Which in our case we have not got.

This is the safety-catch, which is always released
With an easy flick of the thumb. And please do not let me
See anyone using his finger. You can do it quite easy   15
If you have any strength in your thumb. The blossoms
Are fragile and motionless, never letting anyone see
    Any of them using their finger.

And this you can see is the bolt. The purpose of this
Is to open the breech, as you see. We can slide it   20
Rapidly backwards and forwards: we call this
Easing the spring. And rapidly backwards and forwards
The early bees are assaulting and fumbling the flowers:
    They call it easing the Spring.

LESSONS OF THE WAR epigraph: from Horace (with "girls" changed to "war"): "Lately I have lived in the midst of war creditably enough and I have served not without glory." 4 *Japonica:* flowering quince.

They call it easing the Spring: it is perfectly easy   25
If you have any strength in your thumb: like the bolt,
And the breech, and the cocking-piece, and the point of balance,
Which in our case we have not got; and the almond-blossom
Silent in all of the gardens and the bees going backwards and
    forwards,
      For today we have naming of parts.   30

2. *Judging Distances*

Not only how far away, but the way that you say it
Is very important. Perhaps you may never get
The knack of judging a distance, but at least you know
How to report on a landscape: the central sector,
The right of arc and that, which we had last Tuesday,   35
    And at least you know

That maps are of time, not place, so far as the army
Happens to be concerned—the reason being,
Is one which need not delay us. Again, you know
There are three kinds of tree, three only, the fir and the poplar,   40
And those which have bushy tops to; and lastly
    That things only seem to be things.

A barn is not called a barn, to put it more plainly,
Or a field in the distance, where sheep may be safely grazing.
You must never be over-sure. You must say, when reporting: 45
At five o'clock in the central sector is a dozen
Of what appear to be animals; whatever you do,
    Don't call the bleeders *sheep*.

I am sure that's quite clear; and suppose, for the sake of example,
The one at the end, asleep, endeavors to tell us   50
What he sees over there to the west, and how far away,
After first having come to attention. There to the west,
On the fields of summer the sun and the shadows bestow
    Vestments of purple and gold.

The still white dwellings are like a mirage in the heat,   55
And under the swaying elms a man and a woman
Lie gently together. Which is, perhaps, only to say
That there is a row of houses to the left of arc,
And that under some poplars a pair of what appear to be humans
    Appear to be loving.   60

Well that, for an answer, is what we might rightly call
Moderately satisfactory only, the reason being,
Is that two things have been omitted, and those are important.
The human beings, now: in what direction are they, 65
And how far away, would you say? And do not forget
    There may be dead ground in between.

There may be dead ground in between; and I may not have got
The knack of judging a distance; I will only venture
A guess that perhaps between me and the apparent lovers, 70
(Who, incidentally, appear by now to have finished,)
At seven o'clock from the houses, is roughly a distance
    Of about one year and a half.

1946

QUESTIONS

1. In "Naming of Parts," what makes you uneasy when you read the poem the first time?
2. What happens in the fourth and fifth lines of each stanza of the poem?
3. What are the parts being named?
4. Identify the puns in the last two stanzas of "Naming of Parts." How do they contribute to the ironic effect?

ISHMAEL REED
(b. 1938)

BEWARE   :   DO NOT READ THIS POEM 434

    tonite ,   thriller was
    abt an ol woman , so vain she
    surrounded herself w/
        many mirrors

    it got so bad that finally she 5
    locked herself indoors & her
    whole life became the
        mirrors

    one day the villagers broke
    into her house ,   but she was too 10
    swift for them .   she disappeared
        into a mirror

each tenant who bought the house
after that   ,   lost a loved one to
   the ol woman in the mirror   :   15
   first a little girl
   then a young woman
   then the young woman/s husband

the hunger of this poem is legendary
it has taken in many victims   20
back off from this poem
it has drawn in yr feet
back off from this poem
it has drawn in yr legs

back off from this poem   25
it is a greedy mirror
you are into this poem   .   from
   the waist down
nobody can hear you can they   ?
this poem has had you up to here   30
   belch
this poem aint got no manners
you cant call out frm this poem
relax now & go w/ this poem
move & roll on to this poem   35
do not resist this poem
this poem has yr eyes
this poem has his head
this poem has his arms
this poem has his fingers   40
this poem has his fingertips

this poem is the reader & the
reader this poem

statistic :   the us bureau of missing persons reports
that in 1968 over 100,000 people disappeared   45
leaving no solid clues
   nor trace   only
a space   in the lives of their friends

1970

ADRIENNE RICH
(b. 1929)

AUNT JENNIFER'S TIGERS   435

Aunt Jennifer's tigers prance across a screen,
Bright topaz denizens of a world of green.
They do not fear the men beneath the tree;
They pace in sleek chivalric certainty.

Aunt Jennifer's fingers fluttering through her wool   5
Find even the ivory needle hard to pull.
The massive weight of Uncle's wedding band
Sits heavily upon Aunt Jennifer's hand.

When Aunt is dead, her terrified hands will lie
Still ringed with ordeals she was mastered by.   10
The tigers in the panel that she made
Will go on prancing, proud and unafraid.

                                                    1951

A WOMAN MOURNED BY DAUGHTERS   436

Now, not a tear begun,
we sit here in your kitchen,
spent, you see, already.
You are swollen till you strain
this house and the whole sky.   5
You, whom we so often
succeeded in ignoring!
You are puffed up in death
like a corpse pulled from the sea;
we groan beneath your weight.   10
And yet you were a leaf,
a straw blown on the bed,
you had long since become
crisp as a dead insect.
What is it, if not you,   15
that settles on us now
like satin you pulled down
over our bridal heads?

AUNT JENNIFER'S TIGERS 2 *denizens:* inhabitants.

What rises in our throats
like food you prodded in?   20
Nothing could be enough.
You breathe upon us now
through solid assertions
of yourself: teaspoons, goblets,
seas of carpet, a forest   25
of old plants to be watered,
an old man in an adjoining
room to be touched and fed.
And all this universe
dares us to lay a finger   30
anywhere, save exactly
as you would wish it done.

1960

SNAPSHOTS OF A DAUGHTER-IN-LAW   437

1

You, once a belle in Shreveport,
with henna-colored hair, skin like a peachbud,
still have your dresses copied from that time,
and play a Chopin prelude
called by Cortot: *"Delicious recollections*   5
float like perfume through the memory."

Your mind now, moldering like wedding-cake,
heavy with useless experience, rich
with suspicion, rumor, fantasy,
crumbling to pieces under the knife-edge   10
of mere fact. In the prime of your life.

Nervy, glowering, your daughter
wipes the teaspoons, grows another way.

2

Banging the coffee-pot into the sink
she hears the angels chiding, and looks out   15
past the raked gardens to the sloppy sky.
Only a week since They said: *Have no patience.*

SNAPSHOTS OF A DAUGHTER-IN-LAW 5 *Cortot:* Alfred Cortot (1877–1962) who made this remark about one of Chopin's piano preludes.

The next time it was: *Be insatiable.*
Then: *Save yourself; others you cannot save.*
Sometimes she's let the tapstream scald her arm,   20
a match burn to her thumbnail,

or held her hand above the kettle's snout
right in the woolly steam. They are probably angels,
since nothing hurts her anymore, except
each morning's grit blowing into her eyes.   25

3

A thinking woman sleeps with monsters.
The beak that grips her, she becomes. And Nature,
that sprung-lidded, still commodious
steamer-trunk of *tempora* and *mores*
gets stuffed with it all: the mildewed orange-flowers,   30
the female pills, the terrible breasts
of Boadicea beneath flat foxes' heads and orchids.

Two handsome women, gripped in argument,
each proud, acute, subtle, I hear scream
across the cut glass and majolica   35
like Furies cornered from their prey:
The argument *ad feminam,* all the old knives
that have rusted in my back, I drive in yours,
ma semblable, ma soeur!

4

Knowing themselves too well in one another: 40
their gifts no pure fruition, but a thorn,
the prick filed sharp against a hint of scorn . . .
Reading while waiting
for the iron to heat,
writing, *My Life had stood—a Loaded Gun —*   45
in that Amherst pantry while the jellies boil and scum,
or, more often,
iron-eyed and beaked and purposed as a bird,
dusting everything on the whatnot every day of life.

---

29 *tempora and mores:* time and customs. 32 *Boadicea:* queen of ancient Britain who led her people in an unsuccessful revolt against the Romans. 36 *Furies:* avenging spirits. 37 *ad feminam:* play on *ad hominem* ("to the man"), an argument directed against the person rather than according to the rules of reason. 39 *ma semblable, ma soeur:* play on the last line of one of Baudelaire's poems, in which he addresses the "Hypocrite reader, like me, my brother." Here Rich says, "Like me, my sister." 45 *My Life had stood—a Loaded Gun:* from one of Emily Dickinson's poems. 46 *Amherst:* Dickinson's hometown.

5

Dulce ridens, dulce loquens,   50
she shaves her legs until they gleam
like petrified mammoth-tusk.

6

When to her lute Corinna sings
neither words nor music are her own;
only the long hair dipping   55
over her cheek, only the song
of silk against her knees
and these
adjusted in reflections of an eye.

Poised, trembling and unsatisfied, before   60
an unlocked door, that cage of cages,
tell us, you bird, you tragical machine—
is this *fertilisante douleur?* Pinned down
by love, for you the only natural action,
are you edged more keen   65
to prise the secrets of the vault? has Nature shown
her household books to you, daughter-in-law,
that her sons never saw?

7

"To have in this uncertain world some stay
which cannot be undermined, is   70
of the utmost consequence."
                         Thus wrote
a woman, partly brave and partly good,
who fought with what she partly understood.
Few men about her would or could do more,
hence she was labeled harpy, shrew and whore.   75

8

"You all die at fifteen," said Diderot,
and turn part legend, part convention.
Still, eyes inaccurately dream
behind closed windows blankening with steam.
Deliciously, all that we might have been,   80

50 *Dulce ridens, dulce loquens:* Latin from Horace, "sweetly laughing, sweetly talking." 53 *Corinna sings:* first line of a poem by the sixteenth-century poet, Thomas Campion. 63 *fertilisante douleur:* fertilizing pain (French). 69–71 lines from *Thoughts on the Education of Daughters,* by the eighteenth-century writer, Mary Wollstonecraft. 76 *Diderot:* Denis Diderot (1713–1784), French philosopher and author.

all that we were—fire, tears,
wit, taste, martyred ambition—
stirs like the memory of refused adultery
the drained and flagging bosom of our middle years.

9

Not that it is done well, but   85
that it is done at all? Yes, think
of the odds! or shrug them off forever.
This luxury of the precocious child,
Time's precious chronic invalid,—
would we, darlings, resign it if we could?   90
Our blight has been our sinecure:
mere talent was enough for us—
glitter in fragments and rough drafts.

Sigh no more, ladies.
                    Time is male
and in his cups drinks to the fair.   95
Bemused by gallantry, we hear
our mediocrities over-praised,
indolence read as abnegation,
slattern thought styled intuition,
every lapse forgiven, our crime   100
only to cast too bold a shadow
or smash the mold straight off.

For that, solitary confinement,
tear gas, attrition shelling.
Few applicants for that honor.

10

                    Well,   105
she's long about her coming, who must be
more merciless to herself than history.
Her mind full to the wind, I see her plunge
breasted and glancing through the currents,
taking the light upon her   110
at least as beautiful as any boy
or helicopter,
           poised, still coming,
her fine blades making the air wince

85–86 lines based upon Samuel Johnson's remark: "Sir, a woman's preaching is like a dog's
walking on his hinder legs. It is not done well; but you are surprised to find it done at all." 91
sinecure: a position that carries a stipend but requires little work.

but her cargo
no promise then: 115
delivered
palpable
ours.

1963

NECESSITIES OF LIFE   438

Piece by piece I seem
to re-enter the world: I first began

a small, fixed dot, still see
that old myself, a dark-blue thumbtack

pushed into the scene,   5
a hard little head protruding

from the pointillist's buzz and bloom.
After a time the dot

begins to ooze. Certain heats
melt it.
          Now I was hurriedly   10

blurring into ranges
of burnt red, burning green,

whole biographies swam up and
swallowed me like Jonah.

Jonah! I was Wittgenstein,   15
Mary Wollstonecraft, the soul

of Louis Jouvet, dead
in a blown-up photograph.

Till, wolfed almost to shreds,
I learned to make myself   20

unappetizing. Scaly as a dry bulb
thrown into a cellar

NECESSITIES OF LIFE 15 *Wittgenstein:* Ludwig Wittgenstein (1889–1951), Austrian philosopher. 16
Mary Wollstonecraft: eighteenth-century author of *A Vindication of the Rights of Women.* 17 *Louis Jouvet:* French actor.

I used myself, let nothing use me.
Like being on a private dole,

sometimes more like kneading bricks in Egypt.   25
What life was there, was mine,

now and again to lay
one hand on a warm brick

and touch the sun's ghost
with economical joy,   30

now and again to name
over the bare necessities.

So much for those days. Soon
practice may make me middling-perfect, I'll

dare inhabit the world   35
trenchant in motion as an eel, solid

as a cabbage-head. I have invitations:
a curl of mist steams upward

from a field, visible as my breath,
houses along a road stand waiting   40

like old women knitting, breathless
to tell their tales.

1966

ORION   439

Far back when I went zig-zagging
through tamarack pastures
you were my genius, you
my cast-iron Viking, my helmed
lion-heart king in prison.   5
Years later now you're young

my fierce half-brother, staring
down from that simplified west
your breast open, your belt dragged down
by an oldfashioned thing, a sword   10
the last bravado you won't give over
though it weighs you down as you stride

ORION title: a hunter accidentally slain by Diana, who then made him into a constellation. 2
tamarack: a tree found in swamps.

and the stars in it are dim
and maybe have stopped burning.
But you burn, and I know it;   15
as I throw back my head to take you in
an old transfusion happens again:
divine astronomy is nothing to it.

Indoors I bruise and blunder,
break faith, leave ill enough   20
alone, a dead child born in the dark.
Night cracks up over the chimney,
pieces of time, frozen geodes
come showering down in the grate.

A man reaches behind my eyes   25
and finds them empty
a woman's head turns away
from my head in the mirror
children are dying my death
and eating crumbs of my life.   30

Pity is not your forte.
Calmly you ache up there
pinned aloft in your crow's nest,
my speechless pirate!
You take it all for granted   35
and when I look you back

it's with a starlike eye
shooting its cold and egotistical spear
where it can do least damage.
Breathe deep! No hurt, no pardon   40
out here in the cold with you
you with your back to the wall.

1969

PLANETARIUM   440

(Thinking of Caroline Herschel, 1750 – 1848, astronomer, sister of William; and others)

A woman in the shape of a monster
a monster in the shape of a woman
the skies are full of them

23 *geodes:* rocks broken open to reveal crystals within.
PLANETARIUM subtitle: *William Herschel,* royal astronomer to King George III, discovered the planet Uranus. His sister, Caroline, was herself an astronomer.

a woman   'in the snow
among the Clocks and instruments   5
or measuring the ground with poles'

in her 98 years to discover
8 comets

she whom the moon ruled
like us   10
levitating into the night sky
riding the polished lenses

Galaxies of women, there
doing penance for impetuousness
ribs chilled   15
in those spaces   of the mind

An eye,
        'virile, precise and absolutely certain'
        from the mad webs of Uranisborg

                                encountering the NOVA   20

every impulse of light exploding
from the core
as life flies out of us
        Tycho whispering at last
        'Let me not seem to have lived in vain'   25

What we see, we see
and seeing is changing

the light that shrivels a mountain
and leaves a man alive

Heartbeat of the pulsar   30
heart sweating through my body
The radio impulse
pouring in from Taurus

        I am bombarded yet   I stand

I have been standing all my life in the   35
direct path of a battery of signals
the most accurately transmitted most
untranslateable language in the universe

19: *Uranisborg* observatory built by Tycho Brahe.

I am a galactic cloud so deep   so invo-
luted that a light wave could take 15   40
years to travel through me   And has
taken   I am an instrument in the shape
of a woman trying to translate pulsations
into images   for the relief of the body
and the reconstruction of the mind.   45

1971

DIVING INTO THE WRECK   441

First having read the book of myths,
and loaded the camera,
and checked the edge of the knife-blade,
I put on
the body-armor of black rubber   5
the absurd flippers
the grave and awkward mask.
I am having to do this
not like Cousteau with his
assiduous team   10
aboard the sun-flooded schooner
but here alone.

There is a ladder.
The ladder is always there
hanging innocently   15
close to the side of the schooner.
We know what it is for,
we who have used it.
otherwise
it is a piece of maritime floss   20
some sundry equipment.

I go down.
Rung after rung and still
the oxygen immerses me
the blue light   25
the clear atoms
of our human air.
I go down.
My flippers cripple me,

I crawl like an insect down the ladder   30
and there is no one
to tell me when the ocean
will begin.

First the air is blue and then
it is bluer and then green and then   35
black I am blacking out and yet
my mask is powerful
it pumps my blood with power
the sea is another story
the sea is not a question of power   40
I have to learn alone
to turn my body without force
in the deep element.

And now: it is easy to forget
what I came for   45
among so many who have always
lived here
swaying their crenellated fans
between the reefs
and besides   50
you breathe differently down here.

I came to explore the wreck.
The words are purposes.
The words are maps.
I came to see the damage that was done   55
and the treasures that prevail.
I stroke the beam of my lamp
slowly along the flank
of something more permanent
than fish or weed   60

the thing I came for:
the wreck and not the story of the wreck
the thing itself and not the myth
the drowned face always staring
toward the sun   65
the evidence of damage
worn by salt and sway into this threadbare beauty
the ribs of the disaster
curving their assertion
among the tentative haunters.   70

This is the place.
And I am here, the mermaid whose dark hair
streams black, the merman in his armored body.
We circle silently
about the wreck   75
we dive into the hold.
I am she: I am he

whose drowned face sleeps with open eyes
whose breasts still bear the stress
whose silver, copper, vermeil cargo lies   80
obscurely inside barrels
half-wedged and left to rot
we are the half-destroyed instruments
that once held to a course
the water-eaten log   85
the fouled compass

We are, I am, you are
by cowardice or courage
the one who find our way
back to this scene   90
carrying a knife, a camera
a book of myths
in which
our names do not appear.

1973

QUESTIONS

1. This poem uses many pronouns: *I, you, he, she, we, our, their*. Which are you, the reader?
2. Several times the speaker mentions that she must dive alone, yet she frequently refers to "we." Is this a contradiction?
3. What is a myth? What does it have to do with the dive?
4. Why does the speaker dive into the wreck? What is she looking for? What does she find?
5. How is this a dive into something more?

LIVING IN SIN   442

She had thought the studio would keep itself;
no dust upon the furniture of love.
Half heresy, to wish the taps less vocal,
the panes relieved of grime. A plate of pears,

a piano with a Persian shawl, a cat   5
stalking the picturesque amusing mouse
had risen at his urging.
Not that at five each separate stair would writhe
under the milkman's tramp; that morning light
so coldly would delineate the scraps   10
of last night's cheese and three sepulchral bottles;
that on the kitchen shelf among the saucers
a pair of beetle-eyes would fix her own—
envoy from some village in the moldings . . .
Meanwhile, he, with a yawn,   15
sounded a dozen notes upon the keyboard,
declared it out of tune, shrugged at the mirror,
rubbed at his beard, went out for cigarettes;
while she, jeered by the minor demons,
pulled back the sheets and made the bed and found   20
a towel to dust the table-top,
and let the coffee-pot boil over on the stove.
By evening she was back in love again,
though not so wholly but throughout the night
she woke sometimes to feel the daylight coming   25
like a relentless milkman up the stairs.

1975

ORIGINS AND HISTORY OF CONSCIOUSNESS   443

I

Night-life. Letters, journals, bourbon
sloshed in the glass. Poems crucified on the wall,
dissected, their bird-wings severed
like trophies. No one lives in this room
without living through some kind of crisis.   5

No one lives in this room
without confronting the whiteness of the wall
behind the poems, planks of books,
photographs of dead heroines.
Without contemplating last and late   10
the true nature of poetry. The drive
to connect. The dream of a common language.

Thinking of lovers, their blind faith, their
experienced crucifixions,
my envy is not simple. I have dreamed of going to bed   15
as walking into clear water ringed by a snowy wood
white as cold sheets, thinking, *I'll freeze in there.*
My bare feet are numbed already by the snow
but the water
is mild, I sink and float   20
like a warm amphibious animal
that has broken the net, has run
through fields of snow leaving no print;
this water washes off the scent—
You are clear now   25
of the hunter, the trapper
the wardens of the mind—

yet the warm animal dreams on
of another animal
swimming under the snow-flecked surface of the pool,   30
and wakes, and sleeps again.

No one sleeps in this room without
the dream of a common language.

II

It was simple to meet you, simple to take your eyes
into mine, saying: these are eyes I have known   35
from the first. . . . It was simple to touch you
against the hacked background, the grain of what we
had been, the choices, years. . . . It was even simple
to take each other's lives in our hands, as bodies.

What is not simple: to wake from drowning   40
from where the ocean beat inside us like an afterbirth
into this common, acute particularity
these two selves who walked half a lifetime untouching—
to wake to something deceptively simple: a glass
sweated with dew, a ring of the telephone, a scream   45
of someone beaten up far down in the street
causing each of us to listen to her own inward scream

knowing the mind of the mugger and the mugged
as any woman must who stands to survive this city,
this century, this life . . .   50

each of us having loved the flesh in its clenched or loosened beauty
better than trees or music (yet loving those too
as if they were flesh—and they are—but the flesh
of beings unfathomed as yet in our roughly literal life).

III

It's simple to wake from sleep with a stranger,   55
dress, go out, drink coffee,
enter a life again. It isn't simple
to wake from sleep into the neighborhood
of one neither strange nor familiar
whom we have chosen to trust. Trusting, untrusting,   60
we lowered ourselves into this, let ourselves
downward hand over hand as on a rope that quivered
over the unsearched. . . . We did this. Conceived
of each other, conceived each other in a darkness
which I remember as drenched in light.   65
                      I want to call this, life.

But I can't call it life until we start to move
beyond this secret circle of fire
where our bodies are giant shadows flung on a wall
where the night becomes our inner darkness, and sleeps   70
like a dumb beast, head on her paws, in the corner.

1978

EDWIN ARLINGTON ROBINSON
(1869–1935)

MINIVER CHEEVY   444

Miniver Cheevy, child of scorn,
  Grew lean while he assailed the seasons;
He wept that he was ever born,
  And he had reasons.

Miniver loved the days of old   5
  When swords were bright and steeds were prancing;
The vision of a warrior bold
  Would set him dancing.

Miniver sighed for what was not,
    And dreamed, and rested from his labors;   10
He dreamed of Thebes and Camelot,
    And Priam's neighbors.

Miniver mourned the ripe renown
    That made so many a name so fragrant;
He mourned Romance, now on the town,   15
    And Art, a vagrant.

Miniver loved the Medici,
    Albeit he had never seen one;
He would have sinned incessantly
    Could he have been one.   20

Miniver cursed the commonplace
    And eyed a khaki suit with loathing;
He missed the medieval grace
    Of iron clothing.

Miniver scorned the gold he sought,   25
    But sore annoyed was he without it;
Miniver thought, and thought, and thought,
    And thought about it.

Miniver Cheevy, born too late,
    Scratched his head and kept on thinking;   30
Miniver coughed, and called it fate,
    And kept on drinking.

1910

EROS TURANNOS   445

She fears him, and will always ask
    What fated her to choose him;
She meets in his engaging mask
    All reasons to refuse him;
But what she meets and what she fears   5
Are less than are the downward years,
Drawn slowly to the foamless weirs
    Of age, were she to lose him.

MINIVER CHEEVY 11–12 *Thebes . . . Camelot . . . Priam:* Thebes was an ancient Greek city, Camelot a mythical Arthurian land, Priam the king of Troy. 17 *Medici:* Italian Renaissance family under whose rule the arts flourished.

EROS TURANNOS title: "tyrannical love" (Latin). 7 *weir:* fences placed across streams to catch fish.

Between a blurred sagacity
   That once had power to sound him,   10
And Love, that will not let him be
   The Judas that she found him,
Her pride assuages her almost,
As if it were alone the cost.
He sees that he will not be lost,   15
   And waits and looks around him.

A sense of ocean and old trees
   Envelopes and allures him;
Tradition, touching all he sees,
   Beguiles and reassures him;   20
And all her doubts of what he says
Are dimmed with what she knows of days—
Till even prejudice delays
   And fades, and she secures him.

The falling leaf inaugurates   25
   The reign of her confusion;
The pounding wave reverberates
   The dirge of her illusion;
And home, where passion lived and died,
Becomes a place where she can hide,   30
While all the town and harbor side
   Vibrate with her seclusion.

We tell you, tapping on our brows,
   The story as it should be,
As if the story of a house   35
   Were told, or ever could be;
We'll have no kindly veil between
Her visions and those we have seen,
As if we guessed what hers have been,
   Or what they are or would be.   40

Meanwhile we do no harm; for they
   That with a god have striven,
Not hearing much of what we say,
   Take what the god has given;
Though like waves breaking it may be,   45
Or like a changed familiar tree,
Or like a stairway to the sea
   Where down the blind are driven.

1916

THE MILL   446

The miller's wife had waited long,
   The tea was cold, the fire was dead;
And there might yet be nothing wrong
   In how he went and what he said:
"There are no millers any more,"   5
   Was all that she had heard him say;
And he had lingered at the door
   So long that it seemed yesterday.

Sick with a fear that had no form
   She knew that she was there at last;   10
And in the mill there was a warm
   And mealy fragrance of the past.
What else there was would only seem
   To say again what he had meant;
And what was hanging from a beam   15
   Would not have heeded where she went.

And if she thought it followed her,
   She may have reasoned in the dark
That one way of the few there were
   Would hide her and would leave no mark: 20
Black water, smooth above the weir
   Like starry velvet in the night,
Though ruffled once, would soon appear
   The same as ever to the sight.

1920

MR. FLOOD'S PARTY   447

Old Eben Flood, climbing alone one night
Over the hill between the town below
And the forsaken upland hermitage
That held as much as he should ever know
On earth again of home, paused warily.   5
The road was his with not a native near;
And Eben, having leisure, said aloud,
For no man else in Tilbury Town to hear:

"Well, Mr. Flood, we have the harvest moon
Again, and we may not have many more;   10
The bird is on the wing, the poet says,
And you and I have said it here before.

Drink to the bird." He raised up to the light
The jug that he had gone so far to fill,
And answered huskily: "Well, Mr. Flood,   15
Since you propose it, I believe I will."

Alone, as if enduring to the end
A valiant armor of scarred hopes outworn,
He stood there in the middle of the road
Like Roland's ghost winding a silent horn.   20
Below him, in the town among the trees,
Where friends of other days had honored him,
A phantom salutation of the dead
Rang thinly till old Eben's eyes were dim.

Then, as a mother lays her sleeping child   25
Down tenderly, fearing it may awake,
He set the jug down slowly at his feet
With trembling care, knowing that most things break;
And only when assured that on firm earth
It stood, as the uncertain lives of men   30
Assuredly did not, he paced away,
And with his hand extended paused again:

"Well, Mr. Flood, we have not met like this
In a long time; and many a change has come
To both of us, I fear, since last it was   35
We had a drop together. Welcome home!"
Convivially returning with himself,
Again he raised the jug up to the light;
And with an acquiescent quaver said:
"Well, Mr. Flood, if you insist, I might.   40

"Only a very little, Mr. Flood—
For auld lang syne. No more, sir; that will do."
So, for the time, apparently it did,
And Eben evidently thought so too;
For soon amid the silver loneliness   45
Of night he lifted up his voice and sang,
Secure, with only two moons listening,
Until the whole harmonious landscape rang—

MR. FLOOD'S PARTY 20 *Roland:* legendary hero who refused to blow his horn for help in battle until
it was too late.

"For auld lang syne." The weary throat gave out,
The last word wavered; and the song being done, 50
He raised again the jug regretfully
And shook his head, and was again alone.
There was not much that was ahead of him,
And there was nothing in the town below—
Where strangers would have shut the many doors 55
That many friends had opened long ago.

1920

QUESTIONS

1. What do you feel for Mr. Flood? Which images help to evoke that response?
2. Is there humor in this poem? Pathos?
3. Where does the poem veer close to sentimentality? How does it avoid becoming sentimental?
4. Why are there two moons (line 47)?
5. What do Mr. Flood and Mr. Flood toast?
6. What do lines 17–20 contribute to your experience of the poem?

THE SHEAVES   448

Where long the shadows of the wind had rolled,
Green wheat was yielding to the change assigned;
And as by some vast magic undivined
The world was turning slowly into gold.
Like nothing that was ever bought or sold 5
It waited there, the body and the mind;
And with a mighty meaning of a kind
That tells the more the more it is not told.

So in a land where all days are not fair,
Fair days went on till on another day 10
A thousand golden sheaves were lying there,
Shining and still, but not for long to stay—
As if a thousand girls with golden hair
Might rise from where they slept and go away.

1925

THEODORE ROETHKE
(1908–1963)

ELEGY FOR JANE   449

MY STUDENT, THROWN BY A HORSE

I remember the neckcurls, limp and damp as tendrils;
And her quick look, a sidelong pickerel smile;
And how, once startled into talk, the light syllables leaped for her,
And she balanced in the delight of her thought,
A wren, happy, tail into the wind,   5
Her song trembling the twigs and small branches.
The shade sang with her;
The leaves, their whispers turned to kissing;
And the mold sang in the bleached valleys under the rose.

Oh, when she was sad, she cast herself down into such a pure depth,   10
Even a father could not find her:
Scraping her cheek against straw;
Stirring the clearest water.
My sparrow, you are not here,
Waiting like a fern, making a spiny shadow.   15
The sides of wet stones cannot console me,
Nor the moss, wound with the last light.

If only I could nudge you from this sleep,
My maimed darling, my skittery pigeon.
Over this damp grave I speak the words of my love: 20
I, with no rights in this matter,
Neither father nor lover.

1953

THE WAKING   450

I wake to sleep, and take my waking slow.
I feel my fate in what I cannot fear.
I learn by going where I have to go.

We think by feeling. What is there to know?
I hear my being dance from ear to ear.   5
I wake to sleep, and take my waking slow.

Of those so close beside me, which are you?
God bless the Ground! I shall walk softly there,
And learn by going where I have to go.

Light takes the Tree; but who can tell us how?   10
The lowly worm climbs up a winding stair;
I wake to sleep, and take my waking slow.

Great Nature has another thing to do
To you and me; so take the lively air,
And, lovely, learn by going where to go.   15

This shaking keeps me steady. I should know.
What falls away is always. And is near.
I wake to sleep, and take my waking slow.
I learn by going where I have to go.

1953

I KNEW A WOMAN   451

I knew a woman, lovely in her bones,
When small birds sighed, she would sigh back at them;
Ah, when she moved, she moved more ways than one:
The shapes a bright container can contain!
Of her choice virtues only gods should speak,   5
Or English poets who grew up on Greek
(I'd have them sing in chorus, cheek to cheek).

How well her wishes went! She stroked my chin,
She taught me Turn, and Counter-turn, and Stand;
She taught me Touch, that undulant white skin;   10
I nibbled meekly from her proffered hand;
She was the sickle; I, poor I, the rake,
Coming behind her for her pretty sake
(But what prodigious mowing we did make).

Love likes a gander, and adores a goose: 15
Her full lips pursed, the errant note to seize;
She played it quick, she played it light and loose,
My eyes, they dazzled at her flowing knees;
Her several parts could keep a pure repose,
Or one hip quiver with a mobile nose   20
(She moved in circles, and those circles moved).

Let seed be grass, and grass turn into hay:
I'm martyr to a motion not my own;
What's freedom for? To know eternity.
I swear she cast a shadow white as stone.   25
But who would count eternity in days?
These old bones live to learn her wanton ways:
(I measure time by how a body sways).

                                                                   1958

QUESTIONS

1. Describe your first impression of the speaker's attitude toward the woman. Which
   images gave you that impression?
2. What do lines 3, 9–10, 18–21, and 28 have in common? How does the rest of the
   poem develop that motif?
3. What is the effect of the punctuation (the frequent end-stopped lines and the
   parentheses)? How does the punctuation support your reading of the poem?
4. How can the woman be both virtuous (line 5) and wanton (line 27)?

IN A DARK TIME   452

In a dark time, the eye begins to see,
I meet my shadow in the deepening shade;
I hear my echo in the echoing wood—
A lord of nature weeping to a tree.
I live between the heron and the wren,   5
Beasts of the hill and serpents of the den.

What's madness but nobility of soul
At odds with circumstance? The day's on fire!
I know the purity of pure despair,
My shadow pinned against a sweating wall.   10
That place among the rocks—is it a cave,
Or winding path? The edge is what I have.

A steady storm of correspondences!
A night flowing with birds, a ragged moon,
And in broad day the midnight come again!   15
A man goes far to find out what he is—
Death of the self in a long, tearless night,
All natural shapes blazing unnatural light.

Dark, dark my light, and darker my desire.
My soul, like some heat-maddened summer fly,   20
Keeps buzzing at the sill. Which I is *I*?

A fallen man, I climb out of my fear.
The mind enters itself, and God the mind,
And one is One, free in the tearing wind.

1964

CHRISTINA ROSSETTI
(1830–1894)

SONG   453

When I am dead, my dearest,
   Sing no sad songs for me;
Plant thou no roses at my head,
   Nor shady cypress tree:
Be the green grass above me   5
   With showers and dewdrops wet;
And if thou wilt, remember,
   And if thou wilt, forget.

I shall not see the shadows,
   I shall not feel the rain;   10
I shall not hear the nightingale
   Sing on, as if in pain:
And dreaming through the twilight
   That doth not rise nor set,
Haply I may remember,   15
   And haply may forget.

1862

QUESTIONS

1. What do the first two lines lead you to expect? Do you find any surprises?
2. What feeling does the speaker express for the person she calls "dearest"?
3. What is the speaker's attitude toward death?
4. Is it unusual for love and death to be linked so overtly in a poem?

UP-HILL   454

Does the road wind up-hill all the way?
   Yes, to the very end.
Will the day's journey take the whole long day?
   From morn to night, my friend.

But is there for the night a resting-place?   5
   A roof for when the slow dark hours begin.
May not the darkness hide it from my face?
   You cannot miss that inn.

Shall I meet other wayfarers at night?
   Those who have gone before.   10
Then must I knock, or call when just in sight?
   They will not keep you standing at that door.

Shall I find comfort, travel-sore and weak?
   Of labor you shall find the sum.
Will there be beds for me and all who seek?   15
   Yea, beds for all who come.

1862

EVE   455

"While I sit at the door,
Sick to gaze within,
Mine eye weepeth sore
For sorrow and sin:
As a tree my sin stands   5
To darken all lands;
Death is the fruit it bore.

"How have Eden bowers grown
Without Adam to bend them!
How have Eden flowers blown,   10
Squandering their sweet breath,
Without me to tend them!
The Tree of Life was ours,
Tree twelvefold-fruited,
Most lofty tree that flowers,   15
Most deeply rooted:
I chose the Tree of Death.

"Hadst thou but said me nay,
   Adam, my brother,
I might have pined away—   20
   I, but none other:
God might have let thee stay
Safe in our garden,
By putting me away
Beyond all pardon.   25

"I, Eve, sad mother
Of all who must live,
I, not another,
Plucked bitterest fruit to give
My friend, husband, lover.   30
O wanton eyes run over!
Who but I should grieve?—
Cain hath slain his brother:
Of all who must die mother,
Miserable Eve!"   35

Thus she sat weeping,
Thus Eve our mother,
Where one lay sleeping
Slain by his brother.
Greatest and least   40
Each piteous beast
To hear her voice
Forgot his joys
And set aside his feast.

The mouse paused in his walk   45
And dropped his wheaten stalk:
Grave cattle wagged their heads
In rumination;
The eagle gave a cry
From his cloud station: 50
Larks on thyme beds
Forbore to mount or sing;
Bees drooped upon the wing;
The raven perched on high
Forgot his ration;   55
The conies in their rock,
A feeble nation,
Quaked sympathetical;
The mocking-bird left off to mock;
Huge camels knelt as if   60
In deprecation;
The kind hart's tears were falling;
Chattered the wistful stork;
Dove-voices with a dying fall
Cooed desolation   65
Answering grief by grief.

EVE 56 *conies:* rabbitlike animals.

Only the serpent in the dust,
Wriggling and crawling,
Grinned an evil grin, and thrust
His tongue out with its fork.   70

                                                                    1865

AMOR MUNDI   456

"Oh where are you going with your love-locks flowing
    On the west wind blowing along this valley track?"
"The downhill path is easy, come with me an it please ye,
    We shall escape the uphill by never turning back."

So they two went together in glowing August weather,   5
    The honey-breathing heather lay to their left and right;
And dear she was to dote on, her swift feet seemed to float on
    The air like soft twin pigeons too sportive to alight.

"Oh what is that in heaven where gray cloud-flakes are seven,
    Where blackest clouds hang riven just at the rainy skirt?"   10
"Oh that's a meteor sent us, a message dumb, portentous,
    An undeciphered solemn signal of help or hurt."

"Oh what is that glides quickly where velvet flowers grow thickly,
    Their scent comes rich and sickly?"—"A scaled and hooded
        worm."
"Oh what's that in the hollow, so pale I quake to follow?"   15
    "Oh that's a thin dead body which waits the eternal term."

"Turn again, O my sweetest,—turn again, false and fleetest:
    This beaten way thou beatest I fear is hell's own track."
"Nay, too steep for hill-mounting; nay, too late for cost-counting:
    This downhill path is easy, but there's no turning back."   20

                                                                    1875

IN AN ARTIST'S STUDIO   457

One face looks out from all his canvases,
    One selfsame figure sits or walks or leans:
    We found her hidden just behind those screens,
That mirror gave back all her loveliness.
A queen in opal or in ruby dress,   5

AMOR MUNDI title: "love of the world" (Latin).

A nameless girl in freshest summer-greens,
   A saint, an angel—every canvas means
The same one meaning, neither more nor less.
He feeds upon her face by day and night,
   And she with true kind eyes looks back on him,   10
Fair as the moon and joyful as the light:
   Not wan with waiting, not with sorrow dim;
Not as she is, but was when hope shone bright;
   Not as she is, but as she fills his dream.

1896

MURIEL RUKEYSER
(1913–1980)

EFFORT AT SPEECH BETWEEN TWO PEOPLE   458

Speak to me. Take my hand. What are you now?
I will tell you all. I will conceal nothing.
When I was three, a little child read a story about a rabbit
who died, in the story, and I crawled under a chair:
a pink rabbit: it was my birthday, and a candle   5
burnt a sore spot on my finger, and I was told to be happy.

Oh, grow to know me. I am not happy. I will be open:
Now I am thinking of white sails against a sky like music,
like glad horns blowing, and birds tilting, and an arm about me.
There was one I loved, who wanted to live, sailing.   10

Speak to me. Take my hand. What are you now?
When I was nine, I was fruitily sentimental,
fluid: and my widowed aunt played Chopin,
and I bent my head on the painted woodwork, and wept.
I want now to be close to you. I would   15
link the minutes of my days close, somehow, to your days.

I am not happy. I will be open.
I have liked lamps in evening corners, and quiet poems.
There has been fear in my life. Sometimes I speculate
On what a tragedy his life was, really.   20

Take my hand. Fist my mind in your hand. What are you now?
When I was fourteen, I had dreams of suicide,
and I stood at a steep window, at sunset, hoping toward death:
if the light had not melted clouds and plains to beauty,

if light had not transformed that day, I would have leapt, 25
I am unhappy.   I am lonely.   Speak to me.
I will be open.   I think he never loved me:
he loved the bright beaches, the little lips of foam
that ride small waves, he loved the veer of gulls:
he said with a gay mouth: I love you.   Grow to know me. 30

What are you now?   If we could touch one another,
if these our separate entities could come to grips,
clenched like a Chinese puzzle . . . yesterday
I stood in a crowded street that was live with people,
and no one spoke a word, and the morning shone. 35
Everyone silent, moving. . . . Take my hand.   Speak to me.

1935

CARL SANDBURG
(1878–1967)

CHICAGO   459

Hog Butcher for the World,
Tool Maker, Stacker of Wheat,
Player with Railroads and the Nation's Freight Handler;
Stormy, husky, brawling,
City of the Big Shoulders: 5

They tell me you are wicked and I believe them, for I have seen your
  painted women under the gas lamps luring the farm boys.
And they tell me you are crooked and I answer: Yes, it is true I have
  seen the gunman kill and go free to kill again.
And they tell me you are brutal and my reply is: On the faces of
  women and children I have seen the marks of wanton hunger.
And having answered so I turn once more to those who sneer at this
  my city, and I give them back the sneer and say to them:
Come and show me another city with lifted head singing so proud to
  be alive and coarse and strong and cunning. 10
Flinging magnetic curses amid the toil of piling job on job, here is a
  tall bold slugger set vivid against the little soft cities;
Fierce as a dog with tongue lapping for action, cunning as a savage
  pitted against the wilderness,
    Bareheaded,
    Shoveling,

Wrecking,   15
Planning,
Building, breaking, rebuilding,
Under the smoke, dust all over his mouth, laughing with white
    teeth,
Under the terrible burden of destiny laughing as a young man laughs,
Laughing even as an ignorant fighter laughs who has never lost a
    battle,   20
Bragging and laughing that under his wrist is the pulse, and under his
    ribs the heart of the people,
                    Laughing!
Laughing the stormy, husky, brawling laughter of Youth, half-naked,
    sweating, proud to be Hog Butcher, Tool Maker, Stacker of
    Wheat, Player with Railroads and Freight Handler to the Nation.

                                                                    1916

Q U E S T I O N S

1. What one quality of Chicago does the poet emphasize more than others? How would
   you use that to unify a reading?
2. Discuss the complexity of the speaker's attitude toward Chicago? Is he judgmental?
3. Why does the poet use such long sentences? Why, on the other hand, are a few of the
   lines so short?

GRASS   460

Pile the bodies high at Austerlitz and Waterloo.
Shovel them under and let me work—
            I am the grass; I cover all.

And pile them high at Gettysburg
And pile them high at Ypres and Verdun.   5
Shovel them under and let me work.
Two years, ten years, and passengers ask the conductor:
            What place is this?
            Where are we now?

            I am the grass.   10
            Let me work.

                                                                    1918

GRASS 1 *Austerlitz and Waterloo:* Austerlitz was the site of Napoleon's victory over the Russians and
Austrians. Waterloo was the site of Napoleon's defeat. 4 *Gettysburg:* bloody American Civil War
battle. 5 *Ypres and Verdun:* World War I battles.

DELMORE SCHWARTZ
(1913–1966)

DOGS ARE SHAKESPEAREAN,
CHILDREN ARE STRANGERS

461

Dogs are Shakespearean, children are strangers.
Let Freud and Wordsworth discuss the child,
Angels and Platonists shall judge the dog,
The running dog, who paused, distending nostrils,
Then barked and wailed; the boy who pinched his sister,   5
The little girl who sang the song from *Twelfth Night,*
As if she understood the wind and rain,
The dog who moaned, hearing the violins in concert.
—O I am sad when I see dogs or children!
For they are strangers, they are Shakespearean.   10

Tell us, Freud, can it be that lovely children
Have merely ugly dreams of natural functions?
And you, too, Wordsworth, are children truly
Clouded with glory, learned in dark Nature?
The dog in humble inquiry along the ground,   15
The child who credits dreams and fears the dark,
Know more and less than you: they know full well
Nor dream nor childhood answer questions well:
You too are strangers, children are Shakespearean.

Regard the child, regard the animal,   20
Welcome strangers, but study daily things,
Knowing that heaven and hell surround us,
But this, this which we say before we're sorry,
This which we live behind our unseen faces,
Is neither dream, nor childhood, neither   25
Myth, nor landscape, final, nor finished,
For we are incomplete and know no future,
And we are howling or dancing out our souls
In beating syllables before the curtain:
We are Shakespearean, we are strangers.   30

1938

DOGS ARE SHAKESPEAREAN 6 *Twelfth Night:* Shakespeare's play.

THE HEAVY BEAR WHO GOES WITH ME

462

"THE WITHNESS OF THE BODY"

The heavy bear who goes with me,
A manifold honey to smear his face,
Clumsy and lumbering here and there,
The central ton of every place,
The hungry beating brutish one   5
In love with candy, anger, and sleep,
Crazy factotum, dishevelling all,
Climbs the building, kicks the football,
Boxes his brother in the hate-ridden city.

Breathing at my side, that heavy animal,   10
That heavy bear who sleeps with me,
Howls in his sleep for a world of sugar,
A sweetness intimate as the water's clasp,
Howls in his sleep because the tight-rope
Trembles and shows the darkness beneath.   15
—The strutting show-off is terrified,
Dressed in his dress-suit, bulging his pants,
Trembles to think that his quivering meat
Must finally wince to nothing at all.

That inescapable animal walks with me,   20
Has followed me since the black womb held,
Moves where I move, distorting my gesture,
A caricature, a swollen shadow,
A stupid clown of the spirit's motive,
Perplexes and affronts with his own darkness,   25
The secret life of belly and bone,
Opaque, too near, my private, yet unknown,
Stretches to embrace the very dear
With whom I would walk without him near,
Touches her grossly, although a word   30
Would bare my heart and make me clear,
Stumbles, flounders, and strives to be fed
Dragging me with him in his mouthing care,
Amid the hundred million of his kind,
The scrimmage of appetite everywhere.   35

1938

THE HEAVY BEAR WHO GOES WITH ME 7 *factotum:* handyman.

QUESTIONS

1. What does the epigraph contribute to your first reading of the poem? What is the effect of returning to it after you have read the poem? What does it add to your creation of a reading?
2. What is the bear? Describe his actions, his appearance, and the speaker's feelings about him.
3. If not the bear, who is writing the poem? Do his complaints about the bear apply in some way to the poetry-writing process? Do they consider the reader as creator?
4. Why is the bear so afraid (lines 14–19)?

ANNE SEXTON
(1928–1974)

HER KIND   463

I have gone out, a possessed witch,
haunting the black air, braver at night;
dreaming evil, I have done my hitch
over the plain houses, light by light:
lonely thing, twelve-fingered, out of mind.   5
A woman like that is not a woman, quite.
I have been her kind.

I have found the warm caves in the woods,
filled them with skillets, carvings, shelves,
closets, silks, innumerable goods;   10
fixed the suppers for the worms and the elves:
whining, rearranging the disaligned.
A woman like that is misunderstood.
I have been her kind.

I have ridden in your cart, driver,   15
waved my nude arms at villages going by,
learning the last bright routes, survivor
where your flames still bite my thigh
and my ribs crack where your wheels wind.
A woman like that is not ashamed to die.   20
I have been her kind.

1960

THE ABORTION   464

Somebody who should have been born
is gone.

Just as the earth puckered its mouth,
each bud puffing out from its knot,
I changed my shoes, and then drove south.   5

Up past the Blue Mountains, where
Pennsylvania humps on endlessly,
wearing, like a crayoned cat, its green hair,

its roads sunken in like a gray washboard;
where, in truth, the ground cracks evilly,   10
a dark socket from which the coal has poured,

Somebody who should have been born
is gone.

the grass as bristly and stout as chives,
and me wondering when the ground would break,   15
and me wondering how anything fragile survives;

up in Pennsylvania, I met a little man,
not Rumpelstiltskin, at all, at all . . .
he took the fullness that love began.

Returning north, even the sky grew thin   20
like a high window looking nowhere.
The road was as flat as a sheet of tin.

Somebody who should have been born
is gone.

Yes, woman, such logic will lead   25
to loss without death. Or say what you meant,
you coward . . . this baby that I bleed.

                                                        1962

Q U E S T I O N S

1. What do the colors suggest? Be sure to look not only for colors named directly but
   also for colors implicit in certain images.
2. What season of the year is it? How does that contribute to the theme?
3. How does the allusion to Rumpelstiltskin fit into the poem?
4. What are the contrasts the poem explores and develops?
5. What are the speaker's feelings about the abortion?

PAIN FOR A DAUGHTER

Blind with love, my daughter
has cried nightly for horses,
those long-necked marchers and churners
that she has mastered, any and all,
reigning them in like a circus hand—   5
the excitable muscles and the ripe neck;
tending this summer, a pony and a foal.
She who is too squeamish to pull
a thorn from the dog's paw,
watched her pony blossom with distemper,   10
the underside of the jaw swelling
like an enormous grape.
Gritting her teeth with love,
she drained the boil and scoured it
with hydrogen peroxide until pus   15
ran like milk on the barn floor.

Blind with loss all winter,
in dungarees, a ski jacket and a hard hat,
she visits the neighbors' stable,
our acreage not zoned for barns;   20
they who own the flaming horses
and the swan-whipped thoroughbred
that she tugs at and cajoles,
thinking it will burn like a furnace
under her small-hipped English seat.   25

Blind with pain she limps home.
The thoroughbred has stood on her foot.
He rested there like a building.
He grew into her foot until they were one.
The marks of the horseshoe printed   30
into her flesh, the tips of her toes
ripped off like pieces of leather,
three toenails swirled like shells
and left to float in blood in her riding boot.

Blind with fear, she sits on the toilet,   35
her foot balanced over the washbasin,
her father, hydrogen peroxide in hand,
performing the rites of the cleansing.
She bites on a towel, sucked in breath,

sucked in and arched against the pain,   40
her eyes glancing off me where
I stand at the door, eyes locked
on the ceiling, eyes of a stranger,
and then she cries . . .
Oh my God, help me!   45
Where a child would have cried *Mama!*
Where a child would have believed *Mama!*
she bit the towel and called on God
and I saw her life stretch out . . .
I saw her torn in childbirth,   50
and I saw her, at that moment,
in her own death and I knew that she
knew.

1966

FLEE ON YOUR DONKEY   466

> Ma faim, Anne, Anne,
> Fuis sur ton âne . . .
> Rimbaud

Because there was no other place
to flee to,
I came back to the scene of the disordered senses,
came back last night at midnight,
arriving in the thick June night   5
without luggage or defenses,
giving up my car keys and my cash,
keeping only a pack of Salem cigarettes
the way a child holds on to a toy.
I signed myself in where a stranger   10
puts the inked-in X's—
for this is a mental hospital,
not a child's game.

Today an interne knocks my knees,
testing for reflexes.   15
Once I would have winked and begged for dope.
Today I am terribly patient.
Today crows play black-jack
on the stethoscope.

FLEE ON YOUR DONKEY epigraph: "My hunger, Anne, Anne,/Flee on your donkey" (French);
Rimbaud: Arthur Rimbaud (1854–1891), French poet.

Everyone has left me
except my muse,
that good nurse.
She stays in my hand,
a mild white mouse.   20

The curtains, lazy and delicate,
billow and flutter and drop   25
like the Victorian skirts
of my two maiden aunts
who kept an antique shop.

Hornets have been sent.
They cluster like floral arrangements on the screen.   30
Hornets, dragging their thin stingers,
hover outside, all knowing,
hissing: *the hornet knows.*
I heard it as a child   35
but what was it that he meant?
The hornet knows!
What happened to Jack and Doc and Reggy?
Who remembers what lurks in the heart of man?
What did The Green Hornet mean, *he knows?*   40
Or have I got it wrong?
Is it The Shadow who had seen
me from my bedside radio?

Now it's *Dinn, Dinn, Dinn!*
while the ladies in the next room argue   45
and pick their teeth.
Upstairs a girl curls like a snail;
in another room someone tries to eat a shoe;
meanwhile an adolescent pads up and down
the hall in his white tennis socks.   50
A new doctor makes rounds
advertising tranquilizers, insulin, or shock
to the uninitiated.

Six years of such small preoccupations!
Six years of shuttling in and out of this place!   55
O my hunger! My hunger!
I could have gone around the world twice
or had new children—all boys.
It was a long trip with little days in it
and no new places.   60

In here,
it's the same old crowd,
the same ruined scene.
The alcoholic arrives with his golf clubs.
The suicide arrives with extra pills sewn   65
into the lining of her dress.
The permanent guests have done nothing new.
Their faces are still small
like babies with jaundice.

Meanwhile,   70
they carried out my mother,
wrapped like somebody's doll, in sheets,
bandaged her jaw and stuffed up her holes.
My father, too. He went out on the rotten blood
he used up on other women in the Middle West.   75
He went out, a cured old alcoholic
on crooked feet and useless hands.
He went out calling for his father
who died all by himself long ago—
that fat banker who got locked up,   80
his genes suspended like dollars,
wrapped up in his secret,
tied up securely in a straitjacket.

But you, my doctor, my enthusiast,
were better than Christ;   85
you promised me another world
to tell me who
I was.

I spent most of my time,
a stranger,   90
damned and in trance—that little hut,
that naked blue-veined place,
my eyes shut on the confusing office,
eyes circling into my childhood,
eyes newly cut.   95
Years of hints
strung out—a serialized case history—
thirty-three years of the same dull incest
that sustained us both.
You, my bachelor analyst,   100

who sat on Marlborough Street,
sharing your office with your mother
and giving up cigarettes each New Year,
were the new God,
the manager of the Gideon Bible.   105

I was your third-grader
with a blue star on my forehead.
In trance I could be any age,
voice, gesture—all turned backward
like a drugstore clock.   110
Awake, I memorized dreams.
Dreams came into the ring
like third string fighters,
each one a bad bet
who might win   115
because there was no other.

I stared at them,
concentrating on the abyss
the way one looks down into a rock quarry,
uncountable miles down,   120
my hands swinging down like hooks
to pull dreams up out of their cage.
O my hunger! My hunger!

Once,
outside your office,   125
I collapsed in the old-fashioned swoon
between the illegally parked cars.
I threw myself down,
pretending dead for eight hours.
I thought I had died   130
into a snowstorm.
Above my head
chains cracked along like teeth
digging their way through the snowy street.
I lay there   135
like an overcoat
that someone had thrown away.
You carried me back in,
awkwardly, tenderly,
with the help of the red-haired secretary   140

who was built like a lifeguard.
My shoes,
I remember,
were lost in the snowbank
as if I planned never to walk again.   145

That was the winter
that my mother died,
half mad on morphine,
blown up, at last,
like a pregnant pig.   150
I was her dreamy evil eye.
In fact,
I carried a knife in my pocketbook—
my husband's good L. L. Bean hunting knife.
I wasn't sure if I should slash a tire   155
or scrape the guts out of some dream.

You taught me
to believe in dreams;
thus I was the dredger.
I held them like an old woman with arthritic fingers,   160
carefully straining the water out—
sweet dark playthings,
and above all, mysterious
until they grew mournful and weak.
O my hunger! My hunger!   165
I was the one
who opened the warm eyelid
like a surgeon
and brought forth young girls
to grunt like fish.   170

I told you,
I said—
but I was lying—
that the knife was for my mother . . .
and then I delivered her.   175

The curtains flutter out
and slump against the bars.
They are my two thin ladies
named Blanche and Rose.

The grounds outside   180
are pruned like an estate at Newport.
Far off, in the field,
something yellow grows.

Was it last month or last year
that the ambulance ran like a hearse   185
with its siren blowing on suicide—
Dinn, dinn, dinn!—
a noon whistle that kept insisting on life
all the way through the traffic lights?

I have come back   190
but disorder is not what it was.
I have lost the trick of it!
The innocence of it!
That fellow-patient in his stovepipe hat
with his fiery joke, his manic smile—   195
even he seems blurred, small and pale.
I have come back,
recommitted,
fastened to the wall like a bathroom plunger,
held like a prisoner   200
who was so poor
he fell in love with jail.

I stand at this old window
complaining of the soup,
examining the grounds,
allowing myself the wasted life.   205
Soon I will raise my face for a white flag,
and when God enters the fort,
I won't spit or gag on his finger.
I will eat it like a white flower.
Is this the old trick, the wasting away,   210
the skull that waits for its dose
of electric power?

This is madness
but a kind of hunger.
What good are my questions   215
in this hierarchy of death

where the earth and the stones go
Dinn!   Dinn!   Dinn!
It is hardly a feast.   220
It is my stomach that makes me suffer.

Turn, my hungers!
For once make a deliberate decision.
There are brains that rot here
like black bananas.   225
Hearts have grown as flat as dinner plates.
Anne, Anne,
flee on your donkey,
flee this sad hotel,
ride out on some hairy beast,   230
gallop backward pressing
your buttocks to his withers,
sit to his clumsy gait somehow.
Ride out
any old way you please!   235
In this place everyone talks to his own mouth.
That's what it means to be crazy.

Those I loved best died of it—
the fool's disease.

1966

FOR MY LOVER, RETURNING TO HIS WIFE   467

She is all there.
She was melted carefully down for you
and cast up from your childhood,
cast up from your one hundred favorite aggies.

She has always been there, my darling.   5
She is, in fact, exquisite.
Fireworks in the dull middle of February
and as real as a cast-iron pot.

Let's face it, I have been momentary.
A luxury. A bright red sloop in the harbor.   10
My hair rising like smoke from the car window.
Littleneck clams out of season.

FOR MY LOVER, RETURNING TO HIS WIFE **4** *aggies:* agate marbles.

She is more than that. She is your have to have,
has grown you your practical your tropical growth.
This is not an experiment. She is all harmony.
She sees to oars and oarlocks for the dinghy,   15

has placed wild flowers at the window at breakfast,
sat by the potter's wheel at midday,
set forth three children under the moon,
three cherubs drawn by Michelangelo,

done this with her legs spread out   20
in the terrible months in the chapel.
If you glance up, the children are there
like delicate balloons resting on the ceiling.

She has also carried each one down the hall
after supper, their heads privately bent,   25
two legs protesting, person to person,
her face flushed with a song and their little sleep.

I give you back your heart.
I give you permission—

for the fuse inside her, throbbing   30
angrily in the dirt, for the bitch in her
and the burying of her wound—
for the burying of her small red wound alive—

for the pale flickering flare under her ribs,
for the drunken sailor who waits in her left pulse,   35
for the mother's knee, for the stockings,
for the garter belt, for the call—

the curious call
when you will burrow in arms and breasts
and tug at the orange ribbon in her hair   40
and answer the call, the curious call.

She is so naked and singular.
She is the sum of yourself and your dream.
Climb her like a monument, step after step.
She is solid.   45

As for me, I am a watercolor.
I wash off.

1969

WILLIAM SHAKESPEARE
(1564–1616)

SONNET 18   468
[SHALL I COMPARE THEE TO A SUMMER'S DAY?]

Shall I compare thee to a summer's day?
Thou art more lovely and more temperate:
Rough winds do shake the darling buds of May,
And summer's lease hath all too short a date:
Sometimes too hot the eye of heaven shines,   5
And often is his gold complexion dimmed;
And every fair from fair sometimes declines,
By chance or nature's changing course untrimmed;
But thy eternal summer shall not fade,
Nor lose possession of that fair thou ow'st;   10
Nor shall death brag thou wander'st in his shade,
When in eternal lines to time thou grow'st:
So long as men can breathe, or eyes can see,
So long lives this, and this gives life to thee.

1609

SONNET 29   469
[WHEN IN DISGRACE WITH FORTUNE
AND MEN'S EYES]

When, in disgrace with fortune and men's eyes,
I all alone beweep my outcast state,
And trouble deaf heaven with my bootless cries,
And look upon myself, and curse my fate,
Wishing me like to one more rich in hope,   5
Featured like him, like him with friends possessed,
Desiring this man's art and that man's scope,
With what I most enjoy contented least;
Yet in these thoughts myself almost despising,
Haply I think on thee—and then my state,   10
Like to the lark at break of day arising
From sullen earth, sings hymns at heaven's gate;
For thy sweet love remembered such wealth brings
That then I scorn to change my state with kings.

1609

SONNET 18 8 *untrimmed:* stripped of beauty. 10 *ow'st:* ownest.
SONNET 29 3 *bootless:* useless.

SONNET 55
[NOT MARBLE, NOR THE GILDED MONUMENTS]

470

Not marble, nor the gilded monuments
Of princes, shall outlive this powerful rhyme;
But you shall shine more bright in these conténts
Than unswept stone, besmeared with sluttish time.
When wasteful war shall statues overturn,   5
And broils root out the work of masonry,
Nor Mars his sword nor war's quick fire shall burn
The living record of your memory.
'Gainst death and all-oblivious enmity
Shall you pace forth; your praise shall still find room   10
Even in the eyes of all posterity
That wear this world out to the ending doom.
So, till the judgment that yourself arise,
You live in this, and dwell in lovers' eyes.

1609

SONNET 116
[LET ME NOT TO THE MARRIAGE OF TRUE MINDS]

471

Let me not to the marriage of true minds
Admit impediments. Love is not love
Which alters when it alteration finds,
Or bends with the remover to remove.
O no! it is an ever-fixèd mark   5
That looks on tempests and is never shaken;
It is the star to every wand'ring bark,
Whose worth's unknown, although his height be taken.
Love's not Time's fool, though rosy lips and cheeks
Within his bending sickle's compass come.   10
Love alters not with his brief hours and weeks,
But bears it out even to the edge of doom.
    If this be error, and upon me proved,
    I never writ, nor no man ever loved.

1609

QUESTIONS

1. The Anglican Marriage Service reads, "If any of you know cause or just impediment
   why these persons should not be joined together, speak now or forever hold your
   peace." What relationship do you see between these words and the poem?
2. How certain of the truth of his statements is the speaker?

3. Explain "it is an ever-fixèd mark" (line 5). How is this idea ca
   poem?
4. Is love eternal?
5. What is the effect of the repetition of certain words?

SONNET 129
[TH' EXPENSE OF SPIRIT IN A WASTE OF SHAME]

Th' expense of spirit in a waste of shame
Is lust in action; and till action, lust
Is perjured, murderous, bloody, full of blame,
Savage, extreme, rude, cruel, not to trust;
Enjoyed no sooner but despisèd straight: 5
Past reason hunted; and no sooner had,
Past reason hated, as a swallowed bait,
On purpose laid to make the taker mad:
Mad in pursuit, and in possession so;
Had, having, and in quest to have, extreme;   10
A bliss in proof, and proved, a very woe;
Before, a joy proposed; behind, a dream.
All this the world well knows; yet none knows well
To shun the heaven that leads men to this hell.

                                                                      1609

SONNET 138   473
[WHEN MY LOVE SWEARS THAT SHE
IS MADE OF TRUTH]

When my love swears that she is made of truth,
I do believe her, though I know she lies,
That she might think me some untutored youth,
Unlearnèd in the world's false subtleties.
Thus vainly thinking that she thinks me young,   5
Although she knows my days are past the best,
Simply I credit her false-speaking tongue:
On both sides thus is simple truth suppressed.
But wherefore says she not she is unjust?
And wherefore say not I that I am old?   10
Oh, love's best habit is in seeming trust,
And age in love loves not to have years told.
Therefore I lie with her and she with me,
And in our faults by lies we flattered be.

                                                                      1609

PERCY BYSSHE SHELLEY
(1792–1822)

ODE TO THE WEST WIND   474

1

O wild West Wind, thou breath of Autumn's being, A
Thou, from whose unseen presence the leaves dead B
Are driven, like ghosts from an enchanter fleeing, A

Yellow, and black, and pale, and hectic red, B
Pestilence-stricken multitudes: O thou,   5
Who chariotest to their dark wintry bed

The wingèd seeds, where they lie cold and low,
Each like a corpse within its grave, until
Thine azure sister of the Spring shall blow

 *Linked Sonnets*

Her clarion o'er the dreaming earth, and fill   10
(Driving sweet buds like flocks to feed in air)
With living hues and odors plain and hill:

Wild Spirit, which art moving everywhere;
Destroyer and preserver; hear, oh, hear!

2

Thou on whose stream, mid the steep sky's commotion,   15
Loose clouds like earth's decaying leaves are shed,
Shook from the tangled boughs of Heaven and Ocean,

Angels of rain and lightning: there are spread
On the blue surface of thine aëry surge,
Like the bright hair uplifted from the head   20

Of some fierce Maenad, even from the dim verge
Of the horizon to the zenith's height,
The locks of the approaching storm. Thou dirge

Of the dying year, to which this closing night
Will be the dome of a vast sepulcher,   25
Vaulted with all thy congregated might

Of vapors, from whose solid atmosphere
Black rain, and fire, and hail will burst: oh, hear!

ODE TO THE WEST WIND 10 *clarion:* shrill, clear trumpet. 21 *Maenad:* frenzied woman who took part
in the rites of Dionysius, god of wine.

3

Thou who didst waken from his summer dreams
The blue Mediterranean, where he lay,   30
Lulled by the coil of his crystálline streams,

Beside a pumice isle in Baiae's bay,
And saw in sleep old palaces and towers
Quivering within the wave's intenser day,

All overgrown with azure moss and flowers   35
So sweet, the sense faints picturing them! Thou
For whose path the Atlantic's level powers

Cleave themselves into chasms, while far below
The sea-blooms and the oozy woods which wear
The sapless foliage of the ocean, know   40

Thy voice, and suddenly grow gray with fear,
And tremble and despoil themselves: oh, hear!

4

If I were a dead leaf thou mightest bear;
If I were a swift cloud to fly with thee;
A wave to pant beneath thy power, and share   45

The impulse of thy strength, only less free
Than thou, O uncontrollable! If even
I were as in my boyhood, and could be

The comrade of thy wanderings over Heaven,
As then, when to outstrip thy skyey speed   50
Scarce seemed a vision; I would ne'er have striven

As thus with thee in prayer in my sore need.
Oh, lift me as a wave, a leaf, a cloud!
I fall upon the thorns of life! I bleed!

A heavy weight of hours has chained and bowed   55
One too like thee: tameless, and swift, and proud.

5

Make me thy lyre, even as the forest is:
What if my leaves are falling like its own!
The tumult of thy mighty harmonies

---

32 *Baiae's bay:* in Italy.

Will take from both a deep, autumnal tone,   60
Sweet though in sadness. Be thou, Spirit fierce,
My spirit! Be thou me, impetuous one!

Drive my dead thoughts over the universe
Like withered leaves to quicken a new birth!
And, by the incantation of this verse,   65

Scatter, as from an unextinguished hearth
Ashes and sparks, my words among mankind!
Be through my lips to unawakened earth

The trumpet of a prophecy! O Wind,
If Winter comes, can Spring be far behind?   70

1820

TO ——   475

Music, when soft voices die,
Vibrates in the memory—
Odors, when sweet violets sicken,
Live within the sense they quicken.
Rose leaves, when the rose is dead,   5
Are heaped for the belovèd's bed;
And so thy thoughts, when thou art gone,
Love itself shall slumber on.

1824

ENGLAND IN 1819   476

An old, mad, blind, despised, and dying king—
Princes, the dregs of their dull race, who flow
Through public scorn—mud from a muddy spring;
Rulers who neither see, nor feel, nor know,
But leechlike to their fainting country cling,   5
Till they drop, blind in blood, without a blow;
A people starved and stabbed in the untilled field—
An army, which liberticide and prey
Makes as a two-edged sword to all who wield;
Golden and sanguine laws which tempt and slay;   10

ENGLAND IN 1819 title: the poem was written the year before George III's death. 8 *liberticide:* murder of liberty. 10 *sanguine:* bloody.

Religion Christless, Godless—a book sealed;
A Senate—Time's worst statute unrepealed—
Are graves, from which a glorious Phantom may
Burst, to illumine our tempestuous day.

1839

SIR PHILIP SIDNEY
(1554–1587)

FROM ASTROPHEL AND STELLA   477

1

Loving in truth, and fain in verse my love to show,
That the dear she might take some pleasure of my pain,
Pleasure might cause her read, reading might make her know,
Knowledge might pity win, and pity grace obtain,
I sought fit words to paint the blackest face of woe: 5
Studying inventions fine, her wits to entertain,
Oft turning others' leaves, to see if thence would flow
Some fresh and fruitful showers upon my sunburned brain.
But words came halting forth, wanting Invention's stay;
Invention, Nature's child, fled stepdame Study's blows;   10
And others' feet still seemed but strangers in my way.
Thus, great with child to speak, and helpless in my throes,
 Biting my truant pen, beating myself for spite:
 "Fool," said my Muse to me, "look in thy heart, and write."

71

Who will in fairest book of Nature know   15
How virtue may best lodged in beauty be,
Let him but learn of love to read in thee,
Stella, those fair lines which true goodness show.
There shall he find all vices' overthrow,
Not by rude force, but sweetest sovereignty   20
Of reason, from whose light those night birds fly,
That inward sun in thine eyes shineth so.
And, not content to be perfection's heir
Thyself, dost strive all minds that way to move,

[LOVING IN TRUTH, AND FAIN IN VERSE] 1 *fain:* eager. 6 *inventions:* in rhetoric, the process of finding new topics.

Who mark in thee what is in thee most fair.   25
So while thy beauty draws the heart to love,
   As fast thy virtue bends that love to good.
   "But ah," Desire still cries, "give me some food."

1591

LESLIE MARMON SILKO
(b. 1948)

WHERE MOUNTAIN LION LAY DOWN
WITH DEER   478

FEBRUARY 1973

I climb the black rock mountain
  stepping from day to day
         silently.
I smell the wind for my ancestors
    pale blue leaves   5
   crushed wild mountain smell.
Returning
  up the gray stone cliff
  where I descended
         a thousand years ago.   10
Returning to faded black stone
  where mountain lion lay down with deer.
It is better to stay up here
         watching wind's reflection
         in tall yellow flowers.   15
The old ones who remember me are gone
     the old songs are all forgotten
and the story of my birth.
How I danced in snow-frost moonlight
   distant stars to the end of Earth,   20
How I swam away
        in freezing mountain water
narrow mossy canyon tumbling down
      out of the mountain
      out of deep canyon stone   25
   down
     the memory
        spilling out
       into the world.

1974

EDITH SITWELL

(1887–1964)

AUBADE   479

Jane, Jane
Tall as a crane,
The morning light creaks down again;

Comb your cockscomb-ragged hair,
Jane, Jane, come down the stair.   5

Each dull blunt wooden stalactite
Of rain creaks, hardened by the light,

Sounding like an overtone
From some lonely world unknown.

But the creaking empty light   10
Will never harden into sight,

Will never penetrate your brain
With overtones like the blunt rain.

The light would show (if it could harden)
Eternities of kitchen garden,   15

Cockscomb flowers that none will pluck,
And wooden flowers that 'gin to cluck.

In the kitchen you must light
Flames as staring, red and white,

As carrots or as turnips, shining   20
Where the cold dawn light lies whining.

Cockscomb hair on the cold wind
Hangs limp, turns the milk's weak mind. . . .
    Jane, Jane,
    Tall as a crane,   25
    The morning light creaks down again!

1923

QUESTIONS

1. Who is Jane and what does she do? What are her physical characteristics? Her mental capabilities?
2. What is the attitude of the speaker toward Jane? Is this your attitude as you create a reading?

AUBADE title: love song at dawn, expressing regret that the lovers soon must part.

3. What is the effect of the initial triple rhyme, and the rhythm and rhyme of the rest of the poem? How do these devices affect your reading?
4. Discuss the irony of the title.

STEVIE SMITH
(1902–1971)

NOT WAVING BUT DROWNING   480

Nobody heard him, the dead man,
But still he lay moaning:
I was much further out than you thought
And not waving but drowning.

Poor chap, he always loved larking   5
And now he's dead
It must have been too cold for him his heart gave way,
They said.

Oh, no no no, it was too cold always
(Still the dead one lay moaning)   10
I was much too far out all my life
And not waving but drowning.

                                        1957

QUESTIONS

1. Which image captures your attention most quickly? What does it remind you of?
2. How can a dead man moan? What does he say?
3. Who is his audience? What is their response?
4. Why is line 7 a run-on sentence?

WAS HE MARRIED?   481

Was he married, did he try
To support as he grew less fond of them
Wife and family?

No,
He never suffered such a blow.   5

Did he feel pointless, feeble and distrait,
Unwanted by everyone and in the way?

WAS HE MARRIED? 6 *distrait:* absent-minded.

From his cradle he was purposeful,
His bent strong and his mind full.

Did he love people very much   10
Yet find them die one day?

He did not love in the human way.

Did he ask how long it would go on,
Wonder if Death could be counted on for an end?

He did not feel like this,   15
He had a future of bliss.

Did he never feel strong
Pain for being wrong?

He was not wrong, he was right,
He suffered from others', not his own, spite.   20

But there *is* no suffering like having made a mistake
Because of being of an inferior make.

He was not inferior,
He was superior.

He knew then that power corrupts but some must govern?   25

His thoughts were different.

Did he lack friends? Worse,
Think it was for his fault, not theirs?

He did not lack friends,
He had disciples he moulded to his ends.   30

Did he feel over-handicapped sometimes, yet must draw even?

How could he feel like this? He was the King of Heaven.

. . . find a sudden brightness one day in everything
Because a mood had been conquered, or a sin?

I tell you, he did not sin.   35

Do only human beings suffer from the irritation
I have mentioned? learn too that being comical
Does not ameliorate the desperation?

Only human beings feel this,
It is because they are so mixed.   40

All human beings should have a medal,
A god cannot carry it, he is not able.

A god is Man's doll, you ass,
He makes him up like this on purpose.

He might have made him up worse.   45

He often has, in the past.

To choose a god of love, as he did and does,
Is a little move then?

Yes, it is.

A larger one will be when men   50
Love love and hate hate but do not deify them?

It will be a larger one.

1962

W. D. SNODGRASS
(b. 1926)

APRIL INVENTORY   482

The green catalpa tree has turned
All white; the cherry blooms once more.
In one whole year I haven't learned
A blessed thing they pay you for.
The blossoms snow down in my hair;   5
The trees and I will soon be bare.

The trees have more than I to spare.
The sleek, expensive girls I teach,
Younger and pinker every year,
Bloom gradually out of reach.   10
The pear tree lets its petals drop
Like dandruff on a tabletop.

The girls have grown so young by now
I have to nudge myself to stare.
This year they smile and mind me how   15
My teeth are falling with my hair.
In thirty years I may not get
Younger, shrewder, or out of debt.

The tenth time, just a year ago,
I made myself a little list   20
Of all the things I'd ought to know,
Then told my parents, analyst,
And everyone who's trusted me
I'd be substantial, presently.

I haven't read one book about   25
A book or memorized one plot.
Or found a mind I did not doubt.
I learned one date. And then forgot.
And one by one the solid scholars
Get the degrees, the jobs, the dollars.   30

And smile above their starchy collars.
I taught my classes Whitehead's notions;
One lovely girl, a song of Mahler's.
Lacking a source-book or promotions,
I showed one child the colors of   35
A luna moth and how to love.

I taught myself to name my name,
To bark back, loosen love and crying;
To ease my woman so she came,
To ease an old man who was dying.   40
I have not learned how often I
Can win, can love, but choose to die.

I have not learned there is a lie
Love shall be blonder, slimmer, younger;
That my equivocating eye   45
Loves only by my body's hunger;
That I have forces, true to feel,
Or that the lovely world is real.

While scholars speak authority
And wear their ulcers on their sleeves,   50
My eyes in spectacles shall see
These trees procure and spend their leaves.
There is a value underneath
The gold and silver in my teeth.

APRIL INVENTORY 32 *Whitehead:* Alfred North Whitehead (1861–1947), English philosopher. 33
Mahler: Gustav Mahler (1860–1911), Austrian composer.

Though trees turn bare and girls turn wives, 55
We shall afford our costly seasons;
There is a gentleness survives
That will outspeak and has its reasons.
There is a loveliness exists,
Preserves us, not for specialists. 60

1959

QUESTIONS

1. Do you find yourself described as a part of the speaker's world? Can you identify with the speaker on any level?
2. What has the speaker learned and what has he not learned?
3. What does he value? Is it consistent with or at odds with the values of his colleagues?
4. How do the monetary and business metaphors unify his response?
5. What similarities and differences do you find between this poem and A. E. Housman's "Loveliest of Trees"?

WILLIAM STAFFORD
(b. 1914)

TRAVELING THROUGH THE DARK   483

Traveling through the dark I found a deer
dead on the edge of the Wilson River road.
It is usually best to roll them into the canyon:
that road is narrow; to swerve might make more dead.

By glow of the tail-light I stumbled back of the car 5
and stood by the heap, a doe, a recent killing;
she had stiffened already, almost cold.
I dragged her off; she was large in the belly.

My fingers touching her side brought me the reason—
her side was warm; her fawn lay there waiting, 10
alive, still, never to be born.
Beside that mountain road I hesitated.

The car aimed ahead its lowered parking lights;
under the hood purred the steady engine.
I stood in the glare of the warm exhaust turning red; 15
around our group I could hear the wilderness listen.

I thought hard for us all—my only swerving—,
then pushed her over the edge into the river.

1960

QUESTIONS

1. Which of your senses are most affected by the experience of the poem?
2. Identify the verbs. What do they tell you? How do they help to engage the senses?
3. Compare the description of the deer with the description of the car. What do you find?
4. What does the speaker mean by lines 4 and 17?

AT THE BOMB TESTING SITE   484

At noon in the desert a panting lizard
waited for history, its elbows tense,
watching the curve of a particular road
as if something might happen.

It was looking for something farther off   5
than people could see, an important scene
acted in stone for little selves
at the flute end of consequences.

There was just a continent without much on it
under a sky that never cared less.   10
Ready for a change, the elbows waited.
The hands gripped hard on the desert.

1966

WALLACE STEVENS
(1879–1955)

SUNDAY MORNING   485

1

Complacencies of the peignoir, and late
Coffee and oranges in a sunny chair,
And the green freedom of a cockatoo
Upon a rug mingle to dissipate
The holy hush of ancient sacrifice.   5
She dreams a little, and she feels the dark
Encroachment of that old catastrophe,
As a calm darkens among water-lights.
The pungent oranges and bright, green wings
Seem things in some procession of the dead,   10
Winding across wide water, without sound.

The day is like wide water, without sound,
Stilled for the passing of her dreaming feet
Over the seas, to silent Palestine,
Dominion of the blood and sepulchre.   15

2

Why should she give her bounty to the dead?
What is divinity if it can come
Only in silent shadows and in dreams?
Shall she not find in comforts of the sun,
In pungent fruit and bright, green wings, or else   20
In any balm or beauty of the earth,
Things to be cherished like the thought of heaven?
Divinity must live within herself:
Passions of rain, or moods in falling snow;
Grievings in loneliness, or unsubdued   25
Elations when the forest blooms; gusty
Emotions on wet roads on autumn nights;
All pleasures and all pains, remembering
The bough of summer and the winter branch.
These are the measures destined for her soul.   30

3

Jove in the clouds had his inhuman birth.
No mother suckled him, no sweet land gave
Large-mannered motions to his mythy mind
He moved among us, as a muttering king,
Magnificent, would move among his hinds,   35
Until our blood, commingling, virginal,
With heaven, brought such requital to desire
The very hinds discerned it, in a star.
Shall our blood fail? Or shall it come to be
The blood of paradise? And shall the earth   40
Seem all of paradise that we shall know?
The sky will be much friendlier then than now,
A part of labor and a part of pain,
And next in glory to enduring love,
Not this dividing and indifferent blue.   45

4

She says, "I am content when wakened birds,
Before they fly, test the reality
Of misty fields, by their sweet questionings;
But when the birds are gone, and their warm fields

SUNDAY MORNING 35 *hinds:* farmhands.

Return no more, where, then, is paradise?"   50
There is not any haunt of prophecy,
Nor any old chimera of the grave,
Neither the golden underground, nor isle
Melodious, where spirits gat them home,
Nor visionary south, nor cloudy palm   55
Remote on heaven's hill, that has endured
As April's green endures; or will endure
Like her remembrance of awakened birds,
Or her desire for June and evening, tipped
By the consummation of the swallow's wings.   60

5

She says, "But in contentment I still feel
The need of some imperishable bliss."
Death is the mother of beauty; hence from her,
Alone, shall come fulfilment to our dreams
And our desires. Although she strews the leaves   65
Of sure obliteration on our paths,
The path sick sorrow took, the many paths
Where triumph rang its brassy phrase, or love
Whispered a little out of tenderness,
She makes the willow shiver in the sun   70
For maidens who were wont to sit and gaze
Upon the grass, relinquished to their feet.
She causes boys to pile new plums and pears
On disregarded plate. The maidens taste
And stray impassioned in the littering leaves.   75

6

Is there no change of death in paradise?
Does ripe fruit never fall? Or do the boughs
Hang always heavy in that perfect sky,
Unchanging, yet so like our perishing earth,
With rivers like our own that seek for seas   80
They never find, the same receding shores
That never touch with inarticulate pang?
Why set the pear upon those river-banks
Or spice the shores with odors of the plum?
Alas, that they should wear our colors there,   85
The silken weavings of our afternoons,
And pick the strings of our insipid lutes!
Death is the mother of beauty, mystical,
Within whose burning bosom we devise
Our earthly mothers waiting, sleeplessly.   90

7

Supple and turbulent, a ring of men
Shall chant in orgy on a summer morn
Their boisterous devotion to the sun,
Not as a god, but as a god might be,
Naked among them, like a savage source.   95
Their chant shall be a chant of paradise,
Out of their blood, returning to the sky;
And in their chant shall enter, voice by voice,
The windy lake wherein their lord delights,
The trees, like serafin, and echoing hills,   100
That choir among themselves long afterward.
They shall know well the heavenly fellowship
Of men that perish and of summer morn.
And whence they came and whither they shall go
The dew upon their feet shall manifest.   105

8

She hears, upon that water without sound,
A voice that cries, "The tomb in Palestine
Is not the porch of spirits lingering.
It is the grave of Jesus, where he lay."
We live in an old chaos of the sun,   110
Or old dependency of day and night,
Or island solitude, unsponsored, free,
Of that wide water, inescapable.
Deer walk upon our mountains, and the quail
Whistle about us their spontaneous cries;   115
Sweet berries ripen in the wilderness;
And, in the isolation of the sky,
At evening, casual flocks of pigeons make
Ambiguous undulations as they sink,
Downward to darkness, on extended wings.   120

1923

QUESTIONS

1. What does the title lead you to expect? Is that what you find?
2. Identify the details throughout the poem that relate in some way to the title.
3. What is the attitude toward those details? Reverence? Indifference? Cynicism? Regret?
4. Who is the woman and what does her speech reveal about herself?
5. How is death the mother of beauty (sections 5 and 6)? Discuss the limitations of a paradise with no death.
6. Is the poem's final image a note of pessimism, optimism, or resignation? Support your answer with other details from the poem.

THE EMPEROR OF ICE-CREAM   486

Call the roller of big cigars,
The muscular one, and bid him whip
In kitchen cups concupiscent curds.
Let the wenches dawdle in such dress
As they are used to wear, and let the boys   5
Bring flowers in last month's newspapers.
Let be be finale of seem.
The only emperor is the emperor of ice-cream.

Take from the dresser of deal,
Lacking the three glass knobs, that sheet   10
On which she embroidered fantails once
And spread it so as to cover her face.
If her horny feet protrude, they come
To show how cold she is, and dumb.
Let the lamp affix its beam.   15
The only emperor is the emperor of ice-cream.

                                                        1923

THE SNOW MAN   487

One must have a mind of winter
To regard the frost and the boughs
Of the pine-trees crusted with snow;

And have been cold a long time
To behold the junipers shagged with ice,   5
The spruces rough in the distant glitter

Of the January sun; and not to think
Of any misery in the sound of the wind,
In the sound of a few leaves,

Which is the sound of the land   10
Full of the same wind
That is blowing in the same bare place
For the listener, who listens in the snow,
And, nothing himself, beholds
Nothing that is not there and the nothing that is.   15

                                                        1923

THE EMPEROR OF ICE-CREAM 9 *deal:* pine. 11 *fantails:* fantail pigeons.

ANECDOTE OF THE JAR   488

I placed a jar in Tennessee,
And round it was, upon a hill.
It made the slovenly wilderness
Surround that hill.

The wilderness rose up to it,   5
And sprawled around, no longer wild.
The jar was round upon the ground
And tall and of a port in air.

It took dominion everywhere.
The jar was gray and bare.   10
It did not give of bird or bush,
Like nothing else in Tennessee.

1923

THIRTEEN WAYS OF LOOKING AT A BLACKBIRD 489

1

Among twenty snowy mountains,
The only moving thing
Was the eye of the blackbird.

2

I was of three minds,
Like a tree   5
In which there are three blackbirds.

3

The blackbird whirled in the autumn winds.
It was a small part of the pantomime.

4

A man and a woman
Are one.   10
A man and a woman and a blackbird
Are one.

5

I do not know which to prefer,
The beauty of inflections
Or the beauty of innuendoes,   15
The blackbird whistling
Or just after.

6

Icicles filled the long window
With barbaric glass.
The shadow of the blackbird   20
Crossed it to and fro.
The mood
Traced in the shadow
An indecipherable cause.

7

O thin men of Haddam,   25
Why do you imagine golden birds?
Do you not see how the blackbird
Walks around the feet
Of the women about you?

8

I know noble accents   30
And lucid, inescapable rhythms;
But I know, too,
That the blackbird is involved
In what I know.

9

When the blackbird flew out of sight,   35
It marked the edge
Of one of many circles.

10

At the sight of blackbirds
Flying in a green light,
Even the bawds of euphony   40
Would cry out sharply.

11

He rode over Connecticut
In a glass coach.
Once, a fear pierced him,
In that he mistook   45
The shadow of his equipage
For blackbirds.

12

The river is moving.
The blackbird must be flying.

THIRTEEN WAYS OF LOOKING AT A BLACKBIRD 25 *Haddam:* Connecticut town.

13

It was evening all afternoon.   50
It was snowing
And it was going to snow.
The blackbird sat
In the cedar-limbs.

1923

A HIGH-TONED OLD CHRISTIAN
WOMAN   490

Poetry is the supreme fiction, madame.
Take the moral law and make a nave of it
And from the nave build haunted heaven. Thus,
The conscience is converted into palms,
Like windy citherns hankering for hymns.   5
We agree in principle. That's clear. But take
The opposing law and make a peristyle,
And from the peristyle project a masque
Beyond the planets. Thus, our bawdiness,
Unpurged by epitaph, indulged at last,   10
Is equally converted into palms,
Squiggling like saxophones. And palm for palm,
Madame, we are where we began. Allow,
Therefore, that in the planetary scene
Your disaffected flagellants, well-stuffed,   15
Smacking their muzzy bellies in parade,
Proud of such novelties of the sublime,
Such tink and tank and tunk-a-tunk-tunk,
May, merely may, madame, whip from themselves
A jovial hullabaloo among the spheres.   20
This will make widows wince. But fictive things
Wink as they will. Wink most when widows wince.

1923

A HIGH-TONED OLD CHRISTIAN WOMAN 2 *nave:* area in a church where the congregation sits. 5 *citherns:* stringed instruments of the guitar family. A "windy cithern" is probably an Aeolian harp, put in open windows for the wind to play upon. 7 *peristyle:* a row of columns enclosing a space. 8 *masque:* a dramatic court entertainment.

THE IDEA OF ORDER AT KEY WEST 491

She sang beyond the genius of the sea.
The water never formed to mind or voice,
Like a body wholly body, fluttering
Its empty sleeves; and yet its mimic motion
Made constant cry, caused constantly a cry,
That was not ours although we understood,
Inhuman, of the veritable ocean.

The sea was not a mask. No more was she.
The song and water were not medleyed sound
Even if what she sang was what she heard,
Since what she sang was uttered word by word.
It may be that in all her phrases stirred
The grinding water and the gasping wind;
But it was she and not the sea we heard.
For she was the maker of the song she sang.
The ever-hooded, tragic-gestured sea
Was merely a place by which she walked to sing.
Whose spirit is this? we said, because we knew
It was the spirit that we sought and knew
That we should ask this often as she sang.

If it was only the dark voice of the sea
That rose, or even colored by many waves;
If it was only the outer voice of sky
And cloud, of the sunken coral water-walled,
However clear, it would have been deep air,
The heaving speech of air, a summer sound
Repeated in a summer without end
And sound alone. But it was more than that,
More even than her voice, and ours, among
The meaningless plungings of water and the wind,
Theatrical distances, bronze shadows heaped
On high horizons, mountainous atmospheres
Of sky and sea.
                    It was her voice that made
The sky acutest at its vanishing.
She measured to the hour its solitude.
She was the single artificer of the world
In which she sang. And when she sang, the sea,
Whatever self it had, became the self

That was her song, for she was the maker. Then we,   40
As we beheld her striding there alone,
Knew that there never was a world for her
Except the one she sang and, singing, made.

Ramon Fernandez, tell me, if you know,
Why, when the singing ended and we turned   45
Toward the town, tell why the glassy lights,
The lights in the fishing boats at anchor there,
As the night descended, tilting in the air,
Mastered the night and portioned out the sea,
Fixing emblazoned zones and fiery poles,   50
Arranging, deepening, enchanting night.

Oh! Blessed rage for order, pale Ramon,
The maker's rage to order words of the sea,
Words of the fragrant portals, dimly-starred,
And of ourselves and of our origins,   55
In ghostlier demarcations, keener sounds.

1935

OF MODERN POETRY   492

The poem of the mind in the act of finding
What will suffice. It has not always had
To find: the scene was set; it repeated what
Was in the script.
                         Then the theatre was changed
To something else. Its past was a souvenir.   5
It has to be living, to learn the speech of the place.
It has to face the men of the time and to meet
The women of the time. It has to think about war
And it has to find what will suffice. It has
To construct a new stage. It has to be on that stage   10
And, like an insatiable actor, slowly and
With meditation, speak words that in the ear,
In the delicatest ear of the mind, repeat,
Exactly, that which it wants to hear, at the sound
Of which, an invisible audience listens,   15
Not to the play, but to itself, expressed
In an emotion as of two people, as of two
Emotions becoming one. The actor is
A metaphysician in the dark, twanging

An instrument, twanging a wiry string that gives   20
Sounds passing through sudden rightnesses, wholly
Containing the mind, below which it cannot descend,
Beyond which it has no will to rise.
                                        It must
Be the finding of a satisfaction, and may
Be of a man skating, a woman dancing, a woman   25
Combing. The poem of the act of the mind.

                                                                        1942

TO AN OLD PHILOSOPHER IN ROME   493

On the threshold of heaven, the figures in the street
Become the figures of heaven, the majestic movement
Of men growing small in the distances of space,
Singing, with smaller and still smaller sound,
Unintelligible absolution and an end—   5

The threshold, Rome, and that more merciful Rome
Beyond, the two alike in the make of the mind.
It is as if in a human dignity
Two parallels become one, a perspective, of which
Men are part both in the inch and in the mile.   10

How easily the blown banners change to wings . . .
Things dark on the horizons of perception,
Become accompaniments of fortune, but
Of the fortune of the spirit, beyond the eye,
Not of its sphere, and yet not far beyond,   15

The human end in the spirit's greatest reach,
The extreme of the known in the presence of the extreme
Of the unknown. The newsboys' muttering
Becomes another murmuring; the smell
Of medicine, a fragrantness not to be spoiled . . .   20

The bed, the books, the chair, the moving nuns,
The candle as it evades the sight, these are
The sources of happiness in the shape of Rome,
A shape within the ancient circles of shapes,
And these beneath the shadow of a shape   25

TO AN OLD PHILOSOPHER IN ROME title: George Santayana (1863–1952), American philosopher born in
Spain.

In a confusion on bed and books, a portent
On the chair, a moving transparence on the nuns,
A light on the candle tearing against the wick
To join a hovering excellence, to escape
From fire and be part only of that of which   30

Fire is the symbol: the celestial possible.
Speak to your pillow as if it was yourself.
Be orator but with an accurate tongue
And without eloquence, O, half-asleep,
Of the pity that is the memorial of this room,   35

So that we feel, in this illumined large,
The veritable small, so that each of us
Beholds himself in you, and hears his voice
In yours, master and commiserable man,
Intent on your particles of nether-do,   40

Your dozing in the depths of wakefulness,
In the warmth of your bed, at the edge of your chair, alive
Yet living in two worlds, impenitent
As to one, and, as to one, most penitent,
Impatient for the grandeur that you need   45

In so much misery; and yet finding it
Only in misery, the afflatus of ruin,
Profound poetry of the poor and of the dead,
As in the last drop of the deepest blood,
As it falls from the heart and lies there to be seen,   50

Even as the blood of an empire, it might be,
For a citizen of heaven though still of Rome.
It is poverty's speech that seeks us out the most.
It is older than the oldest speech of Rome.
This is the tragic accent of the scene.   55

And you—it is you that speak it, without speech,
The loftiest syllables among loftiest things,
The one invulnerable man among
Crude captains, the naked majesty, if you like,
Of bird-nest arches and of rain-stained-vaults.   60

47 *afflatus:* inspiration.

The sounds drift in. The buildings are remembered.
The life of the city never lets go, nor do you
Ever want it to. It is part of the life in your room.
Its domes are the architecture of your bed.
The bells keep on repeating solemn names   65

In choruses and choirs of choruses,
Unwilling that mercy should be a mystery
Of silence, that any solitude of sense
Should give you more than their peculiar chords
And reverberations clinging to whisper still.   70

It is a kind of total grandeur at the end,
With every visible thing enlarged and yet
No more than a bed, a chair and moving nuns,
The immensest theatre, the pillared porch,
The book and candle in your ambered room,   75

Total grandeur of a total edifice,
Chosen by an inquisitor of structures
For himself. He stops upon this threshold,
As if the design of all his words takes form
And frame from thinking and is realized.   80

1954

MARK STRAND
(b. 1934)

ALWAYS   494

FOR CHARLES SIMIC

Always so late in the day
in their rumpled clothes, sitting
around a table lit by a single bulb,
the great forgetters were hard at work.
They tilted their heads to one side, closing their eyes.   5
Then a house disappeared and a man in his yard
with all his flowers in a row.
The moon was next to go.
The great forgetters wrinkled their brows.
Then Florida went and San Francisco   10
where tugs and barges leave

small gleaming scars across the Bay.
One of the great forgetters struck a match.
Gone were the harps of beaded lights
that vault the rivers of New York.   15
Another filled his glass
and that was it for crowds at evening
under sulphur yellow streetlamps coming on.
And afterwards Bulgaria was gone, and then Japan.
'Where will it end?' one of them said.   20
'Such difficult work, pursuing the fate
of everything known,' said another.
'Yes,' said a third, 'down to the last stone,
and only the cold zero of perfection
left for the imagination.'   25
The great forgetters slouched in their chairs.
Suddenly Asia was gone, and the evening star
and the common sorrows of the sun.
One of them yawned. Another coughed.
The last one gazed at the window: 30
not a cloud, not a tree,
the blaze of promise everywhere.

1983

JONATHAN SWIFT
(1667–1745)

A DESCRIPTION OF THE MORNING   495

Now hardly here and there a hackney-coach
Appearing, showed the ruddy morn's approach.
Now Betty from her master's bed had flown,
And softly stole to discompose her own;
The slip-shod 'prentice from his master's door   5
Had pared the dirt and sprinkled round the floor.
Now Moll had whirled her mop with dext'rous airs,
Prepared to scrub the entry and the stairs.
The youth with broomy stumps began to trace
The kennel-edge, where wheels had worn the place.   10

A DESCRIPTION OF THE MORNING 1 *hackney-coach:* cab drawn by horses. 10 *kennel-edge:* curb.

The small-coal man was heard with cadence deep,
Till drowned in shriller notes of chimney-sweep:
Duns at his lordship's gate began to meet;
And brickdust Moll had screamed through half the street.
The turnkey now his flock returning sees,   15
Duly let out a-nights to steal for fees:
The watchful bailiffs take their silent stands,
And schoolboys lag with satchels in their hands.

1709

A SATIRICAL ELEGY ON THE DEATH
OF A LATE FAMOUS GENERAL   496

His Grace! impossible! what dead!
Of old age too, and in his bed!
And could that mighty warrior fall?
And so inglorious, after all!
Well, since he's gone, no matter how,   5
The last loud trump must wake him now:
And, trust me, as the noise grows stronger,
He'd wish to sleep a little longer.
And could he be indeed so old
As by the newspapers we're told?   10
Threescore, I think, is pretty high;
'Twas time in conscience he should die.
This world he cumbered long enough;
He burnt his candle to the snuff;
And that's the reason, some folks think,   15
He left behind so great a s - - - k.
Behold his funeral appears,
Nor widow's sighs, nor orphan's tears,
Wont at such times each heart to pierce,
Attend the progress of his hearse.   20
But what of that, his friends may say,
He had those honors in his day.
True to his profit and his pride,
He made them weep before he died.

13 *Duns:* bill-collectors. 14 *brickdust:* used for cleaning knives. 15 *turnkey:* jailer.
A SATIRICAL ELEGY ON THE DEATH OF A LATE FAMOUS GENERAL title: the Duke of Marlborough (1650–1722).

Come hither, all ye empty things,   25
Ye bubbles raised by breath of kings;
Who float upon the tide of state,
Come hither, and behold your fate.
Let pride be taught by this rebuke,
How very mean a thing's a Duke;   30
From all his ill-got honors flung,
Turned to that dirt from whence he sprung.

1764

HENRY TAYLOR
(b. 1942)

SOMEWHERE ALONG THE WAY   497

You lean on a wire fence, looking across
a field of grain with a man you have stopped
to ask for directions. You are not lost.
You stopped here only so you could take a moment
to see whatever this old farmer sees   5
who crumbles heads of wheat between his palms.

Rust is lifting the red paint from his barn roof,
and earth hardens over the sunken arc
of his mower's iron wheel. All his sons
have grown and moved away, and the old woman   10
keeps herself in the parlor where the light
is always too weak to make shadows. He sniffs

at the grain in his hand, and cocks an ear
toward a dry tree ringing with cicadas.
There are people dying today, he says,   15
that never died before. He lifts an arm
and points, saying what you already knew
about the way you are trying to go;

you nod and thank him, and think of going on,
but only after you have stood and listened   20
a little while longer to the soft click
of the swaying grain heads soon to be cut,
and the low voice, edged with dim prophecy,
that settles down around you like the dust.

1985

AS ON A DARKLING PLAIN   498

The years pile up, but there rides with you still,
across old fields to which you have come back
to invent your home and cultivate the knack
of dying slowly, to contest your will
toward getting death behind you, to find a hill   5
where you can stop and let the reins go slack
and parse the dark swerve of the zodiac,
a face whose eyes find ways to hold you still.

They hold you now. You turn the chestnut mare
toward the next hill darkening to the west   10
and stop again. The eyes will sometimes change,
but they ride with you, glimmering and vast
as the sweet country you lost once, somewhere
between the Blue Ridge and the Wasatch Range.

1985

THE WAY IT SOMETIMES IS   499

At times it is like watching a face you have just met,
trying to decide who it reminds you of—
no one, surely, whom you ever hated or loved,
but yes, somebody, somebody. You watch the face

as it turns and nods, showing you, at certain angles,   5
a curve of the lips or a lift of the eyebrow
that is exactly right, and still the lost face
eludes you. Now this face is talking, and you hear

a sound in the voice, the accent on certain words—
yes! a phrase . . . you barely recall sitting outside,   10
by a pool or a campfire, remarking
a peculiar, recurring expression. Two syllables,

wasn't it? Doorknob? Bathroom? Shawcross? What the hell
kind of word is shawcross? A name; not the right one.
A couple of syllables that could possibly be   15
a little like something you may once have heard.

AS ON A DARKLING PLAIN 7 *parse:* to discover its various parts.

So the talk drifts, and you drift, sneaking glances,
pounding your brain. Days later a face occurs to you,
and yes, there is a resemblance. That odd word, though,
or phrase, is gone. It must have been somebody else.   20

Yes, it's like that, at times; something is, maybe;
and there are days when you can almost say what it is.

1985

NOT WORKING   500

Whatever he was doing, he looks up
and stares past whatever there is—a lamp,
a window, trees, the shingled garden shed—
as if he were about to think of something
that might have happened to him once, and now   5
refuses to occur to him again.

He stares, then, doing absolutely nothing
for minutes, hours, or a whole afternoon,
as the lamp burns, and sunlight on the shed
brightens and fades; the trees put out their leaves
and let them fall, and seasons wear away   10
the days when what he wanted had a name.

1985

THE FLYING CHANGE   501

1

The canter has two stride patterns, one on the right
lead and one on the left, each a mirror image of the
other. The leading foreleg is the last to touch the
ground before the moment of suspension in the air.
On cantered curves, the horse tends to lead with the   5
inside leg. Turning at liberty, he can change leads
without effort during the moment of suspension, but
a rider's weight makes this more difficult. The aim of
teaching a horse to move beneath you is to remind
him how he moved when he was free.   10

2

A single leaf turns sideways in the wind
in time to save a remnant of the day;
I am lifted like a whipcrack to the moves
I studied on that barbered stretch of ground,
before I schooled myself to drift away   15

from skills I still possess, but must outlive.
Sometimes when I cup water in my hands
and watch it slip away and disappear,
I see that age will make my hands a sieve;
but for a moment the shifting world suspends   20

its flight and leans toward the sun once more,
as if to interrupt its mindless plunge
through works and days that will not come again.
I hold myself immobile in bright air,
sustained in time astride the flying change.   25

                                                    1985

QUESTIONS

1. As you read this poem for the first time, what differences in form and tone do you
   notice between the first and second sections?
2. In which section do the most brilliant images occur? Why?
3. Which words in the first section are repeated in the second section? Do they have
   similar or different meanings in the second section?
4. How does the image of the sieve enlarge the meaning of the poem?

ALFRED, LORD TENNYSON

(1809–1892)

BREAK, BREAK, BREAK   502

Break, break, break,
    On thy cold gray stones, O Sea!
And I would that my tongue could utter
    The thoughts that arise in me.

                                                         5
O, well for the fisherman's boy,
    That he shouts with his sister at play!
O, well for the sailor lad,
    That he sings in his boat on the bay!

And the stately ships go on
  To their haven under the hill;
But O for the touch of a vanished hand,   10
  And the sound of a voice that is still!

Break, break, break,
  At the foot of thy crags, O Sea!
But the tender grace of a day that is dead
  Will never come back to me.   15

1842

ULYSSES   503

It little profits that an idle king,
By this still hearth, among these barren crags,
Matched with an aged wife, I mete and dole
Unequal laws unto a savage race,
That hoard, and sleep, and feed, and know not me.   5
I cannot rest from travel; I will drink
Life to the lees. All times I have enjoyed
Greatly, have suffered greatly, both with those
That loved me, and alone; on shore, and when
Through scudding drifts the rainy Hyades   10
Vext the dim sea. I am become a name;
For always roaming with a hungry heart
Much have I seen and known—cities of men
And manners, climates, councils, governments,
Myself not least, but honored of them all,—   15
And drunk delight of battle with my peers,
Far on the ringing plains of windy Troy.
I am a part of all that I have met;
Yet all experience is an arch wherethrough
Gleams that untraveled world whose margin fades   20
For ever and for ever when I move.
How dull it is to pause, to make an end,
To rust unburnished, not to shine in use!
As though to breathe were life! Life piled on life
Were all too little, and of one to me   25
Little remains; but every hour is saved
From that eternal silence, something more,
A bringer of new things; and vile it were

ULYSSES 10 *Hyades:* five stars in the constellation Taurus, believed to indicate rain when they rose
with the sun.

For some three suns to store and hoard myself, 30
And this gray spirit yearning in desire
To follow knowledge like a sinking star,
Beyond the utmost bound of human thought.
   This is my son, mine own Telemachus,
To whom I leave the scepter and the isle, 35
Well-loved of me, discerning to fulfill
This labor, by slow prudence to make mild
A rugged people, and through soft degrees
Subdue them to the useful and the good.
Most blameless is he, centered in the sphere
Of common duties, decent not to fail 40
In offices of tenderness, and pay
Meet adoration to my household gods,
When I am gone. He works his work, I mine.
   There lies the port; the vessel puffs her sail;
There gloom the dark, broad seas. My mariners, 45
Souls that have toiled, and wrought, and thought with me,
That ever with a frolic welcome took
The thunder and the sunshine, and opposed
Free hearts, free foreheads—you and I are old;
Old age hath yet his honor and his toil. 50
Death closes all; but something ere the end,
Some work of noble note, may yet be done,
Not unbecoming men that strove with gods.
The lights begin to twinkle from the rocks;
The long day wanes; the slow moon climbs; the deep 55
Moans round with many voices. Come, my friends,
'Tis not too late to seek a newer world.
Push off, and sitting well in order smite
The sounding furrows; for my purpose holds
To sail beyond the sunset, and the baths 60
Of all the western stars, until I die.
It may be that the gulfs will wash us down;
It may be we shall touch the Happy Isles,
And see the great Achilles, whom we knew.
Though much is taken, much abides; and though 65
We are not now that strength which in old days
Moved earth and heaven, that which we are, we are,
One equal temper of heroic hearts,
Made weak by time and fate, but strong in will
To strive, to seek, to find, and not to yield. 70

1842

QUESTIONS

1. Where do you feel most strongly the emotion of Ulysses? Why at those points and not at others?
2. What does Ulysses mean when he complains, "I am become a name" (line 11)?
3. In what tone of voice does he say, "As though to breathe were life" (line 24)? What does he mean?
4. Where do symbols appear in the poem and what is their function? Are literal and symbolic meanings separate?
5. Show how metaphor and simile support Ulysses' statements and desires.

TEARS, IDLE TEARS   504

Tears, idle tears, I know not what they mean,
Tears from the depth of some divine despair
Rise in the heart, and gather to the eyes,
In looking on the happy autumn-fields,
And thinking of the days that are no more.   5

Fresh as the first beam glittering on a sail,
That brings our friends up from the underworld,
Sad as the last which reddens over one
That sinks with all we love below the verge;
So sad, so fresh, the days that are no more.   10

Ah, sad and strange as in dark summer dawns
The earliest pipe of half-awakened birds
To dying ears, when unto dying eyes
The casement slowly grows a glimmering square;
So sad, so strange, the days that are no more.   15

Dear as remembered kisses after death,
And sweet as those by hopeless fancy feigned
On lips that are for others; deep as love,
Deep as first love, and wild with all regret;
O Death in Life, the days that are no more!   20

                                                              1847

THE EAGLE   505

He clasps the crag with crooked hands;
Close to the sun in lonely lands,
Ringed with the azure world, he stands.

The wrinkled sea beneath him crawls;
He watches from his mountain walls,
And like a thunderbolt he falls.   5

                                                              1851

CROSSING THE BAR

Sunset and evening star,
  And one clear call for me!
And may there be no moaning of the bar
  When I put out to sea,

But such a tide as moving seems asleep,   5
  Too full for sound and foam,
When that which drew from out the boundless deep
  Turns again home.

Twilight and evening bell,
  And after that the dark!   10
And may there be no sadness of farewell
  When I embark;

For though from out our bourne of Time and Place
  The flood may bear me far,
I hope to see my Pilot face to face   15
  When I have crossed the bar.

1889

DYLAN THOMAS
(1914–1953)

THE FORCE THAT THROUGH THE
GREEN FUSE DRIVES THE FLOWER

The force that through the green fuse drives the flower
Drives my green age; that blasts the roots of trees
Is my destroyer.
And I am dumb to tell the crooked rose
My youth is bent by the same wintry fever.   5

The force that drives the water through the rocks
Drives my red blood; that dries the mouthing streams
Turns mine to wax.
And I am dumb to mouth unto my veins
How at the mountain spring the same mouth sucks.   10

The hand that whirls the water in the pool
Stirs the quicksand; that ropes the blowing wind
Hauls my shroud sail.
And I am dumb to tell the hanging man
How of my clay is made the hangman's lime.   15

The lips of time leech to the fountain head;
Love drips and gathers, but the fallen blood
Shall calm her sores.
And I am dumb to tell a weather's wind
How time has ticked a heaven round the stars.   20

And I am dumb to tell the lover's tomb
How at my sheet goes the same crooked worm.

1934

AND DEATH SHALL HAVE NO DOMINION   508

And death shall have no dominion.
Dead men naked they shall be one
With the man in the wind and the west moon;
When their bones are picked clean and the clean bones gone,
They shall have stars at elbow and foot;   5
Though they go mad they shall be sane,
Though they sink through the sea they shall rise again;
Though lovers be lost love shall not;
And death shall have no dominion.

And death shall have no dominion.   10
Under the windings of the sea
They lying long shall not die windily;
Twisting on racks when sinews give way,
Strapped to a wheel, yet they shall not break;
Faith in their hands shall snap in two,   15
And the unicorn evils run them through;
Split all ends up they shan't crack;
And death shall have no dominion.

And death shall have no dominion.
No more may gulls cry at their ears   20
Or waves break loud on the seashores;
Where blew a flower may a flower no more
Lift its head to the blows of the rain;
Though they be mad and dead as nails,
Heads of the characters hammer through daisies;   25
Break in the sun till the sun breaks down,
And death shall have no dominion.

1936

FERN HILL 509

Now as I was young and easy under the apple boughs
About the lilting house and happy as the grass was green,
    The night above the dingle starry,
      Time let me hail and climb
    Golden in the heydays of his eyes,   5
And honored among wagons I was prince of the apple towns
And once below a time I lordly had the trees and leaves
      Trail with daisies and barley
    Down the rivers of the windfall light.

And as I was green and carefree, famous among the barns   10
About the happy yard and singing as the farm was home,
    In the sun that is young once only,
      Time let me play and be
    Golden in the mercy of his means,
And green and golden I was huntsman and herdsman, the calves   15
Sang to my horn, the foxes on the hills barked clear and cold,
      And the sabbath rang slowly
    In the pebbles of the holy streams.

All the sun long it was running, it was lovely, the hay
Fields high as the house, the tunes from the chimneys, it was air   20
    And playing, lovely and watery
      And fire green as grass.
    And nightly under the simple stars
As I rode to sleep the owls were bearing the farm away,
All the moon long I heard, blessed among stables, the night-jars   25
    Flying with the ricks, and the horses
      Flashing into the dark.

And then to awake, and the farm, like a wanderer white
With the dew, come back, the cock on his shoulder: it was all
    Shining, it was Adam and maiden,   30
      The sky gathered again
    And the sun grew round that very day.
So it must have been after the birth of the simple light
In the first, spinning place, the spellbound horses walking warm
    Out of the whinnying green stable   35
      On to the fields of praise.

FERN HILL 3 *dingle:* small valley. 25 *night-jars:* nocturnal birds. 26 *ricks:* haystacks.

And honored among foxes and pheasants by the gay house
Under the new made clouds and happy as the heart was long,
>   In the sun born over and over,
>   I ran my heedless ways,   40
>   My wishes raced through the house high hay
And nothing I cared, at my sky blue trades, that time allows
In all his tuneful turning so few and such morning songs
>   Before the children green and golden
>   Follow him out of grace,   45

Nothing I cared, in the lamb white days, that time would take me
Up to the swallow thronged loft by the shadow of my hand,
>   In the moon that is always rising,
>   Nor that riding to sleep
>   I should hear him fly with the high fields   50
And wake to the farm forever fled from the childless land.
Oh as I was young and easy in the mercy of his means,
>   Time held me green and dying
>   Though I sang in my chains like the sea.

1946

QUESTIONS

1. Do any of the images or experiences described contain personal associations for you? Do you remember your childhood concept of time? Is it similar or different from what is described here?
2. What phrase is suggested by "once below a time" (line 7)? Why does the speaker say it this way instead?
3. What words and ideas are associated with the word *green* throughout the poem? What is the traditional, symbolic meaning of the word? Is its meaning consistent throughout the poem?
4. What do the following words and phrases indicate to you about the speaker's memories of childhood?

   >   I lordly had the trees and leaves (line 7)

   >   And the sabbath rang slowly
   > In the pebbles of the holy streams (lines 17–18)

   >   it was Adam and maiden (line 30)

   >   fields of praise (line 36)

   What does the phrase "follow him out of grace" (line 45) indicate in this context?
5. Explain the final two lines.

IN MY CRAFT OR SULLEN ART   510

In my craft or sullen art
Exercised in the still night
When only the moon rages
And the lovers lie abed
With all their griefs in their arms,   5
I labor by singing light
Not for ambition or bread
Or the strut and trade of charms
On the ivory stages
But for the common wages   10
Of their most secret heart.

Not for the proud man apart
From the raging moon I write
On these spindrift pages
Nor for the towering dead   15
With their nightingales and psalms
But for the lovers, their arms
Round the griefs of the ages,
Who pay no praise or wages
Nor heed my craft or art.   20

1946

EDWARD THOMAS
(1878–1917)

THE OWL   511

Downhill I came, hungry, and yet not starved;
Cold, yet had heat within me that was proof
Against the North wind; tired, yet so that rest
Had seemed the sweetest thing under a roof.

Then at the inn I had food, fire, and rest,   5
Knowing how hungry, cold, and tired was I.
All of the night was quite barred out except
An owl's cry, a most melancholy cry

Shaken out long and clear upon the hill,
No merry note, nor cause of merriment,   10
But one telling me plain what I escaped
And others could not, that night, as in I went.

And salted was my food, and my repose,
Salted and sobered, too, by the bird's voice
Speaking for all who lay under the stars,   15
Soldiers and poor, unable to rejoice.

                                                                    1917

QUESTIONS

1. As you experience this poem, what encourages you to move from purely personal
   associations to a more universal response?
2. What do the first six lines establish? Why is there so much repetition?
3. Which words in the third stanza establish an opposite picture?
4. What does "salted" mean in lines 13 and 14?

JEAN TOOMER
(1894–1967)

REAPERS   512

Black reapers with the sound of steel on stones
Are sharpening scythes. I see them place the hones
In their hip-pockets as a thing that's done,
And start their silent swinging, one by one.
Black horses drive a mower through the weeds,   5
And there, a field rat, startled, squealing bleeds,
His belly close to ground. I see the blade,
Blood-stained, continue cutting weeds and shade.

                                                                    1923

QUESTIONS

1. Who are the reapers? What else do you associate with that term? How does that
   association fit into the sense of the poem?
2. What does the gesture described in the following lines have to do with the rest of the
   poem?

   I see them place the hones
   In their hip-pockets as a thing that's done (lines 2 and 3)

3. Who and what are plural and who and what are singular? What is the effect?

GEORGIA DUSK   513

The sky, lazily disdaining to pursue
   The setting sun, too indolent to hold
   A lengthened tournament for flashing gold,
Passively darkens for night's barbecue,

A feast of moon and men and barking hounds,   5
   An orgy for some genius of the South
   With blood-hot eyes and cane-lipped scented mouth,
Surprised in making folk-songs from soul sounds.

The sawmill blows its whistle, buzz-saws stop,
   And silence breaks the bud of knoll and hill,   10
   Soft setting pollen where plowed lands fulfill
Their early promise of a bumper crop.

Smoke from the pyramidal sawdust pile
   Curls up, blue ghosts of trees, tarrying low
   Where only chips and stumps are left to show   15
The solid proof of former domicile.

Meanwhile, the men, with vestiges of pomp,
   Race memories of king and caravan,
   High-priests, an ostrich, and a juju-man,
Go singing through the footpaths of the swamp.   20

Their voices rise . . the pine trees are guitars,
   Strumming, pine-needles fall like sheets of rain . .
   Their voices rise . . the chorus of the cane
Is caroling a vesper to the stars. .

O singers, resinous and soft your songs   25
   Above the sacred whisper of the pines,
   Give virgin lips to cornfield concubines,
Bring dreams of Christ to dusky cane-lipped throngs.

1923

EDMUND WALLER
(1607–1687)

SONG   514

   Go, lovely rose!
Tell her that wastes her time and me
   That now she knows,
When I resemble her to thee,
How sweet and fair she seems to be.   5

GEORGIA DUSK 19 *juju:* a charm used by some West African tribes.
SONG 4 *resemble:* compare.

Tell her that's young,
And shuns to have her graces spied,
   That hadst thou sprung
In deserts, where no men abide,
Thou must have uncommended died.   10

   Small is the worth
Of beauty from the light retired;
   Bid her come forth,
Suffer herself to be desired,
And not blush so to be admired.   15

   Then die! that she
The common fate of all things rare
   May read in thee;
How small a part of time they share
That are so wondrous sweet and fair!   20

                                                                     1645

QUESTIONS

1. What are your personal associations with roses? What are the traditional associations?
2. What has the girl been doing? Why? What has the speaker been doing? Why?
3. What are the various instructions the rose is given?
4. What effect does the final stanza have on the tone of the poem? Is there any earlier
   indication that this might be the direction the speaker would veer?

MARILYN WANIEK
(b. 1946)

WOMEN'S LOCKER ROOM   515

The splat of bare feet on wet tile
breaks the incredible luck
of my being alone in here.
I snatch a stingy towel
and sidle into the shower; I'm already soaped   5
by the time a white hand turns the neighboring knob.
I recognize the arm as one that had flashed
for many rapid laps while I dogpaddled at the shallow end.
I dart an appraising glance: She arches down
to wash a lifted heel, and is beautiful.   10
As she straightens, I look into her startled eyes.

For an instant I remember human sacrifice:
the female explorer led skyward,
her blonde tresses loose on her neck;
the drums of my pulse growing louder;   15
the heft of the obsidian knife.
Violets grew in the clefts of the stairs.

I could freeze her name in an ice cube,
bottle the dirt from her footsteps
with potent graveyard dust.   20
I could gather the combings from her hairbrush
to burn with her fingernail clippings,
I could feed her Iago powder.
Childhood taunts, branded ears,
a thousand insults swirl through my memory   25
like headlines in a city vacant lot.

I jump, grimace, divide like an amoeba
into twin rages that stomp around
with their lips stuck out,
then come suddenly face to face.   30
They see each other and know that they
are mean mamas.
Then I burst out laughing
and let the woman live.

1985

R O B E R T   P E N N   W A R R E N
(b. 1905)

GOLD GLADE   516

Wandering, in autumn, the woods of boyhood,
Where cedar, black, thick, rode the ridge,
Heart aimless as rifle, boy-blankness of mood,
I came where ridge broke, and the great ledge,
Limestone, set the toe high as treetop by dark edge   5

Of a gorge, and water hid, grudging and grumbling,
And I saw, in mind's eye, foam white on
Wet stone, stone wet-black, white water tumbling,
And so went down, and with some fright on
Slick boulders, crossed over. The gorge-depth drew night on,   10

WOMEN'S LOCKER ROOM 16 *obsidian:* black, volcanic glass. 23 *Iago:* villain in Shakespeare's *Othello*.

But high over high rock and leaf-lacing, sky
Showed yet bright, and declivity wooed
My foot by the quietening stream, and so I
Went on, in quiet, through the beech wood:
There, in gold light, where the glade gave, it stood.   15

The glade was geometric, circular, gold,
No brush or weed breaking that bright gold of leaf-fall.
In the center it stood, absolute and bold
Beyond any heart-hurt, or eye's grief-fall.
Gold-massy in air, it stood in gold light-fall,   20

No breathing of air, no leaf now gold-falling,
No tooth-stitch of squirrel, or any far fox bark,
No woodpecker coding, or late jay calling.
Silence: gray-shagged, the great shagbark
Gave forth gold light. There could be no dark.   25

But of course dark came, and I can't recall
What county it was, for the life of me.
Montgomery, Todd, Christian—I know them all.
Was it even Kentucky or Tennessee?
Perhaps just an image that keeps haunting me.   30

No, no! in no mansion under earth,
Nor imagination's domain of bright air,
But solid in soil that gave it its birth,
It stands, wherever it is, but somewhere.
I shall set my foot, and go there.   35

                                                            1955

AMERICAN PORTRAIT: OLD STYLE   517

I

Beyond the last house, where home was,
Past the marsh we found the old skull in, all nameless
And cracked in star-shape from a stone-smack,
Up the hill where the grass was tangled waist-high and wind-
        tousled,
To the single great oak that, in leaf-season, hung like   5
A thunderhead black against whatever blue the sky had,

And here, at the widest circumference of shade, when shade was,
Ran the trench, six feet long,
And wide enough for a man to lie down in,
In comfort, if comfort was still any object. No sign there   10
Of any ruined cabin or well, so Pap must have died of camp fever,
And the others pushed on, God knows where.

II

The Dark and Bloody Ground, so the teacher romantically said,
But one look out the window, and woods and ruined cornfields we
    saw:
A careless-flung corner of country, no hope and no history here.   15
No hope but the Pullman lights that swept
Night-fields—glass-glint from some farmhouse and flicker of
    ditches —
Or the night freight's moan on the rise where
You might catch a ride on the rods,
Just for hell, or if need had arisen.   20
No history either—no Harrod or Finley or Boone,
No tale how the Bluebellies broke at the Rebel yell and cold steel.

So we had to invent it all, our Bloody Ground, K and I,
And him the best shot in ten counties and could call any bird-note
    back,
But school out, not big enough for the ballgame,   25
And in the full tide of summer, not ready
For the twelve-gauge yet, or even a job, so what
Can you do but pick up your BBs and Benjamin,
Stick corn pone in pocket, and head out
"To Rally in the Cane-Brake and Shoot the Buffalo"—   30
As my grandfather's cracked old voice would sing it
From days of his own grandfather—and often enough
It was only a Plymouth Rock or maybe a fat Dominecker
That fell to the crack of the unerring Decherd.

III

Yes, imagination is strong. But not strong enough in the face of   35
The sticky feathers and BBs a mother's hand held out.
But no liberal concern was evinced for a Redskin,
As we trailed and out-tricked the sly Shawnees

AMERICAN PORTRAIT: OLD STYLE 21 *Harrod or Finley or Boone:* James Harrod, John Finley, and Daniel
Boone, Kentucky frontiersmen. 22 *Bluebellies:* Union troops. 28 *Benjamin:* overcoat. 33 *Plymouth
Rock:* breed of American chicken; *Dominecker:* from Dominique, a breed of American chicken. 34
Decherd: a firearm.

In a thicket of ironweed, and I wrestled one naked
And slick with his bear grease, till my hunting knife   40
Bit home, and the tomahawk
Slipped from his hand. And what mother cared about Bluebellies
Who came charging our trench? But we held
To pour the last volley at face-gape before
The tangle and clangor of bayonet.   45

Yes, a day is merely forever
In memory's shiningness,
And a year but a gust or a gasp
In the summer's heat of Time, and in that last summer
I was almost ready to learn   50
What imagination is—it is only
The lie we must learn to live by, if ever
We mean to live at all. Times change.
Things change. And K up and gone, and the summer
Gone, and I longed to know the world's name.   55

IV

Well, what I remember most
In a world long Time-pale and powdered
Like a vision still clinging to plaster
Set by Piero della Francesca
Is how K, through lane-dust or meadow,   60
Seemed never to walk, but float
With a singular joy and silence,
In his cloud of bird dogs, like angels,
With their eyes on his eyes like God,
And the sun on his uncut hair bright   65
As he passed through the ramshackle town and odd folks there
With pants on and vests and always soft gabble of money—
Polite in his smiling, but never much to say.

V

To pass through to what? No, not
To some wild white peak dreamed westward,   70
And each sunrise a promise to keep. No, only
The Big Leagues, not even a bird dog,
And girls that popped gum while they screwed.

---

59 *Piero della Francesca:* fifteenth-century Italian painter.

Yes, this was his path, and no batter
Could do what booze finally did: 75
Just blow him off the mound—but anyway,
He had always called it a fool game, just something
For children who hadn't yet dreamed what
A man is, or barked a squirrel, or raised   80
A single dog from a pup.

VI

And I, too, went on my way, the winning and losing, or what
Is sometimes of all things the worst, the not knowing
One thing from the other, nor knowing
How the teeth in Time's jaw all snag backward   85
And whatever enters therein
Has less hope of remission than shark-meat,

And one Sunday afternoon, in the idleness of summer,
I found his farm, and him home there,
With the bird dogs crouched round in the grass
And their eyes on his eyes as he whispered   90
Whatever to bird dogs it was.
Then yelled: "Well, for Christ's sake—it's you!"

Yes, me, for Christ's sake, and some sixty
Years blown like a hurricane past! But what can you say—
Can you say—when *all-to-be-said* is the *done*?   95
So our talk ran to buffalo-hunting, and the look on his mother's face,

And the sun sank slow as he stood there,
All Indian-brown from waist up, who never liked tops to his pants,
And standing nigh straight, but the arms and the pitcher's
Great shoulders, they were thinning to old-man thin.   100
Sun low, all silence, then sudden:
"But, Jesus," he cried, "what makes a man do what he does—
Him living until he dies!"

Sure, all of us live till we die, but bingo!
Like young David at brookside, he swooped down,   105
Snatched a stone, wound up, and let fly,
And high on a pole over yonder the big brown insulator
Simply exploded. "See—I still got control!" he said.

---

105 *David:* when he was a boy, King David slew the giant Goliath with a stone from a sling.

VII

Late, late, toward sunset, I wandered
Where old dreams had once been Life's truth, and where   110
I saw the trench of our valor, now nothing
But a ditch full of late-season weed-growth,
Beyond the rim of shade.
There was nobody there, hence no shame to be saved from, so I
Just lie in the trench on my back and see high,   115
Beyond the tall ironweed stalks, or oak leaves
If I happen to look that way,
How the late summer's thinned-out sky moves,
Drifting on, drifting on, like forever,
From *where* on to *where,* and I wonder   120
What it would be like to die,
Like the nameless old skull in the swamp, lost,
And know yourself dead lying under
The infinite motion of sky.

VIII

But why should I lie here longer?   125
I am not dead yet, though in years,
And the world's way is yet long to go,
And I love the world even in my anger,
And love is a hard thing to outgrow.

1976

CODE BOOK LOST   518

What does the veery say, at dusk in shad-thicket?
There must be some meaning, or why should your heart stop,

As though, in the dark depth of water, Time held its breath,
While the message spins on like a spool of silk thread fallen?

When white breakers lunge at the black basalt cliff, what   5
Does the heart hear, gale lifting, the last star long gone now,

Or what in the mother's voice calling her boy from the orchard,
In a twilight moth-white with the apple blossom's dispersal?

Yes, what is that undeclared timbre, and why
Do your eyes go moist, and a pain of unworthiness strike?   10

CODE BOOK LOST 1 *veery:* thrush.

What does the woman dying, or supine and penetrated, stare at?
Fly on ceiling, or gold mote afloat in a sun-slit of curtains?

Some message comes thus from a world that screams, far off.
Will she understand before what will happen, will happen?

What meaning, when at the unexpected street corner,   15
You meet some hope long forgotten, and your old heart,

Like neon in shore-fog, or distance, glows dimly again?
Will you waver, or clench stoic teeth and move on?

Have you thought as you walk, late, late, the streets of a town
Of all dreams being dreamed in dark houses? What do they signify?   20

Yes, message on message, like wind or water, in light or in dark,
The whole world pours at us. But the code book, somehow, is lost.

1976

QUESTIONS

1. Consider the title apart from its connections with the poem. What personal associations does it bring to mind?
2. Describe the way the lost code book operates as a metaphor in the poem. What are the implications?
3. Identify the types of sentences the poet has chosen to use. What is their effect on the tone of the poem?
4. Describe light and color in the poem. How do they support the theme?

HEART OF AUTUMN   519

Wind finds the northwest gap, fall comes.
Today, under gray cloud-scud and over gray
Wind-flicker of forest, in perfect formation, wild geese
Head for a land of warm water, the *boom,* the lead pellet.

Some crumple in air, fall. Some stagger, recover control,   5
Then take the last glide for a far glint of water. None
Knows what has happened. Now, today, watching
How tirelessly *V* upon *V* arrows the season's logic,

Do I know my own story? At least, they know
When the hour comes for the great wing-beat. Sky-strider,   10
Star-strider—they rise, and the imperial utterance,
Which cries out for distance, quivers in the wheeling sky.

That much they know, and in their nature know
The path of pathlessness, with all the joy
Of destiny fulfilling its own name.   15
I have known time and distance, but not why I am here.

Path of logic, path of folly, all
The same—and I stand, my face lifted now skyward,
Hearing the high beat, my arms outstretched in the tingling
Process of transformation, and soon tough legs,   20

With folded feet, trail in the sounding vacuum of passage,
And my heart is impacted with a fierce impulse
To unwordable utterance—
Toward sunset, at a great height.

                                                                    1976

QUESTIONS

1. What happens to the geese?
2. What do the geese know and not know?
3. What does the speaker know and not know?
4. How does he use the geese to explain his present stance?
5. What might the sunset be a symbol of?

WALT WHITMAN
(1819–1892)

I SAW IN LOUISIANA A LIVE-OAK
GROWING   520

I saw in Louisiana a live-oak growing,
All alone stood it and the moss hung down from the branches,
Without any companion it grew there uttering joyous leaves of dark
        green,
And its look, rude, unbending, lusty, made me think of myself,
But I wonder'd how it could utter joyous leaves standing alone there
        without its friend near, for I knew I could not,   5
And I broke off a twig with a certain number of leaves upon it, and
        twined around it a little moss,
And brought it away, and have placed it in sight in my room,
It is not needed to remind me as of my own dear friends,
(For I believe lately I think of little else than of them,)

Yet it remains to me a curious token, it makes me think of manly
    love;   10
For all that, and though the live-oak glistens there in Louisiana
    solitary in a wide flat space,
Uttering joyous leaves all its life without a friend a lover near,
I know very well I could not.

                                                                  1860

QUESTIONS

1. Read this poem aloud. What do you feel in its rhythms that is different from other
   poems?
2. What about the tree reminds the speaker of himself? What differences does he see?
3. The tree "utters joyous leaves." What does the speaker utter? Are there any
   connections?
4. Explain the last three lines. Do you see any irony in the last statement?

WHEN I HEARD THE LEARN'D ASTRONOMER   521

When I heard the learn'd astronomer,
When the proofs, the figures, were ranged in columns before me,
When I was shown the charts and diagrams, to add, divide, and
    measure them,
When I sitting heard the astronomer where he lectured with much
    applause in the lecture-room,
How soon unaccountable I became tired and sick,   5
Till rising and gliding out I wander'd off by myself,
In the mystical moist night-air, and from time to time,
Look'd up in perfect silence at the stars.

                                                  1865

TO A LOCOMOTIVE IN WINTER   522

Thee for my recitative,
Thee in the driving storm even as now, the snow, the winter-day
    declining,
Thee in thy panoply, thy measur'd dual throbbing and thy beat
    convulsive,
Thy black cylindric body, golden brass and silvery steel,
Thy ponderous side-bars, parallel and connecting rods, gyrating,   5
    shuttling at thy sides,

TO A LOCOMOTIVE IN WINTER 3 *panoply:* complete suit of armor.

Thy metrical, now swelling pant and roar, now tapering in the
distance,
Thy great protruding head-light fix'd in front,
Thy long, pale, floating vapor-pennants, tinged with delicate purple,
The dense and murky clouds out-belching from thy smoke-stack,
Thy knitted frame, thy springs and valves, the tremulous twinkle of
thy wheels,   10
Thy train of cars behind, obedient, merrily following,
Through gale or calm, now swift, now slack, yet steadily careering;
Type of the modern—emblem of motion and power—pulse of the
continent,
For once come serve the Muse and merge in verse, even as here I see
thee,
With storm and buffeting gusts of wind and falling snow,   15
By day thy warning ringing bell to sound its notes,
By night thy silent signal lamps to swing.

Fierce-throated beauty!
Roll through my chant with all thy lawless music, thy swinging
lamps at night,
Thy madly-whistled laughter, echoing, rumbling like an earthquake,
rousing all,
Law of thyself complete, thine own track firmly holding,   20
(No sweetness debonair of tearful harp or glib piano thine,)
Thy trills of shrieks by rocks and hills return'd,
Launch'd o'er the prairies wide, across the lakes,
To the free skies unpent and glad and strong.   25

1881

HAD I THE CHOICE   523

Had I the choice to tally greatest bards,
To limn their portraits, stately, beautiful, and emulate at will,
Homer with all his wars and warriors—Hector, Achilles, Ajax,
Or Shakespeare's woe-entangled Hamlet, Lear, Othello—Tennyson's
fair ladies,
Meter or wit the best, or choice conceit to wield in perfect rhyme,
delight of singers;
These, these, O sea, all these I'd gladly barter,   5
Would you the undulation of one wave, its trick to me transfer,
Or breathe one breath of yours upon my verse,
And leave its odor there.

1889

RICHARD WILBUR
(b. 1921)

THE PARDON   524

My dog lay dead five days without a grave
In the thick of summer, hid in a clump of pine
And a jungle of grass and honeysuckle-vine.
I who had loved him while he kept alive

Went only close enough to where he was   5
To sniff the heavy honeysuckle-smell
Twined with another odor heavier still
And hear the flies' intolerable buzz.

Well, I was ten and very much afraid.
In my kind world the dead were out of range   10
And I could not forgive the sad or strange
In beast or man. My father took the spade

And buried him. Last night I saw the grass
Slowly divide (it was the same scene
But now it glowed a fierce and mortal green)   15
And saw the dog emerging. I confess

I felt afraid again, but still he came
In the carnal sun, clothed in a hymn of flies,
And death was breeding in his lively eyes.
I started in to cry and call his name,   20

Asking forgiveness of his tongueless head.
. . . I dreamt the past was never past redeeming:
But whether this was false or honest dreaming
I beg death's pardon now. And mourn the dead.

1950

LOVE CALLS US TO THE THINGS OF THIS WORLD   525

The eyes open to a cry of pulleys,
And spirited from sleep, the astounded soul
Hangs for a moment bodiless and simple
As false dawn.
                Outside the open window   5
The morning air is all awash with angels.

Some are in bed-sheets, some are in blouses,
Some are in smocks: but truly there they are.
Now they are rising together in calm swells
Of halcyon feeling, filling whatever they wear   10
With the deep joy of their impersonal breathing;

    Now they are flying in place, conveying
The terrible speed of their omnipresence, moving
And staying like white water; and now of a sudden
They swoon down into so rapt a quiet   15
That nobody seems to be there.

                   The soul shrinks

    From all that it is about to remember,
From the punctual rape of every blessèd day,
And cries,   20
        "Oh, let there be nothing on earth but laundry,
Nothing but rosy hands in the rising steam
And clear dances done in the sight of heaven."

    Yet, as the sun acknowledges
With a warm look the world's hunks and colors,   25
The soul descends once more in bitter love
To accept the waking body, saying now
In a changed voice as the man yawns and rises,

    "Bring them down from their ruddy gallows;
Let there be clean linen for the backs of thieves;   30
Let lovers go fresh and sweet to be undone,
And the heaviest nuns walk in a pure floating
Of dark habits,
            keeping their difficult balance."

                           1956

QUESTIONS

1. How do you respond to awakening suddenly out of a sound sleep? How is your reaction similar to or different from the one registered in the first four lines?
2. What are the pulleys used for? Where do you find the first sure confirmation of their function? Where are earlier hints that that may be the case?
3. What is the relationship of soul to body as expressed here? Of motion to stasis? Of lightness to weight?
4. How is the tension resolved?

A BAROQUE WALL-FOUNTAIN IN THE VILLA SCIARRA

526

FOR DORE AND ADJA

Under the bronze crown
Too big for the head of the stone cherub whose feet
   A serpent has begun to eat,
Sweet water brims a cockle and braids down

   Past spattered mosses, breaks   5
On the tipped edge of a second shell, and fills
   The massive third below. It spills
In threads then from the scalloped rim, and makes

   A scrim or summery tent
For a faun-ménage and their familiar goose.   10
   Happy in all that ragged, loose
Collapse of water, its effortless descent

   And flatteries of spray,
The stocky god upholds the shell with ease,
   Watching, about his shaggy knees,   15
The goatish innocence of his babes at play;

   His fauness all the while
Leans forward, slightly, into a clambering mesh
   Of water-lights, her sparkling flesh
In a saecular ecstasy, her blinded smile   20

   Bent on the sand floor
Of the trefoil pool, where ripple-shadows come
   And go in swift reticulum,
More addling to the eye than wine, and more

   Interminable to thought   25
Than pleasure's calculus. Yet since this all
   Is pleasure, flash, and waterfall,
Must it not be too simple? Are we not

   More intricately expressed
In the plain fountains that Maderna set   30
   Before St. Peter's—the main jet
Struggling aloft until it seems at rest

A BAROQUE WALL-FOUNTAIN IN THE VILLA SCIARRA title: park in Rome. 4 *cockle:* shell-shaped basin. 10 *faun-ménage:* faun family. 20 *saecular:* continuing for a long time. 22 *trefoil:* divided into three parts. 23 *reticulum:* netlike pattern. 24 *addling:* muddling. 30 *Maderna:* architect of St. Peter's in Rome.

In the act of rising, until
The very wish of water is reversed,
    That heaviness borne up to burst
In a clear, high, cavorting head, to fill   35

    With blaze, and then in gauze
Delays, in a gnatlike shimmering, in a fine
    Illumined version of itself, decline,
And patter on the stones its own applause?   40

    If that is what men are
Or should be, if those water-saints display
    The pattern of our areté,
What of these showered fauns in their bizarre,

    Spangled, and plunging house?   45
They are at rest in fullness of desire
    For what is given, they do not tire
Of the smart of the sun, the pleasant water-douse

    And riddled pool below,
Reproving our disgust and our ennui   50
    With humble insatiety.
Francis, perhaps, who lay in sister snow

    Before the wealthy gate
Freezing and praising, might have seen in this
    No trifle, but a shade of bliss—   55
That land of tolerable flowers, that state

    As near and far as grass
Where eyes become the sunlight, and the hand
    Is worthy of water: the dreamt land
Toward which all hungers leap, all pleasures pass.   60

1956

THE DEATH OF A TOAD   527

    A toad the power mower caught,
Chewed and clipped of a leg, with a hobbling hop has got
    To the garden verge, and sanctuaried him
    Under the cineraria leaves, in the shade
        Of the ashen heartshaped leaves, in a dim,   5
            Low, and a final glade.

43 *areté:* exemplary characteristics. 52 *Francis:* St. Francis of Assisi.

The rare original heartsblood goes,
Spends on the earthen hide, in the folds and wizening, flows
  In the gutters of the banked and staring eyes. He lies
As still as if he would return to stone,   10
    And soundlessly attending, dies
      Toward some deep monotone,

  Toward misted and ebullient seas
And cooling shores, toward lost Amphibia's emperies.
  Day dwindles, drowning, and at length is gone   15
  In the wide and antique eyes, which still appear
    To watch, across the castrate lawn,
      The haggard daylight steer.

1957

ADVICE TO A PROPHET   528

When you come, as you soon must, to the streets of our city,
Mad-eyed from stating the obvious,
Not proclaiming our fall but begging us
In God's name to have self-pity,

Spare us all word of the weapons, their force and range,   5
The long numbers that rocket the mind;
Our slow, unreckoning hearts will be left behind,
Unable to fear what is too strange.

Nor shall you scare us with talk of the death of the race.
How should we dream of this place without us?—   10
The sun mere fire, the leaves untroubled about us,
A stone look on the stone's face?

Speak of the world's own change. Though we cannot conceive
Of an undreamt thing, we know to our cost
How the dreamt cloud crumbles, the vines are blackened by frost,   15
How the view alters. We could believe,

If you told us so, that the white-tailed deer will slip
Into perfect shade, grown perfectly shy,
The lark avoid the reaches of our eye,
The jack-pine lose its knuckled grip   20

THE DEATH OF A TOAD **14** *Amphibia's emperies:* empire of amphibians.

On the cold ledge, and every torrent burn
As Xanthus once, its gliding trout
Stunned in a twinkling. What should we be without
The dolphin's arc, the dove's return,

These things in which we have seen ourselves and spoken?   25
Ask us, prophet, how we shall call
Our natures forth when that live tongue is all
Dispelled, that glass obscured or broken

In which we have said the rose of our love and the clean
Horse of our courage, in which beheld   30
The singing locust of the soul unshelled,
And all we mean or wish to mean.

Ask us, ask us whether with the worldless rose
Our hearts shall fail us; come demanding
Whether there shall be lofty or long standing   35
When the bronze annals of the oak-tree close.

                                        1959

A LATE AUBADE   529

You could be sitting now in a carrel
Turning some liver-spotted page,
Or rising in an elevator-cage
Toward Ladies' Apparel.

You could be planting a raucous bed   5
Of salvia, in rubber gloves,
Or lunching through a screed of someone's loves
With pitying head,

Or making some unhappy setter
Heel, or listening to a bleak   10
Lecture on Schoenberg's serial technique.
Isn't this better?

Think of all the time you are not
Wasting, and would not care to waste,
Such things, thank God, not being to your taste.   15
Think what a lot

ADVICE TO A PROPHET 22 *Xanthus:* river of Troy.

A LATE AUBADE title *aubade:* dawn love song lamenting the lovers' parting. 7 *screed:* long, monotonous complaint. 11 *Schoenberg:* Arnold Schoenberg, Austrian modernist composer.

Of time, by woman's reckoning,
You've saved, and so may spend on this,
You who had rather lie in bed and kiss
Than anything.

20

It's almost noon, you say? If so,
Time flies, and I need not rehearse
The rosebuds-theme of centuries of verse.
If you *must* go,

25

Wait for a while, then slip downstairs
And bring us up some chilled white wine,
And some blue cheese, and crackers, and some fine
Ruddy-skinned pears.

1968

THE WRITER

530

In her room at the prow of the house
Where light breaks, and the windows are tossed with linden,
My daughter is writing a story.

I pause in the stairwell, hearing
From her shut door a commotion of typewriter-keys
Like a chain hauled over a gunwale.

5

Young as she is, the stuff
Of her life is a great cargo, and some of it heavy:
I wish her a lucky passage.

But now it is she who pauses,
As if to reject my thought and its easy figure.
A stillness greatens, in which

10

The whole house seems to be thinking,
And then she is at it again with a bunched clamor
Of strokes, and again is silent.

15

I remember the dazed starling
Which was trapped in that very room, two years ago;
How we stole in, lifted a sash

And retreated, not to affright it;
And how for a helpless hour, through the crack of the door,
We watched the sleek, wild, dark

20

And iridescent creature
Batter against the brilliance, drop like a glove
To the hard floor, or the desk-top,

And wait then, humped and bloody,   25
For the wits to try it again; and how our spirits
Rose when, suddenly sure,

It lifted off from a chair-back,
Beating a smooth course for the right window
And clearing the sill of the world.   30

It is always a matter, my darling,
Of life or death, as I had forgotten. I wish
What I wished you before, but harder.

                                                                    1971

LYING   531

To claim, at a dead party; to have spotted a grackle,
When in fact you haven't of late, can do no harm.
Your reputation for saying things of interest
Will not be marred, if you hasten to other topics,
Nor will the delicate web of human trust   5
Be ruptured by that airy fabrication.
Later, however, talking with toxic zest
Of golf, or taxes, or the rest of it
Where the beaked ladle plies the chuckling ice,
You may enjoy a chill of severance, hearing   10
Above your head the shrug of unreal wings.
Not that the world is tiresome in itself:
We know what boredom is: it is a dull
Impatience or a fierce velleity,
A champing wish, stalled by our lassitude,   15
To make or do. In the strict sense, of course,
We invent nothing, merely bearing witness
To what each morning brings again to light:
Gold crosses, cornices, astonishment
Of panes, the turbine-vent which natural law   20
Spins on the grill-end of the diner's roof,
Then grass and grackles or, at the end of town
In sheen-swept pastureland, the horse's neck

LYING 14 *velleity:* wish that does not lead to action.

Clothed with its usual thunder, and the stones
Beginning now to tug their shadows in   25
And track the air with glitter. All these things
Are there before us; there before we look
Or fail to look; there to be seen or not
By us, as by the bee's twelve thousand eyes,
According to our means and purposes.   30
So too with strangeness not to be ignored,
Total eclipse or snow upon the rose,
And so with that most rare conception, nothing.
What is it, after all, but something missed?
It is the water of a dried-up well   35
Gone to assail the cliffs of Labrador.
There is what galled the arch-negator, sprung
From Hell to probe with intellectual sight
The cells and heavens of a given world
Which he could take but as another prison: 40
Small wonder that, pretending not to be,
He drifted through the bar-like boles of Eden
In a *black mist low creeping,* dragging down
And darkening with moody self-absorption
What, when he left it, lifted and, if seen   45
From the sun's vantage, seethed with vaulting hues.
Closer to making than the deftest fraud
Is seeing how the catbird's tail was made
To counterpoise, on the mock-orange spray,
Its light, up-tilted spine; or, lighter still,   50
How the shucked tunic of an onion, brushed
To one side on a backlit chopping-board
And rocked by trifling currents, prints and prints
Its bright, ribbed shadow like a flapping sail.
Odd that a thing is most itself when likened: 55
The eye mists over, basil hints of clove,
The river glazes toward the dam and spills
To the drubbed rocks below its crashing cullet,
And in the barnyard near the sawdust-pile
Some great thing is tormented. Either it is   60
A tarp torn loose and in the groaning wind
Now puffed, now flattened, or a hip-shot beast
Which tries again, and once again, to rise.
What, though for pain there is no other word,

42 *boles:* tree trunks. 58 *drubbed:* beaten; *cullet:* pieces of broken glass to be remelted.

Finds pleasure in the cruellest simile? 65
It is something in us like the catbird's song
From neighbor bushes in the grey of morning
That, harsh or sweet, and of its own accord,
Proclaims its many kin. It is a chant
Of the first springs, and it is tributary 70
To the great lies told with the eyes half-shut
That have the truth in view: the tale of Chiron
Who, with sage head, wild heart, and planted hoof
Instructed brute Achilles in the lyre,
Or of the garden where we first mislaid 75
Simplicity of wish and will, forgetting
Out of what cognate splendor all things came
To take their scattering names; and nonetheless
That matter of a baggage-train surprised
By a few Gascons in the Pyrenees 80
Which, having worked three centuries and more
In the dark caves of France, poured out at last
The blood of Roland, who to Charles his king
And to the dove that hatched the dove-tailed world
Was faithful unto death, and shamed the Devil. 85

1987

WILLIAM CARLOS WILLIAMS
(1883–1963)

A LOVE SONG: FIRST VERSION, 1915 532

What have I to say to you
When we shall meet?
Yet—
I lie here thinking of you.

The stain of love
Is upon the world. 5
Yellow, yellow, yellow,
It eats into the leaves,

---

72 *Chiron:* a centaur who was Achilles' tutor. 74 *Achilles:* hero of *The Iliad.* 83 *Roland . . . Charles:* Roland was a legendary defender of Christians and a nephew of Charlemagne (also called Charles the Great).

Smears with saffron
The horned branches that lean
Heavily
Against a smooth purple sky.

10

There is no light—
Only a honey-thick stain
That drips from leaf to leaf
And limb to limb
Spoiling the colors
Of the whole world.

15

I am alone.
The weight of love
Has buoyed me up
Till my head
Knocks against the sky.

20

See me!
My hair is dripping with nectar—
Starlings carry it
On their black wings.
See, at last
My arms and my hands
Are lying idle.

25

30

How can I tell
If I shall ever love you again
As I do now?

1916

LOVE SONG

533

I lie here thinking of you:—

the stain of love
is upon the world!
Yellow, yellow, yellow
it eats into the leaves,
smears with saffron
the horned branches that lean
heavily
against a smooth purple sky!

5

There is no light
only a honey-thick stain   10
that drips from leaf to leaf
and limb to limb
spoiling the colors
of the whole world—
                                                      15
you far off there under
the wine-red selvage of the west!

                                              1917

Q U E S T I O N S

1. What emotion does the color yellow evoke in this poem? What about purple?
2. What do the following words suggest about the speaker's feelings: *stain, eats, smears, heavily, spoiling*?
3. What is the effect of the separation of the first line and the last two lines from the rest of the poem?

DANSE RUSSE   534

If when my wife is sleeping
and the baby and Kathleen
are sleeping
and the sun is a flame-white disc
in silken mists
above shining trees,—   5
if I in my north room
dance naked, grotesquely
before my mirror
waving my shirt round my head
and singing softly to myself: 10
"I am lonely, lonely.
I was born to be lonely,
I am best so!"
If I admire my arms, my face,
my shoulders, flanks, buttocks   15
against the yellow drawn shades,—

Who shall say I am not
the happy genius of my household?

                                              1917

THIS IS JUST TO SAY   535

I have eaten
the plums
that were in
the icebox

and which   5
you were probably
saving for breakfast

Forgive me
they were delicious
so sweet   10
and so cold

1934

RALEIGH WAS RIGHT   536

We cannot go to the country
for the country will bring us no peace
What can the small violets tell us
that grow on furry stems in
the long grass among lance shaped leaves?   5

Though you praise us
and call to mind the poets
who sung of our loveliness
it was long ago!
long ago! when country people   10
would plow and sow with
flowering minds and pockets at ease—
if ever this were true.

Not now. Love itself a flower
with roots in a parched ground.   15
Empty pockets make empty heads.
Cure it if you can but
do not believe that we can live
today in the country
for the country will bring us no peace.   20

1941

RALEIGH WAS RIGHT title: a reference to "The Nymph's Reply to the Shepherd" by Sir Walter Ralegh
(Raleigh).

THE DANCE   537

In Breughel's great picture, The Kermess,
the dancers go round, they go round and
around, the squeal and the blare and the
tweedle of bagpipes, a bugle and fiddles
tipping their bellies (round as the thick-   5
sided glasses whose wash they impound)
their hips and their bellies off balance
to turn them. Kicking and rolling about
the Fair Grounds, swinging their butts, those
shanks must be sound to bear up under such   10
rollicking measures, prance as they dance
in Breughel's great picture, The Kermess.

1944

THE CLOUDS   538

I

Filling the mind
upon the rim of the overarching sky, the
          horses of
the dawn charge from south to north,
          gigantic beasts
rearing flame-edged above the pit,
a rank confusion of the imagination still
          uncured
a rule, piebald under the streetlamps,   5
          reluctant
to be torn from its hold.

                    Their flanks still
caught among low, blocking forms their
          fore-parts
rise lucid beyond this smell of a swamp, a mud
livid with decay and life! turtles   10
that burrowing among the white roots lift
          their green
red-striped faces startled before the dawn.

THE DANCE 1 *Breughel:* Pieter Breughel, sixteenth-century Flemish painter.

A black flag, writhing and whipping at the
　　　staff-head
mounts the sepulcher of the empty bank,
　　　fights
to be free . . .
　　　　　South to north! the direction   15
unmistakable, they move, distinct beyond
　　　the unclear
edge of the world, clouds! like statues
before which we are drawn—in darkness,
　　　thinking of
our dead, unable, knowing no place
where else rightly to lodge them.

　　　　　　　　Tragic outlines   20
and the bodies of horses, mindfilling—but
visible! against the invisible; actual against
the imagined and the concocted; unspoiled
　　　by hands
and unshaped also by them but caressed by
　　　sight only,
moving among them, not that that propels   25
the eyes from under, while it binds:

—upon whose backs the dead ride, high!
undirtied by the putridity we fasten upon
　　　them—
South to north, for this moment distinct
　　　and undeformed,
into the no-knowledge of their nameless   30
　　　destiny.

　　　　　　　　　　II

Where are the good minds of past days, the unshorn?
Villon, to be sure, with his
saw-toothed will and testament? Erasmus
who praised folly and

Shakespeare who wrote so that   35
no school man or churchman could sanction him without
revealing his own imbecility? Aristotle,
shrewd and alone, a onetime herb peddler?

THE CLOUDS *32 Villon:* François Villon, fifteenth-century French poet. *33 Erasmus:* Dutch humanist
and philosopher (1466–1536) who wrote *In Praise of Folly.*

They all, like Aristophanes, knew the clouds and
said next to nothing of the soul's flight   40
but kept their heads and died—
like Socrates, Plato's better self, unmoved.

Where? They live today in their old state because
of the pace they kept that keeps
them now fresh in our thoughts, their   45
relics, ourselves: Toulouse-Lautrec, the

deformed who lived in a brothel and painted
the beauty of whores. These were
the truth-tellers of whom we are the sole heirs
beneath the clouds that bring   50

shadow and darkness full of thought deepened
by rain against the clatter
of an empty sky. But anything to escape humanity!
Now it's spiritualism—again,

as if the certainty of a future life   55
were any solution to our dilemma: how to get
published not what we write but what we would write were
it not for the laws against libelous truth.

The poor brain unwilling to own the obtrusive body
would crawl from it like a crab and   60
because it succeeds, at times, in doffing that,
by its wiles of drugs or other "ecstasies," thinks

at last that it is quite free—exulted, scurrying to
some slightly larger shell some snail
has lost (where it will live). And so, thinking,   65
pretends a mystery! an unbodied

thing that would still be a brain—but no body,
something that does not eat but flies by the propulsions
of pure—what? into the sun itself, illimitedly
and exists so forever, blest, washed, purged   70

and at ease in non-representational bursts
of shapeless flame, sentient (naturally!)—and keeps
touch with the earth (by former works) at least.
The intellect leads, leads still! Beyond the clouds.

---

39 *Aristophanes:* ancient Greek playwright. 42 *Socrates, Plato's better self:* Plato wrote about
Socrates. 46 *Toulouse-Lautrec:* nineteenth-century French painter.

III

(Scherzo)

I came upon a priest once at St. Andrew's
in Amalfi in crimson and gold brocade riding
the clouds of his belief.

It happened that we tourists had intervened
at some mid-moment of the ritual—   80
tipped the sacristan or whatever it was.

No one else was there—porphyry and alabaster,
the light flooding in scented
with sandalwood—but this holy man

jiggling upon his buttocks to the litany   85
chanted, in response, by two kneeling altar boys!
I was amazed and stared in such manner

that he, caught half off the earth
in his ecstasy—though without losing a beat—
turned and grinned at me from his cloud.   90

IV

With each, dies a piece of the old life, which he carries,
a precious burden, beyond! Thus each
is valued by what he carries and that is his soul—
diminishing the bins by that much
unless replenished.

       It is that which is the brotherhood: 95
the old life, treasured. But if they live?
What then?

      The clouds remain
—the disordered heavens, ragged, ripped by winds
or dormant, a caligraphy of scaly dragons and bright moths,
of straining thought, bulbous or smooth,   100
ornate, the flesh itself (in which
the poet foretells his own death); convoluted, lunging upon
a pismire, a conflagration, a . . . .

                               1948

---

75 *Scherzo:* the lively third movement of a musical composition. 81 *sacristan:* an official in charge
of the church sacristy, where the sacred vessels and vestments are kept.

THE SPARROW

(TO MY FATHER)

This sparrow
       who comes to sit at my window
           is a poetic truth
more than a natural one.
       His voice,
           his movements,   5
his habits—
       how he loves to
           flutter his wings
in the dust—   10
       all attest it;
           granted, he does it
to rid himself of lice
       but the relief he feels
           makes him   15
cry out lustily —
       which is a trait
           more related to music
than otherwise.
       Wherever he finds himself
           in early spring,   20
on back streets
       or beside palaces,
           he carries on
unaffectedly
       his amours.   25
           It begins in the egg,
his sex genders it:
       What is more pretentiously
           useless
or about which   30
       we more pride ourselves?
           It leads as often as not
to our undoing.
       The cockerel, the crow
           with their challenging voices   35
cannot surpass
       the insistence
           of his cheep!

Once   40
              at El Paso
                           toward evening,
I saw—and heard!—
              ten thousand sparrows
                           who had come in from   45
the desert
              to roost. They filled the trees
                           of a small park. Men fled
(with ears ringing!)
              from their droppings,   50
                           leaving the premises
to the alligators
              who inhabit
                           the fountain. His image
is familiar   55
              as that of the aristocratic
                           unicorn, a pity
there are not more oats eaten
              nowadays
                           to make living easier   60
for him.
              At that,
                           his small size,
keen eyes,
              serviceable beak   65
                           and general truculence
assure his survival—
              to say nothing
                           of his innumerable
brood.   70
              Even the Japanese
                           know him
and have painted him
              sympathetically,
                           with profound insight   75
into his minor
              characteristics.
                           Nothing even remotely
subtle
              about his lovemaking.   80

          He crouches
before the female,
      drags his wings,
           waltzing,
throws back his head   85
      and simply—
           yells! The din
is terrific.
      The way he swipes his bill
           across a plank   90
to clean it,
      is decisive.
           So with everything
he does. His coppery
      eyebrows   95
           give him the air
of being always
      a winner—and yet
           I saw once,
the female of his species   100
      clinging determinedly
           to the edge of
a water pipe,
      catch him
           by his crown-feathers   105
to hold him
      silent,
           subdued,
hanging above the city streets
      until   110
           she was through with him.
What was the use
      of that?
           She hung there
herself,   115
      puzzled at her success.
           I laughed heartily.
Practical to the end,
      it is the poem
           of his existence   120
that triumphed
      finally;
           a wisp of feathers

flattened to the pavement,
>
> wings spread symmetrically   125
>
>> as if in flight,

the head gone,

> the black escutcheon of the breast
>
>> undecipherable,

an effigy of a sparrow,   130

> a dried wafer only,
>
>> left to say

and it says it

> without offense,
>
>> beautifully;   135

This was I,

> a sparrow.
>
>> I did my best;

farewell.

                                                            1955

WILLIAM WORDSWORTH

(1770 – 1850)

LINES COMPOSED A FEW MILES ABOVE TINTERN ABBEY ON REVISITING THE BANKS OF THE WYE DURING A TOUR. JULY 13, 1798   540

Five years have passed; five summers, with the length
Of five long winters! and again I hear
These waters, rolling from their mountain-springs
With a soft inland murmur. Once again
Do I behold these steep and lofty cliffs,   5
That on a wild secluded scene impress
Thoughts of more deep seclusion; and connect
The landscape with the quiet of the sky.
The day is come when I again repose
Here, under this dark sycamore, and view   10
These plots of cottage ground, these orchard tufts,
Which at this season, with their unripe fruits,
Are clad in one green hue, and lose themselves
'Mid groves and copses. Once again I see

TINTERN ABBEY title *Tintern Abbey:* a ruined monastery on the Welsh–English border. 14 *copses:* thickets.

These hedgerows, hardly hedgerows, little lines   15
Of sportive wood run wild; these pastoral farms,
Green to the very door; and wreaths of smoke
Sent up, in silence, from among the trees!
With some uncertain notice, as might seem
Of vagrant dwellers in the houseless woods,   20
Or of some Hermit's cave, where by his fire
The Hermit sits alone.

                    These beauteous forms,
Through a long absence, have not been to me
As is a landscape to a blind man's eye;
But oft, in lonely rooms, and 'mid the din   25
Of towns and cities, I have owed to them,
In hours of weariness, sensations sweet,
Felt in the blood, and felt along the heart;
And passing even into my purer mind,
With tranquil restoration—feelings too   30
Of unremembered pleasure; such, perhaps,
As have no slight or trivial influence
On that best portion of a good man's life,
His little, nameless, unremembered, acts
Of kindness and of love. Nor less, I trust,   35
To them I may have owed another gift,
Of aspect more sublime; that blessed mood,
In which the burthen of the mystery,
In which the heavy and the weary weight
Of all this unintelligible world,   40
Is lightened—that serene and blessed mood,
In which the affections gently lead us on—
Until, the breath of this corporeal frame
And even the motion of our human blood
Almost suspended, we are laid asleep   45
In body, and become a living soul;
While with an eye made quiet by the power
Of harmony, and the deep power of joy,
We see into the life of things.

                      If this
Be but a vain belief, yet, oh! how oft—   50
In darkness and amid the many shapes
Of joyless daylight; when the fretful stir
Unprofitable, and the fever of the world,

Have hung upon the beatings of my heart—
How oft, in spirit, have I turned to thee,   55
O sylvan Wye! thou wanderer through the woods,
How often has my spirit turned to thee!

   And now, with gleams of half-extinguished thought,
With many recognitions dim and faint,
And somewhat of a sad perplexity,   60
The picture of the mind revives again;
While here I stand, not only with the sense
Of present pleasure, but with pleasing thoughts
That in this moment there is life and food
For future years. And so I dare to hope,   65
Though changed, no doubt, from what I was when first
I came among these hills; when like a roe
I bounded o'er the mountains, by the sides
Of the deep rivers, and the lonely streams,
Wherever nature led—more like a man   70
Flying from something that he dreads than one
Who sought the thing he loved. For nature then
(The coarser pleasures of my boyish days,
And their glad animal movements all gone by)
To me was all in all.—I cannot paint   75
What then I was. The sounding cataract
Haunted me like a passion; the tall rock,
The mountain, and the deep and gloomy wood,
Their colors and their forms, were then to me
An appetite; a feeling and a love,   80
That had no need of a remote charm,
By thought supplied, nor any interest
Unborrowed from the eye.—That time is past,
And all its aching joys are now no more,
And all its dizzy raptures. Not for this   85
Faint I, nor mourn nor murmur; other gifts
Have followed; for such loss, I would believe,
Abundant recompense. For I have learned
To look on nature, not as in the hour
Of thoughtless youth; but hearing oftentimes   90
The still, sad music of humanity,
Nor harsh nor grating, though of ample power
To chasten and subdue. And I have felt
A presence that disturbs me with the joy
Of elevated thoughts; a sense sublime   95

Of something far more deeply interfused,
Whose dwelling is the light of setting suns,
And the round ocean and the living air,
And the blue sky, and in the mind of man:
A motion and a spirit, that impels   100
All thinking things, all objects of all thought,
And rolls through all things. Therefore am I still
A lover of the meadows and the woods,
And mountains; and of all that we behold
From this green earth; of all the mighty world   105
Of eye, and ear—both what they half create,
And what perceive; well pleased to recognize
In nature and the language of the sense
The anchor of my purest thoughts, the nurse,
The guide, the guardian of my heart, and soul   110
Of all my moral being.

                    Nor perchance,
If I were not thus taught, should I the more
Suffer my genial spirits to decay:
For thou art with me here upon the banks
Of this fair river; thou my dearest Friend,   115
My dear, dear Friend; and in thy voice I catch
The language of my former heart, and read
My former pleasures in the shooting lights
Of thy wild eyes. Oh! yet a little while
May I behold in thee what I was once,   120
My dear, dear Sister! and this prayer I make,
Knowing that Nature never did betray
The heart that loved her; 'tis her privilege,
Through all the years of this our life, to lead
From joy to joy: for she can so inform   125
The mind that is within us, so impress
With quietness and beauty, and so feed
With lofty thoughts, that neither evil tongues,
Rash judgments, nor the sneers of selfish men,
Nor greetings where no kindness is, nor all   130
The dreary intercourse of daily life,
Shall e'er prevail against us, or disturb
Our cheerful faith, that all which we behold
Is full of blessings. Therefore let the moon
Shine on thee in thy solitary walk;   135
And let the misty mountain winds be free

To blow against thee: and, in after years,
When these wild ecstasies shall be matured
Into a sober pleasure; when thy mind
Shall be a mansion for all lovely forms,
Thy memory be as a dwelling place
For all sweet sounds and harmonies; oh! then,
If solitude, or fear, or pain, or grief
Should be thy portion, with what healing thoughts
Of tender joy wilt thou remember me,   145
And these my exhortations! Nor, perchance—
If I should be where I no more can hear
Thy voice, nor catch from thy wild eyes these gleams
Of past existence—wilt thou then forget
That on the banks of this delightful stream   150
We stood together; and that I, so long
A worshiper of Nature, hither came
Unwearied in that service; rather say
With warmer love—oh! with far deeper zeal
Of holier love. Nor wilt thou then forget,   155
That after many wanderings, many years
Of absence, these steep woods and lofty cliffs,
And this green pastoral landscape, were to me
More dear, both for themselves and for thy sake!

1798

NUTTING   541

———————————————— It seems a day
(I speak of one from many singled out)
One of those heavenly days that cannot die;
When, in the eagerness of boyish hope,
I left our cottage-threshold, sallying forth   5
With a huge wallet o'er my shoulders slung,
A nutting-crook in hand; and turned my steps
Tow'rd some far-distant wood, a Figure quaint,
Tricked out in proud disguise of cast-off weeds
Which for that service had been husbanded,   10
By exhortation of my frugal Dame—
Motley accoutrement, of power to smile
At thorns, and brakes, and brambles,—and, in truth,
More ragged than need was! O'er pathless rocks,
Through beds of matted fern, and tangled thickets,   15

my way, I came to one dear nook
ited, where not a broken bough
ooped with its withered leaves, ungracious sign
Of devastation; but the hazels rose
Tall and erect, with tempting clusters hung,   20
A virgin scene!—A little while I stood,
Breathing with such suppression of the heart
As joy delights in; and, with wise restraint
Voluptuous, fearless of a rival, eyed
The banquet;—or beneath the trees I sate   25
Among the flowers, and with the flowers I played;
A temper known to those who, after long
And weary expectation, have been blest
With sudden happiness beyond all hope.
Perhaps it was a bower beneath whose leaves   30
The violets of five seasons re-appear
And fade, unseen by any human eye;
Where fairy water-breaks do murmur on
For ever; and I saw the sparkling foam,
And—with my cheek on one of those green stones   35
That, fleeced with moss, under the shady trees,
Lay round me, scattered like a flock of sheep—
I heard the murmur and the murmuring sound,
In that sweet mood when pleasure loves to pay
Tribute to ease; and, of its joy secure,   40
The heart luxuriates with indifferent things,
Wasting its kindliness on stocks and stones,
And on the vacant air. Then up I rose,
And dragged to earth both branch and bough, with crash
And merciless ravage: and the shady nook   45
Of hazels, and the green and mossy bower,
Deformed and sullied, patiently gave up
Their quiet being: and unless I now
Confound my present feelings with the past,
Ere from the mutilated bower I turned   50
Exulting, rich beyond the wealth of kings,
I felt a sense of pain when I beheld
The silent trees, and saw the intruding sky.—
Then, dearest Maiden, move along these shades
In gentleness of heart; with gentle hand   55
Touch—for there is a spirit in the woods.

1800

SHE DWELT AMONG THE UNTRODDEN WAYS   542

She dwelt among the untrodden ways
   Beside the springs of Dove.
A Maid whom there were none to praise
   And very few to love;

A violet by a mossy stone   5
   Half hidden from the eye!
—Fair as a star, when only one
   Is shining in the sky.

She lived unknown, and few could know
   When Lucy ceased to be;   10
But she is in her grave, and, oh,
   The difference to me!

1800

THE SOLITARY REAPER   543

Behold her, single in the field,
Yon solitary Highland Lass!
Reaping and singing by herself;
Stop here, or gently pass!
Alone she cuts and binds the grain,   5
And sings a melancholy strain;
O listen! for the Vale profound
Is overflowing with the sound.

No Nightingale did ever chaunt
More welcome notes to weary bands   10
Of travelers in some shady haunt,
Among Arabian sands;
A voice so thrilling ne'er was heard
In springtime from the Cuckoo bird,
Breaking the silence of the seas   15
Among the farthest Hebrides.

Will no one tell me what she sings?—
Perhaps the plaintive numbers flow
For old, unhappy, far-off things,
And battles long ago;   20

SHE DWELT AMONG THE UNTRODDEN WAYS 2 *Dove:* river in England.

Or is it some more humble lay,
Familiar matter of today?
Some natural sorrow, loss, or pain,
That has been, and may be again?

Whate'er the theme, the Maiden sang   25
As if her song could have no ending;
I saw her singing at her work,
And o'er the sickle bending—
I listened, motionless and still;
And, as I mounted up the hill,   30
The music in my heart I bore,
Long after it was heard no more.

1807

QUESTIONS

1. What is your first response? Does the poem seem like a significant experience at first?
   Do your responses change as you become more familiar with the poem?
2. Why is it that the speaker does not know for sure what the girl is singing?
3. If he does not know what she is singing, how can he be so moved by it?
4. Do you find the ending satisfying? Why or why not?

I WANDERED LONELY AS A CLOUD   544

I wandered lonely as a cloud
That floats on high o'er vales and hills,
When all at once I saw a crowd,
A host, of golden daffodils;
Beside the lake, beneath the trees,   5
Fluttering and dancing in the breeze.

Continuous as the stars that shine
And twinkle on the milky way,
They stretched in never-ending line
Along the margin of a bay: 10
Ten thousand saw I at a glance,
Tossing their heads in sprightly dance.

The waves beside them danced; but they
Outdid the sparkling waves in glee;
A poet could not but be gay,   15
In such a jocund company;
I gazed—and gazed—but little thought
What wealth the show to me had brought:

I WANDERED LONELY AS A CLOUD 16 *jocund:* happy.

For oft, when on my couch I lie
In vacant or in pensive mood,   20
They flash upon that inward eye
Which is the bliss of solitude;
And then my heart with pleasure fills,
And dances with the daffodils.

1807

JAMES WRIGHT
(1927–1980)

LYING IN A HAMMOCK AT WILLIAM
DUFFY'S FARM IN PINE ISLAND,
MINNESOTA   545

Over my head, I see the bronze butterfly,
Asleep on the black trunk,
Blowing like a leaf in green shadow.
Down the ravine behind the empty house,
The cowbells follow one another   5
Into the distances of the afternoon.
To my right,
In a field of sunlight between two pines,
The droppings of last year's horses
Blaze up into golden stones.   10
I lean back, as the evening darkens and comes on.
A chicken hawk floats over, looking for home.
I have wasted my life.

1961

A BLESSING   546

Just off the highway to Rochester, Minnesota,
Twilight bounds softly forth on the grass.
And the eyes of those two Indian ponies
Darken with kindness.
They have come gladly out of the willows   5
To welcome my friend and me.
We step over the barbed wire into the pasture
Where they have been grazing all day, alone.
They ripple tensely, they can hardly contain their happiness
That we have come.   10

They bow shyly as wet swans. They love each other.
There is no loneliness like theirs.
At home once more,
They begin munching the young tufts of spring in the darkness.
I would like to hold the slenderer one in my arms,   15
For she has walked over to me
And nuzzled my left hand.
She is black and white,
Her mane falls wild on her forehead,
And the light breeze moves me to caress her long ear   20
That is delicate as the skin over a girl's wrist.
Suddenly I realize
That if I stepped out of my body I would break
Into blossom.

1963

QUESTIONS

1. Which is the point of strongest emotional impact for you as you read the poem? Why?
2. Describe the relationship of the ponies and the reasons they seem to relate so well to the humans.
3. What is the human response to the ponies—both physically and linguistically?
4. What do the final three lines express?
5. The poet originally entitled this poem "The Blessing." Is the revised title an improvement?

WILLIAM BUTLER YEATS
(1865–1939)

THE LAKE ISLE OF INNISFREE   547

I will arise and go now, and go to Innisfree,
And a small cabin build there, of clay and wattles made:
Nine bean-rows will I have there, a hive for the honey-bee,
And live alone in the bee-loud glade.

And I shall have some peace there, for peace comes dropping slow,   5
Dropping from the veils of the morning to where the cricket sings;
There midnight's all a glimmer, and noon a purple glow,
And evening full of the linnet's wings.

THE LAKE ISLE OF INNISFREE 2 *wattles:* sticks intertwined and woven to make a wall or a roof.

I will arise and go now, for always night and day
I hear lake water lapping with low sounds by the shore;   10
While I stand on the roadway, or on the pavements gray,
I hear it in the deep heart's core.

1892

QUESTIONS

1. Where is the speaker when he says, "I will arise and go now"? How do you know?
2. What does peace sound like to the speaker? How does he hear?
3. How does the following early version of the poem compare with this one? Which do
   you like better?

> I will arise and go now and go to the island of Innisfree
> And live in a dwelling of wattles, of woven wattles and wood-work made.
> Nine bean-rows will I have there, a yellow hive for the honey-bee,
> And this old care shall fade.
>
> There from the dawn above me peace will come down dropping slow,
> Dropping from the veils of the morning to where the household cricket sings;
> And noontide there be all a glimmer, and midnight be a purple glow,
> And evening full of the linnet's wings.

THE WILD SWANS AT COOLE   548

The trees are in their autumn beauty,
The woodland paths are dry,
Under the October twilight the water
Mirrors a still sky;
Upon the brimming water among the stones   5
Are nine-and-fifty swans.

The nineteenth autumn has come upon me
Since I first made my count;
I saw, before I had well finished,
All suddenly mount   10
And scatter wheeling in great broken rings
Upon their clamorous wings.

I have looked upon those brilliant creatures,
And now my heart is sore.
All's changed since I, hearing at twilight,   15
The first time on this shore,
The bell-beat of their wings above my head,
Trod with a lighter tread.

THE WILD SWANS AT COOLE title *Coole:* Coole Park, the estate of Lady Gregory, Yeats' friend.

Unwearied still, lover by lover,
They paddle in the cold   20
Companionable streams or climb the air;
Their hearts have not grown old;
Passion or conquest, wander where they will,
Attend upon them still.

But now they drift on the still water,   25
Mysterious, beautiful;
Among what rushes will they build,
By what lake's edge or pool
Delight men's eyes when I awake some day
To find they have flown away?   30

1917

AN IRISH AIRMAN FORESEES HIS DEATH   549

I know that I shall meet my fate
Somewhere among the clouds above;
Those that I fight I do not hate,
Those that I guard I do not love;
My country is Kiltartan Cross,   5
My countrymen Kiltartan's poor,
No likely end could bring them loss
Or leave them happier than before.
Nor law, nor duty bade me fight,
Nor public men, nor cheering crowds,   10
A lonely impulse of delight
Drove to this tumult in the clouds;
I balanced all, brought all to mind,
The years to come seemed waste of breath,
A waste of breath the years behind   15
In balance with this life, this death.

1919

QUESTIONS

1. Describe the person you visualize speaking these words.
2. Why does the airman fight if he does not have to?
3. The airman says, "I balanced all" (line 13). In what sense does he do just that in the poem?

AN IRISH AIRMAN FORESEES HIS DEATH title: Major Robert Gregory, son of Yeats' friend Lady Gregory, was killed in Italy in 1918. 5 *Kilkartan Cross:* village near the Gregory home.

Iambic Pentameter
English Sonnet

LEDA AND THE SWAN

550

A sudden blow: the great wings beating still
Above the staggering girl, her thighs caressed
By the dark webs, her nape caught in his bill,
He holds her helpless breast upon his breast.

How can those terrified vague fingers push
The feathered glory from her loosening thighs?
And how can body, laid in that white rush,
But feel the strange heart beating where it lies?

A shudder in the loins engenders there
The broken wall, the burning roof and tower
And Agamemnon dead.
                    Being so caught up,
So mastered by the brute blood of the air,
Did she put on his knowledge with his power
Before the indifferent beak could let her drop?

15

1924

SAILING TO BYZANTIUM

551

1

That is no country for old men. The young
In one another's arms, birds in the trees
—Those dying generations—at their song,
The salmon-falls, the mackerel-crowded seas,
Fish, flesh, or fowl, commend all summer long   5
Whatever is begotten, born, and dies.
Caught in that sensual music all neglect
Monuments of unaging intellect.

2

An aged man is but a paltry thing,
A tattered coat upon a stick, unless   10
Soul clap its hands and sing, and louder sing
For every tatter in its mortal dress,

LEDA AND THE SWAN title *Leda:* a mortal loved by Zeus in the form of a swan. Among her children were Helen of Troy and Clytemnestra.
SAILING TO BYZANTIUM title *Byzantium:* ancient city on the site of modern Istanbul.

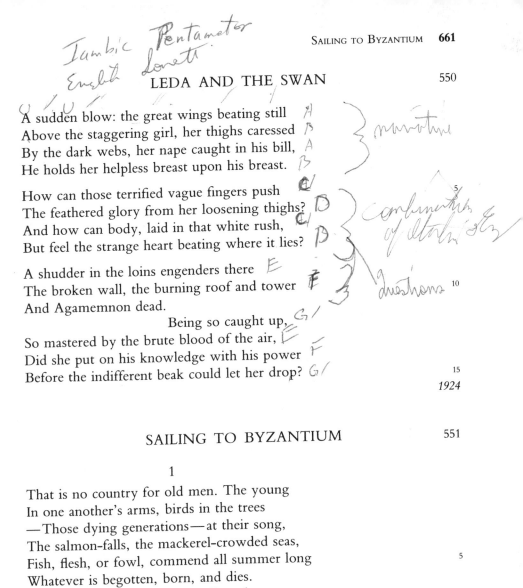

Nor is there singing school but studying
Monuments of its own magnificence;
And therefore I have sailed the seas and come   15
To the holy city of Byzantium.

3

O sages standing in God's holy fire
As in the gold mosaic of a wall,
Come from the holy fire, perne in a gyre,
And be the singing-masters of my soul.   20
Consume my heart away; sick with desire
And fastened to a dying animal
It knows not what it is; and gather me
Into the artifice of eternity.

4

Once out of nature I shall never take   25
My bodily form from any natural thing,
But such a form as Grecian goldsmiths make
Of hammered gold and gold enameling
To keep a drowsy Emperor awake;
Or set upon a golden bough to sing   30
To lords and ladies of Byzantium
Of what is past, or passing, or to come.

1927

AMONG SCHOOL CHILDREN   552

1

I walk through the long schoolroom questioning;
A kind old nun in a white hood replies;
The children learn to cipher and to sing,
To study reading-books and histories,
To cut and sew, be neat in everything
In the best modern way—the children's eyes   5
In momentary wonder stare upon
A sixty-year-old smiling public man.

19 *perne in a gyre:* move in a spiral pattern.

2

I dream of a Ledaean body, bent
Above a sinking fire, a tale that she
Told of a harsh reproof, or trivial event
That changed some childish day to tragedy—
Told, and it seemed that our two natures blent
Into a sphere from youthful sympathy,
Or else, to alter Plato's parable,
Into the yolk and white of the one shell.

3

And thinking of that fit of grief or rage
I look upon one child or t'other there
And wonder if she stood so at that age—
For even daughters of the swan can share
Something of every paddler's heritage—
And had that color upon cheek or hair,
And thereupon my heart is driven wild:
She stands before me as a living child.

4

Her present image floats into the mind—
Did Quattrocento finger fashion it
Hollow of cheek as though it drank the wind
And took a mess of shadows for its meat?
And I though never of Ledaean kind
Had pretty plumage once—enough of that,
Better to smile on all that smile, and show
There is a comfortable kind of old scarecrow.

5

What youthful mother, a shape upon her lap
Honey of generation had betrayed,
And that must sleep, shriek, struggle to escape
As recollection or the drug decide,
Would think her son, did she but see that shape
With sixty or more winters on its head,
A compensation for the pang of his birth,
Or the uncertainty of his setting forth?

10

15

20

25

30

35

40

AMONG SCHOOL CHILDREN 9 *Ledaean body:* as beautiful as Leda's, the mortal loved by Zeus, who visited her in the form of a swan. 15–16 *Plato's parable:* in Plato's *Symposium,* human love is explained as a yearning for the other half of ourselves, illustrated by an egg cut in two. 26 *Quattrocento:* Italian artist of the fifteenth century.

6

Plato thought nature but a spume that plays
Upon a ghostly paradigm of things;
Solider Aristotle played the taws
Upon the bottom of a king of kings;
World-famous golden-thighed Pythagoras   45
Fingered upon a fiddle-stick or strings
What a star sang and careless Muses heard:
Old clothes upon old sticks to scare a bird.

7

Both nuns and mothers worship images,
But those the candles light are not as those
That animate a mother's reveries,   50
But keep a marble or a bronze repose.
And yet they too break hearts—O Presences
That passion, piety or affection knows,
And that all heavenly glory symbolize—   55
O self-born mockers of man's enterprise;

8

Labor is blossoming or dancing where
The body is not bruised to pleasure soul,
Nor beauty born out of its own despair,
Nor blear-eyed wisdom out of midnight oil.   60
O chestnut-tree, great-rooted blossomer,
Are you the leaf, the blossom or the bole?
O body swayed to music, O brightening glance,
How can we know the dancer from the dance?

                                                        1927

BYZANTIUM   553

The unpurged images of day recede;
The Emperor's drunken soldiery are abed;
Night resonance recedes, night-walkers' song
After great cathedral gong;

---

41 *spume:* froth. 43–44 *Aristotle . . . kings:* Aristotle was tutor to Alexander the Great when the latter was a child. As his tutor, he probably had occasion to whip him. 45 *Pythagoras:* sixth-century Greek philosopher, responsible for ideas of cosmic harmony. 62 *bole:* tree trunk.
BYZANTIUM title: ancient city on the site of modern Istanbul.

A starlit or a moonlit dome disdains
All that man is,
All mere complexities,
The fury and the mire of human veins.

Before me floats an image, man or shade,
Shade more than man, more image than a shade;
For Hades' bobbin bound in mummy-cloth
May unwind the winding path;
A mouth that has no moisture and no breath
Breathless mouths may summon;
I hail the superhuman;
I call it death-in-life and life-in-death.

Miracle, bird or golden handiwork,
More miracle than bird or handiwork,
Planted on the starlit golden bough,
Can like the cocks of Hades crow,
Or, by the moon embittered, scorn aloud
In glory of changeless metal
Common bird or petal
And all complexities of mire or blood.

At midnight on the Emperor's pavement flit
Flames that no faggot feeds, nor steel has lit,
Nor storm disturbs, flames begotten of flame,
Where blood-begotten spirits come
And all complexities of fury leave,
Dying into a dance,
An agony of trance,
An agony of flame that cannot singe a sleeve.

Astraddle on the dolphin's mire and blood,
Spirit after spirit! The smithies break the flood.
The golden smithies of the Emperor!
Marbles of the dancing floor
Break bitter furies of complexity,
Those images that yet
Fresh images beget,
That dolphin-torn, that gong-tormented sea.

1932

GLOSSARY

Alexandrine A poetic line of six (usually iambic) feet and twelve syllables.

Alliteration The repetition of an initial consonant sound.

Allusion Indirect references to literary or historical figures, events, artistic works, and so on.

Anapestic See **meter.**

Anaphora The repetition of an initial word or phrase.

Assonance The repetition of similar vowel sounds.

Ballad The ballad stanza consists of four lines of alternating tetrameter and trimeter with a rhyme scheme of *abcb.* The ballad is a narrative poem meant to be sung.

Blank Verse Verse written in unrhymed iambic pentameter.

Caesura A pause in the regular meter of a poetic line.

Cliché An expression that has been used so often that is has become tiresome and hackneyed.

Conceit An exaggerated metaphor which links two extremes in its **tenor** and **vehicle.**

Concrete Poetry Poetry which uses typography in original ways to form an object the poem describes.

Connotation The meaning of a word that is associational, that goes beyond the dictionary definition. For example, *skinny, thin,* and *slim* may mean approximately the same thing, but they suggest differing attitudes; they have different connotations. Compare **denotation.**

Consonance Repetition of the same consonant sounds, usually at the ends of words, although sometimes within the words.

Couplet Two lines of verse, usually rhymed.

Curtal Sonnet See **sonnet.**

Dactylic See **meter.**

Denotation The dictionary or literal definition of a word.

Diction The choice and arrangement of words in a poem.

Dimeter See **meter.**

Dramatic Monologue A poem in which the speaker, or **persona,** relates an event or tells a story to someone else.

Dropped Line The last part of a line of poetry, which drops to the next line. Often used in poems containing dialogue to indicate a change of speakers.

Elegy A formal lyric expressing sorrow over a death.

End Rhymes See **rhyme.**

End-Stopped Lines Poetic lines which end in a period, comma, semicolon, colon, question mark, or exclamation point indicating a brief pause before continuing into the next line. Compare **enjambed lines.**

Enjambed Lines Poetic lines with no punctuation or pause at the end but which continue without stopping to the next line. Compare **end-stopped lines.**

Epic A long narrative poem of elevated style.

Epigram A short, witty poem.

Extended Metaphor A metaphor which is elaborately and completely developed.

Feminine Ending A line of poetry that ends with an extra, unstressed syllable. Compare **masculine ending.**

Foot See **meter.**

Free Verse Poetry which has no formal metrical structure or rhyme scheme.

Haiku A form of Japanese poetry which contains seventeen syllables and/or three lines, usually containing a reference to nature or to the season, and having a spiritual significance.

Heptameter See **meter.**

Heroic Couplet Two rhymed lines of iambic pentameter verse.

Hexameter See **meter.**

Hyperbole An overstatement or exaggeration for ironic effect.

Iambic See **meter.**

Internal Rhymes See **rhyme.**

Irony Irony occurs when an outcome is different from what is expected. Sometimes this occurs when a speaker unwittingly reveals intentions different from stated purposes, but irony can also be the result of a double attitude on the part of the writer or a conscious play of the form of a poem against its subject matter.

Italian Sonnet See **sonnet.**

Light Verse Humorous poetry.

Limerick A short poem in which rhyme, rhythm, and sometimes visual effects create humor.

Lyric Short, concentrated poem expressing personal feeling.

Masculine Ending A line of poetry that ends with a stressed syllable. Compare **feminine ending.**

Metaphor A description of one object, situation or idea through an implicit comparison with another. The two terms of a metaphor are called the **vehicle** and the **tenor.** *Mixed metaphors,* which juxtapose incompatible companions, tend to create a ridiculous effect because their images contradict or undercut each other.

Meter Rhythm or meter is measured in *feet,* units of stressed and unstressed syllables. A line of poetry may be written in *monometer* (having one foot), *dimeter* (two feet), *trimeter* (three feet), *tetrameter* (four feet), *pentameter* (five feet), *hexameter* (six feet), *heptameter* (seven feet), and so on, adhering to any of the following stress patterns:

> *iambic:* ˘ /
> *trochaic:* / ˘
> *anapestic:* ˘ ˘ /
> *dactylic:* / ˘ ˘
> *spondaic:* / /

Metonymy This occurs when an object or characteristic associated with the subject is used in place of the subject, as when *the crown* is used to refer to the monarch or the monarchy.

Metrical Verse Poetry that is measured in stressed syllables.

Monometer See **meter.**

Narrative Poetry Poetry that tells a story.

Negative Capability John Keats used this term to describe the poet's ability to be an objective, passive observer, accepting whatever the senses receive.

Objective Correlative T. S. Eliot's term describing the way in which concrete language evokes feeling in poetry. He said, "The only way of expressing emotion in the form of art is by finding an 'objective correlative'; in other words, a set of objects, a situation, a chain of events which shall be the formula of that *particular* emotion; such that when the external facts, which must terminate in a sensory experience, are given, the emotion is immediately evoked."

Octave An eight-lined stanza.

Ode A lyric written in an elaborate, exalted style.

Off-Rhyme See **rhyme.**

Onomatopoeia Words which sound like the object or action they name.

Ottava Rima An eight-lined stanza written in iambic pentameter with the rhyme scheme *abababcc.*

Paradox A statement which appears to contradict itself.

Parody Intentional imitation of a style or form of poetry for the purposes of ridiculing it.

Pentameter See **meter.**

Perfect Rhyme See **rhyme.**

Persona A character—often the speaker—in a poem.

Personification An inanimate object or quality described as if it were human.

Prose Poem A poem which looks like prose because it has no formal lineation.

Quatrain A stanza of four lines.

Refrain A line, phrase, or verse repeated at intervals throughout a poem.

Rhyme The harmony or echoing effect of words with similar sounds. *Perfect rhymes* are full rhymes in which initial consonants are different, but vowel sounds and final consonants are the same, as in *plain/cane.* *Off-rhymes* or *slant-rhymes* are not full rhymes, but contain elements of sound similar to each other, as in *plain/fame*. *End rhymes* are those which occur at the ends of poetic lines; *internal rhymes* occur within a poetic line or stanza.

Rhyme Scheme Pattern of end rhymes in a poem. See **rhyme.**

Rhythm See **meter.**

Rime Royal An eight-line stanza written in iambic pentameter with the rhyme scheme of *aababbcc.*

Scansion The process of scanning a poem or reading it rhythmically to determine its meter.

Sestet A six-lined stanza.

Sestina A thirty-nine line poem in which the end words of each line of the first stanza are repeated in a particular order throughout the poem.

Shakespearean Sonnet See **sonnet.**

Simile A direct comparison using *like* or *as.* Compare **metaphor.**

Slant-Rhyme See **rhyme.**

Sonnet Usually a fourteen-line poem written in either the Shakespearean style *(abab, cdcd, efef, gg)* or the Italian style *(abba, abba, cdecde),* although some modern and some hybrid forms (such as the *curtal sonnet,* a shortened version of the Italian sonnet) demonstrate variations of the traditional patterns.

Spondaic See **meter.**

Spenserian Stanza A nine-lined stanza with a rhyme scheme of *ababbcbcc.* The first eight lines are written in iambic pentameter, and the last line is in iambic hexameter, an **Alexandrine.**

Substitution A variation of the established meter in a poem whereby one rhythmical pattern is replaced by another for one or more feet in a line.

Syllabic Verse Verse in which the linear unit of measure is the syllable rather than the accent.

Symbol An object which points to a meaning which its strictly denotative definition cannot capture entirely. *Archetypal symbols* are images, patterns, situations which have been repeated so often in the literature, dreams, and myths of all cultures that they lead to immediate associations for the reader. *Traditional* or *general symbols* are those which have acquired meaning within a particular culture. *Private symbols* are those invested with meaning by a particular author.

Synecdoche A poetic device in which a part represents the whole.

Synesthesia The close association of one sensory image with another image perceived by a different sense. For example, "The red geraniums *blare* their color" uses sound to describe a visual image.

Syntax Word order.

Tenor The object being described in a metaphor. Compare **vehicle.**

Tercet A three-lined stanza.

Terza Rima Poem formed from tercets with interlinking rhymes: *aba, bcb, cdc, ded, efe,* and so on.

Tetrameter See **meter.**

Tone The mood of a poem or the attitude expressed in it.

Trimeter See **meter.**

Trochaic See **meter.**

Understatement Subtle or indirect statement, ironically restrained.

Vehicle The object used to describe another in a metaphor. Compare **tenor.**

Villanelle Poem of six stanzas, the first five rhyming *aba,* alternating the first and third lines of the first stanza as the end lines of the next four stanzas. The final stanza rhymes *abaa,* and uses the two repeated lines as a concluding couplet.

PERMISSIONS AND ACKNOWLEDGMENTS

AMY CLAMPITT. "A Procession at Candlemas" from *The Kingfisher* by Amy Clampitt. Copyright © 1983 by Amy Clampitt. Reprinted by permission of Alfred A. Knopf, Inc.

JOHN CLARE. "Badger," The Bodley Head, Ltd.

LUCILLE CLIFTON. "Miss Rosie" from *Good Times* by Lucille Clifton. Copyright © 1969 by Lucille Clifton. Reprinted by permission of Random House, Inc. "Homage to My Hips" and "I Once Knew a Man" reprinted from *Two-Headed Woman* by Lucille Clifton (Amherst: University of Massachusetts Press, 1980) copyright © 1980.

ELIZA COOK. "The Old Arm-Chair" reprinted in *The Stuffed Owl: An Anthology of Bad Verse*, edited by D. B. Wyndham Lewis and Charles Lee, Capricorn Books, 1930, 1962.

GREGORY CORSO. "The Vestal Lady on Brattle," copyright © 1955, 1958 by Gregory Corso. Reprinted by permission of City Lights Books.

HART CRANE. "My Grandmother's Love Letters" and "The Broken Tower" reprinted from *The Complete Poems and Selected Letters and Prose of Hart Crane*, edited by Brom Weber, by permission of Liveright Publishing Corporation. Copyright 1933, © 1958, 1966 by Liveright Publishing Corporation.

ROBERT CREELEY. "A Wicker Basket" and "If you" reprinted with permission of Charles Scribner's Sons, an imprint of Macmillan Publishing Company, from *For Love: Poems 1950–1960* by Robert Creeley. Copyright © 1962 by Robert Creeley. "Mother's Voice" reprinted from *Mirrors*. Copyright © 1983 by Robert Creeley. Reprinted by permission of New Directions Publishing Corporation.

COUNTEE CULLEN. "Incident" and "Heritage" from *On These I Stand*. Copyright © 1925 by Harper & Brothers; copyright renewed 1953 by Ida M. Cullen. Reprinted by permission.

E. E. CUMMINGS. "Spring is like a perhaps hand," "the Cambridge ladies who live in furnished souls," "O sweet spontaneous," and "in Just-" reprinted from *Tulips & Chimneys* by E. E. Cummings, edited by George James Firmage, by permission of Liveright Publishing Corporation. Copyright 1923, 1925, and renewed 1951, 1953 by E. E. Cummings. Copyright © 1973, 1976 by the Trustees for the E. E. Cummings Trust. Copyright © 1973, 1976 by George James Firmage. "silence," "Me up at does," "anyone lived in a pretty how town," and "a salesman is an it that stinks Excuse" reprinted from *Complete Poems, 1913–1962*, by E. E. Cummings, by permission of Liveright Publishing Corporation. Copyright © 1923, 1925, 1931, 1935, 1938, 1939, 1940, 1944, 1945, 1946, 1947, 1948, 1949, 1950, 1951, 1952, 1953, 1954, 1956, 1957, 1958, 1959, 1960, 1961, 1962, by the Trustees for the E. E. Cummings Trust. Copyright © 1961, 1963, 1968 by Marion Morehouse Cummings. "somewhere i have never travelled,gladly beyond" reprinted from *ViVa*, poems by E. E. Cummings, edited by George James Firmage, by permission of Liveright Publishing Corporation. Copyright 1931, 1959 by E. E. Cummings. Copyright © 1979, 1973 by the Trustees for the E. E. Cummings Trust. Copyright © 1979, 1973 by George James Firmage.

WALTER DE LA MARE. "The Listeners" and "Scholars" from *Selected Poems*, Faber & Faber, © 1954. Reprinted by permission of the Literary Trustees of Walter de la Mare and the Society of Authors as their representative.

BABETTE DEUTSCH. "Fireworks" reprinted by permission of the Estate of Babette Deutsch Yarmolinsky.

JAMES DICKEY. "Cherrylog Road" and "The Leap" copyright © 1964 by James Dickey. Reprinted from *Poems 1957–1967* by permission of Wesleyan University Press. "Cherrylog Road" first appeared in *The New Yorker*.

EMILY DICKINSON. "After great pain, a formal feeling comes," "My Life had stood—a Loaded Gun," "I dwell in Possibility," and "In Winter in my Room" from *The Complete Poems of Emily Dickinson* edited by Thomas H. Johnson. Copyright 1914, 1929, 1942 by Martha Dickinson Bianchi. Copyright © renewed 1957 by Mary L. Hampson. By permission of Little, Brown and Company. "A Narrow Fellow in the Grass," "Apparently with no surprise," "Because I could not stop for Death," "I felt a funeral, in my Brain," "I heard a Fly buzz—when I died," "Much Madness is divinest Sense," "My life closed twice before its close," "Tell all the Truth but tell it slant," "The Brain—is wider than the Sky," "The Soul selects her own Society," "There's a certain Slant of light," "This is my letter to the World," and "Wild Nights—Wild Nights!" reprinted by permission of the publishers and the Trustees of Amherst College from *The Poems of Emily Dickinson*, edited by Thomas H. Johnson (Cambridge, MA: The Belknap Press of Harvard University Press). Copyright 1951, © 1955, 1979, 1983 by The President and Fellows of Harvard College.

SUSAN DONNELLY. "Eve Names the Animals" from *Eve Names the Animals* by Susan Donnelly, copyright © 1985 by Susan Donnelly. Reprinted with the permission of Northeastern University Press.

RITA DOVE. "Geometry" reprinted from *The Yellow House on the Corner,* "Dusting," "The Fish in the Stone," "The Zeppelin Factory," and "Roast Possum" from *Thomas and Beulah* by permission of Carnegie-Mellon University Press. © 1980 by Rita Dove.

ALAN DUGAN. "Funeral Oration for a Mouse" copyright © 1961, 1962, 1968, 1972, 1973, 1974, 1983 by Alan Dugan. From *New and Collected Poems, 1961–1983* first published by The Ecco Press in 1983. Reprinted by permission.

ROBERT DUNCAN. "My Mother Would Be a Falconress" reprinted from *Bending the Bow.* Copyright © 1966 by Robert Duncan. First printed in *Poetry.* Reprinted by permission of New Directions Publishing Corporation.

JUDITH DEEM DUPREE. "Nocturne (For Lisa)," Ronald N. Haynes, Inc., reprinted with permission.

RICHARD EBERHART. "Analogue of Unity in Multeity" from *Collected Poems 1930–1986* by Richard Eberhart. Copyright © 1960, 1976, 1988 by Richard Eberhart. Reprinted by permission of Oxford University Press, Inc.

T. S. ELIOT. "Journey of the Magi," "The Love Song of J. Alfred Prufrock," "Preludes," and "Sweeney Among the Nightingales" from *Collected Poems 1909–1962* by T. S. Eliot, copyright 1936 by Harcourt Brace Jovanovich, Inc., copyright © 1963, 1964 by T. S. Eliot, reprinted by permission of Harcourt Brace Jovanovich, Inc.

LAWRENCE FERLINGHETTI. "Constantly Risking Absurdity" and "Sometime During Eternity" reprinted from *A Coney Island of the Mind.* Copyright © 1958 by Lawrence Ferlinghetti. Reprinted by permission of New Directions Publishing Corporation.

CAROLYN FORCHÉ. "Selective Service" copyright © 1981 by Carolyn Forché. "City Walk Up, Winter 1969" copyright © 1980 by Carolyn Forché. From *The Country Between Us* by Carolyn Forché. Reprinted by permission of Harper & Row, Publishers, Inc.

ROBERT FROST. "Acquainted with the Night," "After Apple-Picking," "Birches," "Design," "Fire and Ice," "Forgive, O Lord," "Mending Wall," "Neither Out Far Nor In Deep," "Not to Keep," "Nothing Gold Can Stay," "Out, Out—," "Provide, Provide," "Range-Finding," "Stopping by Woods on a Snowy Evening," "The Gift Outright," "The Oft-Repeated Dream," "The Road Not Taken," and "The Subverted Flower" from *The Poetry of Robert Frost* edited by Edward Connery Lathem. Copyright © 1969 by Holt, Rinehart and Winston, Inc. Copyright © 1962 by Robert Frost. Copyright © 1975 by Lesley Frost Ballantine. Reprinted by permission of Henry Holt and Company, Inc.

ISABELLA GARDNER. "The Widow's Yard" copyright © 1980 by Isabella Gardner. Reprinted from *That Was Then: New and Selected Poems* with the permission of BOA Editions, Ltd.

ALLEN GINSBERG. "America" from *Collected Poems 1947–1980* by Allen Ginsberg. Poem copyright © 1956, 1959 by Allen Ginsberg. *Collected Poems* copyright © 1984 by Allen Ginsberg. Reprinted by permission of Harper & Row Publishers, Inc. "My Sad Self" copyright © 1958 by Allen Ginsberg. From *Collected Poems 1947–1960* by Allen Ginsberg. Both poems reprinted by permission of Harper & Row Publishers, Inc.

NIKKI GIOVANNI. "The Kidnap Poem" from *The Women and the Men* by Nikki Giovanni. Reprinted by permission of William Morrow and Company, Inc. Copyright © 1970, 1974, 1975 by Nikki Giovanni.

LOUISE GLÜCK. "The School Children," and "Poem" copyright © 1971, 1972, 1973, 1974, 1975, by Louise Glück. From *The House on Marshland* first published by The Ecco Press in 1975. Reprinted by permission.

JORIE GRAHAM. "My Garden, My Daylight" and "Mind" from *Erosion.* Copyright © 1983 by Princeton University Press. Reprinted with permission of Princeton University Press.

ROBERT GRAVES. "The Cool Web" and "Down, Wanton, Down!" from *Collected Poems 1975* by Robert Graves. Copyright © 1975 by Robert Graves. Reprinted by permission of Oxford University Press, Inc.

THOM GUNN. "Moly" from *Moly* by Thom Gunn. Copyright © 1961, 1971, 1973 by Thom Gunn. Reprinted by permission of Farrar, Straus and Giroux, Inc.

MARILYN HACKER. "Part of a True Story" and "Open Windows" from *Assumptions* by Marilyn Hacker. Copyright © 1985 by Marilyn Hacker. Reprinted by permission of Alfred A. Knopf, Inc.

THOMAS HARDY. "In Time of 'The Breaking of Nations,'" "The Oxen," and "The Man He Killed" from *The Complete Poems of Thomas Hardy*, edited by James Gibson (New York: Macmillan, 1978).

ROBERT HAYDEN. "Those Winter Sundays" and "Monet's 'Waterlilies'" reprinted from *Angle of Ascent, New and Selected Poems* by Robert Hayden, by permission of Liveright Publishing Corporation. Copyright © 1975, 1972, 1970, 1966 by Robert Hayden.

H. D. (HILDA DOOLITTLE). "Oread" and "We Have Seen Her" reprinted from *The Collected Poems of H.D.* copyright © 1982 by the estate of Hilda Doolittle. Reprinted by permission of New Directions Publishing Corporation.

SEAMUS HEANEY. "Waterfall" and "Docker" from *Death of a Naturalist*, Faber and Faber, Ltd., London. Reprinted by permission.

ANTHONY HECHT. "The Dover Bitch, A Criticism of Life" reprinted with permission of Atheneum Publishers, an imprint of MacMillan Publishing Company, from *The Hard Hours* by Anthony Hecht. Copyright © 1959, 1967 by Anthony E. Hecht. "'More Light! More Light!'" reprinted with permission of Atheneum Publishers, an imprint of Macmillan Publishing Company, from *The Hard Hours* by Anthony Hecht. Copyright © 1961, 1967 by Anthony E. Hecht. "A Lot of Night Music" reprinted with permission of Atheneum Publishers, an imprint of Macmillan Publishing Company, from *Millions of Strange Shadows*. Copyright © 1977 by Anthony E. Hecht.

JOHN HOLLANDER. "Helicon" reprinted with permission of Antheneum Publishers, an imprint of Macmillan Publishing Company, from *Spectral Emanations: New and Selected Poems* by John Hollander. Copyright © 1962, 1963, 1965 by John Hollander.

A. E. HOUSMAN. "Eight O'Clock," copyright 1922 by Holt, Rinehart and Winston and renewed 1950 by Barclays Bank Ltd. Reprinted from *The Collected Poems of A. E. Housman*, by permission of Henry Holt and Company, Inc. "Is My Team Plowing," "Loveliest of Trees," "Terence, This Is Stupid Stuff," "To an Athlete Dying Young," and "With Rue My Heart Is Laden," copyright 1939, 1940, © 1965 by Holt, Rinehart and Winston. Copyright © 1967, 1968 by Robert Symons. Reprinted from *The Collected Poems of A. E. Housman*, by permission of Henry Holt and Company, Inc.

LANGSTON HUGHES. "Brass Spittoons" from *Fine Clothes to the Jew*. Copyright 1927 by Alfred A. Knopf, Inc. Copyright renewed 1955 by Langston Hughes. Reprinted by permission of Harold Ober Associates Incorporated. "Theme for English B" from *Mortgage of a Dream Deferred*. Copyright 1951 by Langston Hughes. Copyright renewed 1979 by George Houston Bass. Reprinted by permission of Harold Ober Associates Incorporated. "Harlem" copyright 1951 by Langston Hughes. Reprinted from *The Panther and the Lash* by Langston Hughes, by permission of Alfred A. Knopf, Inc. "The Negro Speaks of Rivers" copyright 1926 by Alfred A. Knopf, Inc. and renewed 1954 by Langston Hughes; "Sylvester's Dying Bed" copyright 1942 by Alfred A. Knopf, Inc. Reprinted from *Selected Poems of Langston Hughes*, by permission of Alfred A. Knopf, Inc.

TED HUGHES. "The Thought-Fox" copyright © 1957 by Ted Hughes. "Wind" copyright © 1956 by Ted Hughes. "The Bull Moses" copyright © 1959 by Ted Hughes. From *New Selected Poems* by Ted Hughes. Reprinted by permission of Harper & Row, Publishers, Inc.

RICHARD HUGO. "The Hilltop" reprinted from *Making Certain It Goes On, The Collected Poems of Richard Hugo*, by permission of W. W. Norton & Company, Inc. Copyright © 1984 by The Estate of Richard Hugo.

T. R. HUMMER. "The Rural Carrier Stops to Kill a Nine-Foot Cottonmouth" reprinted by permission of Louisiana State University Press from *The Angelic Orders* by T. R. Hummer. Copyright © 1982 by T. R. Hummer.

RANDALL JARRELL. "The Death of the Ball Turret Gunner" from *The Complete Poems* by Randall Jarrell. Copyright © 1945, 1972 by Mrs. Randall Jarrell. Reprinted by permission of Farrar, Straus and Giroux, Inc. "Next Day" reprinted with permission of Macmillan Publishing Company from *The Lost World* by Randall Jarrell, 1963, 1965. Originally appeared in *The New Yorker*.

ROBINSON JEFFERS. "Rock and Hawk" and "The Purse-Seine" reprinted from *Selected Poetry of Robinson Jeffers*, by permission of Random House, Inc. Copyright 1934 and renewed 1962 by Donnan Jeffers and Garth Jeffers.

ILSE JUERGENSEN. "Similes and Metaphors: An Exercise" copyright 1980, American Studies Press.

DONALD JUSTICE. "Tales from a Family Album" and "The Snowfall" copyright © 1960 by Donald Justice. Reprinted from *The Summer Anniversaries* by permission of Wesleyan University Press. "The Suicides" copyright © 1965 by Donald Justice; "Men at Forty" and "The Missing Person" copyright © by Donald Justice. Reprinted from *Night Light* by permission of Wesleyan University Press. "The Suicides," "Men at Forty," and "The Missing Person" first appeared in *Poetry*.

PATRICK KAVANAUGH. "Inniskeen Road: July Evening," permission granted by the Devin-Adair Publishers. Copyright © 1964 by Patrick Kavanaugh.

X. J. KENNEDY. "On a Child Who Lived One Minute" from *Cross Ties*, University of Georgia Press. Reprinted by permission.

GALWAY KINNELL. "First Song" and "For William Carlos Williams" from *What A Kingdom It Was* by Galway Kinnell. Copyright © 1960 by Galway Kinnell. Copyright © renewed 1988 by Galway Kinnell. Reprinted by permission of Houghton Mifflin Company. "The River That Is East" from *Flower Herding on Mount Monadnock* by Galway Kinnell. Copyright © 1964 by Galway Kinnell. Reprinted by permission of Houghton Mifflin Company. "The Burn" from *Body Rags* by Galway Kinnell. Copyright © 1967 by Galway Kinnell. Reprinted by permission of Houghton Mifflin Company. "The Milk Bottle" from *Mortal Acts, Mortal Words* by Galway Kinnell. Copyright © 1980 by Galway Kinnell. Reprinted by permission of Houghton Mifflin Company.

CAROLYN KIZER. "Afternoon Happiness," "Semele Recycled," "The Blessing," "The Copulating Gods," and "Food of Love," copyright © 1984 by Carolyn Kizer. Reprinted from *Yin: New Poems* with the permission of BOA Editions, Ltd.

MAXINE KUMIN. "Morning Swim" from *Our Ground Time Here Will Be Brief* by Maxine Kumin. Copyright © 1965 by Maxine Kumin. All rights reserved. Reprinted by permission of Viking Penguin, a division of Penguin Books USA, Inc. "Woodchucks" and "How It Is" from *Our Ground Time Here Will Be Brief* by Maxine Kumin. Copyright © 1971, 1975 by Maxine Kumin. All rights reserved. Reprinted by permission of Viking Penguin, a division of Penguin Books USA, Inc. "How It Is" originally appeared in *The New Yorker*.

STANLEY KUNITZ. "Father and Son" from *The Poems of Stanley Kunitz, 1928–1978* by Stanley Kunitz. Copyright 1944 by Stanley Kunitz.

PHILIP LARKIN. "Church Going" and "Toads" by Philip Larkin are reprinted from *The Less Deceived* by permission of the Marvell Press, England.

RICHMOND LATTIMORE. "Rise and Shine" reprinted by permission; © 1957, 1985 The New Yorker Magazine, Inc.

D. H. LAWRENCE. "Piano," "Snake," and "Bavarian Gentians" from *The Complete Poems of D. H. Lawrence*, edited and collected by Vivian de Sola Pinto and F. Warren Roberts. Copyright © 1964, 1971 by Angelo Ravegli and C. M. Weekley, Executors of the Estate of Frieda Lawrence Ravagli. All rights reserved. Reprinted by permission of Viking Penguin, a division of Penguin Books USA, Inc.

DENISE LEVERTOV. "Pleasures" reprinted from *Collected Earlier Poems 1940–1960*. Copyright © 1959 by Denise Levertov Goodman. Reprinted by permission of New Directions Publishing Corporation. "Six Variations," "Stepping Westward," "Matins," "The Ache of Marriage," and "The Secret" reprinted from *Poems 1960–1967*. Copyright © 1961 by Denise Levertov Goodman. Reprinted by permission of New Directions Publishing Corporation.

PHILIP LEVINE. "To a Child Trapped in a Barber Shop" copyright © 1966 by Philip Levine; "Animals Are Passing from Our Lives" copyright © 1968 by Philip Levine. Reprinted from *Not This Pig* by permission of Wesleyan University Press.

AUDRE LORDE. "Hanging Fire" reprinted from *The Black Unicorn*, poems by Audre Lorde, by permission of W. W. Norton & Company, Inc. Copyright © 1978 by Audre Lorde. "Conversations in Crisis," "Generation," "Revolution Is One Form of Social Change," "Paperweight," "Love, Maybe," "Black Mother Woman," and "Now That I Am Forever With Child" reprinted from *Chosen Poems, Old and New*, by Audre Lorde, by permission of W. W. Norton & Company, Inc. Copyright © 1982, 1976, 1974, 1973, 1970, 1968 by Audre Lorde.

ROBERT LOWELL. "For the Union Dead" from *For the Union Dead* by Robert Lowell. Copyright © 1956, 1960, 1961, 1962, 1963, 1964 by Robert Lowell. Copyright renewed © 1988 by Harriet Lowell, Sheridan Lowell, Caroline Lowell. Reprinted by permission of Farrar, Straus, and Giroux, Inc. "Skunk Hour" from *Life Studies* by Robert Lowell. Copyright © 1956, 1959 by Robert Lowell. Copyright renewed © 1987 by Harriet Lowell, Sheridan Lowell, Caroline Lowell. Reprinted by permission of Farrar, Straus and Giroux, Inc. "Robert Frost" from *Notebook 1967–68* by Robert Lowell. Copyright © 1967, 1968, 1969 by Robert Lowell. Reprinted by permission of Farrar, Straus and Giroux, Inc. "The Quaker Graveyard in Nantucket" from *Lord Weary's Castle*, Harcourt Brace Jovanovich. Reprinted by permission.

ROGER MCGOUGH. "40—Love" reprinted by permission of the Peters Fraser & Dunlop Group Ltd.

CHARLES MACKAY. "Only a Thought" reprinted in *The Stuffed Owl: An Anthology of Bad Verse*, edited by D. B. Wyndham Lewis and Charles Lee, Capricorn Books, 1930, 1962.

CLAUDE MCKAY. "If We Must Die" copyright 1981 and reprinted with the permission of Twayne Publishers, a division of G. K. Hall & Co., Boston.

ARCHIBALD MACLEISH. "Ars Poetica," "Seafarer," and "You, Andrew Marvell" from *New and Collected Poems 1917–1975* by Archibald MacLeish. Copyright © 1985 by the Estate of Archibald MacLeish. Reprinted by permission of Houghton Mifflin Company.

LOUIS MACNEICE. "London Rain," from *The Collected Poems of Louis MacNeice*, Faber and Faber, Ltd., London. Reprinted by permission.

FRANK MANLEY. "Dead Letters" reprinted from the University of Missouri Press 1980 edition of *Resultances* by Frank Manley, by permission of the author.

WILLIAM MEREDITH. "Weather" reprinted by permission; © 1966 The New Yorker Magazine, Inc. "A Major Work" copyright © 1957 by William Meredith; "A Botanical Trope" copyright © 1956 by William Meredith; "A Korean Woman Seated by a Wall" copyright © by William Meredith. Reprinted from *The Open Sea* by William Meredith, by permission of Alfred A. Knopf, Inc. "Recollections of Bellagio" and "Ideogram" from *The Cheer* by William Meredith. Copyright © 1980 by William Meredith. Reprinted by permission of Alfred A. Knopf, Inc.

W. S. MERWIN. "The Drunk in the Furnace" reprinted with permission of Atheneum Publishers, an imprint of Macmillan Publishing Company, from *The First Four Books of Poems* by W. S. Merwin. Copyright © 1956, 1957, 1958, 1959, 1960 by W. S. Merwin. "For the Anniversary of My Death" reprinted with permission of Atheneum Publishers, an imprint of Macmillan Publishing Company, from *The Lice* by W. S. Merwin. Copyright © 1967 by W. S. Merwin.

JOSEPHINE MILES. "Reason" from *Poems 1930–1960*, Indiana University Press. Reprinted by permission. "As Difference Blends into Identity" copyright © 1965 by Josephine Miles. Reprinted from *Kinds of Affection* by permission of Wesleyan University Press.

EDNA ST. VINCENT MILLAY. "Recuerdo," Sonnet XXXVI of *Fatal Interview*, and "The Return" from *Collected Poems*, Harper & Row. Copyright © 1922, 1931, 1934, 1950, 1958, 1962 by Edna St. Vincent Millay and Norma Millay Ellis. Reprinted by permission. "Counting-out Rhyme" from *Collected Poems*, Harper & Row. Copyright © 1928, 1955 by Edna St. Vincent Millay and Norma Millay Ellis. Reprinted by permission.

MAY MILLER. "The Scream" reprinted from *Dust of Uncertain Journey*, © 1975. Reprinted by permission.

JUDSON MITCHAM. "A Knowledge of Water" from *Notes for a Prayer in June* by Judson Mitcham, State Street Press, Brockport, New York, 1986. Reprinted by permission.

MARIANNE MOORE. "The Fish," "Poetry," "The Monkeys," "Critics and Connoisseurs," and "A Grave" reprinted with permission of Macmillan Publishing Company from *Collected Poems* by Marianne Moore. Copyright 1935 by Marianne Moore, renewed 1963 by Marianne Moore and T. S. Eliot. "The Steeple-Jack" from *The Complete Poems* by Marianne Moore. Copyright 1935, renewed © 1963 by Marianne Moore. All rights reserved. Reprinted by permission of Viking Penguin, a division of Penguin Books USA, Inc. "The Pangolin" reprinted with permission of Macmillan Publishing Company from *Collected Poems* by Marianne Moore. Copyright 1941, and renewed 1969 by Marianne Moore.

EDWIN MUIR. "The Horses" from *Collected Poems* by Edwin Muir. Copyright © 1960 by Willa Muir. Reprinted by permission of Oxford University Press, Inc.

OGDEN NASH. "The Perfect Husband" from *Verses from 1929 On* by Ogden Nash. Copyright 1949 by Ogden Nash.

HOWARD NEMEROV. "Learning by Doing," "The Historical Judas," "The Goose Fish," and "The May Day Dancing" reprinted from *The Collected Poems of Howard Nemerov*, the University of Chicago Press, 1977. Reprinted by permission of the author.

FRANK O'HARA. "Poem," copyright © 1957 by Frank O'Hara. Used by permission of Grove Press, a division of Wheatland Corporation. "Why I Am Not a Painter" copyright © 1958 by Maureen Granville-Smith, Administratrix of the Estate of Frank O'Hara. Reprinted from *The Collected Poems of Frank O'Hara*, by permission of Alfred A. Knopf, Inc. "The Day Lady Died," copyright © 1964 by Frank O'Hara. Reprinted by permission of City Lights Books.

SHARON OLDS. "That Moment" and "Why My Mother Made Me" from *The Gold Cell* by Sharon Olds. Copyright © 1987 by Sharon Olds. Reprinted by permission of Alfred A. Knopf, Inc. "Sex Without Love," "After 37 Years My Mother Apologizes for My Childhood," and "The Size and Sheer Will" from *The Dead and the Living* by Sharon Olds. Copyright © 1983 by Sharon Olds. Reprinted by permission of Alfred A. Knopf, Inc.

MARY OLIVER. From *American Primitive* by Mary Oliver. "Lightning" and "May" copyright © 1983 by Mary Oliver. "Ghosts" copyright © 1983 by Mary Oliver, first appeared in *Native Forum*. "Climbing the Chagrin River" copyright © 1982 by Mary Oliver, first appeared in *Harvard Magazine*. "In the Pinewoods, Crows and Owl" copyright © 1978 by Mary Oliver, first appeared in *Provincetown Poetry Magazine*. By permission of Little, Brown and Company.

WILFRED OWEN. "Anthem for Doomed Youth," "Arms and the Box," "Dulce et Decorum Est" reprinted from *The Collected Poems of Wilfred Owen*. Copyright © 1963 by permission of New Directions Publishing Corporation.

ROBERT PACK. "The Frog Prince" from *Waking to My Name: New Selected Poems*. The Johns Hopkins University Press, Baltimore/London, 1980.

DOROTHY PARKER. "One Perfect Rose" and "Résumé" from *The Portable Dorothy Parker*. Copyright 1927, renewed 1955 by Dorothy Parker. All rights reserved. Reprinted by permission of Viking Penguin, a division of Penguin Books USA, Inc.

AMBROSE PHILIPS. "Ode to Miss Margaret Pulteny" reprinted in *The Stuffed Owl: An Anthology of Bad Verse*, edited by D. B. Wyndham Lewis and Charles Lee, Capricorn Books, 1930, 1962.

MARGE PIERCY. "The Friend" copyright © 1969 by Marge Piercy. Reprinted from *Hard Loving* by permission of Wesleyan University Press. "Barbie Doll" from *Circles on the Water* by Marge Piercy. Copyright © 1982 by Marge Piercy. Reprinted by permission of Alfred A. Knopf, Inc.

SYLVIA PLATH. "Point Shirley" copyright © 1959 by Sylvia Plath; "The Colossus" copyright © 1961 by Sylvia Plath; "Elm" copyright © 1962 by Sylvia Plath. Reprinted from *The Colossus and Other Poems* by Sylvia Plath, by permission of Alfred A. Knopf, Inc. "Ariel" copyright © 1965 by the Estate of Sylvia Plath; "The Arrival of the Bee Box" copyright © 1963 by Ted Hughes; "The Bee Meeting" copyright © 1963 by Ted Hughes; "Black Rook in Rainy Weather" copyright © 1960 by Ted Hughes; "The Couriers" copyright © 1963 by Ted Hughes; "Daddy" copyright © 1963 by Ted Hughes; "Electra on Azalea Path" copyright © 1960 by Ted Hughes; "Getting There" copyright © 1963 by Ted Hughes; "Lady Lazarus" copyright © 1963 by Ted Hughes; "Metaphors" copyright © 1960 by Ted Hughes; "Nick and the Candlestick" copyright © 1966 by Ted Hughes; "Poppies in October" copyright © 1965 by the Estate of Sylvia Plath; "Purdah" copyright © 1963 by Ted Hughes; "Words" copyright © 1965 by the Estate of Sylvia Plath. From *The Collected Poems of Sylvia Plath* by Sylvia Plath. Reprinted by permission of Harper & Row, Publishers, Inc.

EZRA POUND. "The River Merchant's Wife," "Portrait d'une Femme," "A Virginal," "The Return," and "In a Station of the Metro" reprinted from *Personae*. Copyright 1926 by Ezra Pound. Reprinted by permission of New Directions Publishing Corporation.

DUDLEY RANDALL. "Ballad of Birmingham." Broadside Press. Reprinted by permission.

JOHN CROWE RANSOM. "Bells for John Whiteside's Daughter" copyright 1924 by Alfred A. Knopf, Inc. and renewed 1952 by John Crowe Ransom; "Janet Waking" copyright 1927 by Alfred A. Knopf, Inc. and renewed 1955 by John Crowe Ransom; "Piazza Piece" copyright © 1969 by the Estate of John Crowe Ransom. Reprinted from *Selected Poems, Third Edition, Revised and Enlarged* by John Crowe Ransom, by permission of Alfred A. Knopf, Inc.

DONNA RAY. "Journal Entry" reprinted by permission.

HENRY REED. "Lessons of the War" from *A Map of Verona*, Jonathan Cape, Ltd. Reprinted by permission.

ISHMAEL REED. "Beware : Do Not Read This Poem" © 1972 Ishmael Reed. Reprinted by permission.

ADRIENNE RICH. "Aunt Jennifer's Tigers," "A Woman Mourned by Daughters," "Snapshots of a Daughter-in-Law," "Necessities of Life," "Onions," "Planetarium," "Diving into the Wreck," and "Living in Sin" reprinted from *Poems, Selected and New, 1950–1974*, by Adrienne Rich, by permission of W. W. Norton & Company, Inc. Copyright © 1975, 1973, 1971, 1969, 1966 by W. W. Norton & Company, Inc. Copyright © 1967, 1963, 1962, 1961, 1960, 1959, 1958, 1957, 1956, 1955, 1954, 1953, 1952, 1951 by Adrienne Rich. "Origins and History of Consciousness" is reprinted from *The Dream of a Common Language, Poems 1974–1977*, by permission of W. W. Norton & Company, Inc. Copyright © 1978 by W. W. Norton & Company, Inc.

EDWIN ARLINGTON ROBINSON. "Eros Turannos" copyright 1916 by Edwin Arlington Robinson, renewed 1944 by Ruth Nivison; "The Mill" copyright 1920 by Edwin Arlington Robinson, renewed 1948 by Ruth Nivison; "The Sheaves" copyright 1925 by Edwin Arlington Robinson, renewed 1953 by Ruth Nivison and Barbara R. Holt. Reprinted with permission of Macmillan Publishing Company from *Collected Poems* by Edwin Arlington Robinson.

MARY ROBINSON. "The Temple of Chastity" reprinted in *The Stuffed Owl: An Anthology of Bad Verse*, edited by D. B. Wyndham Lewis and Charles Lee, Capricorn Books, 1930, 1962.

THEODORE ROETHKE. "My Papa's Waltz" copyright 1942 by Hearst Magazines, Inc. "Elegy for Jane" copyright 1950 by Theodore Roethke, and "In a Dark Time" copyright © 1960 by Beatrice Roethke as administratrix of the Estate of Theodore Roethke. From *The Collected Poems of Theodore Roethke* by Theodore Roethke. Reprinted by permission of Doubleday, a division of Bantam, Doubleday, Dell Publishing Group, Inc.

MURIEL RUKEYSER. "Effort at Speech Between Two People," reprinted by permission of International Creative Management, Inc. Copyright © 1935 and 1963 by Muriel Rukeyser.

Updike. Reprinted from *Telephone Poles and Other Poems* by John Updike, by permission of Alfred A. Knopf, Inc.

DAVID WAGONER. "Walking in the Snow," from *Collected Poems 1956–1976*, Indiana University Press. Reprinted by permission.

RONALD WALLACE. "Grandmother Grace" first appeared in *New Letters* (Fall 1981). Reprinted by permission of the author.

MARILYN WANIEK. "Women's Locker Room" reprinted by permission of Louisiana State University Press from *Mama's Promises* by Marilyn Nelson Waniek. Copyright © 1985 by Marilyn Nelson Waniek.

ROBERT PENN WARREN. "Gold Glade" copyright © 1957 by Robert Penn Warren. Reprinted from *Selected Poems 1923–1975* by Robert Penn Warren, by permission of Random House, Inc. "American Portrait: Old Style" copyright © 1976 by Robert Penn Warren; "Heart of Autumn" copyright © 1977 by Robert Penn Warren; "Code Book Lost" copyright © 1978 by Robert Penn Warren. Reprinted from *Now and Then: Poems 1976–1978* by Robert Penn Warren, by permission of Random House, Inc.

RICHARD WILBUR. "The Pardon" and "The Death of a Toad" from *Ceremony and Other Poems* (1957); "Love Calls Us to the Things of This World," "A Baroque Wall-Fountain in the Villa Sciarra," from *Things of This World* (1956); "Advice to a Prophet" from *Advice to a Prophet and Other Poems*, Harcourt Brace Jovanovich (originally appeared in *The New Yorker*, 1959); "A Late Aubade" from *Walking to Sleep: New Poems and Translations*, Harcourt Brace Jovanovich (1968; originally appeared in *The New Yorker*); "The Writer" from *The Mind Reader*, Harcourt Brace Jovanovich (1971); "Lying" from *New and Collected Poems*, Harcourt Brace Jovanovich (1987; originally appeared in *The New Yorker*).

WILLIAM CARLOS WILLIAMS. "A Love Song: First Version, 1915," "The Red Wheelbarrow," "Love Song," "This Is Just to Say," and "Dance Russe" reprinted from *Collected Poems, Vol. I, 1909–1939*. Copyright 1938 by New Directions Publishing Corporation. Reprinted by permission of New Directions Publishing Corporation. "The Sparrow," "The Clouds," "The Dance," and "Raleigh Was Right" reprinted from *Collected Poems, Vol. II, 1939–1962*. Copyright 1944, 1948, 1962 by William Carlos Williams. Reprinted by permission of New Directions Publishing Corporation.

JAMES WRIGHT. "A Blessing" and "Lying in a Hammock at William Duffy's Farm in Pine Island, Minnesota" copyright © 1961 by James Wright. Reprinted from *The Branch Will Not Break* by permission of Wesleyan University Press.

WILLIAM BUTLER YEATS. "For Anne Gregory" reprinted with permission of Macmillan Publishing Company from *The Poems of W. B. Yeats: A New Edition*, edited by Richard J. Finneran. Copyright 1933 by Macmillan Publishing Company, renewed 1961 by Bertha Georgie Yeats. "The Wheel" reprinted with the permission of Macmillan Publishing Company from *The Poems of W. B. Yeats: A New Edition*, edited by Richard J. Finneran. Copyright 1928 by Macmillan Publishing Company, renewed 1956 by Georgie Yeats. "The Wild Swans at Coole" and "An Irish Airman Foresees His Death" reprinted with permission of Macmillan Publishing Company from *The Poems of W. B. Yeats: A New Edition*, edited by Richard J. Finneran. Copyright 1919 by Macmillan Publishing Company, renewed 1947 by Bertha Georgie Yeats. "Leda and the Swan," "Sailing to Byzantium," and "Among School Children" reprinted with permission of Macmillan Publishing Company from *Poems of W. B. Yeats: A New Edition*, edited by Richard J. Finneran. Copyright 1928 by Macmillan Publishing Company, renewed 1956 by Georgie Yeats. "Byzantium" reprinted with permission of Macmillan Publishing Company from *Poems of W. B. Yeats: A New Edition*, edited by Richard J. Finneran. Copyright 1933 by Macmillan Publishing Company, renewed 1961 by Bertha Georgie Yeats. "The Second Coming" reprinted with permission of Macmillan Publishing Company from *The Poems of W. B. Yeats: A New Edition*, edited by Richard J. Finneran. Copyright 1924 by Macmillan Publishing Company, renewed 1952 by Bertha Georgie Yeats.

AUTHOR INDEX

TITLE and FIRST-LINE INDEX